SOMEThING ABOUT THe AUThOR®

OUTSTANDING REFERENCE SOURCE

ALA RUSA

Something about the Author *was named an "Outstanding Reference Source,"* the highest honor given by the American Library Association Reference and Adult Services Division.

ISSN 0276-816X

something ABOUT THE author®

**Facts and Pictures about Authors
and Illustrators of Books for Young People**

volume 137

GALE®

THOMSON
GALE

Detroit • New York • San Diego • San Francisco • Cleveland • New Haven, Conn. • Waterville, Maine • London • Munich

Something about the Author, Volume 137

Project Editor
Scot Peacock

Editorial
Katy Balcer, Sara Constantakis, Anna Marie
Dahn, Alana Joli Foster, Natalie Fulkerson,
Arlene M. Johnson, Michelle Kazensky, Julie
Keppen, Joshua Kondek, Thomas McMahon,
Jenai A. Mynatt, Judith L. Pyko, Mary Ruby,
Susan Strickland, Anita Sundaresan, Maikue
Vang, Tracey Watson, Denay L. Wilding,
Thomas Wiloch, Emiene Shija Wright

Research
Michelle Campbell, Sarah Genik, Barbara
McNeil, Tamara C. Nott, Gary J. Oudersluys,
Tracie A. Richardson, Cheryl L. Warnock

Permissions
Debra Freitas, Margaret Chamberlain

Imaging and Multimedia
Dean Dauphinais, Robert Duncan, Leitha
Etheridge-Sims, Mary K. Grimes, Lezlie
Light, Dan Newell, David G. Oblender,
Christine O'Bryan, Kelly A. Quin, Luke
Rademacher

Manufacturing
Stacy L. Melson

LIBRARY OF CONGRESS CATALOG CARD NUMBER 72-27107

ISBN 0-7876-5209-1
ISSN 0276-816X

Printed in the United States of America
10 9 8 7 6 5 4 3 2 1

Contents

Authors in Forthcoming Volumes

Below are some of the authors and illustrators that will be featured in upcoming volumes of *SATA*. These include new entries on the swiftly rising stars of the field, as well as completely revised and updated entries (indicated with *) on some of the most notable and best-loved creators of books for children.

John Agard: Agard's writings are infused with the Caribbean rhythms of his homeland in South America. Agard is highly regarded as a performance poet whose work is most powerful when read aloud but, with numerous volumes of poetry and prose to his credit, he has earned a solid readership as well. Many of Agard's published writings are children's verse collections or stories. In 2002, he coedited a volume titled *Under the Moon and over the Sea: A Collection of Caribbean Poems.*

Tomek Bogacki: Polish-born author and illustrator Bogacki has translated his early love of literature and art into a fruitful career as a creator of children's books. Using such highly textured mediums as oil pastel and tempera, Bogacki has developed a style that incorporates a secondary color palette and an off-kilter sense of perspective. His self-illustrated picture books for young children often deal with friendship by featuring animal characters who overcome their differences, and other works portray events from historic Europe. *Circus Girl* was named to *Smithsonian Magazine*'s Notable Books for Children list in 2001.

*Mary Downing Hahn: A former librarian and artist, Hahn often draws upon her life experiences to write novels for young teens. Her writing is widely praised for its realistic characterizations, well-paced plots, and relevant themes, and effective inclusion of frightening or mysterious elements. Although her books often include serious situations, such as the loss of a parent or the struggle to combine two families when parents re-marry, Hahn's critics single out her gentle humor and sympathetic portrayal of realistic child-characters and their problems as the source of her success. Her young adult novel *Here the Wind Blow* appeared in 2003.

*Syd Hoff: Hoff, who launched his career as a cartoonist in 1928, could easily be ranked as one of the most prolific authors, illustrators, and graphic humorists of the twentieth century. Hoff's work is characterized by simplicity, and he prefers to work in ink, washes, crayon, and watercolor, drawing upon the New York neighborhoods in which he grew up for the characters in his cartoons; however, his humor is not dependent upon cliché or stereotype. *Danny and the Dinosaur,* one of Hoff's earliest books for children, has been translated into half a dozen languages. With more than ten million copies sold, the book has become a classic in children's fare.

*Brian Jacques: Jacques takes as his heroes the small, gentle animals of nature and pits them against rapacious predators in epic fantasy tales of battle and quest, but this fantasy world has become incredibly real to the fans of the "Redwall" series, with over five million books in print. These fantasy novels feature a broad cast of anthropomorphized animals who follow the author's successful good-versus-evil formula that appeals to both young and older readers. 2002 saw the publication of *Triss,* the fifteenth "Redwall" novel.

Barbara Kerley: An author of nonfiction books for children, Kerley has drawn much critical attention since her account of nineteenth-century British artist Waterhouse Hawkins was published as *The Dinosaurs of Waterhouse Hawkins.* The work received a Notable Book citation from the American Library Association and was named an Outstanding Science Trade Book from the National Science Teachers Association. *A Cool Drink of Water* was published in 2002.

Lise Lunge-Larsen: Lunge-Larsen is known fondly as "The Troll Lady," for as a storyteller and author she has focused on the tales of her native Norway, which are replete with trolls and other fantastic creatures. Her 2001 work, *The Race of the Birkebeiners,* was named an American Library Association and *Los Angeles Times* notable book of the year.

*Barry Moser: Moser is an American artist, writer, engraver, designer, and publisher who is acclaimed for his dramatic wood engravings and luminous watercolors, as well as for his unique approach to retellings of classic folk and fairy tales. A prolific illustrator, he has provided the pictures for over 250 books for children and adults. Moser describes himself as a "booksmith" for his careful attention to all aspects of design and production. Viewing each book as a total work of art, Moser designs the whole volume: the cover, the type, the layout, the illustrations, and, for several books, the calligraphy. In 2002 he provided the artwork for Tony Johnston's *That Summer* and Margie Palatini's *Earthquack!*

sean o huigan: During the 1980s and early 1990s, Canadian poet and writer o huigin made a name for himself by writing popular children's poetry collections. The poet struck a cord with grade school children by writing about their concerns and interests in a humorous way. The majority of o huigin's poems deal with dark topics lightened with humor. Though most of o huigin's poems are short, his most celebrated work is the 1983 narrative poem *The Ghost Horse of the Mounties.* It was the first children's poetry book to receive the Canada Council Children's Literature Prize.

David Suzuki: Suzuki, an award-winning zoologist and geneticist, has become a major voice in Canada and across North America in popularizing science and in the battle to protect the environment. Moderator and host of several popular television and radio shows for the Canadian Broadcasting Corporation, Suzuki has become known internationally for his popular show *The Nature of Things,* which airs in over fifty countries. In addition to his academic duties and broadcast ventures, Suzuki also writes books for both children and adults, including the 2002 work *Good News for a Change.*

Carole Boston Weatherford: Weatherford received the Carter G. Woodson Book Award in 2001 for *The Sound that Jazz Makes,* a celebration in rhyme of American music and its roots in African-American history. Weatherford's short poems and the paintings of award-winning artist Eric Velasquez depict a musical journey from the drumbeats of Africa to the drumbeats of rap music in the streets of the city.

*Charlotte Zolotow: Zolotow has been a distinguished contributor to literature for children for nearly sixty years. She is the creator of approximately seventy works, mostly picture books for readers in the early primary grades; in addition, Zolotow is a poet and the compiler of two short story collections for young adults. She also is celebrated for her work in the field of publishing: as an editor at Harper & Row (now HarperCollins) for more than fifty years, Zolotow discovered and fostered the careers of many award-winning writers for young people.

Introduction

Something about the Author (*SATA*) is an ongoing reference series that examines the lives and works of authors and illustrators of books for children. *SATA* includes not only well-known writers and artists but also less prominent individuals whose works are just coming to be recognized. This series is often the only readily available information source on emerging authors and illustrators. You'll find *SATA* informative and entertaining, whether you are a student, a librarian, an English teacher, a parent, or simply an adult who enjoys children's literature.

What's Inside SATA

SATA provides detailed information about authors and illustrators who span the full time range of children's literature, from early figures like John Newbery and L. Frank Baum to contemporary figures like Judy Blume and Richard Peck. Authors in the series represent primarily English-speaking countries, particularly the United States, Canada, and the United Kingdom. Also included, however, are authors from around the world whose works are available in English translation. The writings represented in *SATA* include those created intentionally for children and young adults as well as those written for a general audience and known to interest younger readers. These writings cover the entire spectrum of children's literature, including picture books, humor, folk and fairy tales, animal stories, mystery and adventure, science fiction and fantasy, historical fiction, poetry and nonsense verse, drama, biography, and nonfiction.

Obituaries are also included in *SATA* and are intended not only as death notices but also as concise overviews of people's lives and work. Additionally, each edition features newly revised and updated entries for a selection of *SATA* listees who remain of interest to today's readers and who have been active enough to require extensive revisions of their earlier biographies.

Autobiography Feature

Beginning with Volume 103, *SATA* features two or more specially commissioned autobiographical essays in each volume. These unique essays, averaging about ten thousand words in length and illustrated with an abundance of personal photos, present an entertaining and informative first-person perspective on the lives and careers of prominent authors and illustrators profiled in *SATA*.

Two Convenient Indexes

In response to suggestions from librarians, *SATA* indexes no longer appear in every volume but are included in alternate (odd-numbered) volumes of the series, beginning with Volume 57.

SATA continues to include two indexes that cumulate with each alternate volume: the Illustrations Index, arranged by the name of the illustrator, gives the number of the volume and page where the illustrator's work appears in the current volume as well as all preceding volumes in the series; the Author Index gives the number of the volume in which a person's biographical sketch, autobiographical essay, or obituary appears in the current volume as well as all preceding volumes in the series.

These indexes also include references to authors and illustrators who appear in Gale's *Yesterday's Authors of Books for Children, Children's Literature Review,* and *Something about the Author Autobiography Series.*

Easy-to-Use Entry Format

Whether you're already familiar with the *SATA* series or just getting acquainted, you will want to be aware of the kind of information that an entry provides. In every *SATA* entry the editors attempt to give as complete a picture of the person's life and work as possible. A typical entry in *SATA* includes the following clearly labeled information sections:

- *PERSONAL:* date and place of birth and death, parents' names and occupations, name of spouse, date of marriage, names of children, educational institutions attended, degrees received, religious and political affiliations, hobbies and other interests.

- *ADDRESSES:* complete home, office, electronic mail, and agent addresses, whenever available.

- *CAREER:* name of employer, position, and dates for each career post; art exhibitions; military service; memberships and offices held in professional and civic organizations.

- *AWARDS, HONORS:* literary and professional awards received.

- *WRITINGS:* title-by-title chronological bibliography of books written and/or illustrated, listed by genre when known; lists of other notable publications, such as plays, screenplays, and periodical contributions.

- *ADAPTATIONS:* a list of films, television programs, plays, CD-ROMs, recordings, and other media presentations that have been adapted from the author's work.

- *WORK IN PROGRESS:* description of projects in progress.

- *SIDELIGHTS:* a biographical portrait of the author or illustrator's development, either directly from the biographee—and often written specifically for the *SATA* entry—or gathered from diaries, letters, interviews, or other published sources.

- *BIOGRAPHICAL AND CRITICAL SOURCES:* cites sources quoted in "Sidelights" along with references for further reading.

- *EXTENSIVE ILLUSTRATIONS:* photographs, movie stills, book illustrations, and other interesting visual materials supplement the text.

How a SATA Entry Is Compiled

A *SATA* entry progresses through a series of steps. If the biographee is living, the *SATA* editors try to secure information directly from him or her through a questionnaire. From the information that the biographee supplies, the editors prepare an entry, filling in any essential missing details with research and/or telephone interviews. If possible, the author or illustrator is sent a copy of the entry to check for accuracy and completeness.

If the biographee is deceased or cannot be reached by questionnaire, the *SATA* editors examine a wide variety of published sources to gather information for an entry. Biographical and bibliographic sources are consulted, as are book reviews, feature articles, published interviews, and material sometimes obtained from the biographee's family, publishers, agent, or other associates.

Entries that have not been verified by the biographees or their representatives are marked with an asterisk (*).

Contact the Editor

We encourage our readers to examine the entire *SATA* series. Please write and tell us if we can make *SATA* even more helpful to you. Give your comments and suggestions to the editor:

BY MAIL: Editor, *Something about the Author,* The Gale Group, 27500 Drake Rd., Farmington Hills, MI 48331-3535.

BY TELEPHONE: (800) 877-GALE

BY FAX: (248) 699-8054

Something about the Author Product Advisory Board

The editors of *Something about the Author* are dedicated to maintaining a high standard of excellence by publishing comprehensive, accurate, and highly readable entries on a wide array of writers for children and young adults. In addition to the quality of the content, the editors take pride in the graphic design of the series, which is intended to be orderly yet inviting, allowing readers to utilize the pages of *SATA* easily and with efficiency. Despite the longevity of the *SATA* print series, and the success of its format, we are mindful that the vitality of a literary reference product is dependent on its ability to serve its users over time. As literature, and attitudes about literature, constantly evolve, so do the reference needs of students, teachers, scholars, journalists, researchers, and book club members. To be certain that we continue to keep pace with the expectations of our customers, the editors of *SATA* listen carefully to their comments regarding the value, utility, and quality of the series. Librarians, who have firsthand knowledge of the needs of library users, are a valuable resource for us. The *Something about the Author* Product Advisory Board, made up of school, public, and academic librarians, is a forum to promote focused feedback about *SATA* on a regular basis. The nine-member advisory board includes the following individuals, whom the editors wish to thank for sharing their expertise:

- **Eva M. Davis,** Teen Services Librarian, Plymouth District Library, Plymouth, Michigan

- **Joan B. Eisenberg,** Lower School Librarian, Milton Academy, Milton, Massachusetts

- **Francisca Goldsmith,** Teen Services Librarian, Berkeley Public Library, Berkeley, California

- **Harriet Hagenbruch,** Curriculum Materials Center/Education Librarian, Axinn Library, Hofstra University, Hempstead, New York

- **Monica F. Irlbacher,** Young Adult Librarian, Middletown Thrall Library, Middletown, New York

- **Robyn Lupa,** Head of Children's Services, Jefferson County Public Library, Lakewood, Colorado

- **Eric Norton,** Head of Children's Services, McMillan Memorial Library, Wisconsin Rapids, Wisconsin

- **Victor L. Schill,** Assistant Branch Librarian/Children's Librarian, Harris County Public Library/Fairbanks Branch, Houston, Texas

- **Caryn Sipos,** Community Librarian, Three Creeks Community Library, Vancouver, Washington

Acknowledgments

Grateful acknowledgment is made to the following publishers, authors, and artists whose works appear in this volume.

ALLMAN, BARBARA. Allman, Barbara, photograph. David Gibb Photography. Reproduced by permission.

AVERY, GILLIAN (ELISE). All photographs reproduced by permission of Gillian Avery.

BALCAVAGE, DYNISE. Balcavage, Dynise, photograph by John Baptiste Gatti. Reproduced by permission.

CARBONE, ELISA LYNN. Barnes, Tim, illustrator. From a cover of *Sarah and the Naked Truth,* by Elisa Carbone. Dell Yearling Books, 2002. Reproduced by permission of Random House Children's Books, a division of Random House, Inc.

CARTER, ALDEN R(ICHARDSON). Guillette, Joseph, illustrator. From a jacket of *Crescent Moon,* by Alden R. Carter. Holiday House, 1999. Reproduced by permission./ Young, Dan, photographer. From a photograph in *I'm Tougher Than Asthma!* by Alden R. Carter and Siri M. Carter. Albert Whitman & Company, 1996. Photographs © 1996 by Dan Young. Reproduced by permission./ Young, Dan, photographer. From a cover of *Big Brother Dustin,* by Alden R. Carter. Albert Whitman & Company, 1997. Photographs copyright © 1997 by Dan Young. Reproduced by permission./ Carter, Alden R., photograph. Reproduced by permission.

CHOWN, MARCUS. Jacket of *Afterglow of Creation: From the Fireball to the Discovery of Cosmic Ripples,* by Marcus Chown. University Science Books, 1996. © 1996 by University Science Books. Reproduced by permission./ Jacket of *The Magic Furnace: The Search for the Origins of Atoms,* by Marcus Chown. Oxford University Press, Inc., 2001. Reproduced in the U.K. by permission of John Hawkins & Associates on behalf of the author, in the rest of the world by permission of Oxford University Press, Inc.

CITRA, BECKY. Citra, Becky, photograph. Reproduced by permission.

CREW, LINDA. Kaufman, Stuart, illustrator. From a jacket of *Children of the River,* by Linda Crew. Delacorte Press, 1989. Jacket illustration copyright © 1989 by Stuart Kaufman. Reproduced by permission of Dell Publishing, a division of Random House, Inc./ From a photograph in *Brides of Eden: A True Story Imagined,* by Linda Crew. HarperCollins, 2001. Photograph by the Benton County Historical Society & Museum. Reproduced by permission./ Crew, Linda, photograph by Warren Welch. Reproduced by permission of Linda Crew.

DEETER, CATHERINE. Deeter, Catherine, illustrator. From an illustration in *To Hell with Dying,* by Alice Walker. Harcourt Brace & Company, 1988. Illustrations © 1988 by Catherine Deeter. Reproduced by permission.

DRESCHER, JOAN E(LIZABETH). Drescher, Joan, illustrator. From an illustration in *Your Doctor, My Doctor* by Joan Drescher. Walker and Company, 1987. Illustrations © 1987 by Joan Drescher. Reproduced by permission.

FARLEY, CAROL (J.) Huang, Benrei, illustrator. From an illustration in *Mr. Pak Buys a Story*, by Carol Farley. Albert Whitman & Company, 1997. Illustrations © 1997 by Benrei Huang. Reproduced by permission.

FRASER, MARY ANN. Fraser, Mary Ann, illustrator. From an illustration in *Ten Mile Day and the Building of the Transcontinental Railroad,* by Mary Ann Fraser. Henry Holt & company, 1993. © 1993 by Mary Ann Fraser. Reproduced by permission./ Fraser, Mary Ann, photographer. From a photograph in *In Search of the Grand Canyon,* by Mary Ann Fraser. Henry Holt & Company, 1995. © 1995 by Mary Ann Fraser. Reproduced by permission.

FUSILLO, ARCHIMEDE. Fusillo, Archimede, photograph. Reproduced by permission.

GRIFFIN, KITTY. Wohnoutka, Mike, illustrator. From an illustration in *Cowboy Sam and Those Confounded Secrets,* by Kitty Griffin and Kathy Combs. Clarion Books, 2001. Illustrations © 2001 by Mike Wohnoutka. Reproduced by permission of Clarion Books/Houghton Mifflin Company. All rights reserved.

GRUPPER, JONATHAN. From a photograph in *Destination: Australia,* by Jonathan Grupper. National Geographic Society, 2000. Photograph by Australian Picture Library. © 2000 National Geographic Society. Reproduced by permission.

HIMLER, RONALD (NORBERT). Himler, Ronald, illustrator. From an illustration in *Sadako and the Thousand Paper Cranes,* by Eleanor Coerr. Dell Publishing, 1979. Illustrations copyright © 1979 by Ronald Himler. Reproduced in the U.K. by permission of the artist from Carol Bancroft & Friends, in the rest of the world by permission of G.P. Putnam's Sons, imprint of Penguin Putnam Books for Young Readers, a division of Penguin Putnam Inc./ Himler, Ronald, illustrator. From an illustration in *Why Not Lafayette?* by Jean Fritz. G. P. Putnam's Sons, 1999. Illustrations © 1999 by Ronald Himler. Reproduced by permission of G.P. Putnam's Sons, an imprint of Penguin Putnam Books for Young Readers, a division of Penguin Putnam Inc./ Himler, Ronald, illustrator. From an illustration in *The Caged Birds of Phnom Penh,* by Frederick Lipp. Holiday House, 2001. Illustrations © 2001 by Ronald Himler, Inc. Reproduced by permission./ Himler, Ronald, photograph. Reproduced by permission.

HISCOCK, BRUCE. Hiscock, Bruce, illustrator. From an illustration in *The Big Rivers: The Missouri, the Mississippi, and the Ohio,* by Bruce Hiscock. Atheneum Books for Young Readers, 1997. © 1997 Bruce Hiscock. Reproduced by permission of Atheneum Books for Young Readers, an imprint of Simon & Schuster Children's Publishing Division./ Hiscock, Bruce, illustrator. From an illustration in *Coyote and Badger: Desert Hunters of the Southwest,* by Bruce Hiscock. Caroline House/Boyds Mill Press, 2001. © 2001 Bruce Hiscock. Reproduced by permission.

HONEY, ELIZABETH. All photographs and illustrations reproduced by permission of Elizabeth Honey.

HOOSE, PHILLIP M. Tilley, Debbie, illustrator. From an illustration in *Hey, Little Ant,* by Phillip and Hannah Hoose. Bicycle Press, 1998. Illustrations © 1998 by Debbie Tilley. Reproduced by permission./ From a photograph in *We Were There, Too! Young People in U.S. History,* by Phillip Hoose. Melanie Kroupa Books, 2001. Photograph by New York State Historical Association. Reproduced by permission.

HOROWITZ, ANTHONY. Blackford, John, illustrator. From a cover of *Stormbreaker,* by Anthony Horowitz. Puffin Books, 2002. Cover illustration © 2001 by John Blackford. Reproduced by permission of Philomel Books, an imprint of Penguin Putnam Books for Young Readers, a division of Penguin Putnam Inc./ Horowitz, Anthony, photograph by Bart Beckers. © 2001 Bart Beckers. Reproduced by permission of the author and photographer.

JEFFERS, SUSAN. Jeffers, Susan, illustrator. From an illustration in *The Midnight Farm,* by Reeve Lindbergh. Dial Books for Young Readers, 1987. Illustrations © 1987 by Susan Jeffers. Reproduced in the U.K by permission of Susan Jeffers, the rest of the world by permission of Dial Books for Young Readers, an imprint of Penguin Putnam Books for Young Readers, a division of Penguin Putnam Inc./ Jeffers, Susan, illustrator. From an illustration in *Lassie Come-Home,* retold by Rosemary Wells. Henry Holt, 1995. Illustrations © 1995 by Susan Jeffers. Reprinted by permission of Henry Holt and Company, LLC./ Jeffers, Susan, illustrator. From an illustration in *McDuff Comes Home,* by Rosemary Wells. Hyperion Books for Children, 1997. Cover illustration copyright © 1997 by Susan Jeffers. Reproduced in the U.K. by permission of Susan Jeffers, in the rest of the world by permission of Hyperion Books for Children./ Jeffers, Susan, illustrator. From an illustration in *Rachel Field's Hitty: Her First Hundred Years,* retold by Rosemary Wells and Susan Jeffers. Simon & Schuster, 1999. Illustrations © 1999 by Susan Jeffers. Reproduced by permission of Atheneum Books for Young Readers, an imprint of Simon & Schuster Children's Publishing Division./ Jeffers, Susan, illustrator. From an illustration in *McDuff Saves the Day,* by Rosemary Wells. Hyperion Books for Children, 2002. Illustrations © 1997 by Susan Jeffers. Reproduced in the U.K. by permission of Susan Jeffers, in the rest of the world by permission of Hyperion Books for Children.

KALMAN, MAIRA. Kalman, Maira, illustrator. From a jacket of *Next Stop Grand Central,* by Maira Kalman. G. P. Putnam's Sons, 1999. Jacket art © 1999 by Maira Kalman. Reproduced by permission of G.P. Putnam's Sons, a division of Penguin Young Readers Group, a member of Penguin Group (USA) Inc./ Kalman, Maira, photograph. Reproduced by permission.

LAWLOR, LAURIE. Fisher, Cynthia, illustrator. From an illustration in *The Worst Kid Who Ever Lived on Eighth Avenue,* by Laurie Lawlor. Holiday House, 1998. Illustrations © 1998 by Cynthia Fisher. Reproduced by permission.

LEVIN, BETTY. Levin, Betty, photograph by Jill Paton Walsh. Reproduced by permission of Betty Levin.

MACAULAY, DAVID (ALEXANDER). Macaulay, David, illustrator. From an illustration in *Mill,* by David Macaulay. Houghton Mifflin, 1983. © 1983 by David Macaulay. Reproduced by permission./ Macaulay, David, illustrator. From an illustration in *Building the Book Cathedral,* by David Macaulay. Houghton Mifflin, 1999. © 1999 by David Macaulay. Reproduced by permission./ Macaulay, David, illustrator. From an illustration in *Building Big*, by David Macaulay. Houghton Mifflin, 2000. © 2000 by David Macaulay. Reproduced by permission./ Macaulay, David, illustrator. From an illustration in *Angelo,* by David Macaulay. Houghton Mifflin, 2002. © 2002 by David Macaulay. Reproduced by permission.

MAYER, MERCER. Mayer, Mercer, illustrator. From an illustration in *The Great Brain,* by John D. Fitzgerald. Dial Press, 1967. Illustration copyright © 1967 Mercer Mayer. Reproduced by permission of Dial Books for Young Readers, an imprint of Penguin Putnam Books for Young Readers, a division of Penguin Putnam Inc./ From an illustration in *There's a Nightmare in My Closet,* by Mercer Mayer. Dial Books for Young Readers, 1968. Copyright © 1968 by Mercer Mayer. All rights reserved. Reproduced by permission of Dial Books for Young Readers, an imprint of Penguin Putnam Books for Young Readers, a division of Penguin Putnam Inc.

MCLERRAN, ALICE. Morin, Paul, illustrator. From an illustration in *The Ghost Dance,* by Alice McLerran. Clarion Books, 1995. Illustrations © 1995 by Paul Morin. Reproduced by permission Clarion Books/Houghton Mifflin Company./ Elwell, Tristan, illustrator. From a jacket of *Dragonfly,* by Alice McLerran. Absey & Company, 2000. Jacket illustration © 2000 by Tristan Elwell. Reproduced by permission.

SOMETHING ABOUT THE AUTHOR

ALLMAN, Barbara 1950-

Personal

Born August 7, 1950, in Detroit, MI; daughter of Robert (a sales manager) and Mary (a homemaker) DeFazio; married John Allman (a health care consultant). *Education:* Attended Michigan State University, 1968-70; Oakland University, B.A. (elementary education), 1972, M.A. (teaching), 1978. *Hobbies and other interests:* Singing in a choral group, reading with children at a local elementary school.

Addresses

Home—P.O. Box 1088, Jacksonville, OR 97530. *E-mail*—b.a.reader@barbaraallman.com.

Career

Jim Thorpe Elementary School, Sterling Heights, MI, teacher, 1972-78; Warren Consolidated Schools, Warren, MI, language arts consultant, 1979-82; Frank Schaffer Publications, Torrance, CA, editor, 1984-93; freelance writer, 1993—. Member of the board of directors, Friends of the Jacksonville Library, 2002.

Member

International Reading Association, National Council for the Social Studies, Society of Children's Book Writers and Illustrators, Authors Guild, Music Educators National Conference.

Writings

Teddy Bear, Strong and Healthy, illustrated by Sue Ryono, Frank Schaffer Publications (Palos Verdes Estates, CA), 1985.

Letter and Number Reversals: Grades K-3, illustrated by Marlene Albright, Frank Schaffer Publications (Palos Verdes Estates, CA), 1987.

Maps, Charts and Graphs: Grades 1-2, Frank Schaffer Publications (Palos Verdes Estates, CA), 1988.

Reading Puzzles and Games: Grades 1-2, illustrated by Marlene McAuley, Frank Schaffer Publications (Palos Verdes Estates, CA), 1988.

Reading Puzzles and Games: Duplicating Masters, illustrated by Marlene McAuley, Frank Schaffer Publications (Palos Verdes Estates, CA), 1988.

Famous Black Americans: Grades 1-2, illustrated by Mark Mason, Frank Schaffer Publications (Torrance, CA), 1988.

Prefixes, illustrated by Mark Mason, Frank Schaffer Publications (Torrance, CA), 1988.

Reading and Writing Spanish, illustrated by Sue Ryono, Frank Schaffer Publications (Torrance, CA), 1989.

(With Marsha Elyn Jurca and Peggy Haynes) *Children's Authors and Illustrators,* Volume 3, Frank Schaffer Publications (Torrance, CA), Volume 1, 1991, Volumes 2-3, 1992.

Create with Clay, Instructional Fair (Grand Rapids, MI), 1996.

Create with Paint, Instructional Fair (Grand Rapids, MI), 1996.

Bible Story Activities, Grace Publications (Torrance, CA), 1996.

Barbara Allman

Create with Puppets and Props, Instructional Fair (Grand Rapids, MI), 1996.

Consonants, Frank Schaffer Publications (Torrance, CA), 1996.

Vowels, Frank Schaffer Publications (Torrance, CA), 1996.

Blends, Digraphs and More, Frank Schaffer Publications (Torrance, CA), 1996.

Her Piano Sang: A Story about Clara Schumann, illustrated by Shelly O. Haas, Carolrhoda Books (Minneapolis, MN), 1997.

(Reteller) Robert Louis Stevenson, *Treasure Island,* illustrated by Tani Brooks Johnson, Frank Schaffer Publications (Torrance, CA), 1997.

Social Studies Made Simple, Frank Schaffer Publications (Torrance, CA), 1997.

Developing Character When It Counts, Grades K-1: A Program for Teaching Character in the Classroom, Frank Schaffer, Publications (Torrance, CA), 1999.

Developing Character When It Counts, Grades 2-3: A Program for Teaching Character in the Classroom, Frank Schaffer Publications (Torrance, CA), 1999.

Language Arts Puzzles and Games: A Workbook for Ages 4-6, illustrated by Larry Nolte, Lowell House (Los Angeles, CA), 1999.

A World in Focus: A Unique Text for Social Studies: Central and South America, Blackbirch Press (Woodbridge, CT), 2000.

Dance of the Swan: A Story about Anna Pavlova, illustrated by Shelly O. Haas, Carolrhoda Books (Minneapolis, MN), 2001.

Editor of *Schooldays,* 1984-93; contributor to *Chicken Soup for the Kid's Soul,* Health Communications (Deerfield Beach, FL), 1998, *Let's Play and Learn,* Instructional Fair (Grand Rapids, MI), 1999, *Dance Teacher,* Lifestyle Ventures (New York, NY), 2002.

Sidelights

Barbara Allman told *SATA:* "I am a freelance writer specializing in educational materials and nonfiction for children. My first career was as an elementary teacher and reading consultant in schools in Michigan. I moved to Los Angeles in 1983 and became the editor of *Schooldays,* a magazine of creative ideas for elementary teachers.

"I have written two biographies for middle-grade readers—*Dance of the Swan: A Story about Anna Pavlova* and *Her Piano Sang: A Story about Clara Schumann.* I am currently working on two more. *Her Piano Sang* was selected by the Library of Congress to be published in Braille. I believe biographies make good reading for children because the genre can help children discover what's important in life. The more children learn about people of worth and achievement, the better they come to know themselves. In reading about the lives of people who have made a difference, children come to understand their own potential.

"I have also authored more than seventy teacher's guides, student texts, and activity books, including a supplemental social studies text for fifth grade, *A World in Focus: Central and South America.* My short story titled, 'Grandpa's Bees,' appears in the best-selling book, *Chicken Soup for the Kid's Soul.*

"In writing biographies, I am able to combine three of my main interests: education, writing, and the arts. *Dance of the Swan* tells the story of Anna Pavlova, considered by many to be the greatest ballet dancer ever to grace a stage. With the zeal of a missionary, Pavlova, the petite Russian ballerina, introduced the soaring beauty of classical dance to people the world over.

"As an eight-year-old piano student, I was fascinated by the stories of composers in my piano book. I read every composer's biography I could find in the children's room of the East Detroit Public Library and wondered why there were no biographies written about women composers. Later in life, when I discovered that there *still* were no biographies of women composers written for children, I wrote one about Clara Schumann—*Her Piano Sang.*"

Allman's early interest in the piano came from her mother, whose piano playing saved her sanity when the clamor of seven children (Allman is the oldest) became too much. "[Taking piano lessons] was my idea because my mom played the piano. I always thought that was the greatest thing," Allman told Elisabeth Deffner in the *Independent.* An early interest in biographies also set the stage for Allman's own first biography, *Her Piano Sang.* In this biography for middle-grade readers, Allman brings into focus the life and times of Clara (Wieck) Schumann, whose musical genius—she was performing as a virtuoso at the age of nine—found expression despite the strictures of an overbearing father, a mentally ill husband, and the tasks of running and supporting a household. In addition, the conventions of the era demanded that she give up her career upon marriage, which Schumann refused to do. Critics noted that though more is known about Clara Schumann's husband, composer Robert Schumann, "it is refreshing to read about the Schumanns from Clara's perspective," remarked Mollie Bynum in *School Library Journal.* Likewise, a contributor to *Kirkus Reviews* dubbed *Her Piano Sang* "a fine introduction to a strong, disciplined artist."

Classical music is the common thread between *Her Piano Sang* and *Dance of the Swan,* Allman's next biography for young people. In this biography of the famous Russian ballerina of the nineteenth century—some claim, the most famous ballerina of all time—Allman focuses on the ethereal woman's determination to bring ballet to the four corners of the earth. Writing in *School Library Journal,* Carol Schene called *Dance of the Swan* "clearly written and upbeat," and predicted that "this sensitive portrayal will inspire young readers."

Biographical and Critical Sources

PERIODICALS

Horn Book Guide, fall, 2001, review of *Dance of the Swan: A Story about Anna Pavlova.*

Independent (Irvine, CA), July 18, 1997, Elisabeth Deffner, "Mary DeFazio and Barbara Allman: Mom Inspired Daughter's Writing," pp. 2, 11.

Jacksonville Review Monthly (Jacksonville, OR), October-November, 2001, "Local Author Writes Biography of World-Renowned Ballerina," p. 13.

Kirkus Reviews, December 1, 1996, review of *Her Piano Sang: A Story about Clara Schumann.*

School Library Journal, January, 1997, Mollie Bynum, review of *Her Piano Sang;* July, 2001, Carol Schene, review of *Dance of the Swan.*

OTHER

Barbara Allman Web Site, http://www.barbaraallman.com/ (January 29, 2002).

*   *   *

ASHERON, Sara
See MOORE, Lilian

*   *   *

AUSTIN, Patricia 1950-

Personal

Born November 13, 1950; daughter of Robert L. (a purchasing agent) and June (a singer and library clerk; maiden name Steffen) Austin. *Education:* Agnes Scott College, B.A. (philosophy), 1972; University of New Hampshire, M.A.T., 1973; University of New Orleans, Ph.D. (education), 1987. *Politics:* Democrat. *Hobbies and other interests:* Reading, gardening, tennis.

Addresses

Office—University of New Orleans, Dept. of Curriculum and Instruction, New Orleans, LA 70148. *E-mail*—paustin@uno.edu.

Career

Elementary teacher in Louisiana, Mississippi, and Georgia; Tulane University, New Orleans, LA, assistant professor, 1991-93; University of New Orleans, New Orleans, LA, associate professor of children's literature, 1994—. Coeditor of *Journal of Children's Literature,* a publication of the Children's Literature Assembly of the National Council of Teachers of English, 2000-03.

Member

International Reading Association, National Council of Teachers of English.

Awards, Honors

Muse Medallion, Cat Writer's Association, for *The Cat Who Loved Mozart.*

Writings

The Cat Who Loved Mozart, illustrated by Henri Sorenson, Holiday House (New York, NY), 2001.

Work in Progress

Research on the role of discussion in the classroom, particularly with gifted readers.

Sidelights

Patricia Austin told *SATA:* "For as long as I can remember, stories have been my passion. Some of my favorite books as a child were *The Secret Garden, The Story of Helen Keller,* and biographies about composers. The first piece that I remember writing, at about six years old, was inspired by Charlotte Steiner's "Kiki" series. From the age of nine, I wanted to be a writer, which I recorded for posterity in my *This Is Me* journal. I had a poem published in the *National Poetry Press* in high school and edited the literary journal at Agnes Scott College, but that's as far as my writing dreams seemed to go. I continued to write, but mostly for my own pleasure.

"*The Cat Who Loved Mozart* was inspired by my cat, Dusty, who did indeed love classical music. Dusty was a foundling who followed me home after much cajoling. He did not get along with Musette, my other cat, and resisted my overtures to lavish him with attention. He seemed to have only one hobby—eating. He would jump on the kitchen counter, scrounge scraps in the drain, and try to get into the refrigerator. That is, until I discovered that he loved music. He hopped up beside me whenever I played the piano. Right away, I knew I had a story. I first wrote the manuscript back in 1977, but I did what I did with all my writing—stuffed it in a file drawer. I revived and revised it periodically over the years, illustrating it and creating a book in 1989 when I was working with a group of gifted students. Since I had assigned them to write a book, I figured I'd create one too. I submitted the work for publication and received a bit of positive feedback. I deep-sixed my drawings and continued to submit the manuscript. The tenth submission in 1996 to Holiday House was the charm, and I sold the book in 1997, exactly twenty years since I'd penned the first draft. The answer to the question often posed to writers—how long does it take you to write a book?—can be a bit deceptive. How much time a manuscript languishes in a file is another question altogether.

"For years as an elementary teacher, my happiest moments with my students were spent reading to them. Now I teach children's literature to teachers, and still the best part of my job is sharing picture books."

Biographical and Critical Sources

PERIODICALS

Booklist, May 1, 2001, Gillian Engberg, review of *The Cat Who Loved Mozart,* p. 1688.
School Library Journal, June, 2001, Be Astengo, review of *The Cat Who Loved Mozart,* p. 100.*

*   *   *

AVERY, Gillian (Elise) 1926-

Personal

Born September 30, 1926; daughter of Norman Bates (an estate agent) and Grace Elise (Dunn) Avery; married Anthony Oliver John Cockshut (a university lecturer and writer), August 25, 1952; children: Ursula Mary Elise. *Education:* Attended schools in England. *Religion:* Anglican.

Addresses

Home—32 Charlbury Rd., Oxford, England.

Career

Writer and editor. Worked as a reporter for the *Surrey Mirror,* Surrey, England, during the mid-1940s; secretary at George Newnes (publishers), working on *Chambers's Encyclopaedia,* during the late 1940s; Oxford University Press, Oxford, England, assistant to the illustrations editor, 1950-54.

Awards, Honors

Guardian award and Carnegie Medal runner-up, 1972, for *A Likely Lad.*

Writings

The Warden's Niece, illustrated by Dick Hart, Collins (London, England), 1957, Penguin (New York, NY), 1963, published as *Maria Escapes,* illustrated by Scott Snow, Simon & Schuster (New York, NY), 1992.
Trespassers at Charlcote, illustrated by Dick Hart, Collins (London, England), 1958.
James without Thomas, illustrated by John Verney, Collins (London, England), 1959.
The Elephant War, illustrated by John Verney, Collins (London, England), 1960, Holt, Rinehart and Winston (New York, NY), 1971.
To Tame a Sister, illustrated by John Verney, Collins (London, England), 1961, Van Nostrand (New York, NY), 1964.
The Greatest Gresham, illustrated by John Verney, Collins (London, England), 1962.
The Peacock House, illustrated by John Verney, Collins (London, England), 1963.
The Italian Spring, illustrated by John Verney, Collins (London, England), 1964, Holt, Rinehart and Winston (New York, NY), 1972, published as *Maria's Italian Spring,* illustrated by Scott Snow, Simon & Schuster (New York, NY), 1993.
Call of the Valley, illustrated by Laszlo Acs, Collins (London, England), 1966, Holt, Rinehart and Winston (New York, NY), 1968.
Ellen and the Queen, illustrated by Krystyna Turska, Hamish Hamilton (London, England), 1971, Thomas Nelson (Nashville, TN), 1974.
Ellen's Birthday, illustrated by Krystyna Turska, Hamish Hamilton (London, England), 1971.
A Likely Lad, illustrated by Faith Jaques, Collins (London, England), 1971, Holt, Rinehart and Winston (New York, NY), 1971.
Jemima and the Welsh Rabbit, illustrated by John Lawrence, Hamish Hamilton (London, England), 1972.
Gillian Avery's Book of the Strange and Odd, (nonfiction), illustrated by Michael Jackson, Kestrel Books (London, England), 1975.
Freddie's Feet, illustrated by Krystyna Turska, Hamish Hamilton (London, England), 1976.
Huck and Her Time Machine, Collins (London, England), 1977.
Mouldy's Orphan, illustrated by Faith Jaques, Collins (London, England), 1978.
Sixpence!, illustrated by Antony Maitland, Collins (London, England), 1979.

EDITOR

Juliana Horatia Ewing, *A Flat Iron for a Farthing,* Faith Press (London, England), 1959.
Juliana Horatia Ewing, *Jan of the Windmill,* Faith Press (London, England), 1960.
The Sapphire Treasury of Stories for Boys and Girls, Gollancz (London, England), 1960.
In the Window Seat: A Selection of Victorian Stories, illustrated by Susan Einzig, Oxford University Press (New York, NY), 1960.
Annie Keary, *Father Phim,* Faith Press (London, England), 1962.
Unforgettable Journeys, illustrated by John Verney, Gollancz (London, England), 1965.

Margaret Roberts, *Banning and Blessing,* Gollancz (London, England), 1967.

Andrew Lang, *The Gold of Fairnilee and Other Stories,* Gollancz (London, England), 1967.

Juliana Horatia Ewing, *A Great Emergency, and a Very Ill-Tempered Family,* Gollancz (London, England), 1967.

School Remembered, illustrated by John Verney, Gollancz (London, England), 1967, Funk (New York, NY), 1968.

Charlotte Yonge, *Village Children,* Gollancz (London, England), 1967.

Brenda, *Froggy's Little Brother,* Gollancz (London, England), 1968.

Mary Louisa Molesworth, *My New Home,* illustrated by L. Leslie Brooke, Gollancz (London, England), 1968.

Brenda, Mrs. Gatty, and Frances Hodgson Burnett, *Victoria-Bess and Others,* Gollancz (London, England), 1968, published as *Victorian Doll Stories,* Schocken (New York, NY), 1969.

G. E. Farrow, *The Wallypug of Why,* illustrated by Harry Furniss, Gollancz (London, England), 1968.

The Life and Adventures of Lady Anne, illustrated by F. D. Bedford, Gollancz (London, England), 1969.

Margaret Roberts, *Stephanie's Children,* Gollancz (London, England), 1969.

E. V. Lucas, *Anne's Terrible Good Nature and Other Stories for Children,* Gollancz (London, England), 1970.

Annie Keary, *The Rival Kings,* Gollancz (London, England), 1970.

Red Letter Days, illustrated by Krystyna Turska, Hamish Hamilton (London, England), 1971.

(With Julia Briggs) *Children and Their Books: A Celebration of the Work of Iona and Peter Opie,* Oxford University Press (New York, NY), 1989.

The Everyman Anthology of Poetry for Children, David Campbell Publishers (London, England), 1994, Knopf (New York, NY), 1994.

Russian Fairy Tales, David Campbell Publishers (London, England), 1994, Knopf (New York, NY), 1995.

Charles Dickens, *Holiday Romance and Other Writings for Children,* J. M. Dent (London, England), 1995, Charles E. Tuttle Company (Rutland, VT), 1995.

(With Kimberley Reynolds) *Representations of Childhood Death,* Macmillan (London, England), 1999, St. Martin's Press (New York, NY), 1999.

OTHER

Mrs. Ewing, Bodley Head (London, England), 1961, H. Z. Walck (New York, NY), 1964.

(With Angela Bull) *Nineteenth-Century Children: Heroes and Heroines in English Children's Stories, 1780-1900,* Hodder & Stoughton (London, England), 1965.

Victorian People: In Life and in Literature, Collins (London, England), 1970, Holt, Rinehart and Winston (New York, NY), 1970.

The Echoing Green: Memories of Regency and Victorian Youth, Collins (London, England), 1974, Viking (New York, NY), 1974.

Childhood's Pattern: A Study of the Heroes and Heroines of Children's Fiction, 1770-1950, Hodder & Stoughton (London, England), 1975.

The Lost Railway (fiction), Collins (London, England), 1980.

Onlookers (fiction), Collins (London, England), 1983.

The Best Type of Girl: A History of Girls' Independent Schools, Andre Deutsch (London, England), 1991.

Behold the Child: American Children and Their Books, 1621-1922, Bodley Head (London, England), 1994, John Hopkins University Press (Baltimore, MD), 1995.

(With Marcus A. McCorison) *Origins and English Predecessors of the New England Primer,* American Antiquarian Society (Worcester, MA), 1999.

Cheltenham Ladies: A History of Cheltenham Ladies' College, 1853-2003, James & James (London, England), 2003.

Contributor to volumes such as *The Eleanor Farjeon Book,* Hamish Hamilton, 1966; *Winter's Tales for Children No. 2,* Macmillan, 1966; *Rudyard Kipling,* Weidenfeld & Nicholson, 1972; *Allsorts 5,* Macmillan, 1972; *Jubilee Jackanory,* BBC, 1977; and *Guardian Angels,* Viking Kestrel, 1987. Also contributor of reviews and articles to periodicals, including *London Review of Books, Times Educational Supplement, Review of English Studies, Times Literary Supplement,* and *Horn Book Magazine.*

Sidelights

Gillian Avery has been writing children's novels since the 1950s. Feeling an affinity with children of the Victorian era, she sets most of her work in that period. Avery's most popular books include *The Warden's Niece, The Elephant War,* and *A Likely Lad;* the last garnered her the *Guardian* Award and was a runner-up for the prestigious Carnegie Medal. She has also edited many books for children, including editions of the works of several Victorian children's authors, and has written and edited adult works about children in the Victorian period.

Avery grew up in the town of Redhill, Surrey, England. Although reading was not encouraged by her parents, Avery read Victorian stories and Arthur Mee's *Children's Encyclopedia* as she was growing up. When Avery left school at sixteen, she decided to pursue a career in journalism. In order to learn the skills she would need, such as shorthand and typing, she enrolled in a secretarial school. She did not do well there, and when the bombing of London during World War II necessitated her departure for the safer countryside, Avery left the school, never to return. Her father then found her a temporary position on the *Surrey Mirror,* a newspaper edited by one of his acquaintances. When World War II ended, so did Avery's job, so she found work with publishing firms. She began as a secretary for the illustrations editor at the George Newnes firm, where she worked on *Chambers's Encyclopaedia,* then with Oxford University Press, where she served as the assistant to the illustrations editor of the *Oxford Junior Encyclopedia,* learning the basics of picture research, something to be of great assistance when she needs to find illustrations for her own historical books. While working at Oxford, Avery was introduced to Anthony Oliver John Cockshut, the friend of one of her childhood neighbors. In 1952 she married Cockshut, who was an Oxford scholar interested in the Victorian period.

Avery "came to write," as she put it, when her husband's fellowship at Oxford ended, necessitating a move to Manchester where he got a job as a schoolteacher. Avery disliked Manchester's urban dreariness, and, extremely nostalgic for the pleasant walks of Oxford, she began writing a book about Oxford. This became *The Warden's Niece,* which, after a few rejections and some rewriting, was published in 1957.

Avery continued to write children's novels, mostly with Victorian settings, throughout the 1960s and 70s. *The Elephant War* featured some of the characters from *The Warden's Niece,* involved in a campaign to save a London Zoo elephant from being sold to P. T. Barnum's circus. *The Greatest Gresham* recalled aspects of Avery's own childhood. *A Likely Lad,* set in Manchester, was inspired by anecdotes told by her father-in-law about his Lancashire relations. An interesting exception to Avery's rule of Victorian settings was *Huck and Her Time Machine,* about a modern-day family able to live the lives of their Victorian ancestors through the use of a time machine.

Though she continued to write occasional stories for younger readers, this was Avery's last full-length novel for children, and she began to devote herself to the history of children's books. Since she habitually set her novels in the Victorian period, she had often been asked to write prefaces to works by Victorian children's authors, and in 1960 began to work on a full-length study of these. She was then living in Manchester and research at the libraries with substantial holdings of this material was difficult. In the resultant *Nineteenth-Century Children* (1965) she limited herself to fiction from 1780-1900, and worked largely from books she herself owned. Back in Oxford with all the resources of the Bodleian Library available, she completely recast the book using the same theme—the changing values of writers and their concept of the ideal child. This new work was published in 1975 as *Childhood's Pattern: A Study of the Heroes and Heroines of Children's Fiction 1770-1950.*

Avery wrote no fiction after 1983, but concentrated on the history of childhood and of juvenile books. In 1982 she was invited to Gainesville, Florida to make the presentation speech at the opening of the Baldwin Library, the huge collection of British and American children's books given to the University of Florida by Ruth Baldwin. Browsing among these she was fascinated by the nineteenth-century American books and amazed that apparently no one had yet attempted a full history of the development of these. After repeated visits to the Baldwin Library and other American research centers—the American Antiquarian Society in Worcester, Massachusetts being particularly important for early material—*Behold the Child: American Children and Their Books, 1621-1922* was published in 1994. Mary

M. Burns, reviewing in *Horn Book Magazine,* called the book "more than a chronology" and "a compendium of titles and authors." Burns described the work as a "unique resource" that "will set standards for years to come." Anne Lundin, reviewing in *Library Quarterly,* called *Behold the Child* "a monumental, groundbreaking work" with an "intimate" style, and one that "reads familiarly rather than formally."

During the twelve years that this book took shape, Avery had been teaching a course on the history of children's books at the annual summer school at Christ Church, Oxford, organized under the joint aegis of Oxford and Florida State universities. It was a rewarding experience, and American participants introduced her to many of their own favorite books. Between 1986 and 1988 she had also helped to organize the Opie Appeal to secure for the Bodleian Library Iona and Peter Opie's important collection of 20,000 historical children's books. These arrived in Oxford in 1988 and she and other volunteers unpacked, sorted and shelved them. In 1989 she and Julia Briggs edited *Children and Their Books,* a collection of essays to celebrate the work of the Opies, which raised more money for the appeal. *The Best Type of Girl* (1991), a history of English girls' schools, was followed by a full length history of one of these, Cheltenham Ladies' College—*Cheltenham Ladies* (2003).

Biographical and Critical Sources

BOOKS

Carpenter, Humphrey, and Mari Prichard, *The Oxford Companion to Children's Literature,* Oxford University Press (New York, NY), 1984.

Doyle, Brian, *The Who's Who of Children's Literature,* Schocken (New York, NY), 1968.

Twentieth-Century Children's Writers, fourth edition, St. James Press (Detroit, MI), 1995.

PERIODICALS

Bulletin of the Center of Children's Books, September, 1975.

Growing Point, May, 1985.

Guardian, March 23, 1972.

Horn Book Magazine, August, 1968; April, 1975; July-August, 1993, Ethel L. Heins, review of *Maria's Italian Spring,* p. 457; July-August, 1996, Mary M. Burns, review of *Behold the Child,* p. 483.

Junior Bookshelf, October, 1977.

Library Quarterly, January, 1996, Anne Lundin, review of *Behold the Child,* pp. 96-98.

London Review of Books, August 15, 1991.

New Statesman, November 3, 1967.

New Yorker, December 14, 1968.

Times Literary Supplement, November 26, 1964; March 25, 1977; July 7, 1978.

Washington Post, October 27, 1974.

*   *   *

Autobiography Feature

Gillian Avery

When I was fifteen I wrote my memoirs. "Seated in the firelight, I thought of my childhood whose magic casements had just closed," the introduction says portentously. Written in a round hand at the back of an old school exercise book, crammed up against recitation pieces—poems by Kipling, de la Mare, and Henry Newbolt copied out in an even rounder hand—these forty-odd pages now strike me as very childlike. It is not just the grandiose style, it is the preoccupation with play. Children play with a single-mindedness that borders on fanaticism and I had not then left that behind; I was recalling those games with the same intensity as I had once played them. Looking at that exercise book with its dark blue covers (blue for my schoolhouse, St. Andrew's; St. Patrick's had green books, St. George's had gold) I can, moreover, even now recapture a lot of that intensity and excitement; in many ways those years are far more vivid than much of my subsequent life. And I still have anxiety dreams about being late for school; I still wake on Wednesdays congratulating myself that it is not double geography that morning.

What is curious about the memoirs is that they only record the games that we played with the children next door; there is nothing about my parents (they just have unnamed parts as "irate adults" who make a stand when the games become too noisy), nothing about the school about which my feelings were strong and ambivalent. (I hated it because even as an adolescent I knew that the education it was giving me was deplorable and because I resented the fear that we were made to feel so often, but I loved the buildings and the grounds.) Nor would you ever guess that it was wartime when I was writing, 1941, with the London blitz only just behind us and our own house an air-raid post (the room where I was writing, indeed, was where the air-raid warden on duty spent the night). For World War II affected my brothers and me and our school friends very little; our fathers were too old to fight, our siblings too young. We knew that England would win the war since England always did, and our lives proceeded with the same tranquillity as they had in the decade before. Undoubtedly one had to carry one's gas mask everywhere, bumping uncomfortably on one's back in its cardboard box; one spent a lot of time in air-raid shelters, there was food rationing, and much talk of evacuees. But in many ways life was far safer than today—a fact which is perhaps best illustrated by the instructions that our elders gave us if we were caught away from home when an air-raid warning

Gillian Avery with brother Duncan on Christmas, 1929

sounded. We were to knock immediately on the door of the nearest house and ask if we could shelter until we heard the all-clear. There was no thought then of dangerous strangers or child molesters; adults were benevolent, and the world (except for the unfortunate fact of Nazi Germany) was improving all the time, leaving injustice, misgovernment, and inhumanity behind as things that were recorded in history books but had no part in the present.

This tranquillity and calm optimism, so unimaginable now, was an extraordinary phenomenon of English middle-class childhood in the first decades of this century. All that was unpleasant was concealed from us. We were not encouraged to read newspapers, and the *Children's Newspaper,* which I thought then and still think suffocatingly dull, mostly carried articles about the greatness of the British Empire, the great power for good of Baden-Powell and his Boy Scout movement, and how the League of Nations was saving the world from future war. News items in the *Children Newspaper* were always bland; a headline "New Troubles for Ireland" referred to nothing worse than an outbreak of weevil damage. The threatening shadow that Hitler was throwing over Europe did not reach the young in the comfortable Surrey town where I was growing up. Thus when my father said to me on 15 September 1938, "Mr. Chamberlain is flying to Germany. There may be war," I was dumbfounded. We were on holiday in Somerset, and I was walking with him through a thistly field down to the sea when he suddenly and without any previous warning made this statement.

I was twelve then, about to be thirteen in two weeks, and I vividly remember my feelings of outrage and horror. Wars belonged to history; they were not for now. "The War," also called "the war to end all wars," was the 1914–18 war which ended eight years before I was born, though it might have been eight hundred so remote did it seem. That war did take many by surprise, but by 1938 most perceptive people had long realized that conflict with the Hitler regime would ultimately be inevitable. My father had fought in that first war; he had spent a brief period in Ireland but most of the time he had been in the trenches of Flanders and northern France during the terrible, protracted slaughter that lasted for four years. There were relics of those years in the attic—the camp bed and canvas wash basin, a saddle, his riding boots, his officer's Sam Browne

belt, but without a trace of the fouled mud that must have clung to them when they were in use. And when I took his sleeping bag to Guide camps it never occurred to me to think that this had been through the trenches too; that his adoring mother and sister must have ordered the very best that money could buy (and probably more than they could afford) to try to make a waterlogged, rat-infested dugout bearable. His dressing room was hung three deep with photographs of the Queen's Royal West Surrey Regiment at war and in peace, and the regimental history by his chair in the sitting room carried pictures of the battlefields in northern France, sombre and derelict, full of mud, blasted tree stumps, shattered villages. When he said, "There may be war," it was that landscape that I saw.

My father spoke little about his experiences, and then only about comic or domestic episodes, about the piebald horse who had been trained in a circus and had disconcerting habits, about "Nevins's birthdays"—Nevins being a happy-go-lucky friend who insisted on celebrating birthdays however unsuitable the setting. His account of shaving in his tea was the nearest he got to the horror of what he had really been through, though it was my mother's description of wartime food, and in particular the black bread, that moved us to suppose that war must be truly

Gillian and Duncan with a friend, on a holiday in Devon, 1937

dreadful. Years later I came across the diary he kept when
he first joined up. It was very laconic, but what ran through
almost every entry during his training period and the days
that led up to his first exposure to bombardment, fighting,
and death was his fear of being afraid, and finally his
exultation when, under fire at last, he discovered that he
could bear it.

So many were killed that eventually when fighting
stopped it was he, with the temporary rank of colonel, who
brought the regiment back to its Surrey depot town. There
is a photograph of him on horseback at the head of the
marching men. That, you might say, was the supreme
moment of his life; everything after that was anti-climatic.
He wanted above all else to stay on as a professional
soldier, not because he was a warlike man but because of
his pride in being part of a regiment with a long and
splendid history, and because he enjoyed the male camaraderie and above all the stature that being an army officer
gave him. His family was a very modest one (his own
father had had a small and unsuccessful printing firm), and
in those days the armed services usually drew their officers
from a rather higher class. But there was no permanent
room for him in the regular army. In spite of all his efforts
he found himself after a year of peacetime soldiering back
in civilian life, and working as an estate agent, a member of
an august London firm which specialized in the management of the estates of wealthy and aristocratic clients. My
father's army background went down well with these; some
of them indeed made a personal friend of him, but, like his
own father, he never prospered and never advanced. Life
was always a struggle, a hand-to-mouth affair; in the effort
to keep pace with the bills he had no energy left to make
plans for the future.

Apart from the army, the thing that aroused emotion in
him was Scotland. His mother was a Scotswoman from
Aberdeen, but it was not Aberdeen that he talked about so
much as Ayton, the Berwickshire village where his uncle
had been a Presbyterian minister for fifty years. He and his
sister had spent summer holidays at the manse, and it had a
mystic hold over them both, so much so that when I had my
first bank account at the age of twenty-one, my father
opened it (very inconveniently) at the Bank of Scotland in
Ayton, a place I did not actually visit until long after I had
ceased to bank there. The one positive aspect about the
arrangement was the poetry of the letters I used to get from
the manager (and probably sole member of staff), describing the progress of the seasons in Berwickshire. And when
my father found himself with a little money at the end of
the war, he spent it, not on buying the house which we had
rented so long, but on sending my youngest brother to
boarding school near Ayton, thereby infecting him too with
yearnings for Scotland which have similarly dominated his
life.

This then was the background of my childhood, a
sense that we were clinging precariously to a nationality—
Scots—and more importantly a class that was not properly
our own. And we were very aware that we were a hundred
yards on the wrong side of the boundary that divided the
old market town of Reigate, where the best people lived,
from its inferior and rather sleazy neighbour, Redhill. Our
address was Redhill, but we felt that spiritually we were a
Reigate family. Because my father had been briefly in the
regular army, he kept his rank of major (indeed I always

*The Avery family: (clockwise, from bottom right)
brother Angus, age two; Gillian, age nine; father
Norman; mother Grace; brother Duncan, age seven; on
a visit to Berwickshire, Scotland, 1956*

remember him referred to as "the Major"), and the house
was thick with reminders of his army past. There were of
course the photographs in the dressing room, the accouter-
ments in the attic. On the landing hung the framed
document that had commissioned him as an officer. In the
kitchen the vacuum cleaner was stowed away in a wooden
chest with 2nd Lt. N.B. Avery painted on it. The dining
room walls were festooned with ceremonial swords and
German bayonets arranged like a fan. There were also a lot
of sporting prints, of such upper-class pastimes as fox
hunting and racing. But they didn't really fit this suburban
house that had been put up by a speculating builder in the
garden of the house next door and that always seemed to be
jostling and elbowing its neighbours. Moreover, the house
did not even belong to us, a fact that worried me
increasingly (and with good reason) as I grew older. The
house and my father's devotion to the army form the
background of *The Greatest Gresham* which of all my
books is the one that is closest to my own childhood. Julia
is me, bookish, tiresomely bossy and opinionated and
forever concerned with what other people think. Henry is
my brother Duncan, delicate, timid, but with an underlying
streak of determination. And for some reason I turned my
spirited youngest brother Angus, six years my junior and
for many years the bane of my life (I have always said that
no one who has not had brothers understands what hatred
really is) into a girl. But for the sake of the story I made
Captain Gresham into an ogre which the real Major Avery
certainly was not. He was, it has to be admitted, very
remote from our lives, but this, I think, was due to inertia
and a gentle selfishness; he did not want to be bothered
with our small doings. He left the house at about 7:30 to

travel up to London and he was not back until 7 in the evening; the weekends he spent playing golf. And since he had not married until he was forty he was older than most people's fathers. So it was our mother—very different from the anxious and conciliatory Mrs. Gresham—who really mattered to us, so much so that before we grasped what my father's biological role was, we thought of him as a shadowy irrelevance; we felt the essential family was my mother and us three children.

It was a very happy childhood, chiefly, I suppose, because my mother contrived to make it so, and because Averys are fundamentally cheerful optimists. They may lack judgement and have an uncanny aptitude for making the wrong decision; they certainly are financially inept, but they have a great capacity for contentment. My aunt, my father's sister, having blithely frittered away every penny on frivolities without having made any provision for her old age, and spending her last days in a very unattractive old people's home, used to say how lucky she was and how kind everyone was to her. Thus, in spite of the chronic shortage of money which I must have been aware of from the age of ten or less, and the boredom and frustrations of school, there did seem to be a lot to enjoy—holidays and

Age seventeen

friends and those absorbing games chiefly played with the children next door which I recorded in my memoirs. Rereading a fifteen-year-old's account of them I realize how much we seemed to want to be afraid. Perhaps because of the peacefulness of our lives we craved excitement. There was a game called "The Old Man" where the three of us and Betty, the next-door girl, crouched in the next-door greenhouse while David, her brother, marched round and round the house and in passing banged menacingly on the windows. Our screams were such that the game was eventually forbidden. There was the business of trying to evade the wrath of the Old Lady, an elderly spinster neighbour whom we saw as an ogress because she had once protested about our habit of squatting on the garden wall and staring into her sitting room. Rescuing the balls that went over into her garden was as exciting as braving man-eating tigers. The occupation that kept us busy holiday after holiday was preparing the next-door apple tree, our climbing tree, for siege by David. We envisaged ourselves marooned up there for days on end, so supplies were laid in, and such matters as pencils and papers in case we wanted to send messages, and also quantities of ammunition in the shape of mud bombs baked hard in the sun. As I sadly recorded in my memoirs, David only once stirred himself to attack us and on that occasion the bombs had been left behind. And the game that we played most of all, called, for some unfathomable reason, kicki-peg, a sort of hide-and-seek where those who had been found by the seeker could be "rescued" by those still free, had moments of intense, delirious excitement. It still has; I play it in our present house with all visiting children who can be cajoled into it. Otherwise, what would be the point of having a house with two garden gates and a path all round it?

Games were serious; reading, though equally enjoyable, less so, and indeed seen as self-indulgent; one was discouraged from doing it before lunch, for instance. Books in households such as ours were not regarded as essential. They were the jam rather than the bread of life, and there were not all that many of them around. The only library in our school was about fifty books in a locked cupboard, and such public libraries as there were in our locality were rarely open and consisted almost entirely of reference books; fiction was regarded as a frivolity, and all books had been encased in forbidding library bindings. Even if there had been anything we had wanted to read our parents would have been most reluctant to let us borrow the books; they certainly looked well handled and we were told they were full of germs. So we lent each other books, and also used Boots libraries, found at the back of Boots the chemists. You made your way past the counters of soaps and patent medicines, and in a pleasingly antiseptic atmosphere you chose your book (which was apparently germfree) from the juvenile shelf. Half a crown—approximately twelve pence, three weeks' pocket money—would cover a holiday's reading, only you soon had read all the books available.

But children were better employed in the open air. During the holidays we were chased out-of-doors in the mornings. We could amuse ourselves in our own miserably small garden (but in the back, mind, not in the front where we might offend the neighbours). Or we could go next door, if next door would have us. The family there was more easygoing, and, the father being a schoolmaster, books were held in higher esteem. So I would creep into the room that was given over to the children (it conveniently opened off the garden), and squatting behind the broken-spring armchair I would read David's books. A lot of them were boys' adventures which I did not particularly care for, but there was a set of' Arthur Mee's *Children's Encyclopaedia* and this was my mainstay. I skipped the natural history, the geography, and the astronomy (there was a great deal of those) and read such fiction as there was (like the public libraries of his day, Arthur Mee saw little necessity for fiction, either for himself or for others) and the biographies of great men. Mee was a great believer in self-help and the self-made man, and though it was not he who originally said that genius was only an infinite capacity for taking pains, this was his moral theme. It fired me also to try to be a genius, though the great trouble was that, according to the biographies, signs usually manifested themselves in early youth (look at Mozart, for instance) and so far no sign had been vouchsafed to me. Another perturbing feature of the lives of geniuses was the discomfort in which they lived (Palissy, the great French enameler, burnt up most of his house to fire his furnaces) and the anguish they seemed so frequently to endure; I was specially reluctant to endure an unhappy family life. However, I did discover that very many literary figures had cut their teeth on Walter Scott, that a taste for Scott's novels seemed to be an early sign of literary talent, so I manfully embarked on a course of the Waverley novels (my father possessed them, though he never showed any signs of having read them). Averys are dogged if nothing else, and I did read all that we had, extracting perhaps less enjoyment than anybody else who has read so many. I was defeated by the prolixity, the antiquarian detail and above all the Scots dialect, and still am awestruck by the young Victorians who devoured them so voraciously when they were far younger than I was.

Scott was only one aspect of my quest for self-improvement. There were many things I tried to teach myself; I can remember my struggles with German, Spanish, harmony, heraldry, and Russian history, and there were probably other subjects. When recently I visited one of the best girls' schools in this country and lamented the hopelessness of my own school, the headmistress pointed out how much it had done for my resolve to rise above it. Girls at St. Paul's, she said, tended to accept a good educational background as a fact of life. I could have gone to a better school—that is to say there was an excellent secondary school in our Surrey town which would have cost my father far less than he paid out for the private schooling I was given. But society was intricately stratified in those days and in that sort of milieu. He saw himself as an officer and a gentleman; if he had sent his children to the state schools he would have lost caste, we would have had totally different friends; we would no longer have mixed with the children of his friends. We were just as much aware of it as our parents were, and caste then seemed to be the all-important thing.

So at the age of seven, my mother having taught me my first lessons, I was sent to Dunottar School in Reigate, about a mile away from where we lived. Those were the days when someone with a little capital could buy a house, install a few desks, fix a brass plate on the door, and call it a school. The headmistress had by a curious coincidence begun her school in 1926, the year I was born, in the house where my parents were to live until my father died. It seems to have thrived; it moved four times in the next seven years, each time to a bigger house, and by the time I went there it was in its final home, a splendid Victorian mansion in the classical style, built by a millionaire, who, the story went, had killed himself for love of his dead wife. It stood on twelve acres of very beautiful grounds. There were formal gardens, massed rhododendrons and azaleas, wooded walks, and impressive woodlands, with kitchen gardens and ranges of hothouses for such delicacies as peaches, grapes, and figs. The headmistress ate these, not the pupils.

Looking back at it now, I see that she had probably overreached herself in acquiring these premises, and that this was why the staff was largely unqualified, and why there was so little in the way of books or equipment—there were, for instance, no laboratories, and such science as we did—mostly botany—was mugged up from dictated notes. It was ironical, perhaps significant, that when so little was provided to deck our intellects, outwardly we were conspicuously well-clothed (at the expense of our parents, of course). We were kitted out in elaborate royal blue uniform, a completely different set for each of the three school terms and for all the sports we played, with the school motto embroidered in gold on our blazers: *Do ut des*—I give that thou mayest give.

The headmistress herself seemed to regard the school only as a livelihood. She had apparently no cultural interests, and no particular interest in any of her pupils. She addressed us at morning assembly on the topic of *noblesse oblige* (which appeared to mean that we were specially privileged and it behoved us never to forget it and thereby do such unladylike things as wear our hats on the backs of our heads or go out without our gloves). In my early years she also took junior classes for handwriting lessons, a subject that was treated very, very seriously since neatness was in those days one of the ways to achieve good exam results. We had to write copperplate, probably the most difficult of all writing styles with its loops and pothooks, and failure to make a good pothook meant that our hands were beaten with a ruler. ("Thomas the Taws," she called it; she was a Scotswoman and the taws had been a commonplace in her youth.) Domestic subjects and crafts were not taught. She regarded art, music, and drama as superfluous extras, and the only purpose she appeared to see in English, history, geography, and French was as exam fodder. Because of the neatness we had so painfully acquired and the amount we had committed to memory, Dunottar pupils always obtained very satisfactory results in School Certificate, taken at the end of our school careers; in those days examiners looked for diligence and accuracy rather than for the questing spirit.

Since there seemed to be no shortage of pupils, this type of education must have suited the parents, and it was fairly typical of the small private schools of the day. So was the discipline, the intense concentration on minute details of tidiness and conformity, with bad marks given for such matters as not cleaning out one's paintbox, wearing the wrong shoes in the garden, taking an extra piece of lettuce. Mountains were made out of molehills, and by the time the geography mistress (a dreadful woman) had finished with someone who had, say, handed in an ill-written piece of homework, the weeping transgressor was certain that life had no future for her. When fifteen years later I began writing children's books, it was this memory of Us and Them that I remembered, children versus authority, with an unbridgeable gulf between them. But since by the time that I wrote children no longer seemed to fear the adult world so much as we had done, and were not likely to credit that only twenty years before it had been very different, I transferred the setting to the Victorian period, since everybody seems to accept that the Victorians were strict with their young.

I left school in the summer of 1943. I was sixteen. I had taken School Certificate and passed with glory (it being wartime, examiners were instructed to make allowances for candidates whose schools might have been moved far from their own premises—"evacuated" was the term then used— or who might have had lessons interrupted by air raids). I had spent two placid post-Certificate terms in the company of the one other girl who was left of my contemporaries. Between us we tried to devise a scheme of study to fill the time; we were pathetically anxious to work purposefully, but the school made no provision for sixth form teaching so we didn't get very far, and I was conscious of how ill my parents could afford this unpractical idling. At that stage I did not think of universities; that particular yearning came later. Nobody from Dunottar ever went to a university, nor any girl that I knew then. Though I suppose I must, at some stage, have said wistfully that I wished I could have gone to Oxford because I remember my mother telling me firmly that it made girls narrow-minded. And I also remember, at the age of twenty or so, repeating this glibly, heaven help me, to an Oxford don. It was his incredulity that made me see how preposterous it was to give that as an explanation of why I had no education after the age of sixteen. The fact of the matter was that my parents, who could not possibly have afforded a university for me (in those days there was no state assistance), and in any case saw no necessity whatever for spending money on a girl after she had achieved that goal of School Certificate, had convinced themselves and me, temporarily, that a girl who went in for learning things became an ugly, bespectacled, frumpish spinster, remote from the real world. I was quite enough of a bookworm already, they argued; it was time to shake myself clear and be practical.

Dunottar gave no one career guidance; one's future was never discussed. All the school's energy was concentrated on itself; no other life was seen outside it. It was not that they necessarily expected girls to settle down to wifedom and motherhood—that was, if possible, even less dwelt upon than a future job. My contemporaries seemed to become kindergarten teachers or physiotherapists (which latter training they found very difficult as no science had been taught at school). At this stage I had put my dreams of being a genius behind me. In any case it was musical genius that I had yearned for and with no musical education and no musical instruments at home I had accepted that it was now too late; all I could do was listen and pretend. Such talents as I had seemed to be literary, so I said I wanted to be a journalist. This perplexed my parents, but they took advice and the advice was that I should be sent to a secretarial college. There I would learn shorthand and

Tony and Gillian on their wedding day, August 25, 1952

typing (essential tools for a journalist) and at least I could always get a job with a vaguely literary flavour as secretary to some publisher.

They selected a very chic and expensive London secretarial college, and the one hundred pounds fees (a lot for those days) had to be borrowed from a cousin of my father who had taken a kindly interest in me, the understanding being that I would pay her back out of my future earnings. (This I faithfully did, though it took a long time as my first wages were only a pound a week, and I know I gave up when I was first living away from home because there was no money left after I had paid for board and lodging. I think therefore that the debt could never have been fully repaid.) I well remember my first appearance at Miss Kerr-Sander's college on a September morning in 1943. It was temporarily housed in a suite in a Mayfair hotel. London was then having a lull between bombing attacks, but everybody who could leave the central area had already done so; the hotels were desperate for custom and were glad to accept tenants such as Miss Kerr-Sander. Most of the college had taken up residence at Stanway in the Cotswolds; there was just a nucleus of thirty girls or so who lived in or near London. It was a very hot day, as it often is in September, and I had come up from Redhill in a cotton dress, stockingless, and wearing sandals. (I only had two summer dresses anyway, there being strict clothes rationing; even stockings absorbed precious clothes coupons.) There was a smart secretary who acted as sheepdog and nudged us into some sort of formation, a tense pause and then the door opened and Miss Kerr-

Sander made her state entry. She was a breathtaking and intimidating sight, tall and commanding with short, cropped grey hair. She sported a monocle on a black ribbon, and was immaculately turned out in a man-tailored black suit, a shirt, and tie. (Mercifully, after that we didn't see much of her; she was mostly down at Stanway—a most unlikely sight, surely, in the deep Gloucestershire countryside; could she ever have worn gum-boots?) We grasped her point at once; this was how the perfect secretary was turned out, and dismally conscious of our dishabille we huddled together to try to conceal our naked legs, our less-than-smart footwear. I don't remember that her language was particularly strong, but her crisp tones left us in no doubt whatever that this was positively the last time that we would appear thus, that Kerr-Sander girls never were seen without stockings, and moreover were always hatted and gloved when they walked abroad. We were going to be secretaries, a very different type of person from shorthand typists, and if we didn't wish to be mistaken for this inferior breed we had better take ourselves in hand at once. It was all very like Dunottar where we were always being reminded of the difference between us and the poor wretches who went to grammar schools.

Acquiring a secretarial training was painful, far more difficult than anything else I have subsequently encountered. I was pitiably bad at shorthand, an untidy and inaccurate typist, panicky and inept on the telephone (we had to spend a practice period in the college's office). What I did enjoy was the beautiful emptiness of London. Those of the elegant Mayfair houses that hadn't been bombed were abandoned and boarded up, and I used to explore the streets at lunchtime in a state of dreamy reverie about the past, and in more energetic moods, stride out in the hope of getting further than I had yet been before it was time to come back for the next shorthand lesson, or commercial French (with a French woman who passionately resented all the English), or bookkeeping where I struggled, completely baffled by the double entry system, with company accounts and balance sheets. But London in the hour that we had for lunch was something to be looked forward to daily. The only signs of life then in streets that are now so thronged and noisy used to be in Grosvenor Square, where the Americans even then had taken over most of the buildings, and where one would see members of the U.S. forces in uniforms that always seemed so much more luxurious than the British. The Kerr-Sander plan was that after nine months students would take shorthand and typing speed tests (which of course they would pass) and would then be awarded a diploma and would be helped to find a job. I was becoming apprehensive—it seemed inconceivable that I could ever work my shorthand up to 120 words a minute—when the flying bomb raids came to my rescue. It looked as though the blitz was going to start all over again, and overnight my parents took me away. I never got my diploma and I never communicated with the college again.

It was now that my father's army connections became useful. Without my diploma and without experience I was hardly eligible for a proper secretarial post, and in any case there was no question for the present of my travelling up to London where the good jobs were. So he remembered that the editor of the local paper, the *Surrey Mirror,* had been his orderly in the 1914–18 war, and he persuaded him to

take me on as a junior reporter at the wage of one pound a week. The editor was a great admirer of my father (those who worked under him were always devoted to him), otherwise he would never have given way. The firm had a policy of no women, and there really was no work for me; I was supposed to be standing in for a young man who had departed to the army, but he was experienced and useful whereas I was neither.

There were three men on the reporting staff: Mr. Atkin, Mr. Bingham, and Mr. Bickle. One was too old for army service and the other two were medically unfit. Their kindness and patience, and that of the elderly sub-editor, Mr. Bath, still fills me with awe. It was difficult for them to find jobs I was capable of doing; assignments like the local council meetings and such required rapid and accurate shorthand and considerable knowledge of local politics; so did the sittings of the magistrates' court; inquests were felt to be too harrowing and indelicate for a young woman. As for local drama and music, Mr. Atkin liked doing it himself and did it far better than I ever could—though he generously allowed me to try my hand occasionally. So I spent a lot of time sitting, drooping and yawning, alone in the dusty reporters' room, writing my "copy" on the back of old invoices (there was a severe paper shortage) while the others whirled round Redhill and Reigate on their bicycles, covering local functions. It seemed to be funerals that mostly fell to my share (weddings we did not cover; the bride's mother was expected to send in her own account), and I found these taxing enough. It was my job to stand at the door and take the names of the mourners. But people had a knack of sidling past one and getting lost inside the church, names could be odd and difficult to spell, or I couldn't read my handwriting when I got back. It was very important that the list should be accurate; people complained if their names were omitted or misspelled. But though funerals might cause anxiety they were not harrowing. I used to sit at the back with the undertaker and we both enjoyed the hymns. Far more upsetting was having to call upon next of kin to ask for biographical details; they usually wept and so did I and it often ended in them lending a handkerchief and trying to comfort me. On a more cheerful note I covered all the parties that were given to celebrate first V-E (Victory in Europe) in May 1945 and then V-J (Victory over Japan) that August. Most streets had their own parties with a socking great tea of hoarded delicacies and much patriotic red, white, and blue bunting, and the *Surrey Mirror,* no doubt relieved to find a suitable job for me, sent me to all of them. I travelled round with the Mayor and Mayoress in the mayoral Daimler, one of the very few cars on the road in those fuel-restricted years when most people's cars were jacked up in the garage. It was very hot, and I consumed quantities of trifle and jelly, and caught measles—a great surprise; I had no idea how ill it could make you feel.

I learnt an immense amount from those three years on the *Surrey Mirror.* For one thing I learnt to curb my prose style; Mr. Atkin tactfully rewrote those reports of concerts and amateur dramatics in which I had tried to imitate famous Sunday paper columnists, and showed me how to review books that I disliked without being offensive. And no doubt discomfited by my ignorance, he lent me books, and directed me towards adult education lectures run by the Workers' Educational Association where for the first time I encountered intellectual talk. I used to listen awe-struck to exchanges between the lecturer and the more articulate pupils. (1 was similarly bowled over by the Brains Trust series on the radio just then, where a panel of experts answered listeners' questions. The answers were not usually very enlightening, or even relevant, but people like me had a wonderful sense of eavesdropping at a party where brilliant conversationalists were really enjoying themselves.) But even greater than my intellectual ignorance, if that were possible, was my ignorance of the world. At least I was aware of the first; but I had led such a blinkered existence up till now that I had not the faintest idea of how people lived outside the very narrow circle in which we moved, where everyone seemed profoundly hostile to those who spoke—both literally and metaphorically—with accents different from their own. Nor had I encountered any political opinions different from my father's. Once in my adolescence I had gone through a brief socialist phase (it lasted all of twenty-four hours) and said to my mother that I didn't see why the Royal Family should have lots of palaces and hundreds of servants, why there should be so much difference between them and the rest. My mother pulled herself together enough to say, "You'd better not let Daddy hear anything like that." This sobered me down and I didn't. The *Surrey Mirror* reporters treated me very gently and rarely laughed at my naivety. When the 1945 election swept Labour into office I behaved as though it was Hiroshima (I had supposed that Conservatives would be in power forever, and my father had at some point assured me that this would be so). But Mr. Bickle (who had

voted Labour himself) just said mildly that perhaps it was time for the other chaps to have a go.

My *Surrey Mirror* days did not last much longer than V-J. The young man whose job I was filling came back from the army and I had to find another job. By that stage I must have realized that journalism was not for me. For one thing it all moved too fast; a weekly paper was bad enough, but what would it be like if it were daily? For another, a friend of my aunt had taken me to the Women's Press Club and tried to give me some tips on journalism as a career. The sight of the women's press had daunted me; they were sitting on high stools at the bar in clouds of cigarette smoke, screeching at each other. Besides, I grasped that it would mean serving an apprenticeship in a provincial city like Liverpool or Birmingham, and the thought of leaving home appalled me in those days. So though I wrote round to other Surrey papers asking if they would employ me, I also wrote to magazine publishers. And the firm of George Newnes replied. They published popular women's magazines, but they had a new and most unlikely venture. They had bought *Chambers's Encyclopaedia*, an encyclopaedia of some antiquity which was now hopelessly out-of-date, and Newnes, in an attempt to produce a British rival to the *Britannica* which had departed to Chicago, was all set to revise it from top to toe, calling upon leading British scholars in every field, and recruiting a large editorial and clerical staff to handle all the material as it came in. Alas, there was no chance of my being one of the former, who were all graduates newly returned from the services and looking around for academic posts, but I was allotted to the illustrations editor as a secretary, and for the next three years travelled daily up to London in hat and gloves (I was very mindful of the Kerr-Sanders distinction between secretaries and typists) and worked in the Newnes' offices off the Strand, whose hinterland, though very different, was as fascinating as Mayfair had been; for one thing, it took in the territory where the second-hand book-dealers were concentrated, and I developed a new ambition: I was going to be a great collector. But alas I had not the eye, the talent, or the persistence for this and I never picked up anything of any value. As in the Kerr-Sander days I walked from Victoria Station to work, and used my lunch hours to explore. London, in the later 1940s, was to my eye hauntingly beautiful. It was pathetically shabby, and battered and blasted by air raids, but the disappearance of buildings gave an extraordinary feeling of space in areas which for centuries had been densely crowded. St. Paul's Cathedral, for instance, now stood grandly isolated, all the streets around it having been razed to the ground, and in the summer the bomb sites were purple with rosebay willow herb, and white with its seed in the autumn. And though life had come back to central London in that those businesses that were not bombed out had returned, it was still empty, and I would walk across St. James's Park every morning and see perhaps only three people. I remember from those days, too, the dejected German prisoners of war who had been allocated to the Park as assistant gardeners, staring blankly into space in intervals of sweeping up the leaves on the deserted paths.

The author and her daughter Shenka, age about four

I cannot say that my job at Newnes was scintillating. It mostly consisted of typing and filing and I felt frustrated. As on the *Surrey Mirror* there was not enough to do, nor was there scope for initiative, though towards the end I used to be allowed to compose some of the letters myself. What I did enjoy was writing to Oxford and Cambridge dons with romantic addresses (though I was by that stage so infatuated with academe that even ordinary street names in those university cities sent me into a flutter). Sometimes the encyclopaedia's authors actually called in at the office to discuss their illustrations, and on one or two glorious occasions I was actually sent down to Oxford with a sheaf of drawings to be checked by a historian who benevolently gave me lunch in his college rooms. My sense of having missed out on education became so agonizing that I embarked on a correspondence course for a London University degree in my spare time. Finding the time was not as difficult as the isolation in which I had to study. As it was all done by post, of course I never saw my tutors, and their scribbled corrections on my history essays or Latin proses left so much unsaid, so much that I needed to ask. I passed the hurdle of the first exam but had the sense to realize that I could never manage the rest by correspondence alone. But I had spent more than a year reading and working to a scheme, and doing things that were difficult, which made a pleasant change, even though I had not managed to cross the great divide that existed on *Chambers's Encyclopaedia* between nongraduate and graduate staff.

There was a similar divide at my next job, the Oxford University Press, where I began in February 1950, though here not so much in the work that one did as how one was paid or treated. The encyclopaedia had been eventually completed; all those filing cabinets full of articles and drawings somehow turned into ten blue volumes. The staff drifted away to permanent jobs, the final stage having been the indexing, when the handful of us who were left crouched together in a comradely way working late into the evening as the time grew short. That was easily the best part of the three years I spent there; I always enjoy the sense of a rush job. Then I had written around as before, asking publishers for jobs, and a letter had come from the education department of the OUP saying that their illustrations editor needed an assistant. I was rather afraid that "education" meant schoolbooks, but hoped against hope that it might mean something more grown-up. It did not; the department put out books for backward readers (a particularly dispiriting genre to which one was expected to feel a deep sense of commitment), and geography books and manuals of sewing and so on in which I never learned to take a suitable interest. But it also had embarked on something that was not a textbook, the *Oxford Junior Encyclopaedia,* of which three volumes of the ultimate twelve had already been published, and this was to be my principal concern. It involved tracking down illustrations, and this led me to fascinating places in search of the picture that would really illuminate the text. One day I might be in the Bodleian Library (the university library in Oxford) looking for an early engraving of the Royal Mint, the next in a London flour mill, selecting photographs of manufacturing processes. The trouble was there was not enough work; the volumes only came out at a rate of one a year and, though there might be a temporary spurt while we got

the latest one to the printer, most of the time I was hard pushed to know what to do with myself. A contemporary was driven to learning reams of poetry, but then the man she worked for was out most of the time whereas my editor was there in the same room. In those blank hours at my desk I acquired an intimate knowledge of the bit of the street within range of my window and of the lives of the households who inhabited it.

It was the first time I had lived away from home. I had known I would be homesick and I was. Though I stoutly pretended to my family that the whirl of Oxford life was such that it was difficult to get away, in fact I lived for my third weekend when I had a Saturday off and could go home. One Sunday evening as I drearily made my way towards the train that would take me on the first leg of the tedious journey back, a ticket collector at Redhill Station, whom I had never noticed before, remarked: "Cheer up, miss, it'll soon come round again." I was also fairly pinched for money. Encouraged by my father, I had asked for five pounds a week at my interview with the Secretary of the Press (an urbane man and a learned scholar who later became President of Trinity College). "But I'm afraid we don't pay at that sort of rate here," he had said, adding disarmingly that I would find Oxford a very cheap place to live in. I did not, and I found Oxford landladies rapacious and unscrupulous. They had invested their money in genteel Victorian houses in North Oxford which they filled to capacity with lodgers (they preferred girls, who were more easily bullied in those days), and alternately stressed their own gentle birth ("We are all pukka memsahibs here") and hammered us for more money. They were also alarmingly eccentric; nothing in my sheltered Surrey life had prepared me to cope with any of this, and what with them and my money shortage I was often anxious. My parents could not afford to subsidise me, but my brother Duncan, when he came to see me, used to slip a few coins into my hand. He wasn't earning any more than I was, but at least he was still living at home.

In 1951 I became engaged, to the brother of a girl I had met at my earliest Oxford lodgings. I had never expected to marry. My brothers had assured me not to think of it as a possibility; I hadn't it in me to attract a man. So I had stoutly announced that I was never going to marry. Now here was Jim, a handsome captain in the Royal Artillery, who after not more than half a dozen meetings (nearly always at a ball) had asked me to do so. He proposed in the deserted ladies' drawing room of his London club, underneath a portrait of Nell Gwynne. (I am not clear now why this the most famous of Charles II's mistresses should have found a home in the Army and Navy Club.) Naturally I said yes with alacrity, and we went round to where his mother was staying at her ladies' club to break the news to her. Somewhat to my relief it was too late to find her—it seemed that it ought to be just him and me that evening without dragging in mothers. We were to be married later that year, but I began to wonder whether I really welcomed the idea. There I was in Oxford, the place I had struggled so hard to reach (true, an abyss still divided me from the university, and I rarely met or spoke to anybody who belonged to it, except people who were secretaries at one or other of the colleges); it was going to be a wrench to live in army quarters; I was not sure how much I cared about the regimental spirit which meant so much to Jim and his friends, and I suspected that they cared even less for books than people had in Redhill. I couldn't think what we'd talk about. Still, it would never have occurred to me there was any way out of it, and it came as a thunderbolt when Jim decided that there was and broke off the engagement. I begged him to change his mind but he said that "Mummy" (whose advice he had sought) had agreed he had done the right thing.

Looking back even five years later it was evident that Mummy's advice had been sound; no doubt we both would have made the best of it and struggled on but it could never have been rewarding for either of us. But what now seems a joke, at the time seemed the end of the world. I had given in my notice at the Press and all my plans had been directed towards married life on Salisbury Plain; I had mentally cut off my Oxford life and all my friends and now I was having to creep back and beg for acceptance again. Everybody was extraordinarily kind. The Press let me stay on, and my family and friends searched for ways to divert me. At this stage I realized how very much I did want to be married, but the thought of having to start all over again with the tedious technicalities of courtship was deeply dismaying.

It was at about this period that David, the boy next door, came back into my life. In a sense he had never really been out of it; the family was still living there but, with me being in Oxford which he had left several years before, we met rarely. Nevertheless in 1951 he came back to look up his old college and called to see me, bringing with him a school and college friend with whom he had once shared rooms. I had once met this friend in David's undergraduate days, but though I had been impressed (and somewhat daunted) by him, I could never remember his extraordinary surname. "How is David's friend Tony with the funny name?" I used to say to David's mother. "Oh, Tony's a clever boy," she used to say, "but he's in the army now, doing his National Service." Or "Tony's a clever boy, he's got a research fellowship at Balliol." I was awestruck at finding myself offering coffee to a fellow of Balliol (which regards itself as intellectually the grandest of all the Oxford colleges) but retained sufficient presence of mind to offer to lend him a book (it was that powerful novel of 1824 by James Hogg: *The Private Memoirs and Confessions of a Justified Sinner*) so as to give me a second chance of offering him coffee. My motives were apparently crystal clear, but he always says the ploy was unnecessary; he had decided to come back anyway.

On 25 August 1952, Anthony Oliver John Cockshut, university teacher, married Gillian Elise Avery, publishers' encyclopaedia worker. This is how it appears on the marriage certificate and I suppose that was how I had described my occupation. It seemed to me that we were destined to marry from the moment I had pressed James Hogg on him the previous November, but the formal proposal was not made until 8:20 p.m. on 24 February, on the sofa of the splendid set of rooms he occupied at Balliol. His engagement present was not the usual ring but about twenty books which he thought would please me, and on the flyleaf of each the formula "8.2 p.m., 24.2.52" was inscribed. One was C. S. Lewis's The Allegory of Love which I still have not read, and another was a life of Samuel Johnson which also bears in Tony's writing

Falstaff's sigh before the battle of Shrewsbury: "I would it were bedtime, Hal, and all well." The gift of books was emblematic; most of what I know and certainly my taste for Victorian literature has been derived from him, and when I came to write it was he who pared and sharpened my prose, giving me a horror of unnecessary words.

So life now seemed perfect. Admittedly we were poor; the Press paid very little and Balliol in that era did not expect young research fellows to be so imprudent as to marry when the college provided such comfortable bachelor accommodations. We took in a lodger which helped with the rent of our flat, and thus managed to save; Tony had inherited the thrifty prudence of his Lancashire grandfather, a schoolmaster who had managed to save on an annual income of seventy-five pounds. What I had failed to grasp, with my habitual Avery sanguine optimism, was that when the fellowship came to an end it might be difficult to find another job in Oxford. But it was far worse than I thought; not only were there no jobs in Oxford, there were none at any other university either—the period of university expansion came in the 1960s; in the early 1950s the outlook was even bleaker than it was to become in the 1980s. Tony had used his Balliol years to write a study of Trollope's novels, but it was not accepted for publication in time to make an appearance on the curriculum vitae that I laboriously typed out over and over again, sometimes thinking that no one would be able to resist this array of achievements, sometimes gloomily wondering whether there was anything there that distinguished him from anyone else.

By the summer of 1954 it was clear that he would have to think of something else. He applied for a job teaching English at Manchester Grammar School and got it, and on a bitterly cold, foggy day in November we arrived at the lodgings which David, the boy next door, himself now teaching at MGS, had found for us in a south Manchester suburb. It was too foggy to take in anything of the character of our surroundings, and we found that our landlady had had a severe stroke a few days before. She had stayed, however, to see us in, and that is my one memory of her, welcoming but speechless. She was carried off the next day by her brother and sister-in-law and we never saw her again. At the time it all seemed part of the sadness of our new life. One of the very few things that had made any impact on me in much hated geography lessons was the climate of Manchester. Because of the rain-laden winds that came in over the Atlantic, Manchester and its satellite towns had a permanently wet atmosphere which made it peculiarly suitable for the cotton industry; it was the only question I ever felt competent to answer in exams. By the time we arrived the cotton industry had departed, but the climate was still there—weeping grey skies which rarely allowed any sunshine through, and which trapped the smoke from thousands of domestic chimneys so that the air always smelt sooty. Many of the public buildings in our time were so black that they looked carved out of coal, and a greasy grime coated everything, indoors as well as outside. Perhaps if I had merely been making a whirlwind visit to Manchester I might have been fascinated by the remains of its Victorian grandeur, might have searched out examples of nineteenth-century industrial architecture, but being cooped up there for six months at a time all I wanted was to walk in green fields. But Manchester, unlike Oxford,

Gillian, Shenka, and Tony on Shenka's wedding day, April 1983

is not a place you can walk out of, and there are few parks and open spaces. Fallowfield, where we were living, must have always have been sour, flat country even before it became suburb, and beyond us stretched mile upon mile of housing estate, built in a particularly repellant shiny red brick, used apparently because it was more soot resistant. A country walk is a day's outing and needs much planning, particularly if you have to rely on buses and trains.

Thus, homesick for the paradise we had left, I settled down one February day in 1955 to write about Oxford. By this time we had bought a house, a tall early Victorian affair with extensive cellars that I never cared to investigate after I found tracks of rats in the dust, and with far too much space taken up by passages. We paid for it out of Tony's savings: twelve hundred pounds in pound notes (the vendor for some reason had demanded the money in cash) which he took up to the lawyer's office four miles away one dark and foggy winter afternoon on his bicycle. We had done all that we could afford (very little) to make it comfortable; there were no more curtains to be sewn; the garden would have to be left until the spring, and it came over me that if ever I was going to be a writer I had better make a start. Outside the skies were a dull yellow and sooty snow had temporarily veiled the mounds of rubbish that the previous owners, in their efforts to clear the house, had despairingly tipped into the garden. Oxford weather would probably be as bleak, but I nostalgically remembered its buildings, in particular its sounds: choirs practising in college chapels, the echoing feet in the streets, the bells, the Merton College clock, which at every quarter plays phrases from some ancient plain chant melody. And I wrote about Maria, aged eleven, who in 1875 runs away from her

dreadful school to Oxford, and tells her great uncle, the warden of Canterbury College, that her ambition is to be the first woman professor of Greek. It was not difficult to write about Victorian children; I had read more Victorian than contemporary fiction, and was steeped in biographies and memoirs of the period. Besides, as I have said, I felt that my childhood was Victorian in its attitude toward authority. It was all written with great feeling; I drew on my longing for a proper education and for Oxford. But brothers see through one and are quick to deflate. My youngest brother Angus said: "I suppose you think you were like Maria, Gill. But my God, you weren't, you know."

The book came out in September 1957. No moment in a writer's career can equal the acceptance of the first book. *The Warden's Niece* had had its vicissitudes before it reached that point. In its original form it had been a "going back in time" story, with Maria finding herself in the seventeenth century, and three publishers had sent it back with rejection slips. Then Tony remembered that he had a school friend working at Collins and the manuscript was dispatched there. Robin pointed out that to introduce the seventeenth century into a book about Victorians was too much, but if I cared to dispense with the former, Collins would reconsider it. Unravelling a book and reworking it is one of the most dispiriting things that can be, and at first seemed impossible. But after it had been rejected by yet another publisher I decided that it must be done. I remember nothing of this process, mercifully, but do remember Robin telephoning me in Manchester to tell me that Collins would publish it.

The actual publication date was 5 September, two days after our daughter was born, and I remember lying in the pleasant, small maternity hospital in north London in a state of placid elation on both counts. We had both wanted a daughter so much that, feeling we were bound to be disappointed, we had settled on the names for the son we thought would be inevitable. Hugh Quentin Anthony, he was to be called (the Quentin being thrown in to give him initials that would be instantly recognisable, as Tony's A.O.J.C. has always been). We had resolutely avoided discussing girls' names, until Tony, characteristically all for an immediate decision, sat on my bed saying, "You choose," while I said, "No, you." We each thought that the other wanted Ursula so settled for that, whereas it transpired, when the Hampstead registrar had irrevocably recorded her as Ursula Mary Elise, that really both of us had yearned for her to be Sophia. It proved impossible to call her Ursula—chiefly because we have a close friend of that name and I always supposed that people were referring to her. So she became Ushenka (which we thought sounded like a Russian diminutive—but it doesn't to any Russian), then shortened to Shenka, and this she has been ever since.

Though we always said defiantly at the time that we *loved* Manchester, the fact was that the instant the school term was over we were in a train escaping to the south, to the Avery or the Cockshut homes, and there we stayed until the day before school began. (I had been so determined that Shenka should not be born in Manchester that I gave the hospital Tony's parents' address as ours, and used to go down to London every month for the antenatal clinics.) Probably because of these journeyings she, more than we, always seemed to be an alien in Manchester, and she certainly never throve there nor made friends. Whereas we felt that friends were the great compensation for depressing physical surroundings and a job which Tony often found taxing and exhausting (particularly giving fifteen year olds on the science side their compulsory lessons in English). Manchester was marvellously cosmopolitan and though now the fashion is to live out in far-flung suburbs or in the Cheshire countryside, then most of our friends were in the same few square miles of the city; we saw a lot of them and it was then as Britain gradually emerged from the bleak postwar austerity (there had been food rationing until 1953) that I properly began to indulge my fondness for cooking. Like so many of my contemporaries who had been brought up on the dreary English prewar style of cooking (meat roasted or boiled, two vegetables, and everything blanketed in a white sauce), I was fired by the books of Elizabeth David who described the food of France and the Mediterranean and inspired us all to try to create those smells and tastes which few of us then had experienced firsthand.

By 1964 we had been in Manchester for ten years and supposed that we would be there forever, and at the end of our lives would join the acres of dead buried in the Southern Cemetery, which I passed daily on bus route 42 bringing Shenka home from school. And then Tony's former Oxford tutor wrote suggesting that he should apply for a new lectureship in nineteenth-century English studies that Oxford was setting up. We had long ago stopped hoping that one day he might go back to university teaching; he had been out of it too long even though he had managed to go on writing, and had produced several books. The application was duly made, he went down to Oxford for the interviews. But there was a postal strike at the time and no letter came about the outcome. When it did he was away in Yorkshire with his parents and I slit open the envelope, realizing as I did so that it was far too bulky for a mere note of dismissal. In fact it contained leaflets about pension schemes, and I didn't have to read the accompanying letter to know that we would be going back to Oxford. In thankfulness I went down on my knees in the hall; this was infinitely better than having my first book accepted.

I cannot remember how Tony took the news when he came back the next day, but I do remember telling six-year-old Shenka as I met her outside school, and her saying solemnly, "Papa is going to Ox-ford Un-a-versity." My only regret in leaving Manchester was regret that I could feel none. Our friends gave us a wonderful send-off; there were farewell parties every night for weeks before we left, but all I could think of was that at last we were going home. And I vividly remember that first Oxford walk I took across sparkling frosted fields by the river, under brilliant blue skies, and biking down St. Giles, past St. John's College and thinking, "This is *ours* now; we aren't just visitors."

I n effect this is the end of the story, though it is little more than half my life. Nine of my books had been written from Manchester, eight of them children's books which with only one exception dealt with Oxford or the Oxfordshire countryside, all of them written with nostalgic longing. Once I was back I found the urge had gone. I wrote a few more books for children, mostly shorter ones, and bar two they were set elsewhere. One indeed, *A Likely Lad,* was set in Manchester. I recalled the stories that my

father-in-law had told me about his childhood in East Lancashire, but sited it in Manchester, in a part near the city centre which had already been pulled down by the time we left. A second book, *Call of the Valley,* used both Manchester and the area in the Welsh Marches where we had spent our summer holidays since 1961. I am often asked whether I wrote any of my books with my daughter in mind. But she never read any of them until she was grown-up; she was not a reading sort of child, she preferred music and mathematical problems and books made little impact on her until she was too old for mine. Like nearly all children's writers, I wrote about my own childhood.

Since my books were about young Victorians it began to be supposed that I knew about Victorian books for the young. I had always had a fondness for them, dating from when, during the war, we looked after books for friends who had had to leave their house. Mrs. Ewing's *A Flat Iron for a Farthing* was among them, and I had picked up old children's books in my forays in the Charing Cross Road area. I had been commissioned to do a history of English children's books while we were still in Manchester. I was not then within travelling distance of a suitable library, and had to rely on such books as I possessed and the occasional visit to the British Museum Library when we were staying with Tony's parents. The result was a very scrappy affair with gaps that now appall me. I tried to make amends ten years later, in 1975, when, with the Bodleian Library only a

Carrying two bags of books into Christ Church, 1994

ten-minute bike ride away, I could do a more thorough job. This was *Childhood's Pattern,* which set out to trace the changing ethics that lay behind books written for children. The year before, also working in the Bodleian, I had put together what is possibly my favourite book, and certainly the one that I enjoyed most working on—*The Echoing Green,* which pieces together the progress of the last century through memoirs of childhood; thus it began with a child who remembered hearing the news of the battle of Trafalgar, and finished with one who took part in the celebrations of Queen Victoria's Diamond Jubilee; there were rich children, poor children, a boy who had been a midshipman during the Crimean War, child immigrants to America, a girl who saw her village turn into a London suburb when the railway came. And for this book I did my own picture research, and discovered again all the excitement of the chase that I had experienced in my *Oxford Junior Encyclopaedia* days.

My life has always apparently been shaped by a series of lucky accidents rather than by any conscious purpose on my part. One such was an invitation in 1982 from the University of Florida to speak at the presentation of Ruth Baldwin's vast collection of historical children's books to the university. Looking at the reference section I asked what the best work on the history of American children's books was, and was told there was none. So I thought, why not me? The book is nearly finished now. It has taken me to American libraries every autumn since; to the American Antiquarian Society's library in Worcester, Massachusetts (still my favourite library in the whole world), back to the Baldwin Library, to Chicago, Philadelphia, the Library of Congress, and Boston. The lucky accidents are linked, and start with the fact that I had no education. It was the longing for one that made me write in the first place, and the whim that made me set my books in the last century sent me on to write about books of the past.

> And when I wander here and there,
> then do most go right.
>
> (*The Winter's Tale,* act 4 sc. 3, lines 17-18,
> by William Shakespeare)

POSTSCRIPT

Gillian Avery contributed the following update to *SATA* in 2002:

I see that I ended my earlier entry with a reference to a 1982 visit to the Baldwin Library at the University of Florida which had started my interest in historical American children's books. *Behold the Child: American Children and their Books 1621-1922,* inspired by what I had first encountered in Florida, was published in 1994. It was a great relief to finish it and to have page proofs and at last an index to what had become a very long book.

The intervening twelve years had not been entirely devoted to this. For one thing there was the University of Oxford/Florida State University summer programme, held each summer from 1983 at Christ Church, one of the largest Oxford colleges. Here American students, recruited by Florida State University, did three-week courses in a variety of subjects, including Shakespeare and Winston

Churchill. For twelve years I taught children's literature and its history. If the class had a majority of librarians and teachers, I concentrated more on literary aspects; if they were nurses, medics, or parents, they were more interested in the social history behind the books. This was one of my most rewarding experiences and I made long-standing friends. Many of them helped with *Behold the Child,* sending me books, discussing their favourites. I used to ride my bike the two miles to Christ Church laden with books to lend them, and indeed only gave up in 1994 when the burden of bringing some forty books daily and carrying these through the vast precincts of the college to my teaching room became too great. (And the Oxford traffic had become so much worse.) Much the best two days in each session were when the students came up to our house for the morning class and then lunch.

There were other diversions in the 1980s. In 1986 with a fellow enthusiast, Hugo Brunner, a former Oxford University Press editor, I embarked on a campaign to try to secure for Oxford a magnificent collection of historical children's books made by Iona and Peter Opie, arising out of their work on nursery rhymes, fairy tales, children's games and kindred subjects. They had always been anxious that this should go to Oxford's Bodleian Library, and Iona, on the death of Peter, offered to give the twenty thousand books up to half their value of one million pounds if the other half could be raised by public subscription. It was an appeal to which people responded with an enthusiasm that touched and surprised us. Both small and large donations arrived, and there was help in kind. We had particularly valuable support from the late Sebastian Walker, publisher and founder of Walker Books. He persuaded some of the distinguished artists on his list each to illustrate a separate children's rhyme, Iona selecting these from her archives. The result, *Tail Feathers from Mother Goose: The Opie Rhyme Book,* was published in 1988 with a jacket design by Maurice Sendak, and the art work was later auctioned.

But it was the interest taken by the Japanese in the appeal and their enthusiasm for other Goose rhymes that turned the corner for us. Led by the Crown Princess Michiko (now the Empress), they raised 12,502,066 yen (over 51,000 pounds), and we knew then that we would be successful. Nor was this all; the Bodleian was to benefit four years later from the publication by the Tokyo firm Holp Shuppan of superb facsimiles of twenty-eight outstanding nursery rhyme books in the Opie collection. These were so successful that they followed up with a second series. But, alas, these were only marketed in Japan, never in the West. Each book had a bibliographical introduction contributed by three of us who had worked with the Opie books when they first arrived in Oxford.

We reached our target in April 1988, a few months earlier than the date we had set ourselves, and Bodleian vans brought the books from Hampshire to Oxford, Unpacking these treasures and shelving them was an unforgettable experience. The collection is particularly strong in eighteenth-century works, including some very great rarities, and every day provided new excitement. (But the item that always amused early visitors was the "talking book" where if you pulled the right string a cow would moo or a donkey bray.) To commemorate this great acquisition, the Oxford University Press published in 1989 *Children and their Books: A Celebration of the Work of*

Gillian and Tony in the garden, 2000

Iona and Peter Opie, edited by Julia Briggs and myself, a collection of essays by twenty distinguished scholars on subjects ranging from the Opies as collectors to children's diaries and children's homemade magazines. We were much impressed by the eagerness of people to contribute and the quality of their essays. Further publicity was given by a four-part feature film using the Opie books—*Child's Eye,* shown on Channel 4 television in 1989, but made while we were still unpacking the boxes in the library stacks the previous autumn.

I should add as an Opie postscript that the Empress Michiko paid a private visit to the library in 1998. She has an impressive knowledge of English literature and had sent a list of some of the rarities she would like to see. It would have been impossible to display books in the cramped discomfort of the stacks so we carried them from the New (1930) Bodleian to the Old (1613-24) on the Saturday of her arrival, using the underground passage under Broad Street that links the two buildings. At least, that was the plan. But the aged stack lift, habitually unreliable, had a fit of temperament, and carried three of us and our precious burdens erratically up and down, never where we wanted and only resting between floors. It seemed probable that there would be no books when the Japanese visitors were shown into the curators' room, and possible that we would be stuck there until the stack staff (who didn't work at weekends) came back on Monday. I scrambled out the first time the lift stopped by a door, preferring to walk down so that I could raise the alarm if necessary. (In the end it was not.)

There had not been much time for other work during the months of the appeal. From 1987 to 1989 I was chairman of the Children's Books History Society. The duties were not onerous but did involve finding speakers for the monthly London meetings, ensuring that they turned up, and that they did not overrun the time allotted. The latter was very important as we had undertaken to be out of the Library Association's building by 8 p.m. I remember one fraught occasion when at 7:50 our lecturer, who had begun at 6:30, was still leisurely sketching in preliminary details, and was some seven years away from the date of his subject's birth. "You mean I won't have time for any of this?"—pointing to a huge sheaf of notes. I could only offer him five minutes.

The completion of *Behold the Child* (which had not in the early stages found a publisher) was also delayed by work on a history of British girls' independent schools. This book, *The Best Type of Girl* (the publisher's title, not mine), was commissioned by André Deutsch, who had said that while there had been plenty of such histories of boys' schools, there seemed to be nothing about similar establishments for girls. My agent suggested that I might be the person to do it, since I apparently had an insatiable appetite for listening to people's school experiences. Certainly I once had had a dreamy idea of how fascinating it would be to travel round schools with the pretence of having a daughter to place as a pupil.

So for a few months I had unlimited opportunity to visit any school I was proposing to include. Though time and energy limited the numbers I went to some twenty-five or so, having tried to choose as many different types as possible in a wide variety of localities. Otherwise I had to work from the schools' own accounts of themselves, or from people's memories of their experiences. I enjoyed the visits, particularly when it was possible to meet the pupils. One of the more bizarre experiences was when I had arrived at a very remote boarding school to find that the headmistress was missing. Eventually a secretary hurried in to say that her little dog had got stuck down a rabbit hole and that the whole school was standing around her while the gardeners tried to dig it out. I spent half an hour wondering whether I ought to forego lunch and walk back to the distant railway station, or whether if I stayed I had the skills required to cope with bereavement. In the end all was well, the dog was rescued, and the headmistress was glowing: "All the girls were so supportive." (I knew perfectly well why—they had escaped a Latin vocabulary test, chemistry, hockey, or some other torture.)

A second book came out of *The Best Type of Girl*—a history of Cheltenham Ladies' College, to be published in 2003 to celebrate the school's 150th anniversary. It was a fascinating commission, and for the first time I had research assistants—the college librarian and the archivist, who directed me to material, arranged interviews with people who could help, and found superb illustrations. This book I decided must be my last. No other could be so enjoyable, and I certainly could never expect so much help and companionship in what has usually been a lonely business. And now I would be able to read the books I really wanted—history, but not the history of children's books, nor of schools. And if I decided to spend the whole day gardening, I need not feel guilty!

B

BALCAVAGE, Dynise 1965-

Personal

Born March 14, 1965, in Shenandoah, PA. *Education:* Kutztown University, B.F.A. (visual arts), 1986; Arcadia University, M.A. (English), 1995. *Hobbies and other interests:* Fiber arts, traveling, exercising, gardening.

Addresses

Home—Philadelphia, PA. *Office*—c/o Author Mail, Chelsea House Publishers, 1974 Sproul Rd., Ste. 400, Bromall, PA 19008. *E-mail*—dyniseb@yahoo.com.

Career

Freelance writer and editor, teacher of writing. Arcadia University, Glenside, PA, publicity associate and assistant editor, 1992-94, assistant director, College Relations, 1997-98; Chestnut Hill HealthCare, Philadelphia, PA, associate director, marketing and public relations, and acting director, 1999-2000; editor, Pariscape.com, and freelance editorial consultant, 2000—.

Member

People for the Ethical Treatment of Animals.

Writings

Express (play), performed at Arcadia University, 1994.
Ludwig van Beethoven, Composer, Chelsea House (New York, NY), 1996.
Steroids, Chelsea House (Philadelphia, PA), 2000.
The Great Chicago Fire, Chelsea House (Philadelphia, PA), 2000.
The Federal Bureau of Investigation, Chelsea House (Philadelphia, PA), 2000.
Janis Joplin, Chelsea House (Philadelphia, PA), 2001.
Saudi Arabia, Gareth Stevens Publishers (Milwaukee, WI), 2001.

Dynise Balcavage

Philip Sheridan: Union General, Chelsea House (Philadelphia, PA), 2001.
Gabrielle Reece, Chelsea House (Philadelphia, PA), 2001.
Iowa, Children's Press, (New York, NY), 2002.
Welcome to Saudi Arabia, Gareth Stevens Publishers (Milwaukee, WI), 2002.

Culture Shock! Syria, revised second edition, Times Publishing, Inc. (Singapore, Malaysia), 2002.
Iraq, Gareth Stevens Publishers (Milwaukee, WI), 2003.

Contributor to periodicals, including *Georgia Review, Desktop Publishers Journal, Publish, Dynamic Graphics, Spin-Off, Imprint, Counselor,* and *Vitalcast.com.*

Work in Progress

A book of poetry.

Sidelights

Dynise Balcavage told *SATA:* "When I was a little girl, I spent hours writing and illustrating my own books. I remember impressing my mother with one 'novel' I wrote at age ten. I called it *Disaster 1980,* and it was chock-full of your usual Armageddonesque light fare—hurricanes, tornadoes, earthquakes, floods, droughts, and tidal waves all happening simultaneously. Although I still think the title was good, as you can imagine, the 'book' was poorly written (and illustrated!)—but it didn't matter. I *loved* and *needed* to write. In fact, I've kept a diary since the age of six.

"Not surprisingly, after studying ballet in New York and teaching dance, I ended up working in public relations and marketing. I was happy even when composing advertising copy and press releases, but I especially enjoyed writing magazine articles. Uncovering each individual's unique story and motivation made me feel like an archeologist of tales. While working full time in the public relations office and attending graduate school in English at Arcadia University, I began writing books for young readers and magazine articles on the side.

"In 1999, I 'moved up' and took a position heading a busy public relations and marketing office in a hospital. After attending far too many meetings and feeling jealous whenever I assigned an article or piece of copy to someone else, I realized the job was not for me—I desperately missed writing. Since I had amassed a wealth of contacts from my years of part-time freelancing, I decided to leave the hospital to become a full-time freelance writer, despite the advice of friends and family. Yes, it was a huge risk, but not an uncalculated one. Following my gut instinct has always taken me to the happiest places, and as it turned out, this was no exception.

"I have been a full-time freelance writer and editor for three years now, and I have not looked back. I love the variety and the challenges. I enjoy the solitude of working in my office, but at the same time, I enjoy the camaraderie and collaboration that comes with consulting for various businesses in Philadelphia, nationally, and internationally. I concentrate mainly on magazine work, publishing, and advertising, but I usually complete one or two creative writing projects, mainly for my own fulfillment. No matter which way you slice it, I adore the fact that my work days revolves around words.

"When people hear that I work full-time out of my home office, they often say things like, 'I guess you can sleep until 11:00.' When you think about it, though, if I don't work, I don't get paid—just like any person who has a regular, nine-to-five job. Luckily, I am extremely disciplined. I'm at my desk by 8:00 or 8:30, and I usually work straight through until about 4:00. I keep a notebook in my purse, in the same way that an artist keeps a sketchbook, and I jot down ideas and descriptions while they are fresh (otherwise, I would forget them).

"Although I usually juggle several projects a day—writing an article, for example, working on a book, and developing a marketing plan for a local business—I try never to write and edit on the same day. These two activities use different parts of your brain. After writing something, you need to give the work some space, and then go back and revise it with a sense of objectivity. Hemingway said, 'Sometimes, you have to kill your darlings,' but it's harder to cut them when you've only just written them.

"Why do I write for children? I grew up in a very small coal mining town in Pennsylvania—there were ninety-two in my graduating class—and I felt cut off from the energy and beat of the world. I could not wait to grow up, move to the city, and travel! As a kid, especially if you are creative or intellectually curious, you can feel quite powerless and limited by your surroundings or familial circumstances. Reading, for me, was like taking a free trip to other places and into other people's minds. Books empower children by helping them to escape and to see the possibility and inspiration in life.

"One of my favorite quotes deals with the Buddhist concept of the beginners' mind. 'In the beginner's mind there are many possibilities, but in the expert's mind there are few' (Suzuki). I teach writing, and although I see a lot of talented writers, I also come across many beginners who consider themselves experts and are impatient about getting published. The fact is that we *all* know how to write; we all, of course, learned how to write in school. But being able to type or to form letters with a pencil does *not* make you a writer. It can take a long time for a beginner to understand this. Writing *every* day, on the other hand, seeking out and observing new experiences with an open mind, and being brutally honest with yourself will eventually lead to better writing—and to finding your own voice."

*   *   *

BEGAY, Shonto 1954-

Personal

Born February 7, 1954, near Shonto, AZ; married, wife's name, Cruz; children: three daughters, one son. *Education:* Institute of American Indian Arts (Santa Fe, NM), A.F.A.; California College of Arts and Crafts (Oakland, CA), B.F.A., 1980.

Addresses

Home—Kayenta, AZ 86033. *Agent*—c/o Author Mail, Museum of New Mexico Press, 228 East Palace Ave., Santa Fe, NM 87501. *E-mail*—shonto@shontobegay.com.

Career

Previously herded sheep and drove cattle; National Park Service ranger, Grand Teton National park, 1976-81, Navajo National Monument, 1981-86; artist, illustrator, writer, and speaker, 1981—.

Awards, Honors

Reading Rainbow selection, *The Mud Pony*, 1988; Arizona Author Award, 1993.

Writings

SELF-ILLUSTRATED

Ma'ii and Cousin Horned Toad: A Traditional Navajo Story, Scholastic (New York, NY), 1992.
Navajo: Visions and Voices across the Mesa, Scholastic (New York, NY), 1995.
Strawberry Pop and Soda Crackers, Celebration Press (Glenview, IL), 1996.

ILLUSTRATOR

Caron Lee Cohen, *The Mud Pony: A Traditional Skidi Pawnee Tale*, Scholastic (New York, NY), 1988.
Leigh Casler, *The Boy Who Dreamed of an Acorn*, Philomel (New York, NY), 1992.
White Deer of Autumn, *The Native American Book of Knowledge*, Beyond Words Publishing (Hillsboro, OR), 1992.
White Deer of Autumn, *The Native American Book of Life*, Beyond Words Publishing (Hillsboro, OR), 1992.
White Deer of Autumn, *The Native American Book of Change*, Beyond Words Publishing (Hillsboro, OR), 1992.
White Deer of Autumn, *The Native American Book of Wisdom*, Beyond Words Publishing (Hillsboro, OR), 1992.
Lois Duncan, *The Magic of Spider Woman*, Scholastic (New York, NY), 1996.
Mary Cappellini and Tito Naranjo, *Camila and the Clay-Old-Woman*, Rigby (Crystal Lake, IL), 1997.
Joseph Bruchac, *Navajo Long Walk: The Tragic Story of a Proud People's Forced March from Their Homeland*, National Geographic Society (Washington, DC), 2002.
Charlie Willto, *Collective Willto: The Visionary Carvings of a Navajo Artist*, Museum of New Mexico Press (Santa Fe, NM), 2002.
Ramona Mahler, *Alice Yazzie's Year*, Tricycle Press (Berkeley, CA), 2003.

Sidelights

Shonto Begay is a respected Native-American artist and author whose work reflects both traditional Native and contemporary Euro-American influences. Begay considers himself fortunate to have been raised on the Navajo Indian Reservation in Arizona, where he could discover the beauty of the world around him without the distractions offered by television. He told Faith Clover, who interviewed him for *School Arts* magazine, that he comes from a family of storytellers and that his first canvas was the dirt floor of his family's hogan, where he and his brothers would draw pictures with sticks. Growing up herding sheep on the reservation gave Begay plenty of time to dream. When asked what he would like to say to young artists, Begay told *School Arts:* "I challenge them to find their own story rock, their own sacred space where they can dream, dream, and draw and where they can be creative, think, meditate. The land itself is part of Mother no matter where you are. An empty lot in Los Angeles is just as beautiful, just as sacred as a mesa up here."

Begay's first self-illustrated children's book was *Ma'ii and Cousin Horned Toad: A Traditional Navajo Story.* This is a pourquoi tale that explains why the coyote never bothers the horned toad, whom the Navajo traditionally call "grandfather" and believe embodies great spiritual strength. In this parable, crafty Coyote, or Ma'ii as the trickster is known to the Navajo, goes to his hard-working cousin Horned Toad to get a free meal, ends up eating most of his crops, and then eats the toad himself, in order to take over his farm. "Begay's light-spattered watercolors depict the animals relatively realistically, with expression but with little anthropomorphism," noted Patricia Dooley in *School Library Journal.* Others praised Begay's illustrations for extending the humor of the story, in which the toad gets the last laugh on Coyote by playing tricks on the animal's insides until Coyote releases him. "The tale is told with skill and is well suited for reading aloud," remarked Maeve Visser Knoth in *Horn Book.* In a literature review for the *American Indian Quarterly,* John C. Stott stated: "This is a very strong picture book, with a well-written text and strongly complementary illustrations—a worthy addition to a small, but growing list of illustrated retellings of traditional stories created by Native authors and illustrators."

In *Navajo: Visions and Voices across the Mesa,* Begay showcases twenty paintings, each paired with a free-verse poem describing topics from the spiritual to the commonplace. A recurring theme is the struggle to live in both the Navajo and the American worlds, the struggle to keep life in balance, a traditional Navajo virtue. Likewise, Begay's paintings are executed in a style reminiscent of the Pointillists and the Impressionists, but their coloration reflects the palette of the desert of the Navajo reservation, as Patricia Lothrop Green noted in her review in *School Library Journal.* "Powerful and appealing in both word and image, this reflective book should find a wide audience of sympathetic readers," Green concluded. Although Roger Sutton, who reviewed the book for *Bulletin of the Center for Children's Books,* found the poems less successful than the paintings, especially for a young audience, he nevertheless concluded that "kids will enjoy looking at the pictures and reading the autobiographical anecdotes sprinkled throughout."

The Navajo belief in the necessity of living a balanced life is the subject of *The Magic of Spider Woman,* a picture book written by Lois Duncan and illustrated by Begay. In this story, Weaving Woman becomes so enthralled by her own skill that her spirit becomes trapped in the beautiful blanket she is weaving. She can only be released when her teacher, Spider Woman, pulls out one of the woven strands, and that is why all Navajo weavers purposely weave mistakes into their blankets. "Traditional colors and patterns are employed throughout the art, but special care is taken with the depictions of the Navajo blankets," observed Elizabeth S. Watson in *Horn Book.* A contributor to *Publishers Weekly* remarked that Begay's illustrations, while similar in style to those in his earlier book *Ma'ii and Cousin Horned Toad,* move freely between brightly colored scenes when the story is happy and "darker and often spooky [views] as Weaving Woman traps herself."

Among Begay's other works for children is *Navajo Long Walk: The Tragic Story of a Proud People's Forced March from Their Homeland,* a history of the forced relocation of the Navajo people in the 1860s. Explaining as well the circumstances leading up to the removal, author Joseph Bruchac shares with his readers the story of the 470 mile trek the Navajo were forced to make to a distant reservation. According to a contributor to *Publishers Weekly,* "[Begay's] art reaches a new level of accomplishment and his captions, explaining his use of symbols, will help youngsters interpret the cryptic moments in his work." "Begay's pictures are stunning," wrote *Booklist*'s Hazel Rochman, "and his eloquent captions will challenge readers to look closely."

Biographical and Critical Sources

BOOKS

St. James Guide to Children's Writers, 5th edition, St. James Press (Detroit, MI), 1999, pp. 83-84.

PERIODICALS

American Indian Quarterly, winter, 1995, John C. Stott, review of *Ma'ii and Cousin Horned Toad: A Traditional Navajo Story,* p. 149.

Book Links, July, 1992, Kathleen T. Horning, "Sacred Places: American Indian Literature from Small Presses."

Booklist, December 1, 1992, Karen Hutt, review of *Ma'ii and Cousin Horned Toad,* p. 671; September 1, 1994, Deborah Abbott, review of *The Boy Who Dreamed of an Acorn,* p. 49; April 1, 1995, Karen Hutt, review of *Navajo: Visions and Voices across the Mesa,* p. 1384; March 1, 1996, Carolyn Phelan, review of *The Magic of Spider Woman,* p. 1185; May 1, 2002, Hazel Rochman, review of *Navajo Long Walk: The Tragic Story of a Proud People's Forced March from Their Homeland,* p. 1519.

Bulletin of the Center for Children's Books, October, 1992, Betsy Hearne, review of *Ma'ii and Cousin Horned*

Toad, p. 37; March, 1995, Roger Sutton, review of *Navajo,* p. 228.

Five Owls, September, 1995, Jan Greenberg, review of *Navajo,* p. 5.

Horn Book, January-February, 1993, Maeve Visser Knoth, review of *Ma'ii and Cousin Horned Toad,* p. 94; July-August, 1996, Elizabeth S. Watson, review of *The Magic of Spider Woman,* p. 470.

Instructor, November-December, 1995, Peggy K. Ford, "Let Our Words Be Heard: Native American Stories Passed from Mouth to Ear to Heart," pp. 47-48.

Language Arts, March, 1993, Junko Yokota, review of *Ma'ii and Cousin Horned Toad,* p. 221.

Library Journal, September 15, 2002, Nancy Turner, review of *Collective Willto: The Visionary Carvings of a Navajo Artist,* p. 57.

Publishers Weekly, September 9, 1988, review of *The Mud Pony,* p. 133; December 14, 1992, review of *Ma'ii and Cousin Horned Toad,* p. 55; September 19, 1994, review of *The Boy Who Dreamed of an Acorn,* p. 70; January 9, 1995, review of *Navajo,* p. 64; March 11, 1996, review of *The Magic of Spider Woman,* p. 64; April 22, 2002, review of *Navajo Long Walk,* p. 70.

School Arts, October, 1997, Faith Clover, "Shonto Begay Talks about His Art," p. 23.

School Library Journal, January, 1989, Karen K. Radtke, review of *The Mud Pony,* p. 69; November, 1992, Patricia Dooley, review of *Ma'ii and Cousin Horned Toad,* p. 82; December, 1994, Patricia Lothrop Green, review of *The Boy Who Dreamed of an Acorn,* p. 106; March, 1995, Patricia Lothrop Green, review of *Navajo,* p. 226; March, 1996, Patricia Lothrop, review of *The Magic of Spider Woman,* p. 203; July, 2002, Anne Chapman Callaghan, review of *Navajo Long Walk,* p. 131.

Wilson Library Bulletin, April, 1995, Donnarae MacCann and Olga Richard, review of *The Boy Who Dreamed of an Acorn,* p. 110.

OTHER

Shonto Begay Web Site, http://www.shontobegay.com (January 13, 2003).*

*   *   *

BERG, David 1920-2002

OBITUARY NOTICE—See index for *SATA* sketch: Born June 12, 1920, in Brooklyn, NY; died of cancer May 16, 2002, in Marina del Rey, CA. Cartoonist and author. Berg is best remembered for his contributions to *Mad* magazine, especially for his "The Lighter Side Of" comic strip. A talented artist from a young age, Berg began his formal art education at the age of twelve when he took classes at the Pratt Institute; while in high school he studied at the Cooper Union Art School in New York. His first job as a comic strip artist came when, at the age of twenty, he inked backgrounds for "The Spirit" newspaper comic feature, and he later worked on the "Death Patrol" and "Uncle Sam" comic books. During World War II he was a war correspondent, covering news in Guam, Iwo Jima, Saipan, and, after the war, in

Japan. When he returned home, he was given a job working for Stan Lee at Timely Comics—the predecessor of Marvel—and Archie Comics. He joined the staff at *MAD* in 1955, drawn to the magazine's satirical bent, and his "The Lighter Side Of" debuted in 1961. The comic strip became notable for its satires of human behavior and often featured Berg himself as the character Roger Kaputnik. Berg continued to draw his strip until his death, and his last work was published in the September 2002 issue of *MAD*. In addition to this, Berg published a number of collections of his cartoons in such books as *MAD's Dave Berg Looks at People* (1966) and *MAD's Dave Berg Looks at You* (1982). Actively involved in Little League organizations, the Girl Scouts, and in the B'nai B'rith, where he was a former president of the Marina del Rey branch, Berg also published two humorous looks at religion: *My Friend GOD* (1972) and *Roger Kaputnik and GOD* (1974).

OBITUARIES AND OTHER SOURCES:

PERIODICALS

Los Angeles Times, May 24, 2002, p. B16.
New York Times, May 25, 2002, p. A28.
Washington Post, May 25, 2002, p. B6.

* * *

BERGEL, Colin J. 1963-

Personal

Born August 30, 1963, in Detroit, MI; married, 1988; wife's name, Joyce (a registered nurse); children: Ian, Kayla, Emily. *Education:* Ferris State University, B.A.

Addresses

Home—2095 W. Fox Farm Rd., Manistee, MI 49660. *Agent*—EDCO Publishing, 2648 Lapeer Rd., Auburn Hills, MI 48326. *E-mail*—cjbergel@chartermi.net.

Career

Sea captain and author. U.S. Merchant Marine, third mate, advancing to captain, for Oglebay Norton Co., 1988—. Freelance writer.

Awards, Honors

Michigan Historical Society Merit Award, 2001, and Great Lakes Book Award finalist, both 2001, both for *Mail by the Pail.*

Writings

Mail by the Pail, illustrated by Mark Koenig, Wayne State University Press (Detroit, MI), 2000.
Michigan L.A.P.S. Great Lakes Unit, Colin Bergel's Journal, EDCO Publishing (Auburn Hills, MI), 2002.

Work in Progress

A sequel to *Mail by the Pail;* other children's books.

Sidelights

Colin J. Bergel is a Michigan-based author whose full-time job is as a member of the Merchant Marine, the branch of the U.S. military that pilots commercial ships. His first published book, *Mail by the Pail,* focuses on what he knows best: life as a sailor working on one of the freighters that carries heavy building materials and other goods to the many cities and towns located along the shores of the Great Lakes.

In *Mail by the Pail,* a young girl named Mary decides to send her father a birthday card. While for many children such a task would be simple—just handing a card to Dad during breakfast—Mary has a far greater challenge. Her father works as a sailor on a lake freighter and spends weeks at a time away from home. To reach him, Mary's birthday card must travel to a central post office in Detroit, Michigan, be transferred to a mailboat, and then be hoisted aboard her father's freighter in a metal pail tied to a rope. Readers follow the path of Mary's birthday card as it makes its way to its destination, and learn a little bit about what life is like for sailors and their families along the way.

Bergel told *SATA:* "Originally *Mail by the Pail* was not written for the public. I was missing my children after sailing on a freighter for six weeks. After passing the mailboat and not receiving mail, I was wishing for a letter from home. I decided to write a story for my children to show them where I worked away from home. It took a number of years to find a publisher for this book as it was unique. After finding a publisher, it took another two and a half years to become reality." When Bergel is not working as a freighter captain, he speaks to groups of children and adults about his writing and his experiences sailing the Great Lakes region.

* * *

BRACKETT, Dolli Tingle 1911(?)-1993 (Dolli Tingle)

Personal

Born May 6, 1911(?), in Chicago, IL; died of respiratory failure, December 11, 1993, in Norwalk, CT; daughter of Horace Berchard (an artist) and Mabel (Ermen) Tingle; married Ward Brackett (an artist), May 4, 1940; children: Gordon H. *Education:* Attended Chicago Academy of Fine Arts, American Academy of Fine Arts, and Brooklyn Museum School of Art. *Religion:* Presbyterian.

Career

Artist, illustrator, and designer. Commercial artist; worked as a designer for Whiting and American Artists; U.S. Postal Service, designed eight stamps for Christmas, including 1973 and 1982; rug and book designer. *Exhibitions:* New England Show and Audubon Show, both 1961; Kaymar Gallery, New York, NY, solo exhibition, 1962.

Member

Silvermine Guild of Artists.

Awards, Honors

Woman of the Year, American Needlepoint Guild, 1973, for stamp design; Pablo Picasso Award for painting, New England Show, 1976.

Writings

SELF-ILLUSTRATED; AS DOLLI TINGLE

Our Baby's First Book, C. R. Gibson (Norwalk, CT), 1967.
Expecting?, C. R. Gibson (Norwalk, CT), 1968.
The Little Apple Tree, C. R. Gibson (Norwalk, CT), 1968.
Going to Be a Bride?, C. R. Gibson (Norwalk, CT), 1970.
Look Who's a Grandma!, C. R. Gibson (Norwalk, CT), 1971.
Hello, Daddy, C. R. Gibson (Norwalk, CT), 1978.
And Now You're a New Mom, C. R. Gibson (Norwalk, CT), 1982.

OTHER; AS DOLLI TINGLE

(Preparer) *The Booklover's Map of the British Isles,* R. R. Bowker (New York, NY), 1946.
(Illustrator) Edith Lowe, reteller, *The Valiant Little Tailor,* John Martin's (Kenosha, WI), 1946, published as *The Brave Little Tailor,* Follett (Chicago, IL), 1965, included in *Stories That Never Grow Old,* Random House (New York, NY), 1966.
(Illustrator) *Nursery Rhymes,* S. Lowe (Kenosha, WI), 1948.
(Illustrator) Edith Lowe, reteller, *The Traveling Musicians,* John Martin's (Kenosha, WI), 1948.
(Illustrator) Norah Smaridge, *Your Five Gifts,* C. R. Gibson (Norwalk, CT), 1969.

Sidelights

Dolli Tingle Brackett was a textile and book designer whose wide-ranging creative talents led her from book illustration to stamp design during the 1960s and 1970s; by the 1980s Brackett was able to point to five U.S. Postal Service Christmas issue stamps that were based on her designs. In addition to exhibiting her artwork throughout the East Coast, Brackett created a number of self-penned children's books as well as several books for adult readers, and she also illustrated the stories of other authors, such as Norah Smaridge and fairy-tale adaptor Edith Lowe. Among her books for children are *The Little Apple Tree* and a collection of nursery rhymes. Throughout her career as an author and artist she used her professional name, Dolli Tingle.

Brackett, who lived in southern Connecticut, once noted: "I draw and write at the same time when at work on a new project; I have a need to *see* my characters and how they move." In 1982 she and her husband, portrait artist Ward Brackett, purchased land in Sarasota, Florida, where they had their son design an art studio for use during the cold winter months. "It has great light, a balcony that lets us look out over our property, and a mockingbird that sings his repertoire to us twice a day," the author/illustrator once recalled. Brackett died in 1993.

Obituaries

PERIODICALS

New York Times, December 19, 1993.*

C

CARBONE, Elisa
See CARBONE, Elisa Lynn

*   *   *

CARBONE, Elisa Lynn 1954-
(Elisa Carbone)

Personal

First name is pronounced "ay-lee-za"; born January 2, 1954, in Washington, DC; daughter of Mauro Gregory (a veterinarian) and Lynn (a homemaker; maiden name, Solar) Carbone; married Jeff Nugent, December, 1973 (divorced, 1987); married Jim Casbarian (a photographer); children: (first marriage) Daniel Micah, Rachel Elisa. *Education:* University of Maryland, B.A., 1985, M.A. (speech communication), 1988, (education), 2001. *Religion:* Catholic. *Hobbies and other interests:* Rock climbing, windsurfing, cross-country skiing, white water paddling.

Addresses

Home and office—1324 Canyon Rd., Silver Spring, MD 20904-1406. *Agent*—George Nicholson, 65 Bleecker Street, New York, NY 10012. *Email*—elcarbone@earthlink.net.

Career

Independent consultant and trainer of teaching and communication skills, 1973—; University of Maryland, College Park, MD, lecturer in speech communication, 1985-1998; visiting author at public and private schools, 1993-1998. Part-time writer, 1988-1998, full-time writer, 1998—.

Member

Authors Guild.

Sarah and her friends come to understand that it is essential to show the world your true self by revealing "your naked truth" in Elisa Carbone's novel for young readers. (Cover illustration by Tim Barnes.)

Awards, Honors

Excellence in Teaching Award nomination, University of Maryland, 1990; finalist for Benjamin Franklin

Award, psychology category, Publishers Marketing Association, and nominee for Young Hoosier Book Award, both 1993, both for *My Dad's Definitely Not a Drunk;* Pennsylvania Young Reader's Choice master list, and Children's Literature Choice List, 1999, both for *Starting School with an Enemy;* worthy of special note, Virginia Jefferson Cup Award, Arizona Young Readers Award nominee, Young Hoosier Book Award nominee, Maryland Children's Book Award nominee, Joan Sugarman Award honorable mention, Mark Twain Award Master List selection, Best Book for Young Adults selection, American Library Association (ALA), and EMC Paradigm Masterpiece Series Edition, all for *Stealing Freedom;* Kid's Pick of the Lists, American Booksellers Association, for *Sarah and the Naked Truth;* Books for the Teenage selection, New York Public Library, Best Children's Book, Bank Street College of Education, Notable Children's Book selection, ALA, Junior Library Guild selection, and Jefferson Cup Award, Virginia Library Association, 2002, and Delaware Blue Hen Award nominee, and Virginia Young Readers Middle School List selection, 2003-2004, all for *Storm Warriors.*

Writings

(As Elisa Lynn Carbone) *My Dad's Definitely Not a Drunk,* Waterfront Books (Burlington, VT), 1992, new edition published as *Corey's Story: Her Family's Secret,* illustrated by Sally J. K. Davies, Waterfront Books (Burlington, VT), 1997.

Teaching Large Classes: Tools and Strategies, Sage (Thousand Oaks, CA), 1998.

Starting School with an Enemy, Knopf (New York, NY), 1998.

Stealing Freedom, Knopf (New York, NY), 1998.

Sarah and the Naked Truth, Knopf (New York, NY), 2000.

Storm Warriors, Knopf (New York, NY), 2001.

The Pack, Viking (New York, NY), 2003.

Work in Progress

Night Running, a picture book based on an Underground Railroad story, illustrated by Earl B. Lewis, due in 2004, a historical novel set in Colorado in 1878, due in 2005, and *Heroes of the Surf,* a picture book based on a true United States Life-Saving Service rescue, all for Knopf; a contemporary young adult novel about rock climbing, for Viking; *Many Windows: A Book of Celebrations,* a picture book about the world's five great religions, co-authored with Uma Krishnaswami and Rukhsana Khan.

Sidelights

Elisa Carbone is the author of six novels for young readers, books which both amuse and educate, dealing with subject matter from contemporary school stories to historical fiction. Carbone's award-winning and highly acclaimed *Stealing Freedom* and *Storm Warriors,* in particular, while dealing with topics from African-American history, are also fast-paced and reader-friendly, while her lighter "Sarah" books feature the eponymous, plucky heroine in realistic contemporary novels for middle-grade readers.

"I wrote my first book before I learned how to write," declared Carbone on her author's Web site. Not yet five, Carbone announced to her father that she wanted to dictate a story to him, which she did over the course of the following weeks. The finished product was typed up by her mother with illustrations supplied by the precocious author. "Between age four and a half and my early thirties, which is when I decided to write my second book," Carbone further explained on her Web site, "I had a few adventures." After high school graduation, she lived with relatives in Italy for a time and learned that language. Married as a teenager, Carbone had two children early in her life and has worked variously as a piano, guitar, and dance instructor, as well as a professional dancer. As her children grew up, she found time to get a college education and start a career as a college instructor.

Carbone's first book, *My Dad's Definitely Not a Drunk,* appeared in 1992 and dealt with the difficult problem of adult alcoholism. The book's protagonist, Corey, is a sixth grader who wishes for a normal family life. In her mind, it is only her dad who drinks too much. She just wants him to be like other parents and hold down a job. Carbone deals with many of the dangerous side effects of such a drinking problem, including parental abuse, drunk driving, and employment problems. A reviewer for *Publishers Weekly* found that the author "believably weaves" such elements into Corey's tale, and though the same contributor felt that there was some awkward writing and a too-easy solution, "Carbone's treatment of more complex emotional issues makes up for these shortcomings."

"I wrote *My Dad's Definitely Not a Drunk,* Carbone told *SATA,* "because I wanted to make it clear that alcoholics are not horrible people. I thought there should be a kid's book to explain alcoholism as a disease and help kids understand an alcoholic parent or relative. About one out of six kids in this country is growing up with an alcoholic parent (or two alcoholic parents), so I figured there are a lot of kids who need this book. Also, I think it's always fun to laugh, even when you've got a problem. That's why I made the book funny and light-hearted even though it deals with a serious subject." This novel was reprinted in 1997 as *Corey's Story: Her Family's Secret,* and in a *Horn Book Guide* review of that title, Martha Sibert commented that Carbone's well-executed development of Corey's character "serves to draw readers into her story."

From the subject of alcoholism, Carbone moved on to the problem of school bullies in her next novel for middle-grade readers, *Starting School with an Enemy.* Ten-year-old Sarah, who has just moved with her family from Maine to Maryland, is worried about making friends in her new school, and an incident that happens before school even starts does not help matters. Seeing a small boy on a tricycle when she is riding her bike, Sarah notices that he is about to pedal into the path of a truck. She pulls around him and knocks him over to save him, but the boy's older brother Eric does not understand this. Once school starts, he begins to pick on this girl who he thinks has attacked his brother. Soon the bullying erupts into warfare between the two, and Sarah obsesses on ways to get back at Eric, plots which threaten her new friendship with soccer-playing Christina Perez. Happily, Sarah is able to learn that revenge is not so sweet after all, and her new friendship is saved. "Carbone has a sharp ear for contemporary talk," observed Hazel Rochman in a *Booklist* review of the novel, further noting that the "multicultural cast is a natural part of the story." A contributor for *Publishers Weekly* also praised the book, commenting that "readers will cheer rather than pity spunky Sarah," and lauding the "lifelike" dimensions the author gave her characters as well as the dialogue which, together, make her story "at once comfortably familiar and entirely novel." A critic for *Kirkus Reviews* similarly found that though the story "starts out like any other about playground quarrels, ... [it] briskly moves into some gratifying intricacies about the nature of fighting and winning." The same reviewer concluded that Carbone "delivers a difficult lesson in an exciting tale." And Deborah Stevenson, writing in *Bulletin of the Center for Children's Books,* wrote, "This is eminently satisfying breezy middle-grade fare."

Sarah makes a reprise in *Sarah and the Naked Truth* in which the protagonist has to deal with new challenges after losing much of her hair in a bubble gum accident. Her hair is cut so short that she is taken as a boy on the all-male basketball team she joins. None of the other kids have a clue as to her real identity, even as the team makes it to the finals. However, at this point, Sarah is actually faced with the problem of directly lying to the coach or telling the truth. Meanwhile, Sarah's friend Christina has her own problem, assigned by the teacher to represent Mexico and not her native El Salvador in the school pageant. Another new friend, Olivia, from Trinidad, also has secrets, hiding the fact that she has an artificial leg. Finally the three friends get together and communally figure out how each can tell the truth and thereby learn more about their own character. Critical opinion varied with this title. While a contributor for *Publishers Weekly* felt that fans of Carbone's earlier "Sarah" title might "well be disappointed in this middling sequel," *School Library Journal*'s Linda L. Plevak remarked that "readers will enjoy some of the lighter moments," and that the book would attract "even reluctant readers." Though Rochman had complaints of the "contrived" plot in her *Booklist* review, she also felt that "there's humor and humanity in the friendship depicted."

With *Stealing Freedom,* Carbone explores historical material for young readers, presenting a novel based on actual events in the life of a teenage Maryland slave, Ann Maria Weems. This young girl managed to escape to Canada, disguised as a boy, in the 1850s via the Underground Railroad. Rochman, again writing in *Booklist,* observed that the novel "combines the appeal of exciting escape adventure with authentic details of

time and place." Rochman further praised Carbone's "meticulous" research, though felt at times there was too much "local color" and detail. Elizabeth Bush, however, writing in *Bulletin of the Center for Children's Books,* found that Carbone's "intensive research ... yields enough reliable information to support a credible and far more complete account of a runaway's experiences than is offered in most novels of slave escape." A contributor for *Publishers Weekly* had more unequivocal praise for the book, calling it a "dramatic, often poignant historical novel," and further commenting that the account of Ann's "harrowing escape ... gives youngsters an immediate, at times thrilling account of the workings of the Underground Railroad," the series of safe houses that aided runaway slaves in their journey to freedom in Canada. "This is a fine piece of historical fiction with a strong, appealing heroine," declared Peggy Morgan in a *School Library Journal* review.

Storm Warriors is another piece of historical fiction dealing with African-American themes. In this novel, young Nathan and his father go to live with a grandfather on the Outer Banks of North Carolina after the boy's mother dies. There Nathan lives on Pea Island near a rescue station operated by a crew of African-American members of the United States Life-Saving Service. Soon Nathan has dreams of becoming one of them and sharing their adventures, and this ambition further leads Nathan to take renewed pride in his own heritage, with his grandfather going from slave to free man and his father making his living from fishing. Carolyn Phelan, writing in *Booklist,* called the novel "well-paced" and praised Carbone for being able to balance exciting scenes of "storms, shipwrecks, and rescues" with calmer times of "communication, reflection, and revelation." Lynne T. Burke, writing in *Reading Today,* felt that Nathan's "battle with the ocean is a metaphor for his own family's battle with the Klan," while *Horn Book*'s Mary M. Burns thought that Carbone's book "combines historical figures with created characters in the best traditions of the historical novel," concluding that the "whole is an adventure that brings to life the realities of life for many black people after the Civil War." A reviewer for *Publishers Weekly* called the book an "inspiring and little-known tale," declaring that "suspenseful descriptions of the rescue crew's feats, and the affecting passages between Nathan and his loving grandfather are the novel's greatest strength."

Speaking with Julia Durango in an interview for *By the Book,* Carbone noted that work on historical novels is much more labor intensive than on lighter fiction such as the "Sarah" books. "I researched and wrote the 'Sarah' books in about six months each," she told Durango, "while *Storm Warriors* and *Stealing Freedom* each took nearly three years to research and write. However, Carbone maintains that each book has the same technical requirements. "Whether I'm writing historical or contemporary [fiction], I still have to solve problems with the plot, make characters real, make sure my writing flows in that way; neither type of book is really 'easier.' And both types are wonderfully fun to write, just in different ways."

Biographical and Critical Sources

PERIODICALS

Booklist, September 15, 1998, Hazel Rochman, review of
Starting School with an Enemy, p. 226; January 1,
1999, Hazel Rochman, review of *Stealing Freedom,*
p. 855; February 15, 1999, Hazel Rochman, review of
Stealing Freedom, p. 1068; March 15, 2000, Hazel
Rochman, review of *Sarah and the Naked Truth,*
p. 1376; January 1, 2001, Carolyn Phelan, review of
Storm Warriors, p. 956.

Bulletin of the Center for Children's Books, April, 1998,
Deborah Stevenson, review of *Starting School with an
Enemy,* pp. 276-277; January, 1999, Elizabeth Bush,
review of *Stealing Freedom,* p. 162.

Horn Book, May-June, 2001, Mary M. Burns, review of
Storm Warriors, pp. 319-320.

Horn Book Guide, July-December, 1997, Martha Sibert,
review of *Corey's Story: Her Family's Secret,* p. 69;
July-December, 1998, Henrietta M. Smith, review of
Stealing Freedom, p. 63.

Journal of Further and Higher Education, February, 1999,
Phyllis Creme, review of *Teaching Large Classes,*
pp. 134-136.

Kirkus Reviews, June 1, 1998, review of *Starting School
with an Enemy,* p. 809.

Publishers Weekly, October 12, 1992, review of *My Dad's
Definitely Not a Drunk,* p. 80; June 8, 1998, review of
Starting School With an Enemy, p. 60; December 7,
1998, review of *Stealing Freedom,* p. 61; April 3,
2000, review of *Sarah and the Naked Truth,* p. 81;
December 18, 2000, review of *Storm Warriors,* p. 78;
January 8, 2001, review of *Stealing Freedom,* p. 69.

Reading Today, February, 2001, Lynne T. Burke, review of
Storm Warriors, p. 32.

School Library Journal, November, 1992, Jacqueline Rose,
review of *My Dad's Definitely Not a Drunk,* p. 116;
July, 1998, Eva Mitnick, review of *Starting School
with an Enemy,* p. 92; February, 1999, Peggy Morgan,
review of *Stealing Freedom,* p. 105; April, 2000,
Linda L. Plevak, review of *Sarah and the Naked Truth,*
p. 130.

Stone Soup, July, 1999, Jennie Pernisi, review of *Starting
School with an Enemy,* p. 18.

OTHER

By the Book, http://www.geocities.com/juliadurango/ (August 6, 2002), Julia Durango, "The Amazing Adventures of Elisa Carbone."

Elisa Lynn Carbone Home Page, http://www.elisacarbone.
com/ (October 6, 2002).

*   *   *

CARTER, Alden R(ichardson) 1947-

Personal

Born April 7, 1947, in Eau Claire, WI; son of John
Kelley and Hilda Small (Richardson) Carter; married
Carol Ann Shadis (a photographer), September 14, 1974;
children: Brian Patrick, Siri Morgan. *Education:* University of Kansas, B.A., 1969; Montana State University,
teaching certificate, 1976. *Politics:* Democrat. *Hobbies
and other interests:* Canoeing, camping, hiking, reading.

Addresses

Home and office—1113 West Onstad Dr., Marshfield,
WI 54449. *E-mail*—acarterwriter@tznet.com.

Career

Writer. Taught high school English and journalism in
Marshfield, WI, 1976-80. Speaker at workshops, includ-
ing ALAN Workshop on Young Adult Literature,
American Library Association, International Reading
Association, and National Council of Teachers of
English. *Military service:* U.S. Navy, 1969-74; became
lieutenant senior grade; nominated for Navy Achieve-
ment Medal.

Member

Society of Children's Book Writers and Illustrators,
Writers' Guild, Council for Wisconsin Writers, Sierra
Club.

Awards, Honors

Best Book for Young Adults citation, American Library
Association (ALA), 1984, for *Growing Season;* Best
Book for Young Adults citations, ALA, New York
Public Library (NYPL), Los Angeles Public Library
(LAPL), and the Child Study Association, and Best
Book for Reluctant Readers citation, ALA Young Adult
Services Committee, all 1985, all for *Wart, Son of Toad;*
Best Book for Young Adults citations, ALA and LAPL,
and Best Book for the Teen Age citation, NYPL, all
1987, all for *Sheila's Dying;* Outstanding Science Trade
Book for Children, Children's Book Council and Na-
tional Council of Science Teachers, 1988, for *Radio:
From Marconi to the Space Age;* Best Book citation,
ALA, Best Book for the Teen Age citation, NYPL, and
Editor's Choice citation, *Booklist,* all 1989, and Best of
the Best citation, ALA, 1994, all for *Up Country;* Best
Book for the Teen Age citation, NYPL, and Best
Children's Fiction Book of the Year citation, Society of
Midland Authors, both 1990, both for *RoboDad;* Best
Book for the Teen Age citation, NYPL, 1994, and
American Bookseller Pick of the Lists citation, 1996,
both for *Dogwolf;* Best Book for the Teen Age citation,
NYPL, 1994, for *China Past—China Future;* Best Book
for Young Adults citation, ALA, and Best Book for the
Teen Age citation, NYPL, 1995, both for *Between a
Rock and a Hard Place;* American Booksellers Pick of
the Lists citation, Orbis Pictus nominee, and Cooperative
Children's Book Center Choice, all for *I'm Tougher
Than Asthma!;* Best Book citation, ALA, Top Ten YA
Fiction Books of 1997, ALA, Quick Pick for Reluctant
Readers, ALA, American Bookseller Pick of the Lists
citation, 1997, Heartland Award, and Arthur Tofte
Juvenile Fiction Book Award, Council for Wisconsin
Writers, all for *Bull Catcher;* Gold Seal Award, *Oppen-
heim Toy Portfolio,* Reviewer's Choice, *Sesame Street
Parents,* and Cooperative Children's Book Center

Alden R. Carter

Choice, all for *Big Brother Dustin;* Outstanding Book for Young People with Disabilities, International Board on Books for Youth, Best Children's Book of the Year, Children's Book Council, and Cooperative Children's Book Center Choice, all for *Seeing Things My Way;* Best Book for the Teen Age citation, NYPL, for *Crescent Moon;* Gold Seal, *Oppenheim Toy Portfolio,* for *Stretching Ourselves: Kids with Cerebral Palsy;* Outstanding Achievement Award, Wisconsin Library Association; Best Children's Book of the Year, Children's Book Council, and Archer/Eckblad Award, Council for Wisconsin Writers, both for *I'm Tougher Than Diabetes!;* Notable Wisconsin Author, Wisconsin Library Association, 2002.

Writings

YOUNG ADULT NONFICTION

(With Wayne Jerome LeBlanc) *Supercomputers,* F. Watts (New York, NY), 1985.
Modern China, with photographs by Carol S. and Alden R. Carter, F. Watts (New York, NY), 1986.
(With Wayne Jerome LeBlanc) *Modern Electronics,* F. Watts (New York, NY), 1986.
Illinois, F. Watts (New York, NY), 1987.
Radio: From Marconi to the Space Age, F. Watts (New York, NY), 1987.
The Shoshoni, F. Watts (New York, NY), 1989.
Last Stand at the Alamo, F. Watts (New York, NY), 1990.

The Battle of Gettysburg, F. Watts (New York, NY), 1990.
The Colonial Wars: Clashes in the Wilderness, F. Watts (New York, NY), 1992.
The American Revolution: War for Independence, F. Watts (New York, NY), 1992.
The War of 1812: Second Fight for Independence, F. Watts (New York, NY), 1992.
The Mexican War: Manifest Destiny, F. Watts (New York, NY), 1992.
The Civil War: American Tragedy, F. Watts (New York, NY), 1992.
The Spanish-American War: Imperial Ambitions, F. Watts (New York, NY), 1992.
Battle of the Ironclads: The Monitor and the Merrimack, F. Watts (New York, NY), 1993.
China Past—China Future, F. Watts (New York, NY), 1994.

"AMERICAN REVOLUTION" SERIES; YOUNG ADULT NONFICTION

Colonies in Revolt, F. Watts (New York, NY), 1988.
The Darkest Hours, F. Watts (New York, NY), 1988.
At the Forge of Liberty, F. Watts (New York, NY), 1988.
Birth of the Republic, F. Watts (New York, NY), 1988.

YOUNG ADULT FICTION

Growing Season, Coward-McCann (New York, NY), 1984.
Wart, Son of Toad, Putnam (New York, NY), 1985.
Sheila's Dying, Putnam (New York, NY), 1987.
Up Country, Putnam (New York, NY), 1989.
RoboDad, Putnam (New York, NY), 1990, published as *Dancing on Dark Water,* Scholastic (New York, NY), 1993.
Dogwolf, Scholastic (New York, NY), 1994.
Between a Rock and a Hard Place, Scholastic (New York, NY), 1995.
Bull Catcher, Scholastic (New York, NY), 1996.
Crescent Moon, Holiday House (New York, NY), 1999.

PHOTO-ESSAYS FOR CHILDREN

(With daughter, Siri M. Carter) *I'm Tougher Than Asthma!,* photographs by Dan Young, A. Whitman & Co. (Morton Grove, IL), 1996.
Big Brother Dustin, photographs by Young and Carol S. Carter, A. Whitman & Co. (Morton Grove, IL), 1997.
Seeing Things My Way, photographs by Carol S. Carter, A. Whitman and Co. (Morton Grove, IL), 1998.
Dustin's Big School Day, photographs by Dan Young and Carol S. Carter, A. Whitman and Co. (Morton Grove, IL), 1999.
Stretching Ourselves: Kids with Cerebral Palsy, photographs by Carol S. Carter, A. Whitman and Co. (Morton Grove, IL), 2000.
I'm Tougher Than Diabetes!, photographs by Carol S. Carter, A. Whitman and Co. (Morton Grove, IL), 2001.

OTHER

Contributor to anthologies, including *Connections: Short Stories by Outstanding Writers for Young Adults,* Delacorte (New York, NY), 1989; *Center Stage: One Act Plays for Teenage Readers and Actors,* HarperCollins (New York, NY), 1990; *Join In: Multiethnic Short Stories by Outstanding Writers for Young Adults,*

Delacorte (New York, NY), 1993; *No Easy Answers: Short Stories about Teenagers Making Tough Choices,* Bantam Doubleday Dell (New York, NY), 1997; *Time Capsule,* Bantam Doubleday Dell (New York, NY), 1999; *On the Fringe,* Dial (New York, NY), 2001; and *On the Edge,* Simon & Schuster (New York, NY), 1999.

Sidelights

Author of thirty-five titles for young readers, Alden R. Carter has written books about history, technology, and physical ailments, but is best recognized for his nine award-winning juvenile fiction titles. Writing in *Something about the Author Autobiography Series (SAAS),*

Carter noted, "I like to write for young adults because they have yet to develop the protective layers of emotional experience that desensitize our adult recollection of what it felt like to be teenagers." Praised especially for his mastery of characterization, Carter writes realistically about the personal problems that young people sometimes face as they mature, including serious issues such as death, alcoholism, and mental illness. Aware that these problems might easily overburden his young readers, Carter commented in *SAAS:* "I'm always concerned that my novels sound bleak, when actually there's a fair amount of humor in all of them." This successful balance has earned him and his books recognition from the American Library Association,

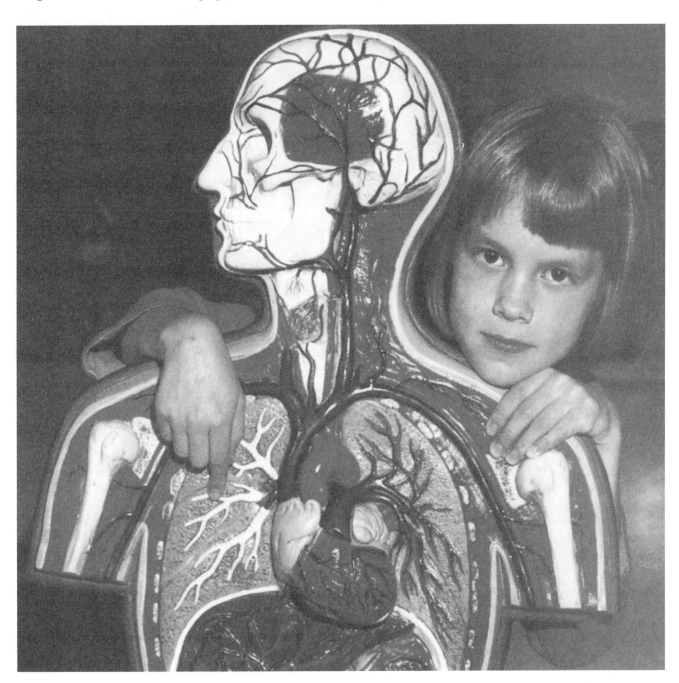

Carter cowrote a picture book with his daughter, Siri, in which they document the affects of Siri's asthma and her determination to overcome her limitations. (From I'm Tougher than Asthma!, *illustrated with photos by Dan Young.)*

library systems around the United States, and several writers' organizations.

Born in 1947, in Eau Claire, Wisconsin, Carter is one of three children. His father was a lawyer and his mother an academic editor who counted passengers of the *Mayflower* among her ancestors. They met and married in Boston, but moved back to Mr. Carter's hometown to start a family and to oversee property left to him by an uncle. Carter remembers his youth as being mostly happy, though his father's heavy drinking frequently disrupted family life. A fair student at school, he took an early and avid interest in reading. Books soon became a haven for him, a safe place away from his father's alcoholism. "I wouldn't learn about the roles played in the 'alcoholic family' until many years later," Carter reported in *SAAS,* "when I began researching a novel, *Up Country,* on the experience of being the child of an alcoholic.... I wish I had known more as a child, because maybe then I wouldn't have felt that we were somehow uniquely flawed.... Like alcoholic families everywhere, we covered up. And, since we didn't talk to outsiders about our problems, we avoided talking about them at home. Instead, we soldiered on, guided by my mother's favorite injunction: 'courage.'"

Carter's parents encouraged his love of books. "My father was never a mean drunk, and he read to me nightly when he was able. We read cowboy books, pirate books, dog books. A lot of it was junk, but he never minded. On family car trips, my mother would read to us. Unlike dad, she would pause to criticize a writer's sloppy work. *The Swiss Family Robinson,* one of my all-time favorites, took a pounding, but from her I learned to distinguish between good and bad writing.

"I started writing down some of my own stories when I was eight or nine. They weren't very good, but I do recall the feeling of amazement and power when my sister cried on hearing my story of an ill-starred racehorse named Percy. I still tell that story when I visit schools but I've added a twist, saving Percy at the last minute and sending him off to live happily ever after.

"Besides books, I enjoyed scouts, movies, camping, canoeing, and sandlot baseball. We owned a cottage in northern Wisconsin and I was always happiest there. Through ninth grade I went to a small school. Eventually, it became pretty claustrophobic and I was delighted to escape to a big high school. I wasn't athletic enough to play sports, but I was a big fan. I wrote for the school newspaper and did most of the typical teenage stuff."

The summer of his sophomore year, Carter and his family vacationed in Europe together. That autumn, his father was diagnosed with throat cancer and died within a matter of months. "It was hard," the author related. "He was a troubled but kind and decent man. He died with a lot of courage. We missed him a lot."

After graduating from high school, Carter spent the summer at the family cabin in northern Wisconsin, where he met his future wife and occasional collabora-

Dustin, a Down's syndrome child, helps his parents find the perfect name for his new baby sister and prepare for her arrival in this picture book, illustrated with photos by Dan Young and Carol S. Carter.

tor, Carol Ann Shadis. That fall he enrolled at the University of Kansas on a ROTC scholarship. "I majored in English and humanities and had the additional load of my naval science classes, so I was busy. During the summers we were in training, either shipboard or with the marines. I enjoyed it."

Upon graduation, Carter was commissioned an ensign in the Navy. He spent the next five years as a line officer with a specialty in communications. He was promoted to lieutenant junior grade and lieutenant senior grade, earning a nomination for the Navy Achievement Medal for his skillful direction of communications during the Department of Defense development project OSDOC II.

His wife joined him during his posting to the naval amphibious base at Little Creek, Virginia, and they married shortly after his discharge. He attended Montana State University to earn a teacher's certificate and took a job teaching English and journalism in Marshfield, Wisconsin, where the Carters have resided since. All during the time he was in college and in the Navy, Carter had never given up a youthful ambition to become a writer. Teaching English, Carter was at least closer to this dream, and during summer vacations, he wrote short stories and an adult novel, none of which sold. Frustrated, Carter decided to quit teaching in 1980 to give full-time writing a chance. "My friends thought I was crazy, and probably with good reason," he says now, "but devoting all my time to writing was something I desperately wanted to do."

It took several years, but finally he published his first novel. *Growing Season* concerns family relationships and the contrasts between city and country life, and it elicited much positive critical response. For instance, in *Voice of Youth Advocates,* Mary K. Chelton praised its "superior characterizations." The novel is told from the perspective of Rick—a straight-arrow teenager whose senior year in high school is disrupted when his family leaves the city for a dairy farm in the country—and recounts his journey into maturity and responsibility. Calling *Growing Season* "a realistic chronicle of agricultural and family life," *Horn Book* contributor Ethel R. Twichell added that "it intertwines closely the narrative about farm life with the theme of family relations." And *School Library Journal* reviewer Hope Bridgewater found it "an honest and sincere portrait of human growth and change," while noting that "the human emotions and situations described are universal."

Carter's second novel, *Wart, Son of Toad,* is the story of the relationship between a father and son whose family has been devastated by the accidental death of the teenage narrator's mother and sister. The father is an unpopular biology teacher whose students refer to him behind his back as "Toad" and to his son as "Wart." A *Kirkus Reviews* contributor found "dramatic power" in the scenes between the father and son. Both are unhappy and "can offer each other neither communication nor comfort," wrote a *Wilson Library Bulletin* contributor, who thought that Carter tells his tale with "just the right amount of humor and compassion." Calling it a "good performance," Robert Unsworth suggested in *School Library Journal* that "Carter is strong on characterization—readers can connect with any of his readily recognizable people."

Sheila's Dying, the story of a young girl diagnosed with a fatal form of uterine cancer, "is a deeply moving story of the illness and death" of the title character, commented Janet Bryan in *School Library Journal.* The story is narrated by boyfriend Jerry, a school basketball player who changes his mind about dumping Sheila in order to devote himself to her throughout her terminal illness. Praising the novel's "sturdy characterization and dialogue," Zena Sutherland added in *Bulletin of the Center for Children's Books* that it "makes a statement about responsibility without moralizing." And according to Susan Ackler in *Voice of Youth Advocates, Sheila's Dying* contains "a memorable cast of characters who are believable and will remain with the reader long after the book is finished." As Stephanie Zvirin stated in *Booklist,* "Carter has written a tough book," one that, as a *Publishers Weekly* contributor suggested, "rings starkly true."

Called "a powerful story, memorably told" by a *Kirkus Reviews* contributor, Carter's 1989 book *Up Country* looks at the troubled life of sixteen-year-old Carl Staggers, who "uses his talent with electronics both to shield himself from his mother's alcoholism and promis-

cuity and to try to make enough money repairing stolen stereos to get into engineering school later," explained *School Library Journal* reviewer Barbara Hutcheson, who called the book "a solid, unpreachy novel." When Carl's mother is arrested after being involved in a hit-and-run accident, he is sent to live with relatives on a country farm, where he encounters "unquestioning acceptance," noted Nancy Vasilakis in *Horn Book.* "Gripping, satisfying, and heart-wrenching—another winner from a talented writer," remarked Stella Baker in *Voice of Youth Advocates.* According to Betsy Hearne in *Bulletin of the Center for Children's Books,* Carter's character and situation will make young adult readers "think about the ways they solve whatever problems loom in their own lives." The selection of *Up Country* to the ALA's Best of the Best list in 1994 was, according to Carter, "the high point of my career."

In *RoboDad,* published in 1990, Carter focuses on a chubby fourteen-year-old girl named Shar, who must contend with the physiological changes of puberty as well as the upheaval in her family caused by her father's altered physical condition. Shar's father has suffered a massive stroke which has transformed him from a loving man into an emotionless and sometimes menacing stranger. Considering *RoboDad* a "fine, sensitive book," Leone McDermott added in *Booklist* that Carter is "extraordinarily, almost painfully, perceptive." A *Bulletin of the Center for Children's Books* contributor remarked: "Powerful and disturbing, the story is told with compassion and honesty." Finding the ending "unsettling" but "refreshingly realistic," Laura L. Lent wrote in *Voice of Youth Advocates* that *RoboDad* "keeps one's attention and leaves an ending that one can muse over for days."

Of his sixth novel, *Dogwolf,* Carter wrote in *SAAS:* "I sometimes think that I have been preparing my whole life to tell the story of Pete LaSavage, Jim Redwing, the dogwolf, and—as Pete describes it—'the fire from the end of the world.' But I do know that, at least for me, *Dogwolf* touches some underlying realities both terrible and wonderful that I have never had the courage or the skill to write about before." *Dogwolf* tells the story of fifteen-year-old Pete, who is partly of Native American descent, as he spends a summer fire-watching on his family's farm in northern Wisconsin. Bonnie Kunzel, writing in *School Library Journal,* noted the "menacing, smoke-filled atmosphere" that frames the story and praised Carter's "fully developed characters." Writing for *Councillor,* published by the Council for Wisconsin Writers, Tom Bontly wrote "I was particularly smitten with Carter's deftness with the language. He's written this book in the muted power and subtle tones of an approaching storm on a thick August night. The strength of Carter's words, much like the forest fire Pete keeps watch for and the struggle that drives him, seethes and churns just below the surface."

A further fiction offering, *Between a Rock and a Hard Place,* is "the ultimate YA survival novel," according to *Booklist*'s Frances Bradburn. The novel tells the story of fifteen-year-old Mark Severson and his diabetic cousin,

Randy, neither of whom are looking forward to their upcoming canoe trip which is a family rite of passage for its young males. Mark is not the outdoor type at all and would rather be spending time with his girlfriend, while Randy's diabetes keeps him from many normal activities. In fact, Mark suspects that his cousin uses the condition to keep him from having to work at all. But out in the canoe, beginning their ten-day trip through the lake country of Minnesota, each realizes that in order for the journey to be any fun at all, they will have to work together. A few easy challenges at the outset, which the two youths easily overcome, give them confidence, and suddenly they are enjoying themselves, fishing and camping along the way. But such an idyll can not last. A bear eats their food, putting Randy's health seriously at risk. But worse is to come. In their hurry to get back to civilization, they chance a dangerous rapids, lose their canoe and Randy's insulin, and are stranded afoot in the dense wilderness. In what Bradburn describes as "a terrifying race for survival," the boys must find a way out before Randy lapses into a fatal coma. Deborah Stevenson, writing in *Bulletin of the Center for Children's Books,* compared Carter's tale to the work of Gary Paulsen, noting that "readers will feel satisfyingly included in the boys' heroic adventure."

Winner of the prestigious Heartland Award, *Bull Catcher* is the story of high school catcher Neil "the bull" Larsen, and his best friend, the team's shortstop and captain, Jeff Hanson. From ninth grade through graduation, the boys' lives revolve around baseball. But there is more to *Bull Catcher* than just games and jock talk. "Unlike many sports novels, *Bull Catcher* does more than pump up its readers for a do-or-die game against the cross-town rivals," remarked Randy Meyer in a *Booklist* review. According to Meyer, Carter takes a "deeper look" at athletics and the requirements for success. While Jeff goes for a scholarship out of high school, Neil, known as Bull, begins to see there are other things in life, and even though his friend wins his scholarship, readers can see that Bull's wider view may in the end make him a better adjusted person. Suzanne Manczuk and Ray Barber, reviewing the book in *Voice of Youth Advocates,* felt that even non-fans of baseball would be "pulled into the relationship between these two [boys]" and their dreams. Randy Brough, also writing in *Voice of Youth Advocates,* noted: "the author clearly knows the game, too. Its dynamics, as played on the high school level, are perfectly delineated.... Baseball fans will certainly enjoy this, and I hope fans of quality writing will step up to the plate as well." The American Library Association named *Bull Catcher* one of the best ten YA novels of 1998.

With the 1999 *Crescent Moon,* Carter turned to historical fiction, writing a story set in his home town of Eau Claire, Wisconsin, in 1912, the year of the last great log drive down the Chippewa River. Thirteen-year-old Jeremy joins his great uncle Mac and an elderly Chippewa, Nathan Two-Horse, in the carving of a life-size sculpture of an Indian maiden to honor her people and the passing of the old ways. Beyond this central motif, *Crescent Moon* paints a colorful picture of life at

the end of a heroic era. Loggers, mill hands, immigrants, child laborers, and a beautiful Indian girl all play a part in the story as Jeremy grows over the course of a summer from a child into a young man. Writing in *Signal,* Elizabeth Poe called the story "a tribute to all the people who helped shape history in this part of the country. Carter crafts his tale as finely as Uncle Mac crafts his statue."

Peter D. Sieruta, reviewing the novel in *Horn Book,* wrote that though the "characters sometimes speak too portentously about their place in history, there is no question that they are living on the cusp of a new era." Carol A. Edwards, writing in *School Library Journal,* found the *Crescent Moon* "good historical fiction, with issues of justice, racism, and the environment woven into the action-packed plot." In *Catholic Library World,* Lisa Prolman called the book "a breathtaking novel that flows like the Chippewa River it describes." She concluded her review: "This book is highly recommended ... especially for fans of the 'Dear America' and 'My Name Is America' books. *Crescent Moon* is a gem that should not be missed."

Carter began writing nonfiction for young people soon after the publication of his first novel. Forming a partnership with his sister's husband, Wayne Jerome LeBlanc, he soon published *Supercomputers* and *Modern Electronics.* Later, with LeBlanc as his advisor, Carter won an Outstanding Science Trade Book for Children citation for *Radio: From Marconi to the Space Age.* With this success behind him, Carter moved to writing nonfiction primarily about American history— "subjects more to my taste," he admitted in *SAAS.* He wrote a series of four books on the American Revolution and six books on America's wars of the eighteenth and nineteenth centuries. Among the latter are *The Colonial Wars: Clashes in the Wilderness, The Mexican War: Manifest Destiny,* and *The Spanish-American War: Imperial Ambitions.* Steven Engelfried, writing in *School Library Journal,* called these three books: "Solid series entries covering three often-overlooked chapters in American history." Writing in the same series, Carter also authored another book on America's struggle for independence. Calling *The American Revolution: War for Independence* a "good introduction," *Booklist*'s Carolyn Phelan remarked that Carter's "perspective and lively writing style make the book quite readable." A further title in the same series, Carter's *Battle of the Ironclads: The Monitor and the Merrimack,* tells the "dramatic story of the race to build the new [ironclad] ships during the Civil War," according to Phelan in *Booklist.* Phelan felt that *Battle of the Ironclads* is one of the best books in the "First Books" series and that Carter manages to draw readers into the story with his explanations, attention to detail, and dialogue.

A 1984 trip with his wife to China inspired Carter's books *Modern China* and *China Past—China Future.* *Voice of Youth Advocates* contributor Suzanne Manczuk called *China Past—China Future* "a concise, current, and thoughtful history." She added that "Carter does a nice job of presenting both facts and issues, in language and format that is accessible to middle school readers." John Philbrook, writing in *School Library Journal,* also found *China Past—China Future* well-balanced, praising Carter for maintaining "admirable impartiality in clear and interesting prose."

Beginning in 1996, Carter began publishing a series of photo-essays for and about children. *I'm Tougher than Asthma!,* narrated by Carter's daughter, Siri, gives a first-person account of her experience with asthma and includes an appendix that answers common questions about asthma and lists resources for families. Carol Baker, reviewing *I'm Tougher than Asthma!* for *Catholic Library World,* found it "great" not only for children with asthma, but "also for all children to learn about the handicaps, feelings, and problems of their classmates." In *Big Brother Dustin* and its sequel, *Dustin's Big School Day,* Carter focuses on a young boy with Down's syndrome, though that fact is never mentioned in the text. *Big Brother Dustin* presents the story of a sibling getting ready for a new baby, in a "low-key" but "never condescending" approach, as *Horn Book*'s Mary M.

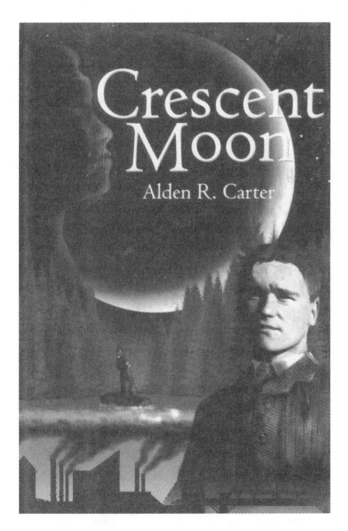

Forward-thinking Jeremy learns to appreciate his uncle's traditional ways when they work together to carve a memorial to the Chippewas in late nineteenth-century Wisconsin. (Cover illustration by Joseph Guillette.)

Burns characterized the book. Reviewing *Dustin's Big School Day* in *School Library Journal,* Lucinda Snyder Whitehurst concluded that the story "is valuable for its depiction of a great kid who has special needs but is integrated completely into the life of his school." *Seeing Things My Way* is a "heartwarming narrative related by a visually impaired child," according to Stephani Hutchinson in *School Library Journal.* With *Stretching Ourselves: Kids with Cerebral Palsy,* Carter provides a "solid introduction" to cerebral palsy, wrote Margaret C. Howell in *School Library Journal,* providing "just enough information for younger children or to begin a discussion." In the 2001 title, *I'm Tougher Than Diabetes!,* Carter's young narrator introduces how she copes with diabetes while living an outgoing life in an "inspirational tale of a family managing a difficult condition," as Helen Rosenberg described the work in a *Booklist* review.

"The reasons why I've written so much nonfiction are varied," Carter commented in *SAAS.* "There are the practical reasons of earning a living and expanding my credit list, but there's more to it. I'm fascinated with history and believe strongly that young people need to learn about the past.... I also enjoy research and the process of expanding and reexamining my own knowledge." But, he later added, "As much as I enjoy writing nonfiction, fiction is my first love, and I think of myself primarily as a novelist."

Although Carter stressed in *SAAS* that he does not "set out to advise kids how to survive the teenage years," he maintains a certain faith that his writing can have some positive influence. "Young adult novels provide no miraculous cure for the age-old problems of growing up," he said. "Yet, a YA novel can offer a respite of sorts. For a few hours, the young adult reader can escape into the lives of fictional young people who are also fighting to make some sense of life: young people who are, in short, proving that the teenage years can be survived."

Biographical and Critical Sources

BOOKS

Authors and Artists for Young Adults, Volume 17, Gale (Detroit, MI), 1995, pp. 39-46.

Children's Literature Review, Volume 22, Gale (Detroit, MI), 1991, pp. 16-23.

Something about the Author Autobiography Series, Volume 18, Gale (Detroit, MI), 1994, pp. 77-94.

Twentieth-Century Young Adult Writers, St. James Press (Detroit, MI), 1993.

Writers for Young Adults, Volume 1, edited by Ted Hipple, Scribner (New York, NY), 1993.

PERIODICALS

Appraisal: Science Books for Young People, spring, 1987, p. 39; fall, 1988, p. 53.

Booklist, July, 1984, p. 1544; May 1, 1985, p. 1247; November 15, 1985, p. 481; June 1, 1986, p. 1458; June 1, 1987, Stephanie Zvirin, review of *Sheila's Dying,* p. 1514; December 15, 1987, p. 703; December 1, 1988, p. 644; October 1, 1989, p. 344; November 15, 1990, Leone McDermott, review of *RoboDad,* p. 653; March 1, 1993, Carolyn Phelan, review of *The American Revolution: War for Independence,* p. 1224; January 15, 1994, Carolyn Phelan, review of *Battle of the Ironclads: The Monitor and the Merrimack,* p. 922; June 1, 1994, Jeanne Triner, review of *China Past—China Future,* p. 1791; January 1, 1995, p. 814; January 1, 1996, Frances Bradburn, review of *Between a Rock and a Hard Place,* p. 828; March 1, 1996, Stephanie Zvirin, review of *I'm Tougher Than Asthma!,* p. 1185; April 15, 1997, Randy Meyer, review of *Bull Catcher,* p. 1420; August, 1997, Ilene Cooper, review of *Big Brother Dustin,* p. 1905; November 15, 1998, Kay Weisman, review of *Seeing Things My Way,* p. 592; February 15, 2000, Roger Leslie, review of *Crescent Moon,* p. 1110; March 15, 2000, GraceAnne A. DeCandido, review of *Stretching Ourselves: Kids with Cerebral Palsy,* p. 1372; December 15, 2001, Ilene Cooper, review of *Sheila's Dying,* p. 729; January 1, 2002, Helen Rosenberg, review of *I'm Tougher Than Diabetes!,* p. 850.

Book Report, January-February, 1986, p. 40; September-October, 1986, p. 50; September-October, 1994, p. 59; March-April, 1996, Cynthia Lee Vallar, review of *Between a Rock and a Hard Place,* pp. 33-34.

Booktalker, September, 1989.

Bulletin of the Center for Children's Books, July-August, 1987, Zena Sutherland, review of *Sheila's Dying,* p. 204; January, 1988, p. 84; July-August, 1989, Betsy Hearne, review of *Up Country,* p. 270; February, 1991, review of *RoboDad,* p. 138; December, 1995, Deborah Stevenson, review of *Between a Rock and a Hard Place,* p. 122; March, 1997, Elizabeth Bush, review of *Bull Catcher,* pp. 242-243.

Catholic Library World, September, 1996, Carol Baker, review of *I'm Tougher than Asthma!;* September, 2000, Lisa Prolman, review of *Crescent Moon.*

Councillor, spring, 1996, Tom Bontly, "The Freedom that Drove it Mad," p. 2.

English Journal, November, 1984, p. 100; October, 1986, p. 84; April, 1989, p. 86.

Horn Book, August, 1984, Ethel R. Twichell, review of *Growing Season,* p. 473; July-August, 1989, Nancy Vasilakis, review of *Up Country,* pp. 486-487; May-June, 1997, Mary M. Burns, review of *Big Brother Dustin,* pp. 303-304; March-April, 2000, Peter D. Sieruta, review of *Crescent Moon,* p. 194.

Horn Book Guide, fall, 1997, Peter D. Sieruta, review of *Bull Catcher,* p. 312.

Kirkus Reviews, November 1, 1985, review of *Wart, Son of Toad,* p. 1197; May 1, 1987, p. 716; October 1, 1988, p. 1466; June 15, 1989, review of *Up Country,* p. 915.

Los Angeles Times Book Review, November 20, 1988, p. 8.

Publishers Weekly, May 8, 1987, review of *Sheila's Dying,* p. 72; February 15, 1999, review of *Between a Rock and a Hard Place,* p. 109.

School Library Journal, September, 1984, Hope Bridgewater, review of *Growing Season,* p. 126; August, 1985, p. 27; February, 1986, Robert Unsworth, review of *Wart, Son of Toad,* pp. 93-94; August, 1986, p. 90; May, 1987, Janet Bryan, review of *Sheila's Dying,* p. 108; March, 1988, p. 205; May, 1988, p. 48;

November, 1988, p. 135; January, 1989, p. 97; May, 1989, p. 115; June, 1989, Barbara Hutcheson, review of *Up Country,* p. 121; November, 1989, p. 42; February, 1993, Steven Engelfried, review of *The Colonial Wars: Clashes in the Wilderness, The Mexican War: Manifest Destiny,* and *The Spanish-American War: Imperial Ambitions,* p. 96; October, 1994, John Philbrook, review of *China Past—China Future,* pp. 131-132; April, 1995, Susan Knorr, review of *Dogwolf,* p. 150; August, 1995, Bonnie Kunzel, review of *Dogwolf,* pp. 37-38; December, 1995, Joel Shoemaker, review of *Between a Rock and a Hard Place,* p. 128; August, 1996, Martha Gordon, review of *I'm Tougher Than Asthma!,* p. 133; May, 1997, Tom S. Hurlburt, review of *Bull Catcher,* p. 131; June, 1997, Maura Bresnahan, review of *Big Brother Dustin,* p. 85; November, 1998, Stephani Hutchinson, review of *Seeing Things My Way,* p. 103; June, 1999, Lucinda Snyder Whitehurst, review of *Dustin's Big School Day,* p. 92; March, 2000, Carol A. Edwards, review of *Crescent Moon,* p. 234; May, 2000, Margaret C. Howell, review of *Stretching Ourselves,* p. 160; May, 2002, Martha Gordon, review of *I'm Tougher Than Diabetes!,* p. 135.

Science Books and Films, March-April, 1987, p. 231.

Signal, fall, 1999-winter, 2000, Elizabeth Poe, review of *Crescent Moon.*

Voice of Youth Advocates, October, 1984, Mary K. Chelton, review of *Growing Season,* p. 195; December, 1985, p. 330; June, 1987, Susan Ackler, review of *Sheila's Dying,* p. 75; February, 1988, p. 294; August, 1989, Stella Baker, review of *Up Country,* p. 155; April, 1990, p. 68; December, 1990, Laura L. Lent, review of *RoboDad,* p. 277; October, 1994, Suzanne Manczuk, review of *China Past—China Future,* p. 229; February, 1995, Francine Canfield, review of *Dogwolf,* p. 336; April, 1996, Judy Sasges, review of *Between a Rock and a Hard Place,* p. 24; October, 1997, Randy Brough, review of *Bull Catcher;* February, 1998, Suzanne Manczuk and Ray Barber, review of *Bull Catcher,* p. 364.

Wilson Library Bulletin, November, 1985, review of *Wart, Son of Toad,* p. 47.

OTHER

Alden R. Carter Web Site, http://www.aldencarter.com (October 9, 2002).

*   *   *

CHOWN, Marcus 1959-

Personal

Born June 9, 1959, in London, England; son of Ronald and Patricia (a homemaker; maiden name, Paradine) Chown; married Karen Chilver, December 24, 1991. *Ethnicity:* "Caucasian." *Education:* University of London, B.S., 1980; California Institute of Technology, M.S., 1984. *Hobbies and other interests:* Swimming, reading.

Addresses

Home—Rose Cottage, Village St., Aldington, Worcestershire WR11 5UB, England; fax: 44 1368 830394. *Agent*—Sara Menguc, 4 Hatch Pl., Kingston-Upon-Thames, Surrey KT2 5NB, England. *E-mail*—mchown@compuserve.com.

Career

Cosmologist, science writer, and science fiction novelist. *New Scientist* magazine, cosmology consultant.

Member

Royal Astronomical Society, Science Fiction & Fantasy Writers of America, Caltech Alumni Association.

Awards, Honors

Science Writers Award, Glaxo-Wellcome, 1994; runner-up, Rhone-Poulenc science book prize, for *Afterglow of Creation: From the Fireball to the Discovery of Cosmic Ripples;* Book of the Year, *New Statesman* and *Asahi Shimbun* (Japan), both for *The Magic Furnace: The Search for the Origins of Atoms;* "Top Ten Sci-Tech Books," *Booklist,* 2002, for *The Universe Next Door: The Making of Tomorrow's Science.*

Writings

(With John Gribbin) *Double Planet* (science fiction novel), Avon Books (New York, NY), 1989.

(With John Gribbin) *Reunion* (science fiction novel), Gollancz (London, England), 1991.

Afterglow of Creation: From the Fireball to the Discovery of Cosmic Ripples, University Science Books (Sausalito, CA), 1996.

The Magic Furnace: The Search for the Origins of Atoms, Oxford University Press (New York, NY), 2001.

The Universe Next Door: The Making of Tomorrow's Science, Oxford University Press (New York, NY), 2002.

Sidelights

Marcus Chown is a scientist who writes both science fiction and books on science fact. His first popular science book, *Afterglow of Creation: From the Fireball to the Discovery of Cosmic Ripples,* describes the events "from the time just before the Big Bang to the year 1992, when the Cosmic Background Explorer satellite (COBE) confirmed that radiation from the Big Bang was still with us in the form of microwaves," according to Anne Fitzgerald in *Astronomy.* Chown "describes the discoveries—and the rediscoveries—that gave birth to the current view of the universe," wrote Jorge A. Lopez in *American Scientist.* Based on his own professional knowledge of cosmology and astrophysics, and on personal interviews with participants, Chown relates "a nicely strung chain of interesting stories told in chronological order" that trace the development of the universe, "from the detection of the expansion of the universe to

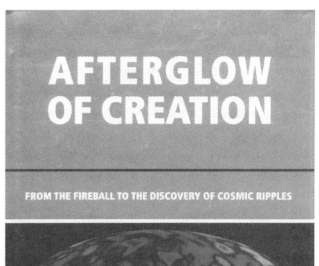

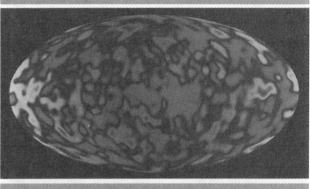

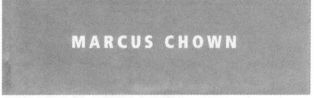

In this work, Marcus Chown examines the discovery of residual energy resulting from the Big Bang explosion fifteen billion years ago, and he outlines the subsequent measurement of the radiation afterglow, including a candid portrayal of the scientists involved.

the measurement of the background 'fossil' radiation," Lopez said.

"Marcus Chown's book is a very good piece of story-telling," wrote Tim Radford in *New Scientist,* "because it patiently pursues not only the story's main thread, but also the wrong turnings, the exasperations and serendipities of the search for the relics of creation." Chown recounts the development of theories of the earliest state of the universe as a densely compact place of nothing but protons, neutrons, and photons which erupted in a "primeval fireball," Lopez said. He also describes the persons and personalities involved in the discoveries, from early theorists and experimenters to Arno Penzias and Robert Wilson, who did not realize that the noise picked up by the first satellite communication antenna was fossil radiation. However, their radioastronomy experiments in 1965 "almost accidentally identified the remnant of the Big Bang," Radford said. They were awarded the Nobel Prize in 1978 for their discoveries in the field. "In the more contemporary part of the story of background radiation, Chown does future generations the favor of untangling the who-did-what," Lopez said.

To Chown's credit, Radford commented, he "writes as if he were addressing his fellow humans." To have discerned a split-second by split-second chronology of the beginning of the universe is a phenomenal achievement, and "only when you reduce the cosmic understanding of the past twenty-five years to something like vernacular English can you begin to appreciate how cosmic it really is."

"I am a science writer, and I have written popular science books, science fiction novels, and a children's book," Marcus Chown once remarked. "I got into writing after being a radio astronomer at the California Institute of Technology in Pasadena. Returning to England, I worked on the staff of the weekly science magazine, *New Scientist.* Now, though, I am freelance. I am the magazine's "cosmology consultant," writing on subjects as diverse as unknowable numbers, multiple universes, and the possibility of time running backwards. Perhaps I should be called the 'no-use-to-man-or-beast consultant' since I generally write about things that are

no use to man or beast! Ideas are what excite me. I suppose I am an ideas junkie. I am constantly amazed that science is so much stranger than anything we could invent."

Afterglow of Creation "was a runner-up for the Rhone-Poulenc science book prize," Chown continued. "In fact, in the UK it's the most-read popular science book after Stephen Hawking's *A Brief History of Time.* I choose my words carefully because 180,000 of those copies were not 'sold' but bought by the magazine *Focus* to give away to its readers. My second popular science book, *The Magic Furnace,* was a 'Book of the Year' in the UK magazine *New Statesman* and also in *Asahi Shimbun,* the second-biggest newspaper in Japan and the world. The English newspaper *Daily Mail* even likened its narrative style to Harry Potter! Perhaps it was the word 'magic' in the title."

In *The Magic Furnace: The Search for the Origins of Atoms,* Chown presents "a series of artfully connected and well-crafted stories" that "trace humanity's 2500-year quest to understand the nature and origin of matter," said Fred Bortz in *Dallas Morning News.* "Ever since Isaac Newton showed that the same gravitational force that pins us to Earth holds the planets in their orbits, we have become more mindful that cosmos and microworld are intricately linked," remarked Martin J. Rees in *Natural History.* "Science Writer Marcus Chown expresses this theme beautifully. He recounts how scientists had to understand atoms before they could understand what made the stars shine, and how this led to the realization that atoms on Earth were themselves forged in ancient stars."

In *Booklist,* reviewer Gilbert Taylor called *The Magic Furnace* "a lucid history" wherein Chown dwells "more closely on the physical experiments, particularly the logic behind them, that intimated atomic structure." Beginning with Democritus, the Greek philosopher who believed that matter could not be subdivided indefinitely, Chown tells the story of "the formation of the elements and interweaves the story of how their stellar origins were pieced together," wrote Jon Turney in *Guardian.* Chown covers subjects as broadly spaced as the discovery of the electron and radioactivity to the conclusive proof that "the Sun, Earth, and stars were made of the same stuff," Rees said. Chown also focuses on the pioneers who made the discoveries, including British astronomer Cecilia Payne, who in 1925 wrote a Ph.D. thesis that contained evidence that hydrogen and helium made up 98 percent of the mass of the sun, but who later downplayed this important discovery because of the skepticism of prominent astrophysicist Henry Norris Russell. Chown also relates the stories of British astronomer Fred Hoyle, who wondered if the entire periodic table could be the result of nuclear transmutations in stars; of George Gamow, who thought that all elements originated with the Big Bang; and Robert Oppenheimer and Hans Bethe, "who calculated the sorts of nuclear reactions stars and supernovae can sustain," Taylor said. The pioneers who sought the true origins of the atom "deserve the same acclaim that is rightly given

Tracing the discovery of the atom from ancient Greece to the present, Chown explains how the origin of matter traces back to the Big Bang and the evolution of stars.

to those who proposed biological evolution," Rees said, and "Marcus Chown's fascinating chronicle of their achievements deserves to be widely read."

But for Chown himself, the reactions of even a single reader can have profound effects on him. "By far the best reaction to the book [*The Magic Furnace*] came from a reader," Chown once recalled. "Her name is Pam. She left school at fourteen with no qualifications. After the book's publication in the UK, she wrote to me to say the book had brought her to tears and inspired her to embark on a university degree in professional writing. In her first year, she has gained 'distinctions' in all her essays. Her three children and husband, a London cab driver, can't believe it. She says I changed her life. I think it could have been anyone. Pam was a powder keg, waiting for someone to light a match, one of so many people with under-utilized potential. But, by chance, I was the one that lit the match. Reaching one reader, changing the life of one person—that's what makes writing worthwhile."

Biographical and Critical Sources

PERIODICALS

American Scientist, November-December, 1997, Jorge A. Lopez, review of *Afterglow of Creation: From the Fireball to the Discovery of Cosmic Ripples,* pp. 565-566.
Astronomy, December, 1996, Anne Fitzgerald, review of *Afterglow of Creation,* p. 102; November, 2001, Nick Nichols, review of *The Magic Furnace: The Search for the Origins of Atoms,* p. 98; June, 2002, Nick Nichols, review of *The Universe Next Door: The Making of Tomorrow's Science,* p. 84.
Booklist, January 1, 2001, Gilbert Taylor, review of *The Magic Furnace,* p. 890; March 1, 2002, Bryce Christensen, review of *The Universe Next Door: The Making of Tomorrow's Science,* p. 1073.
Dallas Morning News, May 6, 2001, Fred Bortz, "To the Center of the Universe: Author Studies Origins of Earth's Mix of Elements," p. 8C.
Guardian, September 2, 2000, Jon Turney, review of *The Magic Furnace,* p. 8.
Natural History, March, 2001, Martin J. Rees, review of *The Magic Furnace,* p. 81.
New Scientist, October 5, 1991, Frederik Pohl, review of *Reunion,* p. 51; July 31, 1993, Tim Radford, review of *Afterglow of Creation,* p. 42; August 19, 2000, "Elemental Us," p. 49.
Science News, April 27, 2002, review of *The Universe Next Door: The Making of Tomorrow's Science,* p. 271.

OTHER

Marcus Chown Web Site, http://www.ourworld.compuserve.com/homepages/MChown/ (January 13, 2003).*

CITRA, Becky 1954-

Personal

Born June 23, 1954, in Vancouver, British Columbia, Canada; married Larry Citra, July 2, 1988; children: Meghan. *Education:* Attended University of British Columbia; Simon Fraser University, teaching certificate. *Hobbies and other interests:* Horseback riding, gardening, hiking, reading.

Addresses

Home—Box 22, Bridge Lake, British Columbia V0K 1E0, Canada. *E-mail*—ercitra@hotmail.com.

Career

Author and teacher. Elementary school teacher in Hazelton, Port Hardy, Chilliwack, and Bridge Lake, all in British Columbia, Canada, 1976—.

Awards, Honors

Rocky Mountain Book Award, 2002, for *Ellie's New Home.*

Writings

My Homework Is in the Mail!, illustrated by Karen Harrison, Scholastic (Richmond Hill, Canada), 1995.
School Campout, Scholastic (Richmond Hill, Canada), 1996.
Ellie's New Home, Orca Book Publishers (Custer, WA), 1999.
The Freezing Moon, Orca Book Publishers (Custer, WA), 2001.
Danger at the Landings, Orca Book Publishers (Custer, WA), 2002.
Dog Days, Orca Book Publishers (Custer, WA), 2003.

Work in Progress

Research on Native Indians and on Canada in the 1880s.

Sidelights

Becky Citra told *SATA:* "My joy of writing began when I was a child. An avid reader of the Hardy Boys and Nancy Drew, I started scribbling my own mystery series at eleven years old. I took a long break from writing when I became a teacher. However, reading wonderful books out loud everyday to young children in schools inspired me one day to give it a try myself—and I've never looked back. My first books drew on experiences right out of the classroom and I still find my students a great source of material! A fascinating story in a magazine about young children immigrating to Upper Canada in the 1800s sparked my interest to do further research and my series on a pioneer family was born. I enjoy writing historical novels and am planning future books about Native Indians and Vikings! I try to write every day, in between a busy teaching career, and love

Becky Citra

the initial stages of a story best when everything is new and full of potential. For breaks, I ride my horse on our ranch, garden, hike, and read, read, read."

Citra's early-reader books are praised for plots filled with suspense and lively action, realistic characters, and child-centered narratives. Her first book, *My Homework Is in the Mail!*, recounts the trials and tribulations of Samantha Higgins (Sam), when her parents move her from urban Vancouver to a farm so far removed from civilization that Sam's school is a correspondence course. "There is much here to interest young readers," remarked Leslie Millar in *CM: Canadian Review of Materials.* "Apprehension about school, moving, and lots of contact with animals will be sure to strike a chord with most youngsters." Sam's mother charges her to find four things she can be grateful for by Thanksgiving, and though Sam devoutly doubts her ability to do this at the start of the book, she comes to appreciate meeting a real cowboy, learning to take care of the farm animals, meeting her eccentric correspondence school teacher in person, and finally making friends. "Citra's writing is tight and graceful, and she definitely knows how kids tick, what pleases them, and what mortifies them," observed Kenneth Oppel in *Quill & Quire.*

Another early reader with a contemporary setting, *School Campout,* was similarly praised for providing a likeable cast of young characters with realistic problems and approaches to solving them. When David's third-

grade class plans a camping trip, David is terrified of the possibilities—getting lost, being attacked by a bear—and when he is paired with the new kid, Bradley, who just moved from the city, he knows he will not find any help there. As the trip unfolds, David learns something about the out of doors, about his friends, and about himself. Anne Louise Mahoney, who reviewed *School Campout* for *Quill & Quire,* enumerated the book's highlights: "This novel gives seven-to-nine-year-olds a fast-paced read with a familiar situation (school), an element of surprise (the camping adventure), and a happy ending."

With *Ellie's New Home,* Citra published her first historical novel. Compared to Laura Ingalls Wilder's "Little House" books for its focus on the pioneer experience, *Ellie's New Home* has a distinctly Canadian flavor. The story centers on nine-year-old Ellie, who emigrates to Canada from England with her father and younger brother, Max, after her mother's death. When they arrive in Canada, Ellie's father leaves her and her brother with another family while he scouts for a location for their new home. Ellie is left to learn the skills that make pioneer life possible from the friendly, but rough, pioneer family. A sequel, *The Freezing Moon,* depicts Ellie and Max's first winter in Upper Canada on their father's homestead. Pioneer life in winter is hard enough, but when their father fails to return from a hunting trip, Ellie and Max must rely on help from a European woodcutter and the Native Indians whose village is nearby, neither of whom they are certain they can trust. Gillian Richardson, writing in *Resource Links,* found much to admire in *The Freezing Moon,* which "quickly engages the reader in a dramatic first chapter encounter with a bear." Though Citra skillfully maintains a high level of action and suspense, "the characters are convincing," and "vivid details bring the wilderness setting into sharp focus," Richardson maintained. Gwyneth Evans, writing in *Quill & Quire,* noted the similarities between Citra's books and the "Little House" series by Laura Ingalls Wilder, concluding: "While Ellie's family and adventures are not so vividly drawn as Laura's they offer an enjoyably Canadian-flavoured version of the pioneer experience."

Biographical and Critical Sources

PERIODICALS

Books in Canada, November, 1995, Phil Hall, review of *My Homework Is in the Mail!,* p. 40.

Quill & Quire, October, 1995, Kenneth Oppel, review of *My Homework Is in the Mail!,* p. 38; November, 1996, Anne Louise Mahoney, review of *School Campout,* p. 48; May, 2001, Gwyneth Evans, review of *The Freezing Moon,* p. 35.

Resource Links, June, 2001, Gillian Richardson, review of *The Freezing Moon,* p. 9.

OTHER

CM: Canadian Review of Materials, www.umanitoba.ca/cm/ (December 8, 1995), Leslie Millar, review of *My Homework Is in the Mail!*

CREW, Linda 1951-

Personal

Born April 8, 1951, in Corvallis, OR; daughter of Warren (a photographer) and Marolyn (an administrative assistant; maiden name, Schumacher) Welch; married Herb Crew (a farmer), June 22, 1974; children: Miles, William and Mary (twins). *Education:* Attended Lewis and Clark College, 1969-70; University of Oregon, B.A., 1973. *Politics:* Democrat. *Religion:* Presbyterian.

Addresses

Home—Wake Robin Farm, 950 Southwest Wake Robin Ave., Corvallis, OR 97333-1609. *Agent*—Robin Rue, Anita Diamant Agency, 310 Madison Ave., New York, NY 10017.

Career

Farmer and writer. Has worked as a receptionist, florist, and substitute mail deliverer.

Member

Authors Guild, Society of Children's Book Writers and Illustrators, Phi Beta Kappa.

Awards, Honors

Golden Kite Honor Book designation, Michigan Library Association Young Adult Honor Book designation, Best Book For Young Adults citation from American Library Association (ALA), and Children's Book Award for older readers, International Reading Association, all 1989, all for *Children of the River;* ALA Notable Book citation, 1991, for *Nekomah Creek.*

Writings

Children of the River, Delacorte (New York, NY), 1989.
Someday I'll Laugh about This, Delacorte (New York, NY), 1990.
Nekomah Creek, illustrated by Charles Robinson, Delacorte (New York, NY), 1991.
Ordinary Miracles (adult novel), Morrow (New York, NY), 1992.
Nekomah Creek Christmas, illustrated by Charles Robinson, Delacorte (New York, NY), 1994.
Fire on the Wind, Delacorte (New York, NY), 1995.
Long Time Passing, Delacorte (New York, NY), 1997.
Brides of Eden: A True Story Imagined, HarperCollins (New York, NY), 2001.

Contributor of articles and stories to periodicals.

Work in Progress

A screenplay version of *Long Time Passing.*

Linda Crew

Sidelights

Linda Crew grounds her fiction for young adults firmly in the real world but also in her own optimistic world view. A native of Corvallis, Oregon, who can boast an ancestor who traveled westward via a wagon train traveling the Oregon Trail in the 1860s, Crew imbues her award-winning novels with a strong sense of place, family, and happy endings. "You like to feel that things are going to turn out okay in the end," the author once commented. "Don't you hate to get invested in characters and then realize, 'Oh, this is going to be one of these stories where the author is going to make me love all these people and then kill them all'?" Crew's upbeat fiction is drawn from her own experience of life, defined by her personal attitude. "I don't just *try* to be optimistic. That's the way I look at life. And besides," she added, "somebody has to write the stories of all the families who stay together but still have problems."

"I'm not one of those who can claim a lifelong determination to be a writer," Crew once admitted, although as a youngster she *was* an avid reader who counted Louisa May Alcott's "Little Women" series, Frances Hodgson Burnett's *The Little Princess,* and classics like *Wuthering Heights* and *The Hunchback of Notre Dame* among her favorite books. She also has always viewed life from a "bookish" perspective. "I don't think that being a writer is just about filling notebooks and notebooks with scribblings all the time," Crew once said. "I think it's kind of a way of looking at life and standing back and saying, 'If this is a story, then I am the main character.' In the books I read as a child, the main character might have had a lot of problems. But she would triumph in the end. And it was kind of a pattern that I've tried to live my whole life." It's also a pattern that appears throughout her fiction.

While Crew enjoyed writing assignments in grade school and even won a Jaycee-sponsored essay contest on "What My Country Means to Me" in middle school, she envisioned a future that was far more glamorous. "I wanted to be an artist or maybe a folksinger," the creative Crew recalled. "Peter, Paul, Mary, and Linda is the sort of thing I had in mind. It only took me two or three years of strumming on the old guitar to figure out that I couldn't sing!" By the time she had reached high school, Crew's career goals had made several shifts: from painter to singer, then to actress. She sustained her acting ambition through high school graduation and even into college, where she enrolled at the University of Oregon with the intention of majoring in dramatic arts. "This dream dissolved rather abruptly somewhere around my sophomore year," Crew remembered. "The fall play was *A Midsummer Night's Dream,* and the fairies were to be topless. As a potential fairy, this did

After leaving her family to escape the Khmer Rouge army in Cambodia, Sundara tries to adapt to America while fighting the feeling that, as she adjusts, she is denouncing her heritage. (Cover illustration by Stuart Kaufman.)

not appeal to me! Also, as a fourth-generation Oregonian, it had begun to dawn on me that perhaps I would not be happy living in New York City or Los Angeles. I took the bus home and told my parents I thought I should change my major. Unfortunately, I didn't have a clue as to which program I should pursue.

"'Well,' my mother said, 'how about journalism? You've always been a pretty good writer.'

"I'm not here to argue that moms always necessarily know best, but taking her advice (for lack of any better idea) certainly worked out well for me in this case. I loved journalism. Because I'd never taken any similar classes in high school, it was all fresh and new—interviewing, researching, marketing, saying what you have to say without a lot of fuss. But my assignments always ended up full of dialogue, and I had this compelling urge to make each story a little better than the way it really happened." By the time Crew graduated from college in 1973, she knew she was destined to write fiction.

In 1974 the young journalism graduate married a farmer named Herb Crew and settled down on a small farm in the town where she, her mother, and her grandmother had all been born and raised. Between helping to manage the farm, raising her family of three—including two active twins—and working on home remodeling projects, it was not always easy to find the opportunity to write. "But," Crew once remarked, "being a writer has certainly fit into all of this better than being an actress would have!"

Crew's first novel, 1989's *Children of the River,* was inspired by events in her own life. "While we Westerners commonly speak of life as a road with various forks to choose, Asians seem more inclined to see it as a river that sweeps the individual along," Crew once explained as a backdrop to her book. "Thus the title of my book, *Children of the River,* refers not only to the close ties of the Cambodian people to their river, the mighty Mekong, but also to their life philosophy." Crew and her husband first became acquainted with Asian culture in 1980, after a Cambodian family came to help harvest fruit and vegetables on their family farm. They were impressed with the Cambodians' strong work ethic, their resolve, and their strong sense of family values. "I'm always looking for something that I feel is *my* story or that there is a reason that I should be writing it as opposed to somebody else," Crew once explained. "I don't write a book just because there needs to be a book on a certain subject. With the Cambodians, it took a while for me to convince myself that I was the person to tell their story. Finally, I thought, 'Maybe I'm the writer who lives on the farm, who met these people. Maybe I'm in the best position to write it.' And the Cambodians aren't going to write their own stories for a couple of decades, because they're just getting used to living here. Someday, of course, they'll write about this time in their lives, and then *Children of the River* will be old hat because of all the things I didn't get right, and that they have better insights into."

Even with the realization that this was a story that she was qualified to tell, Crew invested a lot of time in research before she ever set pen to paper. Fortunately, her background in journalism made the process a little less daunting than it otherwise might have been. "I just read everything I could get my hands on for a whole year before I started even thinking in terms of a fictional plot." She also interviewed many Cambodian refugees and their families. In addition, she was helped by the wealth of information then being issued by the U.S. government in its effort to help Americans understand the culture of these new immigrants.

As *Children of the River* opens, thirteen-year-old Sundara Sovann is visiting her Aunt Soka's home near the banks of Cambodia's Mekong River. It is April of 1975. Suddenly, the political turmoil that had been raging for weeks in the central city of Phnom Phen becomes life-threatening as Khmer Rouge guerilla forces, under Communist leadership, overthrow the country's existing government and take political control of Cambodia. From their comfortable, middle-class existence, Sundara and her relatives suddenly find themselves refugees; carrying but few belongings they flee aboard ship, where Soka's newborn baby dies in a wave of sickness and malnutrition that overtakes the hundreds on board during their long journey. Finally, she and her relatives find their way to a small Oregon town, where they are "adopted" by a local parish and begin to make a life for themselves in an alien culture. In the four years since her arrival in Oregon, Sundara has kept her loneliness and her fears as to the whereabouts of her parents and younger sister hidden from everyone except her immediate relatives. Now seventeen, she is still haunted by fear and guilt—especially from the death of her newborn cousin, who had died on the boat while in the young teen's care. She feels torn between the traditions of her Cambodian culture and the less-restrictive social atmosphere and more carefree lifestyle of her new American peers. When she becomes attracted to classmate Jonathan, a handsome football star, the clash between old and new comes to a head; not allowed to date, Cambodian teens follow the wishes of their parents in decisions regarding marriage, and her aunt and uncle are determined to preserve this tradition even in their new country. Ultimately, Sundara learns that while she may adapt to some American customs, welcoming new ways into her life does not mean that she is rejecting her Cambodian heritage.

Praising Crew's first work of fiction for "its strong storytelling and thorough characterization," Roger Sutton noted in *Bulletin of the Center for Children's Books* that while the character of Jonathan is somewhat idealized, *Children of the River* "is neither sentimental nor sensational: both the horror and the romance are real." Mark Jonathan Harris, writing in the *Los Angeles Times Book Review,* stated, "Sundara's efforts to remain a 'good Cambodian girl,' loyal to her past and family and, at the same time, create a new life for herself in this country is a moving story about the immigrant experience that also provides a fresh perspective on our own culture." Commenting on *Children of the River* in

Based on a true story, **Brides of Eden,** *illustrated with archival photos, depicts sixteen-year-old Eva Mae who becomes one of many in a small town in Oregon at the beginning of the twentieth century who fall under the tragic influence of a charismatic, fanatical preacher.*

Twentieth-Century Young Adult Writers, essayist Suzanne M. Valentic praised the book for highlighting "how the struggle for power often results in the senseless destruction of a people, and how we, as Americans, have learned to take freedom for granted, allowing many of the values we once held dear to disappear."

One of the ways in which *Children of the River* illustrates the cultural division between Sundara and her fellow students is through language. "The interviews gave me a good feel for how the Cambodian immigrants spoke English," Crew once commented. "One girl I spoke to had actually come from Cambodia in the same year, at the same age as Sundara had. She had been well educated. So I figured that any mistakes that she was still making in English were the ones that I should have my character still making." As some readers may realize, Sundara's speech changes when she is in a family setting among her fellow Cambodians. "When the Cambodian characters are speaking within their family, they're speaking Khmer [the language spoken in Cambodia]," the author explained. "Here Sundara's language patterns switch; she doesn't use American idioms or any slang, but she's also not making the grammatical errors she does when speaking to Americans because, of course, she's speaking Khmer." To give an even more vivid sense of the cultural differences, Crew researched short, poetic phrases from a Khmer glossary, which she had her Cambodian characters use in their conversations with each other.

Although the character of Sundara was a composite of many people Crew either met or heard about, she began to quickly take on a life of her own. "There was a girl that I was scheduled to interview. . . . I was well into the book and had already made up the character when I found out about her, and I thought it was my character. And I had this portrait of her: really beautiful and smart—she was a Rose Festival Princess in Portland. But when I met her I knew she wasn't Sundara. She was from a more upper-class background and that really changed it. And after that, I realized that I would never actually meet my character. I know that sounds stupid, but you get so into your writing that you almost begin to believe that this person's out there." Crew has not been the only one wishing to meet the real Sundara. "I've even had letters from Cambodian guys, saying 'Please, give me her address!'"

Crew has also received many letters from young Cambodian women, letters saying, "'That's just like me.' I have heard from a lot of girls that really identify with the character. *Children of the River* is also used for English as a Second Language classes in high school and college, because the reading level is not that advanced. (I'm not trying to dumb it down, but my journalism background is 'short sentences,' 'don't get too flowery.') Even immigrants from Eastern Europe and Russia have written to say that they relate to Sundara's plight, too."

While many books on the plight of Southeast Asian "boat people" focus on the discrimination these immigrants face upon their arrival in the United States, in Crew's book that element is notably absent. "Maybe I'm missing all the terrible things that are happening to these people," Crew once noted, "but sometimes I think that people go out and try and make it more dramatic. And I think that *real life*—as it *really* is—is interesting. Maybe that's my journalism background. I don't think that the sort of discrimination that these people encounter is the blatant, people-making-comments sort of thing. I don't honestly see that going on. And the Cambodians I've talked to didn't seem to be reporting these things. I'm not saying they have an easy time of it. I'm saying it's hard enough, without throwing in drama that is not taken from real life."

Unlike *Children of the River,* which required a great deal of research, Crew's following two books were drawn, for the most part, from her personal experiences. *Someday I'll Laugh about This* has its roots in her childhood and memories of holidays spent at her grandfather's beach cottage in Yachats, on the Oregon coast. In the novel Shelby is looking forward to this year's summer vacation at the family cottage, where she usually spends her time playing with her cousins. Excited about the traditional gathering of aunts, uncles, and assorted other relatives, there is no reason for her to think that this year will be any different than last year, or the year before. But her cousin Kirsten, a year older than Shelby, has reached the transmogrifying age of thirteen; suddenly she is worried about boyfriends, makeup, and keeping the right friends. Rather than spend time with Shelby, Kirsten spends her time with snobby Tanya

Dymond, a new girl in the neighborhood. Meanwhile, for some reason, Shelby's boy cousins will not be caught playing with a girl this year. And her favorite Uncle Jack is no help either; he spends his time with his new fiancée, whom he has brought to meet the whole family. The beach itself is even changing as a stretch of new condominiums springs up along the waterfront. Over the summer Shelby, who narrates the story, overcomes hurt and jealousy and begins to realize that life is about change; that she herself is changing. She also learns to stand up for herself and be an individual. Praising Crew's ability to "capture the pain of growing up, along with its inherent humor," a contributor for *Publishers Weekly* called *Someday I'll Laugh about This* "uplifting."

Nekomah Creek and *Nekomah Creek Christmas* are most closely based on Crew and her family. In fact, she admitted that, by the time 1990 rolled around, *Nekomah Creek*—"the story of a wacky family"—was "the only thing I *could* write, with a nine-year-old, two-year-old twins, and a fun-loving dad underfoot." *Nekomah Creek Christmas* reunites readers with Robby and his rambunctious family. The holiday season is approaching and Robby is growing both excited and nervous about his acting debut in the school Christmas pageant. In the meantime, his parents' mood is shadowed by an impending tax audit, which makes them preoccupied. "The *Nekomah Creek* books were fun," Crew once remarked. "My family gave me a lot of inspiration and the details came so easily. While I was writing, the dialogue was happening right downstairs!"

Crew's 1997 novel *Long Time Passing* is also partially autobiographical. A love story between two high school students that is set in the free-love era of the 1960s, the novel "isn't just hippies and smoking pot, and the thing about sex; the terror of pregnancy," the author explained. "One of the things that's central to the book is the question, 'Is she going to sleep with him or not?' I'm kind of making a plea to young women for sticking up for yourself and just saying no—you don't *have* to have a great reason. You can just decide, 'I don't want to do this yet.'" Including such personally held beliefs in a published work of fiction can feel very emotionally risky, according to Crew. "In books based on your own stuff, when the reviewer writes, 'This character is a little twerp'—you do take it sort of personally. *Children of the River* and *Fire on the Wind* are pretty removed from me. In other books, there are characters that are a lot more a part of me, like Shelby in *Someday I'll Laugh about This* or the young woman in *Long Time Passing.*"

Fire on the Wind, a novel set during a huge forest fire called the Tillamook Burn, is Crew's first historical novel. "I was interested in the trees," she once commented, explaining how the novel came about. "It was 1990, and I was driving to the [Oregon] coast with my kids. We were going to go to the Tillamook County museum and talking about the history of the Burn, imagining the fire coming over the ridge, and I said, 'I wonder what that was like to have been there. I don't think I've ever read a book about that, a novel.' And then I thought,

'Hey, maybe I should write it!' And when we got to the museum I bought a stack of books."

Fire on the Wind is the story of a thirteen-year-old girl named Estora Faye—"Storie" to her friends—who lives at the Blue Star logging camp in the forests of northwestern Oregon. In the dry heat of August 1933, a fire starts near camp. Although loggers and their families are not concerned at first, the blaze quickly grows out of control; small fires eventually converge into an eighteen-mile-long wall of flame that threatens both Storie and her entire community. Storie's consuming concerns about school, her future, and a budding romance with the logger Flynn no longer seem important as her father and Flynn join other loggers in their dangerous attempts to battle the raging inferno while she and the other women and children tense for the worst and wait. Based on a true story about the Tillamook Burn, which destroyed a vast area of Oregon forest in 1933, *Fire on the Wind* creates a vivid atmosphere due to Crew's ability to include small realistic details, provide points of view that alternate between the camp and the sites of the approaching fire, and the effective use of conversation as a way to tell the story. Reviewing the novel in *Horn Book,* Elizabeth S. Watson felt that the novel "is well written with sound character development, authentic dialogue, and just plain good storytelling." *Booklist*'s Merri Monks dubbed the book "first-rate historical fiction ... with a thrilling climax." And a reviewer for *Publishers Weekly* concluded that *Fire on the Wind* was a "gripping, well-researched story."

Again using the history of her native Oregon as backdrop, Crews tells the true story of an early twentieth-century religious cult in the 2001 novel, *Brides of Eden: A True Story Imagined.* Sixteen-year-old Eva Mae Hurt becomes mesmerized by the mysterious stranger, Joshua Creffield, who comes to her Oregon town in 1903. She and many other female followers soon leave husbands, fiancés, and families to follow this self-anointed man of the cloth to an island where he announces that one of the disciples will become the mother of a second Christ. He takes each to his bed, and meanwhile the relatives of these women become increasingly frantic. Finally suicides and murder ensue to break the hold of this cult master. Told in the first person voice of Eva, *Brides of Eden* is a fictionalized account of a real event in Corvallis. Joel Shoemaker, writing in *School Library Journal,* felt that Crew's novel "credibly and engagingly describes the degrees by which common sense and sincere religious belief gradually can be subverted to fanaticism." Shoemaker concluded that most readers will find the book "dramatic, sobering, and sadly all too real." *Booklist*'s Ilene Cooper wrote that Crew "deftly explores religious fanaticism, group thought, and the psychology of victimization, at the same time weaving a strong tale."

Interviewed for *Teenreads.com,* Crew explained that she had long known about the Creffield incident: "The Creffield story has been written about a lot in articles, and a lot of it has taken sort of a smirky tone, as it was

rather amusing how all these men in Corvallis lost control over their wives and daughters. When you look at the impact cult involvement has on families, though, it's not one bit funny; and I wanted to tell the story as it might have seemed to the people actually living it. I wanted to look at it from the female point of view. I've always thought it was an incredibly intriguing story and I wanted to take a shot at telling it in an interesting way."

Even before she became a published writer, Crew made a place for writing within her life. "For me, it's a way of trying to make sense of life," she once commented. "I'm just interested in real life, everything people live through, how things *really* feel as opposed to just hearing the party line about how they feel." After she finished *Children of the River,* her writing made even more demands on her time. "*Children of the River* was rejected sixteen times. I kept working on it, so it wasn't like the *same* book got rejected sixteen times, but that's why I believe in persistence. I was running out of publishers and running out of hope, and my husband said, 'Frankly, honey, I don't know how much longer *I* can support it.' But the passion that I felt for the story was what sustained me." Unlike more prolific young adult authors, Crew doesn't feel pressured to write "just anything," as she once commented. "In a way, I feel that too many books are being published. Unless I have something really worth saying, I think the world can probably go without hearing from me."

Biographical and Critical Sources

BOOKS

Authors and Artists for Young Adults, Volume 21, Gale (Detroit, MI), 1997.
St. James Guide to Young Adult Writers, 2nd edition, St. James Press (Detroit, MI), 1999.
Speaking for Ourselves, Too, edited by Ronald R. Gallo, National Council of Teachers of English (Urbana, IL), 1993.
Valentic, Suzanne M., "Linda Crew," *Twentieth-Century Young Adult Writers,* 1st edition, St. James Press (Detroit, MI), 1994, pp. 156-157.

PERIODICALS

Book, May, 2001, p. 83.
Booklist, March 1, 1989, p. 1128; October 15, 1991, p. 438; December 1, 1992, p. 660; October 15, 1994, p. 413; August, 1995, Merri Monks, review of *Fire on the Wind,* p. 1940; May 15, 2000, p. 1765; December 15, 2000, Ilene Cooper, review of *Brides of Eden: A True Story Imagined,* p. 808.
Bulletin of the Center for Children's Books, February, 1989, Roger Sutton, review of *Children of the River,* pp. 145-146; January, 1996, p. 157.
Horn Book, March-April, 1996, Elizabeth S. Watson, review of *Fire on the Wind,* p. 205; March-April, 2001, p. 206.
Kirkus Reviews, January 15, 1989; September 15, 1995, p. 1348.

Los Angeles Times Book Review, February 26, 1989, Mark Jonathan Harris, review of *Children of the River,* p. 10.

Publishers Weekly, June 8, 1990, review of *Someday I'll Laugh about This,* p. 55; October 30, 1995, review of *Fire on the Wind,* p. 63; July 21, 1997, p. 202; December 18, 2000, p. 80.

School Library Journal, February, 2001, Joel Shoemaker, review of *Brides of Eden,* p. 117.

OTHER

Teenreads.com, http://www.teenreads.com/ (August 22, 2001).*

D

DEETER, Catherine 1947-

Personal

Born November 20, 1947, in Omaha, NE; daughter of Henry Irvin (a broker) and Mare June (Robertson) Deeter; children: Curtis Andrew Reed, Jr., Taage Lander Storey. *Education:* Attended University of Denver, University of Colorado, San Francisco Art Institute, Art Center College of Design, and Los Angeles City College. *Hobbies and other interests:* Gardening, flying small aircraft.

Addresses

Office—P.O. Box 401, Templeton, CA 93465-0401. *Agent*—Linda Pratt, Sheldon Fogelman Agency, 10 East 40th St., New York, NY 10016. *E-mail*—cdeeter@fix.net.

Career

Illustrator and author. Worked in advertising, publishing, and book and product development. Art Center College of Design, Pasadena, CA, instructor.

Writings

Seymour Bleu, Simon & Schuster (New York, NY), 1998.

ILLUSTRATOR

Jane Yolen, *The Robot and Rebecca: The Mystery of the Code-Carrying Kids,* Random House (New York, NY), 1980.
Alice Walker, *To Hell with Dying,* Harcourt (New York, NY), 1988.
Alice Walker, *Finding the Green Stone,* Harcourt (New York, NY), 1991.
(With Maggie Andre) Maggie Andre, *PearBear: The End of Summer Concert,* Oregon Washington California Pear Bureau (Portland, OR), 1994.
Eleanor Farjeon, *Between the Sun and the Earth: Poems,* HarperCollins (New York, NY), 1996.

Arnold Adolf, *The Return of Rex and Ethel,* Harcourt (New York, NY), 2000.
Ruth E. Saltzman, *Poppy Bear: The Garden That Overslept,* Beyond Words (Hillsboro, OR), 2000.
Alice Walker, *Langston Hughes, American Poet,* 2nd edition, HarperCollins (New York, NY), 2000.

Sidelights

Although illustrator Catherine Deeter got her start in the children's book field by illustrating the works of noted writer Alice Walker, she has gone on to make her own mark as an author. Deeter's 1998 picture book, *Seymour Bleu,* tells the story of an artistic feline with blue fur and a strong fashion sense who goes in search of creative inspiration for his next masterwork. Along the way young readers are introduced to the history and use of paint pigments and are presented with some interesting fine-art facts in what *School Library Journal* contributor Julie Cummins dubbed a "clever story that is a tribute to artistic spirit." Through her humorous illustrations, full of saturated, brilliant colors, and her pun-filled text with its "many sly, feline-enhanced nods to the masters," noted a *Kirkus Reviews* critic, Deeter covers not only the artistic process but also presents a short history of art that spans traditional through contemporary painting and sculpture.

In addition to providing artwork for her own text in *Seymour Bleu,* Deeter has illustrated texts by Jane Yolen, Arnold Adolf, and Eleanor Farjeon, as well as by Walker. In Walker's *To Hell with Dying,* published in 1988, she provides a sensitive visual accompaniment to a story about a young African-American girl and the elderly, dying man she befriends. In *School Library Journal,* Patricia Dooley praised Deeter for making "the heroine beautiful through emphasizing her black features," and in her review for *Horn Book,* Elizabeth S. Watson called several of the paintings featured in *To Hell with Dying* "striking and powerful." The illustrator's more recent work on Walker's *Finding the Green Stone* showcases her development as an illustrator. While questioning the consistency of Walker's text

Lovable Mr. Sweet's brushes with death are eased by the affection of a young girl and her brother in To Hell with Dying, *written by Alice Walker and illustrated by Catherine Deeter.*

about personal acts of caring, Dooley praised Deeter's "warm, bright acrylics" as "cheery and attractive." The illustrations Deeter provides for an updated edition of Walker's 1974 juvenile biography *Langston Hughes: American Poet* have also earned praise from critics. "Impressively meshing realism and symbolism ...," noted a *Publishers Weekly* reviewer, Deeter's "period-detailed paintings make creative use of light and texture" in portraying twentieth-century poet Hughes and his life.

Biographical and Critical Sources

PERIODICALS

Horn Book, July-August, 1988, Elizabeth S. Watson, review of *To Hell with Dying,* pp. 504-505.

Kirkus Reviews, November 1, 1998, review of *Seymour Bleu,* p. 1598; November 15, 2001, review of *Langston Hughes: American Poet,* p. 1615.

Publishers Weekly, October 25, 1991, review of *Finding the Green Stone,* p. 66; November 23, 1998, review of

Seymour Bleu, p. 66; November 19, 2001, review of *Langston Hughes: American Poet,* p. 67.

School Library Journal, April, 1988, Patricia Dooley, review of *To Hell with Dying,* p. 92; February, 1992, Patricia Dooley, review of *Finding the Green Stone,* p. 79; December, 1998, Julie Cummins, review of *Seymour Bleu,* p. 82; August, 2001, Gay Lynn Van Vleck, review of *Poppy Bear: The Garden That Overslept,* p. 160; February, 2002, Anne Chapman Callaghan, review of *Langston Hughes: American Poet,* p. 128.*

*   *   *

DODD, Quentin 1972-

Personal

Born June 7, 1972, in Durham, NC; son of Robert (a wildlife biologist) and Suzanne (a teacher; maiden name,

Hevron) Dodd; married Paula Myers (a physical thera-
pist), May 28, 1994. *Education:* Wabash College, A.B.,
1994. *Hobbies and other interests:* Ice hockey, antiques,
B-movies, bonsai trees.

Addresses

Home—1101 Danville Ave., Crawfordsville, IN 47933.
Office—Wabash College, P.O. Box 352, Crawfordsville,
IN 47933. *E-mail*—doddq@quentindodd.com.

Career

Management Consulting and Research, Inc., Dayton,
OH, programmer, 1994-99; Wabash College, Crawfordsville, IN, network administrator, 1999—. Writer,
1998—.

Awards, Honors

Eleanor Cameron Award for best middle grades book,
Golden Duck Awards, 2002, and Books for the Teen
Age selection, New York Public Library, 2002, both for
Beatnik Rutabagas from Beyond the Stars.

Writings

Beatnik Rutabagas from Beyond the Stars, Farrar, Straus
and Giroux (New York, NY), 2001.

Work in Progress

The Princes of Neptune, Farrar, Straus and Giroux (New
York, NY), due 2004.

Sidelights

Quentin Dodd combines a day job as a computer
network administrator with a night career of creating
seriously funny and outlandish books for young readers.
His 2001 title, *Beatnik Rutabagas from Beyond the
Stars,* is the tale of two teens who are spirited away in
alien spaceships to lead competing intergalactic armies.
Walter Nutria, a freshman in high school, is something
of a video junkie, as is his sometimes girlfriend, Yselle
Meridian. Together, they spend hours watching old B-
rated science fiction movies. One day, when he is busy
skipping school, Walter is recruited by aliens to head the
one-spaceship-strong Lirgonian fleet in its efforts to best
their space enemies, the Wotwots. He jumps at the
chance, but one thing Walter does not know is that
Yselle has meanwhile been recruited to lead the Wotwots. Ultimately these two unlikely generals convince
the warring sides that their real enemies are the Space
Mice and the wicked Doctoral Candidate X.

Dodd's first novel earned mostly positive reviews.
While Saleena L. Davidson, writing in *School Library
Journal,* felt that the author "tries too hard to be funny
and neglects character and plot development," other
reviewers were more praiseworthy. A critic for *Publishers Weekly* noted similarities in Dodd's work to Douglas
Adams's "Hitchhiker's Guide" series, dubbing the novel

a "spunky debut," and further noting that Dodd's
"agenda is laughs, and his extravagant imagination
matches well with his flippant writing style." Similarly,
a contributor for *Kirkus Reviews* applauded this "free-
wheeling debut," and commented that it "will draw
chortles from readers who prefer their SF well-larded
with surreal silliness." Greg Hurrell added to the praise
in *Journal of Adolescent and Adult Literacy,* calling the
book a "laugh-a-minute romp across the universe," and
an "excellent first novel."

Dodd, who began his writing career with two novels that
were not published, hopes to continue writing humorous
stories for readers of all ages. For now he is riding the
positive feedback from his first novel and is hard at
work on a second that will combine, as he told Steve
Penhollow in the Fort Wayne, Indiana, *Journal Gazette,*
"the 'my Dad owns a scientific island' genre of
adventure fiction (i.e. Jonny Quest) with an intergalactic
beauty pageant."

"I'm not much for trying to deliver a message," Dodd
told *SATA.* "A lot of books for kids, in my opinion, have
a tendency to moralize excessively, and I think this can
give the impression that reading is Serious Business,
something that can't be done lightly or for enjoyment.
My goal is to be the chocolate sundae of kids' literature:
nutty, messy, and fun."

Dodd further commented to *SATA:* "In writing, what I
find most exciting is taking unrelated ideas and combining them in surprising ways. When I'm working on
something, I rarely use traditional outlines, but instead
cover my desk and my computer monitor with sticky
notes that I can move and arrange into different patterns
as the story takes shape. This means that I tend to
research a lot of things that seem like good ideas at the
time, but never end up on the page. I never throw
anything away, though, and what doesn't fit in one story
is sometimes the perfect ingredient for another."

Biographical and Critical Sources

PERIODICALS

Journal Gazette (Fort Wayne, IN), January 27, 2002, Steve
Penhollow, "Writer Creates Far-Out Aliens Kids Have
Never Eyed Before," pp. E1, E6.
Journal of Adolescent and Adult Literacy, March, 2002,
Greg Hurrell, review of *Beatnik Rutabagas from
Beyond the Stars,* p. 550.
Kirkus Reviews, August 1, 2001, review of *Beatnik
Rutabagas from Beyond the Stars,* p. 1120.
Publishers Weekly, August 20, 2001, review of *Beatnik
Rutabagas from Beyond the Stars,* p. 81.
School Library Journal, October, 2001, Saleena L. David-
son, review of *Beatnik Rutabagas from Beyond the
Stars,* p. 152.

OTHER

Quentin Dodd Web Site, http://www.quentindodd.com/
(October 5, 2002).

DRESCHER, Joan E(lizabeth) 1939-

Personal

Born March 6, 1939, in New York, NY; daughter of Joseph (an artist) and Elizabeth (an artist; maiden name, Straub) McIntosh; married Kenneth Drescher (a printer), June 11, 1960; children: Lisa, Kim, Ken. *Education:* Attended Rochester Institute of Technology, 1957-58, Parsons School of Design, 1958-60, and Art Students League, 1961-62.

Addresses

Home and office—23 Cedar St., Hingham, MA 02043.

Career

Writer and illustrator. Former member of faculty at Cambridge Center for Adult Education, Cambridge Art Association, Massachusetts College of Art, Art Institute of Boston, and Lesley College; currently a fellow of the Mind Body Institute of Lesley University, Cambridge, MA, and an artist-in-residence at Massachusetts General Hospital for Children, Boston, MA; founder, Murals for Healing Environments. *Exhibitions:* Art works have been exhibited in solo shows and special exhibits for children; murals executed at Parents' and Children's Services, Boston, MA, 1982; Memorial Sloan Kettering Hospital, New York, NY, 1986-87; Children's Hospital, Boston, MA, 1988; and St. Anne's Hospital, Fall River, MA, 1988.

Member

Graphic Artists Guild, Authors Guild, Society of Children's Book Writers and Illustrators, New York Society of Illustrators, Boston Society of Illustrators.

Awards, Honors

Younger Honor citation, New York Academy of Sciences, 1980, for *Bubbles and Soap Films;* National Council for the Social Studies Award, National Children's Book Council, 1981, for *Your Family, My Family.*

Writings

SELF-ILLUSTRATED CHILDREN'S BOOKS

What Are Daisies For?, Rand McNally (Chicago, IL), 1975.
(Written with Shirlee Newman) *Tell Me Grandma, Tell Me Grandpa,* Houghton Mifflin (Boston, MA), 1979.
The Marvelous Mess, Houghton Mifflin (Boston, MA), 1980.

In Your Doctor, My Doctor, *Joan E. Drescher demystifies medical personnel by offering young readers information about doctor visits, treatments, and a glimpse at the personal life of those who provide medical care.*

Your Family, My Family, Walker (New York, NY), 1980.

Walter and the Mall, Houghton Mifflin (Boston, MA), 1981.

I'm in Charge, Little, Brown (Boston, MA), 1981.

Max and Rufus, Houghton Mifflin (Boston, MA), 1982.

My Mother's Getting Married, Dial Books (New York, NY), 1986.

Your Doctor, My Doctor, Walker (New York, NY), 1987.

The Birth-Order Blues, Viking (New York, NY), 1993.

ILLUSTRATOR

K. W. Moseley, *Only Birds Have Feathers,* Harvey House (Irvington-on-Hudson, NY), 1973.

Elisabeth Yates, *Skeezer: Dog with a Mission,* Harvey House (Irvington-on-Hudson, NY), 1973.

Jennifer Baroli, *Nonna,* Harvey House (Irvington-on-Hudson, NY), 1975.

Bernice Chesler, *In and Out of Boston with (or without) Children,* Crown (New York, NY), 1975.

Bernice Chesler and Evelyn Kaye, *The Family Guide to Cape Cod,* Crown (New York, NY), 1976.

Nancy Robison, *The Other Place* (science fiction), Walker (New York, NY), 1978.

Bernie Zubrowski, *Bubbles and Soap Films,* Little, Brown (Boston, MA), 1979.

Dale Fife, *Follow That Ghost,* Dutton (New York, NY), 1979.

Barbara Bottner, *Horrible Hannah,* Crown (New York, NY), 1980.

Jane Sutton, *Not Even Mrs. Mazursky,* Dutton (New York, NY), 1984.

David A. Adler, *Eaton Stanley and the Mind Control Experiment,* Dutton (New York, NY), 1985.

OTHER

(With Joan Borysenko) *On the Wings of Light: Meditations for Awakening to the Source,* Warner Books (New York, NY), 1992.

Also author of *The Moon Balloon: A Journey of Hope and Discovery,* 1996.

Sidelights

Joan E. Drescher is an artist and author whose works are often intended to help children, not just entertain them. For example, in her book, *Birth-Order Blues,* a young girl reporter interviews the kids in her neighborhood about the pros and cons of being the oldest, middle, youngest, or only child in the family. The result is both revealing and heartening for adults and children alike, according to reviewers. The author's approach displays both "humor and good sense," claimed Bridget Bennett in the *Horn Book Guide.* Drescher's "lighthearted" illustrations, with bright colors and balloon dialogue, add to the appeal of *Birth-Order Blues,* remarked Ellen Mandel in *Booklist.* Like other reviewers, Janet M. Bair, writing in *School Library Journal,* predicted that most children would see themselves in Drescher's book, which she called "a useful, attractive title for building self-esteem and discussing family relationships."

Drescher's other problem-oriented titles include *Your Doctor, My Doctor,* which a contributor to the *Children's Book Review Service* felt would be a helpful offering to a child with a fear of doctors or facing an appointment with a specialist. A contributor to *Booklist* thought that the simple story of *My Mother's Getting Married* was a similarly "realistic" treatment of the fears and doubts that accompany this momentous occasion. Young children gain a model for growing independence in Drescher's *I'm in Charge,* about a child of working parents, and the variety of types of families and their differing experiences is reassuringly depicted in her *Your Family, My Family.*

In addition to her books for children, Drescher is the founder of Murals for Healing Environments, an effort to decorate the areas for children in hospitals with pictures that allow them to see themselves and help them to express sometimes painful emotions. For a mural for a cancer ward, Drescher told correspondent Judith Montminy, "I would draw kids without hair, with cute hats on. When they look at my art they can see 'somebody knows where I am.'" Her work with hospitalized children inspired *The Moon Balloon: A Journey of Hope and Discovery,* a picture book that encourages children to explore their emotions during stressful times.

Drescher once commented: "Ever since I was a small child, I wanted to write and illustrate books. Lying on my stomach, I would draw until I was cross-eyed. I never stopped making little books and still have many I did when I was a child. Because I feel it is very important to encourage young authors and illustrators, I spend a portion of my time sharing my knowledge of picture books.

"Everyday problems are important to me and appear in many of my books. These problems include what to do when your mother is not home, which I dealt with in *I'm in Charge,* and how to get a boy to clean his room, the subject of *The Marvelous Mess.* I am also concerned with social issues, as in *Your Family, My Family,* and just plain fun: *Max and Rufus* is about a boy and a dog who swap roles. All of these give a young reader plenty to think about."

Biographical and Critical Sources

PERIODICALS

Booklist, July, 1985, review of *I'm in Charge,* p. 1568; December 15, 1988, review of *My Mother's Getting Married* and *Your Family, My Family,* p. 718; August, 1993, Ellen Mandel, review of *The Birth-Order Blues,* p. 2069.

Bulletin of the Center for Children's Books, April, 1986, review of *My Mother's Getting Married,* p. 145.

Children's Book Review Service, January, 1983, review of *Max and Rufus,* p. 41; October, 1987, review of *Your Doctor, My Doctor,* p. 17; September, 1993, review of *The Birth-Order Blues,* p. 2.

Horn Book Guide, spring, 1994, Bridget Bennett, review of *The Birth-Order Blues,* p. 32.

Ms., March, 1981.

Patriot Ledger, July 8, 1976.

Publishers Weekly, February 1, 1980, review of *The Marvelous Mess,* p. 108; October 19, 1980, review of *Horrible Hannah,* p. 73; April 9, 1982, review of *I'm in Charge,* p. 51; December 17, 1982, review of *Max and Rufus,* p. 74; February 22, 1985, review of *My Mother's Getting Married,* p. 157; April 25, 1986, review of *My Mother's Getting Married,* p. 76; February 10, 1989, review of *My Mother's Getting Married,* p. 74; August, 16, 1993, review of *The Birth-Order Blues,* p. 102.

School Library Journal, March, 1980, Susan Cain, review of *Follow That Ghost!,* p. 120; April, 1980, "New York Science Academy Announces '80 Awards,"
p. 13; January, 1981, Brenda Durrin Maloney, review of *The Marvelous Mess,* p. 49; September, 1981, Barbara Hawkins, review of *Your Family, My Family,* p. 106; November, 1981, Elizabeth Holtze, review of *I'm in Charge,* p. 74; December, 1983, Mary Jane Mangini Rossi, review of *Your Family, My Family,* p. 33; May, 1986, Susan Hepler, review of *My Mother's Getting Married,* p. 72; November, 1993, Janet M. Bair, review of *The Birth-Order Blues,* p. 79.

OTHER

Joan Drescher Web Site, http://www.themoonballoon.com/ (April 10, 2002), Judith Montminy, "Through Book and Murals, Artist Strives to Give Children a Healing Force."*

F

FARLEY, Carol (J.) 1936-
(Carol McDole)

Personal

Born December 20, 1936, in Ludington, MI; daughter of Floyd and Thressa Moreen (Radtke) McDole; married Dennis Scott Farley (a professor), June 21, 1956; children: Denise, Elise, Roderick, Jeannette. *Education:* Western Michigan University, teacher's certificate, 1956; Michigan State University, B.A., 1980; Central Michigan University, M.A., 1983.

Addresses

Home—192 Newcastle Ave, Portsmouth, NY 03801.

Career

Freelance writer, teacher, and lecturer, 1957—; language teacher in Seoul, Korea, 1978-79; writer-in-residence in Michigan communities, 1981—; teacher for Institute of Children's Literature, 1983-95.

Awards, Honors

Franklin Watts Mystery Medal, 1966, for *Mystery of the Fog Man;* Golden Kite Award, Society of Children's Book Writers and Illustrators, 1975, and Wel-Met Children's Book Award, Child Study Association of America, 1976, both for *The Garden Is Doing Fine;* Friends of American Writers award, 1978, for *Loosen Your Ears;* Children's Choice Book selection, International Reading Association/Children's Book Council, 1987, for *The Case of the Vanishing Villain.*

Writings

(Under name Carol McDole) *Yekapo of Zopo Land,* Row, Peterson (Evanston, IL), 1958.
Mystery of the Fog Man, Franklin Watts (New York, NY), 1966.

In **Mr. Pak Buys a Story**, *Carol Farley's retelling of a Korean folktale, the servant of a wealthy couple purchases a story that seems worthless until it saves them from being robbed. (Illustrated by Benrei Huang.)*

Mystery in the Ravine, Franklin Watts (New York, NY), 1967.
Sergeant Finney's Family, Franklin Watts (New York, NY), 1969.
The Bunch on McKellahan Street, Franklin Watts (New York, NY), 1971.
The Most Important Thing in the World, Franklin Watts (New York, NY), 1974.

The Garden Is Doing Fine (Junior Literary Guild selection), illustrated by Lynn Sweat, Atheneum (New York, NY), 1975.

Loosen Your Ears, illustrated by Mila Lazarevich, Atheneum (New York, NY), 1977.

Settle Your Fidgets, illustrated by Mila Lazarevich, Atheneum (New York, NY), 1977.

Ms. Isabelle Cornell, Herself, Atheneum (New York, NY), 1980.

Twilight Waves, Atheneum (New York, NY), 1981.

The Mystery of the Fiery Message, illustrated by Carol Newsom, Avon (New York, NY), 1983.

Korea: A Land Divided, Dillon (Minneapolis, MN), 1983.

Mystery of the Melted Diamonds, illustrated by Tom Newsom, Avon (New York, NY), 1986.

The Case of the Vanishing Villain, illustrated by Tom Newsom, Avon (New York, NY), 1986.

The Case of the Lost Lookalike, illustrated by Tom Newsom, Avon (New York, NY), 1988.

The Case of the Haunted Health Club, Avon (New York, NY), 1990.

Songs in the Night, Standard (Cincinnati, OH), 1990.

Korea: Land of the Morning Calm, Dillon (Minneapolis, MN), 1991.

King Sejong's Secret, illustrated by Floyd Cooper, Lothrop (New York, NY), 1995.

Mr. Pak Buys a Story, illustrated by Benrei Huang, Albert Whitman and Company (Morton Grove, IL), 1997.

Tiger! Stories from Old Korea, Lothrop (New York, NY), 1999.

More How They Do That?, HarperCollins (New York, NY), 2001.

The King's Secret: The Legend of King Sejong, illustrated by Robert Jew, HarperCollins (New York, NY), 2001.

Work represented in anthologies, including *2041,* edited by Jane Yolen, Delacorte (New York, NY), 1991; *Stories on Stage,* edited by Aaron Shepard, H. W. Wilson (Bronx, NY), 1993; and *Cross-Roads,* edited by Robert Cormier, Scott, Foresman (Glenview, IL), 1995. Contributor to periodicals, including *Calliope, Cricket, Children's Playmate, Turtle, Spider, Pockets,* and *Challenge.*

Sidelights

"I like to write for young people because they seem less crazy than the adults I know," commented award-winning author Carol Farley in *Fifth Book of Junior Authors and Illustrators.* Farley has penned over twenty books for such young readers, including middle grade novels as well as picture books. Winner of the Golden Kite for her novel *The Garden Is Doing Fine,* Farley has explored a variety of subject matters, including a beloved parent's death from cancer, tall tales, a boy's search for family and meaning, mysteries, folklore, and history, in her popular novels, picture books, and nonfiction books, often using her native Michigan as a setting.

Born in Ludington, Michigan, in 1936, Farley noted in *Fifth Book of Junior Authors and Illustrators* that as a child she was "shy, lonely, homely, and frightened." As

for many such reclusive children, books became a refuge for her where she could "become anybody, could live anywhere, do anything at all." With some surprise, she learned that the authors of the books she loved were just normal people like her, and from there it was a small logical jump to think that she too could write books. By the time she was in high school, she had already filled numerous notebooks with her novels and stories. She transformed the tragedies in her life—the death of her father and of her best friend—in the pages of her fiction into imaginary events or had these people live on in the guise of princes and princesses. Writing, like reading, provided the perfect escape from Farley's imperfect world.

In 1956, after earning a teacher's certificate from Western Michigan University, the author married an Army officer and the couple and their growing family lived and traveled in many places in the United States and around the world, including Michigan, Virginia, Germany, and Korea, where Farley taught English in the late 1970s. In her first twenty-five years of marriage, in fact, Farley and her family moved twenty times.

Her writing career started with the publication of *Yekapo of Zopo Land,* written under her maiden name, Carol McDole. Her subsequent books have all been under the name Carol Farley. Early novels from Farley include mysteries and message-books such as *Mystery of the Fog Man* and *The Most Important Thing in the World.* Farley's first success was with her 1975 title, *The Garden Is Doing Fine,* the story of the final days of Corrie's father, dying of cancer. "The focus is intense," wrote a reviewer for *Booklist,* "as are the characters and relationships." Corrie is in denial that her beloved father is actually dying, giving up her own treats in hopes that such sacrifices will keep him alive. She misses the first basketball game of the year, refuses the lead in the school play, and when her father asks after the garden that he loves, Corrie steadfastly refuses to lie to him and tell him it is fine when actually it has died without his care. She feels that to lie to him about the garden would be to admit that he is not going to be around to see the truth of the matter. However, Corrie finally realizes that no matter what happens, she will always carry him with her in her heart. The same *Booklist* contributor praised the "unsparing, carefully thought out" manner in which the book's central theme is resolved. Mary M. Burns, reviewing the novel in *Horn Book,* found some minor "flaws" in the 1945 setting, but on the whole lauded Farley's skill "in evoking a powerful emotional response to the situation, and her facility in re-creating the dying father's personality through the reminiscences of those who loved him."

Farley moved on to much lighter material in the companion books, *Loosen Your Ears* and *Settle Your Fidgets,* both books narrated by old Josh Hemmer who spins tales about his eccentric Michigan family. Linda Lungheim, reviewing *Loosen Your Ears* in *School Library Journal,* called the stories "colorful" anecdotes and compared them to tall tales. Likewise a contributor for *Booklist* called the same collection of stories "hilarious." More such tales are served up by Josh in *Settle Your Fidgets,* a further gathering of yarns about life on a Michigan farm at the turn of the twentieth century. There is crazy Great Aunt Purity and Uncle Fred who protest that the girls who work at the shoe factory are improper because they wear swimsuits that reveal their elbows at a camping picnic. Susan Sprague, writing in *School Library Journal,* compared the humor to that of Sid Fleischman and forecasted that "kids will find this as funny as its predecessor." "The verbal wool-gathering style is racked with cliches," noted a critic for *Booklist,* "but [is] completely appropriate for this folksy collection."

Farley returns to more serious themes with *Twilight Waves,* the story of one boy's search for his father. Browning's great grandmother has always warned the boy to beware of what he wishes for—it might come true. But Browning can not help himself; his one wish is to find out the truth about his father who supposedly died aboard a ship on Lake Michigan before he was born. When his mother died not long after his birth, Browning went to live with his great-grandmother, but now he has a chance to go to his father's hometown, and he hopes to uncover something about the man. However, what he turns up makes him realize that his real family is actually his great-grandmother, not the myth of a father he has constructed in his head. The novel earned mixed critical reception, with a contributor for *Bulletin of the Center for Children's Books* finding that while the "writing style is sound" and the "characters believable . . ., the pace of the story and its development are weak." However, a *Booklist* reviewer came to a far different assessment, noting that "Farley's keen characterization . . . will earn readers' sympathy."

Farley has also written a number of mysteries, including titles that feature Larry and his friend Kip, as well as those that have Flee Jay at the center of the action. Larry, son of the chief of police, and his cousin Kip set out to find an arsonist in *The Mystery of the Fiery Message,* a "fast-paced mystery," according to a reviewer for *School Library Journal,* who further commented that the two teen detectives "make a good team and readers will want to see more of them." The duo sets out to solve the theft of some diamonds in *Mystery of the Melted Diamonds,* a "neat little surprise package" that "mystery fans will enjoy," according to a *Booklist* contributor. A forty-year-old mystery surrounding the kidnapping of a child is at the heart of *The Case of the Lost Lookalike,* in which Flee Jay and her younger sister play sleuths. A *Booklist* critic praised this mystery as a book that "middle graders will enjoy." Flee Jay and her sister Clarice make reappearances in *The Case of the Vanishing Villain* and its sequel, *The Case of the Haunted Health Club.* Reviewing the latter title, a contributor for *Publishers Weekly* felt that Farley's "comedic tone . . . gives Flee Jay an accessible allure." The same critic also lauded the "gentle sibling rivalry" presented in the subplot.

Farley has also mined the time she spent in Korea as a teacher for material for several books. A departure from

her usual fiction is *Korea: A Land Divided,* which describes the history, culture, geography, customs, and social life of that country, as well as the difficulties posed by the North/South split. Dorothea Hayward Scott, reviewing the title in *School Library Journal,* found the writing style "chatty," and despite a "slight air of condescension," also noted that "on the whole the book reads well." In *Mr. Pak Buys a Story,* Farley retells a Korean folktale in picture book format. Bored in the countryside, a couple send the servant, Mr. Pak, to the city to buy a story for their evening's entertainment. Pak is tricked out of the money with a silly story about the movements of a real stork that the storyteller is watching, but he retells the odd tale and strangely enough it becomes a favorite and ultimately is responsible for foiling a thief who has come to rob the couple. Pam Gosner, writing in *School Library Journal,* found the retelling to be an "enjoyable addition."

More Korean folklore is presented in the 2001 title, *The King's Secret,* a story that tells how the Korean King Sejong attempts to find an easy way for his illiterate countrymen to be able to write their language. It is this fifteenth-century king who has been credited with replacing the 10,000-character Chinese writing method with the twenty-eight symbols of the simplified Hangeul phonetic alphabet. Barbara Scotto, reviewing the picture book in *School Library Journal,* felt Farley's retelling was "well-written," while *Booklist*'s Lauren Peterson praised the "magical ending" as well as the author's note, which "enhances the tale."

Farley once commented: "Writing helps me bring order to what seems to be chaotic existence. I marvel that so many people seem content to float across the surface of life without ever delving deeply or trying to locate a steady anchor. When writing, I'm trying to reach out to others in hope that together we can make sense out of the emotions and events which surround us. Questions help me probe deeply, and putting feelings into words provides a much-needed anchor. I like writing for the young because they're eager to try to understand the unknowable too. Often I use a common genre, such as the mystery, in order to appeal to the most readers."

Biographical and Critical Sources

BOOKS

Fifth Book of Junior Authors and Illustrators, edited by Sally Holmes Holtze, H. W. Wilson (New York, NY), 1983.

Ward, Martha, et al, *Authors of Books for Young People,* 3rd edition, Scarecrow Press (Metuchen, NJ), 1979.

PERIODICALS

Booklist, September 1, 1975, review of *The Garden Is Doing Fine,* p. 39; November 1, 1977, review of *Settle Your Fidgets,* pp. 474-475; December 1, 1981, review of *Twilight Waves,* p. 496; February 15, 1982, review of *Loosen Your Ears,* p. 761; July, 1984, p. 1546; May 1, 1986, review of *Mystery of the Melted Diamonds,* pp. 1309-1310; March 1, 1988, review of *The Case of the Lost Lookalike,* pp. 1188-1189; March 15, 1991,

p. 1502; April 15, 1997, Annie Ayres, review of *Mr. Pak Buys a Story,* p. 1431; September 15, 2001, Lauren Peterson, review of *The King's Secret,* p. 230.

Bulletin of the Center for Children's Books, February, 1982, review of *Twilight Waves,* p. 106.

Horn Book, September-October, 1975, Mary M. Burns, review of *The Garden Is Doing Fine,* p. 462; July-August, 1997, Elizabeth S. Watson, review of *Mr. Pak Buys a Story,* pp. 466-467.

Kirkus Reviews, January 15, 1974, p. 55; July 1, 1975, p. 711; August 15, 1977, p. 850; December 15, 1981, review of *Twilight Waves,* pp. 1523-1524.

Library Journal, September 15, 1974, p. 2266.

Publishers Weekly, January 21, 1974, review of *The Most Important Thing in the World,* p. 85; December 7, 1990, review of *The Case of the Haunted Health Club,* p. 83.

School Library Journal, November, 1977, Susan Sprague, review of *Settle Your Fidgets,* p. 56; May, 1980, pp. 85-86; March, 1981, Linda Lungheim, review of *Loosen Your Ears,* p. 109; May, 1983, review of *The Mystery of the Fiery Message,* p. 92; September, 1984, Dorothea Hayward Scott, review of *Korea: A Land Divided,* p. 116; September, 1986, p. 134; November, 1986, p. 88; December 7, 1990, review of *The Case of the Haunted Health Club,* p. 83; April, 1997, Pam Gosner, review of *Mr. Pak Buys a Story,* p. 122; December, 2001, Barbara Scotto, review of *The King's Secret,* p. 100.*

—*Sketch by J. Sydney Jones*

*   *   *

FINKELSTEIN, Norman H. 1941-

Personal

Born November 10, 1941, in Chelsea, MA; son of Sydney and Mollie (Fox) Finkelstein; married Rosalind Brandt (an electrologist), July 4, 1967; children: Jeffrey, Robert, Risa. *Education:* Hebrew College, B.J.Ed., 1961, M.A., 1986; Boston University, B.S., 1963, Ed.M., 1964, C.A.G.S., 1983. *Religion:* Jewish.

Addresses

Home—56 Greenleaf Circle, Framingham, MA 01701. *Office*—Edward Devotion School, 345 Harvard St., Brookline, MA 02446-2907; c/o Let's Read, P.O. Box 3064, Framingham, MA 01705. *E-mail*—biowriter@hotmail.com.

Career

Brookline Public Schools, Brookline, MA, library media specialist, 1970—; Hebrew College, Brookline, MA, part-time instructor, 1982—; Camp Yavneh, Northwood, NH, teacher, educational director, summers, 1982-89; Massachusetts Corporation for Educational Telecommunications, host of *Thumbs Up—Thumbs Down,* a program on books and media for teachers and librarians, 1990-95.

Member

Society of Children's Book Writers and Illustrators, Foundation for Children's Books (vice president), American Library Association, Association of Jewish Libraries, Massachusetts School Library Media Association, Phi Delta Kappa.

Awards, Honors

National Endowment for the Humanities fellowship, 1980; Holzman Award, Hebrew College, 1985, and Children's Book of the Year selection, Child Study Committee at Bank Street College, both for *Remember Not to Forget: A Memory of the Holocaust;* Children's Book of the Year selection, Child Study Committee at Bank Street College, for *Theodor Herzl: Architect of a Nation;* Brookline Foundation grant, 1987; John F. Kennedy Presidential Library Foundation grant, 1987; Notable Children's Trade Book in the Field of Social Studies, National Council for the Social Studies and Children's Book Council (NCSS and CBC), and Books for the Teen Age selection, New York Public Library, both for *Captain of Innocence: France and the Dreyfus Affair;* Notable Children's Trade Book in the Field of Social Studies, NCSS and CBC, 1989, for *The Other 1492: Jewish Settlement in the New World;* Council for Basic Education fellowship, 1992; Gerald R. Ford Presidential Library grant, 1996; Golden Kite Honor Book, Society of Children's Book Writers and Illustrators, and Honor Book, Society of School Librarians International, both 1997, One Hundred Books for Reading and Sharing and Books for the Teen Age selections, New York Public Library, Notable Children's Trade Book in the Field of Social Studies, NCSS and CBC, 1998, all for *With Heroic Truth: The Life of Edward R. Murrow;* National Jewish Book Award, 1998, for *Heeding the Call: Jewish Voices in America's Civil Rights Struggle;* Books for the Teen Age selection, New York Public Library, Honor Book, Society of School Librarians International, and Notable Social Studies Trade Book, NCSS and CBC, 2000, all for *The Way Things Never Were: The Truth about the "Good Old Days";* National Jewish Book Award, 2002, for *Forged in Freedom: Shaping the Jewish-American Experience.*

Writings

NONFICTION

Remember Not to Forget: A Memory of the Holocaust, illustrated by Lois Hokenson and Lars Hokenson, F. Watts (New York, NY), 1985.

Theodor Herzl: Architect of a Nation, F. Watts (New York, NY), 1985.

The Emperor General: A Biography of Douglas MacArthur, Dillon/Macmillan (New York, NY), 1989.

The Other 1492: Jewish Settlement in the New World, Scribner (New York, NY), 1989.

Captain of Innocence: France and the Dreyfus Affair, Putnam (New York, NY), 1991.

Sounds in the Air: Radio's Golden Age, Scribner (New York, NY), 1993.

Thirteen Days/Ninety Miles: The Cuban Missile Crisis, Simon & Schuster (New York, NY), 1994.

Heeding the Call: Jewish Voices in America's Civil Rights Struggle, Jewish Publication Society (Philadelphia, PA), 1997.

With Heroic Truth: The Life of Edward R. Murrow, Clarion Books (New York, NY), 1997.

Friends Indeed: The Special Relationship of Israel and the United States, Millbrook Press (Brookfield, CT), 1998.

The Way Things Never Were: The Truth about the "Good Old Days," Atheneum (New York, NY), 1999.

Forged in Freedom: Shaping the Jewish-American Experience, Jewish Publication Society (Philadelphia, PA), 2002.

Contributor to professional journals.

Sidelights

Author and children's librarian Norman H. Finkelstein has been fascinated with current events and politics since he was a young boy. As a reader of books, he claims that "fun reading for me is still a good book on politics, diplomacy, or current issues." As a writer, his personal interests dictate his choice of topics. Although many of his books are on Jewish history and biography, Finkelstein believes in recognizing "the struggles and contributions of all people who are part of American society." He enjoys researching his books even more than putting words on paper. The author has strong opinions about children's nonfiction, claiming in an interview with *Boston Sunday Globe* contributor Sean Smith that "young people should be encouraged to enjoy reading for its own sake," and that "nonfiction is the overlooked area of children's literature." Finkelstein's work as a young adult and children's librarian helps him to understand how children think. Crucial in successful writing for children are the following, according to the author: "You can't talk down to them, you don't take anything for granted as far as what they know, and yet you have to present facts with just enough supplementary, anecdotal stuff to make it interesting."

Finkelstein's first book, *Remember Not to Forget: A Memory of the Holocaust,* was an award winner. The realization that there was a lack of literature on the Holocaust for young adults inspired the author to begin work on the book, which covers the history of Jewish persecution, beginning in A.D. 70 and culminating with the murder of six million Jews during the regime of German dictator Adolph Hitler in the twentieth century. In *Theodor Herzl: Architect of a Nation,* Finkelstein writes about a pivotal early twentieth-century Zionist leader. Herzl laid the foundation for what later became the state of Israel. In what Alice Stern, writing in *Voice of Youth Advocates,* called a "well written, readable and interesting" biography, Finkelstein portrays Herzl as both an arrogant young man and a selfless leader devoted to the cause of Zionism, and effectively depicts the anti-Semitism of the day.

In *The Other 1492: Jewish Settlement in the New World,* Finkelstein covers the expulsion of the Jews from Spain

Norman H. Finkelstein outlines the history of the alliance between Israel and the United States throughout the last fifty years and attempts to forecast the possibilities for peace in the Middle East during the twenty-first century. (From Friends Indeed: The Special Relationship of Israel and the United States.*)*

during the time of Columbus. Although the author covers extensive material, Betsy Hearne, writing in the *Bulletin of the Center for Children's Books,* praised Finkelstein's writing as "clear, smooth, and well organized." The "accounts of mob persecution, forced conversion and Inquisition tragedies [are] carefully researched and never overdramatic," Hearne concluded. *Captain of Innocence: France and the Dreyfus Affair* is a look at a famous nineteenth-century espionage case that was motivated by anti-Semitism. Dreyfus, after being accused of espionage, was treated terribly for the next four and one-half years, imprisoned, and court-martialed in a secretive proceeding. Finkelstein places "the reader at the scene wherever possible," according to a contributor to *Publishers Weekly.* Margaret A. Bush of *Horn Book* called *Captain of Innocence* a "capably narrated account, which illuminates history and raises awareness about injustice and the morality of individuals and nations."

Finkelstein writes about the advent of the radio in *Sounds in the Air: Radio's Golden Age.* The author recounts how the popularity of radio mushroomed in the

1920s and eventually replaced vaudeville stage performances as America's preferred source of entertainment. Soon, the radio was host to comedy shows, soap operas, and shows for children, as well as news programs, of which Edward R. Murrow's reports from the front during World War II are considered the hallmark. Finkelstein describes how advertising found a place on radio and compares radio's fast rise to the later rise of television. Judie Porter, writing in *School Library Journal,* called Finkelstein's account of milestones such as the first advertisements "interesting"; similarly, *Booklist* reviewer Carolyn Phelan notes that the author's account of early advertising "might produce nostalgia even among those too young to have heard the shows." A *Horn Book* reviewer concluded that this "solid documentary never loses sight of the excitement generated by this now commonplace medium."

In *Thirteen Days/Ninety Miles: The Cuban Missile Crisis,* the author recounts the events leading up to the 1962 Cuban Missile Crisis. Finkelstein sets the stage for the crisis by explaining the Cold War tension between the United States and the Soviet Union through the U.S.S.R.'s ally, Cuba. "Behind-the-scenes deliberations and strategizing are dramatically related as events unfold," remarked Elizabeth S. Watson in *Horn Book.* Much of the information the author presents was classified until the latter part of the twentieth century, and significantly, Finkelstein carefully details the historical context, "clarifying why the crisis was important and what lessons were learned," according to a contributor to *Kirkus Reviews.* A time line is provided, as well as a description of the major personalities, and black-and-white photographs. "This book dramatically sketches a crucial slice of twentieth-century history," concluded Jack Forman in *School Library Journal.* Likewise, Chris Sherman contended in *Booklist* that "young adult readers who enjoy suspense stories will be hard-pressed to find a more dramatic, well-written account" of these pivotal events.

Finkelstein outlines the life of an important figure in the history of American journalism in *With Heroic Truth: The Life of Edward R. Murrow.* Murrow was known for taking courageous stands on controversial subjects; for example, his comments about Senator McCarthy and the House Un-American Activities Committee almost lost him his passport. Finkelstein's primary source material includes transcripts of Murrow's radio and television broadcasts, which help him create "a sharp, clear portrait of one of the twentieth-century's great journalists," according to David A. Lindsey, writing in *School Library Journal.* Ilene Cooper of *Booklist* called *With Heroic Truth* "a fresh, fascinating subject for biography shelves." Although Susan S. Verner of *Bulletin of the Center for Children's Books* suggested that a book on radio might be difficult to sell to the "CNN generation," she concluded that "budding journalists will take comfort from Murrow's courage and resourcefulness."

The relationship between Jews and African Americans is examined in *Heeding the Call: Jewish Voices in America's Civil Rights Struggle.* Finkelstein points out

parallels in the histories of these groups—in the late 1800s, for example, both groups faced racism and abuse. The author also describes institutions that have been put into place to strengthen relationships between the two groups. In *The Way Things Never Were: The Truth about the "Good Old Days,"* Finkelstein attempts to debunk the popular view of the 1950s and 1960s as a golden era in American life. The author presents myths such as the idea that children were healthier during that era, and by way of refutation cites the polio epidemic of the 1950s, which kept children out of public swimming pools and away from crowds for fear of contagion. The book is heavily illustrated with photographs, and the author's breezy, optimistic attitude toward American history will appeal to young adults, according to Hazel Rochman in *Booklist.* Elizabeth Bush, writing in the *Bulletin of the Center for Children's Books,* however, observed that "in dispelling one set of myths [Finkelstein] inadvertently introduces another, portraying current social conditions as a comparative Camelot." But Cindy Darling Codell, writing in *School Library Journal,* concluded that, "laced with lots of documented information, this concise social history is enticing and accessible."

In *Friends Indeed: The Special Relationship of Israel and the United States,* Finkelstein's ability to write clearly and with interest about history and politics is exemplified once again, according to Malka Keck in *School Library Journal.* This book outlines Israel's turbulent history, focusing on the era since its modern creation in 1958, and dramatizes its special relationship with the United States through lively anecdotes.

The history and role of Jews in the United States is recounted in *Forged in Freedom: Shaping the Jewish-American Experience.* The text is organized chronologically and delves into the history of Jews and how they have influenced American culture. Topics encompass Jews in politics, religion, education, entertainment, their struggle for civil rights, and other issues of major relevance to the American Jewish community. Although the book touches on several topics, Linda Silver of *Jewish Book World* praised Finkelstein's "straightforward and very lucid" writing style while noting that the "selection of detail is cognent and interesting."

Finkelstein once commented: "My first book appeared in 1985—after twenty-six rejections. My twelfth, *Forged in Freedom,* was released in 2002. It's been an amazing experience. My books have all been biographical or historical. The topics are eclectic, from the Holocaust and Israeli-American relations to the Golden Age of Radio and the Cuban Missile Crisis. I've been fortunate. Each of my books has allowed me to pursue a personal interest. As I immerse myself in the subject matter at hand, I sometimes feel as if I'm becoming the world's greatest expert on the topic.

"Readers often want to know what keeps me going as a writer. When I asked the late CBS correspondent Charles Kuralt to share a memory of Edward R. Murrow, about whom I was writing a biography, Kuralt responded: 'Beginners need confidence; of course, I never had the nerve to ask Murrow for advice directly, but if I had, I believe he would have said, "Become good at what you do, and everything else will take care of itself."' I couldn't have said it better myself. I would, however, add two more words, persistence and patience.

"When I speak at schools, I always bring copies of my copyedited manuscripts with the crossing-outs, editor notes, and grammatical corrections. This always impresses my young readers, who sometimes imagine that books are created full-blown out of a writer's mind.

"Along with my writing career, I am also a public school librarian—the best job in any school. I get to admire and read new books and witness my students' reactions to what they read. The library is the perfect laboratory for any writer."

Biographical and Critical Sources

PERIODICALS

Booklist, April 15, 1992, Ellen Mandel, review of *Theodor Herzl: Architect of a Nation,* p. 1517; June 1, 1993, Carolyn Phelan, review of *Sounds in the Air: The Golden Age of Radio,* p. 1833; July, 1994, Chris Sherman, review of *Thirteen Days/Ninety Miles: The Cuban Missile Crisis,* p. 1943; June 1, 1997, Ilene Cooper, review of *With Heroic Truth: The Life of Edward R. Murrow,* p. 1671; August, 1998, Ellen Mandel, review of *Friends Indeed: The Special Relationship of Israel and the United States,* p. 1982; September 1, 1999, Hazel Rochman, review of *The Way Things Never Were: The Truth about the "Good Old Days,"* p. 77; August, 2002, Hazel Rochman, review of *Forged in Freedom: Shaping the Jewish-American Experience,* p. 1943.

Book Report, May-June, 1994, Mary Mueller, review of *Sounds in the Air,* p. 53; November-December, 1994, Pam Whitehead, review of *Thirteen Days/Ninety Miles,* p. 55; September-October, 1997, Marilyn Makowski Heath, review of *With Heroic Truth,* p. 47.

Boston Sunday Globe, June 20, 1993, Sean Smith, interview with Norman Finkelstein, pp. 37, 41.

Bulletin of the Center for Children's Books, May, 1985, p. 164; December, 1989, Betsy Hearne, review of *The Other 1492: Jewish Settlement in the New World,* p. 83; June, 1997, Susan S. Verner, review of *With Heroic Truth,* p. 357; September, 1999, Elizabeth Bush, review of *The Way Things Never Were,* p. 10.

Hadassah, December, 1992, p. 41.

Horn Book, November-December, 1991, Margaret A. Bush, review of *Captain of Innocence: France and the Dreyfus Affair,* p. 753; September-October, 1993, Margaret A. Bush, review of *Sounds in the Air,* pp. 618-620; September-October, 1994, Elizabeth S. Watson, review of *Thirteen Days/Ninety Miles,* pp. 605-606.

Horn Book Guide, July, 1989, p. 139; spring, 1992, p. 134; fall, 1992, p. 328; fall, 1993, p. 362; fall, 1994, p. 391; fall, 1997, p. 380; spring, 1998, Peter D. Sierta, review of *Heeding the Call: Jewish Voices in America's Civil Rights Struggle,* p. 101; fall, 1998, Jackie C. Horne, review of *Friends Indeed,* p. 423.

Jewish Book World, Linda Silver, review of *Forged in Freedom: Shaping the Jewish-American Experience.*

Kirkus Reviews, May 1, 1993, review of *Sounds in the Air,* p. 597; June 15, 1994, review of *Thirteen Days/Ninety Miles,* p. 844; April 15, 1997, review of *With Heroic Truth,* p. 640.

Multicultural Education, spring, 1998, p. 61.

New York Times Book Review, February 25, 1990, p. 33; May 16, 1999, Christine Stansell, "Those Weren't the Days," p. 24.

Publishers Weekly, November 1, 1991, review of *Captain of Innocence,* p. 82; December 13, 1991, p. 51; March 30, 1992, p. 106; May 31, 1999, review of *The Way Things Never Were,* p. 95.

School Library Journal, September, 1985, Gerda Haas, review of *Remember Not to Forget: A Memory of the Holocaust,* p. 132; January, 1988, Jack Forman, review of *Theodor Herzl,* p. 91; February, 1988, p. 30; April, 1989, Eldon Younce, review of *The Emperor General: A Biography of Douglas MacArthur,* p. 111; January, 1990, Susan Kaminow, review of *Captain of Innocence,* p. 111; October, 1991, p. 152; July, 1992, p. 93; July, 1993, Judie Porter, review of *Sounds in the Air,* p. 104; June, 1994, Jack Forman, review of *Thirteen Days/Ninety Miles,* p. 154; July, 1997, David A. Lindsey, review of *With Heroic Truth,* p. 102; June, 1998, Malka Keck, review of *Friends Indeed,* p. 158; July, 1999, Cindy Darling Codell, review of *The Way Things Never Were,* p. 106.

Television Quarterly, spring, 1997, Fritz Jacobi, review of *With Heroic Truth,* p. 92.

Voice of Youth Advocates, June, 1988, Alice Stern, review of *Theodor Herzl,* p. 100; February, 1990, p. 354; December, 1991, p. 335, December, 1992, p. 319.

OTHER

BookPage, http://www.bookpage.com/ (December 29, 1999), Jamie McAlister, review of *The Way Things Never Were: The Truth about the "Good Old Days".*

Norman H. Finkelstein Web Site, http://www.normfinkelstein.com. (January 15, 2003).

*   *   *

FRASER, Mary Ann 1959-

Personal

Born March 6, 1959, in Santa Monica, CA; daughter of Noel (an electrical engineer) and Genevieve (a registered nurse) Damon; married Todd C. Fraser (a certified public accountant); children: Ian, Alex, Brett. *Education:* University of California—Los Angeles, B.A. (summa cum laude), 1981; College of Art and Design (Exeter, England), postgraduate diploma, 1983. *Hobbies and other interests:* Hiking, marble collecting, cooking, camping, nature studying, traveling.

Addresses

Home and office—2270 Rockdale Ave., Simi Valley, CA 93063. *E-mail*—maryann@maryannfraser.com.

Career

Graphic artist, 1982-90; fine artist, 1983—.

Member

Society of Children's Book Writers and Illustrators, Sierra Club, National Wildlife Federation, Southern California Council on Literature for Children and Young People, Children's Authors Network (founding member).

Awards, Honors

Young Reader's Choice, International Reading Association, and Notable Children's Trade Book in the Field of Social Studies, National Council for the Social Studies/ Children's Book Council (NCSS/CBC), both 1991, both for *On Top of the World: The Conquest of Mount Everest;* Rotary International fellowship; Pick of the List, American Booksellers Association, for *Ten Mile Day and the Building of the Transcontinental Railroad;* Book of the Year, *School Library Journal* and *Book- Links,* Outstanding Nonfiction Choice, National Council of Teachers of English (NCTE), 1995, and California Collection for Middle and High Schools selection, 1998, all for *In Search of the Grand Canyon: Down the Colorado with John Wesley Powell;* Notable Children's Trade Book in the Field of Social Studies, NCSS/CBC, 1998, for *A Mission for the People: The Story of La Purisima;* Outstanding Science Trade Book, NCTE, 2000, for *Where Are the Night Animals;* Notable Social Studies Trade Book for Young People, NCSS/CBC, 2000, for *Vicksburg: The Battle That Won the Civil War.*

Writings

On Top of the World: The Conquest of Mount Everest, Holt (New York, NY), 1991.
(And illustrator) *Ten Mile Day and the Building of the Transcontinental Railroad,* Holt (New York, NY), 1993.
One Giant Leap, Holt (New York, NY), 1993.
Sanctuary: The Story of Three Arch Rocks, Holt (New York, NY), 1994.
(And illustrator) *In Search of the Grand Canyon: Down the Colorado with John Wesley Powell,* Holt (New York, NY), 1995.
Forest Fire!, Fulcrum Kids (Golden, CO), 1996.
A Mission for the People: The Story of La Purisima, Holt (New York, NY), 1997.
Vicksburg: The Battle that Won the Civil War, Holt (New York, NY), 1999.
Where are the Night Animals?, HarperCollins (New York, NY), 1999.
How Animal Babies Stay Safe, HarperCollins (New York, NY), 2002.
I. Q. Goes to School, Walker (New York, NY), 2002.

ILLUSTRATOR

Helene Chirinian, *Betsy Bunny's Birthday,* Macmillan (New York, NY), 1988.
Helene Chirinian, *Bobby Bear's Three Wishes,* Macmillan (New York, NY), 1988.
Clement C. Moore, *The Night before Christmas,* Macmillan (New York, NY), 1988.
Sarina Simon (reteller), *The Nutcracker,* Macmillan (New York, NY), 1988.
Helene Chirinian, *Randy Raccoon's Big Mess,* Macmillan (New York, NY), 1988.
Helene Chirinian, *Sally Squirrel's Late Day,* Macmillan (New York, NY), 1988.
Nancy Wright Grossman, *The Duchess Sees Double,* Tor Books (New York, NY), 1989.
Nancy Wright Grossman, *If Wishes Were Horses,* Tor Books (New York, NY), 1989.
Nancy Wright Grossman, *A Leg Up for Lucinda,* Tor Books (New York, NY), 1989.
Nancy Wright Grossman, *The Only Boy in the Ring,* Tor Books (New York, NY), 1989.
Q. L. Pearce, *Armadillos and Other Unusual Animals,* Julian Messner (New York, NY), 1989.
Q. L. Pearce, *Lightning and Other Wonders of the Sky,* Julian Messner (New York, NY), 1989.
Q. L. Pearce, *Quicksand and Other Earthly Wonders,* Julian Messner (New York, NY), 1989.
Q. L. Pearce, *Tidal Waves and Other Ocean Wonders,* Julian Messner (New York, NY), 1989.
Jeffie Ross Gordon, *Little Kids at Home,* Modern (New York, NY), 1989.
Jeffie Ross Gordon, *Little Kids at Play,* Modern (New York, NY), 1989.
Jeffie Ross Gordon, *Little Kids at School,* Modern (New York, NY), 1989.
Jeffie Ross Gordon, *Little Kids in the Neighborhood,* Modern (New York, NY), 1989.
Jean Davis Callaghan, *Patty for President,* Modern (New York, NY), 1990.
Q. L. Pearce, *Tell Me about Nature Dictionary,* Derrydale Books (New York, NY), 1990.
Q. L. Pearce, *Killer Whales and Other Wonders of the Frozen World,* Julian Messner (New York, NY), 1991.
Q. L. Pearce, *Piranhas and Other Wonders of the Jungle,* Julian Messner (New York, NY), 1991.
Q. L. Pearce, *Saber-Toothed Cats and Other Prehistoric Wonders,* Julian Messner (New York, NY), 1991.
Q. L. Pearce, *Tyrannosaurus Rex and Other Dinosaur Wonders,* Julian Messner (New York, NY), 1991.
Q. L. Pearce, *The Stargazer's Guide to the Galaxy,* Tor Books (New York, NY), 1991.
Q. L. Pearce, *My Favorite Dinosaur: Tyrannosaurus Rex,* Lowell House (Los Angeles, CA), 1993.
Jill Smolinski, *Holiday Origami,* photographs by Ann Bogart, Lowell House (Los Angeles, CA), 1995.
Q. L. Pearce, *The Science Almanac for Kids,* co-illustrated by Mary Bryson, Lowell House (Los Angeles, CA), 1998.
Judy Hawes, *Why Frogs Are Wet,* HarperCollins (New York, NY), 2000.

In her self-illustrated Ten Mile Day and the Building of the Transcontinental Railroad, *Mary Ann Fraser discusses the complex engineering of the first railroad to span the North American continent by depicting a single day when crews accomplished the enormous task of completing ten miles of track.*

Also illustrated *Mix and Match Tracing Books,* a series of six books, and *Science Activity Crossword Puzzles,* a series of four books, both for Price, Stern (Los Angeles, CA), 1988; *Science Activity Flashcards,* a series of four books, for ERS, 1988; and *Make Your Own Pop-ups,* a series of four books, for Price, Stern (Los Angeles, CA), 1990. Cover illustrations for four *Word Search Adventures,* for Price, Stern (Los Angeles, CA), 1988.

Sidelights

Author/illustrator Mary Ann Fraser has created a dozen of her own titles as well as illustrating several dozen more picture books by other writers, including Helene Chirinian, Nancy Wright Grossman, Jeffie Ross Gordon, and Q. L. Pearce. Many of Fraser's self-illustrated books are about nature, one of the driving influences in her life, and others deal with historical topics such as the moon landing and the Civil War. She writes both in picture book and longer nonfiction formats, aiming at readers from middle school to high school.

Born in Santa Monica, California, Fraser grew up in the San Francisco Bay area. As she noted in an essay for *Something about the Author Autobiography Series (SAAS),* "My love for adventure began early." She and her brother would be outside as much as they could, but on dismal days she would sometimes stay in and her mother, a nurse and amateur artist, began to teach her the rudiments of illustration. When her mother read to her at night, from Hans Christian Andersen or from the Grimm's fairy tales, Fraser was struck more by the accompanying illustrations than by the stories themselves. Once she began school Fraser was immediately pegged as the class artist, "and for the next eight years they continually drafted me to make posters and drawings," Fraser wrote in *SAAS.*

From the age of eight, Fraser was writing and illustrating her own stories, spending many recesses finishing her latest production, generally an animal tale. "While I may have had an ability to draw, I seriously doubted I could become a writer," Fraser noted in her *SAAS* essay. "Writers seemed godlike. I imagined that they had endless depths of knowledge and everything flowed poetically from their fingertips to the typewriter. They made it look easy, but I already knew better. With the nerve only a kid can possess, I figured anything was possible if you just went at it with enough gusto, even publication." Throughout her grade school years, Fraser's illustrating talents steadily improved, in part aided by advice from her mother, and her writing skills also advanced as her taste in reading matter widened, including such favorites as *Call of the Wild* and *Where the Wild Things Are.*

Pets also started playing a major role in Fraser's life about the time she started kindergarten, and these included snails, rabbits, rats, bullfrogs, hermit crabs, turtles, iguanas, and even two pet chickens. Over the years, her love of animals also grew, engaging in animal collection expeditions when she accompanied her father who loved fly-fishing. Soon Fraser was also fishing with her own rod, using flies she had tied herself. However more than fishing, Fraser enjoyed "poking along the river, observing the animals and drawing" on such expeditions with her father.

Then came her move from private school to public high school where she could actually take an art course. Graduating in 1977, she went on to college at the

Fraser offers readers a detailed account of the three-month exploratory journey of Major John Wesley Powell, who ventured along the uncharted Colorado River in 1869. (From In Search of the Grand Canyon, *illustrated by Fraser.)*

University of California—Los Angeles, intending to study medicine, but soon changed her focus to medical illustration. A class in the history of children's literature planted the seed of becoming a children's book illustrator, but she got no encouragement in this from her instructors. "While I thoroughly enjoyed attending UCLA, I can't say I learned many fundamentals in art," Fraser reported in *SAAS.* In the summer of 1980, Fraser spent seven weeks traveling in Europe, an experience that "drummed home the lessons of my studies in art." Graduating summa cum laude in 1981 with a degree in Fine Art, Fraser won a scholarship to do graduate study in England where she finally made a breakthrough in her art. "Like a small light with a dimmer switch," she wrote in *SAAS,* "my understanding grew in intensity until at last I knew—no, felt—what art was about."

Back in Los Angeles in 1983, Fraser worked in an advertising agency while trying to break into the art market. Her illustration career began as a freelancer for a book packager, illustrating dinosaur books. "I knew ultimately that I wanted to work in children's books," Fraser noted. She married her long-time boyfriend, Todd Fraser, in 1986, and the couple decided to do some traveling before starting a family. Their first major adventure was in India and Nepal, and it was on that trip the author/illustrator first saw Mount Everest and began research on what would become her first self-illustrated title, *On Top of the World: The Conquest of Mount Everest.* In this title, she explored the story of Sir Edmund Hillary and the Sherpa Tenzing in their historic climb.

For her next title, Fraser tackled the huge subject of building the transcontinental railroad in the nineteenth century. The result of months of research and travel, *Ten Mile Day and the Building of the Transcontinental Railroad,* "was the most difficult book I have ever done," Fraser wrote in *SAAS.* "It certainly gave me some of my greatest research challenges. Often the firsthand accounts I managed to unearth contradicted one another. An author can neglect to mention what someone was wearing in a particular scene, but an illustrator can't have everyone running around naked."

Fraser's third title, *One Giant Leap,* was inspired by her own memories of the moon landing in 1969. "I still think of those first footsteps in the lunar dust as man's greatest success in exploration," she noted in *SAAS.* Writing in *Booklist,* Hazel Rochman called the book "fact-filled" and a "step-by-step account of the Apollo II moon mission." Jay Pasachoff, reviewing the title in *Science Books and Films,* praised the "nice illustrations" and Fraser's "explanation of an important historical moment," but was "not clear at what audience the book is targeted." A *Publishers Weekly* critic had fewer reservations about the book, lauding the "thrilling immediacy" of the text, and further calling Fraser's account a "concise" and "fast-paced" chronicle.

From the history of space travel, Fraser returned to her beloved nature for *Sanctuary: The Story of Three Arch Rocks,* the tale of two naturalists in the early twentieth century who, aided by Teddy Roosevelt, helped to save the pristine nature of some rocks off the Oregon coast, known as Three Arch Rocks. *Booklist*'s Kay Weisman felt that the book was a "very readable account that will be of interest to browsers as well as classes studying endangered species." Weisman also noted that Fraser's illustrations were appealing and supplemented the text well. Marilyn Robertson, reviewing *Sanctuary* in *Five Owls,* had further praise. "This is an attractive and useful book for learning about the history of environmental action," Robertson commented. And Amy Adler praised Fraser's "action-packed, full-color illustrations," in a *School Library Journal* review.

Blending history and naturalism, Fraser also recounted the charting of the Grand Canyon in her *In Search of the Grand Canyon: Down the Colorado with John Wesley Powell.* This award-winning volume was dubbed a "thrill-a-minute adventure" by a *School Library Journal* reviewer in that magazine's round-up of the Best Books of 1995. The same reviewer also lauded Fraser's illustrations, which "enliven" the text. *Booklist*'s Chris Sherman also felt that readers "will enjoy her [Fraser's] account."

With *Forest Fire!*, Fraser set out to "show the reader that the world around us is cyclical," as she noted in *SAAS.* "Just as the earth's tectonic plates will continue to shift and weather patterns to alternate, forests and their inhabitants are designed to survive a burn and in fact they are in many ways better for it." Lisa Wu Stowe, writing in *School Library Journal,* thought the text was presented "simply and clearly," while the "richly textured acrylic illustrations take readers from vibrant forest to threatening storm," and on to the lightning-caused fire itself.

History takes center stage again in the 1997 *A Mission for the People: The Story of La Purisima,* set in Santa Barbara, California. The mission's effect on the local indigenous people of the time, the Chumash is described. Fraser continues the story through the destruction of the mission by earthquake in 1812 and the Mexican War of Independence. "In clear, informative prose, Fraser relates the story of this mission," wrote Ann Welton in *School Library Journal.* Annie Ayres, commenting in *Booklist,* felt that Fraser "sensitively relates the complex and interwoven history" of both the Chumash and the Spanish at the mission. Ayres also commented on the illustrations done in "softly colored acrylics."

Where Are the Night Animals? presents an array of nocturnal creatures, including the possum, barn owl, bat, and skunk, in a "good classroom read-aloud," according to *Booklist*'s Carolyn Phelan. A contributor for *Kirkus Reviews* also commented on the "naturalistic illustrations [which] provide stills of each animal against deep blues, teals, and aquamarines." Another book in the same series, *How Animal Babies Stay Safe,* contains watercolors which "aptly illustrate a text" that simply explains how "defenseless the little ones are," according to Nancy Call writing in *School Library Journal.*

Booklist's Phelan also called the book a "solid" entry in the series.

With *Vicksburg: The Battle That Won the Civil War,* Fraser turns her attention back to historical themes, in a "superb introduction to the siege of and battles for Vicksburg," according to Elizabeth M. Reardon in *School Library Journal.* Focusing not only on events, but on the individuals behind the scenes, Fraser's *Vicksburg* is an "attractive little book" and a "fine introduction," *Booklist*'s Phelan noted.

Fraser turned her hand to picture book fiction for the first time in the 2002 title, *I.Q. Goes to School,* the story of an exceedingly smart mouse. The pet mouse in Mrs. Furber's class is desperate to become a student like the boys and girls in the room. He loves story hour and even teaches himself the alphabet and how to read. Thereafter, he determines to get the teacher's attention by joining in the class play and making Mrs. Furber a valentine. A reviewer for *Publishers Weekly* praised Fraser's "tidy drawings from a mouse's point of view," and further commented that young readers who might find their schoolwork daunting "will enjoy reading about an amiable mouse who shares their struggles." Writing in *School Library Journal,* Judith Constantinides felt that Fraser's illustrations "depict the bright, feisty creature eagerly learning typical classroom lessons," while a contributor for *Kirkus Reviews* noted that Fraser's "enthusiasm for children exploring the world is beautifully upheld in all her work."

"Nothing is more exciting than discovering a terrific story to share with others," Fraser once said. "Not only do I love to write and illustrate, but I have been surprised by how much I relish the research. If I can turn history into an adventure for the reader, then I feel I have done my job well." And the author/illustrator further noted in *SAAS:* "When I first began to write children's books, ideas seemed very elusive. Now I find they come to me like hail in a hailstorm. They are falling around me all the time and frequently some hit me in the head so hard it hurts. Those are the ideas I save. If the idea melts before I get to it, then I assume it probably wasn't worth saving. I continue to write books that I hope make a contribution to children's literature."

Biographical and Critical Sources

BOOKS

Something about the Author Autobiography Series, Volume 23, Gale (Detroit, MI), 1997, pp. 79-94.

PERIODICALS

Booklist, October 15, 1993, Hazel Rochman, review of *One Giant Leap,* p. 434; October 15, 1994, Kay Weisman, review of *Sanctuary: The Story of Three Arch Rocks,* p. 429; July, 1995, Chris Sherman, review of *In Search of the Grand Canyon: Down the River with John Wesley Powell,* p. 1875; May 1, 1998, Annie Ayres, review of *A Mission for the People: The Story of La Purisima,* p. 1514; February 15, 1999, Carolyn Phelan, review of *Where Are the Night Animals?,*

p. 1072; March 1, 2000, Carolyn Phelan, review of *Vicksburg: The Battle That Won the Civil War,* p. 1238; February 1, 2002, Carolyn Phelan, review of *How Animal Babies Stay Safe,* p. 942; September 15, 2002, Lauren Peterson, review of *I. Q. Goes to School,* p. 240.

Daily News (Los Angeles, CA), December 30, 1996, Victoria Giraud, "Children's Author Shot for the Moon," p. T1.

Five Owls, January-February, 1995, Marilyn Robertson, review of *Sanctuary,* pp. 62-63.

Horn Book Guide, fall, 1996, p. 336; fall, 1998, p. 429; fall, 1999, Erica L. Stahler, review of *Where Are the Night Animals?,* p. 339.

Kirkus Reviews, December 1, 1998, review of *Where Are the Night Animals?,* p. 1733; July 15, 2002, review of *I.Q. Goes to School,* p. 1031.

Los Angeles Times, August 21, 1996, Kate Folmar, "Books by Mary Ann Foster of Simi Valley Take Kids to Everest and Beyond," p. 2.

Publishers Weekly, November 15, 1993, review of *One Giant Leap,* p. 80; July 29, 2002, review of *I.Q. Goes to School,* p. 71.

School Library Journal, April, 1990, p. 136; October, 1991, p. 138; December, 1991, p. 126; May, 1993, George Gleason, review of *Ten Mile Day and the Building of the Transcontinental Railroad,* p. 114; October, 1993, Margaret M. Hagel, review of *One Giant Leap,* p. 143; November, 1994, Amy Adler, review of *Sanctuary,* p. 114; July, 1995, Julie Halverstadt, review of *In Search of the Grand Canyon,* p. 85; December, 1995, review of *In Search of the Grand Canyon,* p. 21; July, 1996, Lisa Wu Stowe, review of *Forest Fire!,* pp. 77-78; April, 1998, Ann Welton, review of *A Mission for the People,* p. 116; January, 1999, Jackie Hechtkopf, review of *Where Are the Night Animals?,* p. 115; March, 2000, Elizabeth M. Reardon, review of *Vicksburg,* p. 251; February, 2002, Nancy Call, review of *How Baby Animals Stay Safe,* p. 119; September, 2002, Judith Constantinides, review of *I.Q. Goes to School,* p. 190.

Science Books and Films, March, 1994, Jay Pasachoff, review of *One Giant Leap,* p. 51.

OTHER

Children's Authors Network, http://www.childrensauthors network.com/ (October 7, 2002), "Meet Author and Illustrator Mary Ann Fraser."

Mary Ann Fraser Web Site, http://www.maryannfraser. com/ (October 7, 2002).*

—*Sketch by J. Sydney Jones*

*   *   *

FUSILLO, Archimede 1962-

Personal

Born February 19, 1962, in Melbourne, Australia; son of Ruggiero and Iolanda Fusillo; married, 1984; wife's name, Pina; children: Alyssa, Laurence. *Education:* Melbourne University, B.A. (psychology; with honors),

1983. *Politics:* "Personal." *Religion:* Roman Catholic. *Hobbies and other interests:* Flying, sports-car racing, and reading.

Addresses

Agent—Jenny Darling & Associates, P.O. Box 413, Toorak, Victoria 3142, Australia.

Career

Author and teacher. Worked as a secondary school teacher in the late 1980s and early 1990s, teaching English and literature; feature writer for *Vive la Vie* and *Vive la Cuisine* magazines; freelance writer for other magazines; lecturer on literacy and reading throughout Australia.

Member

Australian Society of Authors, Fellowship of Australian Writers, Victorian Writers Centre.

Awards, Honors

Mary Grant Bruce Story Award for Children's Literature, 1989, for "The Farmhouse"; FAW Playwrights Award, 1994, for *A Christmas Dinner;* finalist, Australian BIA Master of Ceremonies Award, 1999; Australian

Archimede Fusillo

Therapists Book of the Year, 2002, for *The Dons;* finalist, Mary Gran Bruce Award for Children's Literature, 2002, for *Uncorked;* finalist, "Italy in the World" Literature Awards; Alan Marshall Short Story Award; Lyndall Hardaw Short Story Award; Henry Savery Short Story Award; finalist, Teacher of the Year Awards.

Writings

Talking to the Moon (picture book), illustrated by Philippa Rickard, Macmillan Australia (South Melbourne, Australia), 1987.

Memories of Sunday Cricket in the Street (picture book), illustrated by Sally Mitrevska, Macmillan Australia (South Melbourne, Australia), 1987.

Short Stories: Reading to Write (young adult textbook), Oxford University Press (Melbourne, Australia), 1996.

Damien Parer: Putting the War on Film (young adult biography), Cardigan Street Publishers (Carlton, Australia), 1996.

Sparring with Shadows (young adult fiction), Penguin Books (Melbourne, Australia), 1997.

Imaginative Writer (textbook), Wizard Books (Ballarat, Australia), 2000.

The Dons (young adult fiction), Penguin Books (Melbourne, Australia), 2002.

Let It Rip ("Aussie Bites" series; picture book), Penguin Books (Melbourne, Australia), 2002.

Game or Not ("Aussie Bites" series; picture book), Penguin Books (Melbourne, Australia), 2003.

An Earful of Static (young adult fiction), Lothian Books (Melbourne, Australia), 2003.

Uncorked (novel), Word Weavers Press (Minneapolis, MN), 2003.

Work in Progress

Short story for new anthology in 2003; "Aussie Bites" titles for publication in 2004.

Sidelights

Archimede Fusillo told *SATA:* "I have always loved the power of stories. As a child I listened to the stories my grandmother (Nonna) and my parents told me—of the war—of the trials of migration—of deprived child-hoods—and of the comic side of life. Stories transported me to other times and places—and in them I saw a way to share with others my own 'take' on the world. Oral stories gave way to reading, and through reading I discovered how lasting a good story could be, and so I tried my hand at writing the sorts of stories that would make me laugh or cry or cringe. I found I loved communicating with an audience and enjoyed their responses.

"With all my writings my aim is to entertain, to take the reader on a journey. If the reader finds some solace, some insight in what they read, that's wonderful; but I write because I have stories I want to tell. I write with my audience in mind—and I write for all sorts of audiences; from young children (as in the "Aussie Bites" books), to teenagers (*The Dons*), to adults (many of my short stories and text books). I read widely and always, from the classics to contemporary works—comic books to novels. My passion is the short story. A good short story requires precision of language, a keen sense of detail, and a ready sense of knowing what to leave out as much as what to include. My earliest success came with my short stories, which dealt with the characters and events of the area where I grew up, short stories set in places I knew intimately and could write about authentically.

"Writers are dreamers. We have to be if we are to see beyond the obvious and create stories which will grab and hold our readers. Writing is a craft which is never fully mastered, but honed through the act of doing, of polishing and refining. My advice to all who want to write is that there is no end point, just new tangents, with every new idea. Writing is as much breathing as it is commitment. I write because I cannot not write."

Biographical and Critical Sources

PERIODICALS

Magpies, November, 2001, Jo Goodman, review of *The Dons,* p. 39.

OTHER

Writers on the Road, http://www.statelibrary.vic.gov.au/ (January 7, 2003).

G

GRIFFIN, Kitty 1951-

Personal

Born July 26, 1951, in Aschafenberg, Germany; adopted daughter of Terence (a naval officer) and Rosemary (a homemaker; maiden name, O'Neill) Griffin; married Gerard Lagorio (a partner in a computer consulting firm); children: Ian Gerard Lagorio (deceased), Danika Lagorio, Beatrice Lagorio. *Education:* Virginia Commonwealth University, B.S. (criminal justice), 1975; Carlow College, teacher certification (secondary social studies), 1989; studied screenwriting at Pittsburgh Filmmakers, 1999-2001. *Religion:* Catholic. *Hobbies and other interests:* Pottery, painting, biking, hiking, gardening, "caring for a Newfoundland dog, a ferret, cats, a canary, and a big, fat angel fish."

Addresses

Home—241 Church Hill Rd., Venetia, PA 15367. *Agent*—Tracey Adams, McIntosh & Otis, 353 Lexington Ave., New York, NY 10016. *E-mail*—klagorio@cobweb.net.

Career

Author. Freelance journalist, 1998—; Community College of Allegheny County, Pittsburgh, PA, instructor, 2000—; Laroche College, Pittsburgh, PA, assistant professor, 2002.

Member

Society of Children's Book Writers and Illustrators, Author's Guild, Carnegie Screenwriters.

Awards, Honors

Honorable mention, best feature (weeklies) and second place, best design (weeklies), Spotlight Award-Keystone State Professional Chapter Society of Professional Jour-

A Texas cowboy is the recipient of too many secrets to keep under his hat in Kitty Griffin's tale Cowboy Sam and Those Confounded Secrets, *cowritten with Kathy Combs and illustrated by Mike Wohnoutka.*

nalists, 1999; honorable mention, children's fiction, *oWriter's Digest* 2001 Writing Competition.

Writings

(With Kathy Combs) *Cowboy Sam and Those Confounded Secrets,* illustrated by Mike Wohnoutka, Clarion (New York, NY), 2001.

(With Kathy Combs) *The Foot-Stomping Adventures of Clementine Sweet,* Clarion (New York, NY), in press.

Work in Progress

Gretel, a novel; several picture books with Kathy Combs, including *Stinker and the Onion Princess,* Dial Books; *When the World Broke—Johnstown, May 31, 1889,* a novel; *Fisheye,* a screenplay.

Sidelights

Kitty Griffin commented to *SATA:* "As a child I often felt out of place, out of time. It was a sense that I was someplace I didn't belong." Later, at age sixteen, she would discover that when she was three she had been adopted from an orphanage in Germany. Indeed, at one time she had another name, another language, another culture. Griffin feels this set her on the path of writing because she had such an intense need to seek out this place where she thought she should be. Where else could she go on her quests but into books and dreams? "I have always loved to read and I read everything—fairy tales, mysteries, suspense, history, science fiction, I'm really not fussy. Here are books that I remember impacting me—*The King's Stilts* (Seuss), *The Roman, The Egyptian, The Etruscan* (all by Mika Walteri), *Foundation* (Asimov), and *Dune* (Herbert)."

In high school her teachers told Griffin that she was a good writer and that she should be a lawyer. So in college she majored in criminal justice thinking she would be the next Perry Mason. Only when she had an opportunity to start interviewing convicts, she realized they were not all oppressed victims of an unjust society—these were real criminals. She ended up working with juveniles and pre-delinquents and found it rewarding and challenging. For the next twenty years, much of her employment involved working with troubled and disadvantaged kids. Although for a couple of years, when she needed a break, she did work as a mailman.

"My daughters were very demanding at bedtime and after reading three stories I'd turn out the light," Griffin recalled. "Then I would make a story up for them. Year after year of doing this released something inside my mind and characters began to take on shape and substance. Finally, these characters begged for more and I had to find out about writing. I was awarded a scholarship to attend a writing for children workshop at Rice University in Houston and that opened the portal. That was in 1991 and I haven't looked back." Even though it took a long time to get that first book published, she felt good about saying she was a writer when people asked what she did.

This scholarship let to her friendship with cowriter Kathy Combs, who lives in Houston, Texas. Their time at Rice University led to their attending other workshops together in different regions, from Indiana to Kentucky, from New York to New Jersey. Both *Cowboy Sam* and their next book, *The Foot-Stomping Adventures of*

Clementine Sweet are Texas stories full of lyrical language. Their third collaboration, *Stinker and the Onion Princess* is a lighthearted "Texas-sized" retelling of the Grimm tale "King Thrushbeard." Instead of a haughty princess, there is a stuck-up son of an oil baron (Big Daddy) and his wife (Big Mama). "Oh whee, does that boy have an adventure as the Onion Princess helps him find his manners," remarked Griffin.

Griffin spent almost two years researching the story of the Johnstown Flood. This horrific event occurred on May 31, 1889, in the Conemaugh Valley just east of Pittsburgh, Pennsylvania. In less than an hour over 2,000 innocent people were brutally killed by a wave that swept down the mountain into the valley after a dam holding back water for a recreational lake broke. A visit to the flood museum in Johnstown left Griffin stunned and overwhelmed and wanting to understand how such a tragedy could happen. Her background as a history teacher turned out to be a valuable asset as she began searching. With the help of several historians at local museums and libraries her new manuscript took shape. She often thinks of a quote from one of the survivors, Reverend David Beale (especially after the events of September 11, 2001), "it were vain to undertake to tell the world how or what we felt, when shoeless, hatless, and many of us almost naked, some bruised and broken, we stood there and we looked upon that scene of death and desolation." What she feels she learned from her study was the remarkable power people have to care for one another, to risk their lives for each other, and to pick up and carry on.

At the suggestion of her friend Kathy Combs, Griffin took a screenwriting workshop and discovered a new and exciting way of looking at story. "Think of a screenplay as sending a series of electric postcards. Each scene has to push the main character further along." She feels that screenwriting has taught her a great deal about character development. That in turn has helped her become a better writer.

"I think of writing like white-water rafting," Griffin stated. "There are days when I am splashing and dashing madly along, and there are days when I'm caught in a whirlpool. Every story is a different adventure. Every story leads into new waters. My advice to those who want to write: Know when to hold on and when to paddle. It's one riot of a ride. The most exciting part is discovering where the story takes you. Of course it's rough, rejection hurts, but you know what? I've finally found where I want to be."

Biographical and Critical Sources

PERIODICALS

Kirkus Reviews, July 15, 2001, review of *Cowboy Sam and Those Confounded Secrets,* p. 1026.
Publishers Weekly, July 16, 2001, review of *Cowboy Sam and Those Confounded Secrets,* p. 180.
School Library Journal, December, 2001, Shara Alpern, review of *Cowboy Sam and Those Confounded Secrets,* p. 103.

GRUPPER, Jonathan 1958-

Personal

Born November 10, 1958, in New York, NY.

Career

Author, film and television writer, producer, and director. New York University Continuing Education Program, instructor in screenwriting.

Awards, Honors

Gold Medal, International Film and Video Festival, Gold Special Jury Prize, WorldFest-Houston, and Silver Medal, WorldFest-Flagstaff, all for *Johnson's List;* nominee, Jackson Hole Best Children's Program, 1999, for *Tales from the Wild;* Cine Golden Eagle Award, 2002, for *The Shape of Life;* five Emmy nominations, including Outstanding Children's Series, for the TV series *Really Wild Animals.*

Writings

Spin's Really Wild Africa Tour, National Geographic Society (Washington, DC), 1996.

Destination: Rain Forest, National Geographic Society (Washington, DC), 1997.

Destination: Polar Regions, National Geographic Society (Washington, DC), 1999.

Destination: Deep Sea, National Geographic Society (Washington, DC), 2000.

Destination: Australia, National Geographic Society (Washington, DC), 2000.

Destination: Rocky Mountains, National Geographic Society (Washington, DC), 2001.

Writer and producer of television programs, including "Ascent: The Story of Hugh Herr," *Profiles,* National Geographic Channel; "Mole People," Discovery Channel; *This Week in History* (twenty-five segments), History Channel; "Niagara Falls: Raging Rapids," Discovery Channel; (and director) *Johnson's List,* History Channel; "Family Life of Animals," Reader's Digest Home Video. Writer of television programs, including *Incredible Journey,* PBS; *Elie Wiesel: First Person Singular,* PBS; "The Andes," Discovery Channel; "Deserts," Discovery Channel; *Mysteries of Deep Space,* PBS; *Barbarians,* History Channel; *Islam: Empire of Faith,* PBS; and *National Geographic Explorer,* Turner Broadcasting System (TBS).

Sidelights

Jonathan Grupper is a prolific writer, producer, and director for television, film, and radio. Grupper is also the author of several books on wildlife for the National Geographic Society. The series' focus on animals, its lush photography, and its conversational, yet informative narratives have led reviewers to recommend the titles as introductory texts for units on various regions. The first volume in the series, *Destination: Rain Forest,* sets the

Tracing the course of one day, Jonathan Grupper leads young readers through the varied habitats of Australia to introduce the animals of the continent in **Destination: Australia.**

standard, with Grupper's narrative directly inviting readers to join in observing the wild variety of plants and animals found in the world's rain forests. Likewise, in *Destination: Deep Sea,* Grupper introduces children to the inhabitants of various levels of the sea, from the surface to the sea bottom, through a text that invites the readers to dive right in and imagine snorkeling around all these fish themselves.

In *Destination: Polar Regions,* Grupper compares and contrasts the Arctic and Antarctic regions, often considered more similar than they actually are. The book employs a longer time frame than the others in the series in order to offer the reader glimpses of the Arctic landscape at various times of the year; in midsummer the reader follows the Arctic tern down to the South Pole, where the calendar is reversed and it is winter. Some reviewers noted the lack of an index and the small amount of space given to any single species, "but for browsing, it's very appealing," concluded Pam Gosner in *School Library Journal.* A contributor to *Kirkus Reviews* concluded that "this attractive volume offers a real sense of the differences between regions often thought of as identical."

In *Destination: Australia,* Grupper "presents Australia as a land of natural wonders," according to Edith Ching in *School Library Journal.* As with the other books in the series, reviewers focused much of their attention on what

Gillian Engberg called in her *Booklist* review, "eye-popping photos," the kind of thing *National Geographic* is famous for. Here again, Grupper employs a second-person narrative, which offers an immediacy to this quick tour of Australia's natural habitat and its strange inhabitants. Readers are invited to imagine what it would feel like to suddenly come upon a Tasmanian devil, for example. Although some reviewers noted that this book was unlikely to offer enough information, and lacks a conducive organization, for report-writing, its format was thought to likely inspire young readers to search further. And William H. Adams, writing in *Science Books and Films,* concluded that "this concise book is made invaluable by its exceptional color photos and informative text."

The reader travels to North America in *Destination: Rocky Mountains* as Grupper leads a whirlwind trek up the mountain, stopping briefly to observe the plants and animals that live at extravagant elevations. Though a contributor to *Kirkus Reviews* found that some readers may have difficulty following the imaginative trek up the mountain due to an occasional disconnect between narrative and photograph, Frieda F. Bustian, writing in the *Horn Book Guide,* contended that "the text and graphics work well together." As always, however, the author was praised for conveying the excitement of discovering his subject to young readers. "Grupper conveys a real feeling for the vastness, variety, and richness of the Rocky Mountains," exclaimed Dona J. Helmer in *School Library Journal.*

Biographical and Critical Sources

PERIODICALS

Appraisal: Science Books for Young People, spring, 2000, review of *Destination: Australia* and *Destination: Polar Regions,* pp. 35-36.

Booklist, November 1, 1997, Carolyn Phelan, review of *Destination: Rain Forest,* p. 464; June 1, 2000, Gillian Engberg, review of *Destination: Australia,* p. 1883.

Catholic Library World, June, 2001, Barbara T. Gould, review of *Destination: Deep Sea,* p. 243.

Horn Book Guide, spring, 2000, Danielle J. Ford, review of *Destination: Polar Regions,* p. 123; January-June, 2001, Frieda F. Bustian, review of *Destination: Rocky Mountains,* p. 361.

Kirkus Reviews, August 15, 1999, review of *Destination: Polar Regions,* p. 1311; March 15, 2001, review of *Destination: Rocky Mountains,* p. 408.

School Library Journal, October, 1997, Kathy Piehl, review of *Destination: Rain Forest,* p. 118; November, 1999, Pam Gosner, review of *Destination: Polar Regions,* p. 143; May, 2000, Edith Ching, review of *Destination: Australia,* p. 161; September, 2000, Frances E. Millhouser, review of *Destination: Deep Sea,* p. 216; May, 2001, Dona J. Helmer, review of *Destination: Rocky Mountains,* p. 166.

Science Books and Films, January-February, 2001, William H. Adams, review of *Destination: Australia,* p. 26.*

H

HIMLER, Ronald (Norbert) 1937-

Personal

Born November 16, 1937, in Cleveland, OH; son of Norbert and Grace (Manning) Himler; married Ann Danowitz, June 18, 1972 (divorced); children: Daniel, Anna, Peer. *Education:* Cleveland Institute of Art, diploma, 1960; graduate study in painting at Cranbrook Academy of Art (Bloomfield Hills, MI), 1960-61, and New York University and Hunter College, 1968-70.

Addresses

Home—11301 East Placita Cibuta, Tucson, AZ 85749.

Career

General Motors Technical Center, Warren, MI, technical sculptor (styling), 1961-63; artist and illustrator, 1963—. Toy designer and sculptor for Transogram Co., New York, NY, 1968, and Remco Industries, Newark, NJ, 1969. Cofounder and headmaster, Blue Rock School, NC, 1982-84. *Exhibitions:* Wolfe Galleries, Tucson, AZ, 1990.

Awards, Honors

Award for Graphic Excellence, American Institute of Graphic Arts, and citation of merit, Society of Illustrators, both 1972, both for *Baby;* Printing Industries of America citation, 1972, for *Rocket in My Pocket;* Children's Book Showcase selection, Children's Book Council, 1975, for *Indian Harvests;* New Jersey Institute of Technology award (with Ann Himler), 1976, for *Little Owl, Keeper of the Trees;* Best of Bias-Free Illustration citation, American Institute of Graphic Arts, 1976, for *Make a Circle, Keep Us In;* Children's Choice selection, International Reading Association/Children's Book Council, 1979, for *Bus Ride;* Best Children's Books, *School Library Journal,* 1979, for *Curly and the Wild Boar,* 1990, for *The Wall,* and 1991, for *Fly Away Home;* Children's Books of the Year selection, Child

Ronald Himler

Study Children's Book Committee at Bank Street College, 1982, for *Moon Song* and *Jem's Island,* and 1992, for *Fly Away Home; Best Town in the World* was exhibited at the Brataslava Biennale of Illustration, 1985; Best Books of 1985, New York Public Library, and Notable Book selection, American Library Association (ALA), 1986, both for *Dakota Dugout;* Pick of the Lists, American Booksellers Association, 1987, for *Nettie's Trip South,* 1990, for *The Wall,* 1991, for *I'm Going to Pet a Worm Today,* and 1992, for *Fly Away Home* and *Katie's Trunk;* Notable Book selection, ALA, 1990, Notable Book selection, Journal of Youth Services in Libraries, 1991, Fanfare Selection, *Horn Book,* 1991, and master list, Texas Bluebonnet Award, all for *The Wall;* One Hundred Titles for Reading and Sharing selection, New York Public Library, 1990, for *The Wall,* and 1992, for *The Lily Cupboard;* Notable Book selection, ALA, 1991, and Editor's Choice, *Booklist,* 1991, both for *Fly Away Home;* Silver Medal, Society of Illustrators, 1992, for best Western painting in book cover art.

Writings

FOR CHILDREN; SELF-ILLUSTRATED

(Compiler) *Glad Day, and Other Classical Poems for Children,* Putnam (New York, NY), 1972.
(With former wife, Ann Himler) *Little Owl, Keeper of the Trees,* Harper (New York, NY), 1974.
The Girl on the Yellow Giraffe, Harper (New York, NY), 1976.
Wake Up, Jeremiah, Harper (New York, NY), 1979.
Six Is So Much Less Than Seven, Star Bright Books (New York, NY), 2002.

ILLUSTRATOR

Robert Burgess, *Exploring a Coral Reef,* Macmillan (New York, NY), 1972.
Carl A. Withers, compiler, *Rocket in My Pocket* (poetry anthology), revised edition, Western Publishing (New York, NY), 1972.
Fran Manushkin, *Baby,* Harper (New York, NY), 1972.
Elizabeth Winthrop, *Bunk Beds,* Harper (New York, NY), 1972.
Millicent Brower, *I Am Going Nowhere,* Putnam (New York, NY), 1972.
Charlotte Zolotow, *Janey,* Harper (New York, NY), 1973.
Marjorie Weinman Sharmat, *Morris Brookside, a Dog,* Holiday House (New York, NY), 1973.
Tom Glazer, *Eye Winker, Tom Tinker, Chin Chopper,* Doubleday (New York, NY), 1973.
Fran Manushkin, *Bubblebath,* Harper (New York, NY), 1974.
William C. Grimm, *Indian Harvests,* McGraw-Hill (New York, NY), 1974.
Robert Burch, *Hut School and the Wartime Homefront Heroes,* Viking (New York, NY), 1974.
Marjorie Weinman Sharmat, *Morris Brookside Is Missing,* Holiday House (New York, NY), 1974.
Betsy Byars, *After the Goat Man,* Viking (New York, NY), 1974.
Polly Curran, *A Patch of Peas,* Golden Press (New York, NY), 1975.
Arnold Adoff, *Make a Circle, Keep Us In,* Delacorte (New York, NY), 1975.
Achim Broger, *Bruno,* Morrow (New York, NY), 1975.
Marty Kelly, *The House on Deer-Track Trail,* Harper (New York, NY), 1976.
Crescent Dragonwagon, *Windrose,* Harper (New York, NY), 1976.
Betty Boegehold, *Alone in the Cabin,* Harcourt (San Diego, CA), 1976.
Yoshiko Uchida, *Another Goodbye,* Allyn & Bacon (Newton, MA), 1976.

When ten-year-old Sadako gets leukemia as a result of the bombing of Hiroshima, her friend reminds her of the belief that a cure will result from making a thousand origami cranes in Eleanor Coerr's account, based on a true story. (From Sadako and the Thousand Paper Cranes, *illustrated by Himler.)*

Richard Kennedy, *The Blue Stone,* Holiday House (New York, NY), 1976.
Jeanette Caines, *Daddy,* Harper (New York, NY), 1977.
Johanna Johnston, *Harriet and the Runaway Book: The Story of Harriet Beecher Stowe and Uncle Tom's Cabin,* Harper (New York, NY), 1977.
Arnold Adoff, *Tornado,* Delacorte (New York, NY), 1977.
Louise Dickerson, *Good Wife, Good Wife,* McGraw-Hill (New York, NY), 1977.
Arnold Adoff, *Under the Early Morning Trees,* Dutton (New York, NY), 1978.
Clyde Bulla and Michael Syson, *Conquista,* Crowell (New York, NY), 1978.
Nancy Jewell, *Bus Ride,* Harper (New York, NY), 1978.
Fred Gipson, *Little Arliss,* Harper (New York, NY), 1978.
Fred Gipson, *Curly and the Wild Boar,* Harper (New York, NY), 1979.
Richard Kennedy, *Inside My Feet: The Story of a Giant,* Harper (New York, NY), 1979.

Carla Stevens, *Trouble for Lucy,* Houghton (Boston, MA), 1979.

Arnold Adoff, *I Am the Running Girl,* Harper (New York, NY), 1979.

Douglas Davis, *The Lion's Tail,* Atheneum (New York, NY), 1980.

Elizabeth Parsons, *The Upside-Down Cat,* Atheneum (New York, NY), 1981.

Linda Peavy, *Allison's Grandfather,* Scribner (New York, NY), 1981.

Byrd Baylor, *Moon Song,* Scribner (New York, NY), 1982.

Katherine Lasky, *Jem's Island,* Scribner (New York, NY), 1982.

Byrd Baylor, *Best Town in the World,* Scribner (New York, NY), 1983.

Thor Heyerdahl, *Kon Tiki: A True Adventure of Survival at Sea,* Random House (New York, NY), 1984.

Ann Turner, *Dakota Dugout,* Macmillan (New York, NY), 1985.

Ellen Howard, *Edith Herself,* Atheneum (New York, NY), 1987.

Ann Turner, *Nettie's Trip South,* Macmillan (New York, NY), 1987.

Susan Pearson, *Happy Birthday, Grampie,* Dial (New York, NY), 1987.

Emily Cheney Neville, *The Bridge,* Harper (New York, NY), 1988.

Alice Fleming, *The King of Prussia and a Peanut Butter Sandwich,* Scribner (New York, NY), 1988.

Susan Nunes, *Coyote Dreams,* Atheneum (New York, NY), 1988.

Ann Herbert Scott, *Someday Rider,* Clarion (New York, NY), 1989.

(With John Gurney) Della Rowland, *A World of Cats,* Contemporary Books (Chicago, IL), 1989.

Crescent Dragonwagon, *Winter Holding Spring,* Macmillan (New York, NY), 1990.

Eve Bunting, *The Wall,* Clarion (New York, NY), 1990.

Dorothy and Thomas Hoobler, *George Washington and Presidents' Day,* Silver Press (Englewood Cliffs, NJ), 1990.

Merry Banks, *Animals of the Night,* Scribner (New York, NY), 1990.

Liza Ketchum Murrow, *Dancing on the Table,* Holiday House (New York, NY), 1990.

Patricia Hubbell, *A Grass Green Gallop,* Atheneum (New York, NY), 1990.

Eve Bunting, *Fly Away Home,* Clarion (New York, NY), 1991.

Constance Levy, *I'm Going to Pet a Worm Today, and Other Poems,* McElderry Books (New York, NY), 1991.

Virginia T. Gross, *The Day It Rained Forever: A Story of the Johnstown Flood,* Viking (New York, NY), 1991.

Kathleen V. Kudlinski, *Pearl Harbor Is Burning,* Viking (New York, NY), 1991.

Shulamith Levey Oppenheim, *The Lily Cupboard,* Harper-Collins (New York, NY), 1992.

Byrd Baylor, *One Small Blue Bead,* Scribner (New York, NY), 1992.

Ann Turner, *Katie's Trunk,* Macmillan (New York, NY), 1992.

Kate Aver, *Joey's Way,* McElderry Books (New York, NY), 1992.

Ann Herbert Scott, *A Brand Is Forever,* Clarion (New York, NY), 1993.

Eve Bunting, *Someday a Tree,* Clarion (New York, NY), 1993.

Virginia Driving Hawk Sneve, *The Sioux,* Holiday House (New York, NY), 1993.

Virginia Driving Hawk Sneve, *The Navajos,* Holiday House (New York, NY), 1993.

Virginia Driving Hawk Sneve, *The Seminoles,* Holiday House (New York, NY), 1994.

Virginia Driving Hawk Sneve, *The Nez Perce,* Holiday House (New York, NY), 1994.

Kathleen V. Kudlinski, *Lone Star,* Viking (New York, NY), 1994.

Kathleen V. Kudlinski, *Earthquake,* Viking (New York, NY), 1994.

Eve Bunting, *A Day's Work,* Clarion (New York, NY), 1994.

Nancy Luenn, *SQUISH! A Wetland Walk,* Atheneum (New York, NY), 1994.

In **Why Not, Lafayette?,** *Himler's illustrations enhance Jean Fritz's portrayal of General Lafayette, zealous advocate of liberty who fought under George Washington in the American Revolution.*

Wendy Kesselman, *Sand in My Shoes,* Hyperion (New York, NY), 1995.

Virginia Driving Hawk Sneve, *The Hopis,* Holiday House (New York, NY), 1995.

Virginia Driving Hawk Sneve, *The Iroquois,* Holiday House (New York, NY), 1995.

D. Anne Love, *Bess's Log Cabin Quilt,* Holiday House (New York, NY), 1995.

D. Anne Love, *Dakota Spring,* Holiday House (New York, NY), 1995.

Sue Alexander, *Sara's City,* Clarion (New York, NY), 1995.

Virginia Driving Hawk Sneve, *The Cherokees,* Holiday House (New York, NY), 1996.

Virginia Driving Hawk Sneve, *The Cheyennes,* Holiday House (New York, NY), 1996.

Eve Bunting, *Train to Somewhere,* Clarion (New York, NY), 1996.

Barbara A. Steiner, *Desert Trip,* Sierra Club Books (San Francisco, CA), 1996.

Ellen Howard, *The Log Cabin Quilt,* Holiday House (New York, NY), 1996.

Linda Oatman High, *A Christmas Star,* Holiday House (New York, NY), 1997.

Virginia Driving Hawk Sneve, *The Apaches,* Holiday House (New York, NY), 1997.

Faye Gibbons, *Hook Moon Night: Spooky Tales from the Georgia Mountains,* Morrow Junior Books (New York, NY), 1997.

Rukhsana Khan, *The Roses in My Carpets,* Holiday House (New York, NY), 1998.

Eve Bunting, *Rudi's Pond,* Clarion Books (New York, NY), 1999.

Eleanor Coerr, *Sadako and the Thousand Paper Cranes,* Putnam (New York, NY), 1999.

Jean Fritz, *Why Not, Lafayette?,* G.P. Putnam's Sons (New York, NY), 1999.

Katherine Kirkpatrick, *Redcoats and Petticoats,* Holiday House (New York, NY), 1999.

Stewart Ross, *Mark Twain and Huckleberry Finn,* Viking (New York, NY), 1999.

Jane Resh Thomas, *The Snoop,* Clarion Books (New York, NY), 1999.

Sherry Garland, *Voices of the Alamo,* Scholastic (New York, NY), 2000.

Steven Kroll, *William Penn: Founder of Pennsylvania,* Holiday House (New York, NY), 2000.

Ellen Howard, *The Log Cabin Christmas,* Holiday House (New York, NY), 2000.

Frederick Lipp, *The Caged Birds of Phnom Penh,* Holiday House (New York, NY), 2001.

Julian Scheer, *By the Light of the Captured Moon,* Holiday House (New York, NY), 2001.

Julian Scheer, *A Thanksgiving Turkey,* Holiday House (New York, NY), 2001.

Ellen Howard, *The Log Cabin Church,* Holiday House (New York, NY), 2002.

Fran Manushkin, *Baby, Come Out!,* Star Bright Books (New York, NY), 2002.

Mike Spradlin, *The Legend of Blue Jacket,* HarperCollins (New York, NY), 2002.

David A. Adler, *A Picture Book of Lewis and Clark,* Holiday House (New York, NY), 2003.

Gwenyth Swain, *I Wonder As I Wander,* Eerdmans (Grand Rapids, MI), 2003.

Betty Ren Wright, *The Blizzard,* Holiday House (New York, NY), 2003.

Several of Himler's books have been translated into other languages, including Dutch and Japanese.

Sidelights

Ronald Himler is one of the most visible artists and illustrators in children's literature, for in addition to his own five self-illustrated books and the hundred-plus books he has illustrated for writers such as Eve Bunting, Virginia Driving Hawk Sneve, Byrd Baylor, and Ellen Howard, he has also created the covers of over a hundred young adult titles. It is hardly possible to go into the juvenile section of a bookshop or library and not see his artwork in some form or another. Himler is known for his work in a variety of artistic media, including watercolor, oils, gouache, and pencil, which he uses to present his imaginative interpretation of popular children's books to young readers. Trained in both painting and illustration, Himler offers characteristically gentle and sensitive depictions of stories and poems that help open the eyes of young children to the world that surrounds them. As Martha E. Ward and Dorothy A. Marquardt noted in *Illustrators of Books for Young People,* Himler's artwork depicts the "essence of child-hood."

Raised in Cleveland, Ohio, Himler spent many child-hood hours immersed in drawing, especially during the weekly trips he took to his grandmother's home, using the dining room table there to create his artwork. Himler has reported that drawing has always been part of his life, and that in fact it is almost as if art chose him rather than vice versa. After graduating from high school, he studied painting at the Cleveland Institute of Art, and went on to attend graduate school at the Cranbrook Academy of Art in Bloomfield Hills, Michigan. Thereafter, Himler worked in various positions as a commercial artist, including a stint as a technical sculptor at the General Motors Technical Center and also as a toy designer and sculptor for two companies.

Early in his career, Himler decided to travel throughout Europe and Scandinavia, doing independent research in such major museums as the Louvre in Paris, the Uffizi Galleries in Florence, and Amsterdam's Rijksmuseum. His tours through some of the world's finest collections of fine art broadened the scope of Himler's own painting, while the contacts he made with people of so many different cultures increased his sensitivity to the diversity of the world's peoples. Upon returning to the United States, Himler was determined to pursue a career as an illustrator of children's books. His first project was a verse anthology called *Glad Day, and Other Classical Poems for Children,* which was published in 1972, the same year he married Ann Danowitz. The *Glad Day* illustrations were quickly followed by others, including drawings to accompany a work of nonfiction entitled *Exploring a Coral Reef.* Requests for illustrations for other books continued to come his way, and Himler found himself working with texts written by a wide variety of popular children's writers, including Betsy Byars, Tom Glazer, Marjorie Weinman Sharmat, and Charlotte Zolotow.

In 1974, Himler and his wife, Ann, collaborated on the children's book *Little Owl, Keeper of the Trees,* with Himler providing the illustrations. Three tales that center on a young owl living high up in a sycamore tree, *Little Owl* weaves magic into the world of forest-dwelling animals through the character of Jonas, a small, friendly monster who possesses special powers. Himler went on to write two other books, including his 1976 publication *The Girl on the Yellow Giraffe,* which features his pencil-sketch illustrations. Calling the book "an affectionate celebration of a child's imaginative powers," *Booklist* reviewer Denise M. Wilms praised the author/illustrator's picture book as an effective portrayal of a child's imaginary world. Himler wrote *The Girl on the Yellow Giraffe* for his daughter, Anna; three years later, he produced *Wake Up, Jeremiah* for his son, Peer. Accompanied by a minimum of text, Himler's impressionist-style, full-color illustrations depict a young boy's excitement at witnessing the start of a new day. Getting up extra early to watch the sunrise from the top of a hill near his home, Jeremiah then rushes home to share this fresh new day with his drowsy parents. "The evolution of dawn—from early murk to resplendent full light—in Mr. Himler's illustrations represent his best, most colorful performance to date," remarked *New York Times Book Review* contributor George A. Woods.

Over two decades were to pass before Himler's next self-illustrated title, *Six Is So Much Less Than Seven.* A contributor for *Kirkus Reviews* called this picture book a "touching tribute to pets and how they enrich our lives," and praised Himler's gentle illustrations and "trademark soft watercolors." The book tells of an elderly man who goes about his daily activities, all the while accompanied by six cats. He rises, eats breakfast, does the housework, repairs his tractor, gives the shed a coat of paint, rests for a bit, fetches the mail, and works around the farmyard, barn, and garden. However, there is an underlying feeling of sadness in the scenes, and the reader learns why toward the end of the day when the man goes to visit the grave of a seventh feline. The somber tone of the book is evened by the last activity of the day when the man goes to visit a cat and her four new kittens. The same critic for *Kirkus Reviews* called the tale "soothing" for anyone getting over the loss of a pet.

Illustrating the works of other authors, Himler has focused on complex emotional issues. In Eve Bunting's *Fly Away Home,* for example, the homeless lifestyle of a young boy and his out-of-work dad is treated by Himler with muted shades of brown and blue watercolor, and the artist places father and son at the edge of his pictures as a way of reflecting their existence on the fringes of airport life. "Himler matches Bunting's understated text with gentle sensibility," noted a *Kirkus Reviews* contributor. Zena Sutherland of the *Bulletin of the Center for Children's Books* similarly noted that "Himler's quiet

paintings echo the economy and the touching quality of the story," and *Horn Book* reviewer Ann A. Flowers commented: "The yearning sadness of the story, ameliorated only by the obvious and touching affection between father and son, is reflected in the subtle, expressive watercolors, dominated by shades of blue."

Other collaborations with Bunting have included the 1990 work *The Wall,* which sensitively presents a boy's impressions of a visit to Washington, D.C.'s Vietnam Memorial. In a review of Bunting's highly regarded *The Wall,* Denise M. Wilms of *Booklist* maintained that "Himler's intense, quiet watercolors capture the dignity of the setting as Bunting's story reaches right to the heart of deep emotions." Himler noted in *Children's Book Illustration and Design* that one of the major problems he had in that book was the depiction of the Vietnam Memorial Wall itself, essentially a dark marble slab that would give each page a "dark, heavy look to it which I did not want." Himler solved this problem by using watercolors and then lightening the wall with both washes and reflections. This in turn allowed him to bring the focus forward to the people in the story, to "evoke thoughtfulness without sentimentality."

Further collaborations with Bunting include the 1993 work *Someday a Tree,* a gentle ecology message for primary graders centering on the fate of one sick tree. In a *Booklist* review of *Someday a Tree,* Hazel Rochman commented favorably on yet another effective Bunting/Himler collaboration, noting that "Himler's watercolors express the quiet harmony of the green shady scene where you can dream and hear leaves whisper and see 'clouds change like smoke.'" A reviewer for *Publishers Weekly* also had praise for this collaborative effort, noting that "Nostalgia and timelessness merge seamlessly in this uncommonly evocative picture book." The same reviewer also lauded Himler's "delicate paintings" which "movingly reinforce" Bunting's message.

Himler again worked with Bunting in *A Day's Work,* the story of a young Mexican-American boy who finds work for his recently arrived grandfather from Mexico. A story of integrity and honesty, as well as one that extols the work ethic, *A Day's Work* was aided by Himler's "expressive, gestural watercolors," according to a reviewer for *Publishers Weekly,* who also felt the artwork "invokes both the harsh and the tender landscapes" of the young boy's world. Bunting and Himler also teamed up on the 1996 *Train to Somewhere,* "Another heartbreaking picture book," according to *Booklist*'s Hazel Rochman. The story of an orphan train that carried New York children to the Midwest in the late nineteenth century, the book focuses on one such orphan, Marianne, the girl nobody wants. "Himler's paintings in watercolor and gouache set the story against a bleak Midwestern fall landscape," Rochman further explained. A contributor for *Publishers Weekly* also had praise for this title, calling it a "characteristically incisive collaboration," and Himler's artwork "at once sobering and uplifting—and assuredly memorable."

A young Cambodian girl who desires good fortune for her impoverished family attempts to buy a bird, believing it will carry her wishes into the sky to be fulfilled in **The Caged Birds of Phnom Penh,** *written by Frederick Lipp and illustrated by Himler.*

While Himler has enjoyed writing and illustrating books for young readers, painting has remained his first love. In 1982, while traveling through the Southwest, the artist was permitted to attend several ceremonial dances performed by Native Americans. The powerful psychological effect of witnessing these traditional dances opened Himler's eyes to a people and a time with which he felt an inexplicable empathy. As a result, he sensed a growing need to understand and give expression to what he perceived as two very different cultures and histories: Plains Indian traditions and the history of the white man who had invaded and altered those traditions. Himler has since worked to capture the essence of Native-American ceremony in oil paintings. Many of these works have won him critical acclaim; Himler's paintings of Native

Americans have been featured in both *Art of the West* magazine and the PBS television program *Arizona Illustrated.*

Such an interest in Native American life has also carried over to his work in children's book illustration. Acknowledged for his beautifully executed illustrations on a variety of topics, another area of interest for Himler is the life and history of the American West. These two reining passions come together in the illustrations he created for "The First Americans," a series of books written by Virginia Driving Hawk Sneve that focus on Native-American tribal culture. Series titles include *The Nez Perce, The Sioux,* and *The Seminoles,* of which *School Library Journal* contributor M. Colleen McDougall noted: "Himler's illustrations are the book's high point.... [His] figures and landscapes are both aesthetically pleasing and pertinent to the discussion." A *Publishers Weekly* reviewer praised "Himler's striking oil paintings" in a review of Sneve's *The Sioux* and *The Navajos,* while *School Library Journal* contributor Jacqueline Elsner, reviewing *The Cherokees,* remarked: "Himler's familiar watercolors, rich, warm, and serene, grace the text." Reviewing *The Cherokees,* Elizabeth S. Watson commented in *Horn Book* that any book that opens with "a wonderfully clear, cleanly drawn map starts out on the right foot." Watson also felt Himler's illustrations both "add detail" and "clarify" the text. Similarly, *Booklist*'s Rochman felt that *The Apaches* provides "a handsomely illustrated overview," and that Himler's "warm watercolors" are full of detail about clothing and daily life.

The ranch stories of Ann Herbert Scott—*Someday Rider* in 1989 and *A Brand Is Forever* in 1993—have also benefitted from Himler's artistic vision; each reflects the artist's sensitivity to Western surroundings. Of *A Brand Is Forever,* Marianne Partridge noted in the *New York Times Book Review* that Himler's illustrations "capture the essentially unchanging nature of ranching while giving [the book] a thoroughly modern flavor." *Horn Book*'s Watson also felt that the "slim volume will please youngsters eager for Western lore," while a contributor for *Publishers Weekly* commented that Himler's "pastel-toned watercolors offer an atmospheric portrayal of open country" and that the "subdued tone" of the artwork also adds to the emotionality of the book. Himler's illustrations for Byrd Baylor's stories of the Southwest have also been hailed by reviewers. A *Publishers Weekly* critic refers to his illustrations for Baylor's *Moon Song* as "harmonious, lovely drawings, dominated by the touching presence of the lonely coyote." Additionally, in *Desert Trip* by Barbara A. Steiner, Himler regales viewers with scenes of the part of the country he has called home for many years. *Booklist*'s Rochman remarked that Himler's watercolors for that book "show the wide open spaces, the astonishing rock formations," and even the amazing detail when viewing a single flower close up.

Himler has also collaborated on two volumes with D. Anne Love dealing with frontier life. In *Bess's Log Cabin Quilt,* he provides artwork for a story of one young girl who is waiting for her father to return to their Oregon frontier home, and in *Dakota Spring,* he focuses on the Dakota prairie with ink drawings that "offer inviting views of the landscape and characters," according to *Booklist*'s Carolyn Phelan. More frontier tales of pioneer life come in collaboration with Ellen Howard. *The Log Cabin Quilt* deals with a family that moves from Carolina to Michigan via wagon train, building a log cabin for their new home. *Booklist*'s Phelan felt this book was "sensitively written and illustrated," and praised Himler's "impressionistic paintings [which] have a rather muted palette." The family's story progresses in *Log Cabin Christmas,* in which Himler's paintings "capture the cramped, rustic, hard-lived conditions in a log cabin," according to a reviewer for *School Library*

Journal. Yet another installment is served up in *The Log Cabin Church,* with illustrations by Himler which "accurately show the life led by pioneers," according to a contributor for *Kirkus Reviews,* who concluded, "An effort doubly blessed."

Early American history comes to the fore in Steven Kroll's *William Penn: Founder of Pennsylvania,* for which Himler provided "elegant illustrations," according to Jackie Hechtkopf in *School Library Journal.* Another bit of Western history is served up in *Voices of the Alamo,* by Sherry Garland. Ruth Semrau, writing in *School Library Journal,* lauded Himler's "outstanding double-page watercolors [which] depict characters, sweeping landscapes, battle scenes, and the Alamo."

Working with Linda Oatman High, Himler moved forward in time to the Depression in *A Christmas Star,* in which a congregation's faith as well as a bit of Yuletide magic come to play in making the season a merry one for one little girl. A contributor for *Publishers Weekly* praised Himler's artwork which "creates a sparse, snowy countryside and a cast of characters." Rochman noted in *Booklist* that Himler's pictures of snow in "blue-toned moonlight" contrast with the interior of the church, "cozy ... in warm shades of brown."

More international in flavor is the picture book *The Roses in My Carpets* by Rukhsana Khan, dealing with a day in the life of a young refugee from Afghanistan, now safe from the aerial bombers which killed his father, but stuck in a destitute situation in an impoverished camp. "Himler paints the family with dignity and warmth," declared a reviewer for *Publishers Weekly,* "enveloping them in earth-colored, rosy tones and the details of daily life." *Booklist*'s Linda Perkins felt that this book "is a rare and welcome glimpse into a culture children usually don't see." Also set international in scope is *The Caged Birds of Phnom Penh,* by Frederick Lipp, featuring the story of eight-year-old Ary who lives in the Cambodian capital and can only dream of the rice fields where the birds fly free. "Himler's appealing art conveys the girl's changeable emotions," noted a contributor for *Publishers Weekly,* while *Booklist*'s Gillian Engberg praised Himler's "lovely ... illustrations [that] help to quiet some of the text's stridency." And *School Library Journal*'s Anne Parker lauded Himler's "outstanding" artwork, which manages to "capture many different kinds of light." Parker further commented that the writing and art "work well together, providing an excellent window into another culture."

Himler has paired with Julian Scheer on two books dealing with topics closer to home. In *By the Light of the Captured Moon,* a group of young children gather fireflies, and eventually one of the children, young Billy, magically pulls the moon into his bedroom. Critics once again praised Himler's watercolor creations. A reviewer for *Publishers Weekly* called them "especially pleasing, conveying the luminescence of the fireflies and the moon's gleaming light as suitably magical," and *Booklist*'s GraceAnne A. DeCandido similarly found that the illustrations provided the "light of hope and imagination." Himler collaborated with Scheer again on *A Thanksgiving Turkey,* the story of one young boy and his grandfather who stalk a wild turkey for several seasons only to come face-to-face with it on Thanksgiving and then decide not to shoot the noble old creature. A *Publishers Weekly* reviewer felt that Himler's artwork evokes "the enchantment of the predawn hours," while Pamela K. Bomboy, writing in *School Library Journal,* praised the "soft, watercolor illustrations" as well as the story which "evoke memories of a time past."

With hundreds of children's books and book cover illustrations to his credit, this master of the soft line and the gentle, tender scene continues to inspire young people through his artistic talents.

Biographical and Critical Sources

BOOKS

Children's Book Illustration and Design, edited by Julie Cummins, PBC/Library of Applied Design (New York, NY), 1992, pp. 70-72.

Kingman, Lee, and others, *Illustrators of Children's Books 1967-1976,* Horn Book (Boston, MA), 1978, p. 126.

Sixth Book of Junior Authors and Illustrators, edited by Sally Holmes Holtze, H. W. Wilson (New York, NY), 1989, pp. 129-130.

Ward, Martha E., and Dorothy A. Marquardt, *Illustrators of Books for Young People,* Scarecrow Press (Metuchen, NJ), 1975, p. 75.

PERIODICALS

Art of the West, January-February, 1989.

Booklist, October 1, 1976, Denise M. Wilms, review of *The Girl on the Yellow Giraffe,* p. 252; September 15, 1979, p. 120; April 1, 1990, Denise M. Wilms, review of *The Wall,* p. 1544; March 1, 1993, Hazel Rochman, review of *Someday a Tree,* p. 1234; April 1, 1993, Ilene Cooper, review of *A Brand Is Forever,* p. 1434; December 15, 1993, p. 759; May 1, 1994, p. 1602; October 1, 1994, p. 331; November 1, 1994, p. 505; February 15, 1995, Kay Weisman, review of *Bess's Log Cabin,* p. 1085; June 1, 1995, Carolyn Phelan, review of *Sand in My Shoes,* p. 1786; October 1, 1995, Stephanie Zvirin, review of *Sara's City,* p. 325; November 15, 1995, Carolyn Phelan, review of *Dakota Spring,* pp. 559-560; February 1, 1996, Hazel Rochman, review of *Train to Somewhere,* p. 930; April 15, 1996, Hazel Rochman, review of *Desert Trip,* p. 1444; December 15, 1996, Carolyn Phelan, review of *The Log Cabin Quilt,* p. 731; April 1, 1997, Hazel Rochman, review of *The Apaches,* p. 1332; September 1, 1997, Hazel Rochman, review of *A Christmas Star,* p. 139; November 15, 1998, Linda Perkins, review of *The Roses in My Carpet,* p. 596; March 1, 1999, Susan Dove Lempke, review of *Mark Twain and Huckleberry Finn,* p. 1210; April 1, 2001, Gillian Engberg, review of *The Caged Birds of Phnom Penh,* p. 1479; May 1, 2001, GraceAnne A. DeCandido, review of *By the Light of the Captured Moon,* p. 1692; September 1, 2001, Hazel Rochman, review of *A Thanksgiving Turkey,* p. 122; October 1, 2002, Kay Weisman,

review of *The Log Cabin Church,* p. 345; November 1, 2002, Linda Perkins, review of *The Legend of Blue Jacket,* p. 489.

Bulletin of the Center for Children's Books, May, 1975, p. 148; February, 1980, p. 111; May, 1991, Zena Sutherland, review of *Fly Away Home,* p. 212; October, 1994, pp. 38-39.

Childhood Education, winter, 2000, Smita Guha, review of *William Penn: Founder of Pennsylvania,* p. 107.

Horn Book, July-August, 1990, pp. 442-443; July-August, 1991, Ann A. Flowers, review of *Fly Away Home,* p. 445; March-April, 1992, p. 193; May-June, 1993, Elizabeth S. Watson, review of *A Brand Is Forever,* pp. 330-331; May-June, 1996, Elizabeth S. Watson, review of *The Cherokees,* p. 353; November-December, 1999, Margaret A. Bush, review of *Why Not, Lafayette?,* p. 756.

Kirkus Reviews, October 15, 1974, p. 1103; February 1, 1991, review of *Fly Away Home,* p. 172; February 15, 1993, p. 223; September 15, 1994, p. 1266; July 15, 2002, review of *Six Is So Much Less Than Seven,* p. 1033; August 1, 2002, review of *The Log Cabin Church,* p. 1133.

New York Times Book Review, June 25, 1972; November 12, 1972; October 28, 1979, George A. Woods, review of *Wake Up, Jeremiah,* p. 18; February 19, 1989; May 30, 1993, Marianne Partridge, review of *A Brand Is Forever,* p. 19.

Publishers Weekly, September 30, 1974, p. 60; May 21, 1982, review of *Moon Song,* p. 76; January 1, 1992, p. 55; March 15, 1993, review of *Someday a Tree,* pp. 86-87; March 29, 1993, review of *A Brand Is Forever,* p. 56; November 8, 1993, review of *The Sioux* and *The Navajos,* p. 80; August 8, 1994, review of *A Day's Work,* pp. 434-435; February 5, 1996, review of *Train to Somewhere,* p. 89; October 6, 1997, review of *A Christmas Star,* p. 55; October 5, 1998, review of *The Roses in My Carpet,* p. 90; September 20, 1999, review of *Why Not, Lafayette?,* p. 89; March 27, 2000, review of *Train to Somewhere,* p. 83; February 26, 2001, review of *By the Light of the Captured Moon,* p. 85; March 5, 2001, review of *The Caged Birds of Phnom Penh,* p. 79; September 24, 2001, review of *A Thanksgiving Turkey,* p. 46.

Quill & Quire, June, 1993, p. 40.

School Library Journal, June, 1991, p. 74; May, 1993, Jacqueline Elsner, review of *Someday a Tree,* p. 81, and Charlene Strickland, review of *A Brand Is Forever,* p. 91; August, 1993, p. 164; October, 1993, p. 147; April, 1994, M. Colleen McDougall, review of *The Nez Perce, The Sioux,* and *The Seminoles,* p. 146; June, 1994, p. 132; January, 1995, p. 82; June, 1995, p. 111; July, 1995, pp. 64, 91; December, 1995, p. 72; March, 1996, pp. 166-167; April, 1996, Jacqueline Elsner, review of *The Cherokees,* p. 130; June, 1996, pp. 1102-1103; October, 1996, Jane Class, review of *The Log Cabin Quilt,* p. 122; July, 1997, pp. 87-88, 95; October, 1997, Jane Marino, review of *A Christmas Star,* p. 42; November, 1998, Diane S. Marton, review of *The Roses in My Carpet,* pp. 87-88; April, 1999, Beth Tegart, review of *Redcoats and Petticoats,* p. 100; May, 1999, Shawn Brommer, review of *Mark Twain and Huckleberry Finn,* p. 142; December, 1999,

Marlene Gawron, review of *Why Not, Lafayette?*, pp. 149-150; April, 2000, Jackie Hechtkopf, review of *William Penn: Founder of Pennsylvania*, p. 122; June, 2000, Ruth Semrau, review of *Voices of the Alamo*, p. 164; October, 2000, review of *The Log Cabin Christmas*, p. 59; March, 2001, Gay Lynn van Vleck, review of *By the Light of the Captured Moon*, p. 220; May, 2001, Anne Parker, review of *The Caged Birds of Phnom Penh*, p. 128; September, 2001, Pamela K. Bomboy, review of *A Thanksgiving Turkey*, p. 205; October, 2002, Margaret Bush, review of *The Log Cabin Church*, p. 112; November, 2002, Dona Ratterree, review of *The Legend of Blue Jacket*, p. 150.

OTHER

Ronald Himler Web Site, http://www.flash.net/~himler/ (October 12, 2002).*

*   *   *

HISCOCK, Bruce 1940-

Personal

Born December 4, 1940, in San Diego, CA; son of Roy Burnett (a doctor) and Clara L. (a homemaker; maiden name, Hauser) Hiscock; married Mary Rebecca Habel (divorced, 1972); married Nancy A. Duffy (divorced, 1988); children: (first marriage) Julia Anne, Frederick William. *Education:* University of Michigan, B.S., 1962; Cornell University, Ph.D., 1966.

Addresses

Home—354 Ballou Rd., Porter Corners, NY 12859.

Career

Dow Chemical Company, Midland, MI, research chemist, 1966-68; Utica College of Syracuse University, Utica, NY, assistant professor of chemistry, 1968-71; Cornell University, Ithaca, NY, laboratory director and equine drug tester at Saratoga Harness Track, 1972-80; Saratoga Springs City Schools, Saratoga Springs, NY, substitute teacher, 1980-90; freelance writer and illustrator, 1990—.

Member

Adirondack Mountain Club, Nature Conservancy, Sierra Club, Northern Alaska Environmental Center, Children's Literature Connection, Wilderness Society, and many arts organizations.

Awards, Honors

Children's Book Council selection for Outstanding Science Trade Book, 1986, for *Tundra: The Arctic Land;* Children's Book Council selection for Outstanding Science Trade Book, 1988, New York Academy of Sciences Younger Honor, 1989, and John Burroughs Association Children's Book Award List selection, all for *The Big Rock;* Children's Book Council selection for

In this self-illustrated work, Bruce Hiscock relates the true story of the 1993 flood along the Mississippi River valley. (From The Big Rivers: The Missouri, the Mississippi, and the Ohio.)

Outstanding Science Trade Book, 1991, for *The Big Tree;* Children's Book Council selection for Outstanding Science Trade Book, 1993, and John Burroughs Association Children's Book Award List selection, for *The Big Storm;* Children's Book Council selection for Outstanding Science and Social Studies Trade Book, 1997, for *The Big Rivers;* National Outdoor Book Award (children's category) and Children's Book Council selection for Outstanding Science Trade Book, both 2001, both for *Coyote and Badger.*

Writings

SELF-ILLUSTRATED CHILDREN'S BOOKS

Tundra: The Arctic Land, Atheneum (New York, NY), 1986.
The Big Rock, Atheneum (New York, NY), 1988.
The Big Tree, Atheneum (New York, NY), 1991.
The Big Storm, Atheneum (New York, NY), 1993.
When Will It Snow?, Atheneum (New York, NY), 1995.
The Big Rivers: The Missouri, the Mississippi, and the Ohio, Atheneum (New York, NY), 1997.
Coyote and Badger: Desert Hunters of the Southwest, Boyds Mills Press (Honesdale, PA), 2001.
Big Caribou Herd: Life in the Arctic National Wildlife Refuge, Boyds Mills Press (Honesdale, PA), 2003.

ILLUSTRATOR

Lorus J. Milne and Margery Milne, *Nature's Great Carbon Cycle,* Atheneum (New York, NY), 1983.

Pat Hughey, *Scavengers and Decomposers: The Cleanup Crew,* Atheneum (New York, NY), 1984.

James Jesperson and Jane Fitz-Randolph, *Rams, Roms, and Robots: The Inside Story of Computers,* Atheneum (New York, NY), 1984.

James Jesperson and Jane Fitz-Randolph, *From Quarks to Quasars,* Atheneum (New York, NY), 1987.

Lorus J. Milne and Margery Milne, *Understanding Radioactivity,* Atheneum (New York, NY), 1989.

James Jesperson, *Looking at the Invisible Universe,* Atheneum (New York, NY), 1990.

Gail Haines, *Sugar Is Sweet: And So Are Lots of Other Things,* Atheneum (New York, NY), 1992.

James Jesperson and Jane Fitz-Randolph, *Mummies, Dinosaurs, and Moon Rocks: How We Know How Old Things Are,* Atheneum (New York, NY), 1995.

Contributor to periodicals, including *American Artist* and *American Kennel Gazette.*

Sidelights

Bruce Hiscock once told *SATA* about how he came to write his first book, *Tundra: The Arctic Land:* "The inspiration for *Tundra* really began when I was eleven

Enhanced with his vibrant watercolor paintings, Hiscock's Coyote and Badger: Desert Hunters of the Southwest *follows two predators on their search for sustenance during a dry season in the Chaco Canyon desert of New Mexico.*

years old and moved from southern Michigan with my mother and stepfather to Shemya, Alaska, a small tundra-covered island in the outer Aleutians. It was a refueling stop for Northwest Airlines flights to Tokyo. For two years I roamed the windswept landscape, watching the Arctic fox, finding tiny flowers, and digging up Aleut artifacts on the beach. I spent my time alone, because there were no other children of school age on the island. I had no thoughts of writing a book at the time and my reading concentrated mainly on practical things, like how to build crystal radios and kites."

"I put off any serious attempts at writing until I was in my thirties. Then I fell off the roof of a house I was building, and, confronted with my own mortality and several months in a cast, I began writing stories and working hard on my drawing. Years would pass before anything was published, but I found the work itself provided a freedom to wander about in my mind. It was completely fascinating.

"Now I live in a little cabin on the edge of the Adirondacks. I built it using stones and trees from the land, and it has turned out to be a composite of my life. It is a scientific design with passive solar heat, but it looks like something from 'The Hobbit.' It is cozy, constantly growing, and a great place to live and work on children's books. In many ways I lead a fairly simple life, but one that is rich in experience. I do a lot of programs with children, helping them write and draw, and I spend time every day in the woods with the birds and animals. At night, I watch the stars with a telescope or make things for my grandchildren. I travel often and far.

"The idea for *Tundra: The Arctic Land* came to me while visiting Rocky Mountain National Park. Looking at the alpine tundra plants, I began to wonder what the Arctic tundra, the land of the caribou, was like. I spent the next several months reading and taking notes on the tundra, but the most important part of my research was a long canoe trip in the barren lands of Canada. The writing did not become real to me until I had come face to face with the caribou, wolves, and musk-oxen. For several weeks I paddled through the unspoiled land, sketching flowers and animals, and slapping mosquitoes, in the twenty-four-hour daylight. After I returned home I spent a year rewriting and illustrating the book.

"*Tundra: The Arctic Land,* proved quite popular and remained in print for many years. When at last it was retired, I wanted to replace it with another book on the Arctic, this time focusing on Alaska. In 1998 I traveled to the Arctic National Wildlife Refuge with the Sierra Club, rafting down one of the rivers and then backpacking across the coastal plain to the Beaufort Sea. Near the ocean we ran smack into half of the famous Porcupine Caribou Herd, about 70,000 animals. This experience became the basis for my picture book, *Big Caribou Herd: Life in the Arctic National Wildlife Refuge.*

"*The Big Rock,* on the other hand, is about this huge boulder that is just down the hill from my house. I was sitting there one day watching the woods and contemplating a story that had just been rejected. Suddenly it came to me, through the seat of my pants I suppose, that I should do a book about the rock itself. I began at once, making sketches and studying geology. I came to know the rock well and gradually pieced together its story over the past billion years."

"My writing, whether fiction or nonfiction, includes several interlocking parts," Hiscock once commented. "First there must be a story line, something real to engage the reader, even in a science book. Then there is information, usually at different levels. Weather is the primary theme of *The Big Storm,* geography the underlying theme. I try to throw in some humor, at least enough to bring on a smile. Writing in *Library Talk,* September/October 1997, a reviewer of *The Big Rivers: The Missouri, the Mississippi, and the Ohio,* noted, 'I know absolutely that I saw Mark Twain and Huckleberry Finn, but I'm pretty sure that Elvis is in here too as a flood victim.' Then I strive to make illustrations that will reflect the writing: beautiful, clean, full of details, but not too fussy. I want kids to feel they can enter the pictures. I work hard to maintain the balance between all of these things. I am not easily satisfied. I spend about two years on a picture book. One of the lessons of the artistic life is accepting yourself and your good effort as enough right now, knowing that five years from now, with practice, your work will be better. On most days I am simply grateful to be able to do the work that I love."

Hiscock is known as an author and illustrator whose science books tell a story, and whose story books teach science. His book, *The Big Rock,* for example, makes geology come alive through the story of the boulder that rests near his home, how it got there before the forest that lives all around it, and how it will likely one day dissolve into sand. The result is "a true geology for the young, based on a single landmark viewed both familiarly and imaginatively," attested Philip and Phylis Morrison in *Scientific American.* In *When Will It Snow?,* on the other hand, Hiscock uses a fictional frame to present his scientific information. Here, a young boy's excitement about the coming of winter leads to his curiosity about how the other animals are preparing for the first snow, and hibernation, the growth of thick new pelts, and nest-building are introduced. *When Will It Snow?* "makes winter exciting and introduces some basic facts about animal adaptation in the cold," remarked Hazel Rochman in *Booklist.*

Coyote and Badger: Desert Hunters of the Southwest is likewise a hybrid title featuring two animals who are traditionally believed to work together in hunting in the desert of New Mexico. Through full-page watercolor illustrations and a comprehensive text, Hiscock tells the story of how badger digs underground for prey, some of which escape aboveground, where coyote is waiting. Cooperating in this way benefits both coyote and badger. "The narrative encompasses dangers from the ground to the sky, a thorough picture of the environment," remarked Mary Elam in *School Library Journal.* Lauren Peterson, writing in *Booklist,* likewise emphasized the scientific value of Hiscock's story, noting its utility in classroom units on animal behavior, the desert, and the Native American culture from which the story originated. "Realistic watercolor illustrations, including some lovely desert scenes, accompany the lengthy text," Peterson concluded.

Biographical and Critical Sources

PERIODICALS

Booklist, July 1, 1986; November 1, 1988; October 1, 1992, Ellen Mandel, review of *Sugar Is Sweet: And So Are Lots of Other Things,* p. 332; November 1, 1993, Kay Weisman, review of *The Big Storm,* p. 517; December 1, 1995, Hazel Rochman, review of *When Will It Snow?,* p. 641; June 1, 1997, Carolyn Phelan, review of *The Big Rivers: The Missouri, the Mississippi, and the Ohio,* p. 1690; April 15, 2001, Lauren Peterson, review of *Coyote and Badger: Desert Hunters of the Southwest,* p. 1564.

Bulletin of the Center for Children's Books, August, 1986; October, 1988.

Childhood Education, winter, 2001, Penny Boepple, review of *Coyote and Badger,* p. 110.

Horn Book, August, 1984, Karen Jameyson, review of *Scavengers and Decomposers: The Cleanup Crew,* p. 485; November-December, 1984, Harry C. Stubbs, review of *Rams, Roms, and Robots: The Inside Story of Computers,* p. 786.

Instructor and Teacher, May, 1984, Allan Yeager, review of *Scavengers and Decomposers,* p. 104.

Reading Teacher, November, 1992, Lee Galda and Pat MacGregor, review of *The Big Tree,* p. 239.

School Library Journal, August, 1984, George Gleason, review of *Scavengers and Decomposers,* p. 74; September, 1986, Ruth S. Vose, review of *Tundra: The Arctic Land,* p. 135; March, 1987, John Peters, review of *From Quarks to Quasars,* p. 172; May, 1989, Jonathan Betz-Zall, review of *Understanding Radioactivity,* p. 130; June, 1989, Joyce Gunn-Gradley, review of *The Big Rock,* p. 99; March, 1991, Martha Topol, review of *The Big Tree,* p. 188; September, 1992, Carolyn K. Jenks, review of *Sugar Is Sweet,* p. 266; September, 1993, Steven Engelfried, review of *The Big Storm,* p. 224; December, 1993, Steven Engelfried, review of *The Big Storm,* p. 106; December, 1995, Susan Chmurynsky, review of *When Will It Snow?,* p. 81; July, 1997, Linda Greengrass, review of *The Big Rivers,* p. 84; August, 2001, Mary Elam, review of *Coyote and Badger,* p. 153.

Scientific American, December, 1989, Philip Morrison and Phylis Morrison, review of *The Big Rock,* p. 150.

Washington Post Book World, November 9, 1986.

OTHER

Bruce Hiscock Web Site, http://www.brucehiscock.com (January 15, 2003).

HONEY, Elizabeth 1947-

Personal

Born 1947; daughter of William (a farmer) and Jean (Tippett) Honey; married to Andrew Clarke (a graphic designer); children: Beatrice, William. *Education:* Attended Swinburne Art School. *Hobbies and other interests:* Reading, music, movies, theater.

Addresses

Home—Melbourne, Australia. *Agent*—c/o Knopf Publishing/Author Mail, 299 Park Avenue, 4th Floor, New York, NY 10171.

Career

Author and illustrator of poetry, picture books, and novels for middle-grade readers.

Awards, Honors

Australian Children's Book of the Year Award, Children's Book Council of Australia, 1997, for *Not a Nibble!;* named Honour Books, Children's Book Council of Australia, for *Honey Sandwich, Don't Pat the Wombat!,* and *45 & 47 Stella Street and Everything That Happened;* Premio Cento Award, Italy, and Young Australians' Best Book Award (YABBA) as Victorian children's selection for older readers, both 1997, both for *45 & 47 Stella Street and Everything That Happened.*

Writings

SELF-ILLUSTRATED

Princess Beatrice and the Rotten Robber (picture book), Puffin (Ringwood, Victoria, Australia), 1988.
Honey Sandwich (poems), Allen & Unwin (St. Leonards, New South Wales, Australia), 1993.
The Cherry Dress, Puffin (Ringwood, Victoria, Australia), 1993.
The Book of Little Books, Allen & Unwin (St. Leonards, New South Wales, Australia), 1994.
45 & 47 Stella Street and Everything That Happened (juvenile novel), Allen & Unwin (St. Leonards, New South Wales, Australia), 1995.
Not a Nibble! (picture book), Allen & Unwin (St. Leonards, New South Wales, Australia), 1996.
What Do You Think, Feezal? (juvenile novel), Allen & Unwin (St. Leonards, New South Wales, Australia), 1997.
Mongrel Doggerel, Allen & Unwin (St. Leonards, New South Wales, Australia), 1998.
Fiddleback (sequel to *45 & 47 Stella Street*), Allen & Unwin (St. Leonards, New South Wales, Australia), 1998, Knopf (New York, NY), 2001.
Remote Man, Knopf (New York, NY), 2002.
The Moon in the Man (poems for children), Allen & Unwin (St. Leonards, New South Wales, Australia), 2002.

ILLUSTRATOR

Manny Clarke, *S.C.A.B.,* 1975.
Morris Lurie, *The Twenty-Seventh Annual African Hippopotamus Race,* Penguin (Ringwood, Australia), 1977.
Meryl Brown Tobin, *Puzzles Galore!,* 1978.
Maureen Stewart, *Snakes Alive!,* 1978.
Bettina Bird, *So What's New?,* 1978.
Phyllis Harry, *Gone Children,* 1978.
Carolyn Marrone, *Gino and Dan,* 1979.
Bettina Bird, *Us Three Kids,* 1979.
Bettina Bird, *Call It Quits,* 1979.
John Jones, *Fame and Misfortune,* 1979.
Laurie Brady, *Feel, Value, Act,* 1979.
Brian McKinlay, *Growing Things: Nature Study Ideas for the Primary School,* 1979.
L. M. Napier, *Mexican Beans,* 1980.
Susan Burke, *All Change at the Station,* 1980.
Judith Worthy, *Barney, Boofer, and the Cricket Bat,* 1980.
Meryl Brown Tobin, *More Puzzles Galore!,* 1980.
Cathy Hope, *Themes through the Year,* 1981.
Jessie Apted, *The Tucker Book,* 1981.
William Mayne, *Salt River Times,* 1982.
Ted Greenwood, *Flora's Treasures,* 1982.
Christobel Mattingley, *Brave with Ben,* 1982.
Brian McKinlay, *History Alive: Introducing Children to History around Them,* 1983.
Michael Dugan, *Melissa's Ghost,* Dent (London, England), 1986.
Roger Vaughan Carr, *Boilover at Breakfast Creek,* 1986.
Helen Higgs, *The Prize,* 1986.
Ted Greenwood, *I Don't Want to Know: Towards a Healthy Adolescence,* 1986.
Brian McKinlay, *Outdoors for Kids,* 1987.
Gilbert Tippett, *Energy for Kids,* 1987.
Ian Edwards, *Trees for Kids,* 1988.
Linda Allen, *Oh No! Not Again,* 1989.
Dream Time: New Stories by Sixteen Award-Winning Authors, edited by Toss Gascoigne, Jo Goodman, and Margot Tyrrell, Houghton Mifflin (New York, NY), 1991.
Christobel Mattingley, *No Gun for Asmir,* Puffin (Ringwood, Australia), 1993.
Christobel Mattingley, *Asmir in Vienna,* Puffin (Ringwood, Australia), 1995.

OTHER

Don't Pat the Wombat!, illustrated by son William Clarke, Allen & Unwin (St. Leonards, New South Wales, Australia), 1996, Knopf (New York, NY), 2000.

Work in Progress

Whitney Chenille Dobbs, a novel for teenagers; *The Ballad of Cauldron Bay* (sequel to *45 & 47 Stella Street* and *Fiddleback*).

Sidelights

Elizabeth Honey grew up on a farm near Wonthaggi in Australia, where her favorite activities were reading books, showing off, drawing, and preparing for a career as a trapeze artist, according to the Web site for her publisher, Allen & Unwin. After art school, Honey traveled through Europe, South America, and the United States, and then embarked on a career illustrating and eventually writing books for children. Her advice to aspiring authors is "Get stuck into your plot early on. Don't waffle for pages then have all the action in the last couple of paragraphs." Honey's own books include award-winning collections of poetry, picture books, and young adult novels which are lauded by critics for the author's ability to capture the essence of childhood through language and image. For children themselves, "it is the wacky humour and exuberant action that make Elizabeth Honey's novels immensely popular," according to *Magpies* reviewer Kevin Steinberger.

Honey's self-illustrated picture books include *Princess Beatrice and the Rotten Robber,* about a young girl whose love of dress-up and wearing jewelry leads to her kidnaping by the Rotten Robber, and, surprisingly, to lots of trouble for the kidnapper. The result is a "jolly romp of a book," according to Judith Sharman in *Books for Keeps.* Honey's picture book *Not a Nibble!* tells of a family vacation almost ruined by the fact that little Susie fails to catch a single fish, until the last day when she catches a glimpse of a mother whale with its young. Honey's watercolor illustrations ably convey the beauty of bright summer days spent by the sea, wrote Alicen Geddes Ward in *School Librarian,* who added: *"Not a Nibble!* is a book which totally captures for me the spirit of childhood holidays and the cherished days of family life."

Honey's novels for the middle grades feature strong, outspoken child characters who get involved in zany, action-packed adventures. In *45 & 47 Stella Street and Everything That Happened,* twelve-year-old Henni and her friends are upset by the arrival of a wealthy, and secretive, new family on Stella Street, and begin to spy on the people they call "the Phonies" in order to uncover the origins of their aloof, and sometimes mean-spirited, behavior. Honey's young characters and their parents "burst from these pages, full of an infectious joy in one another and in their shared lives," attested GraceAnne A. DeCandido in *Booklist.* The story, which is told in the form of Henni's journal, augmented by notes from the Phonies' threatening lawyers and other clues to the mystery, is a testament to the enthusiasm of its narrator for her tale begins on the book's cover and continues on to the title page before moving on into the book proper. While American critics noted that Honey's narrative does contain some Australian vernacular unlikely to be familiar to audiences in the United States, "it doesn't make the book any less delightful," Lucy Rafael remarked in *School Library Journal.* The gang from Stella Street go camping with a heavily pregnant adult in *Fiddleback,* a sequel to *45 & 47 Stella Street and Everything That Happened.* While camping, they find more adventures than they bargained for.

In *Don't Pat the Wombat!,* illustrated by the author's son, William Clarke, a character known as Exclamation Mark tells the story of a week spent at an Australian school camp under the direction of a bullying teacher. "The interaction between teachers, pupils, loners and oddballs is vividly brought out and the dialogue is totally credible," wrote Valerie Caless in *School Librarian.* Honey brings to life another pre-teen protagonist in *What Do You Think, Feezal?,* in which nine-year-old Bean finds a way to interpret the nefarious goings-on around her by reading Honey's picture book, *Princess Beatrice and the Rotten Robber. Magpies* reviewer Kevin Steinberger lauded the author's insight into the "worldview and vernacular of the preteens" she depicts, and concluded that "[Honey's] young fans will certainly be delighted with her latest novel."

Similarly, in a *Magpies* review of Honey's collection of poetry for children, *Mongrel Doggerel,* Steinberger stated: "Elizabeth Honey knows children well. She has the happy knack of being able to convincingly perceive the world through their senses and unfettered imagination." Humor is the point of the poems collected here and in the preceding volume, *Honey Sandwich,* in which a messy room, the daily cleaning of one's ears, a condescending teacher, playing doctor, and getting hurt form the author's subjects. Critics noted that while Honey's verses are indeed "doggerel," their sense of fun would make them appealing to children and would serve as an inviting introduction to the world of more traditional poetry. In his review of *Honey Sandwich* in *Magpies,* critic John Murray concluded: "The verses may not be all that memorable as literature, but they are fun."

In *Don't Pat the Wombat!,* Honey leaves the illustrations to William Clarke and focuses on recounting through young narrator Mark Ryder the doings of sixth graders in school and during summer camp in the Australian "bush." GraceAnne A. DeCandido, writing in *Booklist,* noted, "The sweet, quirky voices of a gaggle of Aussie kids bounce through this account." *School Library Journal* reviewer Marilyn Ackerman concluded, "The humorous short chapters, informal tone, and camaraderie among the boys are sure to make *Wombat!* a hit, even with reluctant readers. In her next book, *Fiddleback,* Honey uses the Australian bush as her backdrop and presents the reader with Henni, a seventh grader who tells the story of her camping trip with family and neighbors. Filled with comic mishaps and adventures, *Fiddleback* is "a book wrought in the same lively spirit" as *Don't Pat the Wombat!,* said a *Publishers Weekly* reviewer. In another recent book, *Remote Man,* Honey again mixes humor with adventure and talks about thought-provoking themes, including the international smuggling of exotic animals.

Honey's writing process "all begins with an idea I find intriguing," she said on publisher Allen & Unwin's Web site. "I know it's a good idea when it follows me around like a stray dog that won't go home. New ideas attach themselves to the first idea and by the time the book is finished hundreds of ideas have been woven through."

Biographical and Critical Sources

PERIODICALS

Booklist, June 1, 1998, GraceAnne A. DeCandido, review of *45 & 47 Stella Street, and Everything That Happened,* p. 1766; May 15, 2000, GraceAnne A. DeCandido, review of *Don't Pat the Wombat!,* p. 1744; September 1, 2001, Kelly Milner Halls, review of *Fiddleback,* p. 104.

Books for Keeps, January, 1991, Judith Sharman, review of *Princess Beatrice and the Rotten Robber,* p. 7.

Horn Book, May, 2000, review of *Don't Pat the Wombat!,* p. 314; September, 2001, review of *Fiddleback,* p. 585.

Magpies, November, 1993, John Murray, review of *Honey Sandwich,* p. 40; March, 1998, Kevin Steinberger, review of *What Do You Think, Feezal?,* p. 33; July, 1998, Kevin Steinberger, review of *Mongrel Doggerel,* p. 19.

Publishers Weekly, July 3, 2000, review of *Don't Pat the Wombat!,* p. 71; June 18, 2001, review of *Fiddleback,* p. 82.

School Librarian, November, 1997, Valerie Caless, review of *Don't Pat the Wombat!,* p. 191; Summer, 1998, Alicen Geddes Ward, review of *Not a Nibble!,* p. 74.

School Library Journal, September, 1998, Lucy Rafael, review of *45 & 47 Stella Street, and Everything That Happened,* p. 204; July, 2000, Marilyn Ackerman, review of *Don't Pat the Wombat!,* p. 105.

OTHER

Allen & Unwin—Authors, http://www.allenandunwin.com/Authors/apHoney.asp (January 16, 2001), "Elizabeth Honey."*

*   *   *

Autobiography Feature

Elizabeth Honey

If I dwell on childhood so be it. The way we were brought up, my family and the country we lived in shaped us, besides I write for children and draw on the experiences of childhood.

My father, William Honey, was a farmer. His forebears came to Australia in the 1840s from Devon and Ireland to take up a variety of enterprises in the new colony, but mainly farming.

My mother, Jean Tippett, became a farmer's wife. Her ancestors came from Cornwall. Through her I claim a distant relationship with Ronaldson Tippett engines. My mother's father died when she was eighteen months old, so she, brother Gilbert, and their frugal, practical mother lived with relatives.

My parents had four children, the fashionable number for the 1940s spaced over ten years and given traditional English names: William, Katherine, Elizabeth, and Mary. When I was born, we lived on a dairy farm called *Yaralla* a few miles south of the coal mining town of Wonthaggi. Our address was Box 2, Wonthaggi, our phone number— Wonthaggi 176.

It came about in this way. In 1943 Uncle Gilbert and Dad had their ears to the ground for affordable land. Mum and Dad, with babies William and Kath, were living in Essendon, Melbourne, where Dad worked as a fitter and turner making Bofor guns, running a farm in time off. Poor sight in one eye precluded him from the services.

Uncle Gilbert was on leave from the air force when an agent told them about four and a half thousand acres of bush near the coast in Gippsland. In foul weather they drove south to inspect it. In the wind and rain they rode around the land on horseback.

The asking price was four pounds an acre. Uncle Gilbert offered one pound an acre. When he heard his offer had been accepted, Uncle Gilbert lent against the wall and said "Strewth!"

"I had a look at that place," said a friend, "but the rabbits scared me off."

"Didn't see the rabbits," said Uncle Gilbert, wondering what he'd done. The love of a bargain's all very well, but this was more than a cheap pair of shoes, it was land, and as everyone knows land shapes your life.

Uncle Gilbert kept a cleared area with a house high on a cliff overlooking the sea, and Dad bought two thousand acres from him at ten shillings an acre. Thus, my parents threw in their lot with country the agent said was only good for raising "a snake to the acre." Wild tea-tree and messmate gums grew on sandy rises, home to kangaroos, wallabies, echidnas, possums, koalas, a great variety of birds, lizards, snakes, stray dogs, and thousands of rabbits.

They needed strong machinery to clear the scrub. Uncle Gilbert and Dad went to Melbourne and bought a steamroller. They rolled it all the way home, but just as they topped the rise overlooking home, the boiler cracked.

It's still there with bees in the firebox and magpies in the chimney.

After the Second World War, there were sales of redundant war materials. Dad bought a blitz, which was a cheap army truck, a two pound antitank gun carrier into which he fitted an old car engine and a few Brengun carriers, the tracks eventually sold for scrap metal. Looking at the relics littered about, you could be forgiven for thinking an artillery battle had been waged on our farm.

Uncle Gilbert bought a tank. They undid the bolts securing the gun turret, chained it to a large gum tree, and drove out from beneath it.

They dozed down the trees, pushed them into piles and burnt them or chopped them up. Dad put sides on the tray of the truck, painted "W. Honey—Wood Merchant" on the door, and sold firewood in Wonthaggi. We were never short of wood.

When I rail in my stories about protecting the environment, I think of my father clearing the land and the habitat lost, but it was different then. He was turning useless scrub into pasture, helping to forge the nation.

He built a dairy and a cottage for a sharefarmer to live in. As soon as the new pasture could feed a herd of cows, Dad, as part of an immigration scheme, sponsored a Dutch sharefarmer and his family. The big cans full of cream were collected from the cream stand on the road and taken to the Archies Creek butter factory.

Our house was a homemade too. First Dad made the cement bricks, and then the house grew in stages from available materials. The large lounge room windows were shop windows.

Dad's workshop was a dark cave of wonders which housed the generator before the electricity arrived and a massive collection of tools and machines: a lathe, jigsaw, drills, vices on the workbench, jacks, jemmies, crowbars, saws, chisels, every conceivable tool, plus iron, wire, timber, rope, and chain. Nothing was ever thrown out.

Dad was more of a developer than an animal or plants farmer, and he was a very good mechanic. He was capable, energetic, and pretty-well did what he wanted all his life. He never swore. "Bother!" was as strong as it got.

My mother married the only son and eldest child. The world of my grandparents on the property *Merrawarp* with its high expectations was one reason my parents went to Wonthaggi, to get away on their own, besides it gave Dad the boy's-own-adventure of his life.

Mum was a gentle, loving person, patient with animals, good with young creatures. She would have made an intelligent nurse or researcher. After a promising beginning as a clever student and the happy time establishing the farm, she became frustrated by the path her life had taken. She impressed on us girls the importance of finding something that gave us satisfaction, an outlet for our talents that allowed independence.

"Why doesn't she practice what she preaches" I grumbled, but I suppose at that time the woman's place was in the home doing never-ending housework, and it's hard to find another path when you're stuck out on a farm with four children. We were the most important thing in her life.

Nevertheless she filled the role of farmer's wife admirably, cooking hearty meals for "the men," bottling fruit, making jam, raising orphaned animals. Mum cooked roast leg of lamb, sausages, chops, stews, occasional

Elizabeth Honey

smoked cod, tripe, liver, oxtail, brains, meat patties called "faces" (which we drew on with tomato sauce), soups in the pressure cooker, eggs poached in bottled tomatoes, custard fruitcake (which I cook), boiled fruitcake, pumpkin fruitcake, raspberry shortbread, cockles (we always had something homemade in our school lunches), steamed pudding, sago pudding, rice pudding, sponge pudding, lemon delicious, dumplings, fritters, junket, custard in all its permutations (plenty of milk and eggs. Mary disliked a custard but could never remember which one. "Do I like thick custard hot?"), and finally to go with the bottled pears or apricots, ice cream made from powdered milk added to fresh milk then frozen rock hard so you could shoot a smooth pellet of it onto your spoon then back into your mouth again and again.

Mum knitted pixies to keep our ears warm and striped jumpers using up scraps of wool and pulled out knitting to reuse the wool. She sewed our clothes from Enid Gilchrist patterns on the treadle Singer. (Our daughter Bea sewed her first costumes on it.) It sounds like a chaff cutter, but this Clydesdale of a sewing machine has faithfully chugged across materials you wouldn't dare feed through the highly strung racehorse machines of today. We grew up in a climate of constant industry, always something in the making and pudding bowls to lick.

Dad gave Mum a TV, perhaps for her birthday, one of those "presents for you that I want." The TV sat in its box in the corner of the lounge and wasn't mentioned for weeks. Maybe Mum thought it would be the end of family life, maybe she was exerting what little power she had. We never heard the arguments, the box simply sat in the corner, and we longed for it to be opened. Mum rarely liked the presents Dad gave her. She complained that what we really needed was a new fly-wire door or the pump fixed.

At last there was a thawing, and the TV came out of the box for us to watch *Disneyland* on Sunday evenings. Little by little the viewing stretched to include *Leave it to Beaver, Seventy Seven Sunset Strip,* and *Father Knows Best* without much visible harm to the family.

Mum was a Sunday school teacher and a Brownie leader. Her spiritual home was Dean, near Ballarat, rich brown dirt potato-growing country where she had spent much of her childhood.

Neither Mum nor Dad drank alcohol, and as a young man Uncle Gilbert took "the pledge." It wasn't until Kath's twenty-first birthday party we had liquor in the house, and most of the guests were worldly wise doctors and foxy nurses who knew all about alcohol.

Poor William was the eldest child and, therefore, "brought up," and burdened with largely unspoken expectations. Like most eldest boys in a farming family, he became my father's apprentice as soon as he was useful. In some ways he had an elevated position, because he was doing a man's job, and his relationship with my father was something us girls never knew. William's future was prescribed.

Kath was the outdoor horsy one, the best rider. I didn't mind being around those large warm animals with floppy bottom lips, but I also liked my horses in books. We belonged to Wonthaggi Pony Club, but it was more important to Kath. She won the ribbons.

Toby, our first pony, was so old and fat it was impossible to hang onto him with our legs, which didn't matter much because he rarely raised a trot. Our saddle was a jockey's pad. Toby was so quiet we could climb up his neck and crawl beneath him.

William had Judy, Kath had Dot and Topsy. Punch was supposed to be my horse, but Punch turned out mean. Lady, the big bay who pulled the sled of skimmed milk to the pigpens, was available when she'd done her work.

My sweet, long-suffering, rosy-cheeked sister Mary was the youngest and put up with all my bossing. As we grow older my sisters and I grow closer.

I was the runt. William could wrap his fingers one and a half times around my wrist. Mum dosed me with Hypol

"The house that Dad built"—the author's painting of her childhood home

and Saunders Malt Extract looking wistfully at the picture of the baby on the label lifting an iron girder. She rubbed my back and feet, and when she thought I looked particularly sallow anointed me with Featherstone's Ointment, which was sponged off with towels as hot as I could stand. Because my body was such a fertile breeding ground for every passing germ, I wasn't sent to school until nearly seven.

When things got too much for Mum, I was sent to stay with Auntie Corrie and Uncle Harve (who subscribed to *Saturday Evening Post*) or better with Dad, to Grandpa and Grandma Honey's for the shearing.

William never teased Mary or Kath the way he teased me, and I in turn took it out on my imaginary friends Big and Little. Maybe I copped the flack because I could take it. I was more argumentative.

The hens (chooks) became my responsibility. Collecting the eggs was a treasure hunt. "I heard a cackle beyond the woodshed near the track to the orchard," Mum might report as I parked my bike, home from school.

Saturday mornings I rode carefully into Wonthaggi for a piano lesson, with a dozen eggs wrapped in newspaper to sell my teacher. The chooks taught me business, swap cards taught me trading, and Monopoly taught me real estate.

As a Girl Guide I sewed my artist's, entertainer's, minstrel's, reader's, and singer's badges on my sleeve, which proves I was a show-off who longed to be famous even though my nose was too big.

As long as we did our chores, we were left to our own devices, free to roam as we pleased. We had trees, sticks, dirt, mud, tadpoles, nests, yabbies, and lizards, nature going full pelt: everything eating, drinking, reproducing, and looking after its own life from the tiniest ant to the tallest gum tree.

On the frequent wet days, we might make papier-mâché puppets with newspaper and clag from Silver Star Starch or stage an art show and charge Mum sixpence to see it.

I had Rabbit and Golly and Tedina, my much-loved honey-coloured bear from Grandma Honey. Tedina has a bald patch where we pounded her squeaker as she slowly lost her squeak. Our best dress-up was a blue crepe number with an elastic bodice and a very full skirt that whizzed up high.

On the subject of best dresses, Kath won the best-dressed doll at the Melbourne Agricultural Show by guessing its name. Jillian was an immaculate dark-haired bride, perfect from her little pearl necklace to her stockinged toes. When I went into Wonthaggi hospital to have my tonsils out, I was allowed to take Jillian, and the nurse said, "Now which one is Elizabeth?"

Being left-handed was never a problem. Kath was made to use her right hand, but by the time I came along a more enlightened attitude prevailed. Later at art school I found myself surrounded by left-handers; we couldn't spell either.

The Wonthaggi State School was shaped like a square donut, a verandah running the four sides of the quadrangle. On rainy days music was piped through the public address system, and we swung round and round folk dancing endlessly like something from *Alice in Wonderland*. The school was notable for its swimming pool. The story probably went like this:

"The Honey family all scrubbed up: William, Elizabeth, Mum, Mary, Kath and Dad in a tie not looking himself at all"

"We're miners. We're good at digging holes. Why don't we dig a pool at the school so our kids can learn to swim?"

All the Honey kids passed their *Herald* newspaper's Learn to Swim Certificate in the pea green water of the school baths.

The highlight of the school year was the fancy dress ball. Mum dyed a hessian sack maroon, and I went as a saveloy, then with Mary in another sack we went as two ends of a clothesline, then in the same sack I went as a bookworm, which was true enough.

Every Monday we stood in rows, saluted the flag, and recited:

I love God and my country
I will honour the flag, serve the Queen
And cheerfully obey my parents, teachers, and the law.

As a member of Junior Red Cross I signed the pledge:

I promise to work loyally for the promotion of Health and the Relief of Suffering and Distress wherever I may find it: to hold in Friendship Boys and Girls of all Nations.

What with Brownies and Girl Guides it was all pledges, oaths, and mottoes!

School library and art were favourite times. Privately I wrote little poems and stories about romantic subjects foreign to my experience (gypsies, snow, skating, circuses) and made up stories to entertain Mary and cousin Margie. My favourite books included *Winnie the Pooh, Milly Molly Mandy, Snugglepot and Cuddlepie, Pipi Longstocking, The Famous Five* (especially George and Timmy), *Eloise, Just William, Pollyanna, The Silver Brumby,* and *Seven Little Australians.*

A children's radio program called *The Argonauts* was TOP PRIORITY. Lying on the floor we listened to the serial *The Muddleheaded Wombat* and the book reading, which was heaven. The whole family, in fact the whole of country Australia, paused every lunch time for the serial *Blue Hills,* which ran for twenty-seven years.

Wonthaggi didn't have a library, but a remote area reading service dispatched books to us by train. These brown paper packages tied up with strings were certainly my favourite things.

When I drew, kids said "You're a good drawer," and I came second in a competition, except they called me Elizabeth Huey. Later when I sang on TV, they called me Elizabeth Howy. They couldn't quite believe it was Honey. Thinking of nominative determinism—Honey has been an excellent name and rhymes with funny, sunny, dunny, and money, although William had the occasional fight when kids teased him about his sissy name.

My father had five sisters. When any of them went overseas, we made the journey to Port Melbourne to see them off, throwing streamers at the retreating liner. When they returned full of travelers' tales, we would watch the slides, look on the maps, and get the presents. Then one after another they married a variety of chaps, and we went to the weddings and saw them in tight little coats with funny hats bundling into Vauxhalls and Standards daubed with paint amid honeymoon hijinks 1950s style, horseshoes, and tin cans. These aunts are feisty individuals, respectable pillars of their various societies.

The family changed when William and Kath went away to boarding schools in Geelong. I remember quite clearly talking to God as I wandered along the farm tracks, not exactly praying, more of a one-way conversation perhaps through loneliness. Maybe that's why Henni prays in *45 & 47 Stella Street.*

"The caravan we built for our journey north to Queensland. From this distance you can't see the insects stuck in the paint."

Here's a piece from my composition book, poor spelling and all:

Lassie

Lassie was given to us as a small furry pup. She was a black and white border collie who came from very good breeding. Even while a puppy her instincts to herd and round things up were very strong. She mostly picked the hens and it was not unusual to see her padding quietly back and forward behind a bewildered bunch of chucks. She was never savage and always playful.

Her favourite game was for us to drag an old wooden hobby horse along while running at full speed. She would then give chase and on catching the bar to which the wheels were attached she would pull furiously and we did the same. The horse bore deep tooth-marks.

Every year when it was shearing time at Grandpa's she would make the journey down to Geelong with Dad to help out.

Oftern when we went to Lorne for the holidays Lassie would come too. Tied securely to the trailer she would lie and bark at every passing car. She loved the beach and would play enthusasticly with us on the sand, thought she would never venture far into the water for fear of the waves. Her bright eyes would shine, and one ear would be pricked even though one only flopped.

Lassie loved little things. She would lie for ages watching a new batch of chickens. Sometimes I think she was more devoted than the Mother. The chickens would scratch around her and oftern peck her small silver registration tag. We wondered what would happen if they tried to peck her tounge. Some-time she even tried to lick them.

Lassie appointed herself mother to a litter of eight little orphan pigs. We fed them on junket through bottles till they were old enough to feed for them selves. Lassie would lick their wiskers and separate any fights, and some times sleep with them.

We always used to leave a drink of milk and a buisket for Santa Clause on the dinning room table. One year as it was hot we left the door open and when mum went in it had gone. Lassie had helped herself.

During her eventful liftime we became very devoted to Lassie and when she died from eating fox bait we were all very sorry.

We attended the Wonthaggi Presbyterian church, which was a major social event for a farmer and his wife who spent much of their time alone. It was hard to converse with the Dutch sharefarmers. Sunday dinner, the roast leg of lamb was popped in the oven in advance, so it was ready when we arrived home full of the word of the Lord and famished.

Off we drove to church dressed in our best, wearing gloves, sitting in the backseat frantically memorising the passage from the Bible set the week before.

Church gave me a bench mark with which to compare all life's boring experiences. The ministers came and went. We had Mr. Anderson whose children's sermon was *The Pilgrim's Progress* laboriously serialised.

"Now where was I up to?" he asked like clockwork each Sunday, peering over his glasses down at us children.

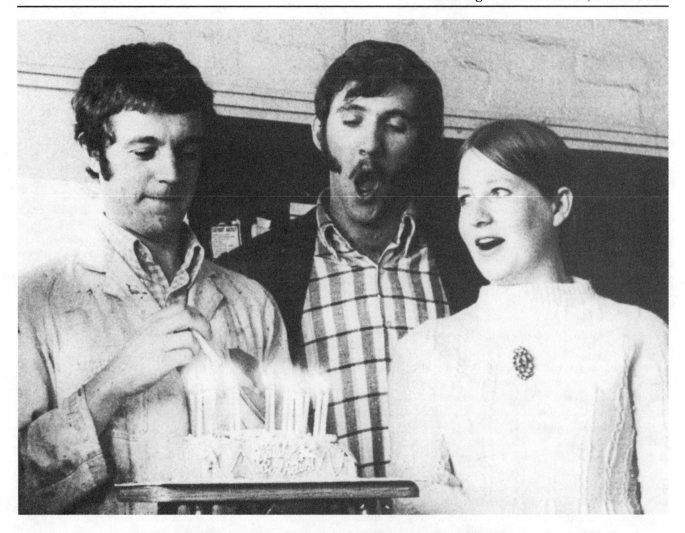

"Andrew, Ian 'Beans' Baker and I (the 68mm revue triumvirate) on Andrew's twenty-first birthday"

Inside I'd be saying "Don't tell him! Don't tell him!" but some goodie goodie like Malcolm McDonald would pipe up "Christian's in the Slough of Despond."

"Ah yes," Mr. Anderson would exclaim with satisfaction, and then he'd clear his throat and Pilgrim would set off again with his burden, which was also our burden.

Sunday school attendance swelled twice a year, before the end-of-year party and prize giving, and the annual picnic. The Sunday school concert was a non-event, because I wasn't cast in a starring role.

For years at bedtime I knelt by my bed and gabbled:

Now I lay me down to sleep
I pray the Lord my soul to keep.
If I should die before I wake
I pray the Lord my soul to take.
God bless—my mother, my father, my sisters, my brother, and all the members of the royal family, my uncles and aunties, Grandpa and Grandma, and all friends, relations, animals, and birds.
Amen.

The prayer finishes with a general cover-all clause and shows the position of the royal family in my esteem. Apparently at a tender age, I announced I was going to

marry Prince Charles and live in sight of Sydney Harbour bridge. But Prince Charles never showed up at our farm, neither did the movie talent scout looking for someone to be Norah of Billabong, or the travelling circus in search of a trapeze artist, so my abundant charm and talent went unnoticed.

William came back from boarding school a heathen. He flatly refused to go to church. Of course this meant he wasn't going to heaven, which was terrible! The whole family was silently upset. That was my perception, but in retrospect it may only have been me who was upset. With bottling-up behaviour, you can never quite tell.

In our family, if you didn't have anything nice to say about someone you didn't say it, you just thought it for a long long time. My mother, who in retrospect was highly strung, was the best bottler-up I've ever known, and if any comment did slip out it was rare and, thus, potent. This behaviour may have come from her living with other families as a child, but it was also popular at the time.

At church we heard stories of believers who answered a "calling" and went to be missionaries in distant, perilous places. I feared this might happen to me and lay in the dark at night scared stiff that God would "call" me. It was such a relief to wake up in the morning and find I didn't have to be a missionary.

William was a tease. Long after we'd gutsed down our Easter eggs, William's would shine brightly in mint condition on his dressing table, but touch them and you'd find your face on the kitchen lino, your arm up behind your back in a hammerlock as he showed his brotherly affection. "Give up, Stinky?" Later I bought a book on judo and tried to teach myself.

When I was confused about the words drover and landdrover, William encouraged me to tell everyone I was going to be a landrover. He also instilled the words pine nuts and coco apples.

As we grew older the physical fights gave way to arguments. William would drop in a hot coal, for example "Art's useless, it's just the icing on the cake," and like a trout I'd rise to the bait. He won at table tennis too, but as the years went by the handicap he gave himself fell. We haven't played for decades. I reckon I could beat him now.

Dad was interested in photography and had an 8 mm camera. We watched ourselves self-consciously waving while sliding down slides, etc. The projector could go backwards too. The aunts' weddings weren't as gripping backwards, but other films were much funnier. We saw in reverse: two early Mickey Mouse cartoons (one where Mickey has only a few hours to repair Pirate Pete's car), "Felix Out of Luck," "The Coronation of Her Majesty Queen Elizabeth II" (where the Queen slides magically like an upright snail backwards out of Westminster Cathedral), and "Swimming and Diving Aces," which was the best. Divers erupted out of the water and miraculously flew backwards like spears to land precisely on the high diving boards. Huge splashes vanished in a flash. It was all silent, so we could give our own commentary. We saw those films backwards as often as we saw them forwards.

The Queen's visit in 1954 was a major event, which shows how boring Australia was in the fifties. I polished my Brownie badge, ironed my tie, and was taken with the pack to Warrigal, a country town, to see the Queen. It was a stinking hot day and lots of people fainted. The ride home, jammed in the back of the ute along a winding road in a thunderstorm, was much more memorable than the Queen.

The beach played a large part in our lives. Our farm was a few miles from a safe little beach called Cape Paterson, and on hot summer evenings when Dad and William finally stopped work, we would pile into the car and drive to Cape Paterson for a swim.

Family holidays provide much of the folklore of a family, when everyone's together and relaxed. Holidays are important, and I'm proud to say Australians are good at holidays.

My grandmother, May Honey, with great foresight and her inheritance, bought four blocks of land in a little town called Lorne, where the forest grew down to the sea on Loutit Bay. In the past, to reach this outpost the traveler made the perilous journey through the Otway Ranges by horse-drawn coach.

During the Depression, Grandpa and Dad, who was nineteen at the time, built a modest practical timber shack, *The Beehive*, where the Honeys went for holidays. It consisted of a small living room with a smoky fireplace, a tiny kitchen, and a bunk room, all lined with cardboard. The wide verandah, which runs along two sides, could accommodate a half dozen on stretchers at a pinch, the best beds in the house being under the mosquito nets at the end

of the verandah. All meals were eaten at a trestle table in the middle of the verandah, and we spat our cherry plum pips over the rail which led to more cherry plums. We were up in the treetops with the kookaburras, parrots, cockatoos, magpies, and honeyeaters!

The ancient fridge didn't have a freezer, so for ice cream a nominated runner would dash to the shop and back timed by the adults, and then the cardboard wrapper on the Neapolitan brick would be unzipped and the ice cream doled out.

We hiked up the Erskine River to the waterfall hopping nimbly from rock to rock. We swam in the surf, read, played shuttlecock, Monopoly, chess and checkers while the record player belted out the new Christmas LP, *Oklahoma, My Fair Lady,* or *South Pacific.* The Lorne roller skating rink played Pat Boone and Frankie Lane while I circled with the skating throng for hours. As teenagers we frequented the jazz joint the Wild Colonial Club and the coffee bar The Arab.

"A Christmas card photo taken outside Stafford Terrace, Kensington, London. Richard Lowe is the tall one. The snow is cotton wool and soap powder."

Later on we each took friends to *The Beehive*. I remember weekends with art school comrades playing Pick Up Sticks, international rules to three thousand points, the huge speakers carried down for the weekend booming out John Handy, Stan Getz, Miles Davis, Otis Redding, and the Supremes singing Rogers and Hart.

Lorne's the setting for my picture book *Not a Nibble!,* and *The Beehive* provided background for the novel *The Ballad of Cauldron Bay.*

The other place us Honey kids could test our independence was the Melbourne Agricultural Show each September. Staying in a caravan within walking distance and using Dad's member's badges, we could come and go freely. For all the wild rides, boxing troupe, and promises of danger, it was safe.

We marveled at the decorated cakes, dolls, perfectly bottled fruit, and coffee tables made from matchsticks by prisoners, saw the show jumping, dog trials, woodchopping, and every breed of goat, pig, horse, cow, dog, ferret, chook, and duck known to man. One year Dad entered competitions for a square foot of pasture and a bale of meadow hay. Another year an announcement came over the loud speaker—"Would Mr. and Mrs. Honey come to the officials' box please?" Kath, at boarding school had appendicitis and needed an operation immediately.

City people, I decided, were different: they had barbeques instead of fires, they bought flowers, they didn't have old clothes called "work clothes," they sat down in cafes and had cups of coffee or tea, which cost a lot of money, instead of filling the thermos and taking some biscuits, they called tea dinner, and dinner tea, they were sissies about spiders, worms, frogs, snakes, leeches, and dead things, they got pocket money, they paid to have their hair cut, they cried if a bull ant bit them, and they thought rabbits were cute.

Dad enjoyed travelling. Wherever he went there was something interesting: pasture, fences, stock, soil type, and even in the city there was the weather. Back home in the shearing shed in the evenings and at weekends, we began to build a caravan for our journey to that mythical paradise, Queensland. That was Dad's way of doing things—build a six berth whale-on-wheels.

The day before blast off we painted the caravan an insipid aqua. My diary begins: "We left Wonthaggi on the 28th of May at 3.45." (Off to an early start!) The paint was still wet as we headed north through Tooradin, a swampy place. We drove into clouds of insects, which stuck to the caravan and came with us to Queensland.

Like a true farmer's daughter, I noted in my diary "Trees were plentiful but still there was a lot of soil erosion" and recorded heights above sea level and the dimensions of lakes. No hint of literary ability. Each entry begins, "We got up, had breakfast and moved on."

In strange towns we window-shopped, on wild beaches we beach-combed. We saw sugar growing, and bananas, peanuts, and cotton. Mary and I didn't fight for the whole six weeks we were away, but as soon as we arrived home, it was business as usual.

W hen I was fifteen, I was sent away to Morongo PGC, the boarding school where Kath and the aunts had gone. My diary records nothing but the food: YMCA

(Yesterday's Muck Cooked Again), Yarra Mud and Dandruff (chocolate Blancmange sprinkled with coconut), Puffballs (deep fried dumplings), Giraffe Meat (stringy stew), Fish Eyes (sago). I plumped out nicely and played tennis every possible second. Shakespeare Day, when each form presented a slice of a play, was a highlight. Overacting as Macbeth, I heard a little girl down the front ask loudly, "What's wrong with her?"

That year Dad bought a farm close to *Merrawarp,* and sold *Yaralla. Merrawarp* was the Honey family seat, an impressive, two-storey house built by my great-great-grandfather out of the sandstone from the hole in which its stands.

It was lovely to visit, very special for us kids. I remember rocking on the rocking horse on the front verandah singing over and over again a song we sang to departing aunts:

Wish me luck as you wave me goodbye,
Cheerio, here I go, on my way

Merrawarp had coloured glass around the front door and stairs, which we slid down every possible way. Water came from a well by the backdoor, like a huge upturned concrete pudding basin, and if we worked the handle of the iron pump, water would eventually gush out.

Descending the stone steps into the house was like entering a cool haven. Things placed on the deep window-sills became beautiful still lifes. Out the front Grandma's English cottage garden spilled over gravel paths. Beneath the house was the damp, creepy cellar.

All was civilised and orderly. Grandpa Honey poured us glasses of his ginger beer. I remember him sitting in his wicker chair on the front verandah with his dog, watching us youngsters. He loved a yarn and could smoke his pipe with one side of his mouth while talking out the other. He was old by the time I came along, and I never saw him do much. In my novel *Fiddleback,* Old Jim is based on Grandpa Honey.

Grandma Honey was practical. One shearing, Grandma decided I needed a haircut, and despite Mum's promise that she'd cut it when I got home, I was taken to the hairdresser for the first time, where my hair was cut against my will.

The one ray of light in boring Geelong was music—folk singing and trad jazz. I saved for a guitar and sang with Crescent City Jazz Band. As a teenager when all that great music was happening—Beach Boys, Beatles, Stones, Motown—I was like the child in the Paul Simon song "Born at the Right Time." When everyone had gone to bed, I danced to the radio in the kitchen.

I always considered my childhood dull, which was confirmed when our friend Laila recounted her adventures returning to the family mansion in France after the war, playing in the gaping holes in the floor where the parquetry had been ripped up and burnt by the occupying German soldiers.

After school what next? With my Commonwealth Scholarship, I could study at university, but I was tired of books. I wanted to *go* somewhere, *do* something, *make* something.

My jigsaw-puzzling friend Jill Glover's father was an art teacher. He had studied at Swinburne Technical College

"'Riding Lady,' an illustration from one of my calendars. It was a long way to the ground." Lady was one of the horses the author's family owned during her childhood.

in Melbourne decades before, so I visited the red brick art school. It was the only building at the college with pretensions to architecture. Friends at university had spreading oaks and hallowed halls, but this place had a row of moth-eaten poplars in pebble pots.

The Honeys regard paying rent as a mug's game, so Mum and Kath, who was now a nurse, bought a little house in the Melbourne seaside suburb of Middle Park. There were four of us living in 211, mostly nurses. They slept at strange hours, told hilarious excruciating tales of deliveries and episiotomies, and threw parties. We watched the TV show *Komotion* and practiced our go-go steps.

Life set sail at Swinburne Art School. The combination of new-found freedom in the city, an extraordinary peer group, inspiring lecturers, and creative studies was intoxicating. For the next three years, I lived and breathed Swinburne.

The first year certificate gave a broad art and design training, and then the following two years students specialised for a Diploma in Advertising, Design, and Illustration.

In 1966 the Film and Television diploma was introduced, the only one in Australia at the time. It emphasised liaison with the industry and learning by doing, which was certainly the case as the lecturers knew little more than we

did. Filming meant everyone was away much of the time. From a letter home:

"Poor Mr. Rob practically rejoices when he sees one of his students. I was talking to him on Friday, and he said he only saw one student on Wednesday and he harried him so much that he went away leaving him with nobody."

We worked on each other's films, starred in each other's films, filmed ourselves filming, and found ourselves featured in the newspapers. With little equipment but boundless enthusiasm, we felt part of something unique.

My folio included three shorts: the diploma film *Readymade* (five minutes, black and white), based on Marshall McLuhan's recently published *The Medium Is the Massage*; *Incommunicado* (three minutes, colour), a modern musical version of "Peter, Peter Pumpkin Eater"; and a commercial for stout. Three films remained unfinished: *The Loaded Dog Weekend, The Mole,* and *Arachnophobia.*

Both graphic design and film students mixed freely in a creative chemistry of eccentric personalities.

Richard Lowe, self proclaimed Earl of Finchwood, was the only child of an eminent ophthalmologist and doting musical mother. With his parents he'd already traveled a fair portion of the globe and knew history, the art movements, antiques, theatre, music, and if he invited you to a ball would design your costume. He was outrageously funny.

When we were set the task of designing a costume, Richard literally shone as Louis XIV parading as an operatic Apollo. ". . . with three-inch red lacquered heels and a gilded full-bottomed wig topped with purple ostrich feathers and gilded wheat ears. The section between was made up from a thermal vest, a very large wire lampshade and a pair of long johns, all sprayed gold, sequined, beribboned, draped, fringed, valanced, swagged, tasseled, and generally made tidy." That's Richard's description for the book *Portrait of a Film School.*

We chose music befitting our costumes and held a parade, which only encouraged us. We staged the melodrama *Temptation Sordid and Virtue Rewarded.*

There was Petsa Kaffens whose name could have been Kalliope Kaffasides but was simplified, her parents Greeks from Constantinople. She's voluptuous, tempestuous, warmhearted, and fiercely opinionated. (Petsa's crazed passionate e-mails inspired Kuza's in *Remote Man.*)

Ann Chambers was a divine Noel Coward heroine-type, giggly, witty, and chic. David Atkinson was quietly funny and clever with sound and animation. (He now heads an animation course.) "Jacko" Graham Jackson had some rat-magic cunning about him in a hobbit-William Dadd way. He carved, potted, drew in miniature with great skill and acid wit, played bouzouki, and made a brilliant short film on false teeth. Jill Stevenson was worldly and visited China during the cultural revolution. (Jill edited *Elizabeth* and *Moulin Rouge.*)

"Beans" Ian Baker was behind the camera from the outset, hardworking, generous, practical yet outrageous. (Beans is cinematographer for most of Fred Schepisi's films.) Strong-willed Alexandra Copeland is an artist in everything she does and one of Australia's leading ceramicists; Peter Dodds is executive producer of the TV soap *Neighbours;* John Golding makes witty pottery in a Mexican-Edward Lear style; Jon Quinn vanished without trace; but more important than anyone else was graphic student Andrew Clarke who left bunches of roses on my desk.

The Melbourne Film Festival, held deep midwinter at the Palais, St. Kilda, showed films from all over the world which otherwise couldn't be seen in Australia. We watched exotic and esoteric films till we couldn't keep our eyes open, then in op shop lapin pranced around like stars in our own foreign films.

Each year the art school whipped itself into a frenzy producing the student revue. In 1967 Jacko and Jon Quinn directed *Braindops,* a creative storm. The following year Andrew Clarke and I directed *68mm,* a name that reflected the emphasis on film. With Beans as producer, it was ambitious with projected props, backgrounds, characters, original dance and music, and many filmed sequences.

From a letter home about the revue film *And now Virdette, Goodbye:*

"We completed it in under three hours—(admittedly it contained only eight shots and a few 'cut-aways') and we were working at a shooting ratio of 1:1 which means *no retakes.* Tuesday night Ian, Andrew, and I superimpose the subtitles (it is a take off on the continental, slow, boring, subtitled bedroom scene), and tomorrow morning we will find out if it has worked."

As director of Student Publications, I edited the weekly Swinburne College rag, *Scrag* (with cartoon *Super Nude,* which became *Super Prude,* then *Super Crude* in which I was Miss Construed), and *Swinopsis,* an annual hodge-podge of dubious literary merit which did, however, reflect the talent of the graphics students. Michael Leunig (Australian cartoonist and conscience) submitted a cartoon which was so apt, that if I'd had the foresight to include it, it would have been the one thing remembered from *Swinopsis.*

I couldn't stop organising things: foundation secretary for Swinburne Film Society, organised The Great Trike Race which resulted in eight arrests, the Psychedelic High (art ball), The Swinburne Premier 1968 (first public showing of our films), and parties at 211 including a Grand Premiere of my 8 mm films.

It was a time of all-round creativity—singing, writing, acting, drawing, designing, and filming. The real world meant choosing and using one talent.

Our films have been lost, borrowed, disappeared, and Ian Baker's house, with all the review material, burnt down in a bush fire. We didn't have money for spare prints, besides, we'd moved on.

Richard escaped abroad to the London Film School where he continued to evolve through Beach Boy to Ziggy Stardust to Brian Ferry.

"Shapes and sizes come and go but the chin never changes on the changeable Lowe,' he scrawled on the back of a photo. He lives in Shaftesbury Avenue, London, and his arrival in Australia heralds a joyous round of parties then he flies home, kilos heavier, as autumn sets in. Richard found his audience at dinner parties. (I found mine in schools.) He's a great correspondent sending hundreds of Christmas cards each October on the cheap rate. Petsa does too. She, too, lives in London, although she always seems to be away at the glamorous launch of some new beauty product.

The film course was valuable. As a writer and illustrator, I'm the director with total control. Sometimes I

hunt for photographs to help create my characters, and I tend to think in pictures and scenes.

I probably laughed more at Swinburne than at any other time, and from such esprit de corps came lasting friendships. They were hilarious, chaotic, creative years.

My first job at the television station ABV2 lasted six months—temporary assistant gramophone operator waiting for the dream job in the film department. I wrote home: "Should be a nice safe job, and if someone above me dies, I might be moved up one and get more money in a couple of centuries." But even as a lowly "grams op," it was cool to be working in a TV studio. When man walked on the moon, I played "Thus Spake Zarathustra" about fifty times.

Andrew Clarke and I were married in the small stone Presbyterian church in the hamlet of Batesford, near Geelong by the Reverend G. S. Sasdy, which made our parents very happy. "Come coloured" said the invitation. Many of the Swinburne crew came tanked as well. Through Andrew I scored the whole Clarke clan whom I adore. Around the Clarke dinner table, everything was discussed loudly and openly. Andrew's mother, Eileen, was feminine

Calendar illustration of the city of Lorne, "'where the forest meets the sea,' except these days we say 'where shopping meets the sea'"

and saucy. Also a good judge of character, she ran a business called Toorak Services, which found domestic staff for rich people.

My next job, thanks to Andrew's boss Philip Adams, was script assistant on the film crew for *The Naked Bunyip,* a colour feature-length documentary for cinema, shot over three months in three states, a lighthearted view of sex in Australia. Produced and directed by John B. Murray, it starred Edna Everage (Barry Humphries) and Graeme Blundell. There were six on the crew, and part of my job was continuity.

Next came a stint in an advertising agency helping sell Hush Puppies and BMW motorbikes. This was a time of indulgence and adjustment living in a small flat atop a Beverly Hills mansion in Darling Street, South Yarra. The vacating tenants left healthy marijuana plants in a wardrobe. "I can't understand it," exclaimed Eileen, "they take such care of the pot plants but they leave the place in such a mess!"

Ever since white man set foot in Australia, he's been flogging back to Europe to have a look. The aunts went. It's a rite of passage for Australians, usually a long one. Our games, rhymes, and children's books were mostly English. We wanted to see what we'd learnt about in History of Art and Richard lived in swinging London. October 1970 we set off with never a care.

In London we found ideal accommodation at 20 Stafford Terrace, Kensington. Owned by a Persian professor, the flat had two large bedrooms, separated by a small storage Hell Hole, which meant Richard could share.

It was coming up to Christmas and the advertising agencies weren't hiring, so I took a job at Derry and Toms the fashion store of Kensington. My wages plus a weekly English lesson for Professor Meshkat paid the rent.

Derry and Toms had a flamingo as its symbol, as it had real flamingos living on its roof garden. During winter the garden was closed, and I always imagined the flamingos were slipped into flamingo-shaped cosies, but come spring the flamingos and the tourists were back.

"Sixth floor. Roof garden please."

First I sold gift vouchers, then after Christmas twinsets at the Pringle Bar. The strange thing was the knitwear we folded endlessly was made from super-soft Geelong lambswool! Then I became a contingent serving wherever needed—soaps and toiletries one day, luggage the next. I wrote copious letters home which Mum numbered and put in bundles. Some excerpts:

*

The postal strike went for seven weeks.

"Postal strike. All the letterboxes are boarded up, gagged. I'm beginning to think a strike of some sort is the status quo and if one had all the luxuries then something was wrong with the workers."

*

Sunday night was bath night.

"Andrew has just come in from his deep deep hot bath and he is so red and white he looks like a cross between an

avid South Melbourne supporter and a prewar Japanese flag. And I look at my legs, and they are pure white with hairs lying limp and disinterested because they haven't seen the day or the sun or had any fresh air for months!"

*

"Richard leapt off down the street saying 'I'm just going out to see if I can stop myself spending some money.'"

*

"Last night I had a lesson with the Professor who had indigestion, so I was able to teach him 'I do not feel well,' and indigestion, stomach pain, etc."

*

"We are waiting for a power cut at the moment. All the maintenance men are on their toes ready to spring into action and light the shop with hurricane lamps and candles. All counters have three or four candles ready. The shop is open, lit by ordinary light, but because the cut is unpredictable, they can't clear the shop, relight, and let customers in again, so everyone has to have eyes open for shoplifters. Apparently there are a couple hanging around down in the electrical department and the 'tech' (store detective) believes they are waiting for the lights to go.

"Each lift has a box of food in it—rations, should the lift be cut off mid-floor."

*

Customers

"Some of the English women are pompous and indirect, for example: 'Well, you know, Phyllis, I don't think I really dislike it,' which means she likes it. 'Do you really think it would go with my peacock blue? I really don't know at all.'

"The most important thing about selling is to agree with anything anyone says.

"'Do you think if I bought half a yard of this, and sewed it around here, would it hide this do you think? Does it match? You don't think it's too bright do you? What do you think, Agnes?'

"I just served a woman with a Princess Margaret scarf and she enunciated so clearly I could see her tonsils for most of the transaction."

*

"On souvenirs again! This morning I had two little French children nosing round the counter and they came across the snow scenes.

"'Regard! Regard Henri! Il neige!' (I understood them! We DID learn French in French!)"

*

"For Christmas I gave Andrew a hamster, which he christened Eileen after his mother. Hamsters are rather blind but have a good sense of smell, can become very tame, and are very inquisitive and live to the ripe old age of two.

"Eileen is really cute when she eats. She holds the food in her little front paws and with whiskers twitching she chews at five thousand chews a second. No wonder she only lives two years when everything is so pepped up.

"Andrew and Richard talk to her like a naughty child, and she's the butt of thousands of corny jokes, e.g.:

"'We'd better take the rubbish down now.'

"'It's very heavy.'

"'Well, Eileen can do it then.'

"Anything to do with hard work or great weights is instantly Eileen's job.

"She is a most convenient pet. Sleeps curled up all the day, is liveliest at night when we are liveliest and at home, and if we should go away for the weekend, this is not a problem because Eileen has her store, and the book on hamsters says they can cheerfully look after themselves for days on end."

*

"When we went to Edinburgh, I had to teach Ali Meshkat what the word 'favour' meant, then ask him for one—to look after Eileen. I was worried as to how Eileen might have fared over the last ten days. But I needn't have worried. As soon as I got inside the front door little Mehnas greeted me with, 'Do you want your mouse now?'

"She was very fat and healthy, in a newly cleaned cage and not at all perturbed."

*

We bought a Morris 1000 van, 1967 model, maroon with seat belts and heater, 245 pounds. Lady Rae (Andrew's Aunt Bunny) gave us the expression "*such* a nice girl," which Richard has used ever since. Richard directed *The Last of the Valerie,* his film of Henry James's short story in which I played an American countess in Rome ca. 1905 doing embroidery and playing the harp. We went to exhibitions and films by the score at the local Gaumont, and a procession of Swinburne friends slept on the kitchen floor.

Then Dad died. He simply vanished from my life. My strong, capable, fix-anything father had gone into hospital for a gall bladder operation, developed a clot, and died. If he could die, what about puny me? I sold ribbons and lace in haberdashery with red eyes. It was hard.

At the Sunday market on Bayswater Road, I tried selling drawings, junk jewellery, and homemade cloth broaches. My pitch was beside Sam and Suzanne who made and sold baby owls.

In January 1972, through the editor of the *Bunyip* film, I landed the job of continuity on the Australian feature film shot in London *The Adventures of Barry McKenzie.*

*

"When Spike Milligan first arrived on the set, which was a filthy and depressing hotel clerk's office, he seemed quite normal, except for the fact that he chuckled all the time, obviously delighted with the set and his part. He emerged from the costume room a grotty little clerk in a cardigan of shapeless grey with buttons missing and pockets that looked as if they'd carried bricks, and very worn old corduroy slippers that he never lifted off the floor

once. He walked with a rocking little shuffle, his head hung forward with a watery-eyed squint.

"The set was the smallest we've worked in yet, and the crew was all packed in on top of each other behind the camera. Someone said something about the overcrowded conditions, and Milligan instantly retorted, 'Ah my man, you wait till we get to the small set!'

"At the beginning of the shot, the clerk sits in his dingy little office reading a newspaper. In the first take (as with all the takes), Milligan began quite simply with something funny: '. . . mumble, mumble, mumble . . . black vicar seaman's false teeth found in doorway, mumble mumble . . . see page eight' (then he has trouble finding page eight) '. . . ah yes, here we are . . . ah yes, ah yes. . . six Guiness and it all went black he told magistrate . . .' With each take it became more outlandish and ridiculously funny. 'Black seaman vicar's false teeth found in nude nun's thigh . . .'

"When he shows Barry, the Australian innocent abroad, up to his horrible, flyspecked, tea-coloured dingy room, Milligan says on take one, 'Show you up to your suite, sir' and by take five (all five takes ruined by actors doubling up with laughter) he was saying, '. . . you have chosen well sir, you have chosen well . . . we are giving you our Winston Churchill luxury memorial suite sir, which means of course no singing, dancing, or laughter on the premises . . .' Behind camera everyone was quite contorted but soundless.

"At the very end of the hotel sequence, Barry dumps his suitcase on the bed which collapses, and quite out of the script, from somewhere in another room, the little clerk's voice yells out, 'That'll be extra!'"

*

"The film gallops on, and the Normal World seems to slip further and further away. The 6:00 a.m. news, the occasional hoarding, the little snatch of gossip is all that's left of the other way of life. Andrew gets a kiss on the cheek before I slip out into the dark of morn, and sometimes I see him at night if he's not at work too. However one good thing about movies, despite the concentrated effort, you always know it's going to end as suddenly as it started."

*

"We finished filming Saturday arvo at 2:00, which allowed me to get all typed up and organised by the time the party began 'half eight' (which is how the Poms say half past eight). We got there to find everyone spruced and cleaned and freshened up and that was novel to see the clean party faces of all the unshaven, disheveled crew. Sometimes we look more like a pack of crooks and ratbags than a film company, very disreputable, Bruce included. So there we were all in Barry Humphrie's flat, he having cleared out to Paris for some sale. (The whole time we were working on the film, he had one eye on the camera and the other on that antique shop across the road.) The party was a fabulous success and the auction of all costumes, sets, props a great feature. . . . Doreen and Norman the caterers did the cooking, and there was music in one room, the auction in another, and in the third various members of the cast and crew debated the eternal topic 'the Australian film industry.'"

"Gig and his friend Sam after a school camp commando course. Some kids tried to avoid the mud but these two added extra." This photo was used on the original Australian cover of **Don't Pat the Wombat!**

*

In 1973 we hitchhiked home via America and Mexico, but that's another collection of letters tied up in bundles. Hitchhiking's an egalitarian way to travel. I swore that when we had a car, I would give hitchhikers a lift and I do. I look them over first of course.

We returned to Melbourne (the ephemara capital of Australia), and settled down, driving an aqua Nappy Wash VW Kombi Dad had planned to convert for his next trip.

"Missa Clarke, dis is gonna be your lucky day!" said Nick Kormas, the Greek real estate agent who sold us our first house in Richmond. He was right.

While working at George Patterson's Advertising Agency, I met copywriter Derrick Warren, a dear friend with a raw irrepressible sense of humour. A compulsive reader, the American writers of the 1930s and 1940s were his compass. Derrick laughed right up to his death. I remember our last phone call. Derrick telling a joke, said, "I'm collecting degenerative diseases." He stopped the conversation. "Wait till I cough up my left lung," he said, went into a rasping coughing fit, then continued the joke.

In 1976 adventures in South America and Europe meant more letters in bundles. On our return I wound myself up in a mohair rug and went freelance, illustrating for *The Age* and *Sydney Morning Herald* newspapers, stamps for *Australia Post* and children's books. Then Andrew went freelance too, both of us working at home. *Notes on Being Invisible,* my first children's story, was published in *Puffinalia* magazine in 1981.

Each November for the next ten years, I published a calendar of illustrations. This peculiar form of masochism, initially to show the talents of Swinburne friends and produce something of my own, had the advantage and disadvantage of being all over in a couple of months. An exhausting exercise, it taught me the difficulties of sales and distribution.

We had plans to see Brazil until our favourite house came on the market. We spent our money on it instead—home base until we're carried out in recycled cardboard boxes. It fits us like a glove, a tight glove. Out the front grows a magnificent tree, a magnolia grandiflora, one of the first species to develop flowers that said to the insects, "You come to me," instead of broadcasting seeds far and wide.

In the backyard grows the apricot tree, which gives us bee-buzzing blossoms in spring. It's a task dealing with the crop. We bottle apricots, freeze them, stew them, and give them away. One year we said "Apricots be damned" and left on holiday. We returned to find a slurry of rotting brown mush covering the whole backyard.

In 1983 Beatrice was born and in 1986 William. (Everyone calls him Gig.) The dictionary defines the word "muse" as "the goddess thought to inspire a poet." My muses are more down to earth. Motherhood made me more passionate, and I'm glad I didn't start to write until the kids came along. Now I'm politically aware and want a better world for them.

I was an elderly primigravida with postnatal euphoria. Women are lucky to bear the babies and have this enforced change in their lives, a precious time to be anticipated and enjoyed.

Bea and Gig loved stories. We were probably Richmond library's best borrowers, returning home time and again triumphant with a feast of books. Their taste was obvious. "I don't want that one! Read *this* one again!" I studied the pile of favourites and tried my hand at writing.

In 1988 my first picture book, *Princess Beatrice and the Rotten Robber,* was published by Penguin.

Then followed a fragmented time when I was involved with the kids, their school, and efforts to save the house of Australian children's author May Gibbs responsible for *Snugglepot and Cuddlepie.* I fell behind on illustrations for a picture book which was cancelled, so I completed *The Cherry Dress* instead.

I'd been jotting down poems to reassure myself that I was still achieving something, polishing them in my head during scraps of quiet time. I sent the collection off, and the following rejection was lucky, because I then sent the manuscript to Rosalind Price, publisher at Allen and Unwin. (People happen to me at the right time: Andrew, Bea, and Gig—both born on March 10th, and now Rosalind.)

Rosalind enjoyed my poems. "Why not call the book *Honey Sandwich?"* Along with many illustrators and writers, I owe a deal to Rosalind who always underplays her achievements. She's a good businesswoman, literary, enthusiastic, and responsible for a rich list of children's books, but besides that she's witty and fun.

Allen and Unwin was an English company whose claims to fame were discovering Tolkien and publishing *The Hobbit,* and being the first to publish Roald Dahl in hardback. Rosalind asked the company if they'd consider a children's list, starting modestly with one or two books a year. They agreed. Later Allen and Unwin became Australian when three employees bought it.

Rosalind doesn't meddle; she says, "Leave well alone," yet she's a great support. She accepts ideas out of left field and always gives a clear reason for her decisions. I've been described as an iconoclast, and when I copped the flack Rosalind supported me. It was her idea to start Allen and Unwin's choir, Word of Mouth. For an hour each Thursday, Sue Johnson, a member of the a cappella group Coco's Lunch, teaches us. Sue turned my poem "All the Wild Wonders" into the most beautiful song.

Bea, our daughter and avid reader, is another reliable sounding board.

"Sit down, Mum," she said seriously after reading the manuscript for *Don't Pat the Wombat!* "I don't think it's very funny."

This came as a shock, and I redoubled my efforts. *Wombat* is the result of my experience as a volunteer at Hawthorn West Primary School. I am a veteran of five school camps.

To illustrate *Wombat,* I tried to draw like Mark, in grade six, but my illustrations looked like an adult trying to draw like a kid. Gig has a sharp sense of humour, so I asked him to do a couple then showed them to Rosalind. With her okay, Gig began the task in earnest, doing a

couple of illustrations a night for a few weeks. It was like a large school project. Sometimes a funny idea came instantly, but when he was stuck we all made suggestions. His drawings match the story perfectly. We were so proud of Gig when the book was short-listed for the Children's Book of the Year Award.

The book *45 & 47 Stella Street* grew over many years. As a kid I loved Enid Blyton's "The Famous Five" series. Basically everyone wants to be part of a cool gang and have thrilling adventures without interfering adults. Bea and Gig were part of a lively bunch in a suburb becoming gentrified. Some new residents didn't want to be friends—The Phonies!

Remote Man grew in a muddled, piecemeal way from a desire to understand the effects of multimedia. Gig took to the internet and chat like a duck to water. Chat is a new way of speaking to each other. Email is like letters but with a character of its own. Play seems to have changed.

At a Children's Book Council conference in Adelaide in 1998, I was asked to speak on the influences of multimedia on children's literature. I invented Remote Man with remotes jangling on his hip like equipment on a New York cop. See how his legs are becoming shorter? He feels interactive with everything. He has all these choices all the time. Books? You can't click on them. He can't stand anything boring. Point. Click! Point. Click! Things obey

"Bea, Andrew, me, a worried Dup and Gig. You can see two leaves from our grand magnolia grandiflora."

him. He wants immediate gratification. He's thirsty now. He wants a drink *now!*

Don't get me wrong. We have a big TV and watch some great programs, but when Gig lies on the couch prowling the channels for hours, I find myself saying to him, "It's stealing your life!"

A character grew, a boy called Ned, keen on reptiles, cars, computers and TV. "Wonder if he could be part of a gang of kids on the net in four interesting places?"

In 1996 Alison Lester, another writer and illustrator, and I received phone calls from Lauris, the agent who organises our school visits. "There's a woman on the phone from an Aboriginal community in the Northern Territory called Gunbalanya. She wants someone for six weeks. Sounds fabulous." We decided to share the job and planned it around school holidays to include our families.

Gunbalanya was hot. Here's a note from a sketch book: "A sudden heat so thick, you have to think to move. You have to make a resolution to do something. It saps your energy and when you first wake, you feel like you've been beaten up, then run over by a bus."

Staying with teachers we found ourselves caught up in the life of the Gunbalanya Community school. It was a rich time, full of new experiences, stories, personalities with nicknames like "The Horse Killer," an assault on the senses, the wildlife, the brumbies around the billabong, the paintings by the local artists. We soaked it up, and with the aboriginal kids we made puppets, wrote stories and illustrated them, drew and painted murals, and everyone had such a good time they invited us back. The second time we all worked together on a pageant based on the seasons.

The Aborigines at Gunbalanya speak Kunwingu. They learn English at school. Their word for white people is "balander," believed to be from the Dutch—Hollander. Most balanders, us included until we went there, have no idea about life in the Top End, let alone Arnhem Land. Our kids had never met an Aborigine except on a bush tucker tourist excursion. Arnhem Land felt wild, the Aboriginies living half between their traditional way of life and western life, dramatic weather, wildlife and landscape, a raw place for us whities. You turn on the tap and a frog comes out. "I should definitely put a character here in the net book," I thought, "a blond girl, daring . . . and as a complete contrast what's ordinary America like? A character in the United States far from cultural coloniser Los Angeles, with old trees? A kid in New England. Jamaicans speak English with a colourful accent. Jamaica has reggae and cricket, they're a bit mad. A kid in Jamaica. Wonder who has computers in Jamaica?"

In 1998 Bea was an exchange student in France in the Loire Valley where the French kings held court in grand chateaux during the Renaissance. Bea boarded at a Catholic school near Tours, spending the weekends with her host family. Her letters and faxes were vivid, so I set a character there based on Bea's experiences.

Mid-1998 we flew to France and stayed with Bea's host family, to London to visit Richard and Petsa, and then Bea and Andrew returned home. Gig and I stayed in London while I finished *Fiddleback.* When I sent those illustrations back to Rosalind, it was a *great* relief. Gig and

I flew to Jamaica, and the researching-the-net-book adventure began.

Jamaica's a Caribbean paradise if you're rich, but for most of its inhabitants, it's an island of grinding poverty. Kingston airport terminal is a huge, hot old shed, and when the assistant at the little tourist desk handed me a carbon copy with the address of a place we might stay, I thought, "How am I going to find a Jamaican kid with access to a computer, let alone one that's on the net!"

It was different travelling as a writer, noting details, looking carefully, taking photos, hoping somehow to make the connection. ("Seek and ye shall find." Matt. 7:8)

In Port Antonia we stayed in Mrs. Victoria Elizabeth Munroe's B 'n' B in Daffodil Drive, Anchovy Gardens. Our room was spartan with a concrete floor, strange and threatening for Gig who sat obstinately on the bed. "I'm not going out there . . . and I'm not staying here either."

We met Mrs. Munroe's grandchildren, Cleverton, Alison, and Colleen who were friendly in an old-fashioned courteous way that was charming. Cleverton later became the basis for the Jamaican character, but I made him older and set him in Kingston.

As for the computer, in the Kingston library just inside the door under the hurricane warning, there was a computer for public access, on the net. What if the boy's grandmother was the cleaner at the library? What if it was holidays and he had to carry something to work for her?

We flew north to United States. Suddenly everything was expensive. A friend had recommended Concord west of Boston as a base, but affordable accommodation seemed impossible to find and ironically, while I worked on the proofs of *Fiddleback,* Gig lay on the huge motel bed for hours watching cable TV!

Then came a stroke of luck. Mona Bornhorst took us in. She had four grown-up children and immediately began to tease Gig and spoil him. The character of Martha is part Mona.

Mona's backyard sloped down to forest. We walked through the conservation lands in the area. Mona hung a bird feeder outside on her deck. The birds came, but after a while so did the squirrels, the chipmunks, and the pesky raccoons.

The local paper reported sightings of a moose in the next county, and deer, and not far from us a bear had been seen raiding bird feeders. I saw a video of the bear, and it was a beautiful black bear with glossy fur. The interface between humans and nature is difficult. Humans want things to be safe. And at the end of our street was a pet shop specialising in expensive, exotic birds. On the net you can buy all sorts of wildlife. What is our attitude to wildlife as we become more urbanised? "If the earth was a rental, we so would not get our bond back," says comedian Will Anderson.

We were lent bikes and a Chevy Cavalier which we christened "Mom's hunk o' junk." We settled down in Massachusetts, mobile and working—Gig at junior high and me researching and writing. We kept in touch with Andrew and Bea back home, by constant email.

Visiting a school I met Bo Levering who introduced me to his corn snakes and provided detail for the characters of Rocky and Ned. Bo was my herpetologist, the snake expert who checked the manuscript to make sure my facts were correct. And on a hike Gig rolled over a rock and there beneath it, what looked like a little rubbery lizard—our first salamander!

Mona included us in her family's Thanksgiving, and the fall happened quietly around us. One of my favourite writing spots was a certain chair in the West Concord library, where looking out a window I could see day by day the leaves of a sugar maple turn a fiery red. After Halloween Gig laid out his loot. He'd never possessed so much candy, and I'm sure he never will again. Kilos!

We arrived home on Christmas Eve. When life had settled down, I began to patch the story together. All my precious research was suffocating the story. Rosalind said, "Keep Ned central to the plot."

The thesaurus entry for "remote" reminded me that the story was about dislocation, a stranger seeing America through Australian eyes, distant. Using colour Post-it Notes, I tracked each character and the plot, striving for a tough tender funny thriller. I wrote the beginning again and again. It's always a good idea to rework your beginning once you've finished the story, and then you can tailor it to what's going to happen.

Slowly the villain, quintessential Los Angeles stuntman, Ross Laana, became real for me, although he's always a shadowy figure.

Remote Man is a patchwork of language in third person to give a godlike overview of the different characters, but Ned's thoughts are shown too, in bold italics.

Had our experiences been different, the story would have been different. It was our experiences woven together with my imagination that became the story. Strangely it didn't really jell until Ned met his cousin in Darwin, and later Rocky in the woods. Once they met in real life, the story took off. The computer became the heroic tool used to set the trap.

I love circling down into a story, going deeper and deeper. When I'm nearing the end, I have the whole thing in my head, all the facts and relationships. I'm saturated with the story, and for the first and last time, know it absolutely inside out. Andrew says I "go mono." I depend on him to keep the home running for those last few months while I sprint to the end. It really is a withdrawal, and then when the manuscript has gone, I soar with relief.

When the book is published I start talking. Over the years I've visited hundreds of schools. The teachers who invite me are kindred spirits, and I've made friends all over Australia.

So here I am living in the same old house with the same old husband, with a new dog just like the old dog and two offspring who will soon spring off, riding my bike around the same old places. We're living in the Information Revolution, part of the generation which pioneered IT, but no matter how we communicate, it's still the friends and relatives that are most dear.

HOOSE, Phillip M. 1947-

Personal

Name is pronounced "hose"; born 1947, in South Bend, IN; son of Darwin Hoose and Patti Williams; married; wife's name Shoshana; children: Hannah, Ruby. *Education:* Attended Indiana University and Yale University School of Forestry and Environmental Studies. *Hobbies and other interests:* Running.

Addresses

Home—Portland, ME. *Agent*—c/o Author Mail, Farrar, Straus, 19 Union Square West, New York, NY 10003. *E-mail*—Hoose@gwi.net.

Career

Author, musician, and conservationist. Nature Conservancy, Portland, ME, staff member, 1977—; songwriter and performing musician, 1984—. Cofounder and member of board of directors, Children's Music Network, 1986—.

Awards, Honors

Christopher Award and American Library Association Notable Book citation, both 1993, both for *It's Our World Too!: Stories of Young People Who Are Making a Difference;* Jane Addams Children's Book Award honor book citation, 1999, for *Hey, Little Ant;* National Book Award finalist, 2001, and "Top Ten Biographies for Youth," *Booklist,* 2002, both for *We Were There Too!: Young People in U.S. History.*

Writings

Building an Ark: Tools for the Preservation of Natural Diversity through Land Protection, Island Press (Covelo, CA), 1981.

Hoosiers: The Fabulous Basketball Life of Indiana, Vintage Books (New York, NY), 1986, revised edition, Guild Press of Indiana (Indianapolis, IN), 1995.

Necessities: Racial Barriers in American Sports, Random House (New York, NY), 1989.

FOR CHILDREN

It's Our World Too!: Stories of Young People Who Are Making a Difference, Joy Street Books (Boston, MA), 1993, new edition published as *It's Our World Too!: Stories of Young People Who Are Making a Differ-*

In rhyming text, Phillip M. Hoose and his daughter, Hannah, outline the wordplay between an ant and the child who is about to step on it. (From Hey, Little Ant, *illustrated by Debbie Tilley.*)

ence: How They Do It—How YOU Can, Too!, foreword by Pete Seeger, Farrar, Straus (New York, NY), 2002.

(With daughter Hannah Hoose) *Hey, Little Ant,* illustrated by Debbie Tilley, Tricycle Press (Berkeley, CA), 1998.

We Were There, Too!: Young People in U.S. History, Farrar, Straus (New York, NY), 2001.

Sidelights

Phillip M. Hoose, a conservationist and musician by profession, was born in South Bend, Indiana, an area famous for the popularity of high school basketball teams. Hoose discusses the history of Indiana basketball in his book *Hoosiers: The Fabulous Basketball Life of Indiana.* He begins at the start of Hoosier basketball just prior to 1900 and continues up to the 1980s. Reviewing the book for *Voice of Youth Advocates,* Hilary King commented, "Hoose has done an admirable job at relaying the tempo and feeling of the remarkable Hoosiers."

In *Necessities: Racial Barriers in American Sports,* Hoose examines the attitudes of players, coaches, managers, owners, and the media toward members of minorities in sports. He interviewed more than one hundred people, including coaches, athletes, and news people, and found that minorities are largely kept out of positions that require decision making such as catchers, managers, or coaches. *Business Week*'s Ron Stodghill II called the book "a hard-hitting analysis of the political and social dynamics that typecast minorities in professional athletics and have helped shape American sports."

Hoose's first book for children, *It's Our World Too!: Stories of Young People Who Are Making a Difference,* became a Christopher Award winner. The book is a collection of fourteen true stories that show how children and teens have stood up and taken action in worthwhile causes, like feeding the homeless, lobbying for a new park, or opposing racism and gang violence. A *Publishers Weekly* reviewer found it a "highly inspirational and engaging book," while *Horn Book*'s Margaret A. Bush noted, "Hoose's upbeat scenarios and practical advice should persuade many that they really can make a difference."

Hey, Little Ant, Hoose's second book for children, was written with his daughter Hannah. The simple tale features an ant who begs for his life when a young child is about to step on him. He has a family at home, the ant pleads. The child, however, has friends who are urging him on, and he does not really believe that ants have feelings. Hoose never reveals if the ant lives or dies, instead he asks the reader to decide. A *Publishers Weekly* reviewer called the book a "parable about mercy and empathy," and Reed Mangels, writing in *Vegetarian Journal,* found it "a great resource for thinking and talking about respecting other beings." The book became a commercial success, was printed in eight languages, and is often used as a teaching tool for tolerance, but it might easily have been buried beneath rejection slips before it got published. Hoose and his daughter originally created the story as a performance piece with music, and it always caught the fancy of their audiences. Hoose felt that the material would make a successful children's book, but it took him more that two years to find an editor who would agree with him—and accept the

story's unresolved ending. As Hoose revealed in a *Peacework* article: "Hannah and I believed to our souls in *Ant.* I didn't give up.... Usually when children want something and they are told no, they don't walk away. They ask, 'Why?' and then listen carefully for a weakness in the defense. Then they adjust and try again. *Hey, Little Ant* became a book because those of us who believed in it most were childlike in our approach and antlike in our persistence."

It took Hoose six years to research and write his next book, *We Were There, Too!: Young People in U.S. History,* his third book for children and a finalist for the National Book Award. The collection of seventy true stories demonstrates that children and teenagers have played an important part in the history of the United States. A reviewer for *Horn Book* commented that whether the author's focus is on an individual or on young people within a group, "Hoose ties lively narratives to larger historical events through cogent chapter introductions." In *Children's Literature,* a reviewer observed, "Written with great care and compassion, this is one of the finest children's books dealing with American history this writer has come across in

In **We Were There, Too!,** *Hoose collects the tales of over seventy young people who helped shape American history as slaves, civil rights workers, and revolutionaries.*

recent years." "A treasure chest of history come to life," noted Herman Sutter in *School Library Journal,* "this is an inspired collection."

Biographical and Critical Sources

PERIODICALS

American Libraries, December, 1986, Bill Ott, review of *Hoosiers: The Fabulous Basketball Life of Indiana,* p. 824.
Booklist, August, 2001, Ilene Cooper, review of *We Were There, Too!: Young People in U.S. History,* p. 2117.
Book World, July 11, 1993, Joe Wakelee-Lynch, *Kids Do the Noblest Things,* p. 11.
Business Week, June 19, 1989, Ron Stodghill II, review of *Necessities: Racial Barriers in American Sports,* p. 16.
Horn Book, September-October, 1993, Margaret A. Bush, review of *It's Our World Too!: Stories of Young People Who Are Making a Difference,* pp. 621-622; September, 2001, review of *We Were There, Too!,* p. 610.
Horn Book Guide, fall, 1999, Carolyn Shute, review of *Hey, Little Ant,* p. 361.
Kirkus Reviews, April 15, 1989, review of *Necessities,* p. 603.
Library Journal, March 15, 1981, Susan Beverly Kuklin, review of *Building an Ark: Tools for the Preservation of Natural Diversity through Land Protection,* p. 671; May 1, 1989, William A. Hoffman, review of *Necessities,* p. 82.
Nation, May 8, 1989, Nicolaus Mills, review of *Necessities,* pp. 634-636.
Peacework, May, 2000, Phillip Hoose, "How 'Hey, Little Ant' Became a Book."
Publishers Weekly, June 7, 1993, review of *It's Our World Too!,* p. 72; September 14, 1998, review of *Hey, Little Ant,* p. 67; August 20, 2001, review of *We Were There, Too,* p. 81.
School Library Journal, December, 1998, Maryann H. Owen, review of *Hey, Little Ant,* p. 98; August, 2001, Herman Sutter, review of *We Were There, Too,* p. 198.
Vegetarian Journal, May, 2001, Reed Mangels, review of *Hey, Little Ant,* p. 31.
Virginia Quarterly Review, spring, 1987, review of *Hoosiers,* p. 68.
Voice of Youth Advocates, April, 1987, Hilary King, review of *Hoosiers,* p. 45; October, 1993, Sari Feldman, review of *It's Our World Too!,* p. 242.

OTHER

BookPage, http://www.bookpage.com/ (January 13, 2002), Ron Kaplan, review of *We Were There, Too!*
Children's Book Council, http://www.cbcbooks.org/ (January 13, 2002), review of *We Were There, Too!*
Children's Literature, http://www.childrenslit.com/ (March 6, 2002), Greg M. Romaneck, review of *We Were There, Too!,* and author biography.
Crimson Bird, http://www.crimsonbird.com/ (January 13, 2002), review of *We Were There, Too!**

HOROWITZ, Anthony 1955-

Personal

Born April 5, 1955, in London, England; son of Mark (a lawyer) and Joyce Horowitz; married Jill Green (a television producer), April 15, 1988; children: Nicholas, Cassian. *Education:* Attended rugby school; University of York, B.A.

Addresses

Office—c/o Greenlit Productions, 13 D'Arblay St., London W1, England. *Agent*—Peters, Fraser & Dunlop, 34-43 Russell St., London WC2B 5HP, England. *E-mail*—ajhorowitz@aol.com.

Career

Writer.

Writings

Enter Frederick K. Bower, Arlington (London, England), 1979.
The Sinister Secret of Frederick K. Bower, illustrated by John Woodgate, Arlington (London, England), 1979.
Misha, the Magician and the Mysterious Amulet, illustrated by John Woodgate, Arlington (London, England), 1981.
The Kingfisher Book of Myths and Legend, illustrated by Frances Mosley, Kingfisher (London, England), 1985, published as *Myths and Mythology,* Little Simon (New York, NY), 1985.
(Adaptor) *Adventurer* (based on a television script by Richard Carpenter), Corgi (London, England), 1986.
(Adaptor with Robin May) Richard Carpenter, *Robin of Sherwood: The Hooded Man* (based on a television play), Puffin (Harmondsworth, England), 1986, published as *The Complete Adventures of Robin of Sherwood,* Puffin (Harmondsworth, England), 1990.
Groosham Grange (also see below), illustrated by Cathy Simpson, Methuen (London, England), 1988.
Starting Out (play), Oberon (London, England), 1990.
Groosham Grange II: The Unholy Grail, Methuen (London, England), 1991, published as *The Unholy Grail: A Tale of Groosham Grange* (also see below), Walker (London, England), 1999.
(Editor) *The Puffin Book of Horror Stories,* illustrated by Daniel Payne, Viking (London, England), 1994.
Granny, Walker (London, England), 1994.
(Editor, and contributor) *Death Walks Tonight: Horrifying Stories,* Puffin (New York, NY), 1996.
The Switch, Walker (London, England), 1996.
Horowitz Horror: Nine Nasty Stories to Chill You to the Bone, Orchard (London, England), 1999.
The Devil and His Boy, Walker (London, England), 1998, Puffin (New York, NY), 2000.
Groosham Grange; and, The Unholy Grail: Two Stories in One, Walker (London, England), 2000.
Mindgame (play), Oberon (London, England), 2000.
More Horowitz Horror: Eight Sinister Stories You'll Wish You'd Never Read, Orchard (London, England), 2000.

The Phone Goes Dead, Orchard (London, England), 2002.
The Night Bus, Orchard (London, England), 2002.
Twist Cottage, Orchard (London, England), 2002.
Burnt, Orchard (London, England), 2002.
Scared, Orchard (London, England), 2002.
Killer Camera, Orchard (London, England), 2002.

Creator of the television series *Midsomer Murders,*
writing the episodes "The Killings at Badgers Drift,"
"Strangler's Wood," "Dead Man's Eleven," and "Judgement Day"; *Murder in Mind,* writing "Teacher," "Echoes," "Mercy," "Torch Song," and other episodes; and
Foyle's War, writing "The German Woman," "The
White Feather," "A Lesson in Murder," and "Eagle
Day." Author of "The Last Englishman" and "Menace,"
for the television series *Heroes & Villains,* British
Broadcasting System (BBC) 1; Has also written television screenplays for *Agatha Christie's Poirot, Crime
Traveller,* and *The Saint.* Also author of a screenplay
based on his novel *Stormbreaker.*

Books by Horowitz have been translated into Spanish,
French, German, Danish, Swedish, Hebrew, Japanese,
Flemish, Italian, and other languages, and published in
Braille editions.

"DIAMOND BROTHERS" SERIES

The Falcon's Malteser (also see below), Grafton (London,
    England), 1986, published as *Just Ask for Diamond,*
    Lions (London, England), 1998.
Public Enemy Number Two, Dragon (London, England),
    1987.
South by South East, Walker (London, England), 1991.
I Know What You Did Last Wednesday, Walker (London,
    England), 2002.
The Blurred Man (published with *The Falcon's Malteser*),
    Walker (London, England), 2002.

"POWER OF FIVE" SERIES

The Devil's Door-Bell, Holt (New York, NY), 1983.
The Night of the Scorpion, Pacer (New York, NY), 1984.
The Silver Citadel, Berkley (New York, NY), 1986.
Day of the Dragon, Methuen (London, England), 1989.

"ALEX RIDER" SERIES; JUVENILE NOVELS

Stormbreaker, Walker (London, England), 2000, Puffin
    (New York, NY), 2001.
Point Blanc, Walker (London, England), 2001, Philomel
    (New York, NY), 2002.
Skeleton Key, Walker (London, England), 2002, Philomel
    (New York, NY), 2003.
Eagle Strike, Walker (London, England), 2003, Philomel
    (New York, NY), 2004.

SCREENPLAYS

The Gathering (based on the novel *Stormbreaker*), Dimen-
    sion Films, 2003.

Adaptations

Stormbreaker was adapted for audiocassette, Listening
Library, 2001; *Point Blanc* is also available on audiocassette.

Anthony Horowitz

Work in Progress

A new "Alex Rider" book, forthcoming in 2004.

Sidelights

The name Anthony Horowitz is well known to young
British fans of horror stories. The editor of *The Puffin
Book of Horror Stories,* Horowitz has also chilled
youngsters' blood for over a decade with such heart-
stopping books as *Death Walks Tonight: Horrifying
Stories* and the novels *Scared* and *Twist Cottage.* More
recently, American readers have been introduced to
Horowitz through his popular series of books featuring
protagonist Alex Rider, the teenage nephew of a former
British secret agent who find himself thrust into a series
of daring adventures. "There are times when a grade-B
adventure is just the ticket for a bored teenager,"
maintained *Booklist* reviewer Jean Franklin, "especially
if it offers plenty of slam-bang action, spying, and high-
tech gadgets." According to Franklin, the "Alex Rider"
novels *Stormbreaker, Point Blanc,* and *Skeleton Key*
provide just that.

Fourteen-year-old Alex Rider makes his fiction debut in
Stormbreaker. When his guardian, Uncle Ian, is killed in
a car wreck, Alex questions whether the police have
correctly classified the death as accidental after he finds
a number of bullet holes in his uncle's car. After his
curiosity over his uncle's death almost gets him killed as

well, Alex discovers Ian was an agent for British Intelligence and decides that joining the agency himself might be the best way to stay alive. Leaving prep school for two weeks of intensive training as an MI6 agent, Alex is given a collection of spy gadgets and sent on his first assignment: to infiltrate a training group run by demented inventor Herod Sayles, who is trying to wipe out Great Britain's children by using biological weapons introduced through an in-school computer system known as "Stormbreaker." Noting that "satirical names abound . . . and the hard-boiled language is equally outrageous," a *Publishers Weekly* reviewer nonetheless wrote that "these exaggerations only add to the fun" for readers. *Stormbreaker* was deemed "an excellent choice for reluctant readers" by *School Library Journal* contributor Lynn Bryant due to its "short cliff-hanger chapters and its breathless pace."

In *Point Blanc,* the second installment in the "Alex Rider" series, the teen operative finds himself back in

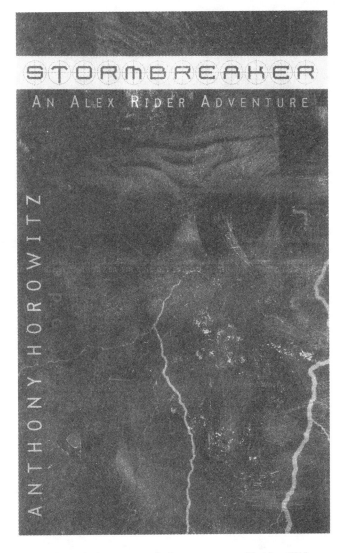

In Horowitz's spy novel, fourteen-year-old Alex Rider suspects his uncle has been killed and attempts to carry out his uncle's treacherous assignment for Britain's top intelligence agency. (Cover illustration by John Blackford.)

prep school, only this time it is an exclusive prep school called Point Blanc that is located in the French Alps and designed to house the young black sheep in Britain's wealthiest families. Run by a South African named Dr. Grief, the school has surprisingly good luck in making these rich teen troublemakers tow the line. But why? After Alex, now trapped at the school, discovers that brainwashing by Grief is only one of the ways these young men are controlled, he begins to worry about his own safety. Fortunately, as a *Kirkus Reviews* critic assured readers, "Horowitz devises a string of miraculous circumstances that keeps Alex alive and spying throughout." Propelled by hidden passages, frightening medical experiments, and a protagonist who barely stays one step away from death, *Point Blanc* was described by Franklin as a "non-stop thriller" in her *Booklist* review.

Many of Horowitz's books feature young teens who find their mundane lives suddenly turned upside down by an evil force. Such is the case in *The Devil's Door-Bell,* one of Horowitz's first novels for young readers. Published in 1983 as the first segment in the "Power of Five" series, it tells the story of thirteen-year-old Martin Hopkins, whose parents' tragic death forces him into the care of a foster mother named Elvira who takes him to live on her country farm in Yorkshire, England. Upset at being newly orphaned and nervous over Elvira's strange demeanor and intimations that Martin's time will also soon be up, the teen realizes that his suspicions are not just due to stress: Elvira is actually a witch, and her coven is planning something that will cause him harm. A clue left by a murdered friend leads Martin and journalist friend Richard Cole to an ancient circle of stones known as the "Devil's Door-Bell" where Elvira's plans to unleash a malevolent supernatural horror energized by a nearby nuclear power station are revealed. Calling *The Devil's Door-Bell* "a satisfyingly scary book," *School Library Journal* contributor Anne Connor added that Horowitz creates a "chilling atmosphere of horror" despite the novel's "sketchy characterization . . . and . . . unbelievable plot." As the author revealed to *SATA*, Horowitz is rewriting *The Devil's Door-Bell* for a new edition.

The "Power of Five" series, which focuses on young people who are fated to do battle with the forces of an ancient evil, continues with *The Night of the Scorpion.* Here Martin and Richard once again find themselves forced to close a portal into hell after a mysterious explosion almost kills a group of Martin's classmates. This time the pair must travel to Peru, where their efforts to battle the demons known as the Old Ones are thwarted by human accomplices who arrest Richard as soon as he gets off the plane. Left alone in a strange country, Martin meets another boy named Pedro, a descendant of the Incas who, like Martin, is destined to do battle with the Old Ones. "Horowitz packs enough suspense and violence into the story to satisfy the most avid thriller fans," according to a *Publishers Weekly* contributor, while *English Journal* reviewer Regina Cowin noted that "the reader is drawn into this story of ancient mysticism just as inexorably as Martin and Pedro are drawn into" their battle against ancient evil.

Other "Power of Five" novels include *The Silver Citadel,* published in 1986, and *Day of the Dragon,* published in 1989.

Horowitz's readers are in for even more travels through time in his novel *The Devil and His Boy.* Set in Elizabethan England, this 2000 novel finds a servant boy named Tom Falconer thrust into an alien world after he is ordered to accompany a friend of his master's to London, but his companion is murdered along the way. Befriended by a pickpocket named Moll, Tom joins a troupe of thespians and suddenly finds himself enmeshed in political intrigue and drawn into the illegal activities of some of his new friends. Cast in a play titled "The Devil and His Boy" which is being produced by the secretive Dr. Mobius, Tom winds up in the lap of the Queen of England herself. "Horowitz paints his characters ... with broad strokes and keeps the melodramatic story moving at a rapid clip," wrote *School Library Journal* contributor Barbara Scotto, dubbing *The Devil and His Boy* a "rollicking good tale that is mostly based on historical fact." Ilene Cooper also cited the historical basis of the novel, adding that, "to his credit, [Horowitz] does not try to pretty up Elizabethan life for his audience.... dirty and disfigured characters are described in detail."

In addition to series and stand-alone novels, Horowitz has published a number of short-story collections, some as editor and some as sole author. In *Horowitz Horror: Nine Nasty Stories to Chill You to the Bone* and its sequel, *More Horowitz Horror: Eight Sinister Stories You'll Wish You'd Never Read,* readers can consider themselves forewarned. Noting that "none will disappoint readers with an appetite for ghoulish happenings," *School Librarian* reviewer Peter Hollindale praised several stories included in the second of the two books, commending Horowitz's creative use of irony, subtlety, and "creepy and surprising variants on familiar themes."

Writing children's books is only one of several areas where Horowitz has used his writing talents; the other is in authoring series and segments for British television, an activity that has helped Horowitz the novelist imbue his stories with a strong cinematic sense and draw even reluctant readers into his tales of horror and suspense. He also oftentimes includes film references in his books, particularly in his "Diamond Brothers" series about the P.I. brothers who star in such novels as *The Falcon's Malteser, Public Enemy Number Two,* and *South by South East.* Calling the books "rattling good yarns," Jo Goodman noted in a *Magpies* review that "*South by South East* contains, amongst others, the windmill scene from [Hitchcock's film] *Foreign Correspondent* and the crop duster from *North by Northwest.*" The Falcon's Malteser references the classic film *The Maltese Falcon* starring Humphrey Bogart, while *Public Enemy Number Two* is a take-off on the gangster film *Public Enemy Number One.*

Horowitz told *SATA:* "It seems that kids who don't like to read love my books! They're written for anyone who loves adventure, excitement, humor, and non-stop action. *Stormbreaker* and *Point Blank,* which are about a fourteen-year-old spy, were both inspired by James Bond, and when you read my books I hope you'll be able to 'see' them—to imagine them as movies. I write a lot for television and the cinema too, particularly horror and murder mystery. There is a dark side to my writing, but mainly I believe in having fun."

Biographical and Critical Sources

PERIODICALS

Booklist, January 1, 2000, Ilene Cooper, review of *The Devil and His Boy,* p. 922; September 1, 2001, Kelly Milner Halls, review of *Stormbreaker,* p. 97; April 1, 2002, Jean Franklin, review of *Point Blank,* p. 1319.
English Journal, October, 1985, review of *The Night of the Scorpion,* p. 82.
Kirkus Reviews, March 15, 2001, review of *Stormbreaker,* p. 410; February 15, 2002, review of *Point Blank,* p. 258.
Magpies, March, 2001, Jo Goodman, "So You Want to Be a Private Investigator?," pp. 14-15.
New Statesman, April 30, 2001, Andrew Billen, "A Few Twists Too Far," p. 49.
Publishers Weekly, March 1, 1985, review of *The Night of the Scorpion,* p. 81; May 21, 2001, review of *Stormbreaker,* p. 109; May 13, 2002, review of *Point Blank,* p. 72.
School Librarian, summer, 2001, Peter Hollindale, review of *More Horowitz Horror,* p. 102.
School Library Journal, April, 1984, Anne Connor, review of *The Devil's Door-Bell,* p. 124; July, 1994, Mary Jo Drungil, review of *Myths and Legends,* p. 124; April, 2000, Barbara Scotto, review of *The Devil and His Boy,* p. 136; June, 2001, Lynn Bryant, review of *Stormbreaker,* p. 150; March, 2002, review of *Point Plank,* p. 232.
Spectator, February 11, 1995, Ian Hislop, "Last of a Kind," p. 47.
Voice of Youth Advocates, April, 2000, review of *The Devil and His Boy,* p. 35.

J–K

JEFFERS, Susan 1942-

Personal

Born October 7, 1942, in NJ; married Steven Cook (a conservation officer); children: Ali. *Education:* Graduated from Pratt Institute, New York, NY, 1964.

Addresses

Home—Westchester County, NY. *Agent*—c/o Hyperion Books for Children, 114 Fifth Ave., New York, NY 10011.

Career

Worked in art departments of three publishing houses, New York, NY, beginning c. 1964; freelance designer; owner, with author-illustrator Rosemary Wells, of design studio, beginning c. 1968; Wiltwyck School for Boys, instructor in art; author and illustrator of children's books.

Awards, Honors

Caldecott Honor Award, American Library Association, 1974, and Golden Apple Award, Biennale of Illustrations Bratislava, 1975, both for *Three Jovial Huntsmen;* Citations of Merit, Society of Illustrators, for *Thumbelina* and *Hansel and Gretel;* awards from Biennale of Illustrations Bratislava, for *Thumbelina* and *Hiawatha;* Golden Kite Award, Society of Children's Book Writers, 1988, for *Forest of Dreams.*

Many of Jeffers's books have been cited by such organizations as the Association of Booksellers, Children's Book Council, Child Study Association, New Jersey Institute of Technology, and American Library Association, and by such periodicals as *American Bookseller, Redbook, Booklist, School Library Journal, Parents' Choice,* and *Horn Book.* Her illustrations have been showcased by the American Institute of Graphic Arts.

In The Midnight Farm, *Susan Jeffers's illustrations complement Reeve Lindbergh's verse depicting a mother and her young son as they visit various farm animals snuggling down for the night.*

Writings

FOR CHILDREN; SELF-ILLUSTRATED

(Adaptor) *Three Jovial Huntsmen* (based on the Mother Goose rhyme of the same name), Bradbury Press (Englewood Cliffs, NJ), 1973.

(Adaptor) *All the Pretty Horses* (based on a song sung by Peter, Paul, and Mary), Macmillan (New York, NY), 1974.

(Adaptor) *Wild Robin* (based on a story in *Little Prudy's Fairy Book* by Sophie May), Dutton Children's Books (New York, NY), 1976.

Using watercolor paintings, many featuring lush depictions of Scottish landscapes, Jeffers illustrated Rosemary Wells's adaptation of **Lassie Come-Home,** *the 1938 classic about an indomitable collie.*

(Adaptor) *If Wishes Were Horses and Other Rhymes,* Dutton Children's Books (New York, NY), 1979.

Little People's Book of Baby Animals, Random House (New York, NY), 1980.

(Adaptor) *Hansel and Gretel* (based on the fairy tale of the same name by Jacob and Wilhelm Grimm), Dial Books for Young Readers (New York, NY), 1980.

I'm Okay ... You're a Brat!, Renaissance Books (Los Angeles, CA), 2000.

ILLUSTRATOR; FOR CHILDREN

Victoria Lincoln, *Everyhow Remarkable,* Crowell-Collier Press (New York, NY), 1967.

Joseph Jacobs, *The Buried Moon,* Bradbury Press (Englewood Cliffs, NJ), 1969.

(With Rosemary Wells) Robert W. Service, *The Shooting of Dan McGrew and the Cremation of Sam McGee,* A & W Publications, 1969.

(With Rosemary Wells) Charlotte Pomerantz, *Why You Look Like You Whereas I Tend to Look Like Me,* Young Scott Books (New York, NY), 1969.

Penelope Proddow, *The Spirit of Spring: A Tale of the Greek God Dionysus,* Bradbury Press (Englewood Cliffs, NJ), 1970.

Harriette S. Abels, *The Circus Detectives,* Ginn (Boston, MA), 1971.

Mary Q. Steele, *The First of the Penguins,* Macmillan (New York, NY), 1973.

Jean Marzollo, *Close Your Eyes* (poem), Dial Books for Young Readers (New York, NY), 1976.

Robert Frost, *Stopping by Woods on a Snowy Evening* (poem), Dutton Children's Books (New York, NY), 1978.

Hans Christian Andersen, *Thumbelina,* retold by Amy Ehrlich, Dial Books for Young Readers (New York, NY), 1979.

Jacob and Wilhelm Grimm, *Snow White and the Seven Dwarfs,* retold by Freya Littledale, Four Winds Press (New York, NY), 1981.

Hans Christian Andersen, *The Wild Swans,* retold by Amy Ehrlich, Dial Books for Young Readers (New York, NY), 1981.

Hans Christian Andersen, *The Snow Queen,* retold by Amy Ehrlich, Dial Books for Young Readers (New York, NY), 1982.

Eugene Field, *Wynken, Blynken, and Nod* (poem), Dutton Children's Books (New York, NY), 1982.

Henry Wadsworth Longfellow, *Hiawatha* (poem), Dial Books for Young Readers (New York, NY), 1983.

Joseph Mohr, *Silent Night* (hymn), Dutton Children's Books (New York, NY), 1984.

Charles Perrault, *Cinderella,* retold by Amy Ehrlich, Dial Books for Young Readers (New York, NY), 1985.

Anna Sewell, *Black Beauty,* adapted by Robin McKinley, Random House (New York, NY), 1986.

In bold illustrations, Jeffers depicts Rosemary Wells's canine protagonist, terrier McDuff, whose adventures comprise the picture book **McDuff Comes Home.**

Reeve Lindbergh, *The Midnight Farm* (poem), Dial Books for Young Readers (New York, NY), 1987.

Rosemary Wells, *Forest of Dreams*, Dial Books for Young Readers (New York, NY), 1988.

Margaret Wise Brown, *Baby Animals*, Random House (New York, NY), 1989.

Reeve Lindbergh, *Benjamin's Barn*, Dial Books for Young Readers (New York, NY), 1990.

Chief Seattle, *Brother Eagle, Sister Sky!: The Words of Chief Seattle*, Dial Books for Young Readers (New York, NY), 1991.

Rosemary Wells, *Waiting for the Evening Star*, Dial Books for Young Readers (New York, NY), 1993.

Rosemary Wells, *Lassie Come-Home*, Holt (New York, NY), 1995.

Rachel Field's Hitty: Her First Hundred Years, retold by Rosemary Wells, Simon & Schuster Books for Young Readers (New York, NY), 1999.

Margaret Wise Brown, *Love Songs of the Little Bear*, Hyperion Books for Children (New York, NY), 2001.

Niki Leopold, *K Is for Kitten*, Putnam (New York, NY), 2002.

ILLUSTRATOR, "McDUFF" SERIES; WRITTEN BY ROSEMARY WELLS

McDuff Moves In, Hyperion Books for Children (New York, NY), 1997.

McDuff Comes Home, Hyperion Books for Children (New York, NY), 1997.

McDuff and the Baby, Hyperion Books for Children (New York, NY), 1997.

McDuff's New Friend, Hyperion Books for Children (New York, NY), 1998.

The McDuff Stories, Hyperion Books for Children (New York, NY), 2000.

McDuff Goes to School, Hyperion Books for Children (New York, NY), 2001.

McDuff Saves the Day, Hyperion Books for Children (New York, NY), 2001.

Adaptations

Black Beauty is available as a book and cassette by Random House.

Sidelights

Susan Jeffers is an award-winning illustrator best known for her pen-and-ink drawings. Specializing in outdoor landscapes populated by both humans and animals, she creates most of her work using the cross-hatch method—an intricate process that involves the intersecting of parallel lines. "I make thousands of little lines to describe form," Jeffers noted in a Dial publicity release. "This looks hard, but it's actually the easiest and most relaxing part." She then washes her detailed artwork in soft, deep colors, using a technique many reviewers believe defines and intensifies her sketches. Her drawings, often extending across two pages, frequently appear in adaptations of classic fairy tales, Mother Goose rhymes, and poetry. Although she has adapted a few tales herself, including her 1974 Caldecott Honor

Retelling Rachel Field's Newbery-winning 1929 tale of the travels and adventures of a wooden doll, Rosemary Wells and illustrator Jeffers recreate the nineteenth-century world from Boston to the South Seas. (From Rachel Field's Hitty: Her First Hundred Years.*)*

Book *Three Jovial Huntsmen,* she primarily illustrates the works of others.

Jeffers discovered art at an early age. "My career as an artist began in a tiny school in Oakland, New Jersey, when I was chosen to paint a history mural," she recalled in *Bookbird.* "I suspect that I was selected as much for my ability to keep poster paint from running—no mean feat—as for my drawing talent. Yet, I was on my way." Her mother became her motivator and guide, teaching her how to mix colors as well as how to add dimension and detail to her work. Most importantly, she inspired in her daughter an enthusiasm for the craft, which helped propel Jeffers toward art studies at New York's Pratt Institute. "When I read my syllabus for my first year I was astounded," Jeffers recalled in the Dial release. "It was eight hours a day of drawing, painting, and sculpture interspersed with English and Psychology. This was heaven."

After graduating in 1964, Jeffers worked at several New York City publishing houses, where she repaired type and designed book jackets. But she found herself drawn to children's books and became increasingly eager to create one of her own. So she began freelancing as a designer and in 1968 began the illustrations for a children's book by Joseph Jacobs titled *The Buried Moon.* Her next project, *Three Jovial Huntsmen,* was a bit harder to realize. Self-illustrated, *Huntsmen* underwent two complete rewrites before being published. The first version, rejected for printing, prompted Jeffers to accept a position teaching art at the Wiltwyck School for Boys. But the urge to rework the book never left, so she tried again. And finally, three years after its inception, *Huntsmen* was published—garnering not only a Caldecott Honor Award, but also the first Golden Apple Award won by an American illustrator.

Adapted from a Mother Goose rhyme, *Huntsmen* follows three bumbling English hunters as they roam the woods in search of game. The lighthearted story focuses on the hunters' foolishness—although readers can spot

the half-hidden forest animals, including opossums, raccoons, and squirrels, the title characters find nothing but a pincushion, a house, and a boat. Drawing praise from reviewers were Jeffers's shadowy woodland scenes, which caused a *Horn Book* contributor to proclaim that *Huntsmen*'s "main attraction lies in [its] physical beauty." According to critics, Jeffers conceals her fauna in a soft-hued forest, which is shaded in reds, blues, yellows, and blacks. The colors are "masterfully blended and differentiated," concluded the reviewer.

Among the works Jeffers has illustrated for other authors are a 1984 edition of Joseph Mohr's *Silent Night* and a

When ants ruin the Fourth of July picnic lunch, resourceful Westie pup McDuff takes charge in Rosemary Wells's **McDuff Saves the Day,** *illustrated by Jeffers.*

1986 version of Anna Sewell's *Black Beauty.* The former is an adaptation of the famous German Christmas hymn honoring the night Jesus Christ was born. Jeffers's "opening scenes are breathtaking in scope," observed a *Publishers Weekly* reviewer. The artist colors the twilight sky in deep violets and blues, then uses a combination of light and shadows to illuminate Jesus' birthplace—a stable—and the joyous angels, shepherds, wise men, and kings who visit. Jeffers's "vision of this favorite carol is ... respectful and majestic," decided Elizabeth M. Simmons in *School Library Journal.* The latter story, *Black Beauty,* is an adaptation of the classic tale of a horse's life. Using half-page to double-page spreads, Jeffers captures the distinct personality of each horse through close attention to such details as muscles, veins, eyes, and body movements. Jeffers's "animals are handsome and symmetrical," wrote a reviewer for *Booklist,* while a contributor to *School Library Journal,* Kathleen Brachmann, found them "intensely yet sensitively wrought."

Well-received too, were Jeffers's illustrations for two books published in the late 1980s—Reeve Lindbergh's *Midnight Farm* and Rosemary Wells's *Forest of Dreams,* winner of the Golden Kite Award. Written in verse, *The Midnight Farm* rejoices in outdoor life as it follows a mother and child through a nighttime tour of the farm. Jeffers offers a peaceful, reassuring portrait of darkness, sketching a variety of domestic and wild animals during their evening activities: a raccoon family preparing for sleep, sheep crowding together for warmth, mice gathering and storing seeds. One scene attracted particular attention from a *Booklist* contributor, who noted that "the serene presence of deer at a pond is captured with inimitable grace." *Forest of Dreams* also celebrates nature and life, portraying the excitement a young girl experiences watching winter turn into spring. Jeffers opens with frosty scenes of snow-covered apple trees, ice-caked marshes, and furry wolves and ermine. By the story's end, the scenery has evolved into a green meadow harboring wild flowers, butterflies, field mice, and blossom-filled apple trees. "Nine glorious double-page paintings illustrate the promise of spring and new beginnings," commented Ruth M. McConnell in *School Library Journal,* adding that "the peaceful, exuberant mood [the book] evokes is refreshing."

Throughout her career Jeffers has illustrated numerous retellings of classic works, including Hans Christian Andersen's *Thumbelina* and *Wild Swans,* Robert Frost's *Stopping by Woods on a Snowy Evening,* and Henry Wadsworth Longfellow's *Hiawatha.* She reached bestseller status for illustrating the 1991 publication of *Brother Eagle, Sister Sky!: The Words of Chief Seattle.*

In her most recent rendering of a children's classic, Jeffers teamed with Rosemary Wells to produce *Rachel Field's Hitty: Her First Hundred Years.* Field's original novel built a loyal following since it won the 1930 Newbery Award, and some reviewers were critical of changes in Hitty's character and changes in the plot that extend the memoirs of the antique-shop doll into contemporary times. Still, the book garnered positive

reviews like Ilene Cooper's in *Booklist:* "Purists will object to the changes, but there is no doubt that Jeffers and Wells have produced a genuinely beautiful book. Jeffers is at the top of her game, offering pictures that are delightful in their detail and charming in their execution."

Jeffers and Wells introduced a popular new series with 1997's *McDuff Moves In.* McDuff, a lovable West Highland terrier, comes on the scene as he escapes from a dogcatcher and searches for a home, which he finally finds with Fred and Lucy. Written for a three-to-six-year-old audience, the series takes up McDuff's problems and adventures, like getting lost while chasing a rabbit and dealing with a new baby in the house. "Jeffers's ability to express a thousand words and emotions with a pair of flattened dog ears," wrote Elizabeth S. Watson in *Horn Book,* "gives McDuff life and character, and the illustrations combine her realistic depictions of flora and fauna with a sleekly forties setting."

Jeffers continues to work from her home, where she is surrounded and inspired by the natural beauty of the neighboring landscape.

Biographical and Critical Sources

BOOKS

Children's Literature Review, Volume 30, Gale (Detroit, MI), 1993.
Silvey, Anita, editor, *Children's Books and Their Creators,* Houghton Mifflin (Boston, MA), 1995.

PERIODICALS

Bookbird, March, 1977, pp. 59-61.
Booklist, December 1, 1986, review of *Black Beauty,* p. 580; September 1, 1987, review of *The Midnight Farm,* pp. 65-66; October 1, 1988; April 15, 1990; April 1, 1997, review of *McDuff Moves In,* p. 1331; June 1, 1997, review of *McDuff Comes Home,* p. 1723; September 15, 1997, review of *McDuff and the Baby,* p. 243; December 1, 1998, review of *McDuff's New Friend,* p. 673; November 15, 1999, Ilene Cooper, review of *Rachel Field's Hitty: Her First Hundred Years,* p. 638.
Bulletin of the Center for Children's Books, November, 1984, p. 52; October, 1988, p. 58.
Christian Science Monitor, November 6, 1987, p. B6.
Horn Book, February, 1974, review of *Three Jovial Huntsmen,* pp. 37-38; April, 1977, pp. 150-151; July-August, 1997, Elizabeth S. Watson, review of *McDuff Comes Home,* p. 446; January-February, 1998, review of *McDuff and the Baby,* p. 65; January, 2000, review of *Rachel Field's Hitty: Her First Hundred Years,* p. 107.
Publishers Weekly, December 6, 1976, p. 62; December 4, 1981, p. 51; October 26, 1984, review of *Silent Night,* p. 104; September 20, 1985; September 26, 1986; July 10, 1987; July 29, 1988; June 8, 1990.
School Library Journal, January, 1977, pp. 82-83; December, 1983, p. 58; October, 1984, Elizabeth M. Simmons, review of *Silent Night,* p. 174; November, 1985;

December, 1986, Kathleen Brachmann, review of *Black Beauty,* pp. 108-109; October, 1987, p. 115; November, 1988, Ruth M. McConnell, review of *Forest of Dreams,* p. 98; June, 1990, p. 103; March, 2001, review of *Love Songs of the Little Bear,* p. 231.
Wilson Library Bulletin, May, 1988, pp. 72-73.*

*　　*　　*

KALMAN, Maira 1949-

Personal

Born 1949, in Tel Aviv, Israel; immigrated to United States, 1953; married Tibor Kalman (a graphic designer and art director; died, 1999); children: Alexander, Lulu. *Education:* New York University, B.A.

Addresses

Agent—c/o Author Mail, Viking Children's Books, 375 Hudson St., New York, NY 10014.

Career

Artist, writer, and illustrator of children's books. Designer, M & Co., New York, NY; designer of fashion mannequins for Ralph Pucci, New York, NY; freelance author/illustrator, 1986—.

Awards, Honors

Parents' Choice Award for Picture Books, Parents' Choice Foundation, 1989, for *Hey Willy, See the Pyramids; New York Times* Best Illustrated Children's Books of the Year citation, 1991, for *Ooh-la-la (Max in Love).*

Writings

(Illustrator) David Byrne, *Stay up Late,* Viking (New York, NY), 1987.
Roarr: Calder's Circus, photographs by Donatella Brun, Whitney Museum of American Art (New York, NY), 1991.
(Coauthor and editor, with husband, Tibor Kalman) *(un)Fashion* (photograph collection), Harry N. Abrams (New York, NY), 2000.
(Editor, with Ruth A. Peltason) Tibor Kalman, *Colors: Tibor Kalman, Issues One-Thirteen,* Harry N. Abrams (New York, NY), 2002.
(With husband, Tibor Kalman) *T. Bor: A Book (to Keep) and Thirty Postcards (to Send),* Little Bookroom (New York, NY), 2002.

SELF-ILLUSTRATED

Hey Willy, See the Pyramids, Viking (New York, NY), 1988.
Sayonara, Mrs. Kackleman, Viking (New York, NY), 1989.
Max Makes a Million, Viking (New York, NY), 1990.
Ooh-la-la (Max in Love), Viking (New York, NY), 1991.
Max in Hollywood, Baby, Viking (New York, NY), 1992.

Chicken Soup, Boots, Viking (New York, NY), 1993.
Swami on Rye: Max in India, Viking (New York, NY), 1995.
Max Doll, Viking (New York, NY), 1995.
Max Deluxe, Viking (New York, NY), 1996.
Next Stop Grand Central, Putnam (New York, NY), 1999.
Where's That Hat? There's That Hat, Whitney Museum of Art (New York, NY), 1999.
What Pete Ate from A-Z: Where We Explore the English Alphabet (in Its Entirety) in Which a Certain Dog Devours a Myriad of Items Which He Should Not, Putnam (New York, NY), 2001.
Fireboat: The Heroic Adventure of the "John J. Harvey," Putnam (New York, NY), 2002.

Sidelights

Artist Maira Kalman can count a cult following among her many fans; she is known for creating picture books that appeal to both children and parents with any eye for the quirky and contemporary. Noted for her witty, stream-of-consciousness prose, Kalman pairs her texts with energetic illustrations full of visual puns and parodies, strong colors and geometric shapes, and exotic locales. Her books are designed to entertain rather than to teach. As Ilene Cooper noted of Kalman's contribution to the David Byrne-penned *Stay up Late* in *Booklist,* the illustrator's "zesty ... totally New Wave" artwork is "filled with numerous asides that parents and kids will find amusing, each on their own level." The ability to entertain both children and adults has remained a Kalman trademark.

Kalman was born in Tel Aviv, Israel, in 1949. When she was four years old, she moved with her family to Riverdale, New York, a section of the Bronx. She got maximum exposure to the arts during childhood, as she explained in a *Publishers Weekly* interview with Elizabeth Devereaux, "My mother decided that we had to have culture—all good girls have to have culture." Having culture meant hours of piano and dance lessons, and attendance at "a million concerts and a million museums." After attending the city's High School of Music and Art, Kalman went to New York University (NYU) to study literature and also indulge a long-held desire to write. It was at NYU in 1968 that Kalman met her future husband, designer Tibor Kalman, then a student of graphic design. After college, Kalman wrote very little, concentrating instead on drawing. When her husband became creative director of bookstore giant Barnes and Noble in the early 1970s, Kalman worked alongside him developing ad campaigns and graphics, and after he founded the graphic design firm M & Co., she created record album covers, textile designs, and movie titles.

In the mid-1980s, Kalman decided to begin creating books for children. The first project she undertook was illustrating the lyrics to the song "Stay up Late" penned by friend Byrne, a member of the New Wave rock group Talking Heads. Questioning whether baby-boomer parents like themselves could still relate to old-fashioned nursery rhymes, Byrne and Kalman decided to experiment with the form. Noting that "the baby-boom generation [was] interested in new forms of art," Kalman explained to Jennet Conant in an interview for *Harper's Bazaar* that her generation "had such a prolonged adolescence that our taste is much closer to our kids' than our parent's was." As a fitting accompaniment to Byrne's lyrics, Kalman created paintings in a style inspired by painters Henri Matisse and Marc Chagal, and incorporated flamboyant colors and an irregular typeface designed by M & Co. Writing in *Booklist,* Cooper deemed *Stay up Late* appropriate "Strictly for the hippest families," while Nicholas Paley commented in *Journal of Youth Services in Libraries* that the postmodernist children's book "zooms around in its own orbit, leaving a collection of question marks and exclamation points scattered in its quirky path." However, not all reviewers were quite so enthusiastic, a *Publishers Weekly* contributor noted that while the book "has a definite appeal for hip adults ... it's not for the literal-minded child."

Kalman's first solo writing effort, *Hey Willy, See the Pyramids,* features Lulu and Alexander, siblings inspired by the author/artist's own children. Patient Lulu tells her little brother nonsense stories when he wakes up in the middle of the night that include family members. Kalman mixes childlike figures with folk art, the seemingly chaotic movement in the illustrations a fitting accompaniment to her surreal tales. The stories in *Hey Willy, See the Pyramids* "make sense in the way that images sliding across the mind as you fall asleep make sense," noted a *Kirkus Reviews* critic, finding the book "outlandish, but born of genuine creativity and understanding." Roger Sutton, writing in *Bulletin of the Center for Children's Books,* described the book as a "new-wave cornucopia of narrative and visual fragments," and felt that "younger readers won't appreciate the hipper-than-thou tone." In *Booklist,* Cooper maintained that "children will probably respond more to the book's wild feel than to the actual content. In any case, for the right child, this could be a mind-stretcher."

Lulu and Alexander continue their adventures in *Sayonara, Mrs. Kackleman,* which finds them touring Japan. Lulu relates fanciful and realistic recollections of slurping "oodles and poodles of noodles," of being packed onto the Tokyo subway like "marshmallows all stuffed together in a bag," and of visiting an outdoor bath and a Noh play, among other activities. In the *New York Times Book Review,* John Burnham Schwartz noted that Kalman "has captured perfectly the child's sense of wonder and has created a funny, exuberant, and inventive introduction to Japan for people of all ages." Schwartz went on to comment that Kalman "fills the page—and our minds—with a wild assortment of colorful images ... in perfect harmony with the way children think, speak, and fantasize." In *Five Owls,* Cathryn A. Camper echoed this sentiment, noting that "this surrealistic travelogue is actually very close to how a real child might record his or her experiences when visiting a foreign country." And Sutton, writing in *Bulletin of the Center for Children's Books,* concluded that "underneath all the zaniness is a true and affectionate portrait of Japan."

Maira Kalman

For Kalman's next book she focused on the friendly beagle named Max Stravinsky, who first appeared in *Hey Willy, See the Pyramids.* In *Max Makes a Million,* the canine sells his book of poetry and is finally able to fulfill his lifelong dream of leaving New York and going to Paris to live the life of a bohemian artist. Bill Ott praised the work in *Booklist,* saying: "In a perfect blending of words and pictures, Kalman creates pages that jump with the syncopated rhythms and Day-Glo colors of city life." Ott called Kalman's detailed paintings a "battleground of competing colors" and recommended the work as "definitely a book for children—and for adults with enough courage and energy to look at life the way Max does."

Readers can continue to follow Max in his travels when Kalman sends him to Paris in search of romance in *Ooh-la-la (Max in Love);* to Tinseltown, accompanied by poodle friend Crepe Suzette, in *Max in Hollywood, Baby;* and to the Far East in search of enlightenment in *Swami on Rye: Max in India.* The "Max" books reveal Kalman's main themes: the lure of the exotic and the safety of home. Reviewing *Max in Hollywood, Baby* in the *New York Times Book Review,* Kurt Andersen called Kalman's books "smart and funny and high-spirited, dense with irony and strangeness in the manner of some hopped-up late-night Dr. Seuss." The critic also conceded that they likely appealed to parents more than children. David Small went further in a *New York Times*

Book Review piece on *Swami on Rye,* noting that Kalman "leaves most young readers out of the joke more often than not." Despite being "beautifully illustrated," Small maintained that her "children's stories are grounded in almost nothing that a child can relate to." In a *School Library Journal* review of *Max in Hollywood, Baby,* Heide Piehler took a middle position, noting that while children might miss Kalman's "mocking of the Golden Age of Hollywood," they would "be caught up in the frenetic rhythms and rhymes of the text."

Kalman addresses the world of work in *Chicken Soup, Boots,* which several reviewers cited as containing more child appeal than her "Max" books. Relatives and friends of the author/illustrator are individually profiled, and their diverse occupations discussed. From short-order cook to architect to photojournalist, "Kalman gives outwardly plain jobs their due," noted a *Publishers Weekly* contributor, "imaginatively depicting many individuals and highlighting the extraordinary attributes they bring to daily tasks." In *Horn Book,* Lolly Robinson was equally enthusiastic, dubbing *Chicken Soup, Boots* "a

new and enjoyable experience all the way to the final endpapers."

Geared toward young readers, Kalman "unleashes her extravagant whimsey" in the "loquacious alphabet book" *What Pete Ate from A-Z,* according to a *Publishers Weekly* reviewer. Pete is a shaggy yellow dog who belongs to the unfortunate Parsley family. Pete's eating habits cause his owners no end of problems as, from an accordion to underpants and beyond, the pooch chomps his way through the alphabet, cheered on by Kalman's alliterative text. Praising the work as a "participatory experience par excellence" in her *School Library Journal* review, Marlene Gawron noted that Kalman's "presentation and ideas are distinctly original and will trigger an imaginative response or awaken innovative thinking" on the part of young readers.

Next Stop Grand Central, published in 1999, finds Kalman focusing on her hometown, specifically on Grand Central Station, the world's biggest railroad station, where 500,000 people enter or leave the city via

The swarming crowd at Grand Central train station is the subject of Kalman's self-illustrated work **Next Stop Grand Central.**

train each day. "Kalman's odd-ball humor is in full evidence here ...," maintained *Horn Book* contributor Lauren Adams, "but the simple silliness of many situations may give the book appeal to a younger-than-usual audience." "The caricatures are as glib as the tongue-in-cheek narration," added a reviewer for *Publishers Weekly*, "yet the author succeeds in recreating the station's frenetic pace and the blurred sense of passers-by." Noting that the book is a "celebration of the city" and a record of the recently renovated station, *Booklist* contributor Hazel Rochman maintained that "even those [readers] far from New York City will recognize the nervous intensity of an airport or train station where hordes rush by you, each individual intent on personal business, each one with a story."

Reviewing *Chicken Soup, Boots* for *Horn Book*, Robinson noted that Kalman's "full-page art shows people and other subjects painted in a way that manages to be irreverent and loving at the same time." It is this combination of irreverence and love that is the basis of Kalman's work. "Good writing liberates you," Kalman told Devereaux in *Publishers Weekly*, "it takes you out of the mundane and to an extremely inspiring and creative level.... It inspires you rather than depresses you.... To me, ninety-nine percent of children's books don't inspire you at any level. They're comforting, and they're nice, but they aren't books that take you over the top in some way."

Biographical and Critical Sources

BOOKS

Byrne, David, *Stay up Late,* illustrated by Maira Kalman, Viking (New York, NY), 1987.
Children's Books and Their Creators, edited by Anita Silvey, Houghton Mifflin (Boston, MA), 1995.
Children's Literature Review, Volume 32, Gale (Detroit, MI), 1994, pp. 176-186.
Kalman, Maira, *Sayonara, Mrs. Kackleman,* Viking (New York, NY), 1989.

PERIODICALS

Booklist, October 1, 1987, Ilene Cooper, review of *Stay up Late,* pp. 390-391; February 1, 1989, Ilene Cooper, review of *Hey Willy, See the Pyramids,* p. 939; October 1, 1990, Bill Ott, review of *Max Makes a Million,* p. 343; October 15, 1991, p. 449; December 1, 1992, Bill Ott, review of *Max in Hollywood, Baby,* p. 675; October 15, 1995, Hazel Rochman, review of *Swami on Rye: Max in India,* p. 404; December 15, 1998, Hazel Rochman, review of *Next Stop Grand Central,* p. 749; September 1, 2001, John Peters, review of *What Pete Ate from A-Z,* p. 115; September 1, 2002, GraceAnne A. DeCandido, review of *Fireboat: The Heroic Adventures of the John J. Harvey,* p. 113.
Bulletin of the Center for Children's Books, September, 1988, Roger Sutton, review of *Hey Willy, See the Pyramids,* pp. 11-12; November, 1989, Roger Sutton, review of *Sayonara, Mrs. Kackleman,* p. 63; January, 1994, Roger Sutton, review of *Chicken Soup, Boots,*

p. 157; March, 1999, Deborah Stevenson, review of *Next Stop Grand Central,* p. 243.
Five Owls, September-October, 1989, Cathryn A. Camper, review of *Sayonara, Mrs. Kackleman,* p. 8.
Harper's Bazaar, March, 1992, Jennet Conant, "Dream Weaver," pp. 179, 191-192.
Horn Book, March-April, 1994, Lolly Robinson, review of *Chicken Soup, Boots,* p. 191; May, 1999, Lauren Adams, review of *Next Stop Grand Central,* pp. 317-318; January-February, 2002, Lauren Adams, review of *What Pete Ate from A-Z,* p. 69; September-October, 2002, Roger Sutton, review of *Fireboat,* p. 596.
Interview, October, 1992, "This Is Not a Picture of Maira Kalman," pp. 76-77.
Journal of Youth Services in Libraries, winter, 1992, Nicholas Paley, "Postmodernist Impulses and the Contemporary Picture Book: Are There Any Stories to These Meanings?," pp. 151-161.
Kirkus Reviews, October 15, 1988, review of *Hey Willy, See the Pyramids,* pp. 1528-1529; October 15, 1992, review of *Max in Hollywood, Baby,* p. 1310; October 1, 1993, p. 1275.
Los Angeles Times Book Review, December 24, 1995, Tobi Tobias, "Talking Pictures," pp. 6-7.
New York, November 23, 1998, James Kaplan, "Tibor Maira," p. 40.
New York Times Book Review, November 12, 1989, John Burnham Schwartz, review of *Sayonara, Mrs. Kackleman,* pp. 25, 49; November 10, 1991, Linda Wertheimer, "An American Dog in Paris," p. 31; December 6, 1992, Kurt Andersen, review of *Max in Hollywood, Baby,* p. 90; November 12, 1995, David Small, "Max Gets a Guru," p. 48.
People, February 1, 1988, Margot Dougherty, review of *Stay up Late,* p. 15.
Publishers Weekly, September 11, 1987, review of *Stay up Late,* p. 89; July 14, 1989, review of *Sayonara, Mrs. Kackleman,* p. 75; October 12, 1990, review of *Max Makes a Million,* p. 60; September 27, 1991, Elizabeth Devereaux, "Maira Kalman's Many Muses," pp. 32-33; October 25, 1991, review of *Ooh-la-la (Max in Love),* p. 64; October 26, 1992, review of *Max in Hollywood, Baby,* p. 68; August 16, 1993, review of *Chicken Soup, Boots,* p. 101; September 18, 1995, review of *Swami on Rye,* p. 130; November 30, 1998, review of *Next Stop Grand Central,* p. 71; July 16, 2001, review of *What Pete Ate from A-Z,* p. 179; July 29, 2002, review of *Fireboat,* p. 71.
School Library Journal, March, 1988, Karen K. Radtke, review of *Stay up Late,* p. 158; September, 1988, David Gale, review of *Hey Willy, See the Pyramids,* p. 167; December, 1990, pp. 80-81; November, 1991, Lisa Dennis, review of *Ooh-la-la (Max in Love),* pp. 98, 100; November, 1992, Heide Piehler, review of *Max in Hollywood, Baby,* pp. 71-72; November, 1993, Lauralyn Persson, review of *Chicken Soup, Boots,* p. 84; November, 1995, Susan Powers, review of *Swami on Rye,* p. 102l; February, 1999, Marcia Hupp, review of *Next Stop Grand Central,* p. 85; September, 2001, Marlene Gawron, review of *What Pete Ate from A-Z,* p. 192; September, 2002, Wendy Lukehart, review of *Fireboat,* p. 214.*

L

LAWLOR, Laurie 1953-

Personal

Born April 4, 1953, in Oak Park, IL; daughter of David (a teacher) and Audrey (a teacher; maiden name, Trautman) Thompson; married John Lawlor (an attorney), June 8, 1974; children: Megan, John. *Education:* Northwestern University, B.S.J., 1975; National-Louis University, M.A.T., 1992. *Hobbies and other interests:* Traveling, reading, camping.

Addresses

Home—2103 Noyes, Evanston, IL 60201. *Agent*—Jane Jordan Browne, Multimedia Product Development, 410 South Michigan, Ste. 724, Chicago, IL 60605. *E-mail*—Laurie@laurielawlor.com.

Career

Freelance writer and editor, 1977-89; teacher of college-level writing courses and coordinating elementary and junior-high school writing workshops throughout the Midwest.

Member

Authors Guild, Authors League of America, Society of Children's Book Writers and Illustrators, Society of Midland Authors, Children's Reading Round Table (Chicago, IL).

Awards, Honors

Children's Literature Award (Utah), 1989, Nebraska Golden Sower Award, 1989, Rebecca Caudill Young Reader's Book Award nomination, 1990, and Iowa Children's Choice Award, 1990, all for *Addie across the Prairie;* KC Three Award, 1990-91, for *How to Survive Third Grade;* Nebraska Golden Sower Award nomination, Iowa Children's Choice Award, and North Dakota Flicker Tale Award, all 1992, all for *Addie's Dakota Winter;* Society of Children's Book Writers and Illustrators/Anna Cross Giblin Nonfiction Grant.

Writings

How to Survive Third Grade, illustrated by Joyce Audy Zarins, A. Whitman (Morton Grove, IL), 1989.

Daniel Boone, illustrated by Burt Dodson, A. Whitman (Morton Grove, IL), 1989.

Second-Grade Dog, illustrated by Gioia Fiammenghi, A. Whitman (Morton Grove, IL), 1990.

The Worm Club, Simon & Schuster (New York, NY), 1994.

Shadow-Catcher: The Life and Work of Edward S. Curtis, Walker Publishing (Morton Grove, IL), 1994.

Little Women (novelization of the movie based on the novel by Louisa May Alcott), Minstrel Books (New York, NY), 1994.

Gold in the Hills, Walker (New York, NY), 1995.

The Real Johnny Appleseed, A. Whitman (Morton Grove, IL), 1995.

Come Away with Me ("Heartland" series), Pocket Books (New York, NY), 1996.

Take to the Sky ("Heartland" series), Pocket Books (New York, NY), 1996.

The Biggest Pest on Eighth Avenue, illustrated by Cynthia Fisher, Holiday House (New York, NY), 1997.

Where Will This Shoe Take You?: A Walk through the History of Footwear, Walker (New York, NY), 1998.

The Worst Kid Who Ever Lived on Eighth Avenue, illustrated by Cynthia Fisher, Holiday House (New York, NY), 1998.

Window on the West: The Frontier Photography of William Henry Jackson, Holiday House (New York, NY), 1999.

Wind on the River, Jamestown Publishers (Lincolnwood, IL), 2000.

Helen Keller: Rebellious Spirit, Holiday House (New York, NY), 2001.

Old Crump: The True Story of a Trip West, illustrated by John Winch, Holiday House (New York, NY), 2002.

Magnificent Voyager: The Story of Captain Cook's Last Expedition, Holiday House (New York, NY), 2002.

"AMERICAN SISTERS" SERIES

West along the Wagon Road, 1852, Pocket Books (New York, NY), 1998.

A Titanic Journey across the Sea, 1912, Pocket Books (New York, NY), 1998.

Adventure on the Wilderness Road, 1775, Pocket Books (New York, NY), 1999.

Crossing the Colorado Rockies, 1864, Pocket Books (New York, NY), 1999.

Voyage to a Free Land, 1630, Pocket Books (New York, NY), 1999.

Down the Rio Grande, 1829, Pocket Books (New York, NY), 2000.

Horseback on the Boston Post Road, 1704, Aladdin (New York, NY), 2000.

Exploring the Chicago World's Fair, 1893, Pocket Books (New York, NY), 2001.

Pacific Odyssey to California, 1905, Aladdin (New York, NY), 2001.

"ADDY ACROSS THE PRAIRIE" SERIES

Addie across the Prairie, illustrated by Gail Owens, A. Whitman (Morton Grove, IL), 1986.

Addie's Dakota Winter, illustrated by Toby Gowing, A. Whitman (Morton Grove, IL), 1989.

Addie's Long Summer, illustrated by Toby Gowing, A. Whitman (Morton Grove, IL), 1992.

George on His Own, illustrated by Toby Gowing, A. Whitman (Morton Grove, IL), 1993.

Luck Follows Me, A. Whitman (Morton Grove, IL), 1996.

Addie's Forever Friend, illustrated by Helen Cogancherry, A. Whitman (Morton Grove, IL), 1997.

Sidelights

Laurie Lawlor told *SATA:* "When I was growing up, we had strange and powerful creatures living in our house. Jack Frost and the Fat Lady were my first attempts at fiction. I'm proud to say that they successfully terrorized my five younger brothers and sisters for years. To this day, no one willingly goes into the attic alone. Why would anyone wish to create such characters? The answer, quite simply, is adventure. It's much more exciting living in a house with witches in the clothes chute than living in a normal house in a normal Chicago suburb. Creating adventure really is at the heart of what I enjoy about writing. I also believe it is at the heart of what children enjoy reading.

"*Addie across the Prairie* began as a personal adventure. For years I had heard stories passed down to my mother by my grandmother about how my Great Aunt Laura and her brothers and sisters traveled from Iowa to Dakota Territory to homestead. This family folklore intrigued but did not satisfy me. Perhaps it was my training as a journalist that made me want to know *exactly* what happened. What was it like to be nine years old, my Great Aunt Laura's age, and leave everything familiar behind? How did her family adjust? How did they survive? Ten lined, yellowed notebook pages launched my search. I discovered an account written by my Aunt Laura when she was married, fifty years old, and struggling to make a go of a homestead west of the

Convinced that their exasperating neighbor is probably a crook, four children team up to play detective and prove his guilt in The Worst Kid Who Ever Lived on Eighth Avenue, *written by Laurie Lawlor and illustrated by Cynthia Fisher.*

Missouri river. On these pages, titled 'Pioneering,' she told in simple, unassuming language the story of her childhood in Dakota. On the last page, her last sentence drifts toward a blot in the bottom corner. 'As I grow older it seems that every year is more like pioneering.' And that was all she wrote.

"The events described in *Addie across the Prairie* occurred more than one hundred years ago. What I particularly enjoy about historical fiction is the way it can explode time barriers. When a period of history is described as realistically and truthfully as a writer knows how, historical fiction allows readers a unique opportunity. They become time travelers, comparing and contrasting their own modern lives with that of a book's characters.

"What struck me again and again as I worked on *Addie* was the marvelous way humans can adapt. When our environment forces us, we can re-learn just about anything; how to find water, how to farm, how to build our houses, how to find fuel. We adjust, we adapt. Think about it. How different is the settlement of remote, hostile parts of the American West from the settlement of remote, hostile parts of our galaxy? The same child reading about Addie's adventures and comparing them with his or her own might one day really experience 'homesteading' in a space colony somewhere. It is this sense of possibility, of adventure, that I hope to convey to readers. What happens to Addie could have—or might one day—happen to them."

Lawlor's books have received high praise for making history, particularly the history of settling the American West in the nineteenth century, come alive for young readers more than a hundred years later. In biographies of real-life legends such as Daniel Boone and Johnny Appleseed, as well as in novels such as the "Addie across the Prairie" and "American Sisters" series, Lawlor teaches children about the social, political, and cultural milieu that makes sense of her characters' lives, and allows her readers to more accurately gauge their struggles as well as their triumphs. While Lawlor is occasionally faulted for paying less attention to character development than to historical context, she has also been praised for composing well-written, exciting historical narratives for children.

In Window on the West, *a biography of William Henry Jackson, Lawlor demonstrates how Jackson's photographs of the American West, taken from 1869 to 1893, captured the natural beauty of the area and the effects of pioneer settlers on the lives of animals and Native Americans.*

Lawlor first became known for her "Addie across the Prairie" series. This series showcases the author's strengths as a writer of historical fiction for children, including a child-centered narrative that is grounded in both a child's reality and in the history of pioneering the West in the 1880s. Other fictional attempts to bring to life this era include *Gold in the Hills* and *Old Crump: The True Story of a Trip West.* In *Gold in the Hills,* a man who has recently lost his wife becomes convinced he can make a fortune panning for gold in the Colorado mountains and leaves his children, Hattie and Pheme, with his cousin Tirzah while he gives it a try. The children's abandonment leaves them vulnerable to the meanness of Tirzah, and Hattie and Pheme are in danger of losing heart until they are befriended by an elderly woodsman. "Readers will be drawn into the mental anguish of these people as they evolve and show some emotional growth," predicted Rita Soltan in *School Library Journal.* Elizabeth Bush, writing in the *Bulletin of the Center for Children's Books,* praised Lawlor's effective characterization as well as her exciting plot, concluding that *Gold in the Hills* should be "as appealing to outdoorsy adventure buffs as it will be to orphan-story fans." *Old Crump: The True Story of a Trip West* is set earlier in the same century, during the long, perilous journey over the mountains and across Death Valley to reach California in 1849. The title character, Old Crump, is the family's faithful ox who tirelessly carries them across the rough terrain and is put out to pasture in gratitude once they arrive. Although a contributor to *Kirkus Reviews* found some factual inaccuracies in the text, a reviewer in *Publishers Weekly* noted that the story is based on period diaries, "making this a solid introduction to the historical journey to the West."

Young readers with a fascination for the world of Laura Ingalls Wilder will likely be attracted to Lawlor's "American Sisters" series, some critics noted. These are novels for middle-grade readers that were inspired by the author's research into pioneer history. Each narrative is interspersed with excerpts from the diaries of the actual people on whom Lawlor based her stories. In *Adventure on the Wilderness Road, 1775,* an eleven-year-old girl narrates her large family's arduous and dangerous journey on Daniel Boone's Wilderness Road to settle in Kentucky. Hazel Rochman, who reviewed the book for *Booklist,* remarked that a greater insight into the barely-glimpsed lives of the Native Americans would have been a welcome addition; yet "Lawlor's research is meticulous, and her narrative is true to the white child's viewpoint of the family adventure." In *West along the Wagon Road, 1852,* the first novel in the series, another eleven-year-old girl, one of seven girls and three boys in the family, narrates her family's journey in a covered-wagon caravan into Oregon Territory. "Lawlor's well-researched text and readable writing style make this book an excellent choice" for young fans of historical fiction, remarked Robin L. Gibson in *School Library Journal.* Two stepsisters appear in *Down the Rio Grande, 1829,* the sixth volume in the series. Although *School Library Journal* critic Betsy Barnett faulted Lawlor's use of magic to rescue her characters

from the worst of their predicaments, she also praised the author's depiction of the boat trip, the topography, and the era, as well as "excellent descriptions of Mexican culture, traditions, language, and people."

Lawlor is also known for her biographies for middle-grade readers. Among these is *Shadow-Catcher: The Life and Work of Edward S. Curtis.* Curtis spent the major part of his life tirelessly photographing the Native Americans of the American West, and while his work—including thirty volumes of haunting photographs and a film—did not garner success during his lifetime, it is now considered a priceless contribution to American history as it provides in many cases the only record of a people, a culture, and a way of life that have since disappeared. "Kids reading the book will get a real sense of the steady erosion of the once all-encompassing civilizations," remarked Deborah Stevenson in *Bulletin of the Center for Children's Books.* Other critics noted that Lawlor refuses to gloss over the less-appealing aspects of Curtis's personal life, sacrificing his relationship with his family in pursuit of his ambition, for example. Through this biography, "the reader will get a feel for the life and dedication of this artist as well as the sacrifices that he made," observed Susan DeRonne in *Booklist.*

A biography of another noted photographer of the nineteenth-century frontier, William Henry Jackson, also garnered critical praise. In *Window on the West: The Frontier Photography of William Henry Jackson,* Lawlor brings to light the last quarter of the nineteenth century, a time of cowboys, Indians, and the ever-expanding railroad. As in her other works, the strength of this book is considered to be its portrait of the America through which her subject walked. As a contributor to the *Horn Book* put it: "The reader gets only quick glimpses of [Jackson], yet the changing world in which he operated is abundantly explored." "This is much more than a look at early photography," proclaimed Randy Meyer in *Booklist,* "it's a memorable, bittersweet valentine to the Old West."

Lawlor investigates a legendary figure in another biography, *The Real Johnny Appleseed.* Here, relying extensively on her knowledge of the history of the era to fill in the gaps in the historical record, the author paints a portrait of John Chapman, who spent much of his life planting apple orchards in pursuit of the Swedenborgian ideal of helping others. "Lawlor's clear narrative style and impeccable scholarship combine to make this . . . an outstanding choice," wrote Susan Scheps in *School Library Journal.* A more recent notable American hero is the subject of another well regarded biography in *Helen Keller: Rebellious Spirit.* As in Lawlor's earlier biographies, her subject's life is well-grounded in its historical context, "making [Keller's] achievements seem all the more astounding given the era's prevailing discrimination against women and the disabled," remarked a contributor to *Horn Book.* And, as in her biography of Edward S. Curtis, reviewers favorably noted Lawlor's willingness to note her subject's flaws along with her virtues.

Lawlor moved out of the nineteenth century and into the twentieth with her "Heartland" series, beginning with *Come Away with Me* and *Take to the Sky,* both set in the early 1900s. Here the stage is set for stories that focus on the conflict between the demands of tradition and the lure of modern innovation, as Emily Kutler noted in *School Library Journal.* In *Come Away with Me,* twelve-year-old Moe gets into some scrapes when two older, more ladylike, cousins come for a visit, and in *Take to the Sky,* Moe and her best friend, Otto, build an airplane. "The books are humorous and well-paced," wrote Kutler.

Lawlor has also written several light-hearted contemporary mysteries, including *The Worst Kid Who Ever Lived on Eighth Avenue* and *The Biggest Pest on Eighth Avenue.* In the *Worst Kid,* the kids on Eighth Avenue become suspicious when they see a man burying something in his parents' backyard. In the *Biggest Pest,* these same kids are constantly annoyed during their preparations for a scary play by the interruptions of pesky little brother Tommy.

Reviewers delighted in Lawlor's history *Where Will This Shoe Take You?: A Walk Through the History of Footwear,* which a contributor to *Child Life* dubbed "a unique and cool way to look at history, one foot at a time." In this book, Lawlor states that throughout history, footwear has been an indicator of social and economic status, political tendencies, and level of power; she also surveys superstitions and traditions related to shoes. "Read this and you'll never look at your old sneakers the same way again," stated Elizabeth Bush in the *Bulletin of the Center for Children's Books.*

Biographical and Critical Sources

PERIODICALS

Booklist, August, 1992, Deborah Abbot, review of *Addie's Long Summer,* p. 2011; September 1, 1993, Kay Weisman, review of *George on His Own,* p. 61; December 1, 1994, Susan DeRonne, review of *Shadow-Catcher: The Life and Work of Edward S. Curtis,* p. 661; June 1, 1995, Frances Bradburn, review of *Gold in the Hills,* p. 1771; September 1, 1995, April Judge, review of *The Real Johnny Appleseed,* p. 71; November 15, 1996, Susan DeRonne, review of *Where Will This Shoe Take You?: A Walk through the History of Footwear,* p. 583; November 15, 1997, Susan Dove Lempke, review of *Addie's Forever Friend,* p. 560; May 1, 1998, Ilene Cooper, review of *The Worst Kid Who Ever Lived on Eighth Avenue,* p. 1524; December 1, 1998, John Peters, review of *West along the Wagon Road, 1852,* p. 667; April 1, 1999, Hazel Rochman, review of *Adventure on the Wilderness Road, 1775,* p. 1426; February 15, 2000, Randy Meyer, review of *Window on the West: The Frontier Photography of William Henry Jackson,* p. 1098; June 1, 2000, Helen Rosenberg, review of *Wind on the River,* p. 1882; April 1, 2001, Ilene Cooper, review of *Exploring the Chicago World's Fair, 1893,* p. 1483; September 1, 2001, Susan Dove Lempke, review of *Helen Keller: Rebellious Spirit,* p. 99.

Book Report, May-June, 1995, Tena Natale Litherland, review of *Shadow-Catcher,* p. 54; March-April, 1996, Pam Whitehead, review of *Gold in the Hills,* p. 36; March-April, 1997, Joan Chezem, review of *Where Will This Shoe Take You?,* p. 58.

Book World, May 7, 1995, Ilan Stavans, review of *Shadow-Catcher,* pp. 13, 18.

Bulletin of the Center for Children's Books, November, 1988, p. 77; December, 1989, p. 87; March, 1990, p. 168; November, 1992, p. 78; February, 1995, Deborah Stevenson, review of *Shadow-Catcher,* p. 205; July-August, 1995, Elizabeth Bush, review of *Gold in the Hills,* p. 388; November, 1995, Elizabeth Bush, review of *The Real Johnny Appleseed,* p. 97; January, 1997, Elizabeth Bush, review of *Where Will This Shoe Take You?,* p. 178.

Child Life, April-May, 1998, review of *Where Will This Shoe Take You?,* p. 20.

Entertainment Weekly, January 27, 1995, A. J. Jacobs, review of *Little Women,* p. 8.

Horn Book, January-February, 1995, Peter D. Sieruta, review of *Shadow-Catcher,* p. 75; March-April, 1997, Elizabeth S. Watson, review of *Where Will This Shoe Take You?,* p. 212; March, 2000, review of *Window on the West,* p. 214; September, 2001, review of *Helen Keller: Rebellious Spirit,* p. 611.

Horn Book Guide, fall, 1995, Martha V. Parravano, review of *Gold in the Hills,* p. 300; spring, 1998, Maeve Visser Knoth, review of *The Biggest Pest on Eighth Avenue,* p. 56; fall, 1998, Maeve Visser Knoth, review of *The Worst Kid Who Ever Lived on Eighth Street,* p. 313; fall, 1999, Bridget McCaffrey, review of *West along the Wagon Road, 1852* and *A Titanic Journey across the Sea,* p. 295.

Kirkus Reviews, February 15, 1998, review of *The Worst Kid Who Ever Lived on Eighth Street,* p. 270; March 1, 2002, review of *Old Crump: The True Story of a Trip West,* p. 337.

New York Review of Books, Alison Lurie, review of *Little Women,* p. 3.

Publishers Weekly, June 10, 1988, review of *How to Survive Third Grade,* p. 80; December 5, 1994, review of *Shadow-Catcher,* p. 78; May 29, 1995, review of *Gold in the Hills,* p. 86; June 24, 1996, review of *Come Away with Me,* p. 61; September 28, 1998, review of *West along the Wagon Road, 1852,* p. 102; January 17, 2000, review of *Window on the West,* p. 58; July 2, 2001, review of *Helen Keller,* p. 77; February 11, 2002, review of *Old Crump,* p. 185.

School Arts, May, 2000, Kent Marantz, review of *Window on the West,* p. 62.

School Library Journal, October, 1986, Elaine Lesh Morgan, review of *Addie across the Prairie,* p. 178; September, 1988, Annette Curtis Klause, review of *How to Survive Third Grade,* p. 184; December, 1988, Katharine Bruner, review of *Daniel Boone,* p. 128; January, 1990, Sylvia S. Marantz, review of *Addie's Dakota Winter,* p. 104; June, 1990, Leslie Barban, review of *Second-Grade Dog,* p. 103; November, 1992, Elizabeth Hamilton, review of *Addie's Long Summer,* p. 95; July, 1993, JoAnn Rees, review of *George on His Own,* p. 86; February, 1995, Nancy E. Curran, review of *Shadow-Catcher,* p. 121; August,

1995, Rita Soltan, review of *Gold in the Hills,* p. 142; January, 1996, Susan Scheps, review of *The Real Johnny Appleseed,* p. 120; November, 1996, Emily Kutler, review of *Come Away with Me* and *Take to the Sky,* p. 108; May, 1997, Wendy D. Caldiero, review of *Where Will This Shoe Take You?,* p. 148; February, 1998, Rosalyn Pierini, review of *Addie's Forever Friend,* p. 86; March, 1998, Sharon R. Pearce, review of *The Biggest Pest on Eight Avenue,* p. 182; April, 1998, Maura Bresnahan, *The Worst Kid Who Ever Lived on Eighth Avenue,* p. 102; December, 1998, Robin L. Gibson, review of *West along the Wagon Road, 1852,* p. 128; November, 1999, Betsy Barnett, review of *Adventure on Wilderness Road, 1775,* p. 160; March, 2000, Steven Engelfried, review of *Window on the West,* p. 256; January, 2001, Betsy Barnett, review of *Down the Rio Grande, 1829,* p. 132; August, 2001, Janie Schomberg, review of *Exploring the Chicago World's Fair, 1893,* p. 185; December, 2001, Kathleen Baxter, "We Could Be Heroes: From an Outspoken Boxer to a Teenage Saint, Four Amazing Lives," p. 39; June, 2002, Ruth Semrau, review of *Old Crump,* p. 98.

Wilson Library Bulletin, April, 1995, Linda Perkins, review of *Shadow-Catcher,* p. 116.

OTHER

Laurie Lawlor Web Site, http://www.laurielawlor.com (January 18, 2003).*

*   *   *

LEVIN, Betty 1927-

Personal

Born September 10, 1927, in New York, NY; daughter of Max (a lawyer) and Eleanor (a musician; maiden name, Mack) Lowenthal; married Alvin Levin (a lawyer), August 3, 1947 (died, 1987); children: Katherine, Bara, Jennifer. *Education:* University of Rochester, A.B. (high honors), 1949; Radcliffe College, M.A., 1951; Harvard University, A.M.T., 1951.

Addresses

Home—Old Winter St., Lincoln, MA 01773. *Agent*—Dorothy Markinko, McIntosh & Otis, Inc., 353 Lexington Ave., New York, NY 10016.

Career

Author, educator, and sheep farmer. Museum of Fine Arts, Boston, MA, assistant in research, 1951-52; part-time teaching fellow, Harvard Graduate School of Education, 1953; creative writing fellow, Radcliffe Institute, 1968-70; Massachusetts coordinator, McCarthy Historical Archive, 1969; Pine Manor Open College, Chestnut Hill, MA, instructor in literature, 1970-75; Minute Man Publications, Lexington, MA, feature writer, 1972; Center for the Study of Children's Literature, Simmons College, Boston, MA, special instructor in children's literature, 1975-77, adjunct professor of

Betty Levin

children's literature, 1977-87; instructor at Emmanuel College, Boston, MA, 1975, and at Radcliffe Seminars. Founding board member and member of steering committee, Children's Literature New England, until 1996.

Member

Authors Guild, Authors League of America, Masterworks Chorale, Children's Books Authors (Boston, MA), Middlesex Sheep Breeders Association.

Awards, Honors

Judy Lopez Memorial Award, 1989, for *The Trouble with Gramary;* Best Book for Young Adults citation, American Library Association, 1990, for *Brother Moose;* Books for the Teen Age selection, New York Public Library, 1993, for *Mercy's Mill;* Parents' Choice Story Book Award, 1994, for *Away to Me, Moss!;* Children's Book of the Year citation, Child Study Association, 1996, for *Gift Horse;* Hope Dean Award, Foundation for Children's Books, 2001.

Writings

NOVELS FOR CHILDREN

The Zoo Conspiracy, illustrated by Marian Parry, Hastings House (New York, NY), 1973.
The Sword of Culann, Macmillan (New York, NY), 1973.

A Griffon's Nest (sequel to *The Sword of Culann*), Macmillan (New York, NY), 1975.

The Forespoken (sequel to *A Griffon's Nest*), Macmillan (New York, NY), 1976.

Landfall, Atheneum (New York, NY), 1979.

The Beast on the Brink, illustrated by Marian Parry, Avon (New York, NY), 1980.

The Keeping-Room, Greenwillow (New York, NY), 1981.

A Binding Spell, Lodestar/Dutton (New York, NY), 1984.

Put on My Crown, Lodestar/Dutton (New York, NY), 1985.

The Ice Bear, Greenwillow (New York, NY), 1986.

The Trouble with Gramary, Greenwillow (New York, NY), 1988.

Brother Moose, Greenwillow (New York, NY), 1990.

Mercy's Mill, Greenwillow (New York, NY), 1992.

Starshine and Sunglow, illustrated by Joseph A. Smith, Greenwillow (New York, NY), 1994.

Away to Me, Moss!, Greenwillow (New York, NY), 1994.

Fire in the Wind, Greenwillow (New York, NY), 1995.

Gift Horse, Greenwillow (New York, NY), 1996.

Island Bound, Greenwillow (New York, NY), 1997.

Look Back, Moss, Greenwillow (New York, NY), 1998.

Creature Crossing, illustrated by Joseph A. Smith, Greenwillow (New York, NY), 1999.

The Banished, Greenwillow (New York, NY), 1999.

Shadow-Catcher, Greenwillow (New York, NY), 2000.

That'll Do, Moss, Greenwillow (New York, NY), 2002.

Shoddy Cove, Greenwillow (New York, NY), 2003.

OTHER

Contributor to books, including *Innocence and Experience: Essays and Conversations on Children's Literature,* compiled and edited by Barbara Harrison and Gregory Maguire, Lothrop (New York, NY), 1987; and *Proceedings for Travelers in Time,* Green Bay Press, 1990. Also contributor of articles to periodicals, including *Harvard Educational Review, Horn Book,* and *Children's Literature in Education.*

Levin's manuscripts are housed in the Kerlan Collection at the University of Minnesota.

Sidelights

Betty Levin transcends time in her young adult novels, often transporting contemporary teens into the past to encounter historical events and at other times weaving elements of myth and fantasy into her novels. Among the real settings Levin employs in her stories are modern-day Maine in *The Trouble with Gramary,* ancient Ireland in *The Sword of Culann,* and the Orkney Islands in *The Forespoken.* Within these settings, her characters often unravel mysteries and reach a higher level of maturity. "Levin is not an easy writer," stated Adele M. Fasick in *Twentieth-Century Children's Writers,* but "readers who are willing to immerse themselves in the strange settings and to struggle to understand the significance of mysterious events will find themselves embarking on an enriching experience."

Born in 1927, Levin grew up with her two older brothers in three different places, moving from a farm in

Bridgewater, Connecticut, to New York City, and then to Washington, D.C. Most summers were spent on the family farm, a place that nourished her affinity for animals. It was here that she first learned of the partnership possible between a human and a dog; and this partnership has helped Levin numerous times throughout her life, especially in her adult career as a sheep farmer. The family's move to Washington, D.C. in 1940 was hard for Levin, who took refuge in books such as *Caddie Woodlawn, Oliver Twist,* and *Gone with the Wind.* "Romanticism saved me from absolute degradation," Levin recalled in an essay for *Something about the Author Autobiography Series* (*SAAS*). "When I discovered Emily Bronte's *Wuthering Heights,* I found even more to satisfy than the sudsy romance of books like *Gone with the Wind.*"

Living through World War II, Levin was very aware of what German Dictator Adolf Hitler was doing and the way it affected her own community; prejudice became a part of daily life. "I had grown up with friends of all backgrounds," Levin revealed in *SAAS.* "I had hardly been aware of racial differences. That first year in Washington was a shock.... I was struggling, and not very well, with the realization that people really can systematically hurt other people." Levin's mother helped during this period of adjustment, taking her daughter to a concert of the great black contralto Marian Anderson and enrolling her in the National Cathedral School. In this place of serious academia, Levin learned with a multicultural student body and was encouraged to pursue her interest in writing.

After graduating from high school, Levin enrolled at the University of Rochester. Originally planning to major in voice, Levin changed her area of concentration to history and literature. Through a circle of literature-minded friends she met Alvin Levin, whom she married the summer before their junior year of college. In 1949 Levin's husband received a scholarship from Harvard Law School and the couple moved to Boston, where Levin also started graduate school. "It was for a seminar on the American city that I wrote a 250-page paper on literature about New York City," recalled Levin in *SAAS.* "I discovered and included children's books in that study. It was the beginning of my interest in the history of children's literature, which I have taught now for so many years."

Levin held several jobs while her husband completed law school, among them a post at the Museum of Fine Arts, a part-time teaching fellowship, and a job as a researcher. Inheriting a bit of money, the couple financed a family trip to Scotland and England—they now had their first daughter, Kathy. On their return home the couple was determined to build their own small farm in Lincoln.

Following the birth of her second child, Bara, Levin was diagnosed with polio during an epidemic of the disease in Boston; her husband contracted the disease two weeks later. Levin was lucky enough to suffer no lasting effects from the disease, but Alvin suffered with it for two years before he was able to return home. When things began to return to normal, Levin had her third child, Jennifer. "But we had to learn new ways of living and being parents, because Alvin never did recover the use of his legs and arms and much of his upper torso," explained Levin in *SAAS*. As the children grew, so did the Levin household as more sheep, puppies, stray cats, and a pony joined the family. For the next few years, most summers were passed on the family farm, where everyone congregated, including Levin's brothers and their families.

During the 1960s and early 1970s, Levin became increasingly active in civil rights and anti-war activities, while her husband served as a delegate at the Democratic Convention. As her political interests brought new friends into Levin's life, so did the sheep and sheep dogs she raised. All these activities and influences, together with a fellowship in creative writing at the Bunting Institute from 1968 to 1970, combined to inspire Levin's early juvenile novels. Beginning with a fantasy trilogy containing elements of Celtic and Norse mythology, Levin has gone on to explore a number of other worlds and historical periods through her fiction.

In the trilogy encompassing *The Sword of Culann, A Griffon's Nest,* and *The Forespoken,* Claudia, who lives on an island off the coast of Maine, travels back in time through the use of an ancient sword hilt. In the first two novels, she is accompanied by her stepbrother Evan, and they both visit medieval Ireland during the historical struggle between Queen Medb and the House of Culann. In *The Forespoken* Claudia travels to the Orkney Islands during the nineteenth century in search of a crow belonging to the old man who originally gave her the sword hilt.

"Levin is skillful in writing of the physical realities of both worlds, especially the cold, dampness, dirt, and hard physical labour," observed Fasick of the trilogy. A *Kirkus Reviews* contributor wrote of *The Sword of Culann:* "The characters are stirring creations, ... and although the plot is labyrinthian it's well worth staying on for the surprises and layered revelations at every turn." Finding the use of symbols, magic, and historical events to be implausible in *A Griffon's Nest,* another *Kirkus Reviews* critic concluded that "for the agile mind" the story is "an unusual adventure in time travel." In his *School Library Journal* review of the final novel in the trilogy, Andrew K. Stevenson found the numerous subplots confusing, but asserted that the "characterization is good, and the mystery and brutality of the islands is powerfully conveyed."

Maine is the setting of Levin's 1984 mystery/fantasy *A Binding Spell.* Unhappy about her family's move to a farm in Maine, Wren seems to be the only one able to see the ghost horse hiding in the mist around the farm. Her investigation of the ghostly vision leads Wren to a neighbor's reclusive Uncle Axel, the original owner of the ghost horse. Through her efforts to bring Axel back into reality, Wren is able to rid him of his haunted past, and the ghost horse disappears. "Levin's characters are

meticulous, and intermittent scenes are quite vivid," noted Denise M. Wilms in *Booklist,* while a *School Library Journal* reviewer maintained that in *A Binding Spell* Levin's "evocative prose ... turns even the commonplace into something magical."

1986's *The Ice Bear* is one of the first fantasy books in which Levin contains her story in a single world. Set in the primitive kingdom of Thyrne, the novel focuses on Wat, a bakeshop boy, and Kaila, a silent girl from the north, as they flee to the forest of Lythe to defend a white Ice Bear. Wat hopes to gain a reward from the king for protecting the precious animal, but Kaila wants only to return to her home in the north with the bear. During the course of their journey, both Wat and Kaila face many dangers, learning the consequences of their actions and the true meaning of freedom. "As always in Levin's work, a poignant tone underlies the action," pointed out Ruth S. Vose in *School Library Journal.* Zena Sutherland asserted in the *Bulletin of the Center for Children's Books* that *The Ice Bear* "has a good pace and sweep; the characters change and grow; the setting is roundly conceived."

Levin has also written a "prequel" to *The Ice Bear* titled *The Banished.* In this 1999 novel, a young girl named Siri helps to free her exiled tribe by aiding in the transport of an ice bear to the king. While making the dangerous voyage to deliver the bear to her ultimately untrustworthy king, Siri learns to respect people of other backgrounds. Calling the novel "an engaging fantasy," *Booklist* contributor Shelle Rosenfeld also lauded Levin for including a discussion of "wonderfully detailed, imaginative cultures and plenty of drama and suspense." In *Kirkus Reviews,* a contributor noted that while the author's "complex, atmospheric morality tale offers no easy answer," it takes place "in a world that is alien and exotic."

Levin's award-winning *Mercy's Mill* is a time-travel story in which three characters—Mercy, who lives in colonial America; Jethro, who is from the nineteenth century; and Sarah, who is a modern teen—find that they are able to interact with each other at an old mill and house in Massachusetts. Jethro and Mercy both have managed to escape their unhappy lives by traveling through time: Mercy traveled through time to meet Jethro, and Jethro moved forward in time to cross paths with Sarah. Sarah, who is unhappy with her own life, including a new stepfather and a home she dislikes, finds the prospect of escaping through time appealing, but as she learns more about the mill and its history, she becomes troubled by Jethro's secrets. Calling *Mercy's Mill* "a gripping tale," a *Publishers Weekly* contributor praised Levin for "masterfully explor[ing] ... the concept of time in an illuminating blend of history and fantasy." In her *Horn Book* review, Maeve Visser Knoth also had praise for the novel, particularly "Levin's ... strong characters, who by force of will lead the reader through the complex, multifaceted story.... [While some] flashbacks are confusing ... good readers will immerse themselves in Sarah's world."

In the same way that Levin does not write a typical time-travel story, Levin's *Away to Me, Moss!* is not just another dog story. Drawing on her extensive knowledge of sheep dogs and herding, Levin creates a "heartfelt and satisfying portrayal" of the bond between dogs and people, according to Wendy E. Betts in *Five Owls*. The novel describes how ten-year-old Zanna Walds's effort to help a Border collie develops into a caring relationship with the dog's owner. Rob Catherwood has suffered a stroke and can no longer give the commands his dog Moss needs to herd sheep; Moss has become unmanageable because of his frustration in not being able to do the work that is so much a part of him. In trying to help Moss and Rob, Zanna learns about sheep herding and discovers that she loves the work. Levin complicates the tale by telling of Zanna's parents' trial separation and how Rob might have to give up Moss to help pay for his rehabilitation. Critics praised Levin's adept handling of such a complicated plot: "the stress of both Zanna's and Rob's families is skillfully paralleled," according to Betsy Hearne in the *Bulletin of the Center for Children's Books*. "Levin sketches adult problems adroitly," remarked a *Kirkus Reviews* contributor, while in *Booklist* Ellen Mandel added that "the end result is not a magically happy resolution but a realistic and satisfying hope for better times for all."

The canine hero in *Away to Me, Moss!* rejoins readers in two sequels, *Look Back, Moss* and *That'll Do, Moss*. *Look Back, Moss* focuses on Jody, an overweight teen burdened by problems in his family, particularly his mother, whose radical animal-rights activities leave him cold. However, when one of his mother's questionable "rescue" efforts to liberate mistreated sheepdogs leaves Moss injured and near death, Jody suddenly finds that he and the struggling dog have a bond. As the dog gains in strength through Jody's care, the boy realizes that he must stand up to his mother and return Moss to his rightful owner so that the dog can continue the work for which he has been trained. In her *Booklist* review of *Look Back, Moss*, Debbie Carton praised Levin's "thoughtful depiction of both sides of the animal rights issue." *Bulletin of the Center for Children's Books* contributor Betsy Hearne also had praise for "the way Jody effects justice without … revealing his mother's part in breaking the law."

Levin has crafted novels such as *The Trouble with Gramary, Starshine and Sunglow, Fire in the Wind,* and *Brother Moose* against realistic backdrops. In *The Trouble with Gramary,* fourteen-year-old Merkka lives in a Maine seaside village with her mother, father, younger brother, and grandmother. As the town develops into a tourist attraction, influential people attempt to force Merkka's family from their home because of the welding business her grandmother, Gramary, runs out of the backyard. Struggling to understand her grandmother's ways, Merkka eventually learns to appreciate her nonconformity. "Although Merkka doesn't always understand her grandmother, the natural affinity between the two is unmistakable," noted Nancy Vasilakis in *Horn Book*. Eleanor K. MacDonald observed in her *School Library Journal* review that *The Trouble with Gramary*

is "a novel in which place, character, and circumstance mesh into a believable and satisfying whole."

Starshine and Sunglow also has a realistic fusing of character and setting. Young Ben, Kate, and Foster come to the rescue when their neighbors, the Flints, decide not to grow sweet corn for the first time in many years. Having supplied corn to the neighborhood for as long as Ben, Kate, and Foster can remember, the Flints are tired of dealing with the numerous animals who raid their fields. So, the children organize the growing of the corn and put together two scarecrows, Starshine and Sunglow, out of an old mop and an old broom. Put at first at opposite ends of the field, as the crops grow, the scarecrows mysteriously move to different locations in the field and are dressed in different clothes. Meanwhile, the children and the rest of the community come together to grow the corn and stop the critters from stealing it. "Accurate information about the challenges of farming are woven into the plot," observed Lee Bock in *School Library Journal*. A *Kirkus Reviews* contributor pointed out that the focus in *Starshine and Sunglow* "is on the nurturing of community spirit," concluding that "Levin has honed her easily read story with a grace and subtle humor." Characterizing the book as "quiet" and "old-fashioned," *Horn Book* contributor Nancy Vasilakis praised Levin's "subdued" prose, noting that it "appropriately reflects the sentiments of this gentle story, in which the characters and plot are sketched rather than filled out, leaving much for the imagination to fill in."

Ben, Kate, and Foster return in Levin's *Creature Crossing,* as Ben discovers a lizard-like creature he is convinced is some sort of dinosaur. When the creature turns out to be an endangered spotted salamander, the children are at first disappointed, then drawn into efforts to preserve the local population, many of which will be run over by traffic as they attempt to migrate. "Lessons about nature are ably handled [and] made part of the story in a gentle, unobtrusive way," commented a *Horn Book* contributor. *Booklist* contributor Shelle Rosenfeld noted that "Readers will enjoy the suspense of learning the creature's identity," calling the follow-up to *Starshine and Sunglow* "engaging." Noting that the novel would be useful for ecology studies, *School Library Journal* reviewer Cheryl Cufari added that "the characters are well defined and light suspense keeps readers interested."

Fire in the Wind takes place in the years following World War II, and focuses on a family who lives in the northern woods of Maine. Meg Yeadon worries that her cousin Orin might be "backward" but does not want to do anything that would force her parents to curtail Orin's way of life. However, after the latest in a series of mysterious fires burns down the family house, Meg is forced to tell her parents that she saw Orin actually lighting a fire nearby that same night. When she finds out that what she actually witnessed was Orin lighting a "backfire" that directed the main fire away from the barn, she realizes that her worries over her cousin are unfounded. *Fire in the Wind*'s "vivid setting and details of life during and after a terrifying fire are memorable," noted *Horn Book* contributor Maeve Visser Knoth, "and the balance of a tense plot with strong characterization makes this a powerful read."

Like *Fire in the Wind, Brother Moose* is a historical novel that focuses on the troubles encountered by many orphaned children during the later nineteenth century. Sent by well-intentioned adoption agencies from the squalid poverty of the eastern cities to a healthy rural environment, many orphaned boys and girls found themselves reduced to little more than slaves, as farm families exploited the orphaned youngsters as a way to gain free farm hands. In other cases, the long trip proved too grueling as many children were in poor health. Levin's story illustrates still another possibility in relating the story of Nell and friend Louisa as they attempt to travel from Canada to northern Maine, Nell to join a new family and Louisa to escape an abusive foster home. Along the way, they find themselves lost in the Maine wilderness. Discovered by a Native American named Joe, the two girls are saved from starvation and aided in finding their adoptive family, despite the fact that Joe has secrets that prevent him from helping the girls directly. Calling the novel "successful," a *Publishers Weekly* contributor praised Levin for "reveal[ing] ... the plight of nineteenth-century orphans and expos[ing] ... the settlers' unfair treatment of Native Americans."

Shadow-Catcher is another historical novel from Levin, this one combining an historical setting and situation with a mystery. It is the 1890s, and budding detective Jonathan Capewell is on a trip across Maine with his elderly grandfather, a photographer, when the two witness a logger in jeopardy on the river. The photographs his grandfather took of the incident soon attract the interest of a stranger named Mr. Whittaker, and Jonathan becomes suspicious of Whittaker's concerted effort to buy the photos. Praising the work as a solid coming-of-age tale in her review for *School Library Journal*, reviewer Carol A. Edwards noted that Levin possesses a "style [that] is well suited to this story that explores family dynamics and social mores as well as the vast difficulties in daily life."

Although Levin's work continues to encompass a variety of settings and themes, the author sees an overall connection. "The themes I'm drawn to and the situations I explore through fiction reflect not only the places and people and ways of life I love, but also the baffling aspects of the human condition—human traits that sadden and trouble me," the author explained in *SAAS*. "I see connections between some of the tiny experiences in my early childhood and unavoidable truths about callousness and cruelty."

Biographical and Critical Sources

BOOKS

Authors and Artists for Young Adults, Volume 23, Gale (Detroit, MI), 1998.
St. James Guide to Children's Writers, 5th edition, St. James Press (Detroit, MI), 1999.

Something about the Author Autobiography Series, Volume 11, Gale (Detroit, MI), 1991, pp. 197-211.
Twentieth-Century Children's Writers, 4th edition, St. James Press (Detroit, MI), 1995.

PERIODICALS

Booklist, November 15, 1984, Denise M. Wilms, review of *A Binding Spell,* p. 449; May 1, 1990, p. 1598; December 1, 1992, p. 670; May 1, 1994, Carolyn Phelan, review of *Starshine and Sunglow,* p. 1598; October 1, 1994, Ellen Mandel, review of *Away to Me, Moss,* p. 327; October 1, 1996, Lauren Peterson, review of *Gift Horse,* p. 352; July, 1997, John Peters, review of *Island Bound,* p. 1819; August, 1998, Debbie Carton, review of *Look Back, Moss,* p. 122; March 1, 1999, Shelle Rosenfeld, review of *Creature Crossing,* p. 1214; August, 1999, Shelle Rosenfeld, review of *The Banished,* p. 2058; May 15, 2000, Shelle Rosenfeld, review of *Shadow-Catcher,* p. 1742; August, 2002, Ellen Mandel, review of *That'll Do, Moss,* p. 1964.
Bulletin of the Center for Children's Books, January, 1976, p. 81; April, 1981, p. 155; July-August, 1985; January, 1987, Zena Sutherland, review of *The Ice Bear,* pp. 91-92; May, 1990, p. 219; December, 1994, Betsy Hearne, review of *Away to Me, Moss!,* pp. 135-136; January, 1996, Elizabeth Bush, review of *Fire in the Wind,* p. 165; November, 1996, Deborah Stevenson, review of *Gift Horse,* p. 105; November, 1997, Deborah Stevenson, review of *Island Bound,* pp. 90-91; October, 1998, Betsy Hearne, review of *Look Back, Moss,* p. 64.
Children's Book Review Service, November, 1997, review of *Island Bound,* p. 35.
Fantasy Review, January, 1987, p. 45.
Five Owls, February, 1995, Wendy E. Betts, review of *Away to Me, Moss!,* pp. 63-64.
Horn Book, February, 1977; December, 1979, pp. 669-670; January-February, 1987, Ethel L. Heins, review of *The Ice Bear,* p. 102; May-June, 1988, Nancy Vasilakis, review of *The Trouble with Gramary,* pp. 353-354; September-October, 1990, Nancy Vasilakis, review of *Brother Moose,* p. 605; January-February, 1993, Maeve Visser Knoth, review of *Mercy's Mill,* p. 92; September-October, 1994, Nancy Vasilakis, review of *Starshine and Sunglow,* pp. 587-588; March-April, 1996, Maeve Visser Knoth, review of *Fire in the Wind,* p. 196; January, 1999, Elizabeth S. Watson, review of *Look Back, Moss,* p. 67; May, 1999, Nancy Vasilakis, review of *Creature Crossing,* p. 331; November, 1999, Jennifer M. Brabander, review of *The Banished,* p. 742; July, 2000, review of *Shadow-Catcher,* p. 461.
Kirkus Reviews, November 1, 1973, review of *The Sword of Culann,* pp. 1212-1213; April 15, 1975, review of *A Griffon's Nest,* p. 465; July 15, 1976, p. 799; August 15, 1992, p. 1064; May 15, 1994, review of *Starshine and Sunglow,* p. 702; October 15, 1994, review of *Away to Me, Moss!,* pp. 1410-1411; August 15, 1996, review of *Gift Horse,* p. 1238; June 15, 1997, review of *Island Bound,* pp. 951-952; July 1, 1999, review of *The Banished,* pp. 1055-1056.
Learning Teacher, May, 1993, p. 33.

People, December 17, 1984, review of *A Binding Spell,* p. 45.

Publishers Weekly, June 18, 1973, p. 70; May 29, 1981, review of *The Keeping Room,* p. 42; May 11, 1990, review of *Brother Moose,* p. 261; September 21, 1992, review of *Mercy's Mill,* p. 95; June 5, 2000, review of *Shadow-Catcher,* p. 95.

Quill & Quire, February, 1991, p. 25.

School Library Journal, September, 1973, p. 71; October, 1973, p. 126; October, 1976, Andrew K. Stevenson, review of *The Forespoken,* p. 118; November, 1979, pp. 89-90; May, 1981, Drew Stevenson, review of *The Keeping Room,* p. 86; December, 1984, review of *A Binding Spell,* p. 101; October, 1986, Ruth S. Vose, review of *The Ice Bear,* p. 192; April, 1988, Eleanor K. MacDonald, review of *The Trouble with Gramary,* p. 102; July, 1990, p. 77; September, 1992, p. 278; June, 1994, Lee Bock, review of *Starshine and Sunglow,* p. 132; November, 1996, Christina Linz, review of *Gift Horse,* p. 108; June, 1999, Cheryl Cufari, review of *Creature Crossing,* p. 100; October, 1999, Patricia A. Dollisch, review of *The Banished,* p. 154; July, 2000, Carol A. Edwards, review of *Shadow-Catcher,* p. 106; October, 2002, Sally Bates Goodroe, review of *That'll Do, Moss,* p. 168.

Times Educational Supplement, June 5, 1987, p. 64.

Times Literary Supplement, July 24, 1987, p. 804.

Voice of Youth Advocates, August, 1981, pp. 29-30; August, 1988, p. 132.

Wilson Library Bulletin, October, 1988, p. 78.*

M

MACAULAY, David (Alexander) 1946-

Personal

Born December 2, 1946, in Burton-on-Trent, England; emigrated to the U.S. in 1957; son of James (a textile machine technician) and Joan (Lowe) Macaulay; married Janice Elizabeth Michel (an organist and choir director), June 13, 1970 (divorced); married Ruth Marris, August 19, 1978 (divorced); married Ruth Ellen Murray, 1997; children: (first marriage) Elizabeth Alexandra, (second marriage) Charlotte Valerie.

Addresses

Home—Rhode Island.

Career

Rhode Island School of Design, Providence, RI, instructor in interior design, 1969-73, instructor in two-dimensional design, 1974-76, adjunct faculty, department of illustration, 1976-90, chair, 1977-79; freelance illustrator and writer, 1979—. Public school art teacher, Central Falls, RI, 1969-70, and Newton, MA, 1972-74; designer, Morris Nathanson Design, 1969-72. Visiting lecturer, Yale University, 1978-79, Simmons College, 1989-90; visiting instructor, Brown University, 1982-86; visiting professor of art, Wellesley College, 1985-87. Worked as a consultant and presenter for television shows produced by Unicorn Projects, Washington, DC, including "Castle," 1982; "Cathedral," 1985; and "Pyramid," 1987; presenter of television show "Sense of Place," WJAR-TV, Providence, RI, 1988. Trustee, Partners for Livable Places, Washington, DC, Slater Mill Historical Site, Pawtucket, RI, and Community Preparatory School, Providence, RI. *Exhibitions:* Works displayed at several exhibitions, including the Annual International Exhibition of Children's Book Illustrations (Bologna, Italy), and *200 Years of American Illustration*, Museum of History, New York, NY; works held in the permanent collections of Cooper Hewitt Museum, Toledo Museum of Art, and Museum of Art, Rhode Island School of Design.

Awards, Honors

New York Times Ten Best Illustrated Books citation, 1973, American Institute of Graphic Arts Children's Book Show citation, 1973-74, Caldecott Honor Book, American Library Association (ALA), and Children's Book Showcase title, both 1974, Jugendbuchpreis (Germany) and Silver Slate Pencil Award (Holland), both 1975, all for *Cathedral: The Story of Its Construction;* Children's Book Showcase title, 1975, for *City: A Story of Roman Planning and Construction;* Christopher Award, and *New York Times* Outstanding Children's Book of the Year, both 1975, *Boston Globe-Horn Book* honor book, and Children's Book Showcase title, both 1976, all for *Pyramid; New York Times* Outstanding Children's Book of the Year, 1976, Children's Book Showcase title, and *School Library Journal* "Best of the Best 1966-1976" citation, 1978, all for *Underground; New York Times Book Review* Outstanding Book of the Year, 1977, New York Academy of Sciences Children's Science Book Award honor, Caldecott Honor Book, ALA, and *Boston Globe-Horn Book* honor book, all 1978, all for *Castle;* Washington Children's Book Guild Award, 1977, for body of work; American Institute of Architects Medal, 1978, for his contribution as "an outstanding illustrator and recorder of architectural accomplishment"; ALA Best Books for Young Adults and New York Public Library's Books for the Teen Age citations, 1980, both for *Motel of the Mysteries; New York Times* Ten Best Illustrated Books, *New York Times Book Review* Notable Book citation, and Parents' Choice Award for illustration in children's books, all 1980, New York Academy of Sciences Award honor, and Parents' Choice Award for Children's Books, both 1981, and Ambassador of Books-across-the-Sea honor book, English-Speaking Union, 1982, all for *Unbuilding; New York Times Book Review* Notable Book of the Year, 1982, for *Help! Let Me Out!; School Library Journal's* Best Books and New York Public Library's Children's Books citations, both 1983, both for *Mill;* nominated for

128

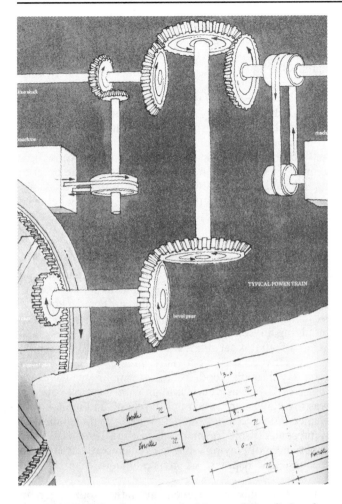

David Macaulay documents the history of four fictional mill buildings in New England, from an early cotton mill of 1810 to a 1974 structure converted into apartments and condominiums. (From Mill, *written and illustrated by Macaulay.*)

Hans Christian Andersen Illustrator Medal, 1984; honorary Doctor of Literature, Rhode Island College, 1987; honorary Doctor of Humanities, Savannah College of Art and Design, 1987; Parents' Choice Award for Children's Books, 1987, for *Why the Chicken Crossed the Road; Times Educational Supplement* Senior Information Book Award, science book prize for under sixteen, The Science Museum/Copus (London, England), and *Boston Globe-Horn Book* Award for best nonfiction book, all 1989, American Institute of Physics Best Science Book of the Year Award, and Charlotte Book Award, both 1990, all for *The Way Things Work;* Caldecott Medal, ALA, 1991, for *Black and White;* Bradford Washburn Medal, Boston Music Society, 1993; Charles Frankel prize, National Endowment for the Humanities, 1995; Chevalier of Order of Arts and Letters (France), 1995.

Writings

SELF-ILLUSTRATED

Cathedral: The Story of Its Construction, Houghton Mifflin (Boston, MA), 1973, revised edition published as

Building the Book Cathedral, Houghton Mifflin (Boston, MA), 1999.

City: A Story of Roman Planning and Construction, Houghton Mifflin (Boston, MA), 1974.

Pyramid, Houghton Mifflin (Boston, MA), 1975.

Underground, Houghton Mifflin (Boston, MA), 1976.

Castle, Houghton Mifflin (Boston, MA), 1977.

Great Moments in Architecture, Houghton Mifflin (Boston, MA), 1978.

Motel of the Mysteries, Houghton Mifflin (Boston, MA), 1979.

Unbuilding, Houghton Mifflin (Boston, MA), 1980.

Mill, Houghton Mifflin (Boston, MA), 1983.

Baaa, Houghton Mifflin (Boston, MA), 1985.

Why the Chicken Crossed the Road, Houghton Mifflin (Boston, MA), 1987.

The Way Things Work, Houghton Mifflin (Boston, MA), 1988; revised and updated edition (with Neil Ardley) *The New Way Things Work,* 1998.

Black and White, Houghton Mifflin (Boston, MA), 1990.

Ship, Houghton Mifflin (Boston, MA), 1993.

Shortcut, Houghton Mifflin (Boston, MA), 1995.

Rome Antics, Houghton Mifflin (Boston, MA), 1997.

Pinball Science (CD-ROM), DK Interactive Learning (New York, NY), 1998.

The Road to Rome: A Rome Antic Journey of the Creative Process (Frances Clarke Sayers Lecture delivered at the University of California—Los Angeles, February 20, 2000), California Center for the Book (Los Angeles, CA), 2000.

Building Big, Houghton Mifflin (Boston, MA), 2000.

Angelo, Houghton Mifflin (Boston, MA), 2002.

Mosque, Houghton Mifflin (Boston, MA), 2003.

Contributor of illustrated articles to magazines, including *Washington Post. The Way Things Work* has been translated into French and Spanish.

ILLUSTRATOR

David L. Porter, *Help! Let Me Out!,* Houghton Mifflin (Boston, MA), 1982.

Bill Sims, *Electricity,* Tennessee Valley Authority (Knoxville, TN), 1983.

Robert Ornstein and Richard F. Thompson, *The Amazing Brain,* Houghton Mifflin (Boston, MA), 1984.

Cartoonist for *Architectural Record,* 1990—.

Adaptations

The following works were adapted and broadcast by PBS-TV: *Castle,* October, 1983; *Cathedral,* 1985; and *Pyramid,* 1987.

Sidelights

David Macaulay is best known for his uncanny ability to explain to young readers how things are built, how gadgets work, and how abstract ideas become concrete reality. An author-illustrator with a background in architecture, Macaulay has won numerous important awards for bringing interest and clarity to the subjects of architecture and technology. *Times Educational Supple-*

ment correspondent Valerie Alderson noted that Macaulay "certainly has a gift for putting across the complexities of construction engineering which should be the envy of most of our writers of children's nonfiction." Likewise, Alvin Eisenman, writing in *Children's Book Showcase,* called Macaulay "a born teacher with an interest in things nobody before had the skill or the courage to try to explain."

Macaulay once told Joseph O. Holmes in *Publishers Weekly:* "I consider myself first and foremost an illustrator, in the broadest sense, someone who makes things clear through pictures and teaches through pictures." Through his line drawings, readers can ascend the heights of a cathedral ceiling and descend into the depths of a city sewer system. Little touches of humor lurk in many illustrations, and human characters provide a sense of perspective. In the *Children's Literature Association Quarterly,* Joyce A. Thomas observed that Macaulay's works "exemplify some of the best in nonfiction illustration.... Macaulay's illustrations are often impressive in themselves, always provide an accurate complement to his text, and extend his words in a way that allows the reader-viewer to live the building of that castle or that cathedral. Instead of passively witnessing, one imaginatively participates."

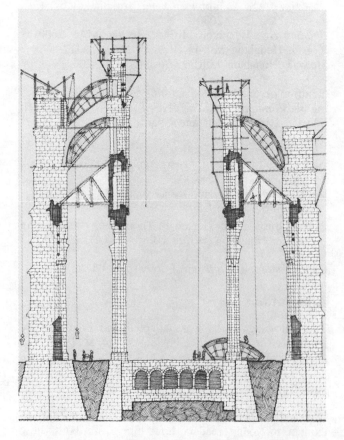

Analyzing the text of his book Cathedral *upon the twenty-fifth anniversary of its publication, Macaulay explains the process of creating the intricate drawings for which he is so well known.* (From Building the Book Cathedral, *written and illustrated by Macaulay.*)

Macaulay was no passive witness even as a child. In an acceptance speech given at the 1991 Caldecott Medal ceremony, the author lovingly recalled his "problem parents," who used the family kitchen as a workshop for their various projects. "We got used to seeing people make things," Macaulay remarked in *Horn Book.* "My siblings and I were systematically and brutally denied mystification of process. We were blatantly encouraged to make things, to understand how things went together and how they came apart. Maybe we didn't know *how* everything was made, but we knew there was an order to it, and we knew there was a right way to do things. By the time we got out of that kitchen, we actually believed that creativity and craftsmanship were desirable—even normal."

Macaulay was born in England, and he remembers his childhood there was particularly happy. He combined an interest in making things with an active imagination, sometimes constructing string-and-cardboard cable car systems in the family sitting room, and sometimes indulging in solitary adventures in the nearby woods. "One of the great things about Bolton, Lancashire, where I lived, was the twenty-minute walk to school each day through woods past a stream," Macaulay once told *SATA.* "I was very familiar with the area, since it was my playground when not in school, and it allowed a chance to let the mind wander. Whenever the opportunity presented itself for me to daydream, I did.... Those experiences of playing alone are remembered as some of the best and happiest of my childhood."

When Macaulay was eleven, his father took a job in America. The family moved to New Jersey—"an incredible shock," as the author once told *SATA.* At first Macaulay was uncomfortable with his American contemporaries, who seemed so much more worldly-wise and mature. "My childhood came to an end between the sixth and seventh grades, but my imagination never stopped protecting me, coming back into play when I needed it," he told *SATA.* After five years in New Jersey, the family moved to Rhode Island, where Macaulay discovered his talent for drawing, amusing himself and his classmates by producing drawings of the Beatles. After high school, Macaulay entered the Rhode Island School of Design to study architecture. "Since then, I have realized that what I was learning in architecture— how to break down an immense problem into its smallest parts and put it back together locally with knowledge, expertise, and imagination—could also be applied to making books," Macaulay told *SATA.*

Macaulay's first attempt at making books was a story about a gargoyle beauty pageant; the illustrations featured the ugly beasts flying around in a Gothic cathedral. The editors at Houghton Mifflin did not care for the gargoyle story, but they were intrigued by Macaulay's drawings of the immense church. They commissioned Macaulay to create a picture book about the construction of a cathedral and sent him off to France to do the research. The result was the award-winning *Cathedral: The Story of Its Construction,* a work that details the building of a great Gothic cathedral

In his Building Big, *Macaulay scrutinized structures such as bridges and domes and details the process of planning, designing, and problem solving in architectural construction.*

in a fictitious town from the conception of the plans to the first service in the finished sanctuary.

Macaulay followed *Cathedral* with a string of similar titles, all done with his meticulous pen-and-ink illustrations: *City: A Story of Roman Planning and Construction, Pyramid, Castle,* and *Mill. Times Literary Supplement* reviewer Mary Furness claimed that the books, with their "beautiful and clear black-and-white line drawings," succeed in making "the most complicated building process comparatively easy to understand." Similarly, in *Children and Books,* Zena Sutherland and May Hill Arbuthnot concluded that "David Macaulay's books on architectural landmarks of the past ... have been for many years and are likely to be for many more, some of the best of their type."

With his reputation solidly established, Macaulay tried some more daring projects. In *Underground,* he explained the complicated system of pipes, subway trains, and sewer drains beneath a city street. *Unbuilding* reverses the building process, showing how New York City's Empire State Building might be dismantled piece by piece at the whim of a rich businessman. *Motel of the Mysteries,* one of the author's humorous works, pokes fun at the unfounded generalizations some archaeologists make when confronted with ancient artifacts. In *Why the Chicken Crossed the Road,* Macaulay poses a series of answers to this old-fashioned riddle using a chicken, a herd of cows, a bridge, a train robber, the fire department, and hydrangea blossoms. A reviewer for the *New York Times Book Review* remarked that "although this is a picture book for young children, there are undoubtedly adults who would be interested in the solution to the age-old question." In contrast, Macaulay's *Baaa* is considered a rather bleak contribution to literature in its depiction of a human race that has disappeared, to be replaced by sheep, who repeat the same mistakes as the humans before them, and also disappear.

Perhaps Macaulay's most ambitious book to date is *The Way Things Work,* first published in 1988. Using humorous line drawings and silly fictitious scientists, the author explains how many gadgets work, from relatively simple things such as zippers and nail clippers to the automatic transmission in a car. In an interview for *Contemporary Authors New Revision Series,* Macaulay said: "We seem to have developed blind spots, and certainly one of them is towards technology.... If *The Way Things Work* does anything, I hope it says to readers, You can figure it out. Follow this through and you'll understand how it works." *The Way Things Work* was a tremendous success, selling more than two million copies over the course of the next decade. Then, in 1998, Macaulay published *The New Way Things Work,* updating the original text and adding nearly a hundred pages of new material, most of it concerning computers. As in all of Macaulay's books, the artwork does much of the work of a narrative explanation. As Stephanie Zvirin observed in a *Booklist* review of *The New Way Things Work,* "The emphasis on the visuals makes the science easier to grasp as well as fun to browse."

In 1991, Macaulay received the Caldecott Medal for *Black and White,* a picture book with four stories that overlap in a collage effect. Liz Rosenberg, writing in the *New York Times Book Review,* remarked that the book is "full of surprises, hidden corners, and revelations.... In its oddity and fixed unfixity it is a genuine original, and may perhaps become a children's puzzle classic." Macaulay told *Horn Book* that recognition of that particular title "tells readers, especially young ones, that it is essential to see, not merely to look; that words and pictures can support each other; that it isn't necessary to think in a straight line to make sense; and finally that risk can be rewarded." Reviewers compared the multiple narratives of *Black and White* to Macaulay's approach in *Shortcut,* in which a number of unrelated characters each engage in a simple act that has enormous repercussions in the life of another character, unbeknownst to them. For example, two farmers travel to market with a load of melons for sale and move a rope that blocks their road; that rope provided mooring for the hot-air balloon of a professor conducting research; the ballast he throws overboard in order to avoid crashing capsizes a boat below, and so forth. "Full of motion and humorous details, the colorful illustrations expand the story with wit and verve," wrote *Booklist* contributor Carolyn Phelan.

A master plasterer finds a wounded pigeon in the facade of the Roman church he is restoring and adopts the bird in Macaulay's self-illustrated **Angelo.**

Another successful example of Macaulay's talent for fiction writing is *Angelo,* a picture book in which an elderly architectural restorer begrudgingly nurses a sickly pigeon back to health only to find he has made a friend who sees him through to the end of his life. Reviewers universally found the story "offbeat" and "charming," but were also quick to point out that Macaulay's illustrations not only contained his signature visual humor, but also his signature tributes to architectural monuments. "Macaulay's watercolor illustrations provide a cornucopia of surprises, architectural details, and humorous touches," remarked Marianne Saccardi in *School Library Journal.* The story itself is a balancing act "of sympathy and silliness," according to a contributor to *Kirkus Reviews,* who concluded that *Angelo* "may be just as important as *Cathedral,* if not as grand."

Macaulay revisited the architecture of Rome from the perspective of a pigeon in another book, *Rome Antics.* Here, a homing pigeon with a message tied to its leg decides to take a detour en route over Rome and visit the city's greatest monuments. "Macaulay's illustrations recall elegant copper-plate engravings from earlier centuries, with every plane delineated by fine lines or fields of cross-hatching that are a marvel of intricacy," remarked David W. Dunlap in the *New York Times Book Review.* A dual perspective also enlivens *Ship,* in which Macaulay simultaneously takes the reader underwater to watch an excavation of a five-hundred-year-old ship, and back in time to a recreation of the ship's original construction in Seville in 1504. Though a work of fiction, *Ship* is built upon the foundation of Macaulay's meticulous research into ancient ship-building techniques and modern archaeological methods. "Fascinating in its dual perspective, *Ship* involves readers through Macaulay's original approach to an intriguing subject," concluded Carolyn Phelan in *Booklist.*

Over the years, the educational thrust and visual vitality of Macaulay's books have made them a natural choice for the producers of the Public Broadcasting System (PBS) to adapt for television, but with the book that eventually became *Building Big,* the television series came first. For this ambitious five-part series, which aimed to introduce its audience to all the major bridges, tunnels, skyscrapers, dams, and domes, the author-artist signed on as executive producer. With filming completed, Macaulay returned to his Rhode Island home to begin writing the book. "I knew that the films would provide the big picture and that I was free to operate on a much smaller scale," he told Sally Lodge in a *Publishers Weekly* interview. "In that sense, the book is my personality, which is nuts and bolts—that is, focusing on what the problem was that people were trying to solve here and how they went about it." This is, indeed, Macaulay's forte, according to reviewers. A contributor to *Publishers Weekly* observed, that "as he delves into the history as well as the mechanics of each project ... Macaulay is in his element, nimbly deploying his gift for making the arcane accessible." Though the book and the television series each stand alone, "together they offer a highly entertaining, instructive glimpse at some of construction's greatest stories, giving young people and

adults the skills to look more closely at the structures around them," concluded Gillian Engberg in *Booklist.*

Biographical and Critical Sources

BOOKS

Alvin Eisenman, editor, *Children's Book Showcase,* Children's Book Council (New York, NY), 1977.
Authors and Artists for Young Adults, Volume 21, Gale (Detroit, MI), 1997.
Children's Literature Review, Gale (Detroit, MI), Volume 3, 1978; Volume 14, 1988.
Dictionary of Literary Biography, Volume 61: *American Writers for Children since 1960: Poets, Illustrators, and Nonfiction Authors,* Gale (Detroit, MI), 1987.
Holtze, Sally Holmes, editor, *Fifth Book of Junior Authors and Illustrators,* H. W. Wilson (New York, NY), 1983, pp. 199-201.
St. James Guide to Children's Writers, 5th edition, St. James Press (Detroit, MI), 1999.
Silvey, Anita, editor, *Children's Books and Their Creators,* Houghton Mifflin (Boston, MA), 1995, p. 424.
Sutherland, Zena, and May Hill Arbuthnot, "Artists and Children's Books: David Macaulay," and "Informational Books: Evaluating Informational Books," in *Children and Books,* 7th edition, Scott, Foresman (Glenview, IL), 1986, pp. 484-487.

PERIODICALS

Architecture, July, 2000, Mickey O'Connor, "PBS Unveils New David Macaulay Film, Book," p. 47.
Booklist, October 15, 1993, Carolyn Phelan, review of *Ship,* p. 437; October 15, 1995, Carolyn Phelan, review of *Shortcut,* p. 412; September 15, 1997, Randy Meyer, review of *Rome Antics,* p. 235; December 1, 1998, Stephanie Zvirin, review of *The New Way Things Work,* p. 674; April 1, 1999, Stephanie Zvirin, review of *The New Way Things Work,* p. 1382, and review of *Rome Antics,* p. 1383; November 15, 1999, Susan Dove Lempke, review of *Building the Book Cathedral,* p. 620; December 1, 1999, Jack O'Gorman, review of *The New Way Things Work,* p. 732; December 15, 2000, Gillian Engberg, review of *Building Big,* p. 808, and "Spotlight on Art," p. 809; July, 2002, Gillian Engberg, review of *Angelo,* p. 1859.
Book Report, May-June, 1989, Alice Benjey, review of *The Way Things Work,* p. 58; May-June, 1995, Barbara Jo McKee, review of *Roman City,* p. 64.
Business Week, December 16, 1996, Karen Pennar, "David Macaulay Explains It All: The Author Is One of a New Breed—Information Architects," p. 68.
Canadian Literature, winter, 1990, Carole Gerson, review of *The Way Things Work,* p. 124.
Chicago Tribune, December 14, 1988.
Childhood Education, summer, 1989, Joan S. Keenan, review of *The Way Things Work,* p. 245.
Children's Literature Association Quarterly, winter, 1981-82, Joyce A. Thomas, review of *Cathedral, Castle, City,* and *Underground,* p. 27.
Discover, October, 2000, Fenella Saunders, review of *Building Big,* p. 100.

English Journal, April, 1984, Dick Abrahamson and Barbara Keifer, review of *Mill,* p. 92; January, 1988, John W. Conner and Kathleen M. Tessmer, review of *Baaa,* p. 101.

Entertainment Weekly, December 3, 1993, Leonard S. Marcus, review of *Ship,* p. 93; October 21, 1994, Leonard S. Marcus, "See Spot ROM," p. 83; December 8, 2000, Clarissa Cruz, "Bound for Glory: A Bevy of Books," p. 85.

Family Life, December 1, 2000, review of *Building Big,* p. 127.

Horn Book, December, 1980, Christine McDonnell, review of *Unbuilding,* p. 655; December, 1983, Ethel R. Twichell, review of *Mill,* p. 726; July-August, 1987, Gertrude Herman, "A Picture Is Worth Several Hundred Words," p. 498; January-February, 1988, Hanna B. Zeiger, review of *Why the Chicken Crossed the Road,* pp. 55-56; March-April, 1989, Elizabeth S. Watson, review of *The Way Things Work,* pp. 226-227; September-October, 1990, Mary M. Burns, review of *Black and White,* p. 593; July-August, 1991, Chris Van Allsburg, "David Macaulay: The Early Years," pp. 422-25, and David Macaulay, "Caldecott Medal Acceptance"; January-February, 1996, Mary M. Burns, review of *Shortcut,* p. 65; January-February, 1998, Mary M. Burns, review of *Rome Antics,* p. 66; September, 1999, Joanna Rudge Long, review of *Building the Book Cathedral,* p. 627; November, 1999, Christine Heppermann, "Cross Purposes," p. 716; January, 2001, Joanna Rudge Long, review of *Building Big,* p.112; May-June, 2002, Joanna Rudge Long, review of *Angelo,* p. 318.

Kirkus Reviews, March 15, 2002, review of *Angelo,* p. 417.

Library Journal, January, 1989, Patty Miller, review of *The Way Things Work,* p. 99.

Los Angeles Times Book Review, November 16, 1980.

New Orleans, October, 2000, review of *Building Big,* p. 114.

Newsweek, December 1, 1980, Jean Strouse, review of *Unbuilding,* p. 104; December 26, 1988.

New Yorker, December 12, 1988, Faith McNulty, review of *The Way Things Work,* p. 158.

New York Times, November 17, 1988; December 27, 1988, Edwin McDonnell, "Explaining the Mysteries of the Familiar," p. B1; September 28, 2000, John Leland, "Engineers' Marvels, Solved in Pictures," pp. F1, F13; November 30, 2000, review of *Building Big,* p. E7.

New York Times Book Review, November 29, 1981, Ray Walters, review of *Cathedral,* p. 47; June 20, 1982, review of *Pyramid,* p. 31; December 5, 1982, review of *Help, Let Me Out!,* p. 18; December 26, 1982, review of *Castle,* p. 19; September 25, 1983; January 8, 1984, review of *City,* p. 34; December 1, 1985; October 18, 1987, review of *Why the Chicken Crossed the Road,* p. 38; June 20, 1988; October 23, 1988; May 20, 1990, Liz Rosenberg, "Stories in Sync," p. 44; November 16, 1997, David W. Dunlap, review of *Rome Antics,* p. 48; December 5, 1999, Steven Heller, "Quicker Than St. John the Divine," p. 16; November 19, 2000, J. D. Biersdorfer, "For the Bridge-and-Tunnel Crowd," p. 60.

Parabola, summer, 1989, Rob Baker, "Necessary Interruptions," p. 42.

Progressive Architecture, October, 1988, Mark Alden Branch, review of *Pyramid,* p. 33.

Public Works, July, 2000, "Television Miniseries Looks at 'Building Big,'" p. 6.

Publishers Weekly, April 10, 1978; January 1, 1982, review of *Cathedral,* p. 51; July 30, 1982, review of *Help! Let Me Out!,* pp. 75-76; June 10, 1983, review of *Underground,* p. 65; August 19, 1983, review of *Mill,* p. 79; July 26, 1985, review of *Baaa,* p. 167; July 24, 1987; August 28, 1987; October 28, 1988, Joseph O. Holmes, "The Way David Macaulay Works," pp. 30-31; February 23, 1990, review of *Black and White,* p. 215; January 25, 1991, "Houghton, Little, Brown Titles Win Caldecott and Newbery Awards," p. 15; September 27, 1993, review of *Ship,* p. 63; October 31, 1994, Joseph O. Holmes, "Making the Leap to CD-ROM," p. 24; July 17, 1995, review of *Shortcut,* p. 228; September 8, 1997, review of *Rome Antics,* p. 76; August 21, 2000, "Work It!," p. 75; October 2, 2000, Sally Lodge, "The Way Big Things Work," p. 30; October 16, 2000, review of *Building Big,* p. 77; January 21, 2002, review of *Angelo,* p. 88.

Reading Teacher, February, 1991, Barbara Kiefer, review of *Black and White,* p. 413.

Saturday Review, October, 1985, Larry McCarthy, "Bright Lights, Big Season," p. 37.

School Library Journal, April, 1980, review of *Motel of the Mysteries,* p. 136; October, 1980, Patricia Homer, review of *Unbuilding,* p. 157; March, 1983, "Awards Announced at Midwinter," p. 80; October, 1983, Jeffrey A. French, review of *Mill,* p. 160; December, 1984, Emmett Corry, review of *Arts Alive,* p. 54; March, 1985, Diana Hirsch, review of *The Amazing Brain,* p. 187; December, 1987, Corinne Camarata, review of *Why the Chicken Crossed the Road,* p. 86; June, 1990, Karen Litton, review of *Black and White,* p. 104; November, 1993, Kenneth Marantz, review of *Ship,* pp. 117-118; May, 1995, Renee Olson, "David Macaulay Talks about the Problems and Promise of CD-ROM," pp. 23-26; September, 1995, Wendy Lukehart, review of *Shortcut,* p. 182; November, 1997, Shirley Wilton, review of *Rome Antics,* p. 121; December, 1998, Shirley Wilton, review of *The New Way Things Work,* p. 140; September, 1999, Beth Tegart, review of *Building the Book Cathedral,* p. 237; November, 2000, Mary Ann Carcich, review of *Building Big,* p. 172; March, 2001, Sarah Flowers, review of *Building Big,* p. 80; May, 2002, Marianne Saccardi, review of *Angelo,* p. 121.

Scientific American, December, 1989, Philip Morrison and Phylis Morrison, review of *The Way Things Work,* p. 147.

Smithsonian, May, 1992, Nathan Cobb, "The Show-and-Tell Tale(s) of the Great Explainer," p. 70.

Technology and Culture, October, 1990, Frederick Allen, review of *The Way Things Work,* p. 911.

Time, October 2, 2000, James Poniewozik, review of *Building Big,* p. 98.

Times Educational Supplement, September 10, 1976, Valerie Alderson, "A Sense of Size and Space," p. 41.

Times Literary Supplement, July 23, 1982, Mary Furness, "The Art of Building," p. 797.

U.S. News and World Report, October 9, 2000, Holly J. Morris, "Giving a Damn about Dams," p. 74;

Washington Post Book World, December 12, 1982; December 11, 1983; September 9, 1985.

Whole Earth, winter, 1989, J. Baldwin, review of *The Way Things Work,* p. 105; summer, 1998, Peter Warshall, review of *Underground,* p. 44.

OTHER

The New Way Things Work, http://www.houghton mifflinbooks.com/ (January 18, 2003).*

* * *

MAYER, Mercer 1943-

Personal

Born December 30, 1943, in Little Rock, AR; married first wife, Marianna (divorced, 1978); married second wife, Jo (divorced); married third wife, Gina; children: four. *Education:* Studied at the Honolulu Academy of Arts and the Art Students League. *Hobbies and other interests:* Guitar playing, painting, walking in the woods, sitting by the river, and listening to opera.

Addresses

Home—Bridgewater, CT. *Agent*—c/o Golden Books, 850 Third Ave., New York, NY 10022.

Career

Author and illustrator of children's books. Has worked as an art director for an advertising agency.

Awards, Honors

Citation of Merit, Society of Illustrators Annual National Exhibit, 1970, for *A Boy, A Dog, and A Frog,* 1975, for *What Do You Do with a Kangaroo?,* and 1976, for *Frog Goes to Dinner;* Children's Book Award, American Institute of Graphic Arts, 1971, for *A Special Trick;* Brooklyn Art Books for Children citation, 1973, for *A Boy, A Dog, and A Frog,* 1975, for *What Do You Do with a Kangaroo?,* and 1977, for *Frog Goes to Dinner;* International Books for Children Award, Association for Childhood Education, 1974, for *A Boy, A Dog, and A Frog;* Best Books of the Year citation, Child Study Association, 1974, for *You're the Scaredy-Cat;* Best Illustrated Books of the Year citation, *New York Times,* Ten Best Books citation, *Learning* magazine, and Irma Simonton Black Award, Bank Street College of Education, all 1977, all for *Everyone Knows What a Dragon Looks Like;* Brooklyn Art Books for Children Award, 1977, for *Frog Goes to Dinner;* Michigan Young Readers Award, 1982, for *Beauty and the Beast;* California Young Reader Medal, 1983, for *Liza Lou and the Yeller Belly Swamp.*

Writings

SELF-ILLUSTRATED

A Boy, a Dog, and a Frog, Dial (New York, NY), 1967.

There's a Nightmare in My Closet, Dial (New York, NY), 1968, published as *There's a Nightmare in My Cupboard,* Dent (London, England), 1976.

Terrible Troll, Dial (New York, NY), 1968.

If I Had . . . , Dial (New York, NY), 1968, published as *If I Had a Gorilla,* Rainbird Publications (Roxbury, CT), 1994.

I Am a Hunter, Dial (New York, NY), 1969.

Frog, Where Are You?, Dial (New York, NY), 1969.

A Special Trick, Dial (New York, NY), 1970.

The Queen Always Wanted to Dance, Simon & Schuster (New York, NY), 1971.

A Silly Story, Parents' Magazine Press (New York, NY), 1972.

Frog on His Own, Dial (New York, NY), 1973.

Bubble, Bubble, Parents' Magazine Press (New York, NY), 1973.

Mrs. Beggs and the Wizard, Parents' Magazine Press (New York, NY), 1973.

Wizard Comes to Town, Rainbird Publications (Roxbury, CT), 1973.

A Frog and a Friend, Golden Books (New York, NY), 1974.

What Do You Do with a Kangaroo?, Four Winds Press (New York, NY), 1974.

Two More Moral Tales (contains *Just a Pig at Heart* and *Sly Fox's Folly*), Four Winds Press (New York, NY), 1974.

Walk, Robot, Walk, Ginn (Lexington, MA), 1974.

You're the Scaredy-Cat, Parents' Magazine Press (New York, NY), 1974.

Frog Goes to Dinner, Dial (New York, NY), 1974.

One Monster after Another, Golden Books (New York, NY), 1974.

The Great Cat Chase: A Wordless Book, Four Winds Press (New York, NY), 1975.

Liza Lou and the Yeller Belly Swamp, Parents' Magazine Press, 1976.

Ah-Choo, Dial (New York, NY), 1976.

Four Frogs in a Box, Dial (New York, NY), 1976.

Hiccup, Dial (New York, NY), 1976.

Oops, Dial (New York, NY), 1977.

Mercer's Monsters, Golden Books (New York, NY), 1977.

How the Trollusk Got His Hat, Golden Books (New York, NY), 1979.

Herbert, the Knightly Dragon, Golden Books (New York, NY), 1980.

East of the Sun and West of the Moon, Four Winds Press (New York, NY), 1980.

Herbert, the Timid Dragon, Golden Books (New York, NY), 1980.

The Sleeping Beauty, Macmillan (New York, NY), 1984.

The Pied Piper of Hamlin, Macmillan (New York, NY), 1987.

There's Something in My Attic, Dial (New York, NY), 1988.

Unicorn and the Lake, Dial (New York, NY), 1990.

Thrills and Spills, Delmar (Albany, NY), 1991.

A Monster Followed Me to School, Golden Books (New York, NY), 1991.

Dog and a Frog, Viking (New York, NY), 1992.

(With J. R. Sansevere) *How the Zebra Lost Its Stripes*, GT Publishing (Vancouver, British Columbia, Canada), 1998.

The Golden Animal Book, Golden Books (New York, NY), 1999.

Shibumi and the Kitemaker, Marshall Cavendish (New York, NY), 1999.

The Rocking Horse Angel, Marshall Cavendish (New York, NY), 2000.

"PROFESSOR WORMBOG" SERIES

Professor Wormbog in Search for the Zipperump-a-Zoo, Golden Books (New York, NY), 1976.

Professor Wormbog's Gloomy Kerploppus: A Book of Great Smells, Golden Books (New York, NY), 1977.

Professor Wormbog's Cut It, Glue It, Tape It, Do-It Book, Golden Books (New York, NY), 1980.

Professor Wormbog's Crazy Cut-Ups, Golden Books (New York, NY), 1980.

"LITTLE MONSTER" SERIES

Little Monster's Word Book, Golden Books (New York, NY), 1977.

Little Monster at Home, Golden Books (New York, NY), 1978.

Little Monster at Work, Golden Books (New York, NY), 1978.

Little Monster at School, Golden Books (New York, NY), 1978.

Little Monster's You-Can-Make-It Book, Golden Books (New York, NY), 1978.

Little Monster's Bedtime Book, Golden Books (New York, NY), 1978.

Little Monster's Alphabet Book, Golden Books (New York, NY), 1978.

Little Monster's Counting Book, Golden Books (New York, NY), 1978.

Little Monster's Neighborhood, Golden Books (New York, NY), 1978.

Little Monster's Library (set of six books), Golden Books (New York, NY), 1978.

Little Monster's Mother Goose, Golden Books (New York, NY), 1979.

Little Monster's Scratch-and-Sniff Mystery, Golden Books (New York, NY), 1980.

Little Monster's Moving Day, Scholastic (New York, NY), 1995.

Little Monster's Sports Fun, Scholastic (New York, NY), 1995.

Little Monster Private Eye Goes on Safari, Inchworm Press/GT Publishing (Vancouver, British Columbia, Canada), 1998.

Little Monster Private Eye Treasure of the Nile, Inchworm Press/GT Publishing (Vancouver, British Columbia, Canada), 1998.

"LITTLE CRITTER" SERIES

Just for You, Golden Books (New York, NY), 1975.

Just Me and My Dad, Golden Books (New York, NY), 1977.

Play With Me, Golden Books (New York, NY), 1982.

Merry Christmas Mom and Dad, Golden Books (New York, NY), 1982.

The New Baby, Golden Books (New York, NY), 1983.

When I Get Bigger, Golden Books (New York, NY), 1983.

I Was So Mad, Golden Books (New York, NY), 1983.

All By Myself, Golden Books (New York, NY), 1983.

Me Too!, Golden Books (New York, NY), 1983.

Just Grandma and Me, Golden Books (New York, NY), 1983.

Just a Snowy Day, Golden Books (New York, NY), 1983.

Gator Cleans House, Random House (New York, NY), 1983.

Bat Child's Haunted House, Random House (New York, NY), 1983.

Little Critter's Holiday Fun Sticker Book, Scholastic (New York, NY), 1984.

Just Me and My Puppy, Golden Books (New York, NY), 1985.

Just Grandpa and Me, Golden Books (New York, NY), 1985.

Just Go to Bed, Golden Books (New York, NY), 1985.

Just Me and My Babysitter, Golden Books (New York, NY), 1986.

Just Me and My Little Sister, Golden Books (New York, NY), 1986.

Astronaut Critter, Simon & Schuster (New York, NY), 1986.

Cowboy Critter, Simon & Schuster (New York, NY), 1986.

Fireman Critter, Simon & Schuster (New York, NY), 1986.

Policeman Critter, Simon & Schuster (New York, NY), 1986.

Sailor Critter, Simon & Schuster (New York, NY), 1987.

Dr. Critter, Simon & Schuster (New York, NY), 1987.

Construction Critter, Simon & Schuster (New York, NY), 1987.

Just a Mess, Golden Books (New York, NY), 1987.

Baby Sister Says No!, Golden Books (New York, NY), 1987.

I Just Forgot, Golden Books (New York, NY), 1988.

Little Critter's Little Sister's Birthday, Golden Books (New York, NY), 1988, also published as *Little Critter's The Best Present*, 2000.

Little Critter's Picnic, Golden Books (New York, NY), 1988.

Staying Overnight, Golden Books (New York, NY), 1988.

This Is My House, Golden Books (New York, NY), 1988.

The Trip, Golden Books (New York, NY), 1988.

These Are My Pets, Golden Books (New York, NY), 1988.

Just My Friend and Me, Golden Books (New York, NY), 1988.

Happy Easter, Little Critter, Golden Books (New York, NY), 1988.

Just Shopping with Mom, Golden Books (New York, NY), 1989.

Little Critter at Play, Golden Books (New York, NY), 1989.

Little Critter's Day, Golden Books (New York, NY), 1989.

This Is My Friend, Golden Books (New York, NY), 1989.

Christmas Book, Golden Books (New York, NY), 1989, new edition, 2001.

Just a Daydream, Golden Books (New York, NY), 1989.

The Fussy Princess, Golden Books (New York, NY), 1989.

Play With Me, Golden Books (New York, NY), 1989.

Just a Nap, Golden Books (New York, NY), 1989.

Just Camping Out, Golden Books (New York, NY), 1989.

Just a Rainy Day, Golden Books (New York, NY), 1990.

Just Me and My Mom, Golden Books (New York, NY), 1990.

Just Going to the Dentist, Golden Books (New York, NY), 1990.

This Is My School, Golden Books (New York, NY), 1990.

Two-Minute Little Critter Stories, Golden Books (New York, NY), 1990.

When I Grow Up, Golden Books (New York, NY), 1991.

Little Critter at Scout Camp, Golden Books (New York, NY), 1991.

Just Me and My Little Brother, Golden Books (New York, NY), 1991.

Little Critter's Jack and the Beanstalk, Green Frog Publishers (New York, NY), 1991.

Little Critter's Little Red Riding Hood, Green Frog Publishers (New York, NY), 1991.

Little Critter's Hansel and Gretel, Random House (New York, NY), 1991.

The exploits of fast-talking, quick-thinking Tom Jenkins are described by his admiring young brother J. D. in John D. Fitzgerald's series of books illustrated with playful pictures by Mayer. (From The Great Brain.*)*

Little Critter's Where Is My Frog?, Random House (New York, NY), 1991.

Little Critter's Where's Kitty?, Random House (New York, NY), 1991.

Where's My Sneaker?, B. Dalton (New York, NY), 1991.

What a Bad Dream, Golden Books (New York, NY), 1992.

Very Special Critter, Golden Books (New York, NY), 1992.

Super Critter to the Rescue, Golden Books (New York, NY), 1992.

Little Critter Colors, Green Frog Publishers (New York, NY), 1992.

Little Critter Shapes, Green Frog Publishers (New York, NY), 1992.

Little Critter Numbers, Green Frog Publishers (New York, NY), 1992.

Little Critter's The Night before Christmas, Green Frog Publishers (New York, NY), 1992.

I Am Helping, Green Frog Publishers (New York, NY), 1992.

I Am Hiding, Green Frog Publishers (New York, NY), 1992.

I Am Playing, Green Frog Publishers (New York, NY), 1992.

I Am Sharing, Green Frog Publishers (New York, NY), 1992.

Little Critter's Camp Out, Golden Books (New York, NY), 1993.

Little Critter's Joke Book, Golden Books (New York, NY), 1993.

Little Critter's Read-It-Yourself Storybook: Six Funny Easy-to-Read Stories, Golden Books (New York, NY), 1993.

This Is My Town, Golden Books (New York, NY), 1993.

Little Critter's Day at the Farm Sticker Book, Scholastic (New York, NY), 1994.

I Said I Was Sorry, Golden Books (New York, NY), 1995.

Little Critter's ABC, B. Dalton (New York, NY), 1995.

Little Critter in Search of the Beautiful Princess, Random House, (New York, NY), 1995.

To Catch a Little Fishy, Random House (New York, NY), 1996.

Bun Bun's Birthday, Random House (New York, NY), 1996.

Little Sister's Bracelet, Random House (New York, NY), 1996.

I Smell Christmas: A Little Critter Scratch-and-Sniff Book, GT Publishing (Vancouver, British Columbia, Canada), 1997.

Just a Bubble Bath, GT Publishing (Vancouver, British Columbia, Canada), 1997.

Just a Magic Trick, GT Publishing (Vancouver, British Columbia, Canada), 1998.

Little Critter Sleeps Over, Golden Books (New York, NY), 1999.

Just a Secret, Golden Books (New York, NY), 2001.

My Trip to the Farm, McGraw-Hill (Columbus, OH), 2001.

A Yummy Lunch, McGraw-Hill (Columbus, OH), 2001.

No One Can Play, McGraw-Hill (Columbus, OH), 2001.

Our Friend Sam, McGraw-Hill (Columbus, OH), 2001.

Our Park, McGraw-Hill (Columbus, OH), 2001.

Snow Day, McGraw-Hill (Columbus, OH), 2001.

Surprise, McGraw-Hill (Columbus, OH), 2001.

Camping Out, McGraw-Hill (Columbus, OH), 2001.
Field Day, McGraw-Hill (Columbus, OH), 2001.
Helping Mom, McGraw-Hill (Columbus, OH), 2001.
The Mixed-up Morning, McGraw-Hill (Columbus, OH), 2002.
Play Ball, McGraw-Hill (Columbus, OH), 2002.
Just Not Invited, Golden Books (New York, NY), 2002.

"LITTLE CRITTER" SERIES; WITH GINA MAYER

Just Me and My Cousin, Golden Books (New York, NY), 1992.
The New Potty, Golden Books (New York, NY), 1992.
This Is My Family, Golden Books (New York, NY), 1992.
Rosie's Mouse, Golden Books (New York, NY), 1992.
This Is My Body, Golden Books (New York, NY), 1993.
Going to the Races, Golden Books (New York, NY), 1993.
It's Mine, Golden Books (New York, NY), 1993.
Just a Gum Wrapper, Golden Books (New York, NY), 1993.
Just a Thunderstorm, Golden Books (New York, NY), 1993.
Just Like Dad, Golden Books (New York, NY), 1993.
Just Me and My Bicycle, Golden Books (New York, NY), 1993.
Just Say Please, Golden Books (New York, NY), 1993.
Just Too Little, Golden Books (New York, NY), 1993.
Taking Care of Mom, Golden Books (New York, NY), 1993.
That's Not Fair, Golden Books (New York, NY), 1993.
Trick or Treat, Little Critter, Golden Books (New York, NY), 1993.
Just Lost!, Golden Books (New York, NY), 1994.
Just Me in the Tub, Golden Books (New York, NY), 1994.
I Didn't Know That, Reader's Digest Kids (Westport, CT), 1995.
I Didn't Mean To, Reader's Digest Kids (Westport, CT), 1995.
I Was So Sick, Reader's Digest Kids (Westport, CT), 1995.
I'm Sorry, Reader's Digest Kids (Westport, CT), 1995.
Just a Bad Day, Reader's Digest Kids (Westport, CT), 1995.
Just a Little Different, Reader's Digest Kids (Westport, CT), 1995.
Just an Airplane, Reader's Digest Kids (Westport, CT), 1995.
Just Leave Me Alone, Reader's Digest Kids (Westport, CT), 1995.
The Loose Tooth, Reader's Digest Kids (Westport, CT), 1995.
My Big Sister, Reader's Digest Kids (Westport, CT), 1995.
The School Play, Reader's Digest Kids (Westport, CT), 1995.
At the Beach with Dad, GT Publishing (Vancouver, British Columbia, Canada), 1998.
Just a New Neighbor, Golden Books (New York, NY), 1999.
Just a Bully, Golden Books (New York, NY), 1999.
Just a Toy, Golden Books (New York, NY), 2000.
Just a Snowy Vacation, Golden Books (New York, NY), 2001.
Just a Piggy Bank, Golden Books (New York, NY), 2001.

When a creature threatens the peaceful bedtime of a little boy, he decides to confront his enemy and is surprised by the outcome in Mayer's self-illustrated **There's a Nightmare in My Closet.**

"LC & THE CRITTER KIDS" SERIES; WITH ERICA FARBER AND J. R. SANSEVERE

Surf's Up, Golden Books (New York, NY), 1994.
The Secret Code, Golden Books (New York, NY), 1994.
Top Dog, Golden Books (New York, NY), 1994.
Ghost of Goose Island, Golden Books (New York, NY), 1994.
Backstage Pass, Golden Books (New York, NY), 1994.
The Mummy's Curse, Golden Books (New York, NY), 1994.
Showdown at the Arcade, Golden Books (New York, NY), 1994.
Circus of the Ghouls, Golden Books (New York, NY), 1994.
The Cat's Meow, Golden Books (New York, NY), 1994.
The Purple Kiss, Golden Books (New York, NY), 1994.
My Teacher Is a Vampire, Golden Books (New York, NY), 1994.
The E-Mail Mystery, Golden Books (New York, NY), 1995.
The Little Shop of Magic, Golden Books (New York, NY), 1995.
The Haunted House, Golden Books (New York, NY), 1995.
Pizza War, Golden Books (New York, NY), 1995.
Swamp Thing, Golden Books (New York, NY), 1995.
The Alien, Golden Books (New York, NY), 1995.
Golden Eagle, Golden Books (New York, NY), 1995.
Jaguar Paw, Golden Books (New York, NY), 1995.
The Prince, Golden Books (New York, NY), 1995.

Octopus Island: An Adventure under the Sea, Golden Books (New York, NY), 1995.

Blue Ribbon Mystery, Golden Books (New York, NY), 1996.

Kiss of the Vampire, Golden Books (New York, NY), 1996.

The Lost Wish, Inchworm Press/GT Publishing (Vancouver, British Columbia, Canada), 1998.

"CRITTERS OF THE NIGHT" SERIES; WITH ERICA FARBER AND J. R. SANSEVERE

Old Howl Hall, Random House (New York, NY), 1996.

No Howling in the House, Random House (New York, NY), 1996.

The Goblin's Birthday Party, Random House (New York, NY), 1996.

If You Dream a Dragon, Random House (New York, NY), 1996.

Kiss of the Mermaid, Random House (New York, NY), 1996.

Purple Pickle Juice, Random House (New York, NY), 1996.

Pirate Soup, Random House (New York, NY), 1996.

Zombies Don't Do Windows, Random House (New York, NY), 1996.

Werewolves for Lunch, Random House (New York, NY), 1996.

Vampire Brides, Random House (New York, NY), 1996.

Midnight Snack, Random House (New York, NY), 1997.

Night of the Walking Dead: Part 1, Random House (New York, NY), 1997.

Night of the Walking Dead: Part 2, Random House (New York, NY), 1997.

No Flying in the Hall, Random House (New York, NY), 1997.

The Roast and Toast, Random House (New York, NY), 1997.

Mummy Pancakes, Random House (New York, NY), 1997.

Love You to Pieces, Random House (New York, NY), 1997.

Ooey Gooey, Random House (New York, NY), 1998.

Zoom on My Broom, Random House (New York, NY), 1998.

Chomp, Chomp, Random House (New York, NY), 1998.

Critters of the Night Glow-in-the-Dark, Random House (New York, NY), 1998.

WITH MARIANNA MAYER

Mine, Simon & Schuster (New York, NY), 1970.

A Boy, a Dog, a Frog, and a Friend, Dial (New York, NY), 1971.

Me and My Flying Machine, Parents' Magazine Press (New York, NY), 1971.

One Frog Too Many, Dial (New York, NY), 1975.

There's An Alligator under My Bed, Dial (New York, NY), 1987.

"TINY TINK! TONK! TALES" SERIES

Tonk in the Land of the Buddy-Bots, Tink Tonk, 1984.

Tink's Subtraction Fair, Tink Tonk, 1984.

Tink's Adventure, Tink Tonk, 1984.

Tuk Goes to Town, Tink Tonk, 1984.

Zoomer Builds a Racing Car, Tink Tonk/Bantam, 1985.

Tinka Bakes a Cake, Tink Tonk/Bantam, 1985.

Tonk Gives a Magic Show, Tink Tonk/Bantam, 1985.

ILLUSTRATOR

John D. Fitzgerald, *The Great Brain,* Dial (New York, NY), 1967.

Liesel M. Skorpen, *Outside My Window,* Harper (New York, NY), 1968.

George Mendoza, *The Gillygoofang,* Dial (New York, NY), 1968.

Sidney Offit, *The Boy Who Made a Million,* St. Martin's Press (New York, NY), 1968.

George Mendoza, *The Crack in the Wall, and Other Terribly Weird Tales,* Dial (New York, NY), 1968.

Sheila LaFarge, *Golden Butter,* Dial (New York, NY), 1969.

John D. Fitzgerald, *More Adventures of the Great Brian,* Dial (New York, NY), 1969.

Kathryn Hitte, *Boy, Was I Mad!,* Parents' Magazine Press (New York, NY), 1969.

Warren Fine, *The Mousechildren and the Famous Collector,* Harper (New York, NY), 1970.

Jean R. Larson, *Jack Tar,* Macrae Smith (Philadelphia, PA), 1970.

Barbara Wersba, *Let Me Fall before I Fly,* Atheneum (New York, NY), 1971.

Jane H. Yolen, *The Bird of Time,* Crowell (New York, NY), 1971.

Jan Wahl, *Margaret's Birthday,* Four Winds Press (New York, NY), 1971.

John D. Fitzgerald, *Me and My Little Brain,* Dial (New York, NY), 1971.

Candida Palmer, *Kim Ann and the Yellow Machine,* Ginn (Lexington, MA), 1972.

Mildred Kantrowitz, *Good-Bye Kitchen,* Parents' Magazine Press (New York, NY), 1972.

Jan Wahl, *Grandmother Told Me,* Little, Brown (Boston, MA), 1972.

John D. Fitzgerald, *The Great Brain at the Academy,* Dial (New York, NY), 1972.

Mabel Watts, *While the Horses Galloped to London,* Parents' Magazine Press (New York, NY), 1973.

John D. Fitzgerald, *The Great Brain Reforms,* Dial (New York, NY), 1973.

Barbara Wersba, *Amanda Dreaming,* Atheneum (New York, NY), 1973.

John D. Fitzgerald, *The Return of the Great Brain,* Dial (New York, NY), 1974.

John D. Fitzgerald, *The Great Brain Does It Again,* Dial (New York, NY), 1975.

John Bellairs, *The Figure in the Shadows,* Dial (New York, NY), 1975.

Jay Williams, *Everyone Knows What a Dragon Looks Like,* Four Winds Press (New York, NY), 1976.

Jay Williams, *The Reward Worth Having,* Four Winds Press (New York, NY), 1977.

Marianna Mayer, reteller, *Beauty and the Beast,* Four Winds Press (New York, NY), reissued, SeaStar Books (New York, NY), 2000.

Nancy Garden, reteller, *Favorite Tales from Grimm,* Four Winds Press (New York, NY), 1982.

OTHER

(Editor) *The Poison Tree and Other Poems,* Scribner (New York, NY), 1977.

Appelard and Liverwurst, illustrated by Steven Kellogg, Four Winds Press (New York, NY), 1978.

Liverwurst Is Missing, illustrated by Steven Kellogg, Four Winds Press (New York, NY), 1982.

Whinnie the Lovesick Dragon, illustrated by Diane Dawson Hearne, Macmillan (New York, NY), 1986.

(Reteller) Charles Dickens, *A Christmas Carol: Being a Ghost Story of Christmas,* Macmillan (New York, NY), 1986.

Adaptations

Works adapted as computer software, including *Tonk in the Land of the Buddy-Bots,* (Atari diskette), Mindscape (Northbrook, IL), 1985; *Tink's Subtraction Fair,* (Atari diskette), Mindscape (Northbrook, IL), 1985; *Tink's Adventure* (Atari diskette), Mindscape (Northbrook, IL), 1985; *Tuk Goes to Town* (Atari diskette), Mindscape (Northbrook, IL), 1985; *Just Grandma and Me* (CD-ROM), Living Books (Novato, CA), 1993; *Little Monster at School* (CD-ROM), Living Books (Novato, CA), 1994; *Just Me and My Dad* (CD-ROM), GT Interactive Software (Vancouver, British Columbia, Canada), 1996; *Just Me and My Mom* (CD-ROM), GT Interactive Software (Vancouver, British Columbia, Canada), 1996; *The Smelly Mystery Starring Little Monster Private Eye* (CD-ROM; adaptation of *Little Monster's Scratch-and-Sniff Mystery*), GT Interactive Software (Vancouver, British Columbia, Canada), 1997; *Just Me and My Grandpa* (CD-ROM), GT Interactive Software (Vancouver, British Columbia, Canada), 1998; *Mercer Mayer's Little Critter and The Great Race* (CD-ROM), Infogrames (New York, NY), 2001; and *The Mummy Mystery Starring Mercer Mayer's Little Monster Private Eye* (CD-ROM), Infogrames (New York, NY), 2001.

Works adapted into video recordings, including *Three Mercer Mayer Stories: Herbert the Timid Dragon, Just for You, How the Trollusk Got His Hat,* Golden Book Video (New York, NY), 1985; *Frog Does to Dinner,* Phoenix Films (New York, NY), 1985; *Shelley Duvall's Bedtime Stories* (includes "There's a Nightmare in My Closet" narrated by Michael J. Fox, "There's an Alligator under My Bed" narrated by Christian Slater, and "There's Something in My Attic" narrated by Sissy Spacek), MCA Home Video (Universal City, CA), 1992; *A Boy, a Dog, and a Frog,* Phoenix Films (New York, NY), 1995; and *Just Me and My Dad,* Sony (New York, NY), 1998.

Works adapted into audio recordings, including *Mercer Mayer's Little Monster Stories* (includes "Little Monster at School," "Little Monster at Home," "Little Monster's Counting Book," and "Little Monster's Alphabet Book"), Listening Library (New York, NY), 1983; *Alligator under My Bed and Other Story Songs,* performed by Mercer Mayer, Big Tuna New Media (Roxbury, CT), 1999; and *The Little Drummer Mouse: A Christmas Story,* narrated by Mercer Mayer, Big Tuna New Media (Roxbury, CT), 1999.

Sidelights

Popular children's author Mercer Mayer is well-known for his versatility, humor, and artistic skill. Noted as one of the first creators of wordless picture books, Mayer also writes and illustrates nonsense fiction, fantasy, and folktales. In both his writing and illustrating, Mayer emphasizes the unconventional; his language can be simple or sophisticated, while his illustrations run the gamut of artistic styles.

Because his father was in the Navy, Mayer moved around a great deal as a child. The family eventually settled in Hawaii, where Mayer attended Theodore Roosevelt High School; upon graduation, he continued his studies at the Honolulu Academy of Arts. In 1964, Mayer moved to New York City for instruction at the Art Students League. Over time, he began to put together an art portfolio, which he hoped to use to land illustration jobs. Unfortunately, Mayer had little luck. He was once told to throw away a portfolio, because the publisher thought his work was so bad. Although initially upset by this evaluation, Mayer decided to take the advice; in his spare time, he began to refine his sketching. Mayer soon quit his job with an advertising agency in order to peddle his artwork to various publishers. Eventually, he was able to secure a number of illustration contracts.

Mayer published his first picture book in 1967. *A Boy, a Dog, and a Frog* was praised by many critics for its imaginative use of pictures. "Mercer [sic] expresses the boy's frustration with economy ... and the range of emotions the frog experiences, bafflement, annoyance, amusement, melancholy, and finally, joy, with a few deft pen strokes," wrote George A. Woods in the *New York Times Book Review.* And Robert Cohen, writing in *Young Readers Review,* called the book "delightful ... most heartily recommended for all picture book collections."

Mayer has repeated the success of *A Boy, a Dog, and a Frog* with numerous other volumes. Also writing in *Young Readers Review,* Phyllis Cohen described *There's a Nightmare in My Closet* as a "magnificently funny book," one that "must be seen to be fully appreciated." Barbara Karlin of the *West Coast Review of Books* praised *Little Monster's Word Book* by saying "Mayer remembers what it was like to be a little kid.... This is a book with which a lot of little people are going to spend many happy hours." "The narrative is smooth.... Illustrations, boldly executed with rich use of color and careful attention to detail, ... are graphically gripping," concluded Barbara Elleman in a *Booklist* review of *East of the Sun and West of the Moon.*

In spite of his own busy writing schedule, Mayer has found time to illustrate books for a number of other authors, including John D. Fitzgerald and his "Great Brain" series. His pictures for Marianne Mayer's retelling of *Beauty and the Beast* were applauded by P. Gila Reinstein of the *Dictionary of Literary Biography* as having a "wealth of detail" that is "full and lavish." And

Bonita Brodt, writing in the *Chicago Tribune,* called Mayer's adaptation of *A Christmas Carol* a "wonderful interpretation ... because it makes the tale accessible to young children and also remains true to the older ones as well." In summing up Mayer's success, Reinstein noted: "Reflecting the world ... from the child's point of view has been a hallmark of [Mayer's] work from the beginning of his career, and whatever changes come in his approach to children and their books, the honesty and emotional intensity that are essential to his work will remain unchanged."

In more than thirty years of illustration, Mayer's work has indeed changed and developed. In the 1960s, he used pen-and-ink drawings for his earliest children's books, like *A Boy, a Dog, and a Frog.* Later, as color publishing became more common, Mayer moved into watercolor painting. Some of those books, like *East of the Sun and West of the Moon,* are in "a lavish, romantic, painterly style," as Anita Silvey observed in *Children's Books and Their Creators.* After the mid-1970s, when he "stumbled on" a funny little character, much of his painting was reserved for the voluminous Little Critter series. Mayer was happily released from the need to paint, which he found "very tedious," as the computer became an accessible publishing tool. An Adobe profile of the artist quoted Mayer: "In the digital world, you can scan and paint and manipulate. You can create environments with lights and forms and shading. I was intrigued by that."

The first book that Mayer illustrated digitally was *Shibumi and the Kitemaker,* the story of the Japanese Emperor's daughter and her brave efforts to help her people. "Mayer says he wasn't sure of what he was trying to achieve," the Adobe profile continued, "and spent a lot of energy experimenting." The final result proved successful. Reviewing *Shibumi and the Kitemaker* for *Booklist,* Stephanie Zvirin pointed out "the strong, unusual artwork that sets his book apart." From small designs that are "subtle and in keeping with the Japanese flavor of the story" to large illustrations that "appear almost three-dimensional," Zvirin found the whole "fascinating; slick but also quite sensitive and expressive." With a better grasp of the process, Mayer embarked on his second digitally illustrated book, *The Rocking Horse Angel,* which a *School Library Journal* review called "visually spectacular ... drenched with color and rich with plush, rough, or silky-smooth textures."

"I want to create images beyond what I could or would want to paint," Mayer said in his profile for Adobe. "Until recently, if you couldn't paint you couldn't do images, but I'm taking the talent that I developed in learning to paint and using it to create digital images that get to the same point without painting."

Biographical and Critical Sources

BOOKS

Children's Literature Review, Volume 11, Gale (Detroit, MI), 1986.

Dictionary of Literary Biography, Volume 61: *American Writers for Children since 1960: Poets, Illustrators, and Nonfiction Authors,* Gale (Detroit, MI), 1987.

St. James Guide to Children's Writers, 5th edition, St. James Press (Detroit, MI), 1999.

Silvey, Anita, editor, *Children's Books and their Creators,* Houghton Mifflin (Boston, MA), 1995.

PERIODICALS

Booklist, November 1, 1980, Barbara Elleman, review of *East of the Sun and West of the Moon,* p. 407; October 15, 1999, Stephanie Zvirin, review of *Shibumi and the Kitemaker,* p. 444.

Chicago Tribune, December 7, 1986, Bonita Brodt, review of *A Christmas Carol,* section 14, p. 3.

New York Times Book Review, November 26, 1967, George A. Woods, review of *A Boy, a Dog, and a Frog,* p. 62; May 1, 1977; May 25, 1980; January 4, 1981; August 16, 1987; November 29, 1987.

Publishers Weekly, June 15, 1992, review of *This Is My Family,* p. 101; May 3, 1993, review of *Little Critter's Read-It-Yourself Storybook,* p. 308; September 12, 1994, review of *Little Critter Grows Up,* p. 33; July 19, 1999, review of *Shibumi and the Kitemaker,* p. 193.

School Library Journal, December, 2000, Catherine T. Quattlebaum, review of *The Rocking Horse Angel,* p. 117.

West Coast Review of Books, September, 1977, Barbara Karlin, review of *Little Monster's Word Book,* p. 55.

Young Readers Review, December, 1967, Robert Cohen, review of *A Boy, a Dog, and a Frog,* p. 12; June, 1968, Phyllis Cohen, review of *There's a Nightmare in My Closet,* p. 10.

OTHER

Adobe, http://www.adobe.com/print/features/mercermayer/ (May, 2001), Anita Dennis, "Mercer Mayer," artist profile and digital illustrations gallery.

Antic Digital, http://www.atarimagazines.com/ (February, 1985), Anita Malnig, review of *Tink's Adventure* and *Tuk Goes to Town* (Atari games).

Apple, http://apple.com/creative/stories/ (November 27, 2001), "Drawing on the Macintosh," details Mayer's digital creation of *Shibumi and the Kitemaker.*

Little Critter Web Site, http://www.littlecritter.com/ (November 14, 2001).

MacCentral, http://maccentral.macworld.com/gaming/reviews/edutain/ (1997), Bonnie Cohen, review of *The Smelly Mystery* (CD-ROM).*

*   *   *

McCLAFFERTY, Carla Killough 1958-

Personal

Born July 11, 1958, in Little Rock, AR; daughter of Raymond (a farmer) and Maxine (a homemaker; maiden name, Rucker) Killough; married Patrick Michael McClafferty (a vice president in electric sales), August 26, 1978; children: Ryan Patrick, Brittney Leigh, Corey Andrew (deceased). *Education:* Graduate of Baptist

Medical Center School of Radiologic Technology, 1978. *Religion:* Baptist.

Addresses

Home—8013 Coleridge Dr., North Little Rock, AR 72116. *E-mail*—c.mcclafferty@comcast.net.

Career

Rebsamen Memorial Hospital, staff radiologic technologist, 1978-83; part-time work in orthopedic clinics, 1983—. Women's Sunday School Teacher, Victory Missionary Baptist Church, 1998—.

Member

Society of Children's Book Writers and Illustrators, Authors Guild, American Society of Radiologic Technologists, American Registry of Radiologic Technicians.

Awards, Honors

Work-in-Progress Grant, Society of Children's Book Writers and Illustrators, 1997; Junior Library Guild Selection and New York Public Library List, both 2002, both for *The Head Bone's Connected to the Neck Bone: The Weird, Wacky, and Wonderful X-Ray;* Children's Book Council selection for Outstanding Science Trade Book, 2002, for *The Head Bone's Connected to the Neck Bone: The Weird, Wacky, and Wonderful X-Ray.*

Writings

Forgiving God: A Woman's Struggle to Understand When God Answers No, Discovery House (Grand Rapids, MI), 1995.
The Head Bone's Connected to the Neck Bone: The Weird, Wacky, and Wonderful X-Ray, Farrar, Straus, & Giroux (New York, NY), 2001.

Contributor to periodicals, including *Cricket, German Life,* and *Radiologic Technologist.*

Work in Progress

A children's book about Marie Curie and radium, working title, *Marie Curie and Her Liquid Sunshine.*

Sidelights

Carla Killough McClafferty first came to writing as a way to cope with her grief over the loss of her fourteen-month-old son. In *Forgiving God: A Woman's Struggle to Understand When God Answers No,* the author describes the spiritual journey that began when her son fell off a backyard swing and died from the injury to his head, which led McClafferty to question her belief in the goodness of God. Coming through on the other side with her faith renewed, McClafferty felt moved to tell her story in the hope of helping others. Along the way, she discovered a love of writing, and soon came *The Head Bone's Connected to the Neck Bone: The Weird, Wacky,*

and Wonderful X-Ray, McClafferty's first children's book. A much different work from her first, this science book for young adults was inspired by McClafferty's first career as an x-ray technologist. It details "the fascinating and often strange history of the X-ray," according to Mary R. Hofmann in *School Library Journal,* beginning with its invention by a German scientist in the nineteenth century to its early medical and entertainment uses, to the important role it currently plays in the medical panoply. A *Book Report* reviewer called *The Head Bone's Connected to the Neck Bone* "a compelling and very readable narrative," while a critic for the *Voice of Youth Advocates* said, "McClafferty presents a clear and amusing discussion of the X-ray." Todd Morning contended in *Booklist,* the strength of the book is in McClafferty's emphasis on "human stories, which makes for fascinating reading."

McClafferty told *SATA:* "Every book begins with a seed of an idea. The seed that grew to become *The Head Bone's Connected to the Neck Bone* was planted with one unanswered question. While working at an orthopedic clinic, I looked up Wilhelm Conrad Roentgen, the man who discovered X-rays, in a book of short medical biographies. The article said Roentgen was expelled from school when he was a boy, but it didn't say why. And I wanted to know why. So I began digging up information about Dr. Roentgen and the early days of X-rays and was fascinated by the funny, sad, and ridiculous stories I found. I just had to write a children's book to share this information. The challenge in writing it came from blending information that covers a wide variety of topics over a period of more than one hundred years, beginning with the discovery and ending with how X-rays are used in science and industry today."

Biographical and Critical Sources

PERIODICALS

Booklist, November 1, 2001, Todd Morning, review of *The Head Bone's Connected to the Neck Bone: The Weird, Wacky, and Wonderful X-Ray,* p. 465.
Book Report, March/April, 2002, review of *The Head Bone's Connected to the Neck Bone,* p. 75.
EPISD Reviews, April 23, 2002, review of *The Head Bone's Connected to the Neck Bone.*
Horn Book, July-December, 2001, review of *The Head Bone's Connected to the Neck Bone,* p. 151.
Louisville Eccentric Observer, June 5, 2002, review of *The Head Bone's Connected to the Neck Bone.*
Reading Teacher, April, 2002, review of *The Head Bone's Connected to the Neck Bone,* p. 700.
School Library Journal, December, 2001, Mary R. Hofmann, review of *The Head Bone's Connected to the Neck Bone,* p. 165.
Voice of Youth Advocates, July, 2002, Linda Perkins, review of *The Head Bone's Connected to the Neck Bone.*

McDOLE, Carol
See FARLEY, Carol (J.)

*   *   *

McLERRAN, Alice 1933-

Personal

Born June 24, 1933, in West Point, NY; daughter of Herbert Bronson (an army officer) and Marian Irene (a teacher and homemaker; maiden name, Doan) Enderton; married Larry McLerran (a physicist), May 8, 1976; children: Stephen Anderson, David Anderson, Rachel Anderson Elandt. *Education:* Attended Stanford University, 1950-51 and 1952-53; University of California—Berkeley, B.A., 1965, Ph.D., 1969; Harvard University, M.S., 1973, M.P.H., 1974, certification in psychiatric epidemiology, 1974. *Hobbies and other interests:* Backpacking, playing harp, traveling.

Addresses

Home—70 South Country Rd., Bellport, NY 11713. *E-mail*—71064.1346@compuserve.com.

Career

State University of New York—Cortland, assistant professor of anthropology, 1969-72; Nursing Home Ombudsman Project, Boston, MA, research analyst, 1974-75; Massachusetts Mental Health Center, Boston, MA, evaluator of children's services, 1975-77, chief of evaluation, 1978; Harvard University, Boston, MA, School of Medicine, lecturer in anthropology, 1977-78, School of Public Health, lecturer in health services, 1978; writer.

Member

Society of Children's Book Writers and Illustrators, Authors Guild, Center for Children's Environmental Literacy, Phi Beta Kappa.

Awards, Honors

Woodrow Wilson fellow, 1965; Southwest Book Award, 1991.

Writings

The Mountain That Loved a Bird, illustrated by Eric Carle, Simon & Schuster (New York, NY), 1985, new edition, Turtleback Books (Madison, WI), 2000.
Secrets (young adult novel), Lothrop (New York, NY), 1990.
Roxaboxen, illustrated by Barbara Cooney, Lothrop (New York, NY), 1991.
Dreamsong, illustrated by Valery Vasiliev, Morrow (New York, NY), 1992.
I Want to Go Home, illustrated by Jill Kastner, Morrow (New York, NY), 1992.

Kisses, illustrated by Mary Morgan, Scholastic (New York, NY), 1993.
Hugs, illustrated by Mary Morgan, Scholastic (New York, NY), 1993.
The Ghost Dance, illustrated by Paul Morin, Clarion Books (New York, NY), 1995.
The Year of the Ranch, illustrated by Kimberly Bulcken Root, Viking (New York, NY), 1996.
The Legacy of Roxaboxen: A Collection of Voices (biography-memoir), Absey (Spring, TX), 1998.
Dragonfly, Absey (Spring, TX), 2000.

A version of *The Mountain That Loved a Bird* was published in Russian, with illustrations by David Khaykin, by Detskaya Literatura, 1989; *The Mountain That Loved a Bird* was published in English and Spanish in a third-grade social studies textbook by Houghton Mifflin; other works have been translated into Japanese, Russian, German, Spanish, and Finnish.

Sidelights

Alice McLerran once told *SATA:* "I was raised in an army family, and 'home' throughout my childhood shifted every year or so—from Hawaii to Germany, from New York to Ecuador. I dropped out of college at the beginning of my junior year but reenrolled as the

Alice McLerran's picture book depicts the Ghost Dance movement, which began as a collaborative effort of Native peoples to reclaim their past but ended in the massacre at Wounded Knee. (From The Ghost Dance, *illustrated by Paul Morin.)*

mother of three children and went on to earn a doctorate in anthropology at the University of California—Berkeley. After a period of teaching and research, with fieldwork in the Andes Mountains, I returned to the student role once more for two years of postdoctoral study at Harvard University's School of Public Health.

"Later, while working in Boston, Massachusetts, as program evaluator for a community mental health center, I met and married a physicist. As we have moved to new homes in California, Washington, Illinois, and Minnesota, my time was at first divided between a series of diverse part-time jobs and equally diverse avocations. I now consider writing to be my job for the indefinite future. I do manage to find time for backpacking, have taught two of our three cats to do tricks, and am myself trying to learn to play the harp. Meanwhile, I follow my physicist-husband on travels that make my earlier life seem sedentary.

"I welcome opportunities to visit schools and libraries to talk with children about the pleasures and challenges of writing. Although my Spanish is not perfect, I am sufficiently fluent in it to enjoy using that language, as well as English, for such visits."

McLerran has published an eclectic collection of books for children. Her *Hugs* and *Kisses,* for example, are two miniature companion books with rhyming texts describing the myriad occasions and accompanying feelings of these human gestures. On the other hand, she has published several picture books based on her family history, including *Roxaboxen* and *The Year of the Ranch.* These books, like McLerran's others, celebrate the joy and comfort of strong family ties and the power of children's imagination to transform a humble environment.

In *The Year of the Ranch,* set in 1919, a man convinces his wife and four daughters to move to the Arizona desert and try to transform it into a farm. The family gamely deals with the lack of civilization by building a tennis court and learns how to cope with scorpions and sandstorms, but at the end of a year, Papa relents and they prepare to move back to the city. The book concludes with a note from the author tracing the historical basis for the story. "This affectionate vignette is peppered with the sort of small details that make it believable and absorbing," claimed a contributor to *Kirkus Reviews.* In *Roxaboxen,* McLerran returns to the desert of her mother's childhood and focuses in on the imaginative play that made the barren desert seem a teeming urban space, filled with cars and stores, a town jail, a place to bake bread, and a place to make war. "McLerran's gentle text is both particular and universal, as she fondly tells this evocative story," remarked a critic in *Publishers Weekly.* In *The Legacy of Roxaboxen: A Collection of Voices,* McLerran parses out the fact and fiction of Roxaboxen, including in the volume a facsimile reproduction of her mother's short stories about the place alongside the memories and photos of other family members.

Jason, his neighbors, and his family vow to keep their pet dragon a secret and to protect her from threats, a promise that involves a move to a deserted island refuge. (Cover illustration by Tristan Elwell.)

McLerran tackles the familiar problem of moving in *I Want to Go Home,* in which little Marta's fretting about her old home, and her dissatisfaction with her new home, are eventually resolved when the family takes in a stray cat who is having problems adjusting to Marta's new home too. Reviewers found this book realistic and reassuring. McLerran's *Dreamsong,* on the other hand, is considered a fairy-tale with European overtones. Here, Pavel is haunted by a song he only hears at night and only half remembers upon waking. One day, he goes off in search of the source of the song, coming upon scraps of it here and there all over the country, until he returns home, falls exhausted into bed, and is asleep before he recognizes the song on his mother's lips. Although some reviewers were puzzled by the significance of the story—"Readers young and old will ask, 'What is this about?'" predicted Susan Hepler in *School Library Journal*—a contributor to *Kirkus Reviews* called *Dreamsong* "a charming bedtime story, sweetly told and set in the long ago and far away."

McLerran is also the author of a pure fantasy in *Dragonfly,* the story of a boy, his family, and their neighbors, who adopt and protect a dragon until the time when he is too big to hide in their garage, whereupon they all set up housekeeping on a deserted island. Secrets of a different kind set the tone for McLerran's young adult novel *Secrets.* When a Russian family moves into the neighborhood, two boys begin to suspect them of espionage. McLerran attempted a story of a different kind in *The Ghost Dance,* which tells of the Native Americans whose lives changed when Europeans invaded North America. "The Ghost Dance" was originally a prayer that the whites would disappear from the land, but McLerran turns it into a plea for environmental responsibility on the part of all humans. "This is a harmonious concept for the twentieth century," remarked Jan Bourdeau Waboose in *Quill & Quire,* "but it was not the intent of the ghost dancers throughout North America, and specifically those who were massacred at Wounded Knee in 1890."

Biographical and Critical Sources

PERIODICALS

Booklist, May 15, 1992, Stephanie Zvirin, review of *I Want to Go Home,* p. 1688; July, 1996, Susan Dove Lempke, review of *The Year of the Ranch,* p. 1830.

Bulletin of the Center for Children's Books, April, 1996, Betsy Hearne, review of *The Year of the Ranch,* pp. 270-271.

Five Owls, November-December, 1994, Gary D. Schmidt, "Places, Real and Imaginary," p. 727.

Horn Book, March-April, 1991, Mary M. Burns, review of *Roxaboxen,* p. 194; July-August, 1996, Maeve Visser Knoth, review of *The Year of the Ranch,* p. 451.

Journal of Adolescent & Adult Literacy, April, 1996, review of *The Ghost Dance,* p. 606.

Kirkus Reviews, June 1, 1992, review of *I Want to Go Home,* p. 727; October 15, 1992, review of *Dreamsong,* p. 1313; December 15, 1992, review of *Hugs,* p. 1574; October 15, 1995, review of *The Ghost Dance,* p. 1496; June 1, 1996, review of *The Year of the Ranch,* pp. 826-827.

Publishers Weekly, April 12, 1991, review of *Roxaboxen,* p. 57; May 11, 1992, review of *I Want to Go Home,* p. 72; November 9, 1992, review of *Dreamsong,* p. 85; December 14, 1992, review of *Hugs* and *Kisses,* p. 55; June 10, 1996, review of *The Year of the Ranch,* p. 98; May 18, 1998, review of *Roxaboxen Remembered,* p. 82; April 10, 2000, review of *The Mountain That Loved a Bird,* p. 101.

Quill & Quire, February, 1996, Jan Bourdeau Waboose, review of *The Ghost Dance,* p. 41.

Reading Teacher, March, 1998, review of *The Year of the Ranch,* p. 504.

School Library Journal, April, 1986, Laura Bacher, review of *The Mountain That Loved a Bird,* p. 75; November, 1990, John Peters, review of *Secrets,* p. 116; February, 1991, Jane Marino, review of *Roxaboxen,* p. 72; June, 1992, Fritz Mitnick, review of *Roxaboxen,* p. 74; August, 1992, Christine A. Moesch, review of *I Want to Go Home,* p. 144; January, 1993, Susan Hepler, review of *Dreamsong,* p. 82, and Linda Wicher, review of *Hugs* and *Kisses,* p. 82; November, 1995,

Ellen Fader, review of *The Ghost Dance,* p. 114; July, 1996, Jody McCoy, review of *The Year of the Ranch,* p. 68; January, 2001, Beth Wright, review of *Dragonfly,* p. 132.

OTHER

Alice McLerran Web Site, http://www.alicemclerran.com/ (December 7, 2002).*

*   *   *

MOORE, Lilian 1909-
(Sara Asheron)

Personal

Born March 17, 1909, in New York, NY; daughter of Aaron and Sarah (Asheron) Levenson; married second husband, Sam Reavin, 1969; children: (first marriage) Jonathan. *Education:* Hunter College, B.A., 1930; graduate study at Columbia University. *Hobbies and other interests:* Chamber music, bicycling, ice skating, gardening, reading, cooking, traveling.

Addresses

Home—Seattle, WA. *Agent*—c/o Author Mail, Henry Holt & Co., 115 West 18th St., New York, NY 10011.

Career

Writer. Worked as elementary school teacher in New York, NY, 1930-37; New York City Bureau of Educational Research, New York, NY, staff member, 1937-50; freelance editorial consultant for children's books, beginning 1950; reading specialist, beginning 1952; Scholastic Book Services, New York, NY, editor of Arrow Book Club, 1957-67; Grosset & Dunlap, Wonder Book division, New York, NY, editor of easy reader series, beginning 1960; editor of history and biography series, 1968-69; series editor for Thomas Y. Crowell, New York, NY; director of Brooklyn Community Counseling Center.

Member

Council on Interracial Books for Children (founding member), PEN, Authors Guild, Authors League.

Awards, Honors

New York Times Best Books of the Year selection, 1960, for *Old Rosie, the Horse Nobody Understood;* Child Study Association Children's Books of the Year selections, 1968, for *Just Right,* 1969, for *Junk Day on Juniper Street, and Other Easy-to-Read Stories,* 1973, for *Sam's Place: Poems from the Country,* 1974, for *To See the World Afresh,* and 1975, for *See My Lovely Poison Ivy, and Other Verses about Witches, Ghosts, and Things;* American Library Association Notable Book citations, 1974, for *To See the World Afresh,* and 1982, for *Something New Begins;* American Library Society Notable Children's Book designation, 1980, for

Think of Shadows; National Council of Teachers of English Award for excellence in poetry for children, 1985; named New York School Library Media Specialist, 1990.

Writings

FOR CHILDREN

A *Child's First Picture Dictionary,* Grosset & Dunlap (New York, NY), 1946.

(With Leon Adelson) *Old Rosie, the Horse Nobody Understood,* illustrated by Leonard Shortall, Random House (New York, NY), 1952.

(With Leon Adelson) *The Terrible Mr. Twitmeyer,* illustrated by Leonard Shortall, Random House (New York, NY), 1952.

The Important Pockets of Paul, illustrated by William D. Haynes, McKay (New York, NY), 1954.

Daniel Boone, illustrated by William Moyers, Random House (New York, NY), 1956.

Wobbly Wheels, illustrated by B. Krush, Abingdon (Nashville, TN), 1956.

The Snake That Went to School, illustrated by Mary Stevens, Random House (New York, NY), 1957.

My Big Golden Counting Book, Golden Press (New York, NY), 1957.

Once upon a Holiday, illustrated by Wesley Dennis, Whittlesey House (New York, NY), 1959.

Tony the Pony, illustrated by Wesley Dennis, Whittlesey House (New York, NY), 1959.

Bear Trouble, illustrated by Kurt Werth, Whittlesey House (New York, NY), 1960.

Everything Happens to Stuey, illustrated by Mary Stevens, Random House (New York, NY), 1960.

Too Many Bozos, illustrated by Susan Perl, Golden Press (New York, NY), 1960.

A Pickle for a Nickel, illustrated by Susan Perl, Golden Press (New York, NY), 1961.

Once upon a Season, illustrated by Gloria Fiammenghi, Abingdon (Nashville, TN), 1962.

(With Leone Adelson) *Mr. Twitmeyer and the Poodle,* illustrated by Leonard Shortall, Random House (New York, NY), 1963.

Papa Albert, illustrated by Gloria Fiammenghi, Atheneum (New York, NY), 1964.

The Magic Spectacles, and Other Easy-to-Read Stories, illustrated by Arnold Lobel, Parents Magazine Press (New York, NY), 1966.

I Feel the Same Way (poems), illustrated by Robert Quackenbush, Atheneum (New York, NY), 1967.

Just Right, illustrated by Aldern A. Watson, Parents Magazine Press (New York, NY), 1968.

I Thought I Heard the City (poems), illustrated by Mary Jane Dunton, Atheneum (New York, NY), 1969.

Junk Day on Juniper Street, and Other Easy-to-Read Stories, illustrated by Arnold Lobel, Parents Magazine Press (New York, NY), 1969.

The Riddle Walk, illustrated by John Pucci, Garrard (Champaign, IL), 1971.

(Reteller) Hans Christian Andersen, *The Ugly Duckling,* illustrated by Mona Barrett, Scholastic (New York, NY), 1972, expanded as *The Ugly Duckling and Two*

Lilian Moore

Other Stories, illustrated by Trina Schart Hyman, 1973.

(Compiler, with Lawrence Webster) *Catch Your Breath: A Book of Shivery Poems,* illustrated by Gahan Wilson, Garrard (Champaign, IL), 1973.

Sam's Place: Poems from the Country, illustrated by Talivaldis Stubis, Atheneum (New York, NY), 1973.

Spooky Rhymes and Riddles, illustrated by Ib Ohlsson, Scholastic (New York, NY), 1973.

(Compiler, with Judith Thurman) *To See the World Afresh* (poems), Atheneum (New York, NY), 1974.

(With Remy Charlip) *Hooray for Me!,* illustrated by Vera B. Williams, Parents Magazine Press (New York, NY), 1975.

See My Lovely Poison Ivy, and Other Verses about Witches, Ghosts, and Things, illustrated by Diane Dawson, Atheneum (New York, NY), 1975.

(Compiler) *Go with the Poem,* McGraw-Hill (New York, NY), 1979.

Think of Shadows (poems), illustrated by Deborah Robinson, Atheneum (New York, NY), 1980.

Something New Begins (poems), illustrated by Mary Jane Dunton, Atheneum (New York, NY), 1982.

I'll Meet You at the Cucumbers (also see below), illustrated by Sharon Wooding, Atheneum (New York, NY), 1988.

Don't Be Afraid, Amanda (sequel to *I'll Meet You at the Cucumbers*), illustrated by Kathleen Garry McCord, Atheneum (New York, NY), 1992.

(Selector) *Sunflakes: Poems for Children,* illustrated by Jan Ormerod, Clarion (New York, NY), 1992.

Adam Mouse's Book of Poems, illustrated by Kathleen Garry McCord, Atheneum (New York, NY), 1992.

I Never Did That Before (poems), Atheneum (New York, NY), 1995.

My First Counting Book, Golden Book (New York, NY), 1997.

Poems Have Roots: New Poems, illustrated by Tad Hills, Atheneum (New York, NY), 1997.

I'm Small, and Other Verses, illustrated by Jill McElmurry, Candlewick Press (Cambridge, MA), 2001.

While You Were Chasing a Hat, illustrated by Rosanne Litzinger, HarperCollins (New York, NY), 2001.

Mural on Second Avenue, and Other City Poems, illustrated by Roma Karas, Candlewick Press (Cambridge, MA), 2004.

Also author of books under the name Sara Asheron, including *Surprise in the Tree,* 1962; *Will You Come to My Party?; Laurie and the Yellow Curtains; The Surprise in the Story Book; Little Gray Mouse and the Train; How to Find a Friend; Little Gray Mouse Goes Sailing; Little Popcorn; The Three Coats of Benny Bunny; Fraidy Cat;* and *Funny Face at the Window.* Contributor to periodicals, including *Humpty Dumpty.*

Drawing upon sensations and experiences from the places she has lived, Moore composed a collection of poems about nature. (Cover illustration by Tad Hills.)

Moore's works are included at the deGrummond Collection at the University of Southern Mississippi.

"LITTLE RACCOON" SERIES; FOR CHILDREN

Little Raccoon and the Thing in the Pool, illustrated by Gloria Fiammenghi, Whittlesey House (New York, NY), 1963.

Little Raccoon and the Outside World, illustrated by Gloria Fiammenghi, Whittlesey House (New York, NY), 1965.

Little Raccoon and No Trouble at All, illustrated by Gloria Fiammenghi, McGraw-Hill (New York, NY), 1972.

Little Raccoon and Poems from the Woods, illustrated by Gloria Fiammenghi, McGraw-Hill (New York, NY), 1975.

Little Raccoon Takes Charge (adapted from *Little Raccoon and No Trouble at All*), illustrated by Deborah Borgo, Western Publishing, 1986.

Little Raccoon's Nighttime Adventure, illustrated by Deborah Borgo, Western Publishing, 1986.

Little Raccoon, illustrated by Doug Cushman, Holt (New York, NY), 2001.

Adaptations

Several books by Moore were adapted into short films, including *Bear Trouble, Too Many Bozos, A Pickle for a Nickel,* and *Tony the Pony.*

Sidelights

Lilian Moore is an editor, educator, poet, and self-styled yarn-spinner who played a significant role in children's literature during the mid- to late twentieth century. As the first editor of the newly established Scholastic's Arrow Book Club from 1957 to 1967, Moore pioneered the program that made quality paperback books accessible and affordable for elementary school children throughout the United States. In addition, she has contributed many stories and poetry collections to the body of available children's literature, and has been honored for her poetry as well as for several of her story books.

Born in New York City in 1909, Moore developed a love of reading and telling stories after she discovered the path to the New York Public Library. In college, she majored in English and planned to teach Elizabethan literature on the college level. However, the nation was in the throes of the Great Depression when she graduated in the 1930s, so she could only find work as a reading teacher for truant children. Although she enjoyed the challenge the job provided, Moore became frustrated over the lack of suitable reading materials and determined that she would eventually write some books to fill this need: books that would be both exciting and easy to read, and that would allow children with reading problems to experience the pleasure of independent reading. While working as an editor for a New York publishing house after her first child was born, Moore began publishing easy-reader books under the pseudonym Sara Asheron. Her first storybook, authored with Leon Adelson, was *Old Rosie, the Horse Nobody*

Understood, an award-winning story that remained in print for several decades after its initial 1952 publication.

The many books Moore has penned since *Old Rosie, the Horse Nobody Understood* have been generally well received by reviewers. Several critics have praised her ability to construct simple but interesting sentences using a basic vocabulary. "Moore is very clever at handling the kind of simple stories that do not discourage those who are still fumbling with the newly acquired ability to read," noted *New York Herald Tribune* contributor M. S. Libby. Many of Moore's stories feature animal characters who, while not totally humanized, embody many of the fears, joys, insecurities, and curiosity experienced by young children. In her highly praised story *I'll Meet You at the Cucumbers,* a young country-loving, poem-scribbling mouse named Adam is fearful to take a trip with his friend into the unfamiliar city. However, by confiding his fears to friend Amanda, Adam is able to confront them and ultimately makes an enjoyable trip into the bustling city. Praising Moore for her strong character development, *School Library Journal* contributor Caroline Ward added that the author's "masterful writing ... manages to achieve a charming simplicity while making profound statements about the human condition." The tables turn for Adam in the sequel, *Don't Be Afraid, Amanda,* as the rural rodent plays host to city friend Amanda and introduces her to the quiet joys of country life. "Moore charms with her lucid narration" and "small, gently characterized creatures," noted a *Kirkus Reviews* contributor in praise of the 1992 book, while in *Horn Book,* Nancy Vasilakis dubbed *Don't Be Afraid, Amanda* "an easy chapter book that will appeal to animal lovers."

In *While You Were Chasing a Hat,* Moore uses poetic prose to trace the path of a girl's windblown hat on a summer day. By linking each place the hat goes— through the park, past trees, and along the edge of a lake—Moore "challeng[es] even the youngest children to understand the connection of things," noted a *Kirkus Reviews* critic, while in *Booklist,* Shelley Townsend-Hudson noted that in Moore's "charming book," young readers will "develop an awareness that unrelated things go on at the same time."

In addition to her prose books, Moore has written several volumes of poetry for young readers and was awarded the National Council of English Teachers' award for excellence in poetry for children in 1985. "Many of the poems have the flavor of haiku and capture the very essence of experience," noted Barbara Gibson in a *School Library Journal* review of Moore's 1967 poetry collection *I Feel the Same Way.* In a review for the *New York Times Book Review,* Alicia Ostricker called Moore "a poet who writes with a child's-eye view that is keen, accurate, and full of vitality." Noting that it is Moore's poetry, rather than prose, that "best combines her understanding of the child's mind and her ability to find beauty in familiar and unexpected places," an essayist in *Children's Books and Their Creators* maintained that the poet's "innovative choice of words and

Eighteen poems by Moore center on the familiar world of childhood with topics like peanut butter, snowsuits, and playing at the beach. (*From* I'm Small, and Other Verses, *illustrated by Jill McElmurry.*)

her vivid imagery ... appeal to the reader's imagination."

Among the many poetry collections credited to Moore are *I Thought I Heard the City,* a 1969 description of the bustling cityscape as seen through a child's eyes; *I'm Small, and Other Verses,* which is geared toward preschooler story time in its focus on everything from peanut-butter sandwiches to finger paints; and *Sam's Place: Poems from the Country,* which contains twenty poems that reflect Moore's love of the natural world as seen from the farm she shares with her second husband in upstate New York. The 1997 collection *Poems Have Roots* contains seventeen poems that continue Moore's sensitive and sometimes humorous examination of nature in what *School Library Journal* contributor Ellen D. Warwick called "minute observations pithily recorded." Frances Phillips noted in *Hungry Mind Review* that in *Poems Have Roots* "Moore has an important ecological message to convey to her young readers. While her formal strategies—simple vocabulary, quirky line breaks, frequent exclamations and questions for emphasis—are not subtle, she is bravely addressing children with a poetry of social action." In *Sunflakes: Poems for Children,* Moore collects the work of other poets to produce an anthology "of seventy-six poems bursting with sound and sense," according to *Bulletin of the Center for Children's Books* reviewer Betsy Hearne. In further praise of the volume, Hearne added that Moore's "consistent selection suggests an ear perfectly tuned to lyrical nuance, on the one hand, and children's sensibilities, on the other."

In her career as both editor and author, Moore has found that her experience in fine-tuning the work of other writers has contributed to her own writing. "I believe that editing is a kind of sculpture," she told Joan I. Glazer in an interview for *Language Arts.* "If there's a line with a bump in it and you have a sense of form, you smooth it and give it shape." The author/poet later expanded on this, telling a *SATA* interviewer: "Good writing is clear thinking and honest feeling; murky feeling produces sentimentality, and muddy thinking produces muddy language.... If a line bounces or bucks, I reshape it, as if I were working on a piece of pottery—until I achieve a line that flows ... without interruption."

Biographical and Critical Sources

BOOKS

Children's Literature Review, Volume 15, Gale (Detroit, MI), 1988, pp. 135-145.

Hopkins, Lee Bennett, *Books Are By People: Interviews with 104 Authors and Illustrators of Books for Young Children,* Citation Press, 1969.

Silvey, Anita, editor, *Children's Books and Their Creators,* Houghton Mifflin (Boston, MA), 1995, pp. 467-468.

Something about the Author, Volume 52, interview with Lilian Moore, Gale (Detroit, MI), 1988.

Ward, Martha E., and Dorothy A. Marquardt, *Authors of Books for Young People,* 2nd edition, Scarecrow Press (Metuchen, NJ), 1971.

PERIODICALS

Booklist, June 1, 1992, Karen Hutt, review of *Don't Be Afraid, Amanda,* p. 1762; September 15, 1992, Carolyn Phelan, review of *Adam Mouse's Book of Poems,* p. 144; November 1, 1995, Leone McDermott, review of *I Never Did That Before,* p. 474; September 1, 1997, Hazel Rochman, review of *Poems Have Roots,* p. 119; April 1, 2001, Shelley Townsend-Hudson, review of *While You Were Chasing a Hat,* p. 1479.

Bulletin of the Center for Children's Books, March, 1988, review of *I'll Meet You at the Cucumbers,* p. 142; February, 1993, Betsy Hearne, review of *Sunflakes: Poems for Children,* p. 186; November, 1997, Deborah Stevenson, review of *Poems Have Roots,* pp. 93-94.

Horn Book, April, 1983, review of *Something New Begins,* p. 179; July-August, 1988, Ethel R. Twitchell, review of *I'll Meet You at the Cucumbers,* p. 492; July-August, 1992, Nancy Vasilakis, review of *Don't Be Afraid, Amanda,* p. 475; March-April, 1993, Hanna B. Zeiger, review of *Sunflakes,* pp. 214-215; May, 2001, Martha V. Parravano, review of *I'm Small, and Other Verses,* pp. 344-345.

Hungry Mind Review, winter, 1997-98, Frances Phillips, review of *Poems Have Roots,* pp. 44-45.

Kirkus Reviews, May 1, 1992, review of *Don't Be Afraid, Amanda,* p. 614; August 15, 1992, review of *Adam Mouse's Book of Poems,* p. 1070; November 1, 1992, review of *Sunflakes,* p. 1382; April 15, 2001, review of *While You Were Chasing a Hat,* p. 590.

Language Arts, October, 1985, Joan I. Glazer, "Profile: Lilian Moore," pp. 647-652.

New York Herald Tribune, April 26, 1959, M. S. Libby, review of *Old Rosie, the Horse Nobody Understood.*

New York Times Book Review, November 14, 1982, Alicia Ostriker, review of *Something New Begins, New and Selected Poems,* pp. 45, 57.

Parnassus, Volume 8, number 2, 1980, pp. 63-82.

Publishers Weekly, May 29, 1987, review of *The Ugly Duckling,* p. 76; March 26, 2001, review of *I'm Small, and Other Verses,* p. 91.

School Library Journal, September, 1967, Barbara Gibson, review of *I Feel the Same Way,* p. 111; February, 1980, Sharon Elswit, review of *Go with the Poem,* p. 58; January, 1981, Maryl Silverstein, review of *Think of Shadows,* p. 53; April, 1988, Caroline Ward, review of *I'll Meet You at the Cucumbers,* p. 82; October, 1992, Susannah Price, review of *Adam Mouse's Book of Poems,* p. 106; October, 1995, Kathleen Whalin, review of *I Never Did That Before,* p. 128; December, 1997, Ellen D. Warwick, review of *Poems Have Roots,* p. 141; May, 2001, Ellen A. Greever, review of *I'm Small, and Other Verses,* p. 145.*

*　　　*　　　*

MURPHY, Claire Rudolf 1951-

Personal

Born March 9, 1951, in Spokane, WA; daughter of Kermit (a lawyer) and Frances Claire (a librarian; maiden name, Collins) Rudolf; married Robert Patrick Murphy (a teacher and principal), June 9, 1979; children: Conor Liam, Megan Frances. *Education:* Santa Clara University, B.A., 1973; University of California—Berkeley, secondary teaching credentials, 1974; University of Alaska—Fairbanks, M.F.A. (creative writing), 1987. *Politics:* Democrat. *Religion:* Catholic. *Hobbies and other interests:* Family outdoor activities, "such as biking, swimming, hiking, and cross-country skiing," running, and tennis; music (piano and voice); community theater.

Addresses

Home—1512 East 19th Ave., Spokane, WA 99203. *E-mail*—mail@clairerudolfmurphy.com.

Career

St. Mary's Mission High School, St. Mary's, AK, teacher of English and drama, 1974-77; Fairbanks Borough School District, Fairbanks, AK, secondary school teacher of English and drama, 1977-83; Fairbanks Correctional Center, Fairbanks, AK, writing instructor, 1984-89; University of Alaska—Fairbanks, instructor in composition, 1990-91; freelance writer, 1991—. Alaska State Writing Consortium teacher consultant, 1984-98, Eastern Washington University, creative writing instructor, 1999—. Member, Fairbanks Light Opera, Immaculate Conception Church, Running

Club North, and Nordale School Parent-Teacher Association.

Member

Alaska Society of Children's Book Writers (co-chair and presenter at 1992 convention), Fairbanks Drama Association.

Writings

Friendship across Arctic Waters: Alaskan Cub Scouts Meet Their Soviet Neighbors, illustrated with photographs by Charles Mason, Lodestar/Penguin (New York, NY), 1991.

To the Summit (young adult novel), Lodestar/Penguin (New York, NY), 1992.

The Prince and the Salmon People, illustrated by Dwayne Pasco, Rizzoli Children's Library (New York, NY), 1993.

A Child's Alaska, Alaska Northwest Books (Anchorage, AK), 1994.

Gold Star Sister (young adult novel), Lodestar/Penguin, 1994, North Star Publishing, 2000.

(With Jane G. Haigh) *Gold Rush Women,* Alaska Northwest Books (Anchorage, AK), 1997.

Caribou Girl, illustrated by Linda Russell, foreword by Jana Harcharek, Roberts Rinehart Publishers (Boulder, CO), 1998.

(With Jane G. Haigh) *Children of the Gold Rush,* Roberts Rinehart Publishers (Boulder, CO), 1999.

(With Jane G. Haigh) *Gold Rush Dogs,* Alaska Northwest Books (Anchorage, AK), 2001.

Gold Rush Winter, illustrated by Richard Waldrep, Golden Books (New York, NY), 2002.

Free Radical, Clarion Books (New York, NY), 2002.

(Editor and contributor, with others) *Daughters of the Desert: Stories of Remarkable Women from Christian, Jewish, and Muslim Traditions,* SkyLight Paths Publishing (Woodstock, VT), 2003.

Sidelights

Claire Rudolf Murphy once told *SATA* about the unusual journey that led to the writing of her first book for children, *Friendship across Arctic Waters: Alaskan Cub Scouts Meet Their Soviet Neighbors.* While trying to sell the story that would eventually become the young adult novel *To the Summit* to *Boys' Life* magazine, Murphy learned about the Nome Alaska Boy Scout troop and their dream of visiting Provideniya, in what was then the Soviet Far East. The troop used the article she wrote about them to convince the American government to let them take the trip, and Murphy went along. "Here I had grown up thinking of the Russians as enemies. In fact, in school during the fifties we used to have air-raid drills and many people in my neighborhood built bomb shelters to protect their families from the terrible Russians. They were our enemies. They didn't believe in God and they wanted to control the earth. Now I had the chance to get to know them for myself. During the visit I found them to be the friendliest, most articulate, and most generous people in the world (next to the Irish, of

course!). Many of them spoke English because English is taught in the schools from the first grade on. They all wanted to know about life in America, our government, what Russian books I had read and movies I had seen. The scouts and the young pioneers were like long-lost buddies. They knew the same games, told the same jokes, and just had fun together."

The beauty of Murphy's adopted state of Alaska was the inspiration for her young adult novel *To the Summit,* the author told *SATA.* "Ever since I first saw Denali (the Athabaskan Indian name for Mount McKinley, meaning 'high one,' a term commonly used by Alaskans) in 1974, it has reached out for me, as it has to many Alaskans. It is the mighty symbol of [Alaska], a magnificent statement about the beauty of our world. . . . [Denali] is one of the wonders of the modern world, so I felt it deserved a novel about climbing it. I wrote *To the Summit* because I believe it speaks to the idea of how much a physical challenge such as climbing Denali can help strengthen a person's inner self. People, teens particularly, can often feel powerless today, and having confidence in one's abilities can help overcome that."

"My third book, *The Prince and the Salmon People,* is very special to me. The salmon is my favorite wild animal, and I am concerned with how endangered they have become today. At the University of Alaska—Fairbanks library, I came upon a set of Tsimshian legends, and included in one volume was the story of the Prince and the Salmon People. After that I found other Tsimshian and Tlingit versions of the same story. . . .

"The Tsimshian learned how to respect and take care of the salmon, so that they would return to them every spring. My hope is that we today can take better care of the salmon so that they will continue to return to us every year, instead of dying out. The book is dedicated to my brother Matt because in 1988 he and I fought the mighty king salmon one July day and it was then that I first said aloud that I wanted to write a book about the salmon.

"I care so much about our incredible state and hopefully this book conveys that love and warmth for young readers everywhere. We have many natural resources up here, as well as a diversity of cultural groups and wild animals, and our job as Alaskans now is to protect all we have for future generations."

With Jane G. Haigh, Murphy wrote a series of heavily illustrated books intended to make Alaskan history come alive for young people. In *Children of the Gold Rush,* for example, the authors collected numerous photographs from the gold rush of the turn of the twentieth century, focusing on children, families, and the objects that were important to them. The book is organized into ten chapters, each featuring an individual child or group of children, telling their stories through letters, diaries, newspaper articles, and memoirs. Featured children are Native Alaskans, mixed Native and Caucasian, and Caucasian children of the invading hordes of gold seekers. Murphy also teamed up with Haigh to create

In Children of the Gold Rush, *Claire Rudolf Murphy and Jane G. Haigh have compiled the stories of numerous children who came to Alaska and the Yukon Territory and learned to conquer the elements in the uncompromising frontier.*

Gold Rush Women. The book celebrates the variety of roles women played in Gold Rush Alaska, from miner to nurse to prostitute, and Murphy's narrative, along with the many contemporary photographs, "create a strong sense of a rugged era," remarked a contributor to *Publishers Weekly.* Hazel Rochman, reviewing the book for *Booklist,* praised the prominent place of Native American women in this history. While finding the book suitable for students writing papers or browsing, Rochman additionally suggested, "recommend it also to adult readers." Murphy and Haigh are also the authors of *Gold Rush Dogs,* a dog-centered history of the early twentieth century in Alaska, when sled dogs still played a pivotal role in daily life. "Action-filled stories; fascinating characters, both human and canine; and great photos should make this ... a winner with both animal lovers and history buffs," concluded Arwen Marshall in *School Library Journal.*

Likewise, in *A Child's Alaska* Murphy provides a brief narrative outlining the variety of ways of life for children in contemporary Alaska. Like the author's other volumes on Alaska, this one is heavily illustrated with photographs, almost to the detriment of the narrative, according to some reviewers. On the other hand, *Booklist* contributor Kay Weisman remarked that "although it is aimed more at browsers than at report writers, this will make an excellent source for units on Alaska." Murphy turned to Alaskan folklore in *The Prince and the Salmon People,* which tells of a young boy's rediscovery of his tribe's forgotten knowledge of caring for the salmon, which are vital to the survival of

the Native Alaskans. Similarly, in *Caribou Girl,* Murphy tells the story of a girl who saves her starving tribe by becoming a caribou and, on her return to human form, teaching her people how to hunt the animals for survival.

Murphy's fascination with history provided fuel for her young adult novel *Gold Star Sister.* Here, thirteen-year-old Carrie gets a lesson in World War II history when her beloved grandmother moves in with Carrie's family while the woman undergoes chemotherapy treatments for her cancer. Gram brings with her a box of correspondence, including letters from a brother who was killed by friendly fire during the war, and whose death was so painful that he was never mentioned again in the family. Among the dead man's effects is a letter, given to him for safekeeping by another soldier, and Carrie decides to make sure, a half-century later, that it is delivered to the man's son. The story of Carrie's reluctant acceptance of her grandmother's impending death is interwoven with Carrie's problems with friends, her sisters, and her parents. Although Elizabeth Bush, who reviewed *Gold Star Sister* for *Bulletin of the Center for Children's Books,* felt that Murphy's story threatens to be toppled by the weight of all its interwoven plot strands, she also concluded that "readers looking for a fresh spin on World War II fiction and those who enjoy a good cry over a family story may find the tale equally enjoyable." *Voice of Youth Advocates* contributor Becky Kornman, however, had no such doubts, calling *Gold Star Sister* "a well-developed, realistic, and thought-provoking novel." Chris Sherman, writing in *Booklist,* similarly found much to praise in this young adult novel, including

Murphy's sensitive characterizations and true-to-life emotions. "The plot unfolds quickly and dramatically," Sherman wrote, "and Murphy's finely crafted depiction of parent-child relationships makes the novel a good family story."

A more recent war forms the backdrop for *Free Radical,* a young adult novel in which teenage Luke must cope with the discovery that his mother once participated in a protest against the Vietnam War that resulted in a man's death. Since then she has lived under an assumed name in Alaska, though her guilt over her responsibility has haunted her all these years and finally drives her to give herself up to the government. Luke himself comes to understand the need for the families of victims to meet with the guilty in order to forgive and encourages his mother to do so. A contributor to *Publishers Weekly* praised the extent of Murphy's evident research for her story, but concluded that the plot relies too "frequently on coincidence ... and contrivance." However, a contributor to *Kirkus Reviews* made a claim for *Free Radical* as a fresh approach for fiction about the Vietnam War. "The author does an excellent job of

Fifteen-year-old Luke faces the dissolution of his placid world in Fairbanks, Alaska when the disclosure of his mother's secret crime impacts their lives. (Cover illustration by Ericka O'Rourke.)

peeling back the layers of consequences and the need for forgiveness that one reckless act carries in its wake," this writer concluded.

Biographical and Critical Sources

PERIODICALS

Bloomsbury Review, May, 1995, review of *A Child's Alaska,* p. 31.

Booklist, May 15, 1992, Chris Sherman, review of *To the Summit,* p. 1674; June 1, 1993, Carolyn Phelan, review of *The Prince and the Salmon People,* p. 1824; November 15, 1994, Chris Sherman, review of *Gold Star Sister,* p. 594; December 1, 1994, Kay Weisman, review of *A Child's Alaska,* p. 666; August, 1997, Hazel Rochman, review of *Gold Rush Women,* p. 1890; March 1, 2000, Stephanie Zvirin, review of *Gold Rush Women,* p. 1248; September 1, 2001, Randy Meyer, review of *Gold Rush Dogs,* p. 95.

Book Report, November-December, 1992, Marion Carmickle, review of *To the Summit,* p. 43; January-February, 1995, Carol Strope, review of *Gold Star Sister,* p. 48; January-February, 1998, Margaret Zinz Jantzen, review of *Gold Rush Women,* p. 46.

Bulletin of the Center for Children's Books, October, 1994, Elizabeth Bush, review of *Gold Star Sister,* p. 59.

Horn Book, July, 1999, Elizabeth S. Watson, review of *Children of the Gold Rush,* pp. 483-484.

Horn Book Guide, spring, 1995, Anne Deifendeifer, review of *A Child's Alaska,* p. 164; fall, 1998, Patricia Riley, review of *Caribou Girl,* p. 301.

Kirkus Reviews, September 15, 1994, review of *Gold Star Sister,* p. 1277; March 15, 1998, review of *Caribou Girl,* p. 408; February 1, 2001, review of *Free Radical,* p. 185.

Kliatt, May, 1999, Claire Rosser, review of *Children of the Gold Rush,* p. 41.

New Advocate, winter, 1994, M. Jean Greenlaw, review of *The Prince and the Salmon People,* p. 63.

Publishers Weekly, August 23, 1993, review of *The Prince and the Salmon People,* p. 71; June 2, 1997, review of *Gold Rush Women,* p. 73; April 6, 1998, review of *Caribou Girl,* p. 77; February 22, 1999, "The Littlest Prospectors," p. 97; January 21, 2002, review of *Free Radical,* p. 91.

School Library Journal, October, 1991, Mollie Bynum, review of *Friendship across Arctic Waters: Alaskan Cub Scouts Meet Their Soviet Neighbors,* p. 140; June, 1992, Joel Shoemaker, review of *To the Summit,* p. 139; November, 1993, Patricia Dooley, review of *The Prince and the Salmon People,* p. 118; November, 1994, Judy R. Johnston, review of *Gold Star Sister,* p. 121; January, 1995, Roz Goodman, review of *A Child's Alaska,* p. 130; November, 1997, Carolyn Lehman, review of *Gold Rush Women,* p. 132; July, 1998, Mollie Bynum, review of *Caribou Girl,* p. 80; September, 1999, Jennifer A. Fakolt, review of *Children of the Gold Rush,* p. 239; September, 2001, Arwen Marshall, review of *Gold Rush Dogs,* p. 251; March, 2002, Coop Renner, review of *Free Radical,* p. 235.

Voice of Youth Advocates, February, 1995, Becky Kornman, review of *Gold Star Sister,* p. 340.

OTHER

Claire   Rudolf   Murphy   Web   Site,   http://www.
clairerudolfmurphy.com (January 15, 2003).*

N

NAPOLI, Donna Jo 1948-

Personal

Born February 28, 1948, in Miami, FL; daughter of Vincent Robert and Helen Gloria (Grandinetti) Napoli; married Barry Ray Furrow (a law professor), December 29, 1968; children: Elena, Michael Enzo, Nicholas Umberto, Eva, Robert Emilio. *Education:* Harvard University, B.A., 1970, Ph.D., 1973.

Addresses

Office—Linguistics Dept., Swarthmore College, Swarthmore, PA 19081. *Agent*—Barry Furrow, Widener University School of Law, Wilmington, DE 19803. *E-mail*—dnapoli1@swarthmore.edu.

Career

Author and educator. Smith College, Northampton, MA, lecturer in philosophy and Italian, 1973-74; University of North Carolina, Chapel Hill, NC, lecturer in mathematics and Italian, 1974-75; Georgetown University, Washington, DC, assistant professor of linguistics, 1975-80; University of Michigan, Ann Arbor, MI, professor of linguistics, 1980-87; Swarthmore College, Swarthmore, PA, professor of linguistics, 1987—.

Member

Society of Children's Book Writers and Illustrators, Authors Guild, Authors League of America, Linguistic Society of America, Società linguistica Italiana.

Awards, Honors

One Hundred Titles for Reading and Sharing selection, New York Public Library (NYPL), 1992, Children's Book of the Year, Bank Street Child Study Children's Book Committee, 1993, and New Jersey Reading Association's Jerry Award, 1996, all for *The Prince of the Pond: Otherwise Known as De Fawg Pin;* Best Book

Donna Jo Napoli

for Young Adults selection, Young Adult Library Services Association (YALSA), 1994, for *The Magic Circle;* Children's Books of the Year, Bank Street Child Study Children's Book Committee, 1995, for *When the Water Closes over My Head,* and 1996, for *Jimmy, the Pickpocket of the Palace;* Leeway Foundation Prize for excellence in fiction, 1995; Pick of the Lists selection, American Booksellers Association (ABA), 1996, for *Zel* and *Song of the Magdalene;* Hall of Fame Sports Book for Kids selection, Free Library of Philadelphia, 1996, for *Soccer Shock;* Notable Children's Trade Book, National Council for the Social Studies and Children's Book Council, Carolyn W. Field Honor Book, Best Books selection, American Library Association (ALA), Golden Kite Award, Society of Children's Book Writers and Illustrators, 1998, Sydney Taylor Book Award,

National Association of Jewish Libraries, 1998, and Best Books for the Teen Age selection, NYPL, 1998, all for *Stones in Water;* Best Books selection, NYPL, for *For the Love of Venice;* Best Books selection, ALA, and Best Books selection, NYPL, both for *Sirena;* Best Books for the Teen Age selection, NYPL, for *Spinners;* Notable Books selection, *Smithsonian* magazine for *Crazy Jack;* Carolyn W. Field Honor Book, for *Beast;* Pick of the Lists selection, ABA, Children's Book Sense Seventy-six List, and Best Children's Books selection, NYPL, 2001, all for *Albert;* Zooba Recommended for Parenting about Grief, and Oppenheim Toy Portfolio Best Book, 2002, both for *Flamingo Dream;* grants and fellowships in linguistics from National Science Foundation, National Endowment for the Humanities, Mellon Foundation, and Sloan Foundation.

Writings

CHILDREN'S FICTION

The Hero of Barletta, illustrated by Dana Gustafson, Carolrhoda Books (Minneapolis, MN), 1988.
Soccer Shock, illustrated by Meredith Johnson, Dutton (New York, NY), 1991.
The Prince of the Pond: Otherwise Known as De Fawg Pin, illustrated by Judith Byron Schachner, Dutton (New York, NY), 1992.
The Magic Circle, Dutton (New York, NY), 1993.
When the Water Closes over My Head, illustrated by Nancy Poydar, Dutton (New York, NY), 1994.
Shark Shock, Dutton (New York, NY), 1994.
Jimmy, the Pickpocket of the Palace, illustrated by Judith Byron Schachner, Dutton (New York, NY), 1995.
The Bravest Thing, Dutton (New York, NY), 1995.
Zel, Dutton (New York, NY), 1996.
Song of the Magdalene, Scholastic (New York, NY), 1996.
Trouble on the Tracks, Scholastic (New York, NY), 1997.
On Guard, Dutton (New York, NY), 1997.
Stones in Water, Dutton (New York, NY), 1997.
Changing Tunes, Dutton (New York, NY), 1998.
For the Love of Venice, Delacorte (New York, NY), 1998.
Sirena, Scholastic (New York, NY), 1998.
Crazy Jack, Delacorte (New York, NY), 1999.
(With Richard Tchen) *Spinners,* Dutton (New York, NY), 1999.
Beast, Atheneum (New York, NY), 2000.
Shelley Shock, Dutton (New York, NY), 2000.
Albert, illustrated by Jim LaMarche, Harcourt (New York, NY), 2001.
(With Richard Tchen) *How Hungry Are You?,* illustrated by Amy Walrod, Atheneum (New York, NY), 2001.
Three Days, Dutton (New York, NY), 2001.
Daughter of Venice, Delacorte (New York, NY), 2002.
Flamingo Dream, illustrated by Cathie Felstead, Greenwillow (New York, NY), 2002.
(With Marie Kane) *Rocky, the Cat Who Barks,* illustrated by Tamara Petrosino, Dutton (New York, NY), 2002.
The Great God Pan, Wendy Lamb Books (New York, NY), 2003.
Breath, Simon and Schuster (New York, NY), 2003.

"ANGELWINGS" SERIES; FOR CHILDREN

Friends Everywhere, illustrated by Lauren Klementz-Harte, Aladdin (New York, NY), 1999.
Little Creatures, illustrated by Lauren Klementz-Harte, Aladdin (New York, NY), 1999.
On Her Own, illustrated by Lauren Klementz-Harte, Aladdin (New York, NY), 1999.
One Leap Forward, illustrated by Lauren Klementz-Harte, Aladdin (New York, NY), 1999.
No Fair!, illustrated by Lauren Klementz-Harte, Aladdin (New York, NY), 2000.
Playing Games, illustrated by Lauren Klementz-Harte, Aladdin (New York, NY), 2000.
Lies and Lemons, illustrated by Lauren Klementz-Harte, Aladdin (New York, NY), 2000.
Running Away, illustrated by Lauren Klementz-Harte, Aladdin (New York, NY), 2000.
April Flowers, illustrated by Lauren Klementz-Harte, Aladdin (New York, NY), 2000.
Partners, Aladdin (New York, NY), 2000.
Left Out, Aladdin (New York, NY), 2000.
Give and Take, illustrated by Lauren Klementz-Harte, Aladdin (New York, NY), 2000.
Know-It-All, illustrated by Lauren Klementz-Harte, Aladdin (New York, NY), 2000.
Happy Holidays, Aladdin (New York, NY), 2000.
New Voices, illustrated by Lauren Klementz-Harte, Aladdin (New York, NY), 2000.
Hang in There, Aladdin (New York, NY), 2001.

ADULT NONFICTION

(Editor) *Elements of Tone, Stress, and Intonation,* Georgetown University Press (Washington, DC), 1978.
(With Emily Rando) *Syntactic Argumentation,* Georgetown University Press (Washington, DC), 1979.
(Editor with William Cressey) *Linguistic Symposium on Romance Languages: 9,* Georgetown University Press (Washington, DC), 1981.
Predication Theory: A Case Study for Indexing Theory, Cambridge University Press (New York, NY), 1989.
(Editor with Judy Anne Kegl) *Bridges between Psychology and Linguistics: A Swarthmore Festschrift for Lila Gleitman,* L. Erlbaum (Mahwah, NJ), 1991.
Syntax: Theory and Problems, Oxford University Press (New York, NY), 1993.
(With Stuart Davis) *Phonological Factors in Historical Change: The Passage of the Latin Second Conjugation into Romance,* Rosenberg & Sellier, 1994.
Linguistics: Theory and Problems, Oxford University Press (New York, NY), 1996.
Language Matters: A Guide to Everyday Questions about Language, Oxford University Press (New York, NY), 2003.

Also contributor to and editor of poetry books, including *The Linguistic Muse, Meliglossa, Lingua Franca,* and *Speaking in Tongues.* Author of numerous professional articles on linguistics. Also author of two short stories, "Sweet Giorgio" and "Little Lella," both in collections compiled and illustrated by Diane Goode and published by Dutton in 1992 and 1997.

Work in Progress

Gracie, the Pixie of the Puddle, a sequel to *The Prince of the Pond: Otherwise Known as De Fawg Pin* and *Jimmy, the Pickpocket of the Palace.*

Sidelights

A professor of linguistics at Swarthmore College, Donna Jo Napoli's passion for language can be seen in her novels for young adults and middle-grade readers. Exploring topics ranging from sports to sharks to fairy tales, Napoli employs both humor and skillful prose to craft stories of hope and inspiration. Noting that her books for young readers "can be broadly divided into two types: contemporary realistic novels and fairy-tale retellings," an essayist in the *St. James Guide to Young Adult Writers* praised the author's "strong points" as her ability to create "genuine, believable characters" and equally believable plots. As the interpreter of stories culled from myth, legend, and biblical sources, she has "forged a brilliant writing career out of making readers see compellingly different interpretations of mythic figures," maintained GraceAnne A. DeCandido in a review of the author's 1998 book *Sirena* for *Booklist.*

Described as "a gifted author" by a *Kirkus Reviews* critic, Napoli did not plan on becoming a writer. As she once told *SATA,* "It just happened to me, when I found that writing helped me through difficult times in my life." The youngest of four children, she was born in Miami, Florida, and by age thirteen she had lived in thirteen different houses that her father, a contractor, built on speculation and subsequently sold. As she wrote in an essay for *Something about the Author Autobiography Series* (*SAAS*), she was a slow learner when it came to reading. When the words finally clicked together for her in the second grade, she began haunting the school library. "We had no books in our house. None whatsoever. We had no magazines. My father read the newspaper. I'm not sure I ever saw my mother read at all. My older siblings had school books. And I had the never-ending library." Napoli blossomed in high school in such subjects as French, Latin, and math. She went on to attend Radcliffe College, where "the world of ideas that I had yearned for in the books I read and gotten a hint of in my high school honors classes opened up to me at last," as she recalled in *SAAS.*

Napoli took her undergraduate degree in mathematics, but switched to Romance linguistics for her doctorate, which was the perfect blend of her interests both in math and in languages. During her junior year she also married, though graduate studies and teaching positions kept her domestic life a challenge for many years. Although she took a course in composition and was encouraged by her instructor to pursue a career in writing, she had no desire "to be a poor writer," as she wrote in *SAAS.* "I wanted to earn money and never have to make my family move and never have to make my children worry about whether there would be food on the table. I was practical."

Napoli held lecturer and assistant professor positions at several colleges while working toward becoming a full professor in linguistics. She attained this position at the University of Michigan in 1984. While as an academic, she published articles in professional publications and eventually began to write poetry and, ultimately, books for children. *The Hero of Barletta,* an adaptation of a traditional Italian tale that became her first book for young readers, was published in 1988. "I felt happy to sell that first story," she explained in *SAAS,* "but I also felt rather strange: the message seemed to be that I could tell traditional stories, but not stories I made up from scratch. It was a mixed message."

Soccer Shock, Napoli's first original tale for young readers, focuses on a sport her children played, particularly Michael. Adam, the ten-year-old protagonist of the novel, discovers that he has magic freckles that can both see and talk, and decides to use this secret to help him earn a place on the school soccer team. "The freckles really steal the show here," commented a *Kirkus Reviews* critic, who described *Soccer Shock* as "a well-written story with an affectionate, tolerant cast." Denise Krell, writing in *School Library Journal,* dubbed the freckles "far-fetched," but decided that even with such a "fantastic twist," this "lighthearted novel succeeds with genuine characters in a believable setting."

Napoli went on to pen several sequels to *Soccer Shock. Shark Shock* finds Adam—a year older and still in communication with his freckles—befriending a blind boy during his summer vacation at the beach. While commenting that Napoli's idea of talking freckles "stretches credibility to the breaking point," Maggie McEwen concluded in *School Library Journal* that "this light read will appeal to children who have an appreciation for the absurd." And in *Shelley Shock,* Adam and his talking freckles have to contend with a girl who makes the team, and the freckles' advice end up creating more trouble than they solve.

Napoli's next book for middle-grade readers, *The Prince of the Pond: Otherwise Known as De Fawg Pin,* employs the fairy tale frog-prince motif, but with a unique twist. A prince is turned into a frog by a hag and is then taken under the protective arm of Jade, a female frog who teaches him the ropes in the pond. Blessed with a prodigious number of spawn, the sensitive frog-prince determines to raise some of them personally. Yet when a princess passes by, the frog-prince leaps to the cheek, kisses her, and becomes a prince once again, leaving Jade and their offspring behind. "The frog prince motif has inspired many books," noted *Booklist* reviewer Carolyn Phelan, "but few as original as this novel." Betsy Hearne of the *Bulletin of the Center for Children's Books* commented both on the point of view—the story is told by Jade, the female frog—and the book's willingness to deal with loss, and concluded that *The Prince of the Pond* is "an animal fantasy that fairy tale readers will relish." A *Kirkus Reviews* critic felt that the author had done her research well: "[This is] a book with an astonishing amount of in-depth natural history cleverly embedded in its endearing, screwball charm." In

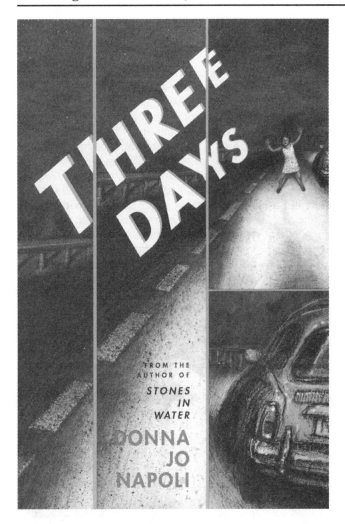

After eleven-year-old Jackie is kidnapped while on a trip to Italy, she comes to understand her captors' motives in Napoli's suspenseful novel. (Cover illustration by Janet Hamlin.)

fact, Napoli spent a great deal of time reading about amphibians and observing pond life. "When I write for children," Napoli explained in *SAAS,* "I am dead serious. If you sit back and think seriously about the frog prince story even just for a moment, you will realize that without a frog to help this prince through the ordeal, he would have been snake meat fast."

To please her fans, who were curious to know what became of the frog family, Napoli wrote a sequel, *Jimmy, the Pickpocket of the Palace.* Attempting to save his pond from the miserable hag, young Jimmy, a frog offspring of the prince, is transformed into a human and does not care much for the change. He inevitably ends up working in the palace where he encounters his father. "This successful successor is certain to satisfy old fans and win new friends to the frog prince and his brood," commented a *Kirkus Reviews* contributor. As the author related to *SATA,* she is working on a third and final book in the series, *Gracie, the Pixie of the Puddle.*

Napoli's *The Magic Circle,* the first of her young-adult novels based on traditional fairy tales, was inspired by

an innocent question posed by the author's daughter, Eva, as to the preponderance of wicked witches and stepmothers in fairy tales, and the dearth of equally evil warlocks and stepfathers. "My little feminist heart beat hard," Napoli recalled in *SAAS,* "and I flipped the pages of my mind through all the fairy tales I knew, looking for the worst woman character I could find. There she was: the witch in Hansel and Gretel." *The Magic Circle* is Napoli's attempt to give a history and motivation to the witch in a prequel to the Hansel and Gretel fairy tale. In her rendition, the witch is a good-hearted healer whom evil spirits have turned into a bad witch with a hunger for children. She takes herself off to the woods where she will not be tempted, until one day two succulent children appear on her doorstep. "Napoli flexes her proven talent for unexpected viewpoints, builds strong pace with compressed vigor, and evokes powerful sensory images," noted Betsy Hearne in a review for the *Bulletin of the Center for Children's Books.* Lisa Dennis, writing in *School Library Journal,* observed "a strongly medieval flavor" in *The Magic Circle* and concluded that "Napoli's writing and the clarity of her vision make this.... a brilliantly conceived and beautifully executed novel that is sure to be appreciated by thoughtful readers." A *Publishers Weekly* reviewer called *The Magic Circle* a young adult novel of "genuine magic and suspense" that would "captivate adults as well."

Napoli's second fairy tale revisioning is based on the Rapunzel story and titled *Zel.* Told alternately from the point of view of Zel held in the tower, the count who wants to save her, and Zel's witch mother who put the girl in the tower, the book plunges into the psychology of the characters. "The genius of the novel lies not just in the details but in its breadth of vision," noted a contributor to *Publishers Weekly.* "Its shiveringly romantic conclusion will leave readers spellbound." In a *Horn Book* review of *Zel,* Roger Sutton commented that the early chapters of the book are a bit of a "wander," but concluded that the novel ultimately "transforms myth without flippancy, honoring the power of its roots."

Crazy Jack, published in 1999, is a somewhat darker version of the "Jack and the Beanstalk" tale. In Napoli's version, nine-year-old Jack is left orphaned after his father gambles away the family farm and then falls off a cliff to his death while trying to rob a wealthy giant. For the next seven years, Jack is obsessed with climbing the cliff that took his father's life, and the boy's strange behavior seems like madness to his mother, especially when he comes home claiming to have acquired magic beans that will aid him in reaching the cliff's summit— and the home of the murderous giant. Noting that Jack's ascent of the beanstalk and stealing a hen that lays golden eggs "can be interpreted as hallucination," *Kliatt* contributor Claire Rosser explained that Napoli enhances the traditional tale with "modern psychological interpretations," including addictive behavior, and maintained that readers "with some basic understanding of the subconscious, will marvel at the neatness of Napoli's narrative" and its "subtle twists of interpretation."

Noting that Napoli "knows traditional folklore," *Bulletin of the Center for Children's Books* contributor Janice M. Del Negro praised *Crazy Jack* as an "old tale [stripped] to bare bones" and supplemented by "newly imagined body, heart, and soul." The author "searches deeply for the emotional motivations" behind the archetypal characters of Jack, his father, and the giant, and works them into a story containing "depth and substance."

Published in 1999, *Spinners* presents the character of Rumpelstiltskin within what *Kliatt* contributor Claire Rosser described as "a morality tale of the crippling reality of greed and vengeance." In the story, which Napoli coauthored with Richard Tchen, Saskia is a young woman who was raised in a troubled home and finds solace in spinning different types of wool and other fibers into beautiful yarns. Into her life comes an embittered man named Rumpelstiltskin. Rumpelstiltskin is a tailor who once passionately loved—and lost— Saskia's mother, who died in childbirth; unknown to her, he is in fact the young woman's father. Greedy for family but unable to love Saskia, the old man places Saskia into a position whereby she will likely lose her own child, the child the old man is determined to gain to create the family he feels was stolen from him. "The novel's emotional content is a stirring mixture of unwise entanglements, foolish father figures, and broken promises," commented Janice M. Del Negro in the *Bulletin of the Center for Children's Books*. Noting that "watching how the tale is unraveled and rewoven is half the fun" of reading one of Napoli's fairy tale adaptations, Chris Sherman commented in *Booklist* that "questions abound" in a story focusing on "love, pride, greed, magic, and revenge: what a wonderful read."

In addition to fantasies, Napoli has authored several works of realistic fiction. *When the Water Closes over My Head* was inspired by her son Michael's fear of drowning. On vacation with grandparents in Iowa, nine-year-old Mikey is continually confronted with his fear of drowning in *When the Water Closes over My Head* and eventually surmounts this phobia. The book is "a funny, easily read story that boys and girls should take to like ducks to water," enthused a *Kirkus Reviews* commentator. Hazel Rochman, writing in *Booklist*, drew attention to Napoli's technique of "tightly structured, cinematic episodes," and use of dialogue that captured the "daily tangle of close relationships," concluding that "kids will want more stories about this family."

Having overcome his fear of drowning, fourth-grader Mikey returns in Napoli's *On Guard*, this time to confront anxieties of another sort. The second of four children, Mikey fears that he will not be special enough in any one way to distinguish himself from his siblings. Mikey discovers the sport of fencing and determines to win the medal his teacher awards weekly to a student who has impressed her with a particular skill, accomplishment, or quality. "Napoli is excellent at depicting Mikey's general tendency towards uncertainty, his frustration at his lack of family stardom, and his passionate attachment to his new field," wrote *Bulletin of the Center for Children's Books* reviewer Deborah

Stevenson. "Especially with its lure of an offbeat and glamorous sport, this will please many young readers."

In *The Bravest Thing*, ten-year-old Laurel has to face the death of her newborn bunnies, an aunt with cancer, and her own diagnosis of scoliosis. "Despite the multitude of hard knocks, this is not a problem novel," noted a *Publishers Weekly* critic. "Napoli . . . inspires the reader to believe that obstacles, no matter how daunting, can be made smaller through courage." Another work of nonfiction focusing on modern young people, *Changing Tunes* finds ten-year-old Eileen dismayed to find that her parents' divorce has disrupted her formerly comfortable home and even her beloved piano is now gone. Ashamed to tell her friends or teachers that her home has been disrupted, she goes in secret to the school's auditorium to practice on the piano there and meets a sympathetic janitor named Mr. Poole who helps Eileen see that "she can't control the family she was born into," according to a *Kirkus Reviews* contributor. "Napoli's characterizations are well-rounded," added Janice M. Del Negro in a *Bulletin of the Center for Children's Books* review, calling *Changing Tunes* a "low-key, gently evolving narrative of a young girl's emotional maturation."

Napoli has also written historical fiction for young people. *Song of the Magdalene*, set in ancient Israel, constructs an account of the life of biblical figure Mary Magdalene from a troubled youth as the daughter of a wealthy Jewish widower in the town of Magdala to her experiences as a helper of Jesus. A *Publishers Weekly* reviewer faulted the work as uneven in many respects, noting, for instance, that "the pacing seems clotted around climactic moments," but nevertheless conceded that "readers may come away with new thoughts about a different era." *Voice of Youth Advocates* contributor Libby Bergstrom offered a more favorable assessment of *Song of the Magdalene*, asserting that "the power of Napoli's investigation into the human psyche will draw YA readers into this book; Miriam [Mary] is a character they will not soon forget." In *Booklist*, Ilene Cooper commented that Napoli's "lyrical writing and layered characterizations" make *Song of the Magdalene* an enjoyable read for a "sophisticated audience."

Moving forward in time, Napoli's *Stones in Water* takes place in Italy during the early twentieth century and focuses on children living in Nazi concentration camps. Motivated by true events, the novel finds thirteen-year-old Roberto, his brother, and friends taken by German soldiers and herded into trains in a surprise roundup of slave laborers that leaves the boys unable to tell their parents what has happened to them. Ultimately, Roberto escapes from his Munich work camp and flees through the Soviet Union and joins a partisan. In what *Voice of Youth Advocates* contributor Janet Mura called a "harrowing tale of inhumanity, strength, and friendship," Napoli recounts the hardships the boys face as some live while others perish. "The honest, understated tone of the narrative . . . makes Napoli's message of the strength which hope and friendship and compassion can impart all the more impressive," maintained an essayist in the *St. James Guide to Young Adult Writers*. Calling *Stones in Water* "an affecting coming-of-age novel with a vivid and undeniable message about the human costs of war," *Horn Book* reviewer Kitty Flynn added that "Napoli's detailed and gripping descriptions bring the incomprehensible tragedy to life for readers."

Other stories that take place in the author's beloved Italy include *For the Love of Venice, Daughter of Venice,* and *Three Days.* The first, a 1998 novel, finds an American teen spending the summer in Venice while his father works on a civil-engineering project. Romance soon enters the picture in the form of a pretty Italian teen, but the relationship becomes complicated when her radical politics are revealed. Citing as the novel's strongest attribute the author's ability to portray "Venice with loving detail," *School Library Journal* contributor Jennifer A. Fakolt added that *For the Love of Venice* "offers a unique slant on contemporary politics and perspectives couched in an exotic romance." Drawing readers back in time to the sixteenth century, *Daughter of Venice* focuses on fourteen-year-old Donata Mocenigo, who desires to break free of the future typical for a younger daughter born to a family of her wealth and station: an adulthood spent in a convent or spent caring for elderly relatives. Disguising herself as a boy, she escapes from her home and ultimately finds romance with a Jewish teen who teaches her to read but whose faith makes him an unsuitable suitor, according to her family. Praising Napoli for avoiding "the easy anachronism," a *Kirkus Reviews* critic explained that the novel's heroine abides by the dictums of her family and polite society, and searches for "a solution to her unhappiness that ... remains essentially true to her culture and its restrictions." Praising the novel as "engrossing and exotic," Lisa Prolman observed in *School Library Journal* that, "While a current trend in historical fiction presents a girl with modern sensibilities chafing under the strict rules of a [former] time, nothing about Donata seems forced."

Often asked where the ideas for her stories come from, Napoli once noted in *SAAS:* "If you keep your eyes and ears and mind and heart open, you will find plenty to write about—more than anyone could ever write in a lifetime." "When I write for children," Napoli added, "I do not hesitate to present them with the sadness of mortality and the horrors of wickedness—but I always try to leave them with a sense that whether or not they can change the problems in life, they can find a way to live decently and joyfully. Hope is an internal matter. I strive to cultivate it in my readers."

While finding material is never a problem for Napoli—who can also count picture books and adult mysteries among her writing accomplishments—finding time in her busy schedule for writing *is* a problem. An organized professional, she even writes in her laundry room so that she can do two tasks at once. Her advice to young writers is simple: write what you know about; write about something that is important; and use good language. A conscientious re-writer, Napoli gets feedback from her editor, family, school children, and even strangers on the street.

Biographical and Critical Sources

BOOKS

Authors and Artists for Young Adults, Volume 25, Gale (Detroit, MI), 1998, pp. 195-200.
Contemporary Literature Review, Volume 51, Gale (Detroit, MI), 1999, pp. 152-168.
Hipple, Ted, editor, *Writers for Young Adults,* Scribner's (New York, NY), 2000, pp. 217-226.
Napoli, Donna Jo, essay in *Something about the Author Autobiography Series,* Volume 23, Gale (Detroit, MI), 1997, pp. 161-178.
St. James Guide to Young Adult Writers, 2nd edition, St. James Press (Detroit, MI), 1999.

PERIODICALS

Booklist, January 15, 1993, Carolyn Phelan, review of *The Prince of the Pond: Otherwise Known as De Fawg Pin,* p. 909; July, 1993, Sally Estes, review of *The Magic Circle,* p. 1957; January 1, 1994, Hazel Rochman, review of *When the Water Closes Over My Head,* p. 827; October 15, 1994, Frances Bradburn, review of *Shark Shock,* p. 427; March 15, 1995, Ilene Cooper, review of *Jimmy, the Pickpocket of the Palace,* p. 1331; October 1, 1995, p. 317; October 1, 1997, Hazel Rochman, review of *Stones in Water,* p. 333; May 1, 1998, Ilene Cooper, review of *For the Love of Venice,* p. 1512; May 15, 1998, John Peters, review of *Changing Tunes,* p. 1627; September 15, 1998, GraceAnne A. DeCandido, review of *Sirena,* p. 221; October 1, 1998, Ilene Cooper, review of *Song of the Magdalene,* p. 341; September 1, 1999, Chris Sherman, review of *Spinners,* p. 124; October 1, 1999, Kay Weisman, review of *Crazy Jack,* p. 355; September 15, 2000, Sally Estes, review of *Beast,* p. 233, and Ellen Mandel, review of *Shelley Shock,* p. 242; September 15, 2001, Michael Cart, review of *How Hungry Are You?,* p. 233; October 1, 2001, GraceAnne A. DeCandido, review of *Three Days,* p. 312; January 1, 2002, Whitney Scott, review of *Beast,* p. 876; March 1, 2002, Lauren Peterson, review of *Rocky, the Cat Who Barks,* p. 1143; April 15, 2002, Ilene Cooper, review of *Flamingo Dream,* p. 1498.
Book Report, March, 2001, Suzanne Manczuk, review of *Beast,* p. 59.
Bulletin of the Center for Children's Books, January, 1993, Betsy Hearne, review of *The Prince of the Pond,* p. 153; April, 1993, Betsy Hearne, review of *The Magic Circle,* p. 260; September, 1994, p. 21; June, 1995, p. 355; October, 1995, p. 64; January, 1997, p. 182; February, 1997, Deborah Stevenson, review of *On Guard,* p. 217; March, 1997, p. 253; February, 1998, Betsy Hearne, review of *Stones in Water,* p. 214; September, 1998, Janice M. Del Negro, review of *Changing Tunes,* pp. 24-25; December, 1998, Janice M. Del Negro, review of *Sirena,* p. 140; September, 1999, Janice M. Del Negro, review of *Spinners,* pp. 25-26; December, 1999, Janice M. Del Negro, review of *Crazy Jack,* pp. 119-120.
Horn Book, September-October, 1996, Roger Sutton, review of *Zel,* p. 603; January-February, 1998, Kitty Flynn, review of *Stones in Water,* p. 77; January, 2000, review of *Crazy Jack,* p. 80; September, 2000,

review of *Beast,* p. 577; January, 2001, Donna Jo Napoli, "What's Math Got to Do with It?, p. 61; March, 2001, Christine Heppermann, "Angel Wings and Hard Knocks," p. 239; September, 2001, review of *Three Days,* p. 590; March-April, 2002, Anita L. Burkam, review of *Daughter of Venice,* p. 216.

Kirkus Reviews, September 15, 1991, review of *Soccer Shock,* p. 1225; October 1, 1992, review of *The Prince of the Pond,* p. 1259; June 15, 1993, p. 789; January 1, 1994, review of *When the Water Closes Over My Head,* p. 72; May 1, 1995, review of *Jimmy, the Pickpocket of the Palace;* January 15, 1997, p. 144; May 15, 1998, review of *Changing Tunes,* p. 741; September 15, 1998, review of *Sirena,* p. 1386; February 15, 2001, review of *Albert,* p. 263; December 15, 2001, review of *Rocky, the Cat Who Barks,* p. 1761, and review of *Daughter of Venice,* p. 1761.

Kliatt, May, 1998, review of *For the Love of Venice,* p. 7; September, 1999, Claire Rosser, review of *Crazy Jack,* p. 12; November, 1999, Claire Rosser, review of *Spinners,* p. 12.

Library Journal, September 1, 1994, Nancy Dice, review of *The Magic Circle,* p. 244.

Los Angeles Times Book Review, April 8, 2001, review of *Albert,* p. 6.

New York Times Book Review, February 11, 2001, review of *Beast,* p. 26.

Publishers Weekly, January 27, 1992, p. 98; November 16, 1992, review of *The Prince of the Pond,* p. 64; June 14, 1993, review of *The Magic Circle,* p. 73; February 21, 1994, review of *When the Water Closes over My Head,* p. 255; June 12, 1995, p. 61; July 3, 1995, p. 62; October 30, 1995, review of *The Bravest Thing,* p. 62; June 17, 1996, review of *Zel,* p. 66; November 4, 1996, review of *Song of the Magdalene,* p. 77; March 23, 1998, review of *For the Love of Venice,* p. 101; June 15, 1998, review of *Changing Tunes,* p. 60; November 2, 1998, review of *Sirena,* p. 84; July 19, 1999, review of *Spinners,* p. 196; November 1,

1999, review of *Crazy Jack,* p. 85, review of *Friends Everywhere,* p. 84; November 8, 1999, review of *Stones in Water,* p. 71; November 6, 2000, review of *Beast,* p. 92; March 5, 2001, review of *Albert,* p. 78; August 20, 2001, review of *How Hungry Are You?,* p. 80; February 18, 2002, review of *Daughter of Venice,* p. 97; March 11, 2002, review of *Flamingo Dream,* p. 72.

School Library Journal, August, 1988, Nancy A. Gifford, review of *The Hero of Barletta,* p. 84; April, 1992, Denise Krell, review of *Soccer Shock,* p. 118; October, 1992, John Peters, review of *The Prince of the Pond,* p. 118; August, 1993, Lisa Dennis, review of *The Magic Circle,* p. 186; March, 1994, Carol Schene, review of *When the Water Closes over My Head,* p. 223; January, 1995, Maggie McEwen, review of *Shark Shock,* p. 109; June, 1995, p. 112; October, 1995, p. 138; November, 1997, Marilyn Payne Phillips, review of *Stones in Water,* p. 122; June, 1998, Jennifer A. Fakolt, review of *For the Love of Venice,* p. 148; July, 2000, Sheila Brown, review of *Crazy Jack,* p. 56; October, 2000, Sharon Grover, review of *Beast,* p. 168; November, 2000, Elaine E. Knight, review of *Shelley Shock,* p. 160; May, 2001, Wendy Lukehart, review of *Albert,* p. 130; August, 2001, B. Allison Gray, review of *Three Days,* p. 186; September, 2001, Barbara Wysocki, review of *Beast,* p. 76; October, 2001, Piper L. Nyman, review of *How Hungry Are You?,* p. 126; March, 2002, Lisa Prolman, review of *Daughter of Venice,* p. 236, and review of *Rocky, the Cat Who Barks,* p. 198; May, 2002, Wendy Lukehart, review of *Flamingo Dream,* p. 124.

Voice of Youth Advocates, August, 1993, p. 169; February, 1997, Libby Bergstrom, review of *Song of the Magdalene,* p. 331; February, 1998, Janet Mura, review of *Stones in Water,* pp. 387-388.

OTHER

Donna Jo Napoli Web site, http://www.donnajonapoli.com.

P

PEET, Bill
See PEET, William Bartlett

*   *   *

PEET, William Bartlett 1915-2002
(Bill Peet)

OBITUARY NOTICE—See index for *SATA* sketch: Born January 29, 1915, in Grandview, IN; died May 11, 2002, in Los Angeles, CA. Animator, illustrator, and author. Peet was a former animator for Walt Disney Studios who later became a popular author and illustrator of children's books. After studying at the John Herron Art Institute from 1933 to 1936, Peet worked briefly for a greeting card company before joining Walt Disney Studios as an illustrator in 1937. While at Disney, he worked on such well-known animated features as *Fantasia* (1940), *Dumbo* (1941), *Song of the South* (1946), *Cinderella* (1950), *Alice in Wonderland* (1951), and *Sleeping Beauty* (1959). Not only was he an artist, but he also outlined many of the stories and directed the actors who voiced the characters. Peet made his first forays into writing when he adapted Dodie Smith's children's book into the 1961 animated film *101 Dalmatians,* and he later also adapted T. H. White's story of King Arthur into *The Sword in the Stone* (1963). Despite his success at Disney, Peet was not happy there because he was tired of collaborative work and because of numerous personal conflicts between himself and Walt Disney. He therefore decided to branch out into children's books on his own. Even before he left the studio in 1964, he had had several books published, including *Goliath II* (1959), *Hubert's Hair-Raising Adventure* (1959), *Huge Harold* (1961), and *The Pinkish, Purplish, Bluish Egg* (1963). Writing sometimes in verse, sometimes in prose, Peet continued to publish children's books into the 1990s, many of which won awards. Some of his many works include *Capyboppy* (1966), *How Droofus the Dragon Lost His Head* (1971), *Cyrus, the Unsinkable Serpent* (1975), *Big Bad Bruce* (1977), *Encore for Eleanor* (1981), *Cock-a-Doodle Dudley* (1990), and his last work, *Abdo and Daughters* (1996), written with J. C. Wheeler. Peet also wrote about his life experiences in *Bill Peet: An Autobiography* (1989), which was a Caldecott honor book. Some of his other honors include an International Reading Association "Children's Choice" award and the Annie Award for distinguished contribution to the art of animation.

OBITUARIES AND OTHER SOURCES:

BOOKS

The Writers Directory, 15th edition, St. James Press (Detroit, MI), 1999.

PERIODICALS

Chicago Tribune, May 16, 2002, Section 2, p. 9.
Los Angeles Times, May 14, 2002, p. B10.
New York Times, May 18, 2002, p. B15.
Times (London, England), May 15, 2002.
Washington Post, May 17, 2002, p. B6.

*   *   *

POLLOCK, Penny 1935-

Personal

Born May 24, 1935, in Cleveland, OH; daughter of William Caswell (a candy maker) and Eleanor (a teacher; maiden name, Cadman) Morrow; married Stewart Glasson Pollock (a state supreme court judge), June 9, 1956; children: Wendy, Stewart, Jeffrey, Jennifer. *Education:* Mount Holyoke College, B.A., 1957; Kean College, M.A., 1973. *Religion:* Society of Friends (Quakers).

Addresses

Home—Brookside, New Jersey. *Agent*—c/o Author Mail, Little, Brown, 1271 Avenue of the Americas, New York, NY 10020. *E-mail*—Penny-StewPollock@world-net.att.net.

Career

Writer and educator. Dogwood School, Chester, NJ, assistant teacher, 1972-73; Village Nursery School, Brookside, NJ, head teacher, 1973-84. Lecturer at schools and libraries, including Fairleigh Dickinson University, 1980. Member, board of trustees, Mendham Township Public Library, 1979-83.

Member

Society of Children's Book Writers and Illustrators, Patricia Lee Gauch Writers' Workshop, New Jersey Press Women, National Association for the Preservation and Perpetuation of Storytelling, New York Storytelling Center.

Awards, Honors

New Jersey Author Award, 1983, for *Keeping It Secret;* Notable Children's Book, *Smithsonian* magazine, 2001, for *When the Moon Is Full: A Lunar Year;* Aesop Accolade Award, for *The Turkey Girl: A Zuni Cinderella Story.*

Writings

Ants Don't Get Sunday Off, illustrated by Lorinda B. Cauley, Putnam (New York, NY), 1978.

A flock of turkeys offer their young caretaker a beautiful new costume and a chance to attend a special dance if she will return home before sunset in this Native American fairy tale. (From The Turkey Girl: A Zuni Cinderella Story, *retold by Penny Pollock and illustrated by Ed Young.)*

Traditional Native American names for each full moon of the year accompany Pollock's poems about the lunar calendar.
(From When the Moon Is Full, *illustrated by Mary Azarian.)*

The Slug Who Thought He Was a Snail, illustrated by Lorinda B. Cauley, Putnam (New York, NY), 1980.

Garlanda: The Ups and Downs of an Uppity Teapot, illustrated by Margot Tomes, Putnam (New York, NY), 1980.

The Spit Bug Who Couldn't Spit, illustrated by Lorinda B. Cauley, Putnam (New York, NY), 1981.

Keeping It Secret, illustrated by Donna Diamond, Putnam (New York, NY), 1982.

Stall Buddies, illustrated by Gail Owens, Putnam (New York, NY), 1984.

Emily's Tiger, illustrated by Judy Morgan, Paulist Press (New York, NY), 1985.

Water Is Wet, photographs by Barbara Beirne, Putnam (New York, NY), 1985.

Summer Captive, Shoe Tree Press (Belvidere, NJ), 1987.

The Turkey Girl: A Zuni Cinderella Story, illustrated by Ed Young, Little, Brown (Boston, MA), 1996.

When the Moon Is Full: A Lunar Year, illustrated by Mary Azarian, Little, Brown (Boston, MA), 2001.

Contributor to periodicals, including *Cricket.*

Work in Progress

A Christmas Journey, illustrated by Richard Jessie Watson, for Little, Brown (Boston, MA), publication expected in 2004.

Sidelights

Penny Pollock is the author of a varied selection of children's books that have in common their focus on the interconnectedness of all life. From teen novels such as *Summer Captive,* in which a high school freshman finds the only bright spot in an otherwise horrible summer to be a young woman he may never see again, to a Native American take on the "Cinderella" story titled *The Turkey Girl,* to the preschool romp *Water Is Wet,* Pollock successfully navigates a number of genres.

Born in Cleveland, Ohio, in 1935, Pollock lived mainly in New Jersey and Pennsylvania but moved several times while growing up. Summers spent in Mexico or Arizona, and winters spent in Florida introduced her to the diversity of life. As she once told *SATA,* "I have inherited my father's taste for adventure and my mother's sense of oneness with all living things. These feelings are important in my writing."

Many of Pollock's books focus on the natural world and feature animal characters. While Pollock noted that writing fictional tales allows her some latitude, because she sets her tales in the real world, in-depth research is frequently required. "It was not enough for me to care about [the animal characters in my books]," she once explained. "I had to know about them too. To learn more about insects, I turned to [university] professors ... for help. To learn more about trotters, I spent days in the barns at a track."

Pollock sometimes draws on Native American traditions due to their rootedness in the natural world, as in *The Turkey Girl,* which provides the author with a good balance between fact and fiction. In this Zuni variant on the European-based "Cinderella" tale, the search for true love is transformed into something more universally resonant: the importance of trust. In Pollock's adaptation, an orphan girl takes care of a flock of turkeys. To thank her for her kindness, the birds decide to give her a gift: they present her with a beautiful doeskin robe so that she can attend the Dance of the Sacred Bird. The only condition is that she return to her flock before sunset. Like Cinderella, the Turkey Girl becomes so caught up in the joys of the Dance that she loses track of time, and by the time she returns to her flock, the sun has risen and the turkeys have departed forever. As Pollock writes in her moral, "Native American versions [of the story] end with the hard truth that when we break our trust with Mother Earth, we pay a price." Unlike Cinderella, the Turkey Girl is never allowed a second chance; nature is far less forgiving than a love-struck prince. Praising the story in *School Library Journal,* Ellen Fader commented on the dreamlike pastel illustrations by Ed Young and added that Pollock's "thoughtful retelling ... gracefully captures the Zuni landscape."

Another book inspired by Native American traditions is *When the Moon Is Full: A Lunar Year,* which contains a series of poems that describe the different moons seen in the night sky throughout the year. Pollock provides the Native American name for different moons and includes information on blue moons, strawberry moons, and other lunar lore. *School Library Journal* reviewer Lisa Gangemi Krapp dubbed *When the Moon Is Full* a "delicate collection" that is "beautifully illustrated" with wood-

cuts by Mary Azarian, while in *Publishers Weekly,* a reviewer called the work a "lovely volume [that] will likely charm readers and inspire them to linger ... under the night-time sky."

"Stories connect us to ourselves and to one another," Pollock once explained. "Fiction has the power to bind humanity together. The more I write, the more I feel the power of fiction. This power grows from such universal feelings as exultation, fear, and love. Children are comforted by shared emotions, and they hunger for stories of human triumph." In Pollock's novel *Keeping It Secret* she focuses on an emotion that overshadowed her own childhood: the fear of alienation due to a handicap—in her case, hearing loss—that she believed might threaten her ability to fit in with others. Jesse Wellington, the thirteen-year-old protagonist of Pollock's 1987 novel *Summer Captive,* has a problem of a different sort: with his mother in the hospital after an accident, he must now learn to deal with a father for whom he has little respect or affection. Fortunately, while the two share the summer working at a resort, Jesse gains a friend who helps him see past his father's stern exterior in a novel that *Voice of Youth Advocates* reviewer Gail Ashe described as an "unusual" work "that may bring ... a few tears to the reader's eyes."

"Writing for children involves the wonderful challenge," concluded Pollock of her craft, "of telling children what it means to be human. The only way to meet this challenge is to share our feelings. This takes courage."

Biographical and Critical Sources

BOOKS

Pollock, Penny, *The Turkey Girl: A Zuni Cinderella Story,* Little, Brown (Boston, MA), 1996.

PERIODICALS

Appraisal, summer, 1986, review of *Water Is Wet,* p. 56.
Booklist, February 15, 1988, review of *Summer Captive,* pp. 1001-1002; April 15, 1996, Janice Del Negro, review of *The Turkey Girl: A Zuni Cinderella Story,* p. 1437; November 1, 2001, Lauren Peterson, review of *When the Moon Is Full: A Lunar Year,* p. 480.
Horn Book, February, 1984, Mary M. Burns, review of *Keeping It Secret,* p. 48.
Publishers Weekly, December 12, 1980, review of *Garlanda,* p. 48; June 14, 1985, review of *Emily's Tiger,* p. 73; April 29, 1996, review of *The Turkey Girl,* p. 71; October 8, 2001, review of *When the Moon Is Full,* p. 63.
School Library Journal, May, 1980, review of *The Slug Who Thought He Was a Snail,* p. 84; November, 1980, Caroline S. Parr, review of *Garlanda,* p. 66; May, 1982, review of *The Spit Bug Who Couldn't Spit,* p. 81; March, 1983, Kathleen Garland, review of *Keeping It Secret,* p. 183; March, 1985, Gayle W. Berge, review of *Stall Buddies,* p. 170; October, 1985, Betty Craig Campbell, review of *Water Is Wet,* p. 159; January, 1988, Robert E. Unsworth, review of *Summer Captive,* p. 87; May, 1996, Ellen Fader, review of *The*

Turkey Girl, p. 107; September, 2001, Lisa Gangemi
Krapp, review of *When the Moon Is Full,* p. 220.
Voice of Youth Advocates, April, 1988, Gail Ashe, review
of *Summer Captive,* pp. 28-29.

OTHER

Penny Pollock Web Site, http://www.home.att.net/~penny-
stewpollock/ (January 10, 2003).*

R

RITTER, John H. 1951-

Personal

Born October 31, 1951, in CA; son of Carl W. (a journalist) and Clara Mae Ritter; married Cheryl B. Ritter (a teacher and curriculum developer), 1972; children: Jolie. *Education:* Attended University of California—San Diego. *Hobbies and other interests:* "Speaking to teachers, students, and writers at conferences and universities about creativity and the writing process; playing baseball in an amateur league; playing guitar and writing songs; walking the streets, observing people, and walking in the country under the stars at night."

Addresses

Home—San Diego, CA. *Agent*—Ginger Knowlton, Curtis Brown, Ltd., Ten Astor Place, New York, NY 10003. *Email*—heyjohn@johnritter.com.

Career

Writer. Speaker in schools and at conferences. Custom painting contractor, 1973-98.

Member

Society of Children's Book Writers and Illustrators, International Reading Association, National Council of Teachers of English (member, Assembly of Literature for Adolescents), Native Cultures Institute of Baja California.

Awards, Honors

Judy Blume Award, Society of Children's Book Writers and Illustrators, 1994; Children's Book Award, International Reading Association (IRA), Best Book for Young Adults, American Library Association (ALA), and Blue Ribbon Book, *Bulletin of the Center for Children's Books,* all 1999, and Young Adult Readers Choice, IRA,

John H. Ritter

2000, all for *Choosing up Sides;* Books for the Teen Age list, New York Public Library, Parents' Guide to Children's Media Award, Shenandoah University, and Texas State Lone Star Book designation, all 2001, all for *Over the Wall.*

Writings

Choosing up Sides, Philomel (New York, NY), 1998.
Over the Wall, Philomel (New York, NY), 2000.

Ritter's work has also appeared in various periodicals, including *Spitball: The Literary Baseball Magazine* and

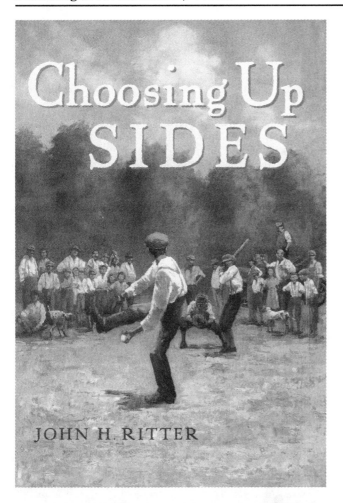

In the early 1920s in a small town in Ohio, budding southpaw Luke Bledsoe must fight the condemnation of his preacher father who fears Satan's presence in Luke's left-handed pitch and the game of baseball. (Cover illustration by Ronald Himler.)

the *Christian Science Monitor.* His short story "Old School/Fu-Char School," appears in the anthology *Big City Cool,* Persea Books (New York, NY), 2002.

Work in Progress

Cruz De La Cruz: The Boy Who Saved Baseball (a true story based on a legend), "novel about a strange boy who shows up to join a ragged baseball team in order to help them win a crucial game and save their small town," publication due in 2003.

Sidelights

"I grew up with my left hand tied behind my back. Well, actually, it was only tied up till I was six or seven." Thus begins John H. Ritter's *Choosing up Sides,* a "debut tale of epiphany and apocalypse," according to Elizabeth Bush in a review for *Bulletin of the Center for Children's Books.* Ritter's 1998 novel introduces readers to the world of fervent baseball, Bible-thumping religion, and a life-altering choice imposed on a young boy with an incredible talent. Ritter's novel is at once

morality tale and sports book, but not an ordinary play-by-play sports book. Winner of the prestigious International Reading Association's (IRA) Children's Book Award as well as an American Library Association Best Book for Young Adults citation, *Choosing up Sides* augured a fine career for the new author. With his second novel, *Over the Wall,* such a promise was fulfilled, according to some critics. As Chris Crowe colorfully put it in a critique for *ALAN Review,* "With his baseball novel *Choosing up Sides* ... rookie YA author John H. Ritter landed a spot on the All Star team.... Ritter's second at bat, *Over the Wall,* will secure him a regular spot in the line up of notable authors writing about sports for young adults."

"I never intended [my books] to be play-by-play sports novels," Ritter told Crowe in an *ALAN Review* interview. "I'm more interested in using baseball scenes as metaphor, or for challenges of character, or to advance the story. I could as easily set the stories in the world of ballet, were I as knowledgeable in that arena. But the thrust would be the same. Kids dealing with hard choices. To me, that's the definition of YA lit." Success with his first two books meant Ritter could quit his day job and go at writing full time. Working for twenty-five years as a painting contractor, he was ready to give painting with words a larger place in his life.

"I grew up in a baseball family," Ritter noted on his Web site. He and his brothers played one-on-one hardball in the dry hills of rural San Diego County, near the Mexican border. But there was more than simply sports in the family background. "We were also a family of musicians and mathematicians, house painters and poets," Ritter explained. John credits his father, a writer from Ohio and former sports editor for the *San Diego Union,* with teaching him both a love for writing and a love for the "holy game of baseball." John's mother, of Irish and Cherokee Indian descent, passed away when John was quite young, but he remembers how she "sang to us constantly, making up a special song for each of her four children. From her, I gained a sense of how to capture a person's spirit in a lyrical phrase."

Another early influence on Ritter was his rural upbringing, the solitude and independence of depending on himself and his siblings for entertainment and friendship. "Out in that country," Ritter explained on his Web site, "the neighbor kids lived so far away, my brothers and I developed a half-real, half-imaginary game where we pitched and hit the ball, then dreamed up the rest, keeping the score, game situations, and full, major league line-ups in our heads." Such games were an early training for Ritter in the art of storyline and plot development.

At school Ritter was, as he described himself to Crowe, a "wild student.... A rabble rouser and a contrarian." Ritter was always looking for the exception to the rule, and in spite or perhaps because of this questioning nature, he was also a high achiever. But he had something of a dual personality in school. "I could be extremely focused one day, then get tossed out of class the next," he admitted to Crowe. "As proof, in high school I was voted both the Senior Class President and the Senior Class Clown." Teachers along the way also discovered that Ritter had a way with words, and they would read his work out to the class as an example of good writing.

Meanwhile, Ritter's father had remarried and two more sisters were added to the Ritter family mix. Baseball continued to dominate his free-time activities; some even thought he might have a chance at playing pro ball. By the time he was in high school, however, Ritter discovered the joys of song writing, heavily influenced by Bob Dylan and Dylan's working-class perspectives. Graduating from high school, Ritter went to college at the University of California—San Diego, carrying around a little notebook in which he would write lyrics for songs, noting riffs and phrases. At school he met his future wife, but by his second year, Ritter knew that he needed to get on with life, that college was not the place he needed to be at that time. "I knew I had to walk the streets, touch life, embrace life, gain experience," he told Crowe. "I wanted to learn from life. To hit the road like Kerouac, Dylan, and Twain. To have something real to write about." So one spring day he filled out a withdrawal card and left the university behind, taking a job as a painter's apprentice with a commercial contractor he had already worked for during the summers. Working for three or four months per year, he could save enough to travel and write the rest of the year. After several years, he married and had a baby daughter; that upped the work year to nine months. However, Ritter always scheduled time for writing.

Ritter struggled with his writing part-time until the late 1980s when he joined a local fiction group led by YA novelist Joan Oppenheimer. Working in this environment of feedback and comment, Ritter soon grew in his abilities. He took extension writing classes, joined another writing group, and in 1994 won the Judy Blume Award for a novel in progress. Though the novel remained unpublished, it did build confidence in the young writer and opened doors with editors. When he settled down to writing another coming-of-age novel, Ritter opted for a baseball setting. He chose such a background for two reasons: not only is this a topic close to his heart, but also baseball carries a heavy and resonant metaphorical value in American culture. Further influences for his first novel came from the author's personal juvenile experiences with prejudice and bias. Growing up in the 1960s, he watched nightly news reports of the civil rights movement, graphic film clips of marchers set upon by snarling dogs, pummeled by police batons, and crushed by sprays of water from fire hoses. Then came the kidnapings and murders in Mississippi. As a ten-year-old country boy, the world seemed to make no sense. About that same time, a teacher put the word "sinister" on the board and asked Ritter and his fellow students the meaning of the word. When the same teacher revealed that, instead of "diabolical" or "evil", it was simply the Latin root for "left" or "left-sided," Ritter learned another lesson in bias. For him and other baseball players, lefties were highly

valued—there was nothing sinister about them. But later in life, these feelings and experiences coalesced in the writing of the novel that became *Choosing up Sides*.

Ritter sets his first novel in southern Ohio in the 1920s, and to research the book he read widely on religious movements, the characteristics of left-handedness, and the Appalachian dialect. He visited relatives in the region who helped with interviewing local people to get to know more intimately customs and culture. Also blended into the stew is a story Ritter's father liked to tell, about a buddy who was so fond of tossing crab apples at a telephone pole that ultimately he became a great pitcher.

The novel's protagonist is thirteen-year-old Luke Bledsoe, the oldest son of a preacher. Born left-handed, Luke is, in the eyes of his Fundamentalist father, a throwback, a potential follower of Satan, for that is the hand of the devil. The authoritarian father, Ezekiel, tries to "cure" Luke of his left-handedness by tying that hand behind his back, but with little luck. Luke's father is the new

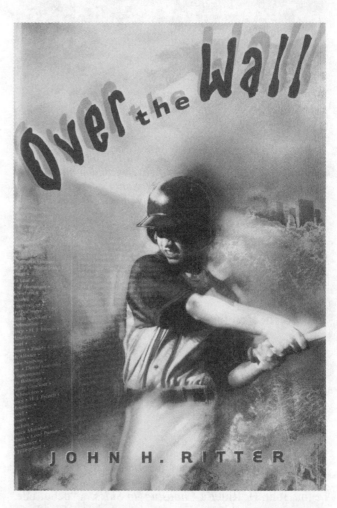

Several factors, including trips to the Vietnam War Memorial, help Tyler Waltern master his temper, develop his budding athletic abilities, and work through his problems with his parents who are devastated by the sudden death of Tyler's sister. (Cover illustration by Cliff Nielsen.)

minister at the Baptist Church in Crown Falls, Ohio, and Luke is the new boy in a town that is baseball crazy. The local team won the county championship the previous year and hopes to do so again this year. But for Luke's father, baseball is, like dancing, a temptation that needs to be resisted. Then one day, while Luke is watching a forbidden game, a ball lands at his feet. Throwing it back with his left hand, he amazes the crowd with his distance and placement. He looks to be the natural the team desperately needs to clinch the championship, and everyone sets about trying to recruit the boy, who has quite accidentally built up his pitching arm by tossing apples.

Classmate and slugger Skinny Lappman counters Ezekiel's religious objections by saying that the wasting of talent such as Luke's is the bigger sin. Also enlisted in the campaign is baseball fanatic Annabeth Quinn, for whom Luke has a strong attraction. Uncle Micah, a sports reporter on his mother's side, also plays a part in this conversion, whisking the talented youngster off to see Babe Ruth, another southpaw, play. Finally Luke gives in and decides to pitch for the team, becoming the local hero until a confrontation with his father leads to a violent beating. His father breaks Luke's pitching arm in the altercation, and the boy vows to run away. Tragically and ironically, Luke's father falls into the Ohio River and Luke is unable to throw a lifeline to him because of his broken arm.

The bare outline of the plot does little to describe a book rich in characterization, nuance, metaphor, and dialogue. Ritter did not commit the first-time writer's mistake of flat characterization, noted critics. Even Luke's father Ezekiel is shown to have his human side; he is not simply a tyrant. Jealous of Luke's bond with Uncle Micah, Ezekiel overcomes his fear of water and takes his son fishing. At one point, he gently touches his son's shoulder with his left hand, indicating to Luke that he too was born left-handed and has had to repress it all these years. The irony of Ezekiel's death is all the stronger not only because he dies because he has broken his son's throwing arm, but also because his favorite hymn for sinners is "Throw out the Lifeline."

Critics and reviewers responded strongly to *Choosing up Sides,* Bush describing it as a novel that "pits fire and brimstone Fundamentalism against a rival religion—Baseball—and treats both with cathartic understanding." Ritter uses an even hand not only in treatment of theme, but in style. Bush further commented, "leavening the sober elements of this morality tale . . . is the pure joy of baseball and, at least in Luke's case, its redemptive power." Patricia K. Ladd, writing in *ALAN Review,* felt that Ritter "addresses themes of autonomy and independence common to young adult readers and portrays plot through authentic dialect and well-developed characters." Ladd went on to note that though the tale was, at first glance, "a simple story of realistic fiction, perhaps even a parable," Ritter's use of dialogue, similes, metaphors and imagery all "add dimensions to the plot that leave readers pondering the book's messages long after turning the final page." Kate Clarke, reviewing the

title in *Book Report,* called it an "entertaining and thought-provoking coming-of-age story" about "being true to one's self and choosing how to live." A reviewer for *Publishers Weekly* noted that, "Despite its somewhat didactic tone, this story offers enough curve balls to keep readers engaged." "Unlike many sports novels, *Choosing up Sides* does more than offer a mere glimpse of the grand old game of baseball—it takes a deeper look at faith, truth, and individuality," maintained Stefani Koorey in her *Voice of Youth Advocates* review, going on to dub the tale a "well-designed study of personal choice" and concluding: "With its wide appeal, this first-person story is a recommended purchase for all public and school libraries." Joel Shoemaker, reviewing *Choosing up Sides* for *School Library Journal,* also praised the writing and theme of Ritter's publishing debut. "Cleverly told in a colloquial first-person twang, this thoughtful tale of authority questioned and dreams denied will be real enough to many readers," Shoemaker wrote. And in announcing the Children's Book Award in *Reading Today,* the IRA committee felt that Ritter's tale was "laced with humor," and presented a "realistic and inspirational picture of a young man torn between two worlds."

News of the IRA award literally brought tears to Ritter's eyes; it was a vindication of his many years of hard work and perseverance. The author, who writes his first drafts longhand and subsequent drafts on the computer, was quick to follow up this initial success with another hard-hitting novel using baseball as a further metaphor for life.

"Writing a book is a lot like growing a plant," Ritter noted in a letter to a young reader posted on the author's Web site. "It starts with a seed, which is only an idea. But like all seeds, it does have the potential to grow into something interesting if you nurture it and are patient. The seed of the idea for *Over the Wall* came from my discovery of two facts. One is that twice as many Vietnam vets died by suicide after the war ended than actually died in the war. The other is that fifty times as many Vietnamese died fighting to save their country as did Americans, but there is no 'wall' for them that lists all of their names. When I realized how unfair and how self-centered that was for Americans to only care about their own people, I realized that the Vietnam War was not really over for many Americans."

In his second novel, Ritter once again takes an historical setting, though one closer to the present, in a story about a boy's journey attempting to reconnect with his father and discover who he is in the process. There are many "walls" in thirteen-year-old Tyler's life: the literal wall of the baseball field he wants to clear with a mighty slam; the Vietnam memorial wall bearing his grandfather's name; and the invisible wall Tyler's dad has built around himself ever since the death of his daughter—Tyler's sister—nine years earlier. When he is invited to spend the summer in New York City with his cousin, Tyler is determined to make it onto the roster of an all-star baseball team. However, Tyler's explosive temper gets in the way of his obvious talent. With the help of his pretty cousin and with the sage advice of his coach, a Vietnam vet, Tyler manages to navigate the risky waters of this passage. The coach helps the boy reconnect with himself and his guilt-ravaged dad. "By the end," noted Todd Morning in a review of *Over the Wall* for *School Library Journal,* "Tyler has gained a level of self-awareness by unraveling some of the tangled stories in his family's past and understanding the intricacies lying beneath the surface of life." Morning concluded, "Sports are just a part of this ambitious work that presents a compelling, multilayered story." A *Publishers Weekly* reviewer found Ritter's second novel to be a "powerful lesson in compassion," and Roger Leslie commented in *Booklist* that *Over the Wall* is a "fully fleshed-out story about compassion and absolution." Connie Russell, reviewing the title for *ALAN Review,* called the book a "poignant and accessible coming-of-age story," while Ladd described the novel as a "profound story of realistic fiction for young and mature adults."

"The driving force behind all my stories comes primarily from finding something that really bugs me," Ritter explained to Crowe. "And so far, it tends to be some sort of injustice. But I refuse to write revenge stories. I hate them. I won't even watch a revenge movie. To me, it's the easy response to injustice, and it lacks integrity.... So I try to look for an alternative solution. That's what spawns my ideas." In an interview with Teri Lesesne in *Teacher Librarian,* Ritter also added insight into the type of novel he enjoys writing: "I don't believe in choosing between character- and plot-driven novels. To me, the greatest stories are a finely woven blend of both. That's what I shoot for. Of the two, character comes easier for me, so I fret more about my plots. That becomes the sand in the oyster—or the ointment—for me. What if a left-handed boy is forced to be right-handed? What's the best thing that could happen? What's the worst? Or what steps, what events would lead an angry and bitter kid to learn to embrace his enemies as a way of freeing himself from the prison of his emotions? How does one get over that wall? These kinds of questions nag at me until I can answer them. That's how my books begin."

Fans of Ritter's first two novels—young readers, critics, and award committees alike—await what other thing might "bug" or "nag" at the author, and result in his next work of fiction. Meanwhile, Ritter carries on with his craft, putting in ten-hour days at the writing desk in hopes of getting just the right word, the right phrase. "I love using that voice to say something I need to say," he concluded on his Web site. "I love the rhythms and the musicality of language. I love discovering a good story, building it, and telling it. And when they all come together between the covers of the book, it's like magic."

Biographical and Critical Sources

BOOKS

Ritter, John H., *Choosing up Sides,* Philomel (New York, NY), 1998.

PERIODICALS

ALAN Review, spring-summer, 2000, Chris Crowe, "An Interview with John H. Ritter," pp. 5-9; spring-summer, 2000, Patricia K. Ladd, "Covering the Bases with Young Adult Literature," pp. 10-17; fall, 2000, Connie Russell, review of *Over the Wall,* p. 33.

Booklist, March 1, 1998, p. 1513; March 15, 1999, p. 1302; April 1, 2000, Roger Leslie, review of *Over the Wall,* p. 1451.

Book Report, March-April, 1999, Kate Clarke, review of *Choosing up Sides,* p. 63.

Bulletin of the Center for Children's Books, June, 1998, Elizabeth Bush, "The Big Picture."

Childhood Education, spring, 1999, p. 174.

Publishers Weekly, April 13, 1998, review of *Choosing up Sides,* p. 76; May 29, 2000, review of *Over the Wall,* p. 83.

Reading Today, June-July, 1999, "IRA Names Award-Winning Children's Books," p. 21.

School Library Journal, June, 1998, Joel Shoemaker, review of *Choosing up Sides,* p. 152; June, 2000, Todd Morning, review of *Over the Wall,* p. 152.

Teacher Librarian, March, 2001, Teri Lesesne, "Complexities, Choices, and Challenges," pp. 44-47.

Voice of Youth Advocates, December, 1998, Stefani Koorey, review of *Choosing up Sides.*

OTHER

John H. Ritter Web Site, http://www.johnhritter.com/ (May 12, 2001).

* * *

ROSEN, Michael (Wayne) 1946-

Personal

Born May 7, 1946, in Harrow, Middlesex, England; son of Harold (a professor) and Connie Ruby (a college lecturer; maiden name, Isakovsky) Rosen; married Elizabeth Susanna Steele, 1976 (divorced, 1987); married Geraldine Clark, 1987 (divorced, 1997); companion of Emma-Louise Williams; children: (first marriage) Joseph Steele, Eddie Steele; (second marriage) Isaac Louis, Naomi Imogen Hill and Laura Clark (step-daughters); (with Williams) Elsie Lavender Ruby. *Education:* Attended Middlesex Hospital Medical School, 1964-65, and National Film School, 1973-76; Wadham College, Oxford, B.A. (English language and literature), 1969; University of Reading, M.A. (children's literature; with distinction), 1993; University of North London, Ph.D., 1997. *Politics:* Socialist. *Religion:* Atheist. *Hobbies and other interests:* "Watching Arsenal F.C."

Addresses

Home—49 Parkholme Rd., London E8 3AQ, England. *Agent*—Peter, Fraser & Dublop Group, Ltd., Drury House, 34-43 Russell St., London WC2B 5HA, England.

Michael Rosen

Career

Writer, poet, playwright, and broadcaster. Has appeared regularly on British Broadcasting Company (BBC) television and radio shows, including *Meridian Books, Treasure Islands,* and *Best Worlds.* Writer in residence at several schools in London, England; presenter of lectures at universities and colleges in the United Kingdom and Canada; presenter at conferences for librarians, teachers, and literature associations in the United Kingdom, Australia, United States, Canada, Singapore, and Italy; performer at various venues in the United Kingdom, including at the Shaw Theatre, National Theatre, Edinburgh Book Festival, and the BBC Children's Poetry Festival.

Member

National Union of Journalists.

Awards, Honors

Best Original Full-Length Play Award, *Sunday Times* National Union of Students Drama Festival, 1968, for *Backbone;* Poetry Award, *Signal,* 1982, for *You Can't Catch Me!;* Other Award, *Children's Book Bulletin,* 1983, for *Everybody Here;* British Book Award runner-up, 1989; Smarties' Best Children's Book of the Year Award and *Boston Globe-Horn Book* Award, both 1990,

and Japanese Picture Book Award, 1991, all for *We're Going On a Bear Hunt;* Cuffies Award for best anthology, *Publishers Weekly,* 1992, and Best Book Award, National Association of Parenting Publications, 1993, both for *Poems for the Very Young;* Glennfiddich Award for best radio program on the subject of food, 1996, for "*Treasure Islands* Special: Lashings of Ginger Beer"; Eleanor Farjeon Award for distinguished services to children's literature, 1997; Play and Learn Award, *Parent* magazine, 1998, for *Snore!;* Talkies Award for best poetry audio tape of the year, 1998, for *You Wait till I'm Older than You;* Sony Silver Award, 2000, for radio feature "Dr. Seuss: Who Put the Cat in the Hat?".

Writings

FOR CHILDREN

Once There Was a King Who Promised He Would Never Chop Anyone's Head Off, illustrated by Kathy Henderson, Deutsch (London, England), 1976.

She Even Called Me Garabaldi, BBC Books (London, England), 1977.

The Bakerloo Flea, illustrated by Quentin Blake, Longman (London, England), 1979.

Nasty!, illustrated by Amanda Macphail, Longman (London, England), 1982, revised edition, Puffin (Harmondsworth, England), 1984.

How to Get out of the Bath and Other Problems, illustrated by Graham Round, Scholastic (New York, NY), 1984.

Hairy Tales and Nursery Crimes, illustrated by Alan Baker, Deutsch (London, England), 1985.

You're Thinking about Doughnuts, illustrated by Tony Pinchuck, Deutsch (London, England), 1987.

Beep Beep! Here Come—The Horribles!, illustrated by John Watson, Walker (London, England), 1988.

Jokes and Verses, illustrated by Quentin Blake, BBC Books (London, England), 1988.

Norma and the Washing Machine, illustrated by David Hingham, Deutsch (London, England), 1988.

Silly Stories (jokes), illustrated by Mik Brown, Kingfisher (London, England), 1988, revised as *Michael Rosen's Horribly Silly Stories,* 1994, revised as *Off the Wall: A Very Silly Joke Book,* Kingfisher (New York, NY), 1994.

The Class Two Monster, illustrated by Maggie King, Heinemann (London, England), 1989.

The Deadman Tapes, Deutsch (London, England), 1989.

The Royal Huddle [and] *The Royal Muddle,* illustrated by Colin West, Macmillan (London, England), 1990.

Clever Cakes, illustrated by Caroline Holden, Walker (London, England), 1991.

Burping Bertha, illustrated by Tony Ross, Andersen (London, England), 1993.

Moving, illustrated by Sophy Williams, Viking (New York, NY), 1993.

Songbird Story, illustrated by Jill Down, Frances Lincoln (London, England), 1993.

The Arabian Frights and Other Gories, illustrated by Chris Fisher, Scholastic (London, England), 1994.

Figgy Roll, illustrated by Tony Ross, Longman (Harlow, England), 1994, published as *Dad's Fig Bar,* Sundance (Littleton, MA), 1997.

Norma's Notebook, illustrated by Tony Ross, Longman (Harlow, England), 1994, Sundance (Littleton, MA), 1997.

Dad, illustrated by Tony Ross, Longman (Harlow, England), 1994, Sundance (Littleton, MA), 1997.

Lisa's Letter, illustrated by Tony Ross, Longman (Harlow, England), 1994, Sundance (Littleton, MA), 1997.

Even Stevens, F.C., illustrated by John Rogan, Collins (London, England), 1995.

This Is Our House, illustrated by Bob Graham, Walker (London, England), Candlewick Press (Cambridge, MA), 1996.

(Author of text) *I Want to Be a Superhero,* score by Robert Kapilow, G. Schirmer (New York, NY), 1998.

Snore!, illustrated by Jonathan Langley, HarperCollins (London, England), 1998.

Mission Ziffoid, illustrated by Arthur Robins, Walker (London, England), Candlewick Press (Cambridge, MA), 1999.

Rover, illustrated by Neal Layton, Bloomsbury (London, England), Random House (New York, NY), 1999.

Lunch Boxes Don't Fly, illustrated by Korky Paul, Puffin (London, England), 1999.

A Thanksgiving Wish, illustrated by John Thompson, Blue Sky Press (New York, NY), 1999.

Shakespeare: His Work and His World (nonfiction), illustrated by Robert Ingpen, Candlewick Press (Cambridge, MA), 2001.

Pinocchio in the Park (play), first performed at Unicorn Theatre (London, England), August 1, 2001.

One Push, illustrated by Martin Olsson, Storycircus (http://www.storycircus.com), 2002.

Lovely Old Roly, illustrated by Priscilla Lamont, Frances Lincoln (London, England), 2002.

Oww!, illustrated by Jonathan Langley, HarperCollins (London, England), 2003.

Howler, illustrated by Neal Layton, Bloomsbury (London, England), 2003.

Also author of short story "Page Twenty-three," in *Round about Six,* edited by Kaye Webb, Frances Lincoln (London, England), 1993.

A young boy unexpectedly lands on what appears to be the planet Ziffoid, where he finds very lively aliens. (From Mission Ziffoid, *written by Rosen and illustrated by Arthur Robins.*)

POEMS; FOR CHILDREN

Mind Your Own Business, illustrated by Quentin Blake, Deutsch (London, England), 1974.

Wouldn't You Like to Know, illustrated by Quentin Blake, Deutsch (London, England), 1977, revised edition, Penguin (Harmondsworth, England), 1981.

Bathtime, BBC Books (London, England), 1979.

(With Roger McGough) *You Tell Me,* illustrated by Sara Midda, Kestrel (London, England), 1979.

You Can't Catch Me!, illustrated by Quentin Blake, Deutsch (London, England), 1981.

Quick, Let's Get out of Here, illustrated by Quentin Blake, Deutsch (London, England), 1983.

Don't Put Mustard in the Custard, illustrated by Quentin Blake, Deutsch (London, England), 1985.

Chocolate Cake, illustrated by Amelia Rosato, BBC Books (London, England), 1986.

When Did You Last Wash Your Feet?, illustrated by Tony Pinchuck, Deutsch (London, England), 1986.

The Hypnotiser, illustrated by Andrew Tiffen, Deutsch (London, England), 1988.

We're Going on a Bear Hunt, illustrated by Helen Oxenbury, Walker (London, England), 1989, Aladdin (New York, NY), 1992.

Freckly Feet and Itchy Knees, illustrated by Sami Sweeten, HarperCollins (London, England), Doubleday (New York, NY), 1990.

Never Mind!, BBC Books (London, England), 1990.

Little Rabbit Foo Foo, illustrated by Arthur Robins, Walker (London, England), Simon & Schuster (New York, NY), 1990.

Who Drew on the Baby's Head?, Deutsch (London, England), 1991.

Mind the Gap, Scholastic (London, England), 1992.

Nuts about Nuts, illustrated by Sami Sweeten, Collins (London, England), 1993.

The Best of Michael Rosen, illustrated by Quentin Blake, RDR Books (Oakland, CA), 1995.

Michael Rosen's ABC, illustrated by Bee Wiley, Macdonald (London, England), 1996.

Smacking My Lips, illustrated by Quentin Blake, Puffin (London, England), 1996.

You Wait till I'm Older than You, illustrated by Shoo Rayner, Viking (London, England), 1997.

The Michael Rosen Book of Nonsense, illustrated by Clare Mackie, Wayland Macdonald (Brighton, England), 1997.

Tea in the Sugar Bowl, Potato in My Shoe, illustrated by Quentin Blake, Walker (London, England), 1998.

Centrally Heated Knickers, illustrated by Harry Horse, Puffin (London, England), 1999.

Even More Nonsense, illustrated by Clare Mackie, Hodder (London, England), 2000.

Views of Notley Green, photographs by Ed Clark, Design Council (London, England), 2000.

Uncle Billy Being Silly, illustrated by Korky Paul, Puffin (London, England), 2001.

No Breathing in Class, illustrated by Korky Paul, Puffin (London, England), 2003.

Also author of *Zoo at Night,* illustrated by Bee Willey, Tradewind Books (Vancouver, Canada). Contributor of ten poems to the Science Museum, Wellsome Gallery (London, England), 2000; twenty-five poems for Maths Year 2000; and twenty phonic cards for Oxford University Press (Oxford, England), 2002.

RETELLINGS; FOR CHILDREN

A Cat and Mouse Story, illustrated by William Rushton, Deutsch (London, England), 1982.

The Wicked Tricks of Till Owlyglass, illustrated by Fritz Wegner, Walker (London, England), 1989.

Peter Pan, illustrated by Francesca Rovira, Firefly (Hove, England), 1989.

Aladdin, illustrated by Jose M. Lavarello, Firefly (Hove, England), 1989.

Alice in Wonderland, illustrated by Francesca Rovira, Firefly (Hove, England), 1989.

Cinderella, illustrated by Agusti Ascensio, Firefly (Hove, England), 1989.

The Three Little Pigs, illustrated by Agusti Ascensio, Firefly (Hove, England), 1989.

Goldilocks and the Three Bears, illustrated by Jose M. Lavarello, Firefly (Hove, England), 1989.

Hansel and Gretel, illustrated by Francesca Rovira, Firefly (Hove, England), 1989.

Little Red Riding Hood, illustrated by Jose M. Lavarello, Firefly (Hove, England), 1989.

Snow White, illustrated by Agusti Ascensio, Firefly (Hove, England), 1989.

The Little Tin Soldier, illustrated by Agusti Ascensio, Firefly (Hove, England), 1990.

The Princess and the Pea, illustrated by Francesca Rovira, Firefly (Hove, England), 1990.

Sinbad the Sailor, illustrated by Francesca Rovira, Firefly (Hove, England), 1990.

The Golem of Old Prague, illustrated by Val Biro, Deutsch (London, England), 1990, illustrated by Brian Simons, Five Leaves (Nottingham, England), 1997.

How the Animals Got Their Colours: Animal Myths from around the World, illustrated by John Clementson, Studio Editions (London, England), Harcourt (New York, NY), 1992.

The First Giraffe, illustrated by John Clementson, Studio Editions (London, England), published as *How Giraffe Got Such a Long Neck ... and Why Rhino Is So Grumpy,* illustrated by John Clementson, Dial (New York, NY), 1993.

The Old Woman and the Pumpkin, illustrated by Bob Hewis, Learning by Design (London, England), 1994.

The Man with No Shadow, illustrated by Reg Cartwright, Longmans (London, England), 1994.

Crow and Hawk: A Traditional Pueblo Indian Story, illustrated by John Clementson, Studio Editions (London, England), Harcourt (New York, NY), 1995.

A Jewish Tale, Longman (Harlow, England), 2002.

Two European Tales, Longman (Harlow, England), 2002.

"SCRAPBOOK" SERIES; POETRY AND PROSE COLLECTIONS; FOR CHILDREN

Smelly Jelly Smelly Fish, illustrated by Quentin Blake, Walker (London, England), Prentice-Hall (New York, NY), 1986.

Under the Bed, illustrated by Quentin Blake, Walker (London, England), Prentice-Hall (New York, NY), 1986.

Hard-Boiled Legs, illustrated by Quentin Blake, Walker (London, England), Prentice-Hall (New York, NY), 1987.

Spollyollydiddilytiddlyitis, illustrated by Quentin Blake, Walker (London, England), 1987, published as *Down at the Doctor's: The Sick Book,* Simon & Schuster (New York, NY), 1987.

NONFICTION; ADAPTED FROM SPANISH; FOR CHILDREN

Fear, the Attic, illustrated by Agusti Ascensio, Firefly (Hove, England), 1989.

Friendship, the Oar, illustrated by H. Elena, Firefly (Hove, England), 1989.

Imagination, the Tree, illustrated by Conxita Rodriguez, Firefly (Hove, England), 1989.

Intelligence, the Formula, illustrated by Carme Peris, Firefly (Hove, England), 1989.

Shyness, Isabel, illustrated by F. Infante, Firefly (Hove, England), 1989.

Lying, the Nose, illustrated by Carme Peris, Firefly (Hove, England), 1989.

"ZOOMABABY" SERIES; FOR CHILDREN

Zoomababy and the Great Dog Chase, illustrated by Caroline Holden, Longman (Harlow, England), 2002.

Zoomababy and the Locked Cage, illustrated by Caroline Holden, Longman (Harlow, England), 2002.

Zoomababy and the Mission to Mars, illustrated by Caroline Holden, Longman (Harlow, England), 2002.

Zoomababy and the Rescue, illustrated by Caroline Holden, Longman (Harlow, England), 2002.

Zoomababy and the Search for the Lost Mummy, illustrated by Caroline Holden, Longman (Harlow, England), 2002.

Zoomababy at the World Cup, illustrated by Caroline Holden, Longman (Harlow, England), 2002.

EDITOR; FOR CHILDREN

Everybody Here (miscellany), Bodley Head (London, England), 1982.

(With Susanna Steele), *Inky Pinky Ponky: Children's Playground Rhymes,* illustrated by Dan Jones, Granada (London, England), 1982.

(With David Jackson) *Speaking to You,* Macmillan (London, England), 1984.

(With Joan Griffiths) *That'd Be Telling,* Cambridge University Press (Cambridge, England), 1985.

The Kingfisher Book of Children's Poetry, illustrated by Alice Englander, Kingfisher (London, England), 1985.

A Spider Bought a Bicycle, and Other Poems for Young Children, illustrated by Inga Moore, Kingfisher (London, England), 1986.

The Kingfisher Book of Funny Stories, illustrated by Tony Blundell, Kingfisher (London, England), 1988.

Culture Shock, Viking (London, England), 1990.

Stories from Overseas/Histoires d'Outre-Mer, Ges-editions (Paris, France), 1990.

Give Me Shelter, Bodley Head (London, England), 1991.

A World of Poetry, Kingfisher (London, England), 1991.

Minibeasties, illustrated by Alan Baker, Firefly (Hove, England), 1991, published as *Itsy-Bitsy Beasties: Poems from around the World,* Carolrhoda Books (Minneapolis, MN), 1992.

Sonsense Nongs, illustrated by Shoo Rayner, A & C Black (London, England), 1992.

South and North, East and West: The Oxfam Book of Children's Stories, Walker (London, England), Candlewick (Cambridge, MA), 1992.

Action Replay, Anecdotal Poems, illustrated by Andrzej Krauze, Viking (London, England), 1993.

Poems for the Very Young, illustrated by Bob Graham, Kingfisher (London, England), 1993.

Pilly Soems, illustrated by Shoo Rayner, A & C Black (London, England), 1994.

A Different Story: Poems from the Past, English and Media Centre (London, England), 1994.

Rap with Rosen, Longmans (London, England), 1995.

Walking the Bridge of Your Nose, illustrated by Chloe Cheese, Kingfisher (London, England), 1996.

The Secret Life of Schools, Channel 4 Learning (London, England), 1997.

Classic Poetry: An Illustrated Collection, illustrated by Paul Howard, Walker (London, England), Candlewick Press (Cambridge, MA), 1998.

Night-Night, Knight, and Other Poems, illustrated by Sue Heap, Walker (London, England), 1998.

Poems Are Crazy, Longman (Harlow, England), 2002.

Poems Are Noisy, Longman (Harlow, England), 2002.

Poems Are Pictures, Longman (Harlow, England), 2002.

Poems Are Private, Longman (Harlow, England), 2002.

Poems Are Public, Longman (Harlow, England), 2002.

Poems Are Quiet, Longman (Harlow, England), 2002.

NONFICTION; FOR ADULTS

Did I Hear You Write?, illustrated by Alan Pinchuck, Deutsch (London, England), 1989.

Goodies and Daddies: An A-Z Guide to Fatherhood, Murray (London, England), 1991.

(Coauthor) *Holocaust Denial: The New Nazi Lie,* Anti-Nazi League (London, England), 1992.

(With Jill Burridge) *Treasure Islands II: An Adult Guide to Children's Writers,* BBC Books (London, England), 1992.

Just Kids: How to Survive the Twos to Tens, illustrated by Caroline Holden, John Murray (London, England), 1995.

(And editor, with Myra Barrs) *A Year with Poetry: Teachers Write about Teaching Poetry,* Centre for Language in Primary Education (London, England), 1997.

(With Simon Elmes) *Word of Mouth,* Oxford University Press (Oxford, England), 2002.

ANTHOLOGIES; FOR ADULTS

Rude Rhymes, illustrated by Riana Duncan, Deutsch (London, England), 1989, revised edition reprinted with *Dirty Ditties* and *Vulgar Verses,* Signet (London, England), 1992.

Dirty Ditties (also see above), illustrated by Riana Duncan, Deutsch (London, England), 1990.

Vulgar Verses (also see above), illustrated by Riana Duncan, Deutsch (London, England), 1991.

(With David Widgery) *The Chatto Book of Dissent,* Chatto & Windus (London, England), 1991.

Penguin Book of Childhood, Penguin (New York, NY), 1994.

Rude Rhymes Two, Signet (London, England), 1994.

POETRY; FOR ADULTS

Bloody L.I.A.R.S., illustrated by Alan Gilbey, privately printed, 1984.

You Are, Aren't You?, Jewish Socialist Group and Mushroom Bookshop (Nottingham, England), 1993.

The Skin of Your Back, Five Leaves Press (Nottingham, England), 1996.

Carrying the Elephant, Penguin (London, England), 2002.

OTHER

Stewed Figs (play), produced at Oxford University, 1966.

Backbone (play; produced at Oxford University, 1967; produced on the West End, 1968), Faber (London, England), 1968.

Regis Debray (radio play), BBC-Radio 4, 1971.

I See a Voice (on poetry), Thames Television-Hutchinson (London, England), 1981.

Mordecai Vanunu: A Reconstruction, performed at Hackney Empire, October, 1993.

Also author of videos, including (as editor) *Why Poetry, Mike Rosen, Count to Five and Say I'm Alive, Poetry Workshop,* and (as editor) *A Poet's Life.* Author of five plays about grandparenting for the British Social Action Unit, BBC Radio, 2000.

Contributor to books, including *There's a Poet behind You!,* edited by Morag Styles and Helen Cook, A & C Black (London, England), 1988; *After Alice: Exploring Children's Literature,* edited by Morag Styles, Victor Watson, and Eve Bearne, Cassell (London, England), 1992; and *Tales, Tellers, and Texts,* edited by Gabrielle Cliff Hodges, Mary Jane Drummind, and Morag Styles, Cassell (London, England), 2000. Contributor to periodicals, including *Guardian, Books for Keeps, Daily Telegraph, Signal, Times Educational Supplement,* and *Children's Literature in Education.*

Author and presenter of radio programs for BBC Radio 4, BBC Radio 3, BBC World Service, and BBC Schools Radio, 1970—, including programs "*Treasure Islands* Special: Lashings of Ginger Beer" and "Dr. Seuss: Who Put the Cat in the Hat?". Writer of television series, including *The Juice Job,* Thames TV, 1981, 1984; *You Tell Me,* Thames TV, 1982; *Everybody Here,* BBC Channel 4, 1982; *Black and White and Read All Over,* BBC Channel 4, 1984; and *Talk Write Read,* Central TV, 1986.

Many of Rosen's books have appeared on audiocassette, performed by the author, including *The Bakerloo Flea, You Can't Catch Me, Quick, Let's Get out of Here, Hairy Tales and Nursery Crimes, Don't Put Mustard in the Custard, Sonsense Nongs, The Wicked Tricks of Till Owlyglass, You Wait till I'm Older than You,* and *Centrally Heated Knickers.*

Sidelights

As *School Librarian* critic Margaret Meek proclaimed, anyone "who has seen Michael Rosen on TV, at work with children in school," or reading to children "testifies to his Pied Piper magic with words." Author Rosen's love of words, his talent for combining them in fresh and exciting ways, and his delightful ability to speak the words of a child in the way a child would speak them has made him one of England's most popular children's poets. Describing *The Best of Michael Rosen,* a collection of over sixty poems from Rosen's work, *Booklist* contributor Carolyn Phelan praised the author for his "excellent descriptions of childhood experiences, sharp insights into people, and ... humor." "Rosen's poetry has become almost a school institution," added an essayist in the *St. James Guide to Children's Writers* describing the poet's influence, particularly in Great Britain during the late twentieth century. Noting that the "humor, accessibility, and child's-eye view" of Rosen's verse "has not only brought children into its spell but has enabled them to enter the world of poetry more widely," the essayist concluded: "That poetry's profile is now higher in schools than in the past, despite the odds currently stacked against it, is due in no small measure to him."

Rosen's love of words is reflected in his enthusiasm for writing, collecting, and sometimes piecing together anecdotes, jokes, songs, folktales, fairytales, vignettes, and nonsense verse, which he has published in informal poetry collections and in the books *Action Replay, Anecdotal Poems* and *That'd Be Telling.* Rosen's habit of collecting stories—or parts of them—is apparent in his novels like *You're Thinking about Doughnuts* and *The Deadman Tapes,* which contain several stories within the larger plot. Rosen once told *SATA* that some "people are worried about whether what I write is 'poetry.' If they are worried, let them call it something else, for example, 'stuff.'"

Rosen realized the importance of pursuing his own style after reading twentieth-century Irish author James Joyce's unconventional novel *Portrait of the Artist as a Young Man* as a teenager. He told an interviewer for *Language Matters,* "That book really came home to me. It was really quite extraordinary, because for the first time I realized that you could actually play around with different ways of saying something. So, for example, you could do a stream of consciousness or you could write about things that happened to you when you were six, and you could do it in the voice of a child of six. So I became absolutely fascinated by this idea and I started to write a few things of that sort."

In college, Rosen developed an interest in performance and theater and wrote a play performed at the Royal Court in London. Later, when he noticed the poems his mother selected for a British Broadcasting Corporation show she helped produce, Rosen decided to write poems for radio and television programs. Although his poems made the air waves, it took longer for them to find a home on the printed page. As Rosen said in *Language*

Matters, publishers rejected his submissions, "saying that 'Children don't like poems written from the child's point of view.'" Then an editor from London publisher Deutsch decided to pair the poet with quirky illustrator Quentin Blake, and in 1974 *Mind Your Own Business* was published.

Since the publication of *Mind Your Own Business,* Rosen's reputation for writing nonsense verse and humorous dialogue has grown. He is especially known for the childlike voice of his poetry, which, as he pointed out in *Language Matters,* is uncommon. While "plenty of people have written about their childhood, they haven't written about it in the kind of speaking voice that is totally accessible to a child, so that they can read it out loud."

According to *Times Educational Supplement* critic Edward Blishen, reviewing the early collections *You Can't Catch Me!* and *Wouldn't You Like to Know,* Rosen's talent lies in his ability to show "how far from being ordinary are the most ordinary of events." Such events are the subjects of the humorous *You Can't Catch Me!;* in one poem a father and child tease one another, in another the joy of sailing is pondered, while yet another focuses on the fear of the dark. Noting the compatibility of Blake's illustrations and Rosen's verse, a reviewer for *Junior Bookshelf* concluded that *You Can't Catch Me!* is a "gorgeous book." Like the poems in *You Can't Catch Me!,* those in *Wouldn't You Like to Know* focus on relationships, fears, and simple joys. As a *Junior Bookshelf* contributor noted, Rosen's verse gives young teens "comforting insights into the problems that can make adults so troublesome."

Similarly, the free-verse poems in *Quick, Let's Get out of Here* recall the events, episodes, and special moments of childhood: fights, birthday parties, tricks and schemes, and the like. As Helen Gregory related in *School Library Journal,* Rosen evokes emotions ranging from the "hysteria of silly joking" to "the agony of breaking a friend's toy." *Horn Book* contributor Ann A. Flowers remarked that, with its "irrepressible" and "outrageous" poems, *Quick, Let's Get out of Here* is a "far cry" from more traditional childhood classics. *You Wait till I'm Older than You* continues Rosen's poetic take on childhood with his characteristic "originality, authenticity, wit and affection," in the opinion of a *Books for Keeps* contributor. Noting that the 1997 collection "fully lives up to expectations," *School Librarian* reviewer Diane Broughton also had praise for Rosen's inclusion of "moments of poignancy" in a series of verses recalling his own childhood, as well as for Shoo Rayner's "appealing" pen-and-ink illustrations. While noting that *Tea in the Sugar Bowl, Potato in My Shoe* is too brief at only twenty-two pages of text and illustrations, *New Statesman* reviewer Michael Glover nonetheless dubbed the 1997 compilation of several previous books "a beautiful piece of work and an exemplary piece of publishing."

Rosen's ability to bring smiles to the faces of his young readers manifests itself in collections of silly verses,

songs, fairytales, and folktales as well as in his poetry. *Freckly Feet and Itchy Knees* presents a list of body parts, describes their owners, and explains their functions in rhythmic verse. Rosen contemplates the nose: "I'm talking about noses / wet noses / warty noses / sleepy noses / when someone dozes." Before the end of the book, children are encouraged to wiggle and jiggle their own body parts. In the opinion of a *Publishers Weekly* reviewer, *Freckly Feet and Itchy Knees* is "always lighthearted" and "ideal for reading aloud." *Nuts about Nuts* contains another list set to rhyme, but this time the focus is on food: sweets like ice cream, cake, and honey as well as staples like bread, eggs, nuts, and rice are, as a *Junior Bookshelf* critic noted, "celebrated and examined." The English alphabet also comes in for a humorous reworking by Rosen in *Michael Rosen's ABC,* as easily recognizable characters like Goldilocks, Rudolph the Red-Nosed Reindeer, Humpty Dumpty, King Kong, and actor Charlie Chaplin team with well-known objects beginning with various letters of the alphabet to parade before readers in what *School Library Journal* contributor Tania Elias characterized as "tongue-twisting" fashion. Describing the text as a "glorious glut of alliterative nonsense," Jill Bennett noted in her *Books for Keeps* review of *Michael Rosen's ABC* that the collection is "peppered with wondrous words."

In addition to his collections of original verses, Rosen has also edited several volumes of poetry for young listeners. *Walking the Bridge of Your Nose,* published in 1996, includes traditional and composed poems that "play with words, their sounds and their spellings, their punctuations," according to *Junior Bookshelf's* Marcus Crouch. Readers will relish the puns, tongue twisters, chants, and quips that Rosen serves up in "demonstrating the peculiarities and foolishness of the English language," as Judith Constantinides noted in a favorable review of *Walking the Bridge of Your Nose* for *School Library Journal.* Other edited anthologies include 1985's *The Kingfisher Book of Children's Poetry,* which contains 250 poems, and *Classic Poetry: An Illustrated Collection,* in which Rosen couples brief biographies of noted English-language poets from William Shakespeare to Langston Hughes with selections from their works. Containing over eighty poems, the volume "reaffirms the English poetry canon familiar to students throughout the English-speaking world since the 1940s," explained a *Magpies* contributor, although the reviewer added that the work would be of greatest value as an historic overview for students.

The works in *Sonsense Nongs*—eight ballads, parodies, and silly songs written by Rosen with contributions from children—are meant to be sung out loud. According to a *Junior Bookshelf* reviewer, *Sonsense Nongs* may help children gain a "deeper understanding of language as well as much fun and laughter." Children may also sing the words to *Little Rabbit Foo Foo,* which is based on the old children's finger-play song in which Little Rabbit Foo Foo bops his helpless victims on the head. Judith Sharman testified in *Books for Keeps* that her son found *Little Rabbit Foo Foo* so charming that she had to

Rosen creates a colorful picture of Shakespeare and his times and discusses some of the Bard's major plays in this book for young readers. *(From* Shakespeare: His Work and His World, *illustrated by Robert Ingpen.)*

"sneak" the book away from him while he slept in order to write her review of it.

From poetry, Rosen also moves into the picture book arena with several illustrated volumes for pre- and beginning readers. In *This Is Our House*, a cardboard box takes on a new life to a group of playground friends, as a young boy learns an important lesson about acceptance. A *Kirkus Reviews* critic dubbed the tale "a

persuasive and entertaining morality play" that reflects the way children think and learn. Praising the "clear and engaging manner" in which Rosen's text illustrates the insecurity and other feelings that cause discrimination, *School Library Journal* reviewer Steven Engelfried added that the author includes "no lectures in the text," leaving the young protagonists to "work out the problem on their own using actions rather than speeches." "Rosen has an instinctive feel for the way children confront one another, ponder, negotiate and form alliances," added a *Publishers Weekly* contributor, commenting that "every word" of Rosen's text "rings true."

Other picture books by Rosen include *Rover, Mission Ziffoid,* and *We're Going on a Bear Hunt,* the last which is based on a traditional motif. In *Rover,* the usual perspective on children and their pets is overturned as the dog tells the story of his pet humans and their daily life. Barbara James praised *Rover* as "bright and breezy" in tone in her review for *Magpies,* adding that young children "will enjoy the leap of imagination of seeing humans from a dog's point of view." In *Books for Keeps,* a reviewer enjoyed Rosen's "deadpan text" while Deborah Stevenson added in her appraisal for *Bulletin of the Center for Children's Books* that "the text adheres firmly to the doggy view of events, ... which keeps the concept from becoming cutesy."

A humorous text also comes in for praise by reviewers reading *Mission Ziffoid,* which Rosen published in 1999. In this offbeat story, a boy builds a faulty spaceship and winds up in the center of a football game played by small, greenish alien beings ... at least, according to the ship-builder's little brother. Praising the text as "laconic and hilarious," a *Magpies* reviewer noted that the story's "imaginative flights of fancy" result from Rosen's care in listening "to young children telling cumulative yarns." Calling *Mission Ziffoid* "a natural readaloud with a generous dose of kid-pleasing hilarity," Janice M. Del Negro added in her review for the *Bulletin of the Center for Children's Books* that "the text zips right along," fueled by Arthur Robins' over-the-top, neon-colored illustrations.

Many children will recognize the story in *We're Going on a Bear Hunt,* which is based on a traditional British children's song. Eager to find a bear, a young family wades through mud, water, grass, and snow and braves the dangers of a forest, a river, and a cave. As they meet each obstacle, they sing "We can't go over it. We can't go under it. Oh, no! We've got to go through it!," and make their way through the muck with joyful noises ranging from "swishy swashy" to "squelch squelch." When the family finally finds the bear, he scares them so much that they turn around and hurry back through each obstacle. As Elizabeth S. Watson commented in *Horn Book,* Rosen's text has "a driving rhythm" and "new sounds" that give the familiar tale added "sparkle."

The fables in *Hairy Tales and Nursery Crimes* are written in verse and lampoon traditional fairy tales. For example, Rosen's version of Hansel and Gretel begins, "Once a plum time, in the middle of a forest, there lived a poor wood-/ nutter and his woof. They lived in a little wooden sausage with their two / children, Handsel and Gristle." In the opinion of George Szirtes, writing in *Times Literary Supplement,* the jokes in these fables "are improved in the telling aloud. Hansel's pocketful of stones ... become a rocket full of phones." According to *School Librarian* reviewer Colin Walter, however, *Hairy Tales and Nursery Crimes* is "not for hearing, and therein lies its secret and appeal."

Rosen's treatment of folktales is tempered by his respect for their origins. His version of an Eastern and Southern African *porquoi* tale, *How Giraffe Got Such a Long Neck ... and Why Rhino Is So Grumpy,* according to *School Library Journal* contributor Lee Bock, is "lively" and "bright." The story tells how Giraffe, originally a small beast, and the much larger Rhino implore Man to help them survive the drought. Although Man instructs Giraffe and Rhino to visit him the next day for help reaching the leaves high in the trees, Rhino does not arrive on time, and Giraffe eats his portion of Man's remedy as well as her own. As a result, Giraffe's neck grows long. Rhino, who feels cheated, only grows grumpy.

The Golem of Old Prague is a collection of stories concerning the legendary Rabbi Loeb of Prague. The stories tell how Rabbi Loeb creates a golem—a huge, strong, but mindless creature—out of clay and gives him life. With the help of the powerful and loyal golem, Rabbi Loeb ensures the Jewish community's survival when they are persecuted by the monk Thaddeus. Writing in *Books for Your Children,* S. Williams concluded that *The Golem of Old Prague* "gives insight to Jewish thinking, customs, and way of life" in sixteenth-century Prague.

South and North, East and West: The Oxfam Anthology of Children's Stories is a collection of twenty-five stories that includes tales from Cyprus, Korea, the Dominican Republic, Bangladesh, China, Jamaica, Malta, Vietnam, and England. Betsy Hearne, writing in *Bulletin of the Center for Children's Books,* found these retellings to be "fresh and colloquial." The royalties from *South and North, East and West* benefit Oxfam, the international organization that establishes self-help development programs in countries disrupted by natural or man-made disasters.

Rosen's work for older children and teenagers frequently addresses serious issues. His poetry collection *When Did You Last Wash Your Feet?,* for example, deals with topics from racism to terminal illness. *Mind the Gap,* a collection Sue Rogers described in *School Librarian* as "brilliant," features "comic, sad," and "controversial" poems, including one that recalls the past as the narrator's mother is dying. *Books for Keeps* critic Adrian Jackson advised librarians to buy many copies: "Teenagers will love it." In *Culture Shock,* a collection of poems Rosen selected from around the world, racism, sexism, love, and hate are also concerns.

Like his poetry, Rosen's fiction for older children often develops around episodes and anecdotes, calls upon his performer's love of dialogue, and insightfully expresses the perspectives of protagonists. The story collection *Nasty!* is narrated by a talkative Cockney cleaning woman known as the Bakerloo Flea Woman. She tells the story of the giant Bakerloo flea, recalls how wasps plagued the residents of London's East End one winter, and remembers how they dealt with the mice that invaded their homes. Although it is a short novel, *You're Thinking about Doughnuts* contains several stories told from strange perspectives. Frank, who is just eight years old, must wait in the dark halls of the museum where his mother works every Friday night. One night, the exhibits, including a skeleton, a space suit, a few Greek statues, and a stuffed tiger, come alive. As these exhibits tell Frank about their lives before they were taken to the quiet museum, Rosen also questions the "honesty and integrity of an institutional building like a museum," according to *School Librarian* contributor Tom Lewis.

Rosen's novel *The Deadman Tapes* also presents a series of stories within a larger plot. When Paul Deadman plays some tapes he has found in the attic of his new house, he is introduced to the voices and stories of eight teens. With occasional interruptions from Paul, these stories make up the novel's text, and like Rosen's more serious poetry, deal with social problems faced by teenagers.

Rosen enjoys sharing the techniques that have made him a successful children's writer. He has published books on writing such as *Did I Hear You Write?*, and also visits schools and libraries. He revealed one of the secrets of his unique style to *Language Matters:* "What I try to do in my mind is to go back and write about my feelings when I was ten.... I write about my experience using the voice of a ten year old. I write in that voice, using what I know as a performer will work, knowing, that is, what children can take off a page."

Biographical and Critical Sources

BOOKS

Children's Literature Review, Volume 45, Gale (Detroit, MI), 1997, pp. 127-152.
Language Matters, Centre for Language in Primary Education (London, England), 1983.
Nettell, Stephanie, editor, *Meet the Authors,* Scholastic (New York, NY), 1994.
Powling, Chris, *What It's Like to be Michael Rosen,* Ginn (Oxford, England), 1990.
Rosen, Michael, *Hairy Tales and Nursery Crimes,* illustrated by Alan Baker, Deutsch (London, England), 1985.
Rosen, Michael, *We're Going on a Bear Hunt,* illustrated by Helen Oxenbury, Walker (London, England), 1989, Aladdin (New York, NY), 1992.
Rosen, Michael, *Freckly Feet and Itchy Knees,* illustrated by Sami Sweeten, HarperCollins (London, England), Doubleday (New York, NY), 1990.
St. James Guide to Children's Writers, 5th edition, St. James Press (Detroit, MI), 1999.
Styles, Morag, and Helen Cook, editors, *There's a Poet behind You,* A & C Black (London, England), 1988.

PERIODICALS

Booklist, December 1, 1993, Elizabeth Bush, review of *How Giraffe Got Such a Long Neck ... and Why Rhino Is So Grumpy,* p. 695; December 15, 1993, Julie Corsaro, review of *Moving,* p. 766; January 1, 1994, Carolyn Phelan, review of *Poems for the Very Young,* p. 821; April 15, 1995, Karen Hutt, review of *Crow and Hawk: A Traditional Pueblo Indian Story,*

p. 1503; February 1, 1996, Carolyn Phelan, review of *The Best of Michael Rosen,* p. 929; November 1, 1996, Carolyn Phelan, review of *This Is Our House,* p. 510; June 1, 1997, Kathleen Squires, review of *Michael Rosen's ABC,* p. 1712; January 1, 1999, Carolyn Phelan, review of *Classic Poetry: An Illustrated Collection,* p. 862; July, 1999, Stephanie Zvirin, review of *Rover,* p. 1953; November 1, 2001, John Peters, review of *Shakespeare: His Work and His World,* p. 477.
Books for Keeps, May, 1981; July, 1988; May, 1992, Judith Sharman, review of *Little Rabbit Foo Foo,* p. 11; September, 1992, Adrian Jackson, review of *Mind the Gap,* p. 13; March, 1996, Jill Bennett, review of *Michael Rosen's ABC,* p. 28; January, 1997, review of *You Wait till I'm Older than You,* p. 25; September, 1999, review of *Rover,* p. 21.
Books for Your Children, autumn-winter, 1991, p. 24; spring, 1991, S. Williams, review of *The Golem of Old Prague,* p. 24.
British Medical Journal, May 2, 1992, Michael Modell, review of *The Chatto Book of Dissent,* p. 1192.
Bulletin of the Center for Children's Books, December, 1992, Betsy Hearne, review of *South and North, East and West,* pp. 121-122; June, 1999, Deborah Stevenson, review of *Rover,* p. 363; November, 1999, Janice M. Del Negro, review of *Mission Ziffoid,* pp. 104-105.
Economist (U.S.), December 7, 1991, review of *The Chatto Book of Dissent,* p. 105.
Horn Book, June, 1984, Anne A. Flowers, review of *Quick, Let's Get out of Here,* p. 345; December, 1989, Elizabeth S. Watson, review of *We're Going on a Bear Hunt,* p. 765; September-October, 1993, Maeve Visser Knoth, review of *How Giraffe Got Such a Long Neck ... and Why Rhino Is So Grumpy,* p. 611; July-August, 1996, Margaret A. Bush, review of *This Is Our House,* p. 454.
Junior Bookshelf, February, 1982, review of *You Can't Catch Me!,* p. 22; October, 1992, review of *Sonsense Nongs,* p. 201; June, 1993, review of *Nuts about Nuts,* p. 100; June, 1995, pp. 93-94; April, 1996, Marcus Crouch, review of *Walking the Bridge of Your Nose,* p. 71; October, 1996, review of *You Can't Catch Me,* p. 194; December, 1996, review of *Wouldn't You Like to Know,* pp. 259-260.
Kirkus Reviews, June 1, 1996, review of *This Is Our House,* p. 829; October 15, 2001, review of *Shakespeare: His Work and His World,* p. 149.
Magpies, March, 1996, review of *Crow and Hawk,* p. 29; November, 1998, review of *Classic Poetry,* pp. 18-19; July, 1999, review of *Mission Ziffoid,* pp. 26-27; November, 1999, Barbara James, review of *Rover,* p. 28.
New Statesman, December 5, 1997, Michael Glover, review of *Tea in the Sugar Bowl, Potato in My Shoe,* p. 63.
Observer (London, England), May 30, 1999, review of *The Kingfisher Book of Children's Poetry,* p. 13.
Publishers Weekly, June 30, 1989, review of *We're Going on a Bear Hunt,* p. 104; June 8, 1990, review of *Freckly Feet and Itchy Knees,* p. 54; September 21, 1992, review of *South and North, East and West,* p. 94; July 26, 1993, review of *How Giraffe Got Such*

a Long Neck . . . and Why Rhino Is So Grumpy, p. 71; October 25, 1993, p. 62; February 27, 1995, review of *Crow and Hawk,* p. 102; October 16, 1995, review of *Walking the Bridge of Your Nose,* p. 61; December 18, 1995, review of *The Best of Michael Rosen,* p. 54; June 24, 1996, review of *This Is Our House,* p. 58; March 3, 1997, review of *Michael Rosen's ABC,* p. 77; December 14, 1998, review of *Classic Poetry,* p. 77; June 7, 1999, review of *Rover,* p. 83; December 3, 2001, review of *Shakespeare: His Work and His World,* p. 61.

School Librarian, March, 1985, Colin Walter, review of *Hairy Tales and Nursery Crimes,* p. 40; May, 1988, Tom Lewis, review of *You're Thinking about Dough-nuts,* p. 59; August, 1988, p. 100; August, 1989, Margaret Meek, review of *Did I Hear You Write?,* p. 128; November, 1990, p. 148; August, 1991, p. 112; November, 1992, Sue Rogers, review of *Mind the Gap,* p. 156; May, 1993, p. 71; February, 1997, Diane Broughton, review of *You Wait till I'm Older than You!,* p. 43; winter, 1999, Anne Rowe, review of *Lunch Boxes Don't Fly,* p. 208.

School Library Journal, May, 1982, review of *You Can't Catch Me,* p. 56; November, 1983, Margaret L. Chatham, review of *A Cat and Mouse Story,* p. 69; October, 1984, Helen Gregory, review of *Quick, Let's Get out of Here,* p. 161; January, 1987, Barbara McGinn, review of *Don't Put Mustard in the Custard,* p. 78; May, 1989, Lucy Young Clem, review of *Down at the Doctor's,* p. 101; February, 1991, JoAnn Rees, review of *Little Rabbit Foo Foo,* p. 74; December, 1992, Karen Wehner, review of *Itsy-Bitsy Beasties,* p. 127; October, 1993, Lee Bock, review of *How Giraffe Got Such a Long Neck . . . and Why Rhino Is So Grumpy,* pp. 121-22; January, 1994, p. 110; March, 1994, Carolyn Noah, review of *Moving,* p. 208; June, 1995, p. 104; July, 1995, Lisa Dennis, review of *Crow and Hawk,* p. 74; January, 1996, Judith Constantin-ides, review of *Walking the Bridge of Your Nose,* p. 105; July, 1996, Steven Engelfried, review of *This Is Our House,* p. 71; March, 1997, Tana Elias, review of *Michael Rosen's ABC,* p. 165; June, 1999, Carol Ann Wilson, review of *Rover,* p. 106; December, 1999, Sally R. Dow, review of *Mission Ziffoid,* p. 112; November, 2001, Patricia Lothrop-Green, review of *Shakespeare: His Work and His World,* p. 184.

Times Educational Supplement, November 20, 1981, Ed-ward Blishen, "Nonsense Not Nauseous," p. 34; April 28, 1995.

Times Higher Education Supplement, May 6, 1994, Colwyn Williamson, review of *The Chatto Book of Dissent,* p. 28.

Times Literary Supplement, March 8, 1985, George Szirtes, review of *Hairy Tales and Nursery Crimes,* p. 270; April 7, 1989, Carol Ann Duffy, review of *Didn't I Hear You Write?,* p. 381; November 24, 1989, D. J. Enright, review of *Rude Rhymes,* p. 1310.

S

SCHULMAN, Janet 1933-

Personal

Born September 16, 1933, in Pittsburgh, PA; daughter of Albert C. (in insurance) and Edith (Spielman) Schuetz; married Lester M. Schulman (a writer and editor), May 19, 1957; children: Nicole. *Education:* Antioch College, B.A., 1956. *Hobbies and other interests:* Tennis.

Addresses

Home—New York, NY. *Office*—Random House, 1540 Broadway, New York, NY 10036.

Career

Writer and publishing company executive. Macmillan Publishing Co., Inc., New York, NY, member of advertising staff, beginning c. 1961, then vice president and juvenile marketing manager, 1965-74; Random House, Inc., New York, NY, manager, 1978, director of library marketing, 1978-80, vice president and editor-in-chief of children's books, beginning 1980, vice president and editor-in-chief of Knopf and Pantheon children's books, beginning 1983, associate publisher, editor-in-chief, and divisional vice president of Books for Young Readers imprint, 1987, publisher and divisional vice president of Knopf, Random House, and Crown juvenile imprints, beginning 1988, editor-at-large of Random House juvenile division, 1994. Worked in advertising in New Orleans, LA, c. 1950s. Member of New York publishing industry committees, including Freedom-to-Read committee, 1980-84, and M.S. Read-a-Thon committee, 1984; Children's Book Council, member of board of directors and president, 1983; consultant to juvenile publishers.

Member

American Library Association.

Writings

The Big Hello, Greenwillow Press (New York, NY), 1976.
Jack the Bum and the Halloween Handout, Greenwillow Press (New York, NY), 1977.
Jack the Bum and the Haunted House, Greenwillow Press (New York, NY), 1977.
Jenny and the Tennis Nut, Greenwillow Press (New York, NY), 1978.
Jack the Bum and the UFO, Greenwillow Press (New York, NY), 1978.
Camp Kee Wee's Secret Weapon, Greenwillow Press (New York, NY), 1979.
The Great Big Dummy, Greenwillow Press (New York, NY), 1979.
(Adaptor) *The Nutcracker,* Dutton (New York, NY), 1979, reprinted with illustrations by Renée Graef, HarperCollins (New York, NY), 1999.
(Selector) *The Twentieth-Century Children's Book Treasury: Celebrated Picture Books and Stories to Read Aloud,* Knopf (New York, NY), 1998.
(Adaptor) Felix Salten, *Bambi,* illustrated by Steve Johnson and Lou Francher, Atheneum (New York, NY), 1999.
(Selector) *You Read to Me and I'll Read to You: Twentieth-Century Stories to Share,* Knopf (New York, NY), 2001.
Countdown to Spring! An Animal Counting Book, illustrated by Meilo So, Knopf (New York, NY), 2002.
A Bunny for All Seasons, illustrated by Meilo So, Knopf (New York, NY), 2003.

Abridger of books, including the "Chronicles of Narnia" series by C. S. Lewis, and other literary classics, for Caedmon Records.

Adaptations

Bambi was recorded on audiocassette by Audio Book-shelf, 2002.

Sidelights

With over four decades working in the publishing industry, Janet Schulman has been in a position to influence the quality and character of twentieth-century children's literature. Beginning her career at Macmillan in New York City, she developed her love of children's books during a job updating jacket copy for a new edition of British author C. S. Lewis's classic "Narnia" books. "When I read the books I thought, 'Wow, if this is what children's literature is like, this is where I want to be,'" she recalled in an interview posted on the Kids@ Random Web site. Schulman has gone on to hold executive positions at Random House and has edited and written a number of well-received works for young readers, working with authors Theodor Geisel ("Dr. Seuss"), Marc Brown, Jack Prelutsky, and Stan and Jan Berenstain.

Born in 1933, Schulman grew up in the shadow of the Great Depression. As she once recalled, "my mother literally counted pennies to put food on the table for us." When the United States entered World War II, her older siblings joined the military, which forced Schulman to "keep a wary eye on reality." Both these experiences shaped the kinds of stories she would later write. "I try to show children operating not in a vacuum but surrounded by circumstances of reality which do affect their lives," she explained. "In *The Big Hello* a little girl moves to California because her father has gone there to find a new job. In *Camp Kee Wee's Secret Weapon* Jill has to go to summer camp because her mother has just gotten a job and Jill is too young to stay home alone during the day. In *Jenny and the Tennis Nut* Jenny's father wants to see Jenny take up tennis enthusiastically because tennis is his game."

Schulman views her editorship of works such as *The Twentieth-Century Children's Book Treasury: Celebrated Picture Books and Stories to Read Aloud* and *You Read to Me and I'll Read to You: Twentieth-Century Stories to Share* as providing a service to parents of preschoolers who would otherwise be lost in a children's book department. The first anthology, which contains forty-four picture books, includes such twentieth-century classics as *Madeline, Curious George, Goodnight Moon, Stellaluna, Millions of Cats,* and *Make Way for Ducklings,* all included in a single volume. Each story is accompanied by selected illustrations from its original publication, making the volume valuable for its collection of artwork by popular illustrators James Marshall, Maurice Sendak, and Quentin Blake, although *Horn Book* reviewer Roger Sutton joined several critics in bemoaning the fact that many illustrations in *The Twentieth-Century Children's Book Treasury* "have gone missing.... making hash out of some selections." "Wouldn't you prefer having [these picture books] ... in their collected, albeit modified, forms to not having them at all?," questioned Karla Kuskin in a review for the *Los Angeles Times Book Review.* "Of course." As Schulman noted on the Kids@Random Web site, "I hope this book will change the tide for many children and send them on the path to a lifelong love of books and reading. But most of all, I hope [*The Twentieth-Century Children's Book Treasury*] ... will bring parents and children closer together."

One of Schulman's most widely reviewed works was her 1999 picture-book adaptation of Felix Salten's 1923 classic *Bambi: A Life in the Woods,* which was later popularized in an animated film directed by Walt Disney in the mid-twentieth century. An Austrian Jew, Salten wrote his novel—originally intended for adults—as a response to the horrors of World War I, and Schulman began to consider the possibility of adapting the original book for young readers as early as 1985. In her adaptation, she worked hard to preserve the language of the original in her abridgement for younger readers, telling *Publishers Weekly* contributor Cindi di Marzo: "I reread the novel a number of times and then I went through and highlighted the dialogue and poignant sentences Salten had written. It was easy for me to work with the text because Salten's language is so poetic."

While the issue of whether such a classic work of literature such as *Bambi* should be rewritten at all is a question about which there continues to be debate among critics and academics, *New York Times Book Review* contributor Elizabeth Spires praised Schulman for "remain[ing] true to the story's original spirit ... by using many of Salten's actual sentences" and preserving the story's "mystical, exultant evocation of nature, and its unwavering depiction of savage human nature." Pleased that Schulman's adaptation did not "sanitize" Salten's novel, *School Library Journal* reviewer Arwen Marshall commented that "the hard realities of life in the wild are still evident, and some of the events may be disturbing to younger, more sensitive children." Noting that the retelling "restores the depth of Bambi's character," a *Publishers Weekly* contributor added that Schulman expresses "the heart of Salten's lessons, namely, the importance of thinking for oneself and of acknowledging that no living creature is all-powerful."

Schulman credits her daughter, Nicole, for helping to shape her career as a children's writer. "I doubt if I would have written the kinds of stories I write if I had not started just at the time Nicole was in the first grade," she once admitted to *SATA.* "I wanted to write stories for her, stories she could read and would like. None of my stories are based directly on anything that has happened in our family, but all of them have grown or been inspired by my daily life with Nicole."

Biographical and Critical Sources

PERIODICALS

Booklist, October 15, 1998, Hazel Rochman, review of *The Twentieth-Century Children's Book Treasury,* p. 428; January 1, 2002, Gillian Engberg, review of *Countdown to Spring! An Animal Counting Book,* p. 861.

Horn Book, August, 1977; November, 1998, Roger Sutton, review of *The Twentieth-Century Children's Book Treasury,* pp. 717-718.

Kirkus Reviews, January 1, 2002, review of *Countdown to Spring!,* p. 50.

Los Angeles Times Book Review, December 6, 1998, Karla Kuskin, review of *The Twentieth-Century Children's Book Treasury,* p. 5.

New York Times Book Review, November 21, 1999, Elizabeth Spires, review of *Bambi,* p. 5.

Publishers Weekly, February 23, 1976; February 28, 1977; September 21, 1998, review of *The Twentieth-Century Children's Book Treasury,* p. 101; September 27, 1999, review of *The Nutcracker,* p. 54; October 18, 1999, review of *Bambi,* p. 80; October 25, 1999, Cindi di Marzo, "A New Look for Bambi," p. 29; August 6, 2001, review of *You Read to Me and I'll Read to You,* p. 89; October 1, 2001, Sally Lodge, "Making the Transition," p. 28; December 24, 2001, review of *Countdown to Spring!,* p. 62; November 25, 2002, review of *A Bunny for All Seasons,* p. 65.

School Library Journal, December, 1998, Margaret Bush, review of *The Twentieth-Century Children's Book Treasury,* pp. 91-92; October, 1999, Arwen Marshall, review of *Bambi,* p. 126, and Lisa Falk, review of *The Nutcracker,* p. 68; December, 2001, Maryann H. Owen, review of *You Read to Me and I'll Read to You,* p. 110; January, 2002, Melinda Piehler, review of *Countdown to Spring!,* p. 124.

OTHER

Kids@Random, http://www.randomhouse.com (March 5, 2002), "Janet Schulman."*

*   *   *

SHANNON, Margaret
See SILVERWOOD, Margaret Shannon

*   *   *

SHEA, Pegi Deitz 1960-

Personal

Born September 22, 1960, in Matawan, NJ; daughter of George A. Deitz (a high school teacher and coach) and Margaret J. (a legal secretary) Devlin; married Thomas F. Shea (a professor of English), July 19, 1986; children: Deirdre Vincena, Thomas Sullivan. *Education:* Rutgers College, Rutgers University, B.A., 1982. *Politics:* Democrat. *Religion:* Roman Catholic.

Addresses

Home and office—27 Fox Hill Dr., Rockville, CT 06066.

Career

Children's book writer and poet. Pegi Deitz Public Relations, president and freelance writer, 1986—.

Member

St. Bernard's Christian Service Committee, Society of Children's Book Writers and Illustrators (member, New England conference planning committee, 1992-93).

Awards, Honors

Evelyn Hamilton Award for Creative Writing, Rutgers College, 1982; Notable Book designation, National Council for the Social Studies/International Reading Association, 1995, for *The Whispering Cloth.*

Writings

Bungalow Fungalow, Clarion (New York, NY), 1991.
The Whispering Cloth: A Refugee's Story, illustrated by Anita Riggio and You Yang, Boyds Mills Press (Honesdale, PA), 1995.
New Moon, illustrated by Cathryn Falwell, Boyds Mills Press (Honesdale, PA), 1996.
Ekaterina Gordeeva, Chelsea House (Philadelphia, PA), 1999.
I See Me!, illustrated by Lucia Washburn, HarperFestival (New York, NY), 2000.
The Impeachment Process ("Your Government and How It Works" series), Chelsea House (Philadelphia, PA), 2000.
(With Cynthia Weill) *Ten Mice for Tet!,* Chronicle Books (San Francisco, CA), 2003.

Contributor of poetry to periodicals, including *Dan River Anthology, Connecticut Writer, College Composition and Communications, Aquarian, Tunxix Review,* and *Connecticut River Review;* contributor of articles to *Millimeter, Television Broadcasting Europe,* and *Videography.*

Work in Progress

More books for children.

Sidelights

Pegi Deitz Shea's first writing appeared as "little poems that I wrote on construction paper for holidays and birthdays," as she once explained to *SATA.* "The sight of those cards up on the mantlepiece, quite a place of honor in our home, inspired me to continue. I won two dollars in a poetry contest when I was in fifth grade and thought, 'Wow, this writing business pays!' While it may not have made me wealthy, writing has opened me up to new lands, new people, new ways of thinking." Growing up to become president of her own freelance writing business based in Connecticut, Shea has continued to write poetry for small-press magazines and has also created a number of books for young readers that share her experiences with new people and new ways of thinking.

Shea's award-winning 1995 novel *The Whispering Cloth: A Refugee Story* takes readers to Thailand in telling the story of Mai, a Hmong girl who lives in a refugee camp with her grandmother after they fled their home in Laos. Despite her impoverished circumstances, Mai finds herself rich in the traditions of her people and learns from other women in the camp how to create a Hmongese pa'ndau, or story cloth. Hoping that the sale of the cloth to tourists will earn her family enough

Set in a Thai refugee camp of the mid-1970s, **The Whispering Cloth** *by Pegi Deitz Shea tells the tale of a young girl who draws upon her personal tragedies to create a pan'dau, or story cloth. (Illustrated by Anita Riggio.)*

money to leave the camp and join relatives in the United States, Mai decides to detail the events of her short life, from her early childhood, the murder of her parents, and her flight through the Mekong carried by her grandmother, to her current life in the camp and her hopes for a brighter future. Illustrated with an actual pa'ndau cloth stitched by Thai refugee You Yang, Shea spins what a *Publishers Weekly* contributor described as a poignant tale that is "bound to elicit many questions" from elementary school-aged readers. You Yang's "stitched pictures ... distance the brutality," noted Hazel Rochman in her *Booklist* review of Shea's "moving" picture

book, "both showing and telling that art can be a powerful force."

Shea has authored several nonfiction books for young readers, among them *The Impeachment Process,* which introduces the process by which a U.S. president can be removed from office. Part of Chelsea House's "Your Government and How It Works" series, *The Impeachment Process* begins with the circumstances prompting the impeachment of former U.S. president Bill Clinton before going on to examine the provisions of the Constitution that govern the impeachment process.

Another nonfiction book by Shea is a biography of Ekaterina Gordeeva, the winner of two Olympic gold medals for figure skating, who was left widowed after her husband and skating partner Sergei Grinkov, died prematurely in 1995. Shea's story of the Russian-born skater's life and efforts to deal with personal tragedy "offers readers hope that although tragic things happen life goes on," according to Barb Lawler in her review of *Ekaterina Gordeeva* for *School Library Journal.*

For the toddler set, Shea has created the board book *I See Me!,* which, through its simple, lyrical text introduces curious minds to the concept of reflection by showing a small child's discovery of her own image in various surfaces. Praising the book's rhythmic text, *Booklist* reviewer Carolyn Phelan found *I See Me!* to be "an appealing picture book for the youngest."

Shea's 1996 effort, *New Moon,* contains colorful cut-paper illustrations by Cathryn Falwell that depict an Hispanic boy and his younger sister as they await the reappearance of "la luna" after several moonless nights. Capturing the affectionate relationship between the two siblings as the brother attempts to explain to his sister why the moon changes shape throughout the month, *New Moon* embodies what a *Children's Book Review Service* contributor dubbed "the magic of discovery,"

After viewing the full moon one night, Vinnie begs her big brother to take her to see it again and he complies in a surprising way. (From New Moon, *written by Shea and illustrated by Cathryn Falwell.)*

while in *Booklist,* Julie Corsaro praised the picture book for its "simple and lyrical seasonal story."

"I feel that to be a good writer, you have to read a lot and read well," Shea once commented to *SATA.* "Reading well doesn't mean reading fast or pronouncing words correctly. It means looking for, AND appreciating, all the different meanings words have. Ask yourself, 'Why or how is this sentence funny or sad? What images does the writer use to make me feel a certain way?' By understanding how a story succeeds, you will understand how to make your own writing succeed."

Biographical and Critical Sources

PERIODICALS

Booklist, January 1, 1995, Hazel Rochman, review of *The Whispering Cloth,* p. 827; January, 1997, Julie Corsaro, review of *New Moon,* p. 870; May 15, 2000, Carolyn Phelan, review of *I See Me!,* p. 1749.
Bulletin of the Center for Children's Books, March, 1995, Elizabeth Bush, review of *The Whispering Cloth,* p. 250.
Children's Book Review Service, September, 1996, review of *New Moon,* p. 6.
Horn Book, July-August, 1991, Ellen Fader, review of *Bungalow Fungalow,* p. 473.
Publishers Weekly, December 12, 1994, review of *The Whispering Cloth,* p. 61.
School Library Journal, June, 1991, Andrew W. Hunter, review of *Bungalow Fungalow,* p. 98; January 1, 1997, Julie Corsaro, review of *New Moon,* p. 879; April, 1999, Barb Lawler, review of *Ekaterina Gordeeva,* pp. 156-157; August, 2000, Linda Beck, review of *The Impeachment Process,* p. 202.*

*   *   *

SHERMAN, Harold (Morrow) 1898-1987

OBITUARY NOTICE—See index for *SATA* sketch: Born July 13, 1898, in Traverse City, MI; died August, 1987, in Mt. View, AR. Writer and radio commentator. Harold Sherman attended the University of Michigan (1918-19). He began his career as a reporter for the *Marion Chronicles,* Marion, IN, in 1921-24, and was the writer and commentator for the *Your Key to Happiness* radio show, produced by CBS-Radio in New York (1935-36) and in Chicago (1943). He was founder, president, and director of the ESP Research Associates Foundation, Little Rock, AR, from 1964 on. He was a free-lance writer for most of his life, beginning in 1924. His first book was *Fight 'em, Big Three* (1926). He wrote some forty books, most on sports or adventure topics, aimed at the juvenile or young adult market, including the "Tahara, Boy King of the Desert" series, and penned another twenty-five books dealing with popular psychology, self-help, and paranormal topics for the adult market. These latter titles were his most popular, and included: *Your Key to Happiness* (1935; repr. Mulvey Books, 1990); *Thoughts Through Space* (with George

Hubert Wilkins) (1942; rev. ed., Amherst, 1983); *How to Use the Power of Prayer* (1958; 2nd ed., Unity Books, 1985); and his last three books, *The Green Man and His Return: An Amazing UFO Pre-Vision of the Coming of the Space People* (Amherst Press, 1979); *Dead or Alive!: They Can and Do Communicate with You!* (Amherst Press, 1981); and *Extra Success Potential: The Art of Out-Thinking and Out-Sensing Others in Business and Everyday Life* (with Al Pollard) (Prentice-Hall, 1981). In addition, he wrote two plays and a screenplay, and made three record albums and two cassette recordings of his more popular self-help titles. He was a life member of the Authors Guild of the Authors League of America, a member of the Dramatists Guild and other fraternal organizations, and co-developer of Blanchard Spring Caverns. He spent the greater part of his life investigating, experimenting on, and lecturing about extra-sensory perception and related topics.

OBITUARIES AND OTHER SOURCES:

BOOKS

The Encyclopedia of Science Fiction, St. Martin's Press, 1993.

* * *

SILVERWOOD, Margaret Shannon 1966-
(Margaret Shannon)

Personal

Born October 10, 1966, in Adelaide, South Australia; daughter of Ernst Tilbrook (a sculptor) and Kathleen O'Neill (a writer). *Education:* University of Auckland. *Politics:* "Vaguely Left Wing." *Religion:* Animist. *Hobbies and other interests:* Reading graphic novels, going to films and theatre, going to the beach, tinkering around the house, patting the cats, playing with life.

Addresses

Agent—c/o Author Mail, Houghton Mifflin, Children's Division, 222 Berkeley, Boston, MA 02116-3764.

Career

Artist, writer, and illustrator.

Awards, Honors

Notable Book citation, Children's Council of Australia, 1992, for *Elvira.*

Writings

UNDER NAME MARGARET SHANNON; SELF-ILLUSTRATED

Elvira, Omnibus Books (Norwood, Australia), 1991, Ticknor & Fields (New York, NY), 1993.
Gullible's Troubles, Houghton Mifflin (Boston, MA), 1998.

The Red Wolf, Houghton Mifflin (Boston, MA), 2002.

Sidelights

Publishing under the name Margaret Shannon, Australian author and illustrator Margaret Shannon Silverwood has created a small but choice body of humorous books for children. In her first book, 1991's *Elvira*, Silverwood's talent was apparent to a *Publishers Weekly* contributor who noted that a "well-honed comic sense" informs Silverwood's "watercolors and her text." "My illustration style is very cartoony," Silverwood once explained to *SATA*, "because I was taught to read with comics. Comics most probably taught me a lot about knitting together pictures and words to tell a story."

Elvira is about a young dragon who does not like to eat princesses or fight like all the other dragons. She likes dressing up and making daisy chains instead. The other dragons tease her unmercifully, but Elvira refuses to give in to peer pressure. Instead, she goes to live with the princesses and learns to make beautiful clothes. Only after her father mistakes her for an oversized—and therefore particularly tasty—princess and tries to eat her do her parents insist she return home. The other dragons now admire Elvira's beautiful clothes and, instead of teasing her, compete to wear her outfits. *Horn Book* contributor Ann A. Flowers described Silverwood's story as "outrageously funny, with energetic pictures of dragons," while Lisa Dennis added in *School Library Journal* that *Elvira*'s illustrations "have a quirky charm and the depiction of the enraged Elvira is extremely well done."

Silverwood has followed *Elvira* with several other equally quirky children's book offerings. *Gullible's Troubles* introduces Gullible Guineapig, who is visiting several distant relatives for a long vacation. Because Gullible is, well, gullible and will believe whatever he is told, members of his family convince him that eating carrots will make him invisible and that there is a terrible monster living in the cellar. When some of their tall tales come true, comedy ensues in what a *Publishers Weekly* contributor dubbed a "witty charmer" of a picture book. Praising *Gullible's Troubles* as a "triumph of good-heartedness over guile," *Horn Book* reviewer Ann A. Flowers praised Silverwood's "expressive illustrations" which, "clearly recording Gullible's emotions, add to the fun."

In 2002's *The Red Wolf*, Silverwood toys with yet another classic fairy story—as well as the works of noted American author/illustrator Maurice Sendak—in relating the tale of a seven-year-old princess named Roselupin who receives a gold basket of yarn for her birthday. Following the instructions on the enclosed card to "Knit what you want," Roselupin knits herself a red wolf suit in the hopes that it will provide a way for her to escape being locked up in the tower by her overprotective father. Remarking that the story's "most inventive heroine celebrates the joy and ... the necessity of freedom," Robin L. Gibson commented in her *School Library Journal* review that Silverwood's "brightly colored illustrations ... enrich this original, delightful tale ... of empowerment." Calling *The Red Wolf* "a cleverly told tale," a *Publishers Weekly* contributor added that the author/illustrator's "antic mixed-media art will have readers howling" while her "sly humor and resourceful heroine are eminently her own." Commending, in particular, Silverwood's illustrations, *Horn Book* reviewer Martha V. Parravano described the book's detailed and evocative artwork as "a lush mix of watercolor, pastel, and colored pencil [that] at times send shivers down the spine" while at other points in the story "convey a lighter mood."

Silverwood once told *SATA:* "Children fascinate me. They are such a mixture of vulnerability, loveliness, and pure obnoxiousness that I love them and want to protect them, but I can't stand to be around them too long. *Elvira* has been my attempt to support kinds in their own beliefs, to help them hold off the pressure to homogenize a few seconds longer—just as my mother did for me."

Biographical and Critical Sources

PERIODICALS

Booklist, August, 1993, Annie Ayres, review of *Elvira,* p. 2071; April, 1998, Hazel Rochman, review of *Gullible's Troubles,* p. 1334.

Horn Book, September-October, 1993, Ann A. Flowers, review of *Elvira,* p. 591; July-August, 1998, Ann A. Flowers, review of *Gullible's Troubles,* p. 481; March-April, 2002, Martha V. Parravano, review of *The Red Wolf,* p. 204.

Kirkus Reviews, February 15, 2002, review of *The Red Wolf,* p. 265.

Magpies, July, 1991, p. 28.

Publishers Weekly, June 28, 1993, review of *Elvira,* p. 76; March 23, 1998, review of *Gullible's Troubles,* p. 98; January 21, 2002, review of *The Red Wolf,* p. 89.

School Library Journal, September, 1993, Lisa Dennis, review of *Elvira,* p. 219; May, 1998, Lauralyn Persson, review of *Gullible's Troubles,* p. 126; May, 2002, Robin L. Gibson, review of *The Red Wolf,* p. 126.

Voice Supplement, September, 1993, p. 24.*

*　　　*　　　*

SPANYOL, Jessica 1965-

Personal

Born March 29, 1965, in Weymouth, Dorset, England; daughter of John (a naval captain) and Jill (an artist; maiden name, Davies) Spanyol; partner of Richard Woods (an artist); children: Milo Spanyol Woods. *Education:* Attended Bath Academy of Art, 1983-84; Brighton Polytechnic, B.A., 1987; Royal College of Art, M.A. (with distinction), 1993.

Addresses

Agent—c/o Author Mail, Candlewick Press, 2067 Massachusetts Ave., Cambridge, MA 02104-1338.

Career

Artist, illustrator, designer, and writer. Royal College of Art, London, England, research fellow, 1993-94; set designer, 1996-97; artist-in-residence, Royal Shakespeare Company, c. 2001. Lectures on art topics at schools, including University of Central England, Birmingham, England; Chelsea College of Art; and Buckingham and Chilterns College. *Exhibitions:* Photographers Gallery, London, England, 1994; Whitechapel Art Gallery, 1994; South Bank Centre, London, England, 1994; 6X4 Gallery, London, England, 1998; Contact Gallery, Norwich, England, solo exhibit, 1998; others.

Awards, Honors

Folio Society Illustration Award; Basil Alkazzi Traveling Scholarship; Painter Stainers Illustration Bursary; Chris Garnham Memorial Prize; Random House Publishing Competition, awards for best book jacket and poster design.

Writings

Carlo Likes Reading, Candlewick Press (Cambridge, MA), 2001.

Carlo Likes Counting, Candlewick Press (Cambridge, MA), 2002.

Carlo Likes Learning (with flash cards), Walker Books (London, England), 2002.

Carlo Likes Colors, Candlewick Press (Cambridge, MA), 2003.

Spanyol's books have been published in France, Germany, Sweden, Denmark, and Spain.

Work in Progress

More "Carlo" storybooks, including *Carlo's New Boots* and *Hello Carlo.*

Sidelights

Jessica Spanyol is the author and illustrator of a series of books featuring a friendly giraffe named Carlo, whose debut in *Carlo Likes Reading* was dubbed "bright, well-conceived, and infectiously enthusiastic" by a *Kirkus Reviews* contributor. With what a *Publishers Weekly* reviewer called a "bright-eyed, plush-toy cuteness," Carlo encourages readers in developing a variety of skills as they follow him through the brightly colored two-page spreads that characterize each book in the continuing series.

The "Carlo" books are based on a character Spanyol wove into a story when she was only six years old. As the author/illustrator told *SATA:* "Originally it was called 'Carlo the Giraffe Who Could Not Read.' The content, as the title suggests, tackled my lack of confidence in my reading ability. The main character was named after my brother's best friend and the idea for the giraffe came from a favorite blow-up toy." In *Carlo Likes Reading,* the bright-eyed giraffe lives in a

Jessica Spanyol

world where every object bears a label spelling out what it is, from the bunny slippers Carlo tucks under his bed at night to the wrench in the garage. Other characters, such as Carlo's cat Crackers, also had their source in these juvenile stories. "My mum helped me write the stories to give me confidence with schoolwork," Spanyol explained, adding that because her mother is no longer alive, the writing process brings back happy memories. "Thirty years after the first version, I was delighted to see *Carlo Likes Reading* in print."

After her first book was published, Spanyol returned to teaching illustration and working on art projects, which, she explained, "included installations for galleries, a short film for a contemporary composer, set designs, and working as an artist-in-residence at the Royal Shakespeare Company." Feeling the need to adjust her busy schedule to accommodate her newborn son, she decided to pull out some more of her childhood storybooks and continue the saga of Carlo the giraffe. Other books in the series include *Carlo Likes Counting* and *Carlo Likes Colors,* with a group of storybooks also in the works.

In creating her illustrations, Spanyol first makes "roughs" by scanning sketches into the computer, then coloring them. Her finished artwork is created using paint and collage. "I hope that my books can tackle learning in a light and enjoyable manner," she noted. "I have always found it useful to work from memories and to think about how I learned things like reading and counting. I hope that my books will help children learn

and have a giggle at the same time. When I make the books I really don't think about children as a mass, anonymous audience; instead, I draw things that make my friends and family laugh."

Spanyol lives in the East End of London with her partner, Richard Woods, and their young son Milo, whose sleep schedule determines his mother's working hours. Ideas for future "Carlo" books "come about by talking to my editors and the designers at Walker Books," she explained. "Meetings about picture books and thinking of new ideas are always fun, and creating children's books is really a great vocation."

Biographical and Critical Sources

PERIODICALS

Booklist, November 1, 2001, Annie Ayres, review of *Carlo Likes Reading,* p. 485; October 1, 2002, Julie Cummins, review of *Carlo Likes Counting,* p. 338.
Good Reading (Australia), September, 2001.
Guardian, October 31, 2001, review of *Carlo Likes Reading.*
Kirkus Reviews, August 1, 2001, review of *Carlo Likes Reading,* p. 1132.
Orlando Sentinel (Orlando, FL), September 9, 2001, "Lively Books Take Learning outside School Walls."
Publishers Weekly, September 3, 2001, review of *Carlo Likes Reading,* p. 86.
School Library Journal, October, 2001, Susan Lissim, review of *Carlo Likes Reading.**

*   *   *

SUTHERLAND, Zena Bailey 1915-2002

OBITUARY NOTICE—See index for *SATA* sketch: Born September 17, 1915, in Winthrop, MA; died of cancer, June 12, 2002, in Chicago, IL. Educator, critic, editor, and author. Sutherland may have possessed a more comprehensive knowledge of children's literature than any living person, without ever having been a "children's author" herself. For nearly thirty years as an editor and reviewer for the *Bulletin of the Center for Children's Books* at the University of Chicago, beginning in 1958, she is credited with reading and reviewing tens of thousands of children's books. Sutherland's reviews differed from the standard fare of her day. She treated her subjects as she would treat adult literature, providing substantive descriptive information and adding her own critical interpretations. Sutherland was also a children's literature columnist for the *Saturday Review* in the 1960s and a children's book editor and columnist for the *Chicago Tribune* in the seventies and eighties. Upon the death of May Hill Arbuthnot in 1969, Sutherland succeeded her as the author of the classic textbook, *Children and Books,* through its ninth edition in 1996. She also wrote *History in Children's Books, The Best in Children's Books,* and *Children and Libraries,* and edited a handful of anthologies. Sutherland taught librarianship at the University of Chicago from 1972 to 1986; the Zena Sutherland lecture series of the University of Chicago and the Chicago Public Library was established in her honor. She also served on the International Board on Books for Young People and judged prestigious literary awards, including the New-bery Award, the Caldecott Award, and the National Book Award.

OBITUARIES AND OTHER SOURCES:

PERIODICALS

Los Angeles Times, June 16, 2002, p. B19.
New York Times, June 15, 2002, obituary by Eden Ross Lipson, p. A27.
Washington Post, June 16, 2002, obituary by Richard Pearson, p. C8.

T

THOMAS, Joyce Carol 1938-

Personal

Born May 25, 1938, in Ponca City, OK; daughter of Floyd David (a bricklayer) and Leona (a housekeeper and hair stylist; maiden name, Thompson) Haynes; married Gettis L. Withers (a chemist), May 31, 1959 (divorced, 1968); married Roy T. Thomas, Jr., (a professor), September 7, 1968 (divorced, 1979); children: Monica Pecot, Gregory Withers, Michael Withers, Roy T. Thomas III. *Education:* Attended San Francisco City College, 1957-58, and University of San Francisco, 1957-58; College of San Mateo, A.A., 1964; San Jose State College (now University), B.A., 1966; Stanford University, M.A., 1967.

Addresses

Home—2422 Cedar St., Berkeley, CA 94708. *Agent*—Anna Ghosh, Scovil-Chichak-Galen Literary Agency, Inc., 381 Park Ave. S., Suite 1020, New York, NY 10016. *E-mail*—author@joycecarolthomas.com.

Career

Worked as a telephone operator in San Francisco, CA, 1957-58; Ravenwood School District, East Palo Alto, CA, teacher of French and Spanish, 1968-70; San Jose State College (now University), San Jose, CA, assistant professor of black studies, 1969-72; Contra Costa College, San Pablo, CA, teacher of drama and English, 1973-75; St. Mary's College, Moraga, CA, professor of English, 1975-77; San Jose State University, San Jose, reading program director, 1979-82, associate professor of English, 1982-83; University of Tennessee, Knoxville, associate professor of English, 1989-92, full professor, 1992-95. Visiting associate professor of English at Purdue University, spring, 1983.

Member

Dramatists Guild, Authors Guild, Authors League of America.

Awards, Honors

Danforth graduate fellow, University of California at Berkeley, 1973-75; Stanford University scholar, 1979-80, and Djerassi fellow, 1982 and 1983; *New York Times* outstanding book of the year citation, American Library Association (ALA) best book citation, and Before Columbus American Book Award, Before Columbus Foundation, all 1982, and American Book Award for children's fiction, Association of American Publishers, both 1983, all for *Marked by Fire;* Coretta Scott King Award, ALA, 1984, for *Bright Shadow;* named Outstanding Woman of the Twentieth Century, Sigma Gamma Rho, 1986; Pick of the Lists, American Booksellers, 1986, and Oklahoma Sequoyah Young Adult Book Award Masterlist, 1988-89, both for *The Golden Pasture;* Arkansas Traveler Award, 1987; Oklahoma Senate and House of Representatives citations, 1989; Chancellor's Award for Research and Creativity, University of Tennessee, and Selected Title for Children and Young Adults, National Conference of Christians and Jews, both 1991, both for *A Gathering of Flowers;* Proclamation, City of Berkeley, 1992, and Kentucky Blue Grass Award masterlist, 1995, both for *When the Nightingale Sings;* 100 Children's Books list, New York Public Library, 1993, Coretta Scott King Honor Book, ALA, Notable Children's Books, National Council of Teachers of English, and Mirrors and Windows: Seeing the Human Family Award, National Conference of Christians and Jews, all 1994, all for *Brown Honey in Broomwheat Tea;* Poet Laureate Award, Oklahoma State University Center for Poets and Writers, 1996-2000; Oklahoma Governor's Award, 1998; Celebrated Storyteller Award, *People* magazine, 1999, for *Gingerbread Days;* Notable Children's Book Award, ALA, Notable Children's Trade Book in Social Studies Award, National Council for the Social Studies/Children's Book Council, Teacher's Choice Award, International Reading Association, and Coretta Scott King Illustrator Honor Book, all 1999, all for *I Have Heard of a Land;* Parents' Choice Award, 2000, and Oklahoma Book Award, 2001, both for *Hush Songs;* Arrell Gibson Lifetime Achievement Award, Oklahoma Center for the Book, 2001, for body of work.

Writings

YOUNG ADULT NOVELS, EXCEPT AS NOTED

Marked by Fire, Avon (New York, NY), 1982.
Bright Shadow, (sequel to *Marked by Fire*), Avon (New York, NY), 1983.
Water Girl, Avon (New York, NY), 1986.
The Golden Pasture, Scholastic (New York, NY), 1986.
Journey, Scholastic (New York, NY), 1988.
When the Nightingale Sings, HarperCollins (New York, NY), 1992.
House of Light (adult novel; sequel to *Marked by Fire* and *Bright Shadow*), Hyperion (New York, NY), 2001.
Abide with Me, Hyperion (New York, NY), 2001.

FOR CHILDREN

Cherish Me (picture book), illustrated by Nneka Bennett, HarperCollins (New York, NY), 1998.
You Are My Perfect Baby (board book), illustrated by Nneka Bennett, HarperCollins (New York, NY), 1999.
The Gospel Cinderella (picture book), illustrated by David Diaz, HarperCollins (New York, NY), 2000.
The Bowlegged Rooster and Other Tales That Signify (short stories), illustrated by Holly Berry, HarperCollins (New York, NY), 2000.
Hush Songs: African American Lullabies (picture book), illustrated by Brenda Joysmith, Hyperion (New York, NY), 2000.
Joy! (board book), illustrated by Pamela Johnson, Hyperion (New York, NY), 2001.
The Angel's Lullabye (board book), illustrated by Pamela Johnson, Hyperion (New York, NY), 2001.

POETRY

Bittersweet, Firesign Press, 1973.
Crystal Breezes, Firesign Press, 1974.
Blessing, Jocato Press, 1975.
Black Child, illustrated by Tom Feelings, Zamani Productions, 1981.
Inside the Rainbow, Zikawana Press, 1982.
Brown Honey in Broomwheat Tea, illustrated by Floyd Cooper, HarperCollins (New York, NY), 1993.
Gingerbread Days, illustrated by Floyd Cooper, Harper-Collins (New York, NY), 1995.
The Blacker the Berry: Poems, illustrated by Brenda Joysmith, HarperCollins (New York, NY), 1997.
I Have Heard of a Land, illustrated by Floyd Cooper, HarperCollins (New York, NY), 1998.
A Mother's Heart, A Daughter's Love: Poems for Us to Share, HarperCollins (New York, NY), 2001.
Crowning Glory: Poems, illustrated by Brenda Joysmith, HarperCollins (New York, NY), 2002.

PLAYS

(And producer) *A Song in the Sky* (two-act), produced in San Francisco, CA, at Montgomery Theater, 1976.
Look! What a Wonder! (two-act), produced in Berkeley, CA, at Berkeley Community Theatre, 1976.
(And producer) *Magnolia* (two-act), produced in San Francisco, CA, at Old San Francisco Opera House, 1977.
(And producer) *Ambrosia* (two-act), produced in San Francisco, CA, at Little Fox Theatre, 1978.

Gospel Roots (two-act), produced in Carson, CA, at California State University, 1981.
I Have Heard of a Land, produced in Oklahoma City, OK, at Claussen Theatre, 1989.
When the Nightingale Sings, produced in Knoxville, TN, at Clarence Brown Theatre, 1991.
(And director) *A Mother's Heart* (two-act), produced in San Francisco, CA, at Marsh Theater, 2001.

OTHER

(Editor and contributor) *A Gathering of Flowers: Stories about Being Young in America* (includes Thomas's short story "Young Reverend Zelma Lee Moses"), HarperCollins (New York, NY), 1990.

Contributor of short story, "Handling Snakes," to *I Believe in Water,* edited by Marilyn Singer, HarperCollins (New York, NY), 2000. Contributor to periodicals, including *American Poetry Review, Black Scholar, Calafia, Drum Voices, Giant Talk,* and *Yardbird Reader.* Editor of *Ambrosia* (women's newsletter), 1980.

Sidelights

Joyce Carol Thomas is a celebrated author of young adult novels, poetry, and picture books, as well as fiction and poetry for adults. The winner of the American Book Award for her first novel, *Marked by Fire,* and the Coretta Scott King Award for her second, *Bright Shadow,* Thomas hit the ground running with her writing career and has never looked back. Using her own unique rural background of Oklahoma and California, she has created a lyrical world of childhood—portraying not only its joys but also its gross injustices—that resonates across the racial lines. In both poetry and fiction, Thomas conjures up stories of African-American heritage, family history, and universal truths. Her language is a compilation of the sounds, imagery, and rhythms of her Oklahoma roots, church-going days, and California connections where she worked side-by-side with Hispanics in the fields. Thomas's background as a migrant farm worker in rural Oklahoma and California thus supplies her with the prolific stock of characters and situations that fill her novels while her love affair with language began with the words and songs she heard in church.

Thomas grew up in Ponca City, Oklahoma, a small, dusty town where she lived across from the school. She has set several of her novels in her hometown, including *Marked by Fire, Bright Shadow, The Golden Pasture,* and *House of Light.* When Thomas was ten years old, the family moved to rural Tracy, California. There Thomas learned to milk cows, fish for minnows, and harvest tomatoes and grapes. Thomas spent long summers harvesting crops, working beside many Mexicans, and she began a long-lasting fascination with their language.

From 1973 to 1978, Thomas wrote poetry and plays for adults, taught in various colleges and universities, and traveled to conferences and festivals all over the world, including Lagos, Nigeria. In 1982, Thomas's career took a turn when she published *Marked by Fire,* a novel for a young adult audience. Steeped in the setting and traditions of her hometown, the novel focused on Abyssinia Jackson, a girl who was born in a cotton field during harvest time. The title refers to the fact that she received a burn on her face from a brush fire during her birth. This leaves her "marked for unbearable pain and unspeakable joy," according to the local healer. The child shows a remarkable talent for singing until she is raped by a member of the church. The story of how she heals from this tragedy fills the rest of the novel.

The book was critically acclaimed and placed on required reading lists at many high schools and universities. Writing in *Black Scholar,* critic Dorothy Randall-Tsuruta noted that Thomas's "poetic tone gives this work what scents give the roses already so pleasing in color." Reviewing this debut novel in *School Library Journal,* Hazel Rochman felt that while the "lack of a fast-paced narrative line and the mythical overtones may present obstacles to some readers, many will be moved" by the story of Abyssinia. *Best Sellers* reviewer Wendell Wray noted that Thomas "captures the flavor of black folk life in Oklahoma." Wray further observed that though she "has set for herself a challenging task ... Thomas' book works." Commenting about her stormy novel, Thomas once stated that "as a writer I work to create books filled with conflict.... I address this quest in part by matching the pitiful absurdities and heady contradictions of life itself, in part by leading the heroine to twin fountains of magic and the macabre, and evoking the holy and the horrible in the same breath. Nor is it ever enough to match these. Through the character of Abyssinia, I strive for what is beyond these, seeking to find newer worlds."

Bright Shadow, a sequel to *Marked by Fire,* was published in 1983. In this work, Abyssinia goes to college and ends up falling in love with Carl Lee Jefferson. The couple work through many problems in order to find their own kind of love. The winner of the Coretta Scott King Award, *Bright Shadow* was called a "love story" and "appealing" by Zena Sutherland, writing in *Bulletin of the Center for Children's Books.* However, as with many of Thomas's books, some critics faulted her for the use of overly epic language. Sutherland for one felt that "the often-ornate phraseology" sometimes weakens the story.

Several of Thomas's more recent books also feature these popular characters from her first two books, including *The Golden Pasture,* which journeys back to Carl Lee's earlier life on his grandfather's ranch, and *Water Girl,* which tells the story of Abyssinia's teenage daughter Amber, given up for adoption. Amber only learns of her biological mother when, after an earthquake, she finds an old letter that speaks of the adoption. Reviewing *The Golden Pasture* in *Publishers Weekly,* a contributor called the book "a spirited, lyrical tale with a memorable cast of characters."

With *Journey,* her fifth novel, Thomas broke new literary ground for herself, mixing fantasy and mystery to come up with a story of crime and family history. Meggie Alexander, "blessed" at birth by a tarantula, has uncommon powers. Reaching adolescence, she investigates the disappearance of several of her friends in the woods, discovering that some of them have been murdered. Meggie herself is soon kidnapped and thrust into horrible danger. Less well received than many of her other novels, *Journey* did earn accolades from a writer for *Kirkus Reviews* who felt that Thomas "dramatically juxtaposes her story's horror with the joy of existence." Other reviewers, such as Starr LaTronica of *School Library Journal,* were less enthusiastic. "This discordant mixture of fantasy and mystery ... never blend[s] successfully," LaTronica wrote.

With *When the Nightingale Sings,* Thomas creates a sort of Cinderella story about young Marigold who is discovered in a swamp and lives with her foster mother, Ruby, and twin stepsisters. As in the fairy tale, this family treats the young girl as a servant rather than a relative. Finally, Marigold turns her attentions away from this abusive foster family and to the local Baptist Church. It is there she finds real salvation, discovering the gift of music in gospel songs. Reviewing this and other books by Thomas in *St. James Guide to Young Adult Writers,* a contributor noted that Thomas's use of language "is exquisite; this craftsmanship provides words that are of music, voice, and song. Her characters are often musical, and the church—the gospel music, rhythm, movement, and harmony—provides not only a backdrop, but a language that expresses the spirit of the community." The same critic went on to observe, "Proverbs, folk wisdom, scripture, and prophecy are liberally scattered among the voices of the characters."

Thomas employs similar techniques and sources in her first adult novel, *House of Light,* which furthers the story of Abyssinia Jackson begun in *Marked by Fire* and continued in *Bright Shadow.* Now a doctor and healer, Abby Jackson-Jefferson is the main narrator of these tales which relate the lives of a myriad of patients in Ponca City, Oklahoma. Reviewing the title in *Booklist,* Hazel Rochman felt that this title "is sure to be popular for the lively dialogue, the sense of community, and yes, the hopeful message." A *Publishers Weekly* contributor called the book "moving" and "marred only by unsubtle repetition, a rhetorical device Thomas relies on too frequently." However, a *Kirkus Reviews* critic offered a different opinion, writing that "Lyrical, earthy prose gives this deceptively simple story depth and richness."

Much of Thomas's talent, energy, and output has been focused on poetry for young readers and on picture books for the very young. Teaming up with illustrator Floyd Cooper, Thomas has created a trio of poetry books aimed at the five- to nine-year-old reading audience. In the award-winning *Brown Honey in Broomwheat Tea,* Thomas gathers a dozen poems dealing with the family, home, and the African-American experience in a "highly readable and attractive picture book," according to a reviewer for *Booklist.* A *Publishers Weekly* contributor called the poems "lyrical" evocations of the African-American heritage. The title poem recalls Thomas's own childhood when broomwheat tea was used as an elixir for anything that ailed the young girl.

Thomas and Cooper again teamed up for *Gingerbread Days,* a picture book containing a dozen poems that "celebrates the passage of a year within the circle of an extended African American family," as Meg Stackpole noted in a *School Library Journal* review. "Like food stored away for winter, this rich harvest of poems contains enough sustenance to last throughout the year," wrote a *Publishers Weekly* reviewer of the same book. "Thomas's simple but touching language describes a hopeful world ... where love is as wonderful as gingerbread, warm and spicy from the oven," the same reviewer concluded. *Horn Book*'s Martha V. Parravano concluded that *Gingerbread Days* was a "worthy companion" to *Brown Honey in Broomwheat Tea,* "made even stronger by Floyd Cooper's glowing, golden illustrations." *I Have Heard of a Land,* which continues the Thomas-Cooper collaboration, is an illustrated book of poems that celebrates the role of African-American women pioneers in the nineteenth-century frontier, largely in Oklahoma. A writer for *Publishers Weekly* called the book a "moving poetic account of a brave black woman," while *Booklist*'s Ilene Cooper dubbed it a "lyrical tribute to the pioneer spirit."

Thomas has also worked with illustrator Nneka Bennett on two books for very young children, *Cherish Me* and *You Are My Perfect Baby.* Reviewing the first title in *Booklist,* Kathy Broderick called Thomas's poem "compelling" and described the book as a "winning offering." Another title for the very young is *Hush Songs,* a book designed for adults to sing to babies and preschoolers, collecting ten African-American lullabies, including three written by Thomas, under one cover. Claiming that "the songs themselves are timeless," *Booklist* reviewer Rochman wrote that the lullabies "touch all of us." With *A Mother's Heart, A Daughter's Love,* Thomas honors the bond between those two family member with poems from the point of view of each. In the *Bowlegged Rooster and Other Tales That Signify,* she serves up five short stories for young readers featuring Papa Rooster and his chick, all set in Possum Neck, Mississippi. "Although the plots are not always terrifically involving," wrote Steven Engelfried in *School Library Journal,* "the animals' personalities and the bustling atmosphere of the barnyard make these tales appealing." Shelley Townsend-Hudson, writing in *Booklist,* felt these tales are "a joy to hear as well as to read."

With her imagination and ability to bring authenticity to her novels, Thomas has been highly praised and often compared to other noted black women authors, including Maya Angelou, Toni Morrison, and Alice Walker. Thomas takes scenes and characters from her youth and crafts them into powerful fiction. "If I had to give advice to young people," Thomas commented in her autobiographical essay, "it would be that whatever your career choice, prepare yourself to do it well. Quality takes talent and time. Believe in your dreams. Have faith in yourself. Keep working and enjoying today even as you reach for tomorrow. If you choose to write, value your experiences. And color them in the indelible ink of your own background."

"I work for authenticity of voice," Thomas commented in *SAAS,* "fidelity to detail, and naturalness of developments." It is this authenticity that critics say sings out in all of Thomas's work, and that allows her fiction and poetry to transcend race, gender, and geography. "I treasure and value the experiences that include us all as people." Thomas concluded in *SAAS.* "I don't pay any attention to boundaries."

Thomas told *MAICYA:* "I am happiest around sunlight, flowers, and trees. I like quiet, comfortable places to think. I especially like to encourage my children, my grandchildren and all young people. I enjoy the process of writing. It starts within the imagination. What a wonderful place is the mind. So welcoming! ... I hope you [readers] will be happy in whatever direction you choose to take your life. And if you come across a book of mine, I wish you happy reading."

Biographical and Critical Sources

BOOKS

Authors and Artists for Young Adults, Volume 12, Gale (Detroit, MI), 1994.
Children's Literature Review, Volume 19, Gale, 1990.
Contemporary Literary Criticism, Volume 35, Gale, 1985.
Dictionary of Literary Biography, Volume 33: *Afro-American Fiction Writers after 1955,* Gale, 1984.
St. James Guide to Young Adult Writers, 2nd edition, edited by Tom Pendergast and Sara Pendergast, St. James, 1999.
Thomas, Joyce Carol, *Marked by Fire,* Avon (New York, NY), 1982.

PERIODICALS

African American Review, spring, 1998, pp. 139-147.
Best Sellers, June, 1982, Wendell Wray, review of *Marked by Fire,* pp. 123-124.
Black Issues Review, May, 2001, Althea Gamble, review of *House of Light,* p. 23.
Black Scholar, summer, 1982, Dorothy Randall-Tsuruta, review of *Marked by Fire,* p. 48.
Booklist, February 15, 1986, pp. 861-862; February 15, 1994, review of *Brown Honey in Broomwheat Tea,* p. 1081; September 15, 1995, p. 176; March 15, 1997, p. 1249; February 15, 1998, Ilene Cooper, review of *I Have Heard of a Land,* p. 1009; January 1, 1999, Kathy Broderick, review of *Cherish Me,* p. 891; October 1, 2000, Shelley Townsend-Hudson, review of *The Bowlegged Rooster and Other Tales That Signify,* p. 342; December 15, 2000, Hazel Rochman, review of *Hush Songs,* p. 823; February 15, 2001, Hazel Rochman, review of *House of Light,* p. 1101.
Bulletin of the Center for Children's Books, February, 1984, Zena Sutherland, review of *Bright Shadow,* p. 119; June, 1998, pp. 376-377.
English Journal, April, 1991, p. 83; October, 1993, p. 81.
Horn Book, March-April, 1996, Martha V. Parravano, review of *Gingerbread Days,* pp. 219-220.
Kirkus Reviews, September 15, 1988, review of *Journey,* p. 1410; February 1, 2001, review of *House of Light.*
Publishers Weekly, July 25, 1986, review of *The Golden Pasture,* p. 191; September 9, 1988, p. 140; October 11, 1993, p. 87; September 25, 1995, review of

Gingerbread Days, p. 57; January 8, 1996, review of *Brown Honey in Broomwheat Tea,* p. 70; April 6, 1998, review of *I Have Heard of a Land,* p. 77; October 19, 1998, p. 83; February 19, 2001, review of *House of Light,* p. 69.

School Library Journal, March, 1982, Hazel Rochman, review of *Marked by Fire,* p. 162; January, 1984, pp. 89-90; August, 1986, p. 107; October, 1988, Starr LaTronica, review of *Journey,* p. 165; October, 1990, p. 145; February, 1993, pp. 106-107; November, 1993, p. 103; January, 1996, Meg Stackpole, review of *Gingerbread Days,* p. 107; December, 1998, p. 116; August, 1999, p. 132; November, 2000, Steven Engelfried, review of *The Bowlegged Rooster and Other Tales That Signify,* p. 135.

Variety, September 9, 1987, p. 75.

OTHER

Joyce Carol Thomas Web site, http://www.joycecarolthomas.com/ (January 24, 2003).

* * *

Autobiography Feature

Joyce Carol Thomas

I must have fallen in love with words when I was still in the womb. Probably because my mother fairly lived in the church house while she was pregnant with me.

In that little wooden white chapel on an Oklahoma hillrise even the spoken words were sung with a kind of lilting sweetness, measured in breaths that rose and fell; words, chanted back and forth from the preacher, the deacon, and the female missionaries. In my writing I try to recreate this music on the printed page. Sing the way those people used to speak.

My mother was such an avid churchgoer that one night while she was tarrying on the altar, our house burned down. She didn't get up off her knees to go put out the fire or to try to save any of our worldly possessions. Maybe she already had the fire described in the lyrics by the gospel quartet groups, "Holy Ghost, it's like fire shut up in my bones." She didn't need to look at the flames or try to control the fire. She moved about the world like that, letting things happen; for I think that in her mind, one thing happening was as good or as bad as another. She allowed life. She and my father built another house.

She told me that when she married my father, she owned a rag doll. My father threw the doll in the garbage can. "You want a baby girl, I'll give you a baby girl," he promised.

They had a gang of children. Gave birth to thirteen, nine of us lived. They kept having boys, she wanted a girl. Fifth of the nine, I was born on May 25, 1938. And the first girl. My sister, Flora, born the year after me, was the second and last daughter. More brothers followed.

My mother studied the Bible a lot, reading it silently and aloud, at home and in church. Sitting up under her I learned to follow along when she sang out the words in her perfect-pitch voice for the preacher to repeat and interpret. I learned to read by listening to and looking at what my mother read.

Hers wasn't a singing voice. Even though there was a melody to her words when she spoke. My father was the singer.

He sang with an *a capella* choir at radio station WBBZ on the Sunday morning broadcast. I remember sitting with one ear glued to the cloth-covered speaker at the bottom of the Emerson radio, hugging the long thin mahogany legs of the floor model trying to listen to every bend of the liquid notes that curled and turned this way and that as they flooded the room. It seemed to me that even the plainest lyric sounded sweet when sung in four-part harmony.

We lived in a small Oklahoma town called Ponca City. Although it was called Ponca City, there was no city there. Its size qualifies it as a town. Still the place was the world to me when I was young. It was only later that I understood, through comparison, what a quaint place Ponca City was—and is. Our house at 1028 South Twelfth Street is no longer standing; all that remains is the backyard cottonwood tree I climbed at dusk to hide among its leaves in a game of hide-and-seek, the annoying white cotton from the cottonwood tree falling, getting caught like lint in my black cotton braids.

Ponca City is the setting for much of my fiction, including three of my novels: *Marked by Fire, Bright Shadow,* and *The Golden Pasture.* Although now I live half a continent away from my hometown, when it comes to my writing I find that I am still there.

We stayed in Ponca until I was in the fourth grade.

Our house sat directly across the street from the school. Crispus Attucks School was named after the African-American hero, first soldier to die in the Boston Massacre, 1770. My character Abyssinia Jackson attends a school with the same name.

Although we lived almost in the school's front door, I was forever anxious about getting to class on time. Not so much because I would be scolded, but because I didn't want to miss anything. My mother had all these other children to attend to, my younger sister's hair to braid, for instance. And there I was impatiently hopping from one foot to the other, waiting my turn to bow down, ducking and cringing under Mama's exacting comb as I watched the clock inch up relentlessly to bell time.

Sometimes I'd brush yesterday's braids in place and rush away, much to my mother's chagrin, for she was the hairdresser of the community and here I was looking like a wild child: hair sticking out every which way on my head.

I learned to braid my own hair when I was about seven, freeing my mother of one of her many duties and easing my own anxiety about punctuality. I felt relieved to be seated in my chair before the bell rang. Didn't want to be late for a lesson or catching the school clown wrestling pigs in the school yard or to miss seeing the principal getting thrown out the window by an irate teenager. Thank goodness the ground was only one level away and the window was open!

Getting ready for school included not only hair braiding, but also eating a good breakfast. Because we didn't have much money, my mother was a genius at "making do." If times were hard she'd do a head for twenty-five cents in order to buy groceries. ("Doing a head" meant straightening and/or curling one of the Ponca women's hair.)

Every school morning we had hot Quaker oatmeal or Cream of Wheat or Malt-o-Meal for breakfast, with Pet milk poured over the steaming cereal. And homemade biscuits.

"Light bread" (store-bought, white sliced bread) was a luxury to eat. Little did I know that I would yearn many a day for my mother's fragrant home-baked buttermilk biscuits, piping hot from the oven. If there was dough left over, she made a hoecake, fought over by my brothers and cousin. At noon we ate "beans and corn bread." On alternate days the menu changed and we lunched on "corn bread and beans." Changing the order of the words was the only way to give that meal variety, I tell you.

Dinner could be anything, but usually vegetables—corn, tomatoes, okra, sometimes hot-water corn bread. Not much meat.

But Sunday meals were different. A delight. We dined on Wonder bread and Post Toasties cornflakes for breakfast. Dinner, most of it cooked on Saturday night, might be roast chicken and sage dressing, pan gravy, Kentucky Wonder string beans, Sunday yams, and "monkey bread"— so called because these yeast rolls were so feathery light and buttery good you made a monkey of yourself eating too many of them. And the white coconut cake, moist, jump-in-the-mouth tender, was a mouth-watering delicacy with the blackberry jam filling the middle. Add company and the number of desserts increased accordingly. Out-of-town guests? Then nothing would do but to add sweet-potato pies, peach and pear cobblers. Is there any wonder midwestern and southern folks took naps after such a feast?

Many readers have commented about the importance of food in my novels. Food, they say, occupies almost as much of a place as setting. I suppose the food's joyous inclusion and fragrant presence comes from having a mother who was known as the best cook in town and from having seven competing brothers and one cousin who staged eating contests. Because in such a home food was another language for love, my books are redolent of sugar

Joyce Carol Thomas, c. 1991

and spice, kale and collards. Having watched my mother, I know what it means to do a thing well, to cook with a loving/knowing hand scooped into a flour barrel so expert at the art of baking that no measuring cup is needed.

In just about all my novels, broom wheat tea is steeped, poured, sipped. When I had a headache or caught chicken pox or measles, my mother would go into the weed fields and pick the tea leaves and serve me a steaming cup from the crushed golden blossoms. "Good for what ails you," she would assert. Once my brother accidentally scalded my leg with a pan of boiling water in which he'd boiled eggs. I zipped out of the kitchen through the house, flew out the front door, and raced around the yard, too pained to scream. Just ran, whistling in pain. A technicolored agony. I didn't think anything could hurt that badly. The burn scar still remains. Perhaps it was my mother's and Mother Nature's loving care that made me better and not the tea. Who knows? They're inseparable. Broom wheat tea and caring! When I write it gives me comfort to see this elixir steeped in an imaginary cup and drunk by one of my characters.

The small towns, the rural settings in which I grew up, have affected my life and my writing. I need and like open space. I like trees and flowers and the earth. And so do my characters. The cotton field is an important place for me and my Abyssinian people. At a little place outside of Ponca City, a place called Red Rock, my family and I picked and chopped cotton. To keep us from being economically exploited too much, my mother kept the books. The look and feel of cotton in the early morning when the dew still glistens on it is a memory of my childhood that I will carry forever. My character Abyssinia Jackson was born in the cotton patch. Telling her story lets me go there once again. Not only to the hard work but to the place where the ghost stories were told, to the place where night was so dark my favorite brother ran into a tree and gashed his forehead wide open.

Staunching the blood was not easy and under the candlelight I wanted to bleed for him, his eyes looked so scared. Yet away from electrical lights, the stars sparkled like a sky-sized chandelier. Red Rock is a place where the night sounds were those of crickets, and the night-lights, fireflies. Where soft sounds came from nature and the sound of the Arkansas River, a lulling wonder or an awful thing especially in the years when the floods came to Ponca and drove people out of their houses. The people who lived near the river bottom, beyond Boone's Grocery Store, let things happen. The Arkansas River followed its natural path; in seasons of heavy rains the swollen river forced folks with their chickens and goats and cows to flee to higher ground. Once the flood waters receded, the people moved back home again. To the same place that the river was sure to flood again.

The Ponca people gave themselves over into the hands of Mother Nature. They took what she dished out, waiting to be bopped upside the head by a tree, run off by a flood, or gifted with a harvest of spring peppergrass greens.

Joyce (right), and her sister, Flora, the only girls among nine children, 1946

And the spiders. One year in the cotton fields my mother was bitten by a black widow spider. She had to keep her leg up so the poison would not go deeper. It took forever to heal. And there was even talk of her losing the leg. Thank goodness they didn't have to cut her leg off. Something so tiny as a black widow spider can be so deadly. A black widow's venom, measure for measure, contains more poison than that of a rattlesnake. Still, spiders fascinated me and there are awesome spiders in my novel *Journey*. Mostly good spiders.

Maybe I wanted those powerful creatures to be on my side.

When we migrated to California (I had my tenth birthday on the train), we moved again to a small town, settling in a rural area five miles out of Tracy. Can't get much more country than that.

Tracy is also the setting for *Water Girl*. In rural Tracy I fished for minnows in the creek, hunted jackrabbits, milked cows, fed chickens, slopped hogs, listened to crickets chirping. When we found another house, we moved a little closer to town, just three miles out—a house full of spiders. We couldn't get rid of them. Black widow spiders stayed under my bed. Every weekend, while cleaning, I would look and the spiders would be nesting under the mattress. The red spot glowing like a badge of danger. They must have affected my sleep. How, I cannot say. Sleeping with the threat of danger is a different kind of slumber, I suspect.

Add to the spiders, wasps. When we were in Oklahoma, one of my older brothers used to frighten me and my sister with wasps. And I think this brother, like many "responsible" siblings, punished us because he resented having to take care of us, maybe for our being younger or girls. And when my sister told our parents about his staying out late or some other devilment, he punished both of us, putting us in a dark closet (with little light trickling in from the outside) that had a wasp nest in the ceiling corner. This was in Oklahoma. I remember the two of us crouched sweating on the closet floor as the wasps swarmed above us. The fear of being stung uppermost in our minds. Hoping, praying, for our parents to return and save us. I never told. My mother often remarked on my fear of hornets and wasps. Sometimes she would say, "Sister, the wasps won't hurt you, but looks like they'll make you hurt yourself just getting out of the way." She said this as she watched me falling over chairs, bruising an arm, twisting a foot, stubbing a toe, leaping out of the way of the worrisome wasps.

I put wasps in *Marked by Fire*. I wanted to write something scary for my character to deal with, so I figured wasps would do it. Two years ago I gave a talk to some Oakland schoolchildren in the library. The librarian was gone and there was no one in the room but me and the students. In the middle of my talk a wasp flew into the room. I stopped, panicked, and was braced to run. Then I realized I was the only adult there. Not everyone could panic. I looked at the wasp, looked at the children, and decided to stand my ground. I then realized the wasp wouldn't hurt me. The wasps of my childhood had been used as an instrument to terrify me. The wasps were innocent. Today, I'm happy to report I can sit in a room with wasps, bees, and hornets. However, I still don't *choose* to go into a room with any stingers.

A book is a safe place to experience fear. Maybe that's why we like to read scary novels too, don't you think?

Well, the spiders that I feared/fear have become my friends. At least in books!

Flowers are safe friends. I am at home with them. I trust them in my yard, on my table. Before I was ten, I remember that our neighbor down the road kept a garden that was so beautiful, I often asked to run errands that sent me by her yard. It was a country of flowers. Of marigolds and hemlocks. Of daffodils and blue irises. Sunflowers and tiger lilies. Now, if I should see the same garden, it probably would not look as immense. But then some of the flowers were taller than I was. Looked like trees of color. I would linger. Smelling all the perfumes mixed-up together. Delighted with delicious color. My senses overwhelmed. The touch of the rose petals, so delicate, so bright, so wonderful. Pure intoxication!

When we moved to Tracy we continued to harvest crops. This time tomatoes, mainly. And sometimes yellow onions, and the sweet black grapes of the San Joaquin Valley vineyards. I like grapes and especially liked to enjoy their juicy clusters as I worked. But the main summer job was picking tomatoes. Teenagers of all types worked the fields, but our numbers consisted mostly of Blacks and the Mexicans who crossed the California border in the summer to make enough money from the tomato harvest to carry back to Mexico where the money went further. I have never seen anybody work any harder than my workmates, running down the fields with the boxes of red, red tomatoes, working against time, sweat maps on the backs of their shirts. Working with poor people in the fields I have never believed poor people are lazy. I know better. And the mariachi songs, languid, wafting, harmonious, filled the air and made me wonder at the language, at the souls of the people who made such music. I think the music made the work go easier, faster. Much the way the songs in the cotton fields of Oklahoma lightened our loads. And like the people in the church I grew up attending, even when the Spanish speakers talked they seemed to sing.

That language I wanted to know. And so, when I selected foreign languages in high school, I chose Spanish and Latin. I learned the syntax, the spelling, the grammar of the language in school, but I learned the ethos of the language in the fields with the migrant workers. In college too, I majored in Spanish and minored in French. I found foreign languages the language of the church, and that of the Ponca and Tracy people to be a fitting foundation for writing. The music of the word is what I wanted to be able to master in my study of languages. The music of the word is what I want to create in my writing of books.

From this base of languages I taught myself all I know about writing. I have never taken a creative-writing course. My formal education includes a bachelor of arts degree with distinction from California State University, San Jose, graduating with a major in Spanish and a minor in French. And a master of arts degree from Stanford University: education major with an emphasis on Spanish.

I taught foreign language in my first teaching positions in Jordan Junior High and in the middle schools of the Ravenswood City School District. My last teaching positions were as visiting associate professor of English at Purdue University and visiting associate professor of

Graduating from Stanford, with an M.A. in Education, June, 1967

creative writing at the University of California at Santa Cruz.

After I graduated from California State University I took my first trip abroad to Guadalajara, Mexico, where while enjoying my vacation I tested my ability to speak Spanish. Much to my delight, nobody was at a loss to understand my accent when I ordered *enchiladas, arroz con pollo,* and other culinary delights from the menu. It was Spanish that I spoke *regateando* in the marketplace. And I felt welcome from *la gente.* In addition, I was heartened to find that some of the Mexican people had skin as dark as mine. Others would smile and say, *Que negrita bonita.* I was flattered at the hospitality and goodwill extended to me at every turn. But the phrase I cherished most was *hablas como un loro,* you speak like a native.

That first trip to Guadalajara went so well that over the years I have felt at home in other parts of the world: Nigeria, Hong Kong, Saipan, Rome, Haiti.

Often one of the needs of a writer is the need to be alone. All my life I certainly have had that need. But it was an unfulfilled yearning.

It was not possible to be alone for long in my early years being part of a family of eleven. Especially in our small house where we slept four to a twin-sized bed. Our house in Oklahoma was built a little up off the ground (maybe because of the fear of flooding). Under the house was the only place I could be alone for a spell. I would go there and find some solitude. I made up songs in my head in the rare quiet. And sang them there, clothed them with melodies. Nobody bothered me or asked me questions or commanded me to do anything in my special hideaway.

I could very easily turn into a recluse. Well, almost. Decades later when I was invited to finish up a Pamela Djerassi Fellowship at the Djerassi Foundation in Woodside, I had an entire country house to myself. Nobody came to visit unless I invited them. I wouldn't have houseguests very often. And when friends did come, often I couldn't

Representing North America in poetry at the International Arts Cultural Festival, Lagos, Nigeria, with poet Angela Johnson (right), 1977

wait for them to leave. I was ashamed at my delight at being left alone!

This was the first time I had been alone for any extended period of time. Right after high school I had left my huge family to get married and begin to raise a family of my own.

Some of my friends observe that I am alone even in a crowd of people. And that's probably true, too. I think a writer has to be able to go inside herself in order to create. Yet I enjoy talking to students, teachers, librarians, and readers about my work. Perhaps I need the mountains and the multitudes.

I am a nester. My surroundings are important to my spirit. I have created most of my novels here in this house in Berkeley.

My first novel, *Marked by Fire,* was written here. It's a wonderful space in which to meditate and write. There are windows that open to generous light. There is a fantastic water view of the three bridges and the San Francisco Bay from my study. The backyard is a miniforest of pines, avocado, lemon, and apple trees with blackberry and loganberry bushes gracing the landscape. And through the trees I can glimpse the campanile from which the university clock is a time reminder so gentle that if I do not listen carefully, I miss hearing the bells chiming the hour.

Here in my little house I like to think that I have the best of both worlds: my front windows look out onto the front yard and onto the street, with cars coming and going, with sidewalks leading to grocery stores, banks, the cleaners, and the post office. In my backyard the country and in my front yard the city. Until a year ago in the back cottage there lived a dog named Redwood; he was so playful and friendly that I placed him as a character in my fifth novel, *Journey.* I have a cat too, named Smokey, who is the color of smoke; he is a Persian with copper-colored eyes. Other cats, Abyssinian, Himalayan, and Siamese have lived here. I celebrate cats in *Bright Shadow.* In this book the mysterious cat, Opia, reminds Abyssinia that in a world of weeds, flowers are still blooming.

A few summers ago on a trip to Shawnee, Oklahoma, to visit my aunt Mary and uncle Ben who still raise horses for the Boley Rodeo, I saw an Appaloosa who let me ride him. He became the Appaloosa horse named Thunderfoot in *The Golden Pasture.*

I try to remember as I write my fiction that not only do we share the world with other races and nationalities but also with other creatures and critters—horses, cats, dogs, deer, snakes, spiders. So there is the hungry snake in *Marked by Fire,* the dancing deer in *Water Girl,* the mysterious Appaloosa horse in *The Golden Pasture,* the magical cat in *Bright Shadow,* the plotting spiders in *Journey,* and Redwood, the faithful mongrel, also in *Journey.*

I'm often asked about the naming of my characters. How, for instance, did Amber get her name? Amber is a jewel that the sages of ancient time said was a soothing, healing stone. Because Amber is a Black girl, I wanted the dark amber to be the jewel in the mind of the reader, so the epigram to *Water Girl* describes her color and suggests that she is appealing to behold. It reads:

Creating **Marked by Fire** *in 1978*

Amber: the reddish-brown jewel the color of mountains in Indian summer, a creation of resin from pine trees plunging long ago to the bottom of the sea, buried there for ages, collecting beauty til washed ashore by that ancient midwife Water.

Abyssinia, the name used by the shero of *Marked by Fire,* is the old name for Ethiopia. I happen to like Abyssinian cats. And too there are Black churches named Abyssinia, and the name is poetic to me.

I wanted my character to have a name that nobody else had used. It had to be distinctive, arresting, fresh, with a meaning I could embellish. I wanted the original meaning to be shaped by the personality of the character. The person Abyssinia is someone who triumphs over tragedy, who is a healer, a lover and respecter of people and nature. A believer in God. A humanitarian, a sister of light.

The name had to be musical sounding. The five vowels could be the notes to a song, depending upon how they are spoken. *Abyssinia.* I heard them that way and when I read excerpts from the Abyssinian books, I automatically say her name in a way that I hope suggests music. I have always known that words have power and I try to be careful with what comes out of my mouth and with the names I bestow upon my characters. Once when I was writing the fifth draft of *Marked by Fire* I needed to create a sinister, mean, spiteful character. I reached back into my childhood and came upon a man we used to call Trembling Slim. He trembled when he moved and we used to run when he walked the streets. Now I understand that Mr. Slim probably suffered from some devastating illness, but we children were not told this. If I wasn't good, I was told, "All right, we're going to give you to Trembling Slim." Or: "Trembling Slim's gonna get you!" Scared us half to death. So I named this character Trembling Slim. Along about the fifth draft, the character began to talk in a female voice. She said, "My name's not Trembling Slim, this here's Trembling Sally." Okay, I thought, and from that point on Trembling Sally, a fierce, mad woman, made her presence known.

Patience, Abyssinia's mother, got her name from a quality that my mother possessed. Leona Haynes's life mirrored an incomparable patience. I often wonder how she managed to raise nine children and one nephew. A steadfast, sweet-spirited woman, she possessed amazing tolerance. She's gone now but I think of her when life gets

trying. It is then that the memory of her fortitude sustains me.

Strong, Abyssinia's father, was so named because I wanted to demonstrate his resilience. He made mistakes in the novel; for example, he abandoned his family when they needed him most. Although he made this monstrous error, he was strong enough to turn around and go back home. There is no test if nothing terrible ever happens to us. And there are no perfect situations. We can always act better. As Aretha Franklin sings, "I need a little time to pray. I've been in the storm way too long," then dips between lines ad-libbing, "I know what I'm talking about, I've been there myself." Life is not always sunshine, so when the storms come and lay Strong low, as they do so devastatingly in *Marked by Fire* and in *Bright Shadow,* he pulls himself

The author at a family birthday party in 1983, "celebrating the fruit of my family-raising years": (from left) granddaughter Maria, held by son-in-law Herman; Joyce, holding granddaughter Crystal; son Roy; daughter Monica, with granddaughter Aresa

together, gets on up off the ground, and rises again to meet whatever challenge is laid at his doorstep. Strong is strong enough to understand that when life knocks him down, to get back up, go back home, begin again. Again and again.

*

More recently, during the writing of *Journey,* another of my characters changed her name. This time I had sent the final draft off to my editor, Jean Feiwel, and proceeded to relax. Eleven drafts and finally done. I had put the manuscript in the mail and sent *Journey* on its journey to New York.

Well, now, about two nights later, I woke up out of a deep sleep. The clock said 2:30 a.m. "What's going on?" I wondered. I'm a sound sleeper. Rarely do I have insomnia.

"My name," said the woman standing at the foot of my bed.

"What?"

"My name is not Margarite. It's Memory."

"Memory?"

She nodded.

I got up. Who wouldn't? Went into the study. Turned on the computer and gave the command that allows me to change a word throughout the manuscript. The machine finds the old word for me and makes the change I type in. The computer found "Margarite." "Change to?" it asked with its green light. "Memory," I typed. And the computer began its search and blinked for me to hit the *Y* (for yes) key for the change to "Memory." I hit *Y* until all the "Margarites" changed to "Memory."

Once this was done, the character started talking. Telling me more. She said I'd left out the part about Meggie's grandmother, whose name was Midnight. I put that in. She went on all through the manuscript. My goodness, by the time she was finished with me I had a new draft. I got on the phone the next day and called my editor. I said, "That last *Journey* draft I sent you? That's not it. Another's on the way."

When she had read the Memory draft of *Journey,* she called back to say, "Why this is incredible!" (She uses incredible to mean amazing.) "Incredible!"

You're telling me, I thought. A visitation is not to be taken lightly.

Names are important.

My own name also. My aunt Mary named me Joyce Carol for joyful song. Everything I write—no matter how gruesome or horrible the conflict, the pain, the suffering—has to turn out with a positive resolution. If there is no joy, I can't use it. I want/need peace and happy endings. Well, I say to myself, I'm the creator. If a happy ending is what I want, I write one.

What wakes up my wit? What triggers my imagination? Why do I choose to pick up a pen to write? I'm not sure what the answers to those questions are. But I know that I write in spite of everything that is going on around me. I have written with tears rolling down my cheeks and with laughter, running through the house like a child. More than once when I was an adolescent I was so intent on scribbling down words that I was absentminded. For example, there's the question of what happened to my father's hat.

I was forever running into difficulty with my imagination. I loved to read and create songs, stories, poems. This enchantment with the written word was sometimes so engrossing that I paid scant attention to some of my household duties. I don't think I was lazy, just obsessed.

On the occasion of my father's hat question, my chore was to clean the kitchen, clear the breakfast table, wash the dishes, wipe off the stove and refrigerator, sweep and mop the floor.

I hurried through these tasks for I was intent upon completing a poem I'd started before breakfast.

Just about the time I'd finished the kitchen and plopped down comfortably on the couch with my pad and pencil, my father came in to announce he could not find his hat. He thought he'd left it on the top of the refrigerator, but it was nowhere to be found.

My mother looked and looked but we could not find the hat. Under the table, no hat. Behind the refrigerator, no hat. In the living room, no hat. In the closet, no hat.

Finally, my father, who would not leave the house without his hat, which he wore everywhere, gave up. Realizing he would be late for work, he decided to brew a nerve-settling pot of coffee. He poured himself a cup and opened the refrigerator to get the Pet milk. Then I heard him yell to my mother, "Come here, Leona, and see what this gal's done!"

Of course I swiftly followed my mother into the kitchen to see what the matter was.

My father was standing glaring into the refrigerator. There, as neatly placed as you please, next to the cream, the butter, the eggs, and the orange juice, sat my father's hat.

Walking around in a daze, dreaming while awake, characterizes my state of mind when I'm writing. Dreams play an important role in my work. My first play, *A Song in the Sky,* started out as a poem, called "Blessing"—the stanzas became the acts. I dreamed the poem about 3:00 a.m. one morning and got up and wrote all the verses down and went right back to sleep. One year later the poem blossomed into a play.

I'm sometimes asked if I'm the same person as my character Abyssinia. Yes and no. Yes, because we share a hometown, elementary school, joys, hurts, recoveries from the myriad sufferings life may offer. No, because Abyssinia can do many things that I wish I could do and can't. She can sing, I can't.

Before I began writing novels I wrote poetry. Another writer remarked that wings are mentioned throughout my work. It is a persistent motif that I had not noticed until she pointed it out to me.

Wings probably mean many things to me. Freedom to fly away, lightness, joy. My son-in-law told me that when he was dating my daughter, he thought he could fly. After leaving her here at the house, he said he would walk up to Holy Hill, a nearby hill of seminaries close to the University of California campus, and be tempted to jump and fly into the sky. Love does that. Makes us feather light. The winged moments of life are like that. Wings, invisible wings, brush my shoulders when I see the flash of wind poppies, look deeply into the dancing eyes of children, watch the sun rise and set, hear Aretha Franklin sing gospel, or listen to the multicolored birds lift their multicolored voices outside my morning window ... Well, I could go on and on. An artist I met at the Djerassi

Gathering of Flowers *was honored as the millionth volume to be researched by the University of California, Santa Cruz University Library, at the dedication of the campus's new Science Library, 1991*

Foundation painted my portrait once; when I went to the opening of her show at Stanford University, I saw she had sketched, above me where I sat in a chair, just behind my shoulders, an angel woman with wings. I don't think my artist-friend had read any of my poetry at the time. I like her portrait for all the happy reasons I mentioned above.

The prominence of the church in my writing stems from my family's living under the wing of the church. Both literally and figuratively. We lived a half block from the sanctuary and we spent many weekday evenings, as well as almost all day Sunday, in the corner building.

I saw some amazing things there. There was an evangelist, Brother Edwards, who used to travel from town to town, holding revivals. The man could close his eyes and dance the backs of pews from the front of the church to the back, spin around on the shoulder of the back pew, and skip his way back to the front altar without falling.

There his happy acrobatics performed while praising the Lord astonished me, even though I was used to seeing all kinds of strange and wonderful goings-on at the services.

My first published poems happened because the Brother Edwards memory of the 1950s was stirred by a woman shouting a holy dance at a James Cleveland concert at the San Jose Civic Center in 1972. At the time I was a professor at San Jose State University. As I was being transported back in time to an event that many intellectuals would consider unsophisticated, I marveled at the clarity of the connection.

I know a few folks who won't own up to the fact that they're from the backwoods of Mississippi or a long way from Georgia or rural Alabama. They think it marks them as poor and ignorant. They are scared of being thought of as "country bumpkins." I can think of worse things to be.

My background is an ink coloring the rich landscape of my settings, the flightful joys and arduous sufferings of Oklahoma adventures, the starts and turns of the rural California of my fiction.

That woman's shouting (holy dancing) gave rise to three poems in me—"Church Poem," "Shouting," and "The James Cleveland Concert." I mention them here because they were pivotal to my publishing career. They mark my awakening as a woman who willingly and sometimes unwillingly walks the subconscious halls of memory and writes.

Instead of feeling the shame that some folks feel about rural southern or midwestern roots, I find cause for celebration. I felt elated after writing that poem. In fact, I felt I could fly!

When the work has gone well I feel an indescribable ecstasy. At the end of an especially good poem or chapter, I say a humble prayer of thanks.

My aunt Corine has a saying that I try to follow: "Children, keep God in your business."

My aunts, Aunt Corine, Aunt Annie Mae, Aunt Birdtee, sisters to my mother, have played supporting roles in my career as writer. Also, my aunt Mary, my father's sister, is a continuing source of inspiration and influence.

I write something every day. My hours are from eight until two in the afternoon, in general. Given other needs, family, speaking engagements, business appointments, the "office" hours may change. Now the characters who wake me up out of sound sleep, I must tell you, are no respecters of office hours either. They come and go when they choose. I am at their mercy and I have been known to write well past my two o'clock closing time. How long does it take me to write a novel? My answer to that is two to three years and all my life. Two to three years of crafting ten to twelve drafts of the novel and all the memories and events that my life holds.

Beyond the writing of the books, the muse still works. Imagination plays a global role in all my storytelling and fiction writing. I was surprised by the persistent subliminal part that imagination played even in the naming of my novels. For me the discovery was a pristine glimpse of the entire vision. A glimmer lodged in the secret wheels of the subconscious mind.

When my fourth novel, *The Golden Pasture,* came in the mail in 1986 I unwrapped it from its crating, studied its cover with the Black boy proudly seated on his horse, and then held this nicely bound edition close to me. Then I lined up the four novels on the stone fireplace mantel, from the first to the fourth, *Marked by Fire, Bright Shadow, Water Girl,* and *The Golden Pasture.* Here were fire, air, water, and earth. A small storytelling miracle. A world of fire, air, water, and earth, shaped by the imagination, illuminated by the muse.

At this writing a musical has been made from my first novel, *Marked by Fire.* How did this happen?

The book, published January 1982, had been out less than a year when I received a letter from Ted Kociolek of New York City. There was something funny about the envelope the letter came in though. It was addressed to Joyce Carol Thomas, San Jose State University, Berkeley, California. Now San Jose State University is located in the city of San Jose, about fifty miles from Berkeley. That I should receive the letter at all was a miracle, but I received it at my desk on campus in San Jose. Mr. Kociolek wrote that he wanted to fly out and talk to me about the possibility of obtaining the dramatic rights to *Marked by Fire.* I called him and asked why he had addressed the letter the way he had. He said he'd tried to reach me through my agent but couldn't and that he'd noticed, in the back of the novel, a short bio that read "the author teaches at San Jose State where she lives in Berkeley." So much for my eastern publishers' understanding of California geography! That error was in one of the first printings.

Ted Kociolek, who was working on another New York show, flew out on an 8:00 p.m. flight and had to return on a twelve midnight flight. Clearly our time was limited. Still I was curious about his ideas. I picked him up at the airport. My first impressions as he walked toward me at Oakland International were: "Here he is, he's so young, he's white, he's redheaded, he's obviously male. What could he possibly know about Abyssinia, a Black girl from Oklahoma?" It turns out he knew quite a lot. Imagine my surprise when we reached my house and he sat down at the piano, pulled out a script with score, and began to play, sing, and act the parts of the characters of a show he'd written based on *Marked by Fire.* You could have knocked me over with a feather. He had risked quite a bit. In the first place, one usually gets permission first on a copyrighted work before making any adaptations. And I could have very easily said, "No thank you." But I was astounded that he had captured the spirit of the book, and I liked the direction in which his musical was leading.

I asked him why he had gone ahead and written the play.

He said he'd found the *Marked by Fire* novel in a Philadelphia bookstore, started reading it, couldn't put it down, and became obsessed with setting it to music. He could not help himself.

I understood. I'd been there myself in my own work. When the muse calls, one simply answers.

Then he added that while working on the musical he had experienced a healing.

I didn't ask him what he meant by that. But whatever it was I looked in his eyes and realized he was telling the truth. I asked him to call my agent, Mitch Douglas, when he returned to New York. He did so, and six years later the musical was on stage, ably directed by the gifted Tazewell Thompson, who moves the story along with subtlety and passion.

The all-Black musical is now titled *Abyssinia* after our central character in *Marked by Fire*. In its showcase and tryout productions in New York and Connecticut the show continues to receive outstanding reviews.

Well, it's a divine play is all I can tell you.

How does it feel to see my words performed on stage? I enjoy looking into the faces of the audiences and feeling their responses. Blacks, Whites, Gentiles, and Jews relate to Abyssinia's story about faith in an emotional heartfelt way. And I suppose that is what we hope for in the arts, that we all share a little bit of the humanity, that we all laugh and cry during the emotional scenes, for life gives us her acts and we, actors and audience, play them as best we can.

It has taken six years for the play to reach where it is today. I don't think the success it's having could have come overnight.

I'm an intuitive person. I rarely go wrong when I follow my "right mind." I'm glad I said Yes to young Ted Kociolek.

On tour for **Gingerbread Days and Brown Honey,** *with illustrator Floyd Cooper, 1995*

*

I continue to write every day. Poems come between chapters of my fiction. I stop to record them. Characters change their names, in the middle of drafts and in the middle of the night. I enjoy writing. I don't know what else I'd rather be doing. I give it time. The talent part is a gift. When I speak to students I say to them that writing is a process. I don't just sit down and start from page one and type until I reach the end. I think about scenes. I see them. I describe what I see at the time. In later drafts I see more, I write more. I am open to the muse. Sometimes I sit in my study waiting for inspiration to come. Sometimes she lets me sit here. But when she comes I am grateful. Being here in my study is important. When inspiration calls I want to be present. When she calls I answer.

Sometimes ideas don't come in the quiet of the study but they come when I'm driving down the road. Or on an airplane. They rear their heads between speaking engagements. When no pen is in sight and my hands are wet washing dishes, here comes a story. I walk early in the morning to clear my mind before I sit down at my desk. Characters all dressed up in their bright clothing and their country accents walk beside me as I hike up and down the Berkeley hills, inhaling the fresh air. Conversations with my aunts often stir up memories or possibilities. Church services keep my spirits up, especially the singing. Barbershop visits with my son remind me of the rhythms of my deceased father's voice when the men tease each other and gossip. These are the rhythms I hear when my male characters Carl Lee and Strong speak.

I have written this short autobiography in a spiral and not a straight line. Circles within circles, and not straight lines, describe my way of creative thinking and I remember the turning wheels within the middle of a wheel as I tell you something of my life, linking past and present, people and places who have helped and inspired my work.

If I had to give advice to young people, it would be that whatever your career choice, prepare yourself to do it well. Quality takes talent and time. Believe in your dreams. Have faith in yourself. Keep working and enjoying today even as you reach for tomorrow. If you choose to write, value your experiences. And color them in the indelible ink of your own background.

And when you come across a book of mine I wish you mainly this: happy reading.

POSTSCRIPT

Joyce Carol Thomas contributed the following update to *SATA* in 2002:

The educational tradition carries forward from my aunt Mary and my uncles, who graduated from Langston University, in Langston, Oklahoma. Their parents also earned college degrees. I thought I'd be different and choose another profession. But teaching was in my blood.

The legacy of teaching continued in California. I taught for twenty-five years, my son teaches math and science at a high school, my granddaughters, one who graduated from University of California, Berkeley, with a bachelor of arts in political science in May 2002, and the other who graduated with a juris doctor, cum laude from Harvard Law School in June 2002, continue to expand their own horizons. I wouldn't be surprised if they chose teaching as one of their professions.

I continue to discover much about my family's history. Because my maternal grandmother died so young, I thought that a vital part of my ancestral legacy was lost.

I didn't know enough about the family women who lived long before my time. Female caregivers, that I saw and see all around me, were and are the storytellers, the designers of quilt patches, source workers who knew and know the family roots of who begot whom. They are and were the keepers of family Bibles, with dates of births and deaths and names scribbled with a flourish in blue ink calligraphy.

Way back history. For me, as for so many African-Americans, links were missing.

In 1993 my aunt Corine revealed to me a few of the missing ancestral roots. What she shared led me to write my historical poetry book, *I Have Heard of a Land.* Aunt Corine Coffey told me that my great-grandparents, Charlie and Judy Graham, made the treacherous journey westward from Tennessee to Oklahoma, known then as the Territory. They traveled by wagon train to run for free land that the government had set aside. The year was 1893 and they traveled with about three hundred other families who left the South fleeing the horrors of lynching and burnings that still continued after the Emancipation Proclamation was passed.

My paternal Haynes ancestors left Mississippi in that same period. They, too, staked their claim to 160 acres in the Oklahoma territory.

The late 1800s was a time when owning land was another name for freedom. This was a time when Native Americans, White Americans, and African-Americans cooperated as they fought to survive in a hard, and sometimes frozen, land. They lived in sod huts, homes carved out of the heart of the earth. Those dugouts served as temporary housing until the pioneers were able to build log cabins. They cooperated, worked together to grow vegetables, to raise horses, cows, and goats. They built shelters and stored food before winter's beginning.

When I make author visits to schools, I sometimes read from the poetry book *I Have Heard of a Land.* Students ask many question about this daring and dangerous adventure of moving so far from the known to the unknown. I suggest that each student interview a senior relative or important older friend: grandparent, great-grandparent, great uncle, great aunt, or senior neighbor, about the family's journey to the student's particular state.

Students then may choose to write an essay or a poem about some aspect of the journey.

I recently visited students at a juvenile hall in a city near my Berkeley home. I was told to expect the students to be non-attentive, since the librarian noticed I had a soft voice. I began the program by reading poetry from my picture book, *Brown Honey in Broomwheat Tea* (illustrated by Floyd Cooper). The girls sat up prouder. Backs straightened, they leaned forward. In preparation for my visit, their librarian had given them copies of *Marked by Fire.*

One young woman, I was saddened to hear, had committed no crime, yet was locked up there because her mother had no place to keep her. Her mother, homeless, lived on the streets.

Receiving the Coretta Scott King Honor for **Brown Honey in Broomwheat Tea,** *1996*

I saw a room full of hope and possibilities in the faces of these young women.

The boys, who were supposed to be among the "troublemakers," were equally attentive. One row of students asked to see a picture of the grandmother in the *Brown Honey* book. I had noticed that every time a poem mentioned the word "mother" their faces took on longing and wistful expressions. They missed their families. They missed the bonding members of those families, their elders (many had been raised by grandmothers and great-grandmothers and grandfathers).

In addition, the young man and young woman who had introduced me gave two of the most insightful student analyses of *Marked by Fire* that I had ever heard. It was the first novel either of them had ever read all the way through.

My granddaughter who graduated first from Stanford and then from Harvard Law School invited me to her Harvard graduation and to read for her hairdresser's book club while I was in Boston. It was a pleasure to read from their chosen book, *House of Light.* Their next choice will be *Marked by Fire,* enjoyed evidently by a readership that spans from the young adults to the older adults, like the eighty-five-year-old matriarch in the Church Book Club audience, who said, "Just call me Auntie C." She reminded me of my Aunt Corine, also eighty-five. She asked deep questions about the *House of Light* characters, especially the feisty and independent Zenobia Butterfield.

Because I write books for the entire family, my titles include baby books: *Joy, The Angel's Lullabye, You Are My Perfect Baby,* and *Cherish Me;* children's books: *Brown Honey in Broomwheat Tea, Gingerbread Days, I Have Heard of a Land,* and *Crowning Glory;* teen or young adult novels: *Marked by Fire, Bright Shadow, The Golden Pasture,* and *Journey.* My collection of poetry *A Mother's Heart, A Daughter's Love: Poems for Us to Share* is read by every age group, to babies, by children, by teens, and by adults

One of my newer titles is *House of Light,* my debut adult novel, written twenty years ago. Published in 2001, it took two decades to find the right publisher. *House of Light* continues the story of Abyssina Jackson, first met by readers twenty years ago in *Marked by Fire.*

The saga of Abyssinia Jackson continues to haunt me; her stories follow me into my dreams. Upon waking up in the middle of the night, I head for my study and continue writing the fiction that she and her characters dictate.

At least one more novel, inspired by Abyssinia Jackson, will follow.

A Mother's Heart, A Daughter's Love: Poems for Us to Share illuminates the lifelong relationship between mothers and daughters, from the cradle and beyond. I see many women raising their grandchildren and their great-grandchildren. They are the triple-deck sandwich generation, caretakers of their children, their children's children,

as well as their own parents. These women are courageously committed to family and to the future. Students sometimes experience the book like a play, the young woman reading the mother's part, thereby glimpsing how her mother might see the relationship.

The Bowlegged Rooster, a chapter book, is what my granddaughter calls "the first signifying book for children using sweet and gentle language." When he's hatched, the little Bowlegged Rooster teaches us one of life's lessons. Other lessons follow at the Baldheaded Buzzard's baptism, Grandpa Goose's funeral, Crow's wedding, and during the Barnyard Christmas celebration where that fiddle-playing Lizard and the Bullfrog Quartet provide the music.

In the creation of *Hush Songs: African American Lullabies,* I chose old standards as well as composed new songs that soothe our babies and young children. My author's note tracks the journey of music sung by slaves to the White and Black babies in the long ago to that sung to all children now.

Crowning Glory celebrates in poetry the many wonderful ways that Black girls and women wear their hair: braided, curled, dreadlocked, and free. The book, ten years in the making, was a collaboration with my friend, the studio artist Brenda Joysmith. My granddaughters modeled for the paintings. This collaboration, in many ways, makes *Crowning Glory* a family book.

Family gathering, Thanksgiving, 2002: (front, from left) Granddaughter Aresa Pecot; the author; granddaughters Maria and Chrystal Pecot; (middle, from left) sons Gregory and Roy T. Thomas, and Michael Withers; (back, from left) cousins Cory and Irving Herbert

I am often asked about the anthology *A Gathering of Flowers: Stories about Being Young in America,* which was honored as the millionth volume at the UCSC Library in "keeping with the University of California, Santa Cruz's silver-anniversary motto, 'UCSC: Where Innovation is Tradition.'"

The volume reflected the growing diversity of UCSC's student population.

The librarian's choice also mirrored my intentions in the creating of the collection and in the reason I wanted it to exist.

In my teaching students and in directing a reading program at San Jose State University, I was frustrated by the lack of books and stories I might assign to students from diverse backgrounds. My classes consisted of Spanish-speakers, Asian students, Pacific Islanders, African-Americans, and Whites.

The books on the shelves were favorites of mine, from Shakespeare to Poe, yet I wanted a book that would include stories with characters that might be more familiar to the students sitting before me. I checked, not one such anthology existed.

Years later when invited to publish anything I chose, I chose to publish *A Gathering of Flowers: Stories about Being Young in America.* I called award-winning authors of the backgrounds of those students in that study hall and told them the concept of the book.

When all the writers replied affirmatively, I looked at the list and saw I had achieved a balance of skilled authors from various ethnic backgrounds—White, Black, Native American, Spanish American, Asian-American.

The contributors include Gerald Vizenor, Lois Lowry, Al Young, Ana Castillo, Kevin Kyung, Jeanne Wakatsuki Houston, Gerald Haslam, Maxine Hong Kingston, and Rick Wernli, two of whom were my creative writing students at University of California, Santa Cruz. I described this book's intent in the introduction as "A sampling of the rich colors and voices that make up today's America."

My next anthology, titled *Linda Brown, You Are Not Alone: Brown vs. the Board of Education,* will be a collection commemorating the 1954 Supreme Court decision. Ten contributors will share their experiences in short stories, memoirs, poetry, and essays. The selected Black authors and White authors—those affected most deeply by this decision—are mature enough to have lived through this historic period. This list of award-winning and best-selling contributors includes Michael Cart, Jean Craighead George, Eloise Greenfield, Lois Lowry, Katherine Paterson, Ishmael Reed, Jerry Spinelli, Quincy Troupe, Leona Welch, and myself.

My traveling has enhanced my sense of the world. I have visited, spoken at conferences, and/or taught English to educators in Italy, Nigeria, Saipan, Mexico, Hong Kong, New Zealand, Australia, Jamaica, Cancun, Haiti, and Ecuador.

Further background that aids me in my writing includes my education and what I have chosen to do with it: I earned a bachelor of arts degree with distinction from San Jose State University in 1966. I earned a master's degree in education, with a concentration in foreign languages from Stanford University in 1967. After graduating from Stanford, I taught Spanish and French in Palo Alto and East Palo Alto California middle schools.

Following the middle school teaching years, I received an appointment as assistant professor at San Jose State University. I went on to teach creative writing at St. Mary's College; at the University of California, Santa Cruz; at Purdue University; and as a full professor, teaching creative writing in the Department of English at the University of Tennessee, Knoxville.

Marked by Fire was adapted for stage by Ted Kociolek and Jim Racheef, and it has enjoyed productions across the country. I think my "Abyssinia" characters are delighted to see their stories told in lights. The rave reviews depict the show's journey so far from New York to Dallas. Everywhere I speak, readers want to know about the musical. I hope "Abyssinia" continues on her journey, telling the story that is based on my book.

In the meantime, I am dedicated to writing. I devote my time to books for the entire family, from baby books to children's books to teen books to adult novels.

I have been fortunate to work with such gifted book illustrators as Nneka Bennett, Holly Berry, Floyd Cooper, Pamela Johnson, and Brenda Joysmith, as well as with a brilliant array of literary agents and editors.

I now write full time near my family in Berkeley, California, where I have lived for more than fifty years.

Please look for forthcoming titles on your library and bookstore shelves, and on the Internet.

When people ask, "How can you stand being in a room alone?" My answer is I need a certain peace when I create. Like the Ponca Indians of Oklahoma, and like my mother, I try to live a life of peace. I pray, "Peace be with me in every word I speak, in every decision I make, in the guiding of my children, so that they will be disciplined in their education, in their understanding of the ways of the world, and in the ways of love.

"That I be thoughtful and quiet, not boisterous, loud, or disruptive. That I meditate day and night, think before acting, and choose to live in the blessing places of my heart."

TINGLE, Dolli
See BRACKETT, Dolli Tingle

W

WAIT, Lea 1946-

Personal

Born May 26, 1946, in Boston, MA; daughter of George (an accountant) and Sally (an artist and antiques dealer; maiden name, Smart) Wait; children: Caroline Wait Childs, Alicia Wait Gutschenritter, Rebecca Wait Wynne, Elizabeth Wait. *Education:* Chatham College, B.A., 1968; New York University, M.A., 1974, doctoral studies, 1974-77.

Addresses

Home—P.O. Box 225, Edgecomb, ME 04556. *E-mail*—leawait@clinic.net.

Career

Author and antiques dealer. A. T. & T., New York, NY, and New Jersey, public relations manager, 1968-98; M. A. H. Antiques, owner, 1977—. Adoptive Single Parents of New Jersey, president, 1978-92.

Member

Authors Guild, Mystery Writers of America, Sisters in Crime, Society of Children's Book Writers and Illustrators, Maine Writers and Publishers Alliance (Board of Trustees), National Council for Single Adoptive Parents (Board of Trustees).

Awards, Honors

Notable Children's Book designation, *Smithsonian* magazine, and Best Children's Books selection, Bank Street College of Education, both 2001, both for *Stopping to Home.*

Lea Wait

Writings

FOR CHILDREN

Stopping to Home, Simon & Schuster (New York, NY), 2001.
Seaward Born, Simon & Schuster (New York, NY), 2003.
Wintering Well, Simon & Schuster (New York, NY), 2004.

208

OTHER

Shadows at the Fair: An Antique Print Mystery, Scribner
    (New York, NY), 2002.
Shadows on the Coast of Maine: An Antique Print Mystery,
    Scribner (New York, NY), 2003.

Work in Progress

A historical novel about two young Scottish immigrants
who face a moral dilemma in 1850s New England.

Sidelights

Lea Wait has drawn on her love of New England and its
history to author a number of books for young readers.
In novels such as *Stopping to Home* and *Seaward Born,*
she focuses on self-reliant young people living in the
early nineteenth century who overcome difficult circumstances and gain knowledge and maturity. A search for
family and security runs through each of Wait's novels,
as well as a strong sense of the past. Reviewing *Stopping
to Home* in *Publishers Weekly,* a reviewer praised Wait
for "effectively" evoking the past by weaving in the
"customs . . . , language and geography that capture" life
in a coastal town in Maine.

Wait was born in Boston, Massachusetts, in 1946, and
spent winters at her home in suburban New Jersey and
summers in Maine with her grandparents. "My grandmother was the first person to take me to a library, or
encourage me to read," Wait told *SATA.* "She had me
read Shakespeare's plays out loud to her and encouraged
me to read and talk about adult books when I was just in
grade school. Many of the books she suggested I read
were nineteenth-century novels about brave women or
girls, many of them without families, who succeeded
through hard work and gumption. She taught me that
possibilities were unlimited and that books could lead
you to them."

Wait's grandmother was an antique dealer as well as an
avid reader; as Wait grew up she decided that she
wanted to follow the same path and be a writer too. She
served as editor of her high school newspaper, and then
studied English and drama at Chatham College in
Pittsburgh, Pennsylvania. Following college, she got a
job with A. T. & T., and worked in their public relations
department for many years. "I did start an antique print
business," she added, "but my mother ran it, since my
life quickly became very busy." Wait also decided to
adopt several children; as she noted, "Ever since I had
read those nineteenth-century novels about abandoned
children, I had planned to adopt, and when I was in my
late twenties I decided it was the right time." She soon
found herself the single mother of four older girls, and
her experiences as a single adoptive parent prompted her
involvement in adoption advocacy.

In the late 1990s, Wait left her corporate job to attend to
her lifelong dreams of following her grandmother's lead.
Moving to Maine, she became active in her antique print
business and started writing. Her first published book for
young readers was *Stopping to Home,* published in 2001.

Taking place in Wiscasset, Maine, during the first
decade of the nineteenth century, the novel finds eleven-
year-old Abigail Chambers taking care of her four-year-
old brother after her mother dies of smallpox. With her
father, a sailor, likely lost at sea, Abigail must bring in
enough money to keep the children out of the orphanage,
but as the smallpox epidemic lingers on, work becomes
more difficult to find. Fortunately, a pregnant teen
widow opens her home to the two Chambers children,
and a bond develops that creates a new family, in a
novel that *Horn Book* contributor Martha V. Parravano
called "quietly compelling" and Hazel Rochman praised
in a *Booklist* review as "a moving first novel that finds
drama in ordinary life."

Other novels for young readers include *Seaward Born,*
which finds thirteen-year-old slave Michael Lautrec
working on the docks in Charleston and dreaming of
freedom. The year is 1805, and when the opportunity to
take the chance and run away comes, Michael bravely
takes flight, realizing that it is a risk worth taking.
Wait's *Wintering Well* returns readers to Maine, as Will
Ames must deal with life as a cripple after he loses a leg
in a farming accident. With dreams of a future as a
farmer now dashed, the young man determines to deal
with life on his own rather than stay in the care of his
parents. In addition to her works for children, Wait is the
author of a series of adult mystery novels focusing on
the antiques business.

Biographical and Critical Sources

PERIODICALS

Book, March-April, 2001, review of *Stopping to Home,*
    p. 81.
Booklist, November 15, 2001, Hazel Rochman, review of
    Stopping to Home, p. 567; June 1, 2002, Sue O'Brien,
    review of *Shadows at the Fair,* p. 1692.
Horn Book, January-February, 2002, Martha V. Parravano,
    review of *Stopping to Home,* p. 85.
Kirkus Reviews, September 15, 2001, review of *Stopping to
    Home,* p. 1371; May 1, 2002, review of *Shadows at
    the Fair,* p. 623.
Library Journal, June 1, 2002, Rex E. Klett, review of
    Shadows at the Fair, p. 200.
Publishers Weekly, November 5, 2001, review of *Stopping
    to Home,* p. 69; June 24, 2002, review of *Shadows at
    the Fair,* p. 42.
School Library Journal, October, 2001, Sue Sherif, review
    of *Stopping to Home,* p. 174.

OTHER

Lea Wait Home Page, http://www.leawait.com (May 24,
    2002).

*   *   *

WOLFF, Alexander (Nikolaus) 1957-

Personal

Born February 3, 1957, in Wilmington, DE; son of
Nikolaus (a chemist) and Mary (a musician; maiden

name, Neave) Wolff; married Vanessa James, June 20, 1998; children: one son. *Education:* Princeton University, B.A. (cum laude), 1980.

Addresses

Home—Cornwall, VT. *Office*—*Sports Illustrated,* 135 West 50th St., New York, NY 10020-1201. *E-mail*—thehooplife@aol.com.

Career

Sports journalist. *Sports Illustrated,* New York, NY, reporter, 1980-81, writer, 1981-82, staff writer, 1982-85, senior writer, beginning 1985. Olympics commentator for Cable News Network (CNN) and CNNSI.com, 1996. Young Writers Institute mentor-through-the-mail, 1991; Institute for International Sports, Kingston, RI, sports ethics fellow, 1992; commentator for British Broadcasting Corp. at Atlanta Olympics, 1996; Ferris Professor of Journalism, Princeton University, 2002.

Member

Professional Basketball Writers Association, U.S. Basketball Writers Association (president, 1999-2000), National Sportscasters and Sportswriters Association, U.S. Tennis Writers Association, Association Internationale de la Presse Sportive.

Awards, Honors

Four writing awards from U.S. Basketball Writers Association; award from *Sporting News,* 1990; sports journalism award, Women's Sports Foundation, 1997; numerous other professional awards.

Writings

(With Chuck Wielgus) *The In-Your-Face Basketball Book,* Everest House (New York, NY), 1980.
(With Chuck Wielgus) *The Back-in-Your-Face Guide to Pick-up Basketball,* Dodd (New York, NY), 1986.
(With Chuck Wielgus and Steve Rushin) *From A-Train to Yogi: The Fan's Book of Sports Nicknames,* Harper (New York, NY), 1987.
(With Armen Keteyian) *Raw Recruits,* Pocket Books (New York, NY), 1990.
One Hundred Years of Hoops: A Fond Look Back at the Sport of Basketball, Oxmoor House (Menlo Park, CA), 1991.
A March for Honor, photographs by Damian Strohmeyer, Masters Press (Indianapolis, IN), 1997.
Big Game, Small World: A Basketball Adventure, Warner Books (New York, NY), 2002.

Contributor to *1990 Best Sports Stories,* edited by Dave Sloan, Sporting News, 1990.

Sidelights

Alexander Wolff is a sports journalist who has worked at *Sports Illustrated* for much of his career and has

Compiling facts and stories from sixteen different countries, Alexander Wolff forms a picture of the game of basketball and the global popularity of this prominent sport. (Cover photo by Darren Robb.)

sidelined as an author in order to further explore his favorite sports. "Sports have always fascinated me," Wolff once told *SATA* in recalling his year as a club basketball player in Switzerland, "but as I got older, I followed sports more and more for the opportunities they presented a writer—insights into people and how they go about pursuing the goals they set." A writer first and a sportswriter second, Wolff searches out stories that overlap the two arenas. "No matter how much you love sports, you will be a better sportswriter if you bring to your writing about the games a well-rounded sensibility." Several of these overlapping stories have found their way into books such as *Raw Recruits* and *Big Game Small World: A Basketball Adventure.*

In *Raw Recruits,* Wolff joins coauthor and fellow sports journalist Armen Keteyian for a look at the influence sponsorship money now wields in college sports. Focusing their attention on the ways in which colleges recruit top high school basketball stars, the authors use Los Angeles as an example of the way sneaker companies, camps, and other interested parties seduce inner-city African Americans with potential—but ultimately illusory—financial security. Describing the book as "rather like an extended series of magazine exposés," *New York Review of Books* contributor Arthur Kempton noted the presence of "coaches and players with price tags attached and bills of lading sticking out of their pockets.... people who have something valuable to sell for the first time in their lives and ... other people who see their chance in helping them to make the deal." Calling the book "important," a *Kliatt* reviewer described *Raw Recruits* as a "cynical, desperate look at the recruitment process" motivated by the authors' "desire to somehow save the game before it is too late."

Published in 2002, *Big Game, Small World* finds Wolff traveling through sixteen countries—including Angola, Brazil, Bhutan, and Lithuania—and across several states in search of evidence to support his thesis that professional basketball—by 2000 second only to soccer and rising as the world's most popular game—is a reflection of "American cultural power." In his role as what a *Publishers Weekly* reviewer dubbed a "roundball anthropologist," Wolff "proves that the game's essence transcends national boundaries," his "knack for finding fascinating people to interview" viewed by *Library Journal* contributor Will Hepfer as "go[ing] far in humanizing basketball in a global context." Calling *Big Game, Small World* a "wonderful book," *Booklist* reviewer Wes Lukowsky noted that the author's "passion for the game burns as feverishly as it did twenty years ago, when he was looking for pickup games."

Because of his high profile as a nationally known sportswriter, Wolff is often asked how he became a journalist. "I did it by writing," he explained to *SATA*. His advice to budding sportswriters? "Write at every opportunity; show your work to others for feedback; don't be discouraged by criticism. There are a few blessed geniuses for whom writing comes easily, but for most of us it's a painstaking undertaking, rife with trial, error, and discouragement. What makes it worthwhile is a finished product that somehow works."

Biographical and Critical Sources

PERIODICALS

Book, March-April, 2002, Tom LeClair, review of *Big Game, Small World: A Basketball Adventure,* p. 76.
Booklist, January 1, 2002, Wes Lukowsky, review of *Big Game, Small World,* p. 793.
Kliatt, January, 1991, review of *Raw Recruits,* p. 55.
Library Journal, June 1, 1980, Robert L. Rice, review of *The In-Your-Face Basketball Book,* p. 1323; February 1, 2002, Will Hepfer, review of *Big Game, Small World,* p. 108.
New York Review of Books, April 11, 1991, Arthur Kempton, "Native Sons," pp. 57-59.
Publishers Weekly, December 24, 2001, review of *Big Game, Small World,* p. 57.
School Library Journal, December, 1980, Eileen D. Burt, review of *The In-Your-Face Basketball Book,* p. 83.

WOLFF, Virginia Euwer 1937-

Personal

Born August 25, 1937, in Portland, OR; daughter of Eugene Courtney (a lawyer and farmer) and Florence (a teacher and farmer; maiden name, Craven) Euwer; married Art Wolff, July 19, 1959 (divorced, July, 1976); children: Anthony Richard, Juliet Dianne. *Education:* Smith College, A.B., 1959; graduate study at Long Island University, 1974-75, and Warren Wilson College.

Addresses

Home—Parkdale, OR. *Agent*—Marilyn Marlowe, Curtis Brown Ltd., 10 Astor Pl., Floor 3, New York, NY 10003-6982.

Career

English teacher at junior high school in Bronx, NY, 1959-60; Miquon School, Philadelphia, PA, elementary school teacher, 1968-72; Fiedel School, Glen Cove, NY, elementary school teacher, 1972-74; Hood River Valley High School, Hood River, OR, English teacher, 1976-86; Mt. Hood Academy, Government Camp, OR, English teacher, 1986-98. Lecturer on techniques of fiction writing at Willamette Writers' Conference, 1977. Swimming teacher and lifeguard. Violinist with Mid-Columbia Sinfonietta and other orchestral groups.

Member

Society of Children's Book Writers and Illustrators, Chamber Music Society of Oregon.

Awards, Honors

First prize in poetry from Long Island University, 1976; awards from Oregon Teachers as Writers for poems and from *Willamette Week* for story "Pole Beans for Rent," both 1979; International Reading Association Award, young adult division, and PEN-West Book Award, both 1989, and Best Book for Young Adults selection, American Library Association (ALA), all for *Probably Still Nick Swansen;* award from Child Study Children's Book Committee at Bank Street College, and Golden Kite Award, Society of Children's Book Writers and Illustrators, both 1993, Oregon Book Award, Young Reader's category, 1994, Young Reader's Choice Award nominee, Canadian Library Association, 1996, Notable Book selection and Best Book for Young Adults selection, both ALA, *Booklist* Editor's Choice and Top of the List winner, *School Library Journal* Best Books List, and *Parents* Magazine's Reluctant Young Adult Readers list, all for *Make Lemonade;* Notable Book and Best Book for Young Adults, ALA, and Janusz Korczak Literary Competition honorable mention citation, Anti-Defamation League Braun Center for Holocaust Studies, all for *The Mozart Season;* National Book Award for young people's literature, 2001, for *True Believer.*

Writings

Rated PG (novel), St. Martin's (New York, NY), 1980.
Probably Still Nick Swansen, Holt (New York, NY), 1988.
The Mozart Season, Holt (New York, NY), 1991.
Make Lemonade, Holt (New York, NY), 1993.
Bat 6, Scholastic (New York, NY), 1998.
(Author of foreword) *We're Alive and Life Goes On: A Theresienstadt,* Holt (New York, NY), 1998.
True Believer, Atheneum (New York, NY), 2001.

Contributor of stories and poems to magazines, including *Ladies' Home Journal* and *Seventeen.*

Sidelights

Virginia Euwer Wolff came to young adult literature relatively late in life—approaching age fifty—but in a very short time and with four novels, the author has created her own niche in the genre. "I major in disappointment," Wolff told *Booklist*'s Stephanie Zvirin in an interview, and indeed she is known for her incisive takes on outsiders, for kids who face and deal with disappointment, who confront confusing and disorienting experiences. From special education student Nick in *Probably Still Nick Swansen,* to Jolly, the single teenage mom in *Make Lemonade,* Wolff's protagonists face an uphill battle in life. And even when the way seems relatively smooth, as for the young violinist Allegra in *The Mozart Season,* the outsider status still pertains—in this case a gifted individual set apart from the quotidian. An essayist for the *St. James Guide to Young Adult Writers* noted: "Wolff introduces young adult readers to worlds of adolescence they may have never considered. Whether learning disabled or precocious, affluent or poor, her protagonists must learn to fit into a world that frequently lacks accommodations for those who are atypical."

Language is paramount in a Wolff novel. "We live by language," Wolff observed in a 1997 speech delivered at a children's literature conference and reprinted in *Horn Book.* "Incendiary and insightful. The language of the In-group, the Out-group—and always the potential for hostile fire between them." For Wolff, the type of language used either separates or includes: the language of education, of poverty, of music, of inchoate longing. The use of a particular form of speech or code sets a person in his or her world as firmly as does their economic or physical condition. "Insider and Outsider language are always a fragile, trembling balance," Wolff noted in her 1997 address. It is not surprising then that she has also declared that "Words have probably guided my life."

Wolff was born in Portland, Oregon, on August 25, 1937, the second of two children. Her father, Eugene Courtney Euwer, was a lawyer in Pennsylvania before abandoning the rat race to move to the Pacific Northwest and grow fruit. Her mother, Florence, was a teacher. Though the Euwers lived in a hand-built log house without electricity, theirs was not a simple back-to-nature life; it was not a rejection of civilization but an

Virginia Euwer Wolff

enlargement on it. "I was born into a loved and loving home," Wolff recalled in *Horn Book.* "From our backyard we had a towering view of Mt. Hood, 11,235 feet high, with snow on it all year round. From our front lawn on a clear day we could see three more of the Cascades, including Mt. St. Helens." Surrounding the house were orchards and old growth Douglas fir, and inside "we had a grand piano, a huge stone fireplace, and a house full of books and paintings." Wolff grew up listening to Chopin and Beethoven, and learned early the pleasure of books, with Winnie the Pooh a constant companion.

This idyllic childhood was drastically altered with the death of her father when Wolff was five. "Suddenly the world that had just the day before made sense to us went kerplooey," she noted in *Horn Book.* Wolff's mother determined to continue working the farm, a gutsy decision for a single woman in 1942. The life of music and art continued for both Wolff and her older brother. Going to school was a shock for the young Wolff, for here she came into contact with peers who spoke another sort of language—the direct speech of the playground. And trips to New York introduced her to still another reality—the world of museums and theater. Under the influence of a New York cousin, Wolff requested to learn the violin and her passion for music won her another vocabulary, one that she has continued to enlarge upon all her life.

At sixteen, Wolff was sent to boarding school far from the forests of Oregon, and from there she went on to study English at Smith College. During these years she fell under the influence of language masters such as the poets Gerard Manley Hopkins and Dylan Thomas, novelists like James Joyce and Nikolai Gogol, and of course Shakespeare. "I am in love with the English sentence," Wolff told Zvirin in her *Booklist* interview. The works of these writers helped to foster that love.

Wolff married directly out of college and was introduced to the world of the theater, the world of her husband. For the next seventeen years she was a wife and mother of two children. Off-Broadway, regional, and repertory theaters on the Atlantic seaboard became her new reality, and the family moved twelve times in these years, living in Philadelphia, New York City, Long Island, Washington, D.C., Ohio, and Connecticut. She also taught English at both public and private schools. When her son and daughter were teenagers, she began to

Fourteen-year-old LaVaughn takes a job babysitting the two children of a teenage mother and soon learns that all three need her to help them move toward a better life. (Cover illustration by Denise Crawford.)

try to write. An M.F.A. program in writing put her on track for the long-distance job of novel writing, but she left two-thirds of the way through without finishing the degree.

Divorced in 1976, Wolff returned to her native Oregon, more an Easterner than a member of the Pacific Northwest community. Language differences were symbolic of how she had become an outsider to her own roots: "I said ahpricot, but had not gone as far as tomahto," she recalled in *Horn Book.* She taught at a public high school in Hood River, Oregon, for ten years. During that time she published her first and only adult novel, *Rated PG.* Karen Pate of *Oregon* magazine remarked that Wolff "succeeds in capturing the confusion and excitement of youth and first love in language characterized by surprising and appropriate metaphor.... Writing in a lively and engaging style, Virginia Euwer Wolff offers sensitive insights into the way people act and why, without resorting to pat resolutions and neatly happy endings." "I don't admire the book," Wolff told *Booklist*'s Zvirin. "I guess first novels are always embarrassing." It was another seven years until she turned her hand to novel writing again, and this time she had in mind a story dealing with the young people whom she worked with daily as a teacher.

Wolff's first YA title, *Probably Still Nick Swansen,* deals with a learning-disabled student, a sixteen-year-old boy who is ridiculed by other students and also haunted by the death of his beloved sister who drowned seven years earlier. Room Nineteen, the special education room, is the center of his school universe, but there are other challenges as well: learning to drive and learning to deal with emotional pain. Stood up by a former special education student, Shana, whom he has asked to the prom, he comes to understand the complexities of the world. Though Shana has mainstreamed from Room Nineteen, she is still considered stupid by the others and still lives in turmoil and self-doubt. Over the several weeks in Nick's life that the novel covers, "the reader becomes immersed ... in Nick's world," according to Barbara A. Lynn, writing in *Voice of Youth Advocates.* Lynn concluded that this "is an exceptional novel for junior and senior high teens." Wolff also manages, through her close and detailed writing of character, to make Nick's problems not just those of a special education student. As Constance A. Mellon noted in *School Library Journal,* the book "stresses the similarities between Nick and other teens rather than highlighting the differences."

Wolff next turned to music and a twelve-year-old protagonist for her second YA title, *The Mozart Season.* Instead of an outsider, she chose someone very much on the inside of her chosen specialty. Allegra Shapiro is preparing for a music competition in which she will play Mozart's Fourth Violin Concerto in D. The way in which Allegra spends the summer mastering the work of a nineteen-year-old composer who wrote two centuries before her "is the basis of a sturdy, engrossing novel," according to a critic in the *New York Times Book Review.* "With a clear, fresh voice that never falters,

Wolff gives readers a delightful heroine, a fully realized setting, and a slowly building tension that reaches a stunning climax," according to Connie C. Rockman in *School Library Journal.* Along the way, Allegra also wrestles with what it means to be herself versus what her parents—both concert musicians—want her to be, as well as trying to come to terms with her Jewish identity.

Friends and relatives help Allegra: she learns of love from a singer friend of her mother; a homeless man, Mr. Trouble, seeks her help in assuaging the wounds of his past; her friends Jessica and Sarah not only challenge her but also make her have fun; and her parents and brother lend their support. Rachel Gonsenhauser, writing in *Voice of Youth Advocates,* felt that "Wolff's story is mesmerizing" and went on to note that the author "conveys eloquently the fragility of life, and the importance of heritage." A reviewer for *Publishers Weekly,* while commenting on parts that seemed "slightly flawed," concluded that "it is a pleasure to have a novel of ideas for young adults that describes the delicate dance between honoring traditions of the past and being your own person in the present." Julie Jaffee Nagel, writing in *American Music Teacher,* found that "this book provides not only an interesting and well-written story but also an example of how music can be an integral part of one's life."

Like her character Allegra, Wolff, too, is a violinist who has played with several community orchestras and both amateur and professional chamber ensembles. Teri S. Lesesne, writing in *Writers for Young Adults,* remarked that a strong influence in Wolff's fiction "is her own love of music. As a violinist, she believes music is very powerful.... The uncertainty of playing and performance is yet another facet of music that affects Wolff's work. Never being quite sure what the next note will sound like is somewhat akin to the writing of a novel. What comes next, what will happen next to the characters in the story, is not always planned. Wolff, for example, notes that she was not sure whether Allegra from *The Mozart Season* would win the music competition; that not knowing kept her writing."

Wolff noted in her 1997 speech that after this second YA book "I needed to go in a different direction. I thought I could do something more dangerous." In *Make Lemonade,* partly inspired by a television series about the poor who fall into the cracks of the system and remain there for generations, Wolff decided to focus on several such individuals and most emphatically not make them victims. LaVaughn is fourteen and a bright student, saving money for college. Her mom is widowed and hard-working, but LaVaughn knows that if she wants an education, she is going to have to pay for it herself. To this end, she takes a job babysitting two young children, Jeremy and Jilly, offspring of a seventeen-year-old single parent, Jolly. When Jolly loses her job after rebuffing the sexual advances of her supervisor, LaVaughn is drawn more closely into Jolly's world, ultimately prompting the older girl to go back to school. A critic in *Publishers Weekly* noted that this story, "radiant with hope" and told in a "meltingly lyric blank

In her second novel about LaVaughn, Wolff depicts the girl's fifteenth year, with the tribulations of first love, shaky friendships, and a strained mother-daughter relationship. (Cover illustration Russell Gordon.)

verse," was a "stellar addition to YA literature." Barbara Gorman, writing in *Kliatt,* noted in particular the format of the book, divided into sixty-six brief chapters "set up like a blank verse poem." A *Kirkus Reviews* contributor observed that *Make Lemonade* provided a "spare, beautifully crafted depiction of a fourteen-year-old whose goal of escaping poverty is challenged by friendship with a single teenage mother," and went on to remark that while the protagonists could be from almost any ethnic group or inner city, "their troubles—explored in exquisite specificity—are universal. Hopeful—and powerfully moving." Writing in *School Library Journal,* Carolyn Noah called the book "a triumphant, outstanding story."

In *True Believer,* "Wolff continues the story of the vulnerable, resilient LaVaughn," according to Roger Sutton in *Horn Book.* In this story, LaVaughn assumes center stage as she develops a crush on a boy, drifts apart from her two best friends, and sees her widowed mother begin to date. Wolff told Sutton that she had to write a sequel to *Make Lemonade* because "I became very interested in the questions that the first book raised, and I guess I just really got interested in LaVaughn. Thanks to my editor, Brenda Bowen, LaVaughn became a solid character in *Make Lemonade,* and I've been thinking about her ever since." Speaking of the religious theme in *True Believer,* Wolff told an interviewer for *Publishers Weekly:* "I would be so untethered without my personal faith. I wouldn't be able to go through a day—but that's my own experience.... I found it difficult to write about religion with lucidity; I wanted to be fair, strenuously fair. Readers have their own religious beliefs and questions. The teenage years are the years to examine faith—the need to be independent and the need to be anchored."

Gillian Engberg, writing in *Booklist,* found the novel to be "transcendent, raw, and fiercely optimistic." A critic for *Publishers Weekly* concluded: "In delving into LaVaughn's life, Wolff unmasks the secret thoughts adolescents hold sacred and, in so doing, lets her readers know they are not alone." A *Horn Book* reviewer commented that *True Believer* is "a heartbreaking story, truthful in its pain but buoyed by LaVaughn's resilient spirit and by a redemptive and earned ending." *True Believer* earned the National Book Award for young people's literature in 2001.

Wolff is a self-confessed procrastinator. As she told *Booklist*'s Zvirin, "I'm able to delay and delay and delay, and even sabotage a book." Indeed, Wolff's books are slow in coming. Her fourth YA title, *Bat 6,* appeared in 1998, five years after *Make Lemonade. Bat 6* once again is a complete departure from Wolff's previous work. The book uses a softball game in 1949 between the sixth grade girls of two small Oregon towns to explore the meanings and echoes of prejudice. "None of the twenty-one girls emerges unchanged from what happens during that fateful encounter nor, one predicts, will most readers of this powerful novel," wrote Michael Cart in *Booklist.* Told as a series of flashbacks by various players, the central conflict develops between Aki, a Japanese American, and Shazam, whose father was killed at Pearl Harbor. Once again, Wolff employed the rhythms and vernacular of actual everyday speech to build her narrative. A *Kirkus Reviews* critic remarked that "Through the first-person narrations of the twenty-one girls of the two teams, the story emerges ... their emotions and perspectives ring true." Bill Mollineaux, writing in *Voice of Youth Advocates,* stated that the author "paints a picture of small-town America in the Forties that shows its beliefs, attitudes, and values." *School Library Journal* contributor Luann Toth observed that "Wolff delves into the irreversible consequences of war and the necessity to cultivate peace and speaks volumes about courage, responsibility, and reconciliation—all in a book about softball."

Wolff explained to Sutton why she used so many narrators in *Bat 6:* "It was nothing but imitating Faulkner. I don't care how many children's and YA authors have done that before, we're all just imitating Faulkner. None of us made it up. With twenty-one narrators, I knew I was straining the reader's patience, but I wanted—you know, it takes a village to raise a child? I wanted a village to tell a story." Speaking of

how she writes a book, she told Sutton: "Katherine Anne Porter always wrote the last page first, evidently. I can't do that; I don't have any idea where it's going. Well, *Bat 6* came because I looked up in my brain and saw a whole crowd of people rushing toward first base, and I knew there was a crisis there. And so in a sense I wrote around that event, but that's not the end of the book. No, I never know how it's going to end." In describing to the *Publishers Weekly* interviewer how she created the character LaVaughn in *Make Lemonade* and *True Believer,* Wolff admitted that she used a kind of interview process herself: "You sit down with pen and paper—some people use a tape recorder—and interview her. I type a lot of questions and [LaVaughn] answers them: What do you like to do? What are your hobbies? At first [while writing *Make Lemonade*] she was stubborn: "Why should I talk to you now—you weren't interested in me in the first draft?" I work early in the morning, before my nasty critic gets up—he rises about noon. By then I've put in much of a day's work."

Wolff is untroubled by the fact that her books take years to complete, for writing is not her only interest; she takes violin lessons, for instance. She also takes pleasure in her children—her son, a jazz guitarist with a degree in religious studies, and her daughter, a psychotherapist and a mother in her own right—and in her grandchild. Life, in many ways, has come full circle for Wolff, for she is once again living in the shadow of Mt. Hood, just as she did as a child. Language is still paramount for her, but in the final analysis, as she concluded to Zvirin, "I guess I'd rather write fewer books and have them be unusual ... than write quantity."

Wolff once observed, "My obsession with human perception constantly finds itself fused with my obsession with music. Some of my guides in the trek toward vision are Shakespeare, Chekhov, Mozart, Wagner, Gogol, Brahms, Steinbeck, Welty, Sibelius, and Salinger. I've approached writing chiefly through a third art form, the theatre. In a highly ironic age, I'm coming to believe that irony isn't the only thing that matters. One of my editors has tended to lean in a similar direction; I'm grateful to her. In retrospect, I'm also extremely grateful for my Smith education, which taught me essentially what Maya Angelou says: 'Preparation is rarely easy, and never beautiful.'

"I have taught school during most of my adult life, students from age five to twenty-one, kindergarten through undergraduate. My daughter once asked me which age was my favorite to teach, and I realized that the answer was 'whatever age I happen to be teaching when you ask me.' During the Vietnam era I was also active in Another Mother for Peace."

Biographical and Critical Sources

BOOKS

Authors and Artists for Young Adults, Volume 26, Gale (Detroit, MI), 1999.
Children's Literature Review, Volume 62, Gale (Detroit, MI).

St. James Guide to Young Adult Writers, 2nd edition, St. James Press (Detroit, MI), 1999.

Writers for Young Adults, Scribner's (New York, NY).

PERIODICALS

ALAN Review, spring, 1991, Virginia Euwer Wolff, "Rarely Easy and Never Beautiful," pp. 2-3.

American Music Teacher, April-May, 1992, Julie Jaffee Nagel, review of *The Mozart Season,* p. 84.

Booklist, November 15, 1988, Stephanie Zvirin, review of *Probably Still Nick Swansen,* p. 567; June 1, 1991, Hazel Rochman, review of *The Mozart Season,* p. 1869; June 1-15, 1993, Stephanie Zvirin, review of *Make Lemonade,* p. 1813; March 1, 1994, Stephanie Zvirin, "The *Booklist* Interview: Virginia Euwer Wolff," pp. 1250-1251; May 1, 1998, Michael Cart, review of *Bat 6,* p. 1517; February 1, 2001, Gillian Engberg, review of *True Believer,* p. 1051.

Books for Keeps, July, 1995, Wendy Cooling, review of *Make Lemonade,* p. 28; p. 28; November, 1996, p. 11.

Bulletin of the Center for Children's Books, July-August, 1991, p. 279; July-August, 1993, p. 361; June, 1998, pp. 378-379.

English Journal, January, 1990, Alleen Nilsen and Ken Donelson, review of *Probably Still Nick Swansen,* p. 89.

Horn Book, September-October, 1991, Ellen Fader, review of *The Mozart Season,* p. 599; September-October, 1993, Ellen Fader, review of *Make Lemonade,* pp. 606-607; May-June, 1998, Virginia Euwer Wolff, "If I Was Doing It Proper, What Was You Laughing At?," pp. 297-308; July-August, 1998, Nancy Vasilakis, review of *Bat 6,* pp. 500-501; January, 2001,

review of *True Believer,* p. 98; May, 2001, Roger Sutton, "An Interview with Virginia Euwer Wolff," p. 280.

Kirkus Reviews, May 15, 1993, review of *Make Lemonade,* p. 670; May 1, 1998, review of *Bat 6,* p. 666.

Kliatt, November, 1994, Barbara Gorman, review of *Make Lemonade,* p. 16.

New York Times Book Review, August 4, 1991, review of *The Mozart Season,* p. 21; October 17, 1993, p. 33.

Oregon, April, 1981, Karen Pate, review of *Rated PG.*

Publishers Weekly, May 24, 1991, review of *The Mozart Season,* p. 59; May 31, 1993, review of *Make Lemonade,* p. 56; July 11, 1994, p. 80; April 20, 1998, review of *Bat 6,* p. 67; December 18, 2000, review of *True Believer,* p. 79, and *"PW* Talks with Virginia Euwer Wolff," p. 79.

School Library Journal, December, 1988, Constance A. Mellon, review of *Probably Still Nick Swansen,* p. 124; November, 1989, pp. 42-43; July, 1991, Connie C. Rockman, review of *The Mozart Season,* p. 91; July, 1993, Carolyn Noah, review of *Make Lemonade,* p. 103; December, 1993, p. 28; May, 1998, Luann Toth, review of *Bat 6,* p. 150.

Times Educational Supplement, September 1, 1995, Geraldine Brennan, review of *Make Lemonade,* p. 24.

Voice of Youth Advocates, June, 1989, Barbara A. Lynn, review of *Probably Still Nick Swansen,* p. 109; December, 1991, Rachel Gonsenhauser, review of *The Mozart Season,* p. 320; October, 1993, p. 220; June, 1998, Bill Mollineaux, review of *Bat 6,* pp. 126-127.

Wilson Library Bulletin, June, 1989, p. 101; November, 1989, p. 11.*

Z

ZAUNDERS, Bo 1939-

Personal

Born June 5, 1939, in Sweden; son of Erik Johansson (a farmer and banker) and Thea Zaunders (a milliner); married Anna-Stina Erhardt, 1962 (divorced, 1963); married Roxie Munro (an artist), 1986. *Education:* Attended Folkhögskola in Sweden; studied with surrealist painter Waldemar Lorentzon. *Hobbies and other interests:* Travel, literature, cooking.

Addresses

Home and office—20 Park Ave., New York, NY 10016. *E-mail*—zaundersnyc@aol.com.

Career

Art director, photographer, illustrator, and author. Young & Rubicam (advertising agency), art director in Stockholm, Sweden, Madrid, Spain, Paris, France, London, England, and New York, NY, 1965-79; freelance illustrator, 1980—; freelance photographer and writer, 1985—; art director and creative director in advertising for New York agencies, beginning 1989. *Military service:* Swedish Navy; served as medic.

Member

Players Club (New York, NY).

Awards, Honors

Georgia Children's Picture Storybook Award, 1988, for *Max, the Bad-Talking Parrot* by Patricia B. Demuth; Children's Book Council Outstanding Book of the Year, National Council for the Social Studies, 1999, for *Crocodiles, Camels, and Dugout Canoes: Eight Adventurous Episodes;* Best Book of the Year designation, *School Library Journal,* and Best Book of the Year List, *Center for Children's Books,* both 2002, both for *Feathers, Flaps, and Flops: Fabulous Early Fliers.*

Writings

Crocodiles, Camels, and Dugout Canoes: Eight Adventurous Episodes, illustrated by Roxie Munro, Dutton (New York, NY), 1998.
Feathers, Flaps, and Flops: Fabulous Early Fliers, illustrated by Roxie Munro, Dutton (New York, NY), 2001.

ILLUSTRATOR

Patricia B. Demuth, *Max, the Bad-Talking Parrot,* Dodd, Mead (New York, NY), 1986.
Joanne Oppenheimer, adaptor, *One Gift Deserves Another,* Dutton (New York, NY), 1992.

Work in Progress

Two children's books: *Gargoyles, Girders, and Glass Houses,* a book about architecture, and *Ule,* a book about a Swedish troll.

Sidelights

On the heels of a long career in advertising that took him from his native Sweden to New York City and many other places in between, Bo Zaunders began a second career as a children's book writer in the late 1990s. Working with his illustrator wife Roxie Munro, he has published two nonfiction titles that showcase the daring of men and women from history and benefit from what a *Horn Book* contributor called his "fast-paced descriptive narration and an innate sense of history." *Crocodiles, Camels, and Dugout Canoes: Eight Adventurous Episodes* and its follow-up, *Feathers, Flaps, and Flops: Fabulous Early Fliers,* contain brief biographical portraits that place each of Zaunders' subjects into their technological and historic context.

Crocodiles, Camels, and Dugout Canoes introduces readers to such people as nineteenth-century British explorer Richard Burton, mid-twentieth-century cross-Europe cyclist Dervla Murphy, and early twentieth-century mountaineer Annie Smith Peck. Beginning each section with what *Booklist* contributor Susan Dove

Bo Zaunders recounts the stories of early aviators and their daring exploits in Feathers, Flaps, and Flops: Fabulous Early Fliers, *illustrated by Roxie Munro.*

Lempke characterized as "a particularly thrilling moment," Zaunders relates the career of these amateur explorers, revealing their motives to be intense curiosity rather than a quest for fame or riches. According to a *Publishers Weekly* reviewer, the enthusiasm of the husband-and-wife team—"and their subjects' own intrepid spirits—shine through the pages of this absorbing picture book." Calling *Crocodiles, Camels, and Dugout Canoes* "informative and supremely entertaining," the *Publishers Weekly* contributor concluded that Zaunders "demonstrates that reading can be a great adventure, too."

A new batch of adventurers take to the air in *Feathers, Flaps, and Flops*, as Zaunders and Munro once more tantalize young readers with their stylish nonfiction. Early twentieth-century African-American pilot Bessie Coleman, the Montgofier brothers and their development of the hot-air balloon, dirigible innovator and pilot Alberto Santos-Dumont, and "Wrong-Way" Corrigan and his memorable 1938 flight to Ireland are among the airborne luminaries whose life stories are "told in a lively manner," according to Louise L. Sherman in her *School Library Journal* review. In addition to citing Munro's water color and ink drawings, *Booklist* contributor Carolyn Phelan praised *Feathers, Flaps, and Flops* as "an eclectic and appealing introduction to early fliers" while in *Horn Book*, Zaunders was praised for including a thorough biography and an introduction that "highlights the span of aviation history."

In addition to his work as an author, Zaunders has also illustrated several books for other authors. Reviewing his illustrations for Patricia B. Demuth's *Max, the Bad-Talking Parrot*, a *Publishers Weekly* reviewer praised Zaunders for his "expressive" and "quirky" contribution to the humorous picture book, while the watercolor cartoon illustrations he contributed to Joanne Oppenheim's adaptation of *One Gift Deserves Another* were praised by a *Publishers Weekly* reviewer. Noting that the illustrations "heighten the humor, by comically exaggerating" story elements, the reviewer remarked upon Zaunders' use of bright color and "engaging peripheral touches."

"I've always loved books," Zaunders told *SATA*. "By age eleven I had read every single one in my father's library—some with a flashlight, long after I was supposed to be asleep. Now, being involved with actually creating books is tremendously exciting. I can think of nothing more satisfying."

Biographical and Critical Sources

PERIODICALS

Booklist, October 15, 1998, Susan Dove Lempke, review of *Crocodiles, Camels, and Dugout Canoes: Eight Adventurous Episodes*, p. 420; August, 2001, review of *Feathers, Flaps, and Flops: Fabulous Early Fliers*, p. 2118.

Horn Book, January, 1999, review of *Crocodiles, Camels, and Dugout Canoes,* p. 85; July, 2001, review of *Feathers, Flaps, and Flops,* p. 480.

Publishers Weekly, April 25, 1986, review of *Max, the Bad-Talking Parrot,* p. 73; October 5, 1992, review of *One Gift Deserves Another,* p. 69; August 31, 1998, review of *Crocodiles, Camels, and Dugout Canoes,* p. 76.

School Library Journal, November 1, 1998, Patricia Manning, review of *Crocodiles, Camels, and Dugout Canoes,* p. 144; July, 2001, Louise L. Sherman, review of *Feathers, Flaps, and Flops,* p. 101.

*   *   *

ZEINERT, Karen 1942-2002

Personal

Born February 28, 1942, in Superior, WI; died, August 15, 2002; daughter of Richard (a telephone company employee) and Burdella (a homemaker; maiden name, Hestikin) O'Neil; married John A. Zeinert (a history teacher), August 13, 1966. *Education:* Wisconsin State University—Eau Claire, B.A., 1964. *Hobbies and other interests:* Traveling, reading, gardening.

Career

Educator and author of nonfiction for children. English/ social studies teacher in Oshkosh, Neenah, and Hortonville, WI, 1960-74; buyer of teaching aids and materials for Appleton School Suppliers, 1974-81; medical claims processor, 1976-78; freelance writer, 1981—.

Member

Society of Children's Book Writers and Illustrators, Council for Wisconsin Writers.

Awards, Honors

School Library Journal Top Children's Book, 1989, for *The Salem Witchcraft Trials;* Council for Wisconsin Writers' Top Children's Nonfiction Book designation, and Society of School Librarians Best of the Year selection, both 1993, New York Public Library Books for the Teen Age selection, 1994, and Child Study's Children's Books of the Year selection, all for *The Warsaw Ghetto Uprising;* New York Public Library Books for the Teen Age selection, 1995, for *Those Incredible Women of World War II,* 1996, for *Captured by the Indians: The Narrative of Mary Jemison, Elizabeth Van Lew: Southern Belle, Union Spy,* and *Free Speech: From Newspapers to Music Lyrics,* and 2000, for *The Lincoln Murder Plot; Voice of Youth Advocates* Top Forty Nonfiction Books for Young Adults designation, 1996, for *Across the Plains in the Donner Party;* Council for Wisconsin Writers Children's Nonfiction Award, 1996 and 1999; New York Public Library Titles for Reading and Sharing selection, 1997, *Book Links* Lasting Connections list, and Society for Midland Authors Children's Nonfiction Award, all 1997, all for

Karen Zeinert traces a story of human rights lost and won in her informational book The Amistad Slave Revolt and American Abolition, *illustrated by Nathaniel Jocelyn.*

The Amistad Slave Revolt and American Abolition; National Council for the Social Studies notable book, 1999, for *Those Courageous Women of the Civil War,* and 2000, for *The Valiant Women of the Vietnam War; Voice of Youth Advocates* Nonfiction Honor List, 2000, for *The Lincoln Murder Plot.*

Writings

All about Chinchillas, TFH Publications (Neptune City, NJ), 1986.

The Salem Witchcraft Trials, F. Watts (New York, NY), 1989.

The Warsaw Ghetto Uprising, Millbrook Press (Brookfield, CT), 1993.

(Editor) *The Memoirs of Andrew Sherburne, Patriot and Privateer of the American Revolution,* illustrated by Seymour Fleishman, Linnet (Hamden, CT), 1993.

Those Incredible Women of World War II, Millbrook Press (Brookfield, CT), 1994.

Free Speech: From Newspapers to Music Lyrics, Enslow (Springfield, NJ), 1995.

Elizabeth Van Lew: Southern Belle, Union Spy, Dillon (Parsippany, NJ), 1995.

(Editor) *Captured by the Indians: The Narrative of Mary Jemison,* Linnet (North Haven, CT), 1995.

Victims of Teen Violence, Enslow (Springfield, NJ), 1996.

Those Remarkable Women of the American Revolution,
    Millbrook Press (Brookfield, CT), 1996.
The Ancient Persians, Marshall Cavendish (Tarrytown,
    NY), 1996, published as *The Persian Empire,* Bench-
    mark (Tarrytown, NY), 1997.
(Editor) James Frazier Reed and Virginia Reed Murphy,
    Across the Plains in the Donner Party, Linnet (North
    Haven, CT), 1996.
Wisconsin, Marshall Cavendish (Tarrytown, NY), 1997.
Cults, Enslow (Springfield, NJ), 1997.
The Amistad Slave Revolt and American Abolition, Linnet
    (North Haven, CT), 1997.
Those Courageous Women of the Civil War, Millbrook
    Press (Brookfield, CT), 1998.
*McCarthy and the Fear of Communism in American
    History,* Enslow (Springfield, NJ), 1998.
The Lincoln Murder Plot, Linnet (North Haven, CT), 1999.
Suicide: Tragic Choice, Enslow (Springfield, NJ), 1999.
The Valiant Women of the Vietnam War, Millbrook Press
    (Brookfield, CT), 2000.
To Touch the Stars: A Story of World War II, Jamestown
    (Lincolnwood, IL), 2000.
Those Extraordinary Women of World War I, Millbrook
    Press (Brookfield, CT), 2001.
Tragic Prelude: Bleeding Kansas, Linnet (North Haven,
    CT), 2001.
Women in Politics: In the Running, Twenty-first Century
    Books (Brookfield, CT), 2002.
The Brave Women of the Persian Gulf War, Millbrook
    Press (Brookfield, CT), 2003.

Author of articles published in children's magazines,
including *Cobblestone* and *Cricket.* Creator of teaching
materials for Badger House Publications and McDougal,
Littell.

Sidelights

Karen Zeinert's nonfiction books for young adults have
garnered praise for the author's prose style and her use
of original sources, footnotes, and bibliographies, as
well as her attention to the role of women, children, and
minorities in the histories she recounts. Outstanding
among her large body of work are her profiles of notable
American women during wartime included in such
books as *Those Remarkable Women of the American
Revolution* and *The Valiant Women of the Vietnam War,*
as well as her editorship of diaries, letters, and other
primary materials in a way that make voices from
America's past comprehensible to modern readers. "My
goal is to highlight people who have been forgotten in
history," Zeinert once told *SATA.* Her books on fourteen-year-old Revolutionary War foot soldier Andrew
Sherburne and Civil War spy Elizabeth Van Lew focus
on people who "made contributions to causes that were
so important to them, they risked their lives many times.
Yet, few even know their names." Through her writing,
Zeinert attempted to correct the historic record.

"I began my writing career with Badger House Publications in Green Bay, [Wisconsin]," Zeinert, a former
teacher, once told *SATA.* "I was working as a buyer for
teaching aids when I first approached this company,

looking for Wisconsin history materials for my employer's stores. When I found out the publisher was looking
for former teachers to prepare materials for use in
history classes—something I had always thought I might
like to do—I offered to submit some work. The
company folded about four months later, but by that
time I knew I wanted to spend the rest of my life
writing."

Most of Zeinert's books focused on American history. In
The Salem Witchcraft Trials, Zeinert placed the events
of 1692 in Salem, Massachusetts, when nineteen people
were hanged as witches, in their historical context,
taking into consideration the tenets of the Puritan
religion and the isolation of colonial America. She
discussed the causes of the mass hysteria that gripped
Salem in the late 1600s in terms of psychology, history,
and sociology. Reviewing *The Salem Witchcraft Trials*
for *School Library Journal,* Mary Mueller lauded the
work as a "good analysis" and mentioned its "emphasis
on explaining how the hysteria happened."

In *The Amistad Slave Revolt and American Abolition,*
Zeinert reviewed an early nineteenth-century occurrence

*Covering the role of American women at home and on
the front, Zienert recognizes their contributions to the
war in Vietnam, as well as the protests against
American involvement. (From* The Valiant Women of
the Vietnam War.*)*

that was almost forgotten prior to the release of a feature film by director Steven Spielberg. After a group of fifty slaves broke free while on board a Cuban ship bound for Havana, they reached the coast of Long Island, and disembarked in New Haven, Connecticut. Court battles over the legal status of these Africans resulted in their freedom, but not before many eminent orators spoke out or wrote in support of both sides of the abolition issue. In her book, "Zeinert skillfully delineates the odd cast of characters who became involved with the Amistad trials," explained *New York Times Book Review* contributor Eric Foner, and "expertly sketches the national context regarding slavery." She continued her focus on slavery in *Tragic Prelude: Bleeding Kansas,* a profile of the Kansas Territory as abolitionists and pro-slavery factions battled during the late 1850s in an effort to influence the future of slavery in America. Zeinert incorporated a wealth of letters, diaries, photographs, and other primary documents, creating a history that *Booklist* reviewer Marta Segal characterized as "readable" and "engaging."

Zeinert left the United States and drew readers to Europe and the rise of the Jewish resistance during World War II in *The Warsaw Ghetto Uprising.* She presented a detailed account of the creation of the Jewish ghetto in Warsaw, Poland, and included a thumbnail history of the rise of Nazism and anti-Semitism in Europe in the 1920s and 1930s. Reviewers praised Zeinert's inclusion of information regarding everyday life in the ghetto, unusual methods of survival, and individual acts of heroism. David A. Lindsey of *School Library Journal* called *The Warsaw Ghetto Uprising* "a concise history that's packed with information." Esther Sinofsky of *Voice of Youth Advocates* dubbed Zeinert's history "riveting" and "an excellent addition to the Holocaust shelf," while in *Booklist,* Kay Weisman praised the book's emphasis on "the actions of those Jews [who] helped to turn the tide of war" against Germany and sent "signals of hope" to prisoners of the Third Reich.

The role of women throughout history has served as the focal point of several books by Zeinert, and her work in this area has done much to enlighten young historians as to the significant contributions made by women from many walks of life. Beginning with a discussion of the role of women in eighteenth-century America that *Booklist* reviewer Susan Dove Lempke predicted would be "an eye-opener for today's young readers," Zeinert's *Those Remarkable Women of the American Revolution* profiles spies, soldiers, and politicians on both side of the battle between Great Britain and her upstart American colony. *Those Courageous Women of the Civil War* transports readers to the mid-1800s and introduces them to not only well-known women such as Red Cross-founder Clara Barton and abolitionist Harriet Tubman, but also lesser-known women living both North and South of the battle lines that fractured the United States. Praising the book as "readable," Carolyn Phelan remarked in a *Booklist* review on the inclusion of "quotations from firsthand accounts" that bring "the war into sharper focus" for young readers. In *School Library Journal,* contributor Elizabeth Reardon called *Those*

Courageous Women of the Civil War "well-written," "well-researched," and "a solid work that is sure to open the eyes of many readers."

Zeinert took her examination of women in wartime to the twentieth century and the onset of what was first called the Great War. *Those Extraordinary Women of World War I* retains the same format—including brief biographies, bibliography, timeline, and a wealth of primary source documents—in its examination of women who supported their nation as nurses, factory workers, members of the press corps, military personnel, and the like. "Zeinert emphasizes the broader connection between women's entry into the work force and peripheral military roles," commented *Bulletin of the Center for Children's Books* contributor Elizabeth Bush. Zeinert ends her work with a discussion of the war's effect on passage of the Nineteenth Amendment granting women the right to vote. In *Those Incredible Women of World War II,* she again assembled archival photos, newspaper clips, advertisements, and other writings to supplement the accounts of women who aided in the war effort during the 1940s. Praising the "highly readable text," *Booklist* contributor Ellen Mandel added that Zeinert's inclusion of short biographical essays about Eleanor Roosevelt, physician Emily Barringer, and other notable women contributes to her "tightly written war perspective." Praising the book as "a fascinating view of a pivotal time in U.S. history," *School Library Journal* contributor Louise L. Sherman predicted that *Those Incredible Women of World War II* "is so readable that it should find an audience" even among general readers.

The Valiant Women of the Vietnam War continues Zeinert's history series by discussing the contributions of the 11,000 women who served in the U.S. military or in civilian jobs in support of the war in Southeast Asia during one of the nation's most controversial conflicts. The book "portrays an aspect of the war about which many adults, much less students, remain unaware," commented Leah J. Sparks, adding in her *School Library Journal* review that Zeinert's book holds special value due to its coverage of the effects of the war on Vietnamese women who experienced the horrors of the battlefield first-hand.

Zeinert believed that the best start for beginning writers is at their local library. "You should read everything you can about the writing business," she once commented to *SATA,* as well as "samples of published work in the area/areas in which you hope to publish. Then sort through all the advice and pick out what makes sense to you. Don't take shortcuts. Send for those sample copies, study publishers' guidelines, rewrite until you think your work is perfect, then rewrite it once more. Above all, be patient."

Biographical and Critical Sources

PERIODICALS

Booklist, March 1, 1993, Kay Weisman, review of *The Warsaw Ghetto Uprising,* p. 1222; May 15, 1993, Sheilamae O'Hara, review of *The Memoirs of Andrew*

Sherburne, p. 1685; January 15, 1995, Ellen Mandel, review of *Those Incredible Women of World War II,* p. 911; April 1, 1995, Hazel Rochman, review of *Free Speech: From Newspapers to Music Lyrics,* p. 1387; September 1, 1995, Karen Hutt, review of *Captured by Indians,* p. 52; June 1, 1996, Hazel Rochman, review of *Across the Plains in the Donner Party,* p. 1692, and Anne O'Malley, review of *Victims of Teen Violence,* p. 1688; December 1, 1996, Susan Dove Lempke, review of *Those Remarkable Women of the American Revolution,* p. 654; July, 1997, Anne O'Malley, review of *The Amistad Slave Revolt and American Abolition,* p. 1810; June 1, 1998, Carolyn Phelan, review of *Those Courageous Women of the Civil War,* p. 1763; March 1, 1999, Roger Leslie, review of *The Lincoln Murder Plot,* p. 1202; December 15, 1999, Roger Leslie, review of *Suicide: Tragic Choice,* p. 788; April 1, 2000, Gillian Engberg, review of *The Valiant Women of the Vietnam War,* p. 1461; June 1, 2001, Marta Segal, review of *Tragic Prelude: Bloody Kansas,* pp. 1861-1862; November 15, 2001, Hazel Rochman, review of *Those Extraordinary Women of World War I,* p. 564; December 1, 2002, Ilene Cooper, review of *Women in Politics: In the Running,* p. 655.

Bulletin of the Center for Children's Books, April, 1989, p. 212; April, 1995, Roger Sutton, review of *Free Speech,* pp. 262-263; May, 1999, Janice Del Negro, review of *The Lincoln Murder Plot,* pp. 334-335; January, 2002, Elizabeth Bush, review of *Those Extraordinary Women of World War I,* p. 189.

Catholic Library World, March, 1999, Charlotte Decker, review of *McCarthy and the Fear of Communism in American History,* p. 51.

Horn Book, July, 1999, review of *The Lincoln Murder Plot,* p. 488.

Kirkus Reviews, February 1, 1993, p. 156.

Kliatt, January, 1998, Mary T. Gerrity, review of *The Amistad Slave Revolt and American Abolition,* p. 32.

New York Times Book Review, August 31, 1997, Eric Foner, review of *The Amistad Slave Revolt and American Abolition,* p. 13.

School Library Journal, June, 1989, Mary Mueller, review of *The Salem Witchcraft Trials,* p. 132; January, 1993, David A. Lindsey, review of *The Warsaw Ghetto Uprising,* p. 141; July, 1993, Elaine Fort Weischedel, review of *The Memoirs of Andrew Sherburne,* p. 97; February, 1995, Louise L. Sherman, review of *Those Incredible Women of World War II,* p. 111; June, 1995, Donna Weisman, review of *Free Speech,* pp. 139-140; July, 1995, Joyce Adams Burner, review of *Captured by Indians,* p. 103; September, 1995, Elizabeth M. Reardon, review of *Elizabeth Van Lew,* p. 230; July, 1996, Carol Fazioli, review of *Victims of Teen Violence,* p. 106; August, 1996, David A. Lindsay, review of *Across the Plains in the Donner Party,* p. 174; March, 1997, David N. Pauli, review of *The Persian Empire,* p. 212; June, 1997, Elizabeth M. Reardon, review of *The Amistad Slave Revolt and American Abolition,* p. 150; August, 1998, Elizabeth M. Reardon, review of *Those Courageous Women of the Civil War,* p. 186; December, 1998, William C. Schadt, review of *McCarthy and the Fear of Communism in American History,* p. 144; May, 1999, Mary Mueller, review of *The Lincoln Murder Plot,* p. 144; May, 2000, Leah J. Sparks, review of *The Valiant Women of the Vietnam War,* p. 189; September, 2000, Linda Binder, review of *To Touch the Stars: A Story of World War II,* p. 233; June, 2001, Eldon Younce, review of *Tragic Prelude,* p. 182; October, 2001, Cathy Coffman, review of *Those Extraordinary Women of World War I,* p. 192; November, 2002, Linda Beck, review of *Women in Politics,* p. 193.

Voice of Youth Advocates, October, 1989, p. 242; June, 1993, Esther Sinofsky, review of *The Warsaw Ghetto Uprising;* August, 1996, Cynthia L. Blinn, review of *Victims of Teen Violence,* p. 186; April, 1997, Maura Bresnahan, review of *Those Remarkable Women of the American Revolution,* p. 64; October, 1997, Vicky Burkholder, review of *Cults,* p. 262.

OTHER

Sternig & Byrne Literary Agency, http://www.sff.net/people/jackbyrne (January 20, 2003).*

Cumulative Indexes

Illustrations Index

(In the following index, the number of the *volume* in which an illustrator's work appears is given *before* the colon, and the *page number* on which it appears is given *after* the colon. For example, a drawing by Adams, Adrienne appears in Volume 2 on page 6, another drawing by her appears in Volume 3 on page 80, another drawing in Volume 8 on page 1, and so on and so on....)

YABC

Index references to *YABC* refer to listings appearing in the two-volume *Yesterday's Authors of Books for Children,* also published by The Gale Group. *YABC* covers prominent authors and illustrators who died prior to 1960.

Castro, Antonio *84:* 71
Catalano, Dominic *94:* 79
Catalanotto, Peter *63:* 170; *70:* 23; *71:* 182;
    72: 96; *74:* 114; *76:* 194, 195; *77:* 7; *79:*
    157; *80:* 28, 67; *83:* 157; *85:* 27; *108:*
    11; *113:* 30, 31, 33, 34, 36; *114:* 27, 28,
    29; *117:* 53; *124:* 168
Catania, Tom *68:* 82
Cather, Carolyn *3:* 83; *15:* 203; *34:* 216
Catrow, David *117:* 179
Cauley, Lorinda Bryan *44:* 135; *46:* 49
Cayard, Bruce *38:* 67
Cazet, Denys *52:* 27; *99:* 39, 40
Cecil, Randy *127:* 132, 133
Cellini, Joseph *2:* 73; *3:* 35; *16:* 116; *47:*
    103
Cepeda, Joe *90:* 62; *109:* 91; *134:* 172
Chabrian, Debbi *45:* 55
Chabrian, Deborah *51:* 182; *53:* 124; *63:*
    107; *75:* 84; *79:* 85; *82:* 247; *89:* 93;
    101: 197
Chagnon, Mary *37:* 158
Chalmers, Mary *3:* 145; *13:* 148; *33:* 125;
    66: 214
Chamberlain, Christopher *45:* 57
Chamberlain, Margaret *46:* 51; *106:* 89
Chamberlain, Nigel *78:* 140
Chambers, C. E. *17:* 230
Chambers, Dave *12:* 151
Chambers, Jill *134:* 110
Chambers, Mary *4:* 188
Chambliss, Maxie *42:* 186; *56:* 159; *93:*
    163, 164; *103:* 178
Champlin, Dale *136:* 124
Chan, Harvey *96:* 236; *99:* 153
Chandler, David P. *28:* 62
Chang, Warren *101:* 209
Chapel, Jody *68:* 20
Chapman, C. H. *13:* 83, 85, 87
Chapman, Frederick T. *6:* 27; *44:* 28
Chapman, Gaynor *32:* 52, 53
Chappell, Warren *3:* 172; *21:* 56; *27:* 125
Charles, Donald *30:* 154, 155
Charlip, Remy *4:* 48; *34:* 138; *68:* 53, 54;
    *119:*29, 30
Charlot, Jean *1:* 137, 138; *8:* 23; *14:* 31;
    48: 151; *56:* 21
Charlot, Martin *64:* 72
Charlton, Michael *34:* 50; *37:* 39
Charmatz, Bill *7:* 45
Chartier, Normand *9:* 36; *52:* 49; *66:* 40;
    74: 220
Chase, Lynwood M. *14:* 4
Chast, Roz *97:* 39, 40
Chastain, Madye Lee *4:* 50
Chatterton, Martin *68:* 102
Chauncy, Francis *24:* 158
Chee, Cheng-Khee *79:* 42; *81:* 224
Chen, Chih-sien *90:* 226
Chen, Tony *6:* 45; *19:* 131; *29:* 126; *34:*
    160
Cheney, T. A. *11:* 47
Cheng, Judith *36:* 45; *51:* 16
Chermayeff, Ivan *47:* 53
Cherry, David *93:* 40
Cherry, Lynne *34:* 52; *65:* 184; *87:* 111;
    99: 46, 47
Chesak, Lina *135:* 118
Chess, Victoria *12:* 6; *33:* 42, 48, 49; *40:*
    194; *41:* 145; *69:* 80; *72:* 100; *92:* 33,
    34; *104:* 167
Chessare, Michele *41:* 50; *56:* 48; *69:* 145
Chesterton, G. K. *27:* 43, 44, 45, 47
Chestnutt, David *47:* 217
Chesworth, Michael *75:* 24, 152; *88:* 136;
    94: 25; *98:* 155
Chetham, Celia *134:* 34
Chetwin, Grace *86:* 40
Chevalier, Christa *35:* 66
Chew, Ruth *7:* 46; *132:* 147
Chewning, Randy *92:* 206

Chichester Clark, Emma *72:* 121; *77:* 212;
    78: 209; *87:* 143; *117:* 37, 39, 40
Chifflart *47:* 113, 127
Child, Lauren *119:* 32
Chin, Alex *28:* 54
Cho, Shinta *8:* 126
Chodos, Margaret *52:* 102, 103, 107
Chollick, Jay *25:* 175
Choma, Christina *99:* 169
Chorao, Kay *7:* 200-201; *8:* 25; *11:* 234;
    33: 187; *35:* 239; *69:* 35; *70:* 235; *123:*
    174
Chowdhury, Subrata *62:* 130
Christelow, Eileen *38:* 44; *83:* 198, 199; *90:*
    57, 58
Christensen, Bonnie *93:* 100
Christensen, Gardell Dano *1:* 57
Christiana, David *90:* 64; *135:* 13
Christiansen, Per *40:* 24
Christie, Gregory *116:* 107; *127:* 20, 21
Christy, Howard Chandler *17:* 163-165, 168-
    169; *19:* 186, 187; *21:* 22, 23, 24, 25
Chronister, Robert *23:* 138; *63:* 27; *69:* 167
Church, Frederick *YABC 1:* 155
Chute, Marchette *1:* 59
Chwast, Jacqueline *1:* 63; *2:* 275; *6:* 46-47;
    11: 125; *12:* 202; *14:* 235
Chwast, Seymour *3:* 128-129; *18:* 43; *27:*
    152; *92:* 79; *96:* 56, 57, 58
Cieslawksi, Steve *101:* 142; *127:* 116
Cirlin, Edgard *2:* 168
Clairin, Georges *53:* 109
Clapp, John *105:* 66; *109:* 58; *126:* 7;
    *129:*148; *130:* 165
Clark, Brenda *119:* 85
Clark, David *77:* 164; *134:* 144, 145
Clark, Emma Chichester *See* Chichester
    Clark, Emma
Clark, Victoria *35:* 159
Clarke, Gus *72:* 226; *134:* 31
Clarke, Harry *23:* 172, 173
Clarke, Peter *75:* 102
Claverie, Jean *38:* 46; *88:* 29
Clayton, Robert *9:* 181
Cleaver, Elizabeth *8:* 204; *23:* 36
Cleland, T. M. *26:* 92
Clemens, Peter *61:* 125
Clement, Charles *20:* 38
Clement, Rod *97:* 42
Clement, Stephen *88:* 3
Clementson, John *84:* 213
Clevin, Jörgen *7:* 50
Clifford, Judy *34:* 163; *45:* 198
Clokey, Art *59:* 44
Clouse, James *84:* 15
Clouse, Nancy L. *78:* 31; *114:* 90
Coalson, Glo *9:* 72, 85; *25:* 155; *26:* 42;
    35: 212; *53:* 31; *56:* 154; *94:* 37, 38,
    193
Cober, Alan E. *17:* 158; *32:* 77; *49:* 127
Cober-Gentry, Leslie *92:* 111
Cocca-Leffler, Maryann *80:* 46; *136:* 60
Cochran, Bobbye *11:* 52
CoConis, Ted *4:* 41; *46:* 41; *51:* 104
Cocozza, Chris *87:* 18; *110:* 173; *111:* 149
Coerr, Eleanor *1:* 64; *67:* 52
Coes, Peter *35:* 172
Cogancherry, Helen *52:* 143; *69:* 131; *77:*
    93; *78:* 220; *109:* 204; *110:* 129
Coggins, Jack *2:* 69
Cohen, Alix *7:* 53
Cohen, Sheldon *105:* 33, 34
Cohen, Vincent O. *19:* 243
Cohen, Vivien *11:* 112
Coker, Paul *51:* 172
Colbert, Anthony *15:* 41; *20:* 193
Colby, C. B. *3:* 47
Cole, Babette *58:* 172; *96:* 63, 64
Cole, Brock *68:* 223; *72:* 36, 37, 38, 192;
    127: 23; *136:* 64, 65
Cole, Gwen *87:* 185
Cole, Herbert *28:* 104

Cole, Michael *59:* 46
Cole, Olivia H. H. *1:* 134; *3:* 223; *9:* 111;
    38: 104
Colin, Paul *102:* 59; *123:* 118; *126:* 152
Collicott, Sharleen *98:* 39
Collier, Bryan *126:* 54
Collier, David *13:* 127
Collier, John *27:* 179
Collier, Steven *50:* 52
Collins, Heather *66:* 84; *67:* 68; *81:* 40; *98:*
    192, 193; *129:* 95, 96, 98
Colon, Raul *108:* 112; *113:* 5; *117:* 167;
    *134:*112
Colonna, Bernard *21:* 50; *28:* 103; *34:* 140;
    43: 180; *78:* 150
Comport, Sally Wern *117:* 169
Conde, J. M. *100:* 120
Condon, Grattan *54:* 85
Cone, Ferne Geller *39:* 49
Cone, J. Morton *39:* 49
Conklin, Paul *43:* 62
Connolly, Howard *67:* 88
Connolly, Jerome P. *4:* 128; *28:* 52
Connolly, Peter *47:* 60
Conoly, Walle *110:* 224
Conover, Chris *31:* 52; *40:* 184; *41:* 51;
    44: 79
Contreras, Gerry *72:* 9
Converse, James *38:* 70
Conway *62:* 62
Conway, Michael *69:* 12; *81:* 3; *92:* 108
Cook, G. R. *29:* 165
Cook, Joel *108:* 160
Cookburn, W. V. *29:* 204
Cooke, Donald E. *2:* 77
Cooke, Tom *52:* 118
Coomaraswamy, A. K. *50:* 100
Coombs, Charles *43:* 65
Coombs, Patricia *2:* 82; *3:* 52; *22:* 119; *51:*
    32, 33, 34, 35, 36-37, 38, 39, 40, 42, 43
Cooney, Barbara *6:* 16-17; *50:* 12; *42:* 13:
    92; *15:* 145; *16:* 74, 111; *18:* 189; *23:*
    38, 89, 93; *32:* 138; *38:* 105; *59:* 48, 49,
    51, 52, 53; *74:* 222; *81:* 100; *91:* 25; *96:*
    71, 72, 74; *100:* 149; *YABC 2:* 10
Cooper, Floyd *79:* 95; *81:* 95; *84:* 82; *85:*
    74; *91:* 118; *96:* 77, 78; *103:* 149
Cooper, Heather *50:* 39
Cooper, Helen *102:* 42, 43, 44
Cooper, Mario *24:* 107
Cooper, Marjorie *7:* 112
Cope, Jane *61:* 201; *108* 52
Copelman, Evelyn *8:* 61; *18:* 25
Copley, Heather *30:* 86; *45:* 57
Corbett, Grahame *30:* 114; *43:* 67
Corbino, John *19:* 248
Corcos, Lucille *2:* 223; *10:* 27; *34:* 66
Corey, Robert *9:* 34
Corlass, Heather *10:* 7
Cornell, James *27:* 60
Cornell, Jeff *11:* 58
Cornell, Laura *94:* 179; *95:* 25
Corrigan, Barbara *8:* 37
Corwin, Judith Hoffman *10:* 28
Cory, Fanny Y. *20:* 113; *48:* 29
Cosgrove, Margaret *3:* 100; *47:* 63; *82:* 133
Costabel, Eva Deutsch *45:* 66, 67
Costanza, John *58:* 7, 8, 9
Costello, Chris *86:* 78
Costello, David F. *23:* 55
Cote, Nancy *126:* 139
Couch, Greg *94:* 124; *110:* 13
Councell, Ruth Tietjen *79:* 29
Courtney, Cathy *58:* 69, 144; *59:* 15; *61:*
    20, 87
Courtney, R. *35:* 110
Counihan, Claire *133:* 106
Cousineau, Normand *89:* 180; *112:* 76
Couture, Christin *41:* 209
Covarrubias, Miguel *35:* 118, 119, 123, 124,
    125
Coville, Katherine *32:* 57; *36:* 167; *92:* 38

Fregosi, Claudia *24:* 117
French, Fiona *6:* 82-83; *75:* 61; *109:* 170; *132:*79, 80, 81, 82
Frendak, Rodney *126:* 97, 98
Freynet, Gilbert *72:* 221
Friedman, Judith *43:* 197; *131:* 221
Friedman, Marvin *19:* 59; *42:* 86
Frinta, Dagmar *36:* 42
Frith, Michael K. *15:* 138; *18:* 120
Fritz, Ronald *46:* 73; *82:* 124
Fromm, Lilo *29:* 85; *40:* 197
Frost, A. B. *17:* 6-7; *19:* 123, 124, 125, 126, 127, 128, 129, 130; *100:* 119; *YABC 1:* 156-157, 160; *2:* 107
Frost, Kristi *118:* 113
Fry, Guy *2:* 224
Fry, Rosalie *3:* 72; *YABC 2:* 180-181
Fry, Rosalind *21:* 153, 168
Fryer, Elmer *34:* 115
Fuchs, Bernie *110:* 10
Fuchs, Erich *6:* 84
Fuchshuber, Annegert *43:* 96
Fufuka, Mahiri *32:* 146
Fujikawa, Gyo *39:* 75, 76; *76:* 72, 73, 74
Fulford, Deborah *23:* 159
Fuller, Margaret *25:* 189
Fulweiler, John *93:* 99
Funai, Mamoru *38:* 105
Funk, Tom *7:* 17, 99
Furchgott, Terry *29:* 86
Furness, William Henry, Jr. *94:* 18
Furukawa, Mel *25:* 42

G

Gaadt, David *78:* 212; *121:* 166
Gaadt, George *71:* 9
Gaber, Susan *99:* 33; *115:* 57, 58
Gaberell, J. *19:* 236
Gabler, Mirko *99:* 71
Gackenbach, Dick *19:* 168; *41:* 81; *48:* 89, 90, 91, 92, 93, 94; *54:* 105; *79:* 75, 76, 77
Gad, Victor *87:* 161
Gaetano, Nicholas *23:* 209
Gaffney-Kessell, Walter *94:* 219
Gag, Flavia *17:* 49, 52
Gág, Wanda *100:* 101, 102; *YABC 1:* 135, 137-138, 141, 143
Gagnon, Cécile *11:* 77; *58:* 87
Gal, Laszlo *14:* 127; *52:* 54, 55, 56; *65:* 142; *68:* 150; *81:* 185; *96:* 104, 105
Galazinski, Tom *55:* 13
Galdone, Paul *1:* 156, 181, 206; *2:* 40, 241; *3:* 42, 144; *4:* 141; *10:* 109, 158; *11:* 21; *12:* 118, 210; *14:* 12; *16:* 36-37; *17:* 70-74; *18:* 111, 230; *19:* 183; *21:* 154; *22:* 150, 245; *33:* 126; *39:* 136, 137; *42:* 57; *51:* 169; *55:* 110; *66:* 80, 82, 139; *72:* 73; *100:* 84
Gallagher, S. Saelig *105:* 154
Gallagher, Sears *20:* 112
Galloway, Ewing *51:* 154
Galouchko, Annouchka Gravel *95:* 55
Galster, Robert *1:* 66
Galsworthy, Gay John *35:* 232
Galvez, Daniel *125:* 182
Gamble, Kim *112:* 64, 65; *124:* 77
Gammell, Stephen *7:* 48; *13:* 149; *29:* 82; *33:* 209; *41:* 88; *50:* 185, 186-187; *53:* 51, 52-53, 54, 55, 56, 57, 58; *54:* 24, 25; *56:* 147, 148, 150; *57:* 27, 66; *81:* 62, 63; *87:* 88; *89:* 10; *106:* 223; *126:*2; *128:* 71, 73, 74, 77
Gamper, Ruth *84:* 198
Gampert, John *58:* 94
Ganly, Helen *56:* 56

Gannett, Ruth Chrisman *3:* 74; *18:* 254; *33:* 77, 78
Gantschev, Ivan *45:* 32
Garafano, Marie *73:* 33
Garbot, Dave *131:* 106
Garbutt, Bernard *23:* 68
Garcia *37:* 71
Garcia, Manuel *74:* 145
Gardner, Earle *45:* 167
Gardner, Joan *40:* 87
Gardner, Joel *40:* 87, 92
Gardner, John *40:* 87
Gardner, Lucy *40:* 87
Gardner, Richard *See* Cummings, Richard
Gargiulo, Frank *84:* 158
Garland, Michael *36:* 29; *38:* 83; *44:* 168; *48:* 78, 221, 222; *49:* 161; *60:* 139; *71:* 6, 11; *72:* 229; *74:* 142; *89:* 187; *93:* 183; *104:* 110; *131:* 55
Garland, Peggy *60:* 139
Garland, Sarah *62:* 45; *135:* 67, 68
Garn, Aimee *75:* 47
Garner, Joan *128:* 170
Garneray, Ambroise Louis *59:* 140
Garnett, Eve *3:* 75
Garnett, Gary *39:* 184
Garns, Allen *80:* 125; *84:* 39
Garraty, Gail *4:* 142; *52:* 106
Garrett, Agnes *46:* 110; *47:* 157
Garrett, Edmund H. *20:* 29
Garrett, Tom *107:* 194
Garrick, Jacqueline *67:* 42, 43; *77:* 94
Garrison, Barbara *19:* 133; *104:* 146; *109:* 87
Garro, Mark *108:* 131; *128:* 210
Garvey, Robert *98:* 222
Garza, Carmen Lomas *80:* 211
Gates, Frieda *26:* 80
Gaughan, Jack *26:* 79; *43:* 185
Gaver, Becky *20:* 61
Gawing, Toby *72:* 52
Gay, Marie-Louise *68:* 76-77, 78; *102:* 136; *126:* 76, 78, 81, 83; *127:* 55, 56
Gay, Zhenya *19:* 135, 136
Gaydos, Tim *62:* 201
Gazsi, Ed *80:* 48
Gazso, Gabriel *73:* 85
Geary, Clifford N. *1:* 122; *9:* 104; *51:* 74
Gee, Frank *33:* 26
Geer, Charles *1:* 91; *3:* 179; *4:* 201; *6:* 168; *7:* 96; *9:* 58; *10:* 72; *12:* 127; *39:* 156, 157, 158, 159, 160; *42:* 88, 89, 90, 91; *55:* 111, 116
Gehm, Charlie *36:* 65; *57:* 117; *62:* 60, 138
Geisel, Theodor Seuss *1:* 104-105, 106; *28:* 108, 109, 110, 111, 112, 113; *75:* 67, 68, 69, 70, 71; *89:* 127, 128; *100:* 106, 107, 108
Geisert, Arthur *92:* 67, 68; *133:* 72, 73, 74
Geldart, William *15:* 121; *21:* 202
Genia *4:* 84
Gentry, Cyrille R. *12:* 66
Genzo, John Paul *136:* 74
George, Jean *2:* 113
George, Lindsay Barrett *95:* 57
Geraghty, Paul *130:* 60, 61
Gérard, Jean Ignace *45:* 80
Gérard, Rolf *27:* 147, 150
Gerber, Mark *61:* 105
Gerber, Mary Jane *112:* 124
Gerber, Stephanie *71:* 195
Gergely, Tibor *54:* 15, 16
Geritz, Franz *17:* 135
Gerlach, Geff *42:* 58
Gerrard, Roy *47:* 78; *90:* 96, 97, 98, 99
Gershinowitz, George *36:* 27
Gerstein, Mordicai *31:* 117; *47:* 80, 81, 82, 83, 84, 85, 86; *51:* 173; *69:* 134; *107:* 122
Gervase *12:* 27
Getz, Arthur *32:* 148
Gewirtz, Bina *61:* 81

Giancola, Donato *95:* 146
Gibbons, Gail *23:* 78; *72:* 77, 78, 79; *82:* 182; *104:* 65
Gibbs, Tony *40:* 95
Gibran, Kahlil *32:* 116
Gider, Iskender *81:* 193
Giesen, Rosemary *34:* 192-193
Giffard, Hannah *83:* 70
Giguère, George *20:* 111
Gilbert, John *19:* 184; *54:* 115; *YABC 2:* 287
Gilbert, W. S. *36:* 83, 85, 96
Gilbert, Yvonne *116:* 70; *128:* 84
Gilchrist, Jan Spivey *72:* 82, 83, 84-85, 87; *77:* 90; *105:* 89, 91; *130:* 63, 64
Giles, Will *41:* 218
Gili, Phillida *70:* 73
Gill, Margery *4:* 57; *7:* 7; *22:* 122; *25:* 166; *26:* 146, 147
Gillen, Denver *28:* 216
Gillette, Henry J. *23:* 237
Gilliam, Stan *39:* 64, 81
Gillies, Chuck *62:* 31
Gilliland, Jillian *87:* 58
Gillman, Alec *98:* 105
Gilman, Esther *15:* 124
Gilman, Phoebe *104:* 70, 71
Ginsberg, Sari *111:* 184
Ginsburg, Max *62:* 59; *68:* 194
Giovanopoulos, Paul *7:* 104; *60:* 36
Giovine, Sergio *79:* 12; *93:* 118
Githens, Elizabeth M. *5:* 47
Gladden, Scott *99:* 108; *103:* 160
Gladstone, Gary *12:* 89; *13:* 190
Gladstone, Lise *15:* 273
Glanzman, Louis S. *2:* 177; *3:* 182; *36:* 97, 98; *38:* 120, 122; *52:* 141, 144; *71:* 191; *91:* 54, 56
Glaser, Milton *3:* 5; *5:* 156; *11:* 107; *30:* 26; *36:* 112; *54:* 141
Glass, Andrew *36:* 38; *44:* 133; *48:* 205; *65:* 3; *68:* 43, 45; *90:* 104, 105
Glass, Marvin *9:* 174
Glasser, Judy *41:* 156; *56:* 140; *69:* 79; *72:* 101
Glattauer, Ned *5:* 84; *13:* 224; *14:* 26
Glauber, Uta *17:* 76
Gleeson, J. M. *YABC 2:* 207
Glegg, Creina *36:* 100
Glienke, Amelie *63:* 150
Gliewe, Unada *3:* 78-79; *21:* 73; *30:* 220
Gliori, Debi *72:* 91
Glovach, Linda *7:* 105
Gobbato, Imero *3:* 180-181; *6:* 213; *7:* 58; *9:* 150; *18:* 39; *21:* 167; *39:* 82, 83; *41:* 137, 251; *59:* 177
Goble, Paul *25:* 121; *26:* 86; *33:* 65; *69:*68-69; *131:* 79, 80
Goble, Warwick *46:* 78, 79
Godal, Eric *36:* 93
Godfrey, Michael *17:* 279
Goembel, Ponder *42:* 124
Goffe, Toni *61:* 83, 84, 85; *89:* 11; *90:* 124
Goffstein, M. B. *8:* 71; *70:* 75, 76, 77
Golbin, Andrée *15:* 125
Goldfeder, Cheryl *11:* 191
Goldsborough, June *5:* 154-155; *8:* 92, *14:* 226; *19:* 139; *54:* 165
Goldsmith, Robert *110:* 77
Goldstein, Leslie *5:* 8; *6:* 60; *10:* 106
Goldstein, Nathan *1:* 175; *2:* 79; *11:* 41, 232; *16:* 55
Goldstrom, Robert *98:* 36
Golembe, Carla *79:* 80, 81; *136:* 91
Golin, Carlo *74:* 112
Gómez, Elizabeth *127:* 70; *133:* 76
Gomi, Taro *64:* 102; *103:* 74, 76
Gon, Adriano *101:* 112
Gonzalez, Maya Christina *104:* 3; *136:* 92
Goodall, John S. *4:* 92-93; *10:* 132; *66:* 92, 93; *YABC 1:* 198

Q

R

X

Y

Z

Author Index

The following index gives the number of the volume in which an author's biographical sketch, Autobiography Feature, Brief Entry, or Obituary appears.

This index includes references to all entries in the following series, which are also published by The Gale Group.

YABC—*Yesterday's Authors of Books for Children: Facts and Pictures about Authors and Illustrators of Books for Young People from Early Times to 1960*
CLR—*Children's Literature Review: Excerpts from Reviews, Criticism, and Commentary on Books for Children*
SAAS—*Something about the Author Autobiography Series*

Author Index

S

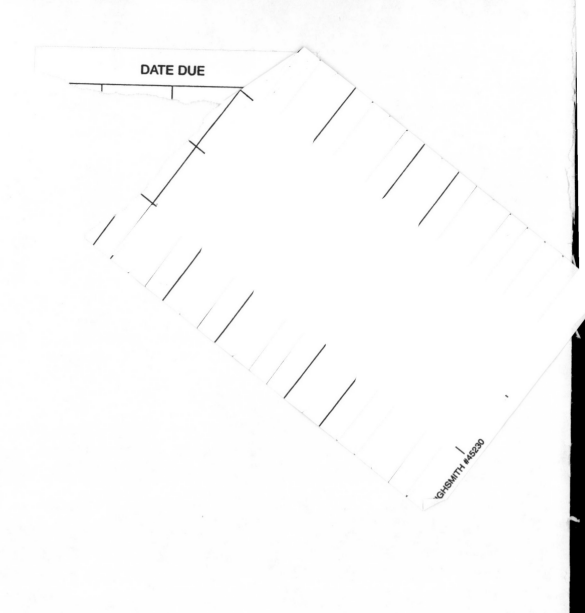

DATE DUE

GHSMITH #45230